Multiobjective Decision Making:

Theory and Methodology

NORTH-HOLLAND SERIES IN

SYSTEM SCIENCE AND ENGINEERING

Andrew P. Sage, *Editor*

1	**Wismer and Chattergy**	Introduction to Nonlinear Optimization: A Problem Solving Approach
2	**Sutherland**	Societal Systems: Methodology, Modeling, and Management
3	**Šiljak**	Large-Scale Dynamic Systems
4	**Porter et al.**	A Guidebook for Technology Assessment and Impact Analysis
5	**Boroush et al.**	Technology Assessment: Creative Futures
6	**Rouse**	Systems Engineering Models of Human–Machine Interaction
7	**Sengupta**	Decision Models in Stochastic Programming: Operational Methods of Decision Making Under Uncertainty
8	**Chankong and Haimes**	Multiobjective Decision Making: Theory and Methodology

Multiobjective Decision Making:
Theory and Methodology
Series Volume 8

Vira Chankong
Khon Kaen University

and

Yacov Y. Haimes
Case Western Reserve University

North-Holland
New York • Amsterdam • Oxford

Elsevier Science Publishing Co., Inc.
52 Vanderbilt Avenue, New York, NY 10017

Distributors outside the United States and Canada:
Elsevier Science Publishers B.V.
P.O. Box 211, 1000 AE Amsterdam, The Netherlands

Library of Congress Cataloging in Publication Data

Vira Chankong.
Multiobjective decision making.
(North Holland series in system science and engineering; 8)

Includes bibliographical references and index.
1. Decision-making—Mathematical models. I. Haimes, Yacov Y.
II. Title. III. Series.
HD30.23.V57 001.53′8 82-2536
ISBN 0-444-00710-5 AACR2

Manufactured in the United States of America

to our wives,
Pornpituk and Sonia,
and our children,
Dohm,
Yosi, and Michelle

Contents

Foreword

This is an excellent work in the theory and methodology of systems engineering as it relates to the evaluation of alternative courses of action and associated decision making. It is increasingly being recognized that there are competing concerns associated with evaluation and selection from among competing alternatives. These concerns involve multiple, conflicting, noncommensurate criteria against which decisions must be evaluated. By treating criteria as multidimensional, rather than scalar, it becomes possible to move normative theories of decision analysis, which describe how one should exercise judgment, one step closer to a behavioral theory of decision making, describing how decisions are actually made.

This important contemporary work begins with a description of the fundamental rational decision-making process. Following this introductory discussion of the systemic approach to judgment and decision, two chapters are devoted to psychological value measurements, utility, and classical decision analysis. A chapter concerning vector optimization theory concludes Part I by providing quantitative theory in vector optimization and associated mathematical programming concepts that serve as a fundamental basis of the multiobjective decision-making methodologies to follow.

Four of the five chapters in Part II concern methods of assessing and evaluating alternatives. A variety of these are discussed, including both noninteractive and interactive methods, among them the ε-constraint and surrogate worth trade-off methods that owe much of their development to the research of Professor Haimes. The final chapter presents a brief taxonomy and comparative evaluation of the methods discussed.

This work admirably fullfills the goals (multiple, of course) of this series in systems science and engineering. It is an advanced, definitive work in a scholarly area of much interest. At the same time, the material is pedagogically sound and eminently teachable to beginning- and intermediate-level graduate students in quantitative areas of systems engineering, operations research, and management science.

Andrew P. Sage
Series Editor
University of Virginia

Preface

This book is intended for students of, researchers in, and practitioners of multiobjective problem solving who are interested in a conceptual point of view. It draws together contributions from a number of disciplines in a cohesive framework that should serve two primary purposes. For beginners about to embark on the study of this interesting field, the book may be used as an introduction to multiobjective theories and techniques. For readers who already have their favorite specialties, the book will serve as a convenient reference to related theories and techniques that they may find necessary to call upon.

We have attempted to emphasize *why* and *how* the concepts and steps are introduced. In so doing, we have liberally borrowed fundamental concepts and principles from various basic disciplines. In particular, we have assumed that the reader has an adequate background in undergraduate mathematics, particularly set theory, linear and matrix algebra, probability theory, and linear programming. A familiarity with elementary concepts in mathematical analysis is also helpful. Some of the more advanced background topics that will prove useful in reading this book are presented in Chapter 2. The reader who is not interested in technical details may skip some of the proofs, concentrating on the underlying concepts and results.

In Chapter 1 we define a general multiobjective decision problem and identify its key elements as a coordinating framework for the presentation to follow. A variety of theories (Part I) and techniques (Part II) in multiobjective decision making are then presented. The two main multiobjective theories, namely multiattribute utility theory and vector optimization theory, are discussed in Chapters 3 and 4, respectively. Chapter 5 presents a collection of assessment and evaluation techniques, focusing mainly on formalizing the structure of a decision maker's preferences. Chapter 6 presents a class of programming techniques, concentrating on generating noninferior (Pareto-optimal) solutions. Several programming techniques, both noninteractive and interactive, for generating the best-compromise solution are outlined in Chapter 7. Chapter 8 develops and summarizes the surrogate worth trade-off (SWT) method and its extensions. Finally, several criteria for making comparative evaluations of multiobjective techniques are discussed in Chapter 9.

Some of the material used in this book was originally prepared for regular graduate courses at Case Western Reserve University and Khon Kaen University, Thailand. The book is based on current research results published in the literature as well as on notes used since 1972 for the Case Western Reserve University annual short course titled "A Hierarchical–Multiobjective Approach in Water Resources Planning and Management."

Numerous individuals and institutions have contributed both directly and indirectly to the writing and the completion of this book. We are particularly grateful to Warren A. Hall for his invaluable inspiration and his contribution to the development of the SWT method; Andrew P. Sage for encouraging us to write this book and including it in the North-Holland series on systems science and engineering; Jared Cohon for his most helpful review of and comments on the early manuscripts of this book; Leon S. Lasdon for his evaluation of the early manuscripts; W. Scott Nainis, Takashi Shima, and Kyosti Tarvainen for their constructive comments; Eric L. Asbeck for his judicious and relentless effort in working with us on proofreading the edited manuscript; Kenneth J. Wallenstein for his most valuable contribution in reading galley proofs; Mark Leach for doing the tedious work of preparing the subject and author indexes and for his dedicated effort in reading galley proofs; our graduate students Peter Zwick, Jacob Thadathil, and Fernando Gomide for their valuable comments; Virginia Benade for her most conscientious and outstanding editorial contribution; Joyce Martin for so skillfully typing and retyping the manuscript; and Mary Ann Pelot for actually managing and coordinating our work on this book with patience, professional skill, and a pleasant attitude.

Special thanks should be extended to the National Science Foundation (grant ENG79-03605), the U.S. Department of Energy (contracts EL-77-S-01-2124 and DEACO-180-RA-50256), Case Western Reserve University, and Khon Kaen University for supporting, in part, much of the research that resulted in this book. However, we, the authors, and not the above agencies and institutions, take responsibility for the results and ideas presented here.

The authors are indebted to the following faculty members: Rector Kawee Tungsubutra and Dean Rangsri Nantasarn of the faculty of engineering of Khon Kaen University, for their courteous support that allowed Vira Chankong to complete the book, and the faculty of the systems engineering department of Case Western Reserve University—Professors

Irving Lefkowitz, Stephen Kahne, Mihajlo Mesarovic, Soroosh Sorooshian, Kenneth Loparo, Marc Buchner, and Howard Chizeck.

The authors would further like to thank the *IEEE Transactions on Systems, Man, and Cynbernetics*, *Automatica*, and the Pergamon Press for permission to use material from published papers. The authors would also like to express their gratitude to the editorial staff of Elsevier for their cooperativeness and most supportive effort.

Finally, we would like to thank our wives, Pornpituk and Sonia, for their support and patience, which made the completion of this book possible.

PART I
THEORY

Chapter 1

Elements of Multiobjective Decision Problems

1.1 Introduction

Decision making is an integral part of our daily lives. It ranges in scope from the individual to the largest groups and societies, including nations and, ultimately, organization at the global level. It considers situations ranging in complexity from the simple to the most complex involving multiple objectives. This book is primarily concerned with large, multiple-objective decision-making problems at the level of organizations or higher.

Because of the diversity of situations in which multiobjective decision problems can arise and because of the multiplicity of factors that are involved, the literature on the subject produced since the early 1960s is large, as well as diverse in emphasis and style of treatment, and the general indication is that this trend will continue. Theoretical and methodological developments have been based on a number of different viewpoints, reflecting the breadth of disciplines involved. If researchers are to direct and streamline their future research so that practicing managers and decision makers can best select from among the available multiobjective techniques, the different viewpoints must be fully appreciated. A coherent account of existing theories and techniques related to multiobjective decision problems is therefore appropriate.

The aim of this book is modest. We hope to draw together various contributions so as to provide such an account of multiobjective theories and methodologies. It should provide readers about to embark on a study of this important field with some of the concepts necessary to more advanced research and applications. It should also serve as a reference for those already working in the field. Hence our focus is on fundamental ideas, and existing methodologies are discussed from a conceptual viewpoint. However, important results will also be presented, to give interested readers greater insight into related theoretical developments, and simple, mostly hypothetical, examples will illustrate and clarify various points.

1.2 The Multiobjective Decision Problem

The approach of this volume is to consider explicitly five key components of a multiobjective decision problem: a *decision-making unit*, a *decision situation*, a set of *objectives*, a set of *attributes*, and a *decision rule*. Most of these terms, unfortunately, do not have a universally acknowledged definition. In what follows we shall describe these (and other related terms) in an informal manner. This, however, will be preceded by a discussion of the multiobjective decision-making process as a whole and the role of value judgments.

1.2.1 The Multiobjective Decision-Making Process

The term *multiobjective decision-making process* refers to the entire process of problem solving, consisting essentially of the five steps depicted in Figure 1.1.[1] The process begins when the decision maker perceives the need to alter the course of the system[2] about which he is concerned.[3] The situation is then diagnosed,[4] and general statements of overall needs or objectives[5] are stated. The problem-formulation step then begins. Various tasks involved in this step normally include a) translating vaguely stated overall objectives into a more operational set of specific multiple objectives and b) specifying clearly all essential elements in the system (or problem), system boundary, and system environment.

Once the system, its environment, and the set of objectives are well defined, appropriate models are constructed. By a "model" is meant a collection of key variables and their logical (or physical) relationships that together facilitate effective and meaningful comprehensive analysis of the pertinent aspects of the system. There are various forms of models, including simple mental models, graphic models (e.g., a chart), complex physical models, and mathematical models. They have several functions, one of which is to generate available alternative courses of action.

Since alternatives need to be compared, a set of attributes or objective measures[6] must be clearly specified. The levels of these attributes, measured in an appropriate scale for a given alternative, serve as yardsticks by which the degree of attainment of the particular objectives (and hence the overall

---

[1] Clearly there are other ways of describing the multiobjective decision-making process. See, for example, Easton [1973] or Harrison [1975].

[2] Generally, a system is a collection of parts and their coordination to accomplish a set of goals.

[3] For a more detailed discussion of the triggering mechanism of a decision process, the reader may refer to Easton [1973, pp. 54–55] or Segev [1976].

[4] For a more detailed discussion of diagnosis, see Easton [1973, pp. 56–61 and references on p. 66].

[5] The term "objective" will be defined more precisely shortly.

[6] Other terms used interchangeably with these in the literature include "performance measure," "performance index," "performance criteria," "decision criteria," and "objective function."

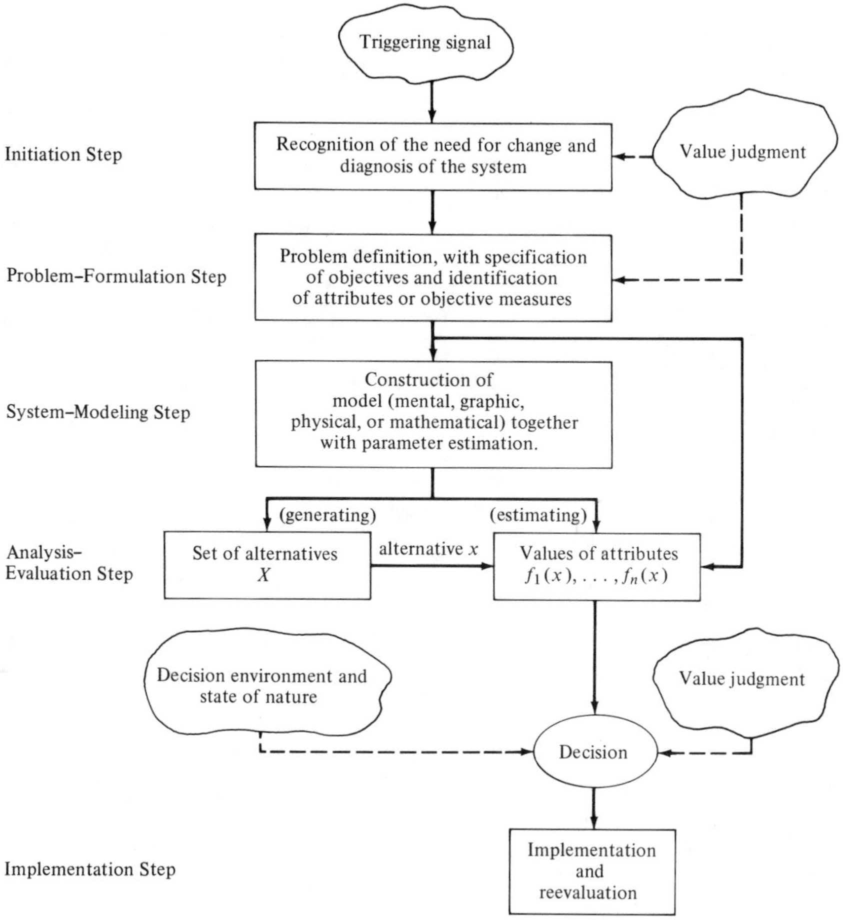

Figure 1.1 Typical multiobjective decision-making process.

objectives) specified in the preceding step can be assessed. The (measured) values of these attributes for a given alternative can be obtainable either from the model or through subjective judgments.

To complete the analysis and evaluation step, each alternative is evaluated relative to others in terms of a prespecified decision rule or set of rules used to rank the available alternatives. The alternative having the highest rank according to the decision rule is then chosen for implementation.

The process may end here, in which case it is known as an *open-loop pr cess*. Alternatively, if the current result is found to be unsatisfactory, we may use information about the observed output (obtained from implementing the chosen alternative) to return to the problem-formulation step. We then speak of a *closed-loop process*.

1.2.2 Judgment and the Value System

In every decision process and in any decision situation, there are *factual elements* and *value elements*. Factual elements are those that can be verified scientifically and subjected to scientific machinery that lead to other verifiable elements. Value elements, on the other hand, defy all forms of scientific verification and treatment. A collection of value elements and their sources constitutes *the value system*. *Judgment*, which signifies the act of giving an opinion, is the most common value element in any decision-making process.

There has been debate on the emphasis and extent to which a value system, particularly the element of judgment, should be incorporated in the actual decision-making process.[7] On one hand are those who tend to ignore value judgments altogether and who justify this "rational" approach by claiming that value systems are the main source of "irrationality." A hard-line manager or administrator, on the other hand, may make decisions based solely on intuition, experience, and good judgment. It is not our intention here to weigh the arguments. It is more fruitful to identify those tasks in the multiobjective decision-making process (Figure 1.1) in which judgment is an integral part.

In the initiation step, for example, recognizing the need for change and perceiving the overall objectives to be achieved are purely subjective processes, involving soul-searching for "needs" and "wants." Other tasks in the multiobjective decision-making process that are mostly subjective include

- defining clearly the statement of the problem, the system boundary, and the system environment (problem-formulation step);
- articulating the set of specific objectives[8] and identifying appropriate attributes (problem-formulation step);
- choosing the type of model to be used (modeling step);
- choosing key variables to be incorporated in the model[9] (modeling step); and
- choosing the set of decision rules[10] (analysis and evaluation step).

Some examples of tasks that may require value judgments are the following:

- developing logical relationships among the chosen decision variables, as well as between variables and the chosen attributes (modeling step).

---

[7]See, for example, the preface of Easton's book [1973] (or papers by Black [1975]).

[8]After the set of specific objectives is well defined, graphic techniques, such as those described by Sage [1977], can be used as an aid to arranging the hierarchy of objectives, if one exists.

[9]The procedure called "brainstorming," as described, for example, by Sage [1977], may be quite useful when the problem is large and complex.

[10]See, for example, Rigby [1964]. More will be said about this when we discuss the decision rule.

This may be either purely subjective, if only mental models are involved, purely analytical or quantitative, in cases where mathematical models are appropriate representations of the system, or a mixture of both if some other forms of models (such as the accounting chart) are used.

evaluating the impact of each alternative, i.e., calculating the value of each attribute and assessing the relationship between attributes and objectives (analysis and evaluation step). This depends on the type of model and the type of attributes used. More will be said about this when we discuss attributes and objectives.

applying the decision rule to arrive at the final decision (analysis and evaluation step). This depends on the type of the decision rule used, as will be discussed later.

Attempts have been made to deal with the judgments involved in these tasks. Experimental psychologists and behavioral scientists seek to understand through empirical studies the psychology underlying judgment. Management scientists, operations researchers, and systems engineers, on the other hand, are more interested in finding appropriate guidelines for effectively combining judgment with some formal procedures. Perhaps the most successful treatment of judgment in multiobjective decision problems is in the area of the preference structure of the decision maker. This type of judgment is required in the evaluation step, outlined in Figure 1.1. Unidimensional utility theory, multiattribute utility theory, and other related topics all represent attempts to formalize the preference structure of the decision maker. We shall return to a discussion of these theoretical developments in a later chapter.

What we have tried to accomplish here is to identify how and where judgment is required in the multiobjective decision-making process. Indirectly, therefore, we can also identify those tasks that can be carried out through formal procedures. In this way it is hoped that we can strike a proper balance between objectivity and subjectivity in solving multiobjective decision problems.

We now describe the five key components of a multiobjective decision problem.

1.2.3 The Decision-Making Unit and the Decision Maker

As noted by Rigby [1964], the term "decision maker" is difficult to define precisely. Churchman [1968] refers to the decision maker[11] as "the person who has the ability to change the system, i.e., the responsibility and authority for such a change." More specifically, and more appropriate to the

---

[11] See Churchman [1968, p. 184].

context with which we shall be concerned, we shall take the *decision maker* to be an individual or a group of individuals who directly or indirectly furnishes the final value judgment that may be used to rank available alternatives, so that the "best" choice can be identified. Implicit in this statement is that whenever final value judgments need to be made concerning the "goodness" or "badness" of a given choice, they are to be made by the decision maker.

A *decision-making unit* consists of the decision maker and possibly a collection of men and machines which together act as an information processor which performs the following functions:

receives input information;

generates information within itself;

processes information into intelligence; and

produces the decision.

Thus the smallest decision-making unit is the decision maker himself. A larger unit may, for example, consist of the decision makers, system analysts, and computing and graphic instruments. We intentionally make this distinction between the decision maker and the decision-making unit so that we can be more flexible in our subsequent discussion on the boundary of the decision situation. This flexibility will be useful, as we shall later see, in understanding the nature of various multiobjective decision-making techniques.

1.2.4 Objectives and Attributes

An understanding of the meaning, structure, and properties of the terms *objectives* and *attributes* is crucial if one hopes to capture the essence of a complex multiobjective decision problem. Keeney and Raiffa [1976] give an excellent account of this topic, with numerous illustrative examples. Much of what follows summarizes and illustrates the basic concepts involved.

Definitions and the Hierarchical Structure of Objectives Inasmuch as the decision-making unit and the decision situation are essential ingredients of a decision problem, a multiobjective decision problem must also have objectives; otherwise, it would be vacuous or poorly defined. Essentially, an *objective* is a statement about the desired state of the system under consideration toward which the decision maker strives. Thus, in a multiobjective decision problem, there are several statements expressing the decision maker's desired state of the system. Objectives are statements of "wants" and thus may or may not be achievable. Nonetheless, they are the goal toward which the system should be proceeding and they are standards against which the quality or performance of a given alternative may be evaluated.

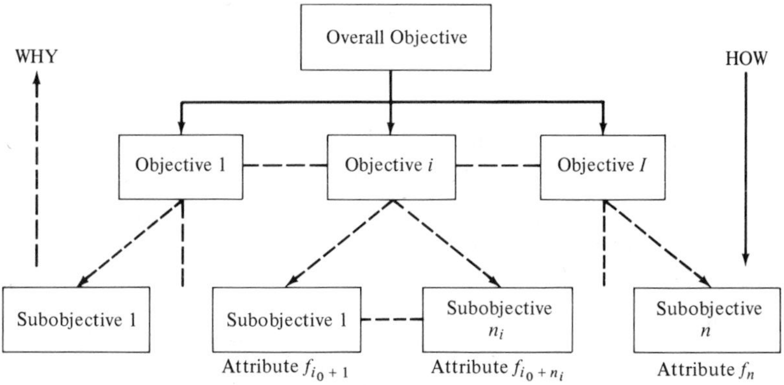

Figure 1.2 Typical hierarchical structure of objectives.

A well-defined set of objectives often exhibits a hierarchical structure, as illustrated in Figure 1.2. The highest level of this structure generally represents the broad overall objectives that are instrumental in initiating the multiobjective decision problem in the first place. These objectives are, however, often vaguely stated and, hence, unoperational. As we go down the hierarchical level, objectives at the lower level are more specific and more operational than those in the higher level and are perceived as means to achieving higher ends represented by objectives in the higher level. Thus objectives at the lowest level of the hierarchy are "most specific" and "most operational."

An objective is operational if there is a practical way to assess the level of achieving such an objective. To facilitate this practical method, a set of attributes is assigned to each objective in the lowest level. An *attribute* is a measurable quantity whose (measured) value reflects the degree of achievement for a particular objective (to which the attribute is ascribed). We assume that each attribute is comprehensive and measurable, as we shall discuss later.

As mentioned, articulating lower-level objectives and identifying the appropriate set of attributes for a given set of objectives, as required in the first two steps in Figure 1.1, is a creative process requiring ingenuity, experience, and creative judgment. A guideline for this process normally begins with the generation and articulation of ideas through the process called "brainstorming" or "brainwriting."[12] After this process is completed, one hopes that a set of pertinent objectives, not necessarily in hierarchical structure, will be created. A graphic tool, such as the subcoordination

[12] See, e.g., Sage [1977].

matrix described in Sage [1977], can then be used to establish the hierarchical levels of such objectives. Appropriate attributes are then assigned to each objective at the lowest level.

To illustrate, consider a planning model of water and land resources for the Maumee River Basin developed by Haimes et al. [1979]. The overall objective of such planning is to improve the quality of life in the region through water and land resources development. To accomplish this objective, according to the *Principles and Standards* for water and land resources planning set by the Water Resources Council, two (second-level) objectives were identified:

to enhance regional (national) economic development by increasing the value of the region's (nation's) output of goods and services and improving the regional (national) economic efficiency; and

to enhance the quality of the environment by the management, conservation, preservation, creation, restoration, and improvement of the quality of certain natural and cultural resources and ecological systems.

Toward fulfilling these objectives, the following more specific objectives are chosen:

to enhance water quality;

to reduce erosion, sedimentation, and phosphorus from nonpoint sources;

to enhance recreation opportunities;

to protect wildlife habitats;

to reduce flood damage;

to protect agricultural land and increase agricultural production; and

to minimize the cost of water and land resources management.

Figure 1.3 displays the hierarchical structure of these objectives and the attributes associated with objectives in the lowest (third) level.

The Proxy Attribute In many instances, the value of an attribute (or attributes) will give an obvious and direct indication of the degree of achieving an associated objective. For example, the attribute "net profit measured in terms of dollars" is a direct measurement of the degree of achieving the objective "maximizing profit." For some problems, it may be possible to formulate accurately the multiobjective decision problem in such a way that objectives and attributes are related only by direct relationships. This type of direct relationship between objectives and attributes is, indeed, what we would like to have. The idea of articulating objectives into hierarchical levels is, in fact, a way of achieving this goal. For each objective in the lowest level there should ideally exist an attribute (or a set of attributes) whose value is a direct measurement of the level of achieving that objective.

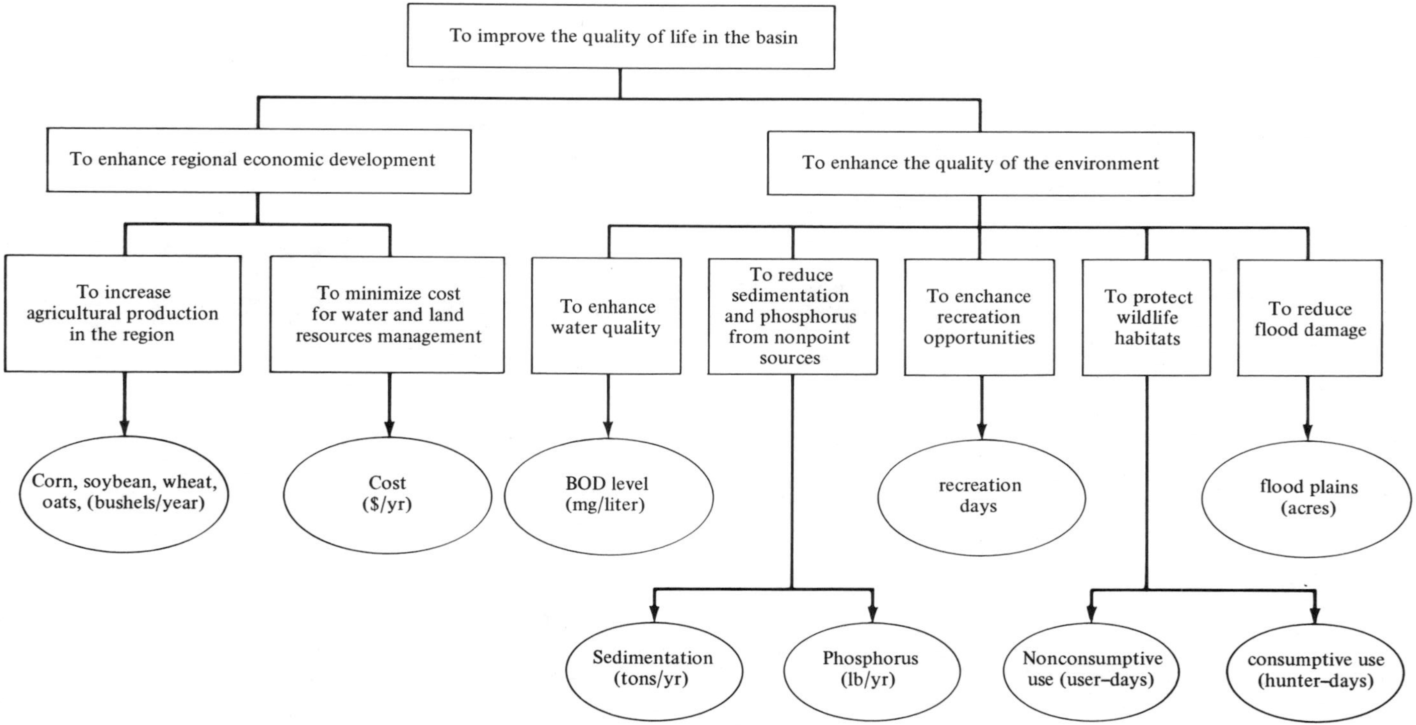

Figure 1.3 Hierarchical structure of objectives and attributes of a water-resources planning model. (1 recreation-day is a visit by one individual to a recreational development or area for recreational purposes during a reasonable portion or all of a 24-hr period. 1 user-day is the participation of one individual in the uses of a wildlife resource that do not reduce the supply, such as bird-watching or nature photography, during a reasonable portion or all of a 24-hr period—a proxy attribute.)

For some cases, however, there may be an objective (particularly if associated with ethics or values) for which there is no obvious attribute or set of attributes to measure the level of achievement directly. However, an attribute (or set of attributes) that is more convenient to measure and that indirectly reflects the level of achieving the objective may exist. Such an attribute is referred to by Keeney and Raiffa [1976] as a *proxy attribute*. Whenever an objective is indirectly measured by a proxy attribute, an indirect relationship is implied implicitly between such an objective and the corresponding proxy attribute. By indirect relationship we mean that an additional activity involving value judgment by the decision maker is needed to complete the final evaluation of the level of achievement for the objective in terms of the value of the proxy attribute. For example, one of the objectives of water-resources planning for a river basin given earlier reads, "to enhance recreation opportunities in the basin area." There is no obvious attribute (or set of attributes) for this objective. A common proxy attribute used for this objective is the number of *recreation-days*, where 1 recreation-day is defined as one visit by one individual to a recreational development or area for recreation purposes during a reasonable portion or all of a 24-hr period.[13] The implicit value judgment implied here is that the higher the number of recreation-days, the better the recreation opportunity in the basin.

The Properties of an Attribute To assign an attribute (or set of attributes) to a given objective, two properties should be satisfied, comprehensiveness and measurability. An attribute is *comprehensive* if its value is sufficiently indicative of the degree to which the objective is met. It is *measurable* if it is reasonably practical to assign a value in some scale to the attribute for a given alternative. Although both requirements are intuitively clear, the *scale* of measurement has in some quarters received less attention than it deserves.

An attribute may have a natural unit that can be measured in the so-called ratio scale. In such a case, we have complete freedom in performing any mathematical operation on the value of such attribute without destroying or distorting the information it contains. Because of such freedom and because of our familiarity with numbers and measurements in such a scale (particularly in engineering and natural sciences), there is a general tendency to create (in the modeling process) artificial attributes together with an artificial set of rules for measuring those (created) attributes in the ratio scale, hoping that, by doing so, existing sophisticated analytical tools can be utilized. Sometimes this is done without regard for practicality and reality. Much thought may be required to ensure that the proxy attributes reflect accurately the level of achieving the overall objectives. This step may

[13] See Great Lakes Basin Commission [1976].

involve "extreme subjectivity," the inaccuracy and uncertainty of which may lead to even greater skepticism regarding the final result.

Generally, there are other ways to treat this type of problem. An attribute does not always have to be measured in a ratio scale to be useful. Although an attribute measured in another scale[14] does not entertain the full spectrum of mathematical operations, thus limiting the application of some existing sophisticated techniques, other equally successful but less demanding techniques are available or may be developed. Measurement of attributes in other scales normally requires subjective evaluation, but since there are no artificially imposed conditions, these attributes usually have some practical meanings that the decision maker can relate to his experience and intuition so that he can perform this subjective task more easily and more meaningfully. Measurement will be discussed in further detail in Chapter 2. The fact that attributes can be measured in various scales and that there are various ways in which measurement can be carried out (e.g., direct calculation from a mathematical model or the use of subjective value judgment and mental models) is one factor responsible for the diversity of approaches in both theoretical and methodological developments involving multiobjective decision making.

The Properties of a Set of Attributes Just as an attribute assigned to a given objective should be comprehensive and measurable, a set of attributes representing the entire multiobjective decision problem should also possess some desirable properties. Keeney and Raiffa [1976] list five such properties: A set of attributes must be complete, operational, decomposable, nonredundant, and minimal. A set of attributes for a given multiobjective decision problem is *complete* if all pertinent aspects of the decision problem are represented by the attributes. It is *operational* if it can be utilized in some meaningful manner in the ensuing analysis. It is *decomposable* if simplification of the evaluation process is possible by disaggregating the decision problem into parts. It is *nonredundant* if no aspect of the decision problem is accounted for (by the attributes) more than once. Finally, it is *minimal* if there is no other complete set of attributes representing the same multiobjective decision problem with a smaller number of elements.

1.2.5 The Decision Situation

Fundamental to a multiobjective decision problem is a lucid description of the corresponding decision situation that defines the problem structure and the decision environment of the decision problem. To describe the decision situation, the boundary and the basic components of the decision problem

---

[14] For example an interval, ordinal, or even nominal scale. See Chapter 2 for greater detail.

must be clearly identified. In particular, a good description of a decision situation should clearly specify the type and amount of inputs needed and those which are available; the set of decision variables and the set of attributes, and the scales in which they are measured; the relationships among these variables and the means–ends relationships between decision variables and the attributes; the set of alternatives; and, finally, the states of the decision environment.

Structurally, both the (multiobjective) decision process and the decision situation can be viewed as a black box requiring some input information and producing a decision as one of its outputs. While the boundary and the type of inputs required for the former are fixed, the boundary and, hence, the type of inputs required for the latter varies and depends upon the nature of the problem. The smallest boundary that a decision situation can have coincides with the assessment and evaluation step (Figure 1.1) and contains an explicit list of alternatives, a set of attributes that also serve as decision variables, and a description of the state of nature. In this type of decision situation, the inputs required are those which can be used to compute the consequences (the values of the attributes) for each alternative for a given state of nature. In this case, the decision-making unit consists only of the decision maker himself. A newly married couple buying a house, a new graduate choosing from various job offers, and a handicapper deciding on which horse to bet are only a few typical examples of decision problems having this type of decision situation. At the other extreme, we may have a decision situation whose boundary embraces the whole problem-solving process as depicted in Figure 1.1. The corresponding decision problem is usually typified by

1. large numbers of decision variables with complex causal interrelationships;
2. complex means–ends relationships between decision variables and attributes or objectives; and
3. a set of alternatives that cannot be narrowed down to an explicit list and, thus, must be given implicitly in the form of causal and means–ends relationships.

A large amount of raw input data is normally required to calibrate the whole system. In that case, the decision-making unit consists of the decision maker and all man–machine units that are involved in the entire process. Designing parameters for large-scale engineering systems, planning water-resources systems, and planning regional or national economic development are some examples of decision problems of this nature.

The flexibility gained by describing the decision situation in this way makes it easier to compare different multiobjective techniques. Each technique is designed for a particular decision situation. Thus in searching for a suitable method for solving a certain multiobjective decision problem, we must first find out the type of decision situation that is most appropriate for that problem. For example, in buying a house, where the choices (houses) are explicit and the attributes (such as cost, location from work, neighborhood) are well known, multiobjective techniques that concentrate on measuring the decision maker's preference, such as the multiattribute utility function approach, should prove advantageous. On the other hand, in designing parameters for a large engineering system, a problem characterized by a large complex of decision variables and relationships, techniques that facilitate man–machine interaction may be more appropriate. While the nature of the decision situation determines the suitable multiobjective methodology, there is no formal guideline for choosing an appropriate decision situation for a particular decision problem. The design situation depends on the nature of the problem and on the experience, ingenuity, and judgment of all concerned.

1.2.6 The Decision Rule

In making a decision, one tries to choose the "best" available alternative. This implicitly implies ranking all available alternatives according to their performance or quality measured in terms of the values of all attributes selected for the multiobjective decision problem. A set of rules that facilitate a complete ranking of alternatives will be referred to as the *decision rule*. Part of the decision rule is often implied by the statements of objectives. The statement of objectives may even completely specify the decision rule. For example, in the classical theory of the firm, the decision problem consists of the single objective, "to maximize profit," and the attribute "net profit measured in terms of dollars" is used to measure the performance of a given alternative. The decision rule clearly implied in this case is, "Choose an alternative having the maximum possible profit." For some other decision problems, the decision rule needs to be explicitly stated apart from the statements of objectives. For example, in a water-quality model for a river, the single objective may read, "to improve the water quality of the river," and the attribute "BOD[15] level measured in mg/liter" is used to measure the performance of a given alternative. In this case, it is not clear from the statement of the objective itself how alternatives should be ranked. A decision rule that may be used for this purpose may read, "Choose any alternative with BOD level below 5 mg/liter."

In connection with the decision rule the concept of a goal is important. The goal of an attribute is the value of that particular attribute perceived as a standard of acceptability. A set of goals (one goal for each attribute in the

---

[15] BOD (biochemical oxygen demand) level of 1 mg/liter means that 1 mg of dissolved oxygen is used by microorganisms in the biochemical oxidation of the organic matter in 1 liter of water.

decision problem) furnishes a mechanism for ranking alternatives by means of partitioning the set of alternatives into a subset of "acceptable" attributes and a subset of "not acceptable" ones. A given alternative is, therefore, either acceptable or not acceptable. Thus, specification of goals in some decision problems is, in effect, an implicit specification of the decision rule.

The need for explicit specification of the decision rule becomes more apparent in multiobjective decision problems. For example, with reference to Figure 1.2, statements of objectives may read, "maximize each objective f_j, $1 \leq j \leq n$." (n is the number of attributes and is greater than 1 in a multiobjective decision problem.) It may happen that there exists an alternative having the highest possible value for each and every attribute $f_1, \ldots, f_n$. Thus, according to the statements of objectives (which form a part of the decision rule itself), that particular alternative (which is commonly associated with the concept of *dominance*) will be chosen and no further set of rules is required. However, so simple a case is rare. Application of the set of rules implied by the above statements of objectives generally leads, at best, to a set of Pareto-optimal[16] alternatives. A further set of rules is required to choose the "best" Pareto-optimal alternative. This may read "choose a Pareto-optimal alternative that best satisfies the decision maker." In this case, explicit consideration of the decision maker's preference becomes an integral part of the multiobjective problem solving.

How do various theoretical and methodological developments differ from one another? Part of the answer[17] lies in implicit assumptions about the decision rule itself. The goal-programming approach, for example, implicitly assumes the following decision rule (in the traditional version): "Given a set of goals and priorities on goals, choose an alternative having the minimum combined[18] deviation from the specified goals."

Thus, in order to select a suitable multiobjective decision technique for a given multiobjective decision problem, one must first determine whether the decision rule implied in a technique is suitable for that particular problem. This is a creative process and should be left to the ingenuity and experience of the decision maker and the decision analyst of the problem concerned.

In practice, decision rules fall roughly into two categories: the *optimizing* rule and the *satisficing*[19] rule. A decision rule in the optimizing category is a set of rules that orders all available alternatives into a *complete* ranking. In a

---

[16] This term will be defined more precisely later on. Roughly speaking, an alternative is said to be Pareto optimal (with respect to attributes $f_1, \ldots, f_n$) if there is no feasible alternative that will improve one attribute without degrading at least one other attribute.

[17] As we pointed out earlier, different forms of decision making units and decision situations and different scales of measurement for attributes all constitute parts of the answer.

[18] To be precise, this decision rule should also specify how individual "goal-performance" deviation should be combined to form a single indicator.

[19] The satisficing behavior of individuals was brought into focus by H. A. Simon [1960].

complete ordering, there is always a best alternative with respect to a certain criterion implied by a decision rule. On the other hand, a decision rule in the satisficing category is not ambitious. It merely seeks a "satisfactory" alternative in the sense specified in the satisficing rule, which sacrifices "optimality" in favor of simplicity and possible substantial savings in time and cost. Application of a satisficing rule leads to a partitioning of the set of all available alternatives into a manageable number of ordered subsets (e.g., two subsets labeled acceptable, unacceptable; or four subsets labeled good, acceptable, poor, unacceptable). Clearly, two alternatives from different subsets are always comparable in the sense that one can always be identified as "better" than the other according to the pertinent satisficing rule. On the other hand, two alternatives from the same subset are indistinguishable (or not comparable) by such a rule.

Further subdivisions of the above two categories of the decision rules also exist. For example, for a decision problem whose decision situation is embedded in the uncertain environment of an unknown probability distribution, the optimistic rule, the pessimistic rule, the Laplace or rationality rule, etc., are all possible candidates that can be chosen as a suitable optimizing decision rule for such a problem. In Chapter 2, when we review traditional decision analysis for a decision problem with a single objective and under uncertainty, we shall discuss these types of decision rules in more detail.

1.3 Symbolic Representation of the Multiobjective Decision Problem

We summarize the foregoing discussion in symbolic form and give a few examples: To describe a multiobjective decision problem (MDP), one needs to specify clearly

- the decision-making unit (DMU), one of whose components is the decision maker (DM);
- a set of objectives and its hierarchy (OBJ);
- an appropriate set of attributes (ATT) and complete objective–attribute relationships—if they are not obvious (OBJ–ATT);
- the decision situation (DS); and
- the decision rule (DR).

The output of an MDP is a decision. The inputs of an MDP consist of a trigger telling the DMU that a decision is required and the data required to complete a description of the DS. Figure 1.4 schematically illustrates a typical multiobjective decision problem.

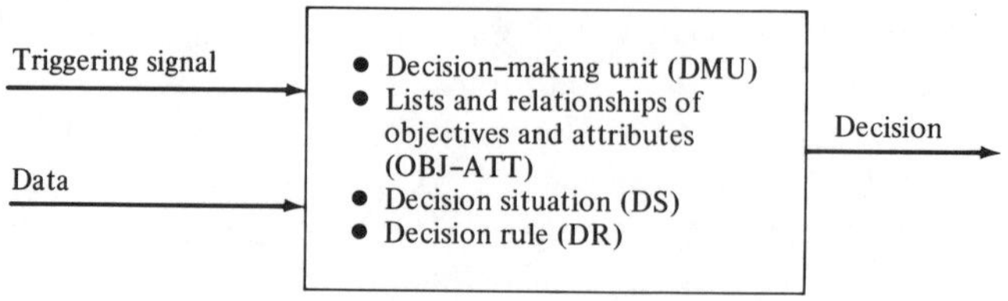

Figure 1.4 Typical multiobjective decision problem.

Essentially, to specify a DS, the following are needed:

the set of alternatives X, which is a set of N-dimensional vectors of decision variable $\mathbf{x}$ (an alternative is completely specified by specifying the value of $\mathbf{x}$);

$f_1(\mathbf{x}),\ldots,f_n(\mathbf{x})$, the set of rules by which the value of each attribute $f_1,\ldots,f_n$ is evaluated for a given alternative $\mathbf{x}$;

a description of the decision environment—certainty, uncertainty with known probability distribution (risk analysis), or uncertainty with an unknown probability distribution.

The specification of X may be explicit, as is the case when the DS covers only the analysis and evaluation step in the multiobjective decision-making process shown in Figure 1.1. It may also be in implicit form (i.e., in terms of causal relationships and constraints on available resources, etc.), as is normally the case when the DS covers both the system modeling and the analysis and evaluation steps. In the latter case, a more complex mathematical model is often used, and formal quantitative procedures, such as those of operations research and systems engineering, may be useful for a comprehensive analysis. These are the two types of DS most commonly treated in the literature.[20]

A multiobjective decision problem MDP may be written in a more operational form: Given the description of environment and the DMU, solve

$$\underset{\mathbf{x}\in X}{\mathrm{DR}}\left[f_1(\mathbf{x}),\ldots,f_n(\mathbf{x})\right], \tag{1.1}$$

where (1.1) is to be interpreted, "Apply the decision rule DR to choose the best alternative in X according to the values of attributes $f_1,\ldots,f_n$."

[20] There are a few techniques dealing with the DS that treat the problem-formulation, the system modeling, and the analysis and evaluation steps. One of these is the technique developed by the Water Resources Research Centers of the 13 Western States [1974] for dealing with water-resources planning. In this technique, the emphasis is placed upon the formulation of objectives in the problem-formulation step, i.e., articulating objectives and ranking them, and identifying appropriate attributes. Other, more general, techniques can be found in Sage [1977].

Table 1.1 A Typical Tabulated Attribute–Alternative Relation Required for Example 1

x	$f_1(x)$	$f_2(x)$	$\cdots$	$f_n(x)$
1	$f_1(1)$	$f_2(1)$	$\cdots$	$f_n(1)$
2	$f_1(2)$	$f_2(2)$	$\cdots$	$f_n(2)$
$\vdots$	$\vdots$	$\vdots$		$\vdots$
r	$f_1(r)$	$f_2(r)$	$\cdots$	$f_n(r)$

Example 1: Discrete MDP involving risk.

DMU: the DM only.

OBJ–ATT: $\{f_1,\ldots,f_n\}$—no proxy attributes.

DS (covering the analysis–evaluation step in Figure 1.1): A set of alternatives is explicitly specified as $X=\{1,2,3,\ldots,r\}$, where r is a positive integer. The decision variable x is an integer between 1 and r inclusive. The state of nature is uncertain but with known probability distribution. For a given x and the state of nature, the value of each f_j, $j=1,\ldots,n$, is obtained from a table such as Table 1.1.

DR: Step 1—Assume the existence of multiattribute utility function. Step 2—Choose an alternative having the maximum expected utility value.

NOTE: Step 2 could also be the pessimistic rule, the optimistic rule, the minimization of regret rule, etc., as will be discussed in Chapter 2.

Example 2: Discrete MDP under certainty and with a satisficing rule. In this type of MDP, the decision-making unit, the decision situation, and typical objective–attribute relationships are as specified in Example 1 except that the state of nature is now known with certainty.

A decision rule DR may read as follows: "Choose an alternative $\mathbf{x}$ which minimizes f_1 while maintaining the values $f_2,\ldots,f_n$ below a given standard $f_2^0,\ldots,f_n^0$." This is equivalent to solving an optimization problem of the form

$$\begin{aligned} &\min_{\mathbf{x}\in X} \quad f_1(\mathbf{x}) \\ &\text{subject to} \quad f_j(\mathbf{x})\leq f_j^0, \quad j=2,\ldots,n. \end{aligned} \tag{1.2}$$

An alternative DR for this example may read, "Choose any alternative $\mathbf{x}$ which has the values $f_1,\ldots,f_n$ below a given standard $f_1^0,\ldots,f_n^0$."

Both of these decision rules represent the satisficing behavior we mentioned earlier.

Example 3: Continuous MDP under certainty with an optimizing rule.

DMU: DR, analyst, and computers, if necessary.

OBJ–ATT: $\{f_1,\ldots,f_n\}$, no proxy attribute.

DS (covers modeling and analysis–evaluation steps): The set of alternatives is $X=\{\mathbf{x}|\mathbf{x}\in R^N,\ g_i(\mathbf{x})\leqslant 0,\ i=1,\ldots,m\}$, where the decision variable $\mathbf{x}$ is an N-dimensional vector in Euclidean space and $g_i(\ )$ is a real-valued function defined on R^N. For a given $\mathbf{x}$, the value of each attribute f_j, $j=1,\ldots,n$, is calculated from a real-valued function $f_j(\mathbf{x})$, $j=1,\ldots,n$. The state of nature is known with certainty.

DR: Step 1—First try to minimize each $f_1,\ldots,f_n$ individually. Step 2—If an alternative having the lowest possible value for each $f_1,\ldots,f_n$ exists, select that alternative. Step 3—If an alternative described in Step 2 does not exist, choose an alternative that is noninferior or Pareto-optimal and best satisfies the DM.

The application of Step 1 leads to the concept of noninferiority (or Pareto-optimum) and to vector-optimization theory. Specifically, the application of Step 1 is equivalent to solving a vector-optimization problem of the form

$$\min_{\mathbf{x}\in X}\left[f_1(\mathbf{x}),\ldots,f_n(\mathbf{x})\right]. \tag{1.3}$$

To solve (1.3) is to find the set of noninferior alternatives X^*. If X^* is a singleton, then Step 2 tells us to choose that particular element in X^* as the final decision. If X^* is not a singleton, which is normally the case, Step 3 must be applied.

Step 3 requires explicit treatment of the DM's structure of preference and, hence, is a process involving value judgments. In several multiobjective decision-making techniques to be discussed in this book (particularly interactive ones), major efforts are centered around this process. One approach is to modify Step 3 to read, "Assume that the DM's preference structure is characterized by a multiattribute utility function $u[f_1(\mathbf{x}),\ldots,f_n(\mathbf{x})]$. Choose a noninferior alternative that maximizes $u(\ )$." This is equivalent to solving

$$\max_{\mathbf{x}\in X^*} u\left[f_1(\mathbf{x}),\ldots,f_n(\mathbf{x})\right]. \tag{1.4}$$

A procedure can then be developed to solve (1.3) and (1.4) iteratively and interactively.

Example 4: Continuous MDP under certainty with a pseudo-optimizing rule.

In this example, DMU, OBJ–ATT, and DS are the same as in Example 3.

DR: Choose an alternative having the minimum combined deviation from the given goals $f_1^0,\ldots,f_n^0$; the priorities for each goal are $P_1,\ldots,P_n$ and the rule of combination is

$$\min_{\mathbf{x}\in X} \sum_{i=1}^{n} P_j | f_i - f_i^0 |. \tag{1.5}$$

This type of decision problem is known as the goal-programming problem.

1.4 Outline of the Book

The remaining chapters of this book present a variety of theories (Part I) and methodologies (Part II) that have been developed to deal with various types of multiobjective decision problems—including those described in Examples 1–4 of Section 1.3.

Chapter 2 presents a capsule review of selected background topics, which include the scale of measurement in measurement theory, (statistical) decision analysis, and selected topics in mathematical programming. This background material will provide added insight and understanding for subsequent chapters. We pointed out earlier that the scale of measurement for attributes (and for alternatives) plays a significant role in determining the kind of theories and techniques required for a particular multiobjective decision problem. Decision analysis [which is a formal technique for solving a decision problem in the form of Example 1, but with a single objective and a single attribute (i.e., $n=1$)] is reviewed here for two reasons: First, some of the multiobjective techniques to be discussed later on are extensions of decision analysis to the multiple objectives case; second, it provides a good opportunity to introduce some of the decision rules commonly found for MDPs in an uncertain environment. Selected topics on mathematical programming, particularly those related to the Kuhn–Tucker conditions for optimality and the so-called sensitivity theorem, are discussed here in preparation for the material to be presented in later chapters (most notably Chapter 4).

Of the existing theoretical developments, the most common fall roughly into two categories. First, there are those, most notably multiattribute utility theory, which attempt to formalize the DM's preference structure. These are discussed in Chapter 3. The second category concerns vector optimization and the concept of noninferiority which, as we have pointed out, may be pertinent when dealing with multiobjective decision problems of the form described in Example 3 of Section 1.3. Vector optimization theory is presented in Chapter 4.

Part II of the book focuses on the methodological aspects of multiobjective problem solving. The primary concern will be to translate the theoretical constructs described in Part I into operational procedures. Since there has been a proliferation of these procedures during the past two decades, a classification scheme is needed before they can be discussed and compared meaningfully. Previous efforts in developing such schemes have been numerous. We shall not discuss them until Part II, Chapter 9. Although there is no one universally accepted scheme, the most common criteria upon which most schemes are based are associated with the extent and the mechanics of the decision maker's involvement in the decision-making process. We believe that for a classification scheme to have significant practical implication such as furnishing a preliminary selection guide, it should be based on the following criteria:

1. the extent to which the decision maker is involved in the solution process;
2. the manner in which the decision maker is involved (e.g., direct questioning; noninteractive or interactive; prior to, during, or after the process);
3. the kind of information being given to and elicited from the decision maker;
4. the way in which information, particularly from the decision maker, is processed;
5. the number of decision makers involved; and
6. the problem structure (as discussed in the preceding sections).

With these criteria we could have developed an elaborate classification scheme, similar to that used by MacCrimmon [1973], and organized the material in this part of the book accordingly. Instead, we feel that a simple classification strategy based mainly on (6), which groups various methods into either outcome-oriented or process-oriented classes, is quite adequate as a preliminary classification scheme. Appropriate subcategorization in each class according to criteria (1)–(5) can then be carried out.

The organization of material in Part II is in accordance with the above simple preliminary two-class categorizations of multiobjective methodologies. Chapter 5 discusses available techniques designed to handle multiobjective decision problems of the form described in Example 1. These are characterized by explicit specification of the set of alternatives and uncertain environment. Since alternatives have already been explicitly given, these methods then concentrate on assessing the values of outcomes in the preference (or utility) scale and evaluating the resulting assessment in order to obtain a final decision. Chapters 6–8 describe various methods that fall into a group which can be characterized as process-oriented or mathematical-programming techniques in which the set of alternatives is implicitly specified in terms of resources-constraint equations. These methods are designed for multiobjective decision problems of the form given in either of Examples 3 and 4. The principal tasks in some of these techniques involve 1) identification of noninferior or feasible alternatives from the feasible set, and 2) using some kind of assessing and evaluating procedure to identify the best compromise alternative from those that are noninferior. In presenting

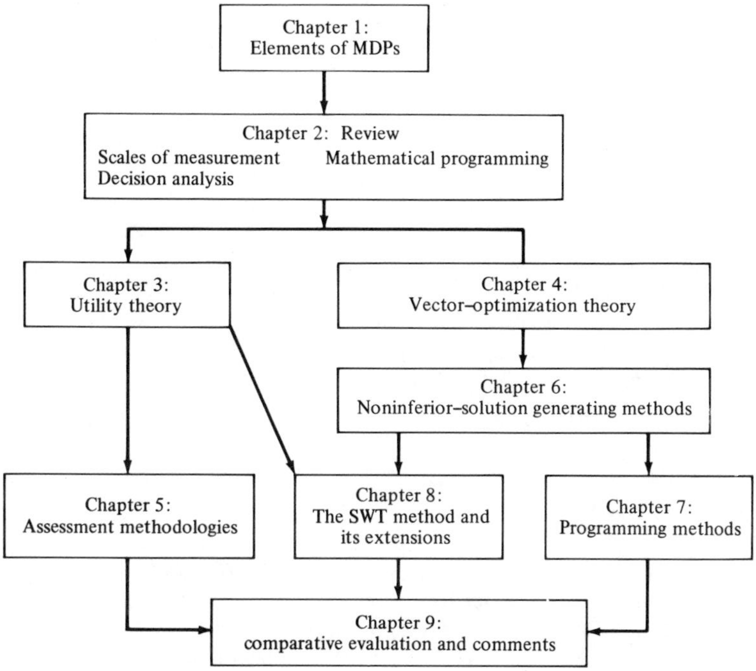

Figure 1.5 Interdependence of the chapters of this book.

these techniques, we shall follow a strategy similar to that used by Cohon [1978]. The generating techniques discussed in Chapter 6 focus on task 1 and leave task 2 to be done elsewhere. Chapter 7 presents a collection of techniques that attempt to complete both tasks in a variety of ways. The development of the surrogate-worth trade-off (SWT) method and its extension is presented in Chapter 8. The book closes with Chapter 9, in which the relative merits of different methods are considered based on several criteria for comparative evaluation. The interdependence of these chapters is illustrated in Figure 1.5.

References

Black, M., ed. (1975). *Problems of Choice and Decision*, proceedings of a colloquium in Aspen, Colorado, 24 June–6 July 1974, Cornell University Program on Science, Technology, and Society, Ithaca, New York.

Churchman, C. W. (1968). *The Systems Approach*, Dell, New York.

Cohon, J. L. (1978). *Multiobjective Programming and Planning*, Academic, New York.

Easton, A. (1973). *Complex Managerial Decisions Involving Multiple Objectives*, Wiley, New York.

Great Lakes Basin Commission (1976). Maumee River Basin Level-B Study: Alternative Plans for Public Action, January, Ser. No. 7.

Haimes, Y. Y., Das, P., and Sung, K. (1979). Level-B multiobjective planning for water and land, *Journal of the Water-Resources Planning and Management Division* 105, 385–401.

Harrison, E. F. (1975). *The Managerial Decision-Making Process*, Houghton Mifflin, Boston.

Keeney, R. L., and Raiffa, H. (1976). *Decisions with Multiple Objectives: Preferences and Value Tradeoffs*, Wiley, New York.

MacCrimmon, K. R. (1973). An overview of multiple-objective decision making, in *Multiple Criteria Decision Making* (J. L. Cochrane and M. Zeleny, eds.), University of South Carolina Press, Columbia, pp. 18–44.

Rigby, F. D. (1964). Heuristic analysis of decision situations, in *Human Judgements and Optimality* (M. W. Shelly II and G. L. Bryan, eds.), Wiley, New York.

Sage, A. P. (1977). *Methodology for Large-Scale Systems*, McGraw–Hill, New York.

Segev, E. (1976). Triggering the strategic decision-making process, *Management Decision* 14, 229–238.

Simon, H. A. (1960). *The New Science of Management Decision*, Harper and Row, New York.

The Technical Committee of the Water Resources Research Centers of the 13 Western States (1974). Water Resources Planning, Social Goals, and Indicators: Methodological Development and Empirical Test, PRWG 131-1, Utah Water Research Laboratory, Utah State University, Logan, Utah.

Chapter 2

Fundamentals: Selected Background Topics

In this chapter we give a brief account of three separate background topics. The purpose is to provide readers in brief with some basic concepts that help in understanding the theories and techniques of multiobjective decision making. These three topics are scales of measurement, elementary decision analysis, and optimality conditions in mathematical programming. Specific motivation for discussing these three topics has already been given in Section 1.4.

2.1 Scales of Measurement

Fundamental to all forms of scientific inquiry is the process of measurement. Through measurement a proposed scientific theory can be linked with empirical evidence so that scientific verification of the theory is possible. Without empirical import, a theory might be void of scientific value.

There are a number of definitions for the term *measurement*.[1] According to Stevens [1951, p. 22], "Measurement is the assignment of numerals to objectives or events according to rules of some kind... ." According to this definition, both objects and their properties can be measured.[2] The most common form of measuring objects is what is normally known as classification or identification. The number of each player on a football team (which is used for identification purposes) is an example of measurement of this type. Measurement of properties of objects is probably more familiar. Weight, height, and other physical statistics of each player are examples of measurement of properties of objects (players).

---

[1]Apart from Stevens's definition quoted here, other well-known definitions are those of Russell [1938, p. 176] and Campbell [1938, p. 126].

[2]Some prefer to restrict the use of the term "measurement" to the measurement of properties of objects only. See, e.g., Campbell [1938, p. 126] and Torgerson [1963].

2.1.1 Logical Foundation of the Theory of Scales

The primary purpose of measurement is to establish isomorphic relationships between the pertinent characteristics of the "things" we are measuring (whether they be properties of objects or the objects themselves) and the characteristics of the corresponding number system. By so doing, we hope to deduce relevant empirical properties of the "things" we are measuring from formal properties of the number system which we are using. For example, suppose we are interested in making comparison of lengths of three sticks, A, B, and C, which have been measured to be 12.2, 6.1, and 2.0 in. respectively. We can conclude that

1. B is longer than C and that A is longer than both B and C since $12.2>6.1>2.0$,
2. A is exactly twice as long as B since $12.2=2\times 6.1$ or $12.2/6.1=2$,
3. the difference in length between A and B is more than the difference in length between B and C since $12.2-6.1>6.1-2.0$, and
4. the combined length of B and C is still less than the length of A since $6.1+2<12.2$.

In the above example, lengths (of objects) are measured in real numbers. In fact, the real number system is one of the most familiar number systems utilized in measurement. It is also richest in structure. Under the usual arithmetic addition, multiplication, and allied operations, all common fundamental algebraic laws (such as closure, associativity, commutativity, the existence of a unique identity element and inverses, etc.) and the underlying axiom of choice hold very neatly in the real number system. However, not all quantities have the same wealth of properties and structure as the real numbers, even if they are designated by real numbers. For example, we may assign numbers 30, 20, and 15 to three football players P, Q, and R respectively. Although $30=2\times 15$, we cannot conclude that P has twice as much talent as R, nor can we say that the combined talent of Q and R is "better" than that of P—despite the fact that $20+15>30$. The only property of real numbers preserved in this type of designation is that P, Q, and R are different players with distinct "names" 30, 20, and 15.

Consider another example. Suppose that temperatures of three rooms X, Y, and Z, are 72°, 54°, and 36°F respectively. In this case, we can say that Y is cooler than X and that Z is cooler than both X and Y since $36<54<72$. We can also say that the difference in temperature between X and Y is the same as the difference in temperature between Y and Z. However, it is not meaningful to infer that X is twice as warm as Z just because $72/36=2$; nor does it make any sense to say that Y and Z combined are warmer than X because $68+36>72$.

What, then, are the factors determining these different restrictions? The answer lies in the fact that not all empirical characteristics of objects or properties of objects to be measured have isomorphic relationships with all of the formal properties of the real number system. Because of this, we are led to construct different scales of measurement for different types of quantities. To facilitate classifying different scales of measurement, we introduce the following concepts related to the number system which are important in the theory of measurement, namely: *identity*, *order*, *distance*, and *origin*.[3] We shall introduce these concepts informally[4] in the course of our discussions.

Let A be a collection of empirical elements. The set A can be a set of objects, or a set of *magnitudes* associated with measurable properties of objects, or a set of *quantities*[5] associated with measurable properties of objects.

There are four common scales that we can use to measure elements of A, namely *nominal*, *ordinal*, *interval*, and *ratio* scales.

2.1.2 Nominal Scales

The lowest form of measurement is the nominal scale. It involves the use of numbers or names for identification or classification purposes. To construct a nominal scale, one must specify a binary relation called the coincidence relation C which satisfies all of the identity axioms. These axioms are

1. the reflexive property (any element $x \in A$ must coincide with itself),
2. the symmetric property (if x coincides with y, then y coincides with x),
3. the transitive property (if x coincides with y and y coincides with z, then x coincides with z), and
4. the connected property (for any x and y in A, x either does or does not coincide with y).

With the existence of a coincidence relation, each element of A has its own *identity* to be distinguished from other elements. A classic coincidence relation is "$=$" defined in any number system. Numbers assigned players on a football team, or call numbers of books in a library, or even names of individuals are examples of measurements in nominal scales.

Although a real number may be used to represent a value measured in a nominal scale, permissible arithmetic and statistical operations are very

---

[3]We add the "identity" concept to Torgerson's list to accommodate the so-called nominal scale.

[4]A formal discussion of these concepts can be found in Luce and Suppes [1965].

[5]As Torgerson [1963] pointed out, the distinction between the terms "magnitude" and "quantity" should be made clear. According to Torgerson "a magnitude is a particular amount of a measurable property of an object and a quantity is a particular instance of a particular magnitude." For example, we talk about a measurable property of an object (e.g., a stick) called length. We can say that a stick has a length of magnitude 8 in. If two sticks P and Q both have the same magnitude of length 8 in., we can say that the quantity "8 in., which is the magnitude of length of stick P" is equal to the quantity "8 in., which is the magnitude of length of stick Q."

restricted. In fact, none of the arithmetic operations are meaningful, and only operations concerning modes and frequency counting are legitimate statistical operations on numbers in a nominal scale. However, nominal scales are the least restricted in terms of invariant mathematical transformation. In fact, any mathematical transformation in the permutation group, i.e., any one-to-one transformation, leaves the nominal scale invariant.

2.1.3 Ordinal Scales

We can enrich the structure of nominal scales by imposing an ordering relation. In addition to the coincidence relation C, which is used for *distinguishing* purposes, we can impose the precedence relation P, which compares two elements for *ordering* purposes. The relations C and P can be combined to form yet another binary relation, R. For any x and y in A, xRy if and only if x coincides with or precedes y. If R is reflexive, transitive, and connected, then R defines the so-called weak-ordering relation; we say elements in A are measured in a weak-order scale, which is one type of ordinal scale.

As an example, suppose we want to use integer numerals to name (or to measurefour different water-resources projects in terms of their priorities. We can define the relation C as "has the same priority as" and the relation P as "has a higher priority than." More compactly, the weak ordering relation R implied by C and P is read, "has at least the same priority as." We again observe that R is reflexive, transitive, and connected. The relation R will now be used in this measurement. Suppose that, of the four projects, two projects are of equal and highest priority. Using R, we assign the numeral 1 to the project with the lowest priority, the numeral 2 to the second lowest, and the numeral 3 to the two highest priority projects, thereby completing the measurements in an ordinal scale which arranges the four projects in an increasing priority order as 1, 2, 3, 3.

A variation of the weak-order scale is a strict-order scale in which P is transitive and connected. In this case, the relation P itself is called a strict-ordering relation, and an ordinal scale defined by P is called a strict-order scale. It is clear that two elements cannot have the same value (ties are not allowed) in a strict-order scale; hence, C is not required to define such a scale.

In the preceding example, suppose that we can further discriminate the two projects both originally labeled 3 and find that one project has in fact a higher priority. To the highest priority project we assign the numeral 4 to complete measurement in a strict-order scale 1, 2, 3, 4.

Other types of ordering relations will be discussed in Section 3.6.3.

An ordinal scale (whether weak or strict) may not have a natural origin (zero point) as in the foregoing example, although it may if one has specified the rule for a binary operation, assigning to each pair of elements in the set a distinct element in the set. As Torgerson [1963] noted, many of the scales of experimental esthetics, in which the order of the numbers corresponds to the order of pleasantness of a set of stimuli, are of this latter type.

As one may observe, the construction of an ordinal scale does not require specification of a binary operation for combining two elements. Not all basic arithmetic operations on measured values are permitted on an ordinal scale. In addition to modes and frequency counting (which are admissible operations for nominal scales, however), medians, percentiles, and order correlation are all permissible. Furthermore, any mathematical transformation in the "isotonic" group of monotonic functions leaves this scale invariant.

2.1.4 Interval Scales

The next step in strengthening the structure of the scale of measurement is to introduce the rule for combining two elements in the form of the "distance" binary operation $\circ$. Intuitively, for any two elements x and y in A, $x \circ y$ represents the distance or difference between x and y. A typical example of a distance operation in the set of real numbers is subtraction.

A scale constructed by introducing the distance operation $\circ$ and a (weak) ordering relation[6] R, weakly ordering both the elements in A and the differences of elements in A, is known as the *interval scale*. In the physical sciences measurements in interval scales (such as temperature) are normally carried out by derivative procedures, wherein a variable (or attribute) is measured in terms of its relation with other variables (e.g., temperature may be measured in terms of volume and pressure). In the psychological and social sciences, on the other hand, measurements (in interval scales) are normally based on the concept of the equal interval (distance), where quantities are measured at points of equal spacing. One important property of an interval scale to be observed is its *lack of natural origin*.

Although the interval scale has a zero element, the zero does not necessarily have the null property. A good example of this, again, is temperature. It is clear that 0°F and 0°C represent entirely different levels of temperature. As a result, the ratio of any two measured values in interval scales varies with the choice of scales. For example, the ratio 32°F/212°F is not the same as the ratio 0°C/100°C although 0°C and 32°F represent the same temperature, as do 212°F and 100°C.

The mathematical transformation that leaves the interval scale invariant is restricted to the linear form $y = ax + b$ where $a \neq 0$. Not all arithmetic operations are permitted for interval scales, but they are valid for the

[6]See Luce and Suppes [1965] for a precise set of axioms serving this purpose.

distances or differences if a "zero" can be set. The zero point of time, for example, is set by convention. As such, time measured in hours can be added and subtracted, even though time is actually an interval scale. The common statistical operations (including mode, frequency counting, median, percentile, order correlation, mean, standard deviation, product-moment skewness, and correlation) are meaningful for interval scales with the exception of coefficient of correlation, whose value depends on the location of the origin.

2.1.5 Ratio Scales

The most restrictive but most powerful scale of measurement is the ratio scale. Intuitively, it is an interval scale with natural origin. All arithmetic and statistical operations in a ratio scale are valid. Because a ratio scale has a natural origin, the ratio of two measurements remains unchanged if the scale is changed. The ratio of lengths 1 in. to 2 in. is equal to the ratio of lengths 2.54 cm. to 5.08 cm. The most general mathematical transformation that leaves the descriptive accuracy of the ratio scale unchanged is that of the form $y = ax$, where $a \neq 0$. This type of scale is most common in physical and other natural sciences but is quite rare in social sciences. Length, weight, and area are but a few examples of quantities that can be measured in ratio scales.

2.1.6 Multidimensional Scales

When several attributes of different types, such as those in multiobjective decision problems, are measured, various scales of measurement may be required. Multidimensional scaling deals with ways of combining measured values of different attributes to form a single index of measurement (e.g., by weighting or using distance functions). Since multidimensional scaling overlaps the study of multiobjective decision making, we shall be discussing it in more detail.

2.2 Elementary Decision Analysis

Decision analysis is a formal procedure to aid the decision maker in solving certain types of decision problems, where 1) the set of alternative actions is finite and prespecified, 2) only one attribute or objective function is to be optimized, and 3) the environment or state of nature is uncertain. After a decision problem has been properly defined, decision analysis entails

assessing the probability of each event (each possible state of nature);

assessing the value of the outcome in monetary or utility terms for each alternative and each possible event;

choosing a proper decision criterion;

formulating a payoff table (for single-stage decision problem) or a decision tree (for multistage decision problem); and

carrying out an appropriate optimization procedure to choose the best alternative action.

Apart from probability theory and utility theory, the underlying principles of decision analysis are based on common sense. While we assume that the reader is already familiar with the basic concepts of probability theory, utility theory (the formal study of the structure of the decision maker's preference) will be discussed in some detail in Chapter 3.

2.2.1 Model of the Decision Problem

We adopt the following standard form [Sage, 1977, p. 311] of a decision problem for decision analysis.[7] The decision maker is faced with

1. a set of r alternative actions $A=\{a_1, a_2,\ldots,a_r\}$;
2. a set of q states of nature $S=\{s_1, s_2,\ldots,s_q\}$ where s_i is usually treated as a random variable whose probability of occurrence $P(s_i)$ may be known;
3. a set of rq outcomes or results of his actions, which is denoted by an action–environment pair (a_i, s_j), i.e., $Q=\{(a_1, s_1),\ldots,(a_i, s_j),\ldots,(a_r, s_q)\}$;
4. a set of rq payoff values, which may be in terms of monetary values or utility, $U=\{u_{11},\ldots,u_{ij},\ldots,u_{rq}\}$, where $u_{ij}=\omega(a_i, s_j)$ and ω is the payoff function defined on the outcome set Q;
5. the decision criterion to be optimized, $f(a_j)$, where f is a real-valued function defined on A.

The decision maker is confronted with the problem of choosing an alternative action a_i that optimizes the decision criterion $f(a_j)$. An action a_i may be a simple and explicit alternative [such as choosing among several different projects $(1,2,3,\ldots,r)$] or it can be more complex (such as choosing a strategy, which is a rule for taking action based on the information about the environment). A state of nature s_j is an aggregate representation of all relevant uncontrollable (by the decision maker) factors surrounding the decision problem. A particular outcome (a_i, s_j) comprises controllable and uncontrollable parts and results from taking a particular action a_i (controllable) in a particular state of nature s_j (uncontrollable). A value or payoff for each outcome u_{ij} or $\omega(a_i, s_j)$ reflects the decision maker's preference for

---

[7]See also Anderson et al. [1977].

that particular outcome. More precisely, the payoff value is a measurement of the decision maker's preference for each outcome. This may be done subjectively or objectively and may be measured in either interval or ratio scales depending upon the nature of the alternative actions. A useful compact form of presenting A, S, Q, and U is the *payoff matrix*:

	s_1	s_2	$\cdots$	s_q
a_1	u_{11}	u_{12}	$\cdots$	u_{1q}
a_2	u_{21}	u_{22}	$\cdots$	u_{2q}
$\vdots$	$\vdots$	$\vdots$		$\vdots$
a_r	u_{r1}	u_{r2}	$\cdots$	u_{rq}

Finally, a decision rule for choosing the "best" available action is specified, in this case in terms of the decision criterion f to be optimized. There is a variety of common decision rules, which will be discussed in Section 2.2.4.

2.2.2 *Example: Developing a New Product*[8]

A company is considering launching a new product. The marketing manager of the company, after gathering and considering a considerable amount of data, projects that there is about a 75% chance that the demand for the product will increase by 20% from the current level within a one-year period and about 25% chance that the demand will fall by 5% from the current level within the same period. The managing director of the company is considering three possible alternative actions:

1. do nothing;
2. operate with the existing machines in the plant, but put employees on overtime; or
3. buy additional machines.

After possible levels of demand and responses to them have been identified, the accounting department of the company makes a thorough cost–benefit estimation for each option and each level of demand, yielding the following estimates of profits or payoff: If the level of demand actually rises at the projected rate, the profits for next year will be \$1.5, \$2.0, and \$2.1 million for options 1, 2, and 3, respectively. On the other hand, if the level of demand falls at the projected rate, the estimated profits for next year will be \$1.4, \$1.4, and \$1.0 million for options 1, 2 and 3, respectively.

What we have just described is the situation of a decision problem that is amenable to the decision-analysis procedure. In terms of our standard

[8] This example is inspired by the "Rev Counter" problem of Moore and Thomas [1976].

Table 2.1 Payoff Matrix for the Example

Action	Level of demand (millions of $)	
	s_1 [$P(s_1)=0.75$]	s_2 [$P(s_2)=0.25$]
a_1	1.5	1.4
a_2	2.0	1.4
a_3	2.1	1.0

terminology, this decision problem can be written in a compact form. For alternative action $A=\{a_1, a_2, a_3\}$, where a_1 denotes continue to operate as before, a_2 institute overtime, and a_3 buy additional machines; and states of nature $S=\{s_1, s_2\}$, where s_1 denotes the level of demand rises by 20% and s_2 the level of demand falls by 5%, we have the payoff matrix shown in Table 2.1.

If the philosophy of the company is to maximize profit, an appropriate decision rule that can be used is to maximize expected monetary value (EMV). That is, we shall choose a course of action which yields the maximum expected profit.

From the payoff matrix, the expected profit for option a_1 is

$$0.75\times 1.5+0.25\times 1.4=1.475,$$

for option a_2 is

$$0.75\times 2.0+0.25\times 1.4=1.85, \leftarrow \text{maximum}$$

and for option a_3 is

$$0.75\times 2.1+0.25\times 1.0=1.825.$$

Hence, according to the specified decision rule, the company would choose option a_2 (overtime), which yields the highest EMV. Several other commonly used decision rules could have been used, as will be discussed in a later section.

2.2.3 Types of Decision Problems

In the above example, it is implicitly assumed that the probability distributions of the states of nature can be completely determined either subjectively or from available data. In practice, the degree of difficulty in estimating such probabilities ranges from very trivial (e.g., in the case of certainty), to simple (e.g., tossing a coin or throwing a die), to complex (e.g., those probabilities which have to be determined subjectively), and finally, to so complex that it may not be worthwhile, or possible, to determine probabilities. The range of difficulty and the manner in which these probabilities are estimated lead to the following classification of decision problems for decision analysis.

Decision making under certainty corresponds to the case where it is known with certainty that one and only one of r states of nature occurs. In particular, that is the case in which $P(s_j)=1$ or 0 for all $j=1,\ldots,r$ and $\Sigma_{j=1}^{r}P(s_j)=1$, reducing the decision problem to a deterministic one. This is obviously a special case of the standard formulation given earlier. In the above example, if it is known for certain that the level of demand is going to rise at the projected rate, i.e., $P(s_1)=1$ and $P(s_2)=0$, the decision problem would reduce to

$$\max_{1\leqslant i\leqslant r} \quad u_{i1},$$

whose solution is a_3 (purchase additional machines).

Decision making under risk arises when it is possible to estimate the probability of occurrence of each state of nature $P(s_j)$ either subjectively or objectively. As the name implies, the risk can be quantified and analyzed explicitly, if we so desire. In many instances, the estimation of $P(s_j)$ for each s_j is carried out based on past data or on a purely subjective basis. During the decision-analysis process, additional information about the environment aimed at improving the original estimates of $P(s_j)$ may be available. The utility, cost, and procedures for synthesizing additional information in this manner are the subject of Bayesian decision analysis, and the updated probabilities so constructed are called a posteriori probabilities.

Decision making under uncertainty is a class of decision problems where it is not possible to estimate the probabilities of the states of nature. In such a problem, risk can no longer be quantified or analyzed explicitly, although the element of risk remains. The most common way of coping with risk in this case is through proper selection of decision rules. Some of these rules are of the risk-prone type while others may be of either the risk-aversion or the risk-neutral type. More will be said about these rules subsequently.

Decision making under conflict is a class of decision problems in an environment consisting of rational opponents with conflicting interest. In terms of the payoff matrix, each column represents a counter-strategy of one of the rational opponents. This type of decision making is studied in game theory.

2.2.4 Choosing a Decision Rule

As we mentioned in Chapter 1, an integral part of a decision problem of any kind is the statement of the decision rule. The choice of decision rules is not a trivial matter for it depends on the decision maker's attitude or the norms or policies of the governing organization. We present several common decision rules. Further discussion on how well these decision rules perform can be found in Luce and Raiffa [1957, pp. 286–298].

Decision Rules for Making Decisions Under Certainty In a payoff matrix with only one column, if each payoff value truly represents the decision maker's preference for the corresponding alternative, an obvious choice of decision rule would be to choose an alternative which maximizes the payoff. In other words, this decision problem under certainty becomes a simple optimization problem of the form

$$\max_{1 \leqslant i \leqslant r} \quad u_i,$$

where u_i is the payoff for alternative a_i.

In some instances, the number of available alternatives may be so numerous (or even infinite) that it is not possible to write out the payoff matrix completely. Consequently, direct search or complete enumeration, such as above, may not be possible; more advanced techniques, such as linear programming, branch and bound, and others may have to be used. In other instances, it may not be practical to perform an extensive search for the optimal alternative. A *satisficing* decision rule, in which we merely search for an alternative yielding the payoff above a prespecified threshold, would perhaps be more appropriate. Many individual decisions such as buying a house or looking for a job are of this type.

Decision Rules for Making Decisions Under Risk The most common decision rule for making decisions under risk is to maximize the expected payoff value. If the payoff is expressed in monetary terms, the corresponding decision rule would be to maximize the expected monetary value (EMV), which leads to

$$\max_{1 \leqslant i \leqslant r} \quad \sum_{j=1}^{q} P(s_j) u_{ij}.$$

In our example, the maximum-EMV decision rule leads to the selection of alternative a_2 (overtime), as we have shown earlier.

Instead of EMV, we may also use the *expected opportunity loss* (EOL), also known as *expected regret*, as our decision criterion. An opportunity loss (or regret) is defined as the loss incurred due to failure to select the best alternative available. One can easily convert the payoff table to a regret table by replacing each entry of the payoff table by $M_j - u_{ij}$, where $M_j = \max_{1 \leqslant i \leqslant r} u_{ij}$. Thus in our example, the corresponding regret table is shown in Table 2.2.

Using the minimization of EOL decision rule leads to the selection of a_2, which is the same as when maximizing EMV. It can be easily shown that the two rules just described are in fact equivalent. This can be easily seen from

Table 2.2 Regret Table for the Example

Action	Level of demand	
	$s_1\,[P(s_1)=0.75]$	$s_2\,[P(s_2)=0.25]$
a_1	0.6	0
a_2	0.1	0
a_3	0	0.4

the following identity:

$$\max_{1\leqslant i\leqslant r}\sum_{j=1}^{q}P(s_j)u_{ij}=\sum_{j=1}^{q}P(s_j)M_j+\min_{1\leqslant i\leqslant r}\left[-\sum_{j=1}^{q}P(s_j)u_{ij}\right]$$

$$=\min_{1\leqslant i\leqslant r}\left[\sum_{j=1}^{q}P(s_j)(M_j-u_{ij})\right].$$

The value judgment implied in using the EMV (or EOL) decision criterion would be that the higher the monetary payoff (or the lower the value of opportunity loss) we can expect, the better the alternative action. Note that utility is always assumed to be a monotonic function and that the attitude toward risk is invariant with respect to the size of the payoff. Such a premise is, however, frequently subjected to criticism since the element of risk is not considered. One effective way to incooperate risk in the analysis is through explicit quantification of risk.

To be specific, we define risk associated with choosing an alternative a_i as the probability that the actual payoff falls below a prespecified level β given that an alternative a_i is selected. Denote this probability by ρ_i. Clearly, ρ_i can be easily computed from the formula

$$\rho_i=\sum_{j\in J_i}P(s_j)\qquad\text{where}\quad J_i=\{j\,|\,1\leqslant j\leqslant n,\,u_{ij}\leqslant\beta\}.$$

By convention, $\rho_i=0$ if J_i is empty (i.e., all $u_{ij}\geqslant\beta$), in which case there is no risk that the payoff will fall below a given value if alternative a_i is chosen. The probability ρ_i can be computed for each alternative. We can then modify the EMV decision rule to read,"Choose any alternative that maximizes EMV and has ρ_i no greater than a prespecified risk level α," which solves the following problem:

$$\max_{1\leqslant i\leqslant r}\quad\sum_{j}P(s_j)u_{ij}$$

$$\text{subject to}\quad\rho_i\leqslant\alpha.$$

In our example, suppose we set the lower limit of payoff β to be \$1.2 million and the highest permissible level of risk at $\alpha = 0.20$. Clearly, alternative a_3 would not qualify, despite the fact that it has the highest possible payoff value, since $\rho_3 = 0.25 > \alpha$. Both a_1 and a_2 are possible candidates since $\rho_1 = \rho_2 = 0$. But EMV of a_2 is greater than that of a_1, which leads to the selection of a_2 according to the modified EMV decision rule.

A different way of treating risk is by means of another form of value judgment. In this approach, monetary values are replaced by *utility*, which measures the decision maker's preference in an interval scale. Using utility as a measure of reward or gain, the corresponding decision rule would be to maximize the expected value of utility (EVU). The rationale of this approach is that the same amount of money may be valued differently by different individuals under different circumstances. A classic example that will help illustrate this point is a simple coin-tossing game. Suppose B challenges A to play the following simple game. A fair coin is tossed once. If a head turns up, B will pay A \$400, and if tails turns up, A must pay B \$200. Should A play the game? If A is an EMVer, he should clearly play the game since EMV for playing is

$$\tfrac{1}{2}(\$400) + \tfrac{1}{2}(-\$200) = \$100,$$

which is greater than EMV for not playing (namely, zero). However, there is also a 50% chance that A will lose \$200. If A is a risk-conscious individual, then he would consider the value of \$200 against his financial status. If the loss of \$200 has minimal effect on his finances, then he would probably play the game. On the other hand, A may have only a small bank account, which he put aside for emergencies. He may want to avoid any risk of losing \$200, even with an EMV of \$100. The theoretical basis for representing preference by utility will be discussed in Chapter 3.

Decision Rules for Making Decisions Under Uncertainty When each $P(s_j)$ is unknown, it is not possible to use any of the maximization or minimization of expectation criteria nor is it possible to analyze risk explicitly. The following decision rules are common for this situation. They treat risk implicitly by reflecting the DM's attitude or intuitive feeling toward risk.

The pessimistic rule (*maximin* criterion) takes a pessimistic view of the environment: it assumes that no matter what alternative action a_i is selected, the worst situation for that alternative action will prevail. A natural cause of action would be to make sure that the largest possible payoff or utility under such circumstances is assured by maximizing the minimum payoff or utility (hence the name "maximin"). Thus we solve

$$\max_i \left(\min_j \ u_{ij} \right).$$

The pessimistic view and the maximin procedure reflect risk-aversion behavior of the decision maker. Applying the maximin rule to the payoff table

(Table 2.2) of our example, where $P(s_1)$ and $P(s_2)$ are now assumed to be unknown, yields the following:

$$a_1:\quad \min_j u_{1j} = 1.4, \leftarrow \text{maximum}$$

$$a_2:\quad \min_j u_{2j} = 1.4, \leftarrow \text{maximum}$$

$$a_3:\quad \min_j u_{3j} = 1.0.$$

Hence, $\max_i(\min_j u_{ij}) = 1.4$, which corresponds to either alternative a_1 or a_2.

The optimistic rule (*maximax* criterion), on the other extreme, takes an optimistic view of the environment: it assumes that whatever action is taken, the maximum possible payoff or utility will result. Under such an assumption, it is natural to maximize the maximum payoff, i.e.,

$$\max_i \left(\max_j \; u_{ij} \right).$$

This is obviously a risk-prone situation. Applying the optimistic rule to the example yields

$$a_1:\quad \max_j u_{1j} = 1.5,$$

$$a_2:\quad \max_j u_{2j} = 2.0,$$

$$a_3:\quad \max_j u_{3j} = 2.1. \leftarrow \text{maximum}$$

Hence, $\max_i(\max_j u_{ij}) = 2.1$, which corresponds to alternative a_3.

The Hurwitz rule (optimistic index-α criterion) compromises between the two extreme viewpoints through the use of the index α. The decision maker will express his degree of optimism by specifying the value of α between 0 and 1, forming a linear combination between the maximin and maximax criteria for each alternative a_i:

$$u_i(\alpha) = \alpha \min_j u_{ij} + (1-\alpha) \max_j u_{ij} \qquad (0 < \alpha < 1).$$

For a given value of α, the alternative yielding the maximum $u_i(\alpha)$ is then selected. That is, we solve

$$\max_i \quad u_i(\alpha).$$

Applying the Hurwitz rule to our example yields

$$a_1:\quad u_1(\alpha) = 1.4\alpha + 1.5(1-\alpha) = 1.5 - 0.1\alpha$$

$$a_2:\quad u_2(\alpha) = 1.4\alpha + 2.0(1-\alpha) = 2.0 - 0.6\alpha$$

$$a_3:\quad u_3(\alpha) = 1.0\alpha + 2.1(1-\alpha) = 2.1 - 1.1\alpha.$$

Hence, we would select a_2 if $0.2 \leqslant \alpha \leqslant 1$, but would select a_3 if $0 \leqslant \alpha \leqslant 0.2$. We would never select a_1 irrespective of the value of α.

The minimax regret rule is a variation of the pessimistic rule which takes opportunity loss or regret into account rather than gain or payoff. The maximum possible loss for a given action is assumed. It would be wise, therefore, to minimize the maximum opportunity loss in these circumstances. In other words, if $M_j = \max_i u_{ij}$, we solve

$$\min_i \left[\max_j \left(M_j - u_{ij} \right) \right].$$

Applying this rule to the regret table (Table 2.2) of the example again yields the selection of a_2, since

$$a_1: \quad \max_j \left(M_j - u_{ij} \right) = 0.6,$$

$$a_2: \quad \max_j \left(M_j - u_{2j} \right) = 0.1, \leftarrow \text{minimum}$$

$$a_3: \quad \max_j \left(M_j - u_{3j} \right) = 0.4.$$

Decision Rules for Decision Making Under Conflict As far as the payoff matrix and knowledge of the probability of each strategy of our rational opponent are concerned, the basic calculations for decision under conflict are quite similar to those under risk or uncertainty. Thus, the set of decision rules for decision making under conflict is the same as that listed above.

2.2.5 Decision Trees

Thus far the basic calculations have been simple. It is evident that the payoff table alone is an adequate graphic aid in such calculations. For complex problems involving *sequential decision making* under risk or conflict, a *decision tree* may be useful (Raiffa [1968]).

A decision tree consists of *decision nodes* and *outcome nodes*, *action branches* which emanate from the decision nodes, and *outcome branches* which emanate from outcome nodes. A decision tree always begins with an initial decision node and ends with outcome branches. A column of decision nodes signifies the beginning of the next stage of decision. Figure 2.1 depicts a typical two-stage decision tree. In a decision-tree diagram, a decision node is represented by a square and an outcome node by a circle.

To draw a decision tree, start with the initial decision node and draw as many action branches as there are available alternative actions in the first stage. At the end of each of these branches, assign an outcome node. From each of these outcome nodes, draw as many outcome branches as there are possible states of nature in the first stage. The probability of each corresponding stage of nature is then assigned to each outcome branch. A

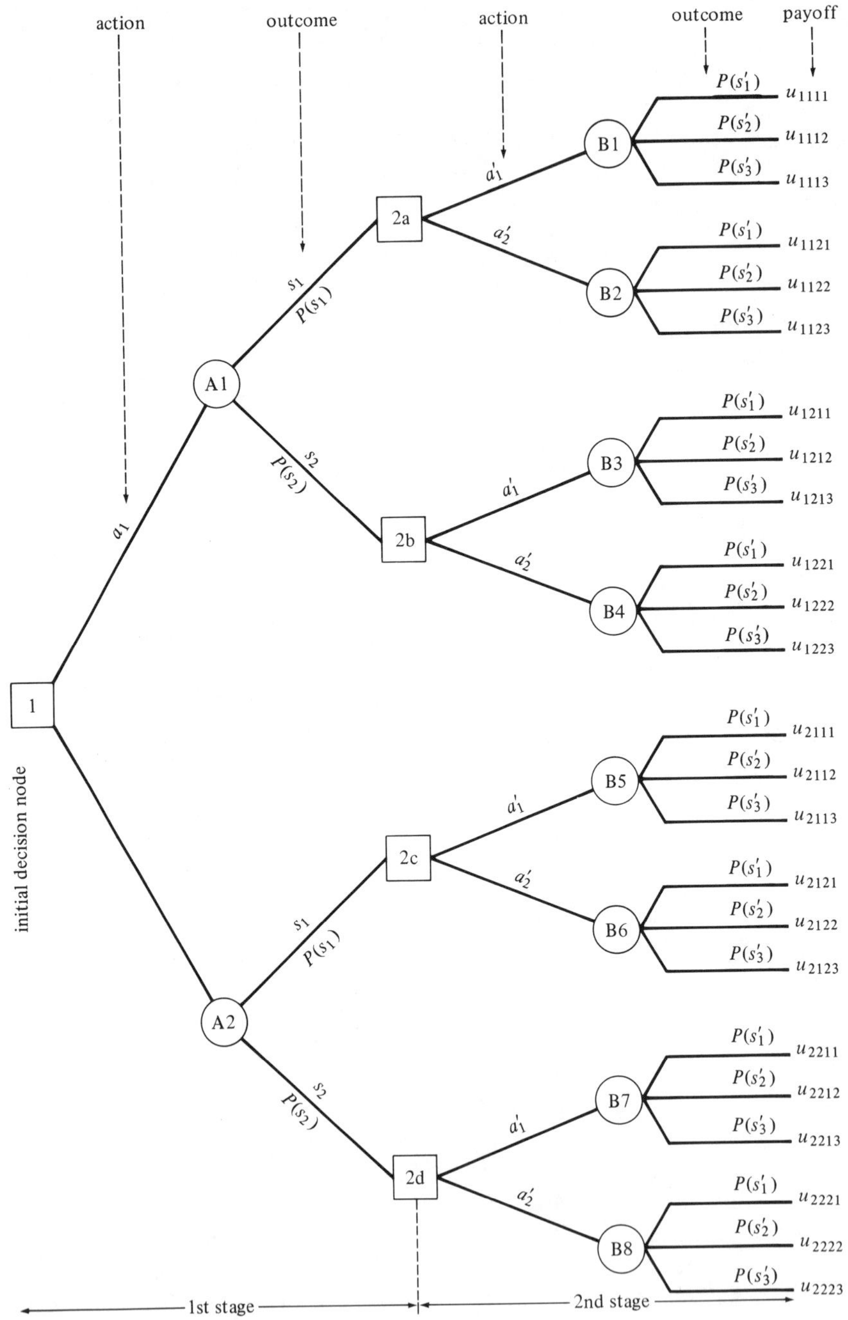

Figure 2.1 Typical two-stage decision tree.

decision node is also assigned at each outcome branch, to begin the next stage. The procedure just described is repeated at each decision node until the final stage. Finally, at the tip of each outcome branch in the final stage, assign the corresponding payoff or utility.

The decision tree of our new-product example in Section 2.2.2 is illustrated in Figure 2.2. We now demonstrate how to use a decision tree. In the above example, suppose that we want to use maximum EMV as our decision rule.

First we write at the tip of each outcome branch the corresponding payoff, which can be readily obtained from the payoff table. Then, at each outcome node, we compute and write the corresponding EMV that we can expect, should the action and preceding events lead to that outcome. For example, at the outcome node A1, which is at the end of the action branch a_1,

$$\text{EMV}(a_1) = 0.75 \times 1.5 + 0.25 \times 1.4 = 1.475.$$

Similar calculations can be made for nodes A2 and A3, and the corresponding results are shown in Figure 2.2. Finally, at the initial decision node 1, we look for an action leading to an outcome node having the maximum EMV, which is node A2 in this case.

The simplicity of this example does not permit illustration of the full potential of a decision tree as a graphic aid in decision analysis. We shall, therefore, extend the example of Section 2.2.2 a little further.

Suppose that the company now wants to plan not one but two years ahead. For convenience, we shall eliminate alternative a_1 (continue to operate at the existing level) from further considerations since it can be

Figure 2.2 One-stage decision tree of the example in Section 2.2.2.

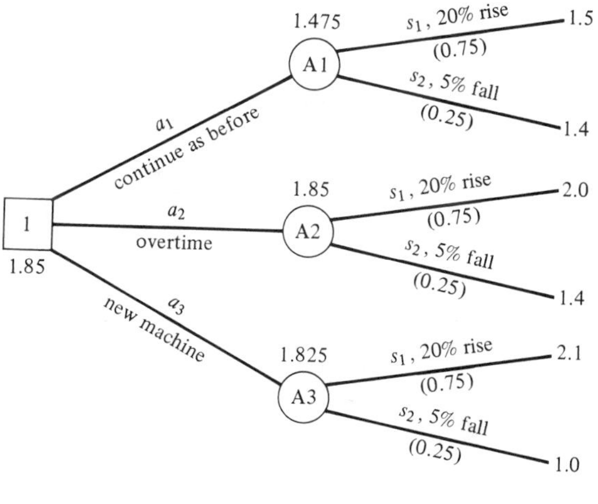

shown that it consistently produces inferior results to the other two alternatives. Suppose, furthermore, that it can be determined that there are three possible levels of demand in the second year: high, medium, and low. The probabilities of these three possible levels of demand are estimated to be 0.2, 0.7, and 0.1, respectively. The two-stage decision tree of this example is shown in Figure 2.3. Also shown in Figure 2.3 are the payoff possibilities in the second year for each possible action–outcome–action–outcome combination.

As one may observe, it is inconvenient, if not impossible, to write the payoff information in the form of a single payoff table for a multistage decision-analysis problem. The decision tree becomes the most convenient and useful means available for such a purpose. The steps in using a decision tree as a graphic tool in decision analysis are similar to those in backward dynamic programming. We start at the end of the tree and work backward to the initial decision node. This procedure is commonly known as *average out and fold back* procedure (see, e.g., Raiffa [1968]).

To illustrate, let us again use the maximum EMV as our decision rule. For decision node $2a$, the EMV values at outcome nodes B1 and B2 are, respectively,

$$\text{EMV(B1)} = 0.2\times4.8 + 0.7\times4.0 + 0.1\times3.5 = 4.11,$$
$$\text{EMV(B2)} = 0.2\times4.3 + 0.7\times4.2 + 0.1\times3.5 = 4.15.$$

Thus the maximum EMV at the decision node 2a is given by

$$\max\{\text{EMV(B1)}, \text{EMV(B2)}\} = 4.15.$$

Similar calculations at other decision nodes in the second stage can be carried out, yielding values as indicated in Figure 2.3. Having completed the second stage of calculations, we repeat similar calculations for the first stage, taking the EMV values at each decision node for the second stage as the (expected) payoff for the first stage. Figure 2.3 shows the completed decision tree for this example. It is clear from the decision tree that the best strategy for the company according to the maximum-EMV decision rule is to install new machines for the first year and institute the overtime alternative in the second year. The EMV for this strategy is seen to be maximum at \$3.975 million for the two-year planning period.

To summarize the main steps involved in decision analysis under risk or conflict using a decision tree and the average out and fold back procedure, we list the following steps, which follows Sage [1977, p. 312]:

1. draw the decision tree;
2. assign payoffs at the tip of outcome branches at the end of the decision tree;
3. assign probabilities at all outcome branches; and
4. carry out the average out and fold back procedure.

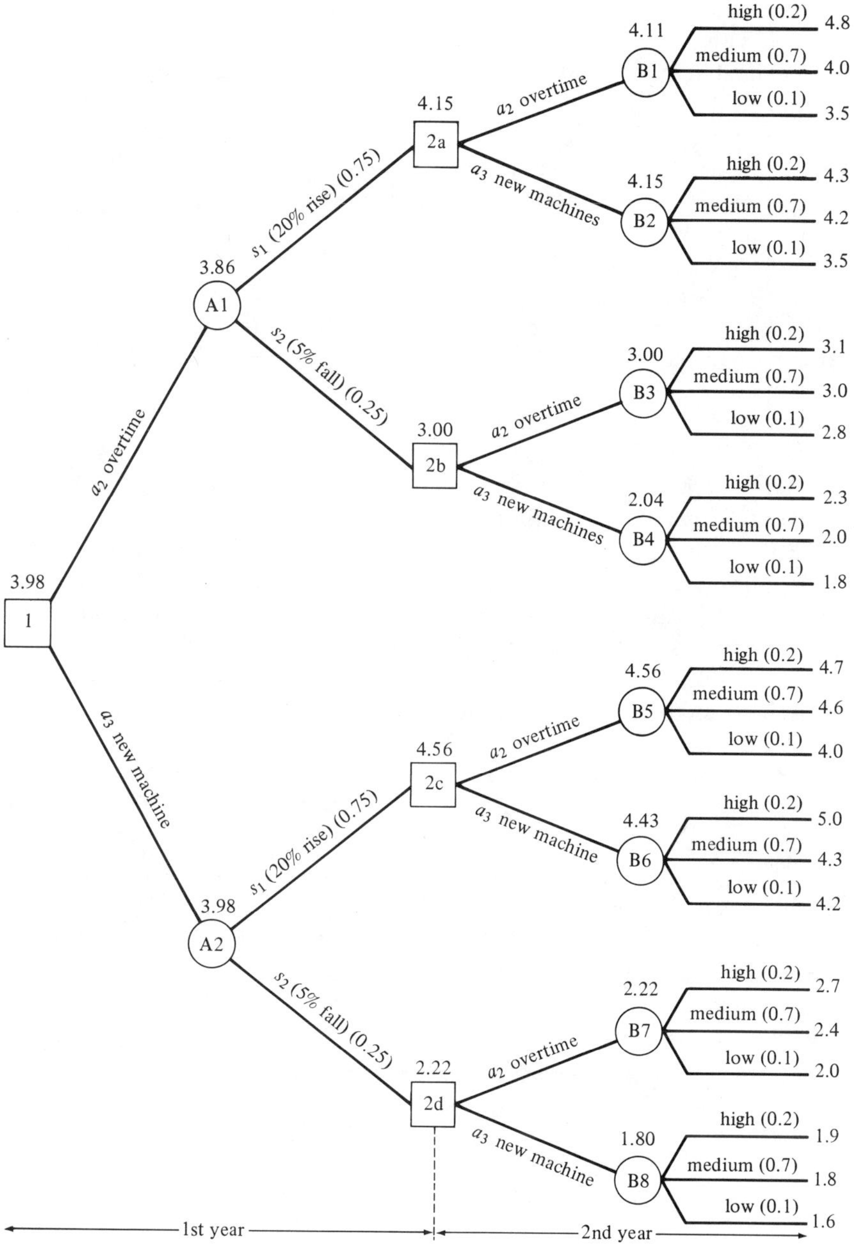

Figure 2.3 Decision tree of the extended example.

The calculation using a decision tree can also be carried out in a forward manner. This may be useful when not all probabilities are known, and they have to be determined subjectively. By proceeding in a forward manner (i.e., beginning at the initial decision node), these subjective determinations of probability may be deferred until the end, which avoids unnecessary potential errors and makes it easier to see the sensitivity of the solutions to probabilities. The complexity of the decision tree will grow to the unmanageable level very rapidly as the number of decision stages, alternative actions, and states of nature increase. To avoid writing out and making calculations for every possible node, procedures such as *branch and bound* or *probe forth* (Chen and Patton [1970]) may be utilized (hence saving cost and effort for collecting data). (For further detail see there or Sage [1977].)

2.2.6 Using Additional Information

The preceding calculating procedures (involving risk or conflict) use predetermined (*a priori*) probabilities of events, which may be obtained either subjectively or from past data. During the course of calculation, additional information may become available and this information may be useful in updating the values of a priori probabilities. The adjusted probability incorporating new information is called *a posteriori probability*.

The underlying statistical concept for synthesizing additional information in decision analysis is known as Bayes's theorem. The study in this area is called "Bayesian decision analysis."

Suppose that there is a certain random activity V whose outcome will affect the probability of occurrence of the state of nature in a decision problem. Suppose further that there are l possible outcomes of this activity denoted $v_1,\ldots,v_k,\ldots,v_l$. The probability of each outcome v_k is also known and is denoted $P(v_k)$. Thus the probability that s_j is the state of nature given that event $V=v_k$ has already occurred is given by Bayes's formula:

$$P(s_j|V=v_k)=P(s_j)P(v_k|s_j)/P(v_k),$$

where:

$P(s_j)$	is the a priori probability of event s_j;
$P(s_j\|V=v_k)$	is the a posteriori probability of event s_j knowing that the event $V=v_k$ has already occurred;
$P(v_k\|s_j)$	is the conditional probability of event $V=v_k$, given that the event s_j has already occurred; and
$P(v_k)$	is, as defined earlier, the probability of event $V=v_k$ and can be computed from $P(v_k\|s_j)$ and $P(s_j)$ by the formula

$$P(v_k)=\sum_{j=1}^{q} P(s_j)P(v_k|s_j).$$

The role of a posteriori probabilities in decision analysis is the same as that of a priori probabilities. Using the former, however, usually leads to a decision with higher EMV (or EVU) than might be expected had the additional information not been utilized. If extra information can be easily obtained without cost, then there is no reason not to obtain such information and incorporate it in the analysis. In practice, however, obtaining information incurs a cost. One must therefore make a trade-off between the cost incurred and the increase in EMV.

A useful quantity for evaluating the value of information is the *expected value of sample information* (EVSI), which is defined as the difference in optimal EMV (or EVU or EOL) between using and not using the extra information. Clearly if EVSI <0, the information is not worth obtaining. A more useful quantity is the so-called expected net gain of sampling information (ENGSI), which is defined as

$$\text{ENGSI} = \text{EVSI} - (\text{cost of information}).$$

The sampling information would be worth obtaining if and only if ENGSI >0 and vice versa.

To illustrate calculations involving the value of information, we extend the "new-product" example further.

Suppose that the company acquires a service of an outside consulting company for a fee of $15,000 to do a thorough research on the next year's market condition for the new product. The consultant is to report whether the market will be favorable or unfavorable. In judging the reliability of the consultant's report, the marketing manager feels that the consultant is 90% reliable. More precisely, if the level of demand for next year actually rises, there is 90% chance that the consultant will report correctly (i.e., favorable conditions) and 10% chance that the consultant will report unfavorable conditions. On the other hand, if the level of next year's demand actually falls, there is a 90% chance that the consultant will report unfavorable conditions and 10% chance that the consultant will report favorable conditions.

We use this information to see how it would affect the decision for a one-year period. Let F denote the event that the consultant will report favorable market conditions and U denote the event that the consultant will report unfavorable market conditions. Thus the probability that the consultant will report favorable market conditions is

$$\begin{aligned} P(F) &= P(F|s_1)P(s_1) + P(F|s_2)P(s_2) \\ &= 0.9\times 0.75 + 0.1\times 0.25 = 0.7, \end{aligned}$$

and the probability that the consultant will report unfavorable conditions of the market is

$$\begin{aligned} P(U) &= P(U|s_1)P(s_1) + P(U|s_2)P(s_2) \\ &= 0.1\times 0.75 + 0.9\times 0.25 = 0.3. \end{aligned}$$

Using Bayes's formula, we can now compute the following a posteriori probabilities. The probability that the level of demand will rise by 20% next year given that the consultant reports favorable condition is

$$\begin{aligned} P(s_1|F) &= P(F|s_1)P(s_1)/P(F) \\ &= 0.9\times 0.75/0.7 = 0.964. \end{aligned}$$

Likewise

$$\begin{aligned} P(s_2|F) &= P(F|s_2)P(s_2)/P(F) \\ &= 0.1\times 0.25/0.7 = 0.036, \\ P(s_1|U) &= P(U|s_1)P(s_1)/P(U) \\ &= 0.1\times 0.75/0.3 = 0.25, \end{aligned}$$

and

$$\begin{aligned} P(s_2|U) &= P(U|s_2)P(s_2)/P(U) \\ &= 0.9\times 0.25/0.3 = 0.75. \end{aligned}$$

We now draw a decision tree, as shown in Figure 2.4. From the decision tree the following conclusions are evident.

1. With new information, the optimal strategy for the one-year period would be to purchase new machines. The optimal EMV before the consulting fee (or sampling cost) is \$1.907 million and the net optimal EMV after the consulting fee is \$1.895 million.
2. The expected value of sampling information EVSI $= 1.907 - 1.85 =$ \$0.057 million.
3. The expected net gain of sampling information ENGSI $= 1.892 - 1.85$ $=$ \$0.042 million.

Another concept useful for analyzing the value of information is that of the *expected value of perfect information* (EVPI), which reflects the maximum expected worth of sampling information. If we know for certain that event s_j will occur, it would be natural to choose an alternative a_i such that the payoff u_{ij} is maximum. Based on this philosophy, the expected payoff under perfect information would be

$$\sum_{j=1}^{q} P(s_j)\left(\max_i u_{ij}\right).$$

EVPI is then defined as the difference between the expected payoff under perfect information as defined above and the optimal expected payoff without sampling information. From our example:

$$\begin{aligned} \text{EVPI} &= [P(s_1)u_{31} + P(s_2)u_{12}] - \text{EMV(without information)} \\ &= 0.75\times 2.1 + 0.25\times 1.4 - 1.85 \\ &= 0.075. \end{aligned}$$

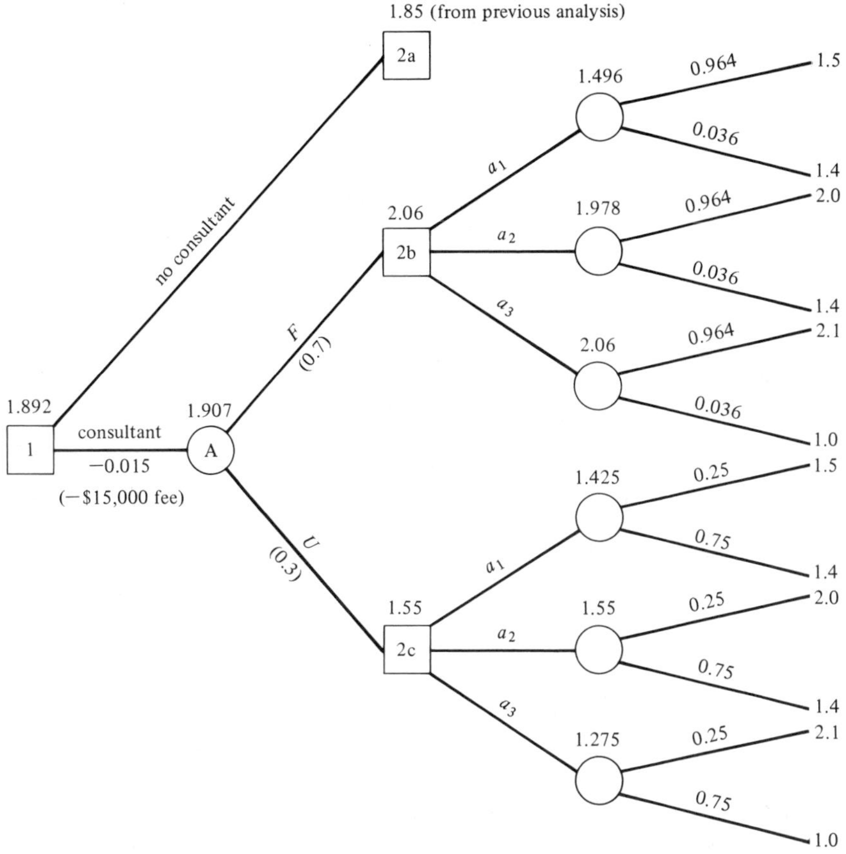

Figure 2.4 Decision tree of the example, with consultation added.

Thus the expected worth of sampling information can be at most \$0.075 million in this example.

2.3 Optimality Conditions in Mathematical Programming

Mathematical programming seeks to select values for finite-dimensional decision variables that minimize an objective function subject to a set of constraints. In particular, mathematical programming typically is concerned with solving an optimization problem of the form[9]

$$\begin{aligned} &\min \quad f(\mathbf{x}) \\ &\text{subject to} \quad \mathbf{x} \in X, \end{aligned} \tag{2.1}$$

[9]Note that all other mathematical models can be converted to the form described in (2.1).

where $\mathbf{x}$ is an N-vector of decision variables, f is a real-valued function of $\mathbf{x}$, and X is a feasible set, defined as

$$X \triangleq \{\mathbf{x} | \mathbf{x} \in R^N, h_i(\mathbf{x}) = 0, i = 1, \ldots, l, g_j(\mathbf{x}) \leq 0, j = 1, \ldots, m\},$$

where h_i and g_j are real-valued functions defined on X.

Solving (2.1) involves finding $\mathbf{x}^* \in X$ such that

$$f(\mathbf{x}^*) \leq f(\mathbf{x}) \qquad \text{for all} \quad \mathbf{x} \in X. \tag{2.2}$$

The point $\mathbf{x}^*$ is said to be a *global optimum* (minimum) of (2.1). If strict inequality holds in (2.2), $\mathbf{x}^*$ is the *unique* global optimum of (2.1). If (2.2) holds only for some neighborhood of $\mathbf{x}^*$, then $\mathbf{x}^*$ is a *local* or *relative optimum* (minimum) of (2.1), while it is *strict local optimum* if strict inequality holds in (2.2) in a neighborhood of $\mathbf{x}^*$. It is well-known that if X is a convex set and f is a convex function on X, then every local minimum of (2.1) is also a global minimum of (2.1).[10]

When $X = R^N$, i.e., when there is no constraint on $\mathbf{x}$, (2.1) becomes an unconstrained optimization problem. A useful special form of (2.1) is when f, h_i, and g_j are linear, whereby the model becomes a linear programming model. A typical linear programming model is of the form

$$\begin{aligned} &\min \quad \mathbf{cx} \\ &\text{subject to} \qquad A\mathbf{x} \geq \mathbf{b}, \quad \mathbf{x} \geq \mathbf{0}, \end{aligned} \tag{2.3}$$

where $\mathbf{c}$ is an N-vector of cost coefficients, A is an $m \times n$-coefficient matrix of constraints, and $\mathbf{b}$ is an m-vector of resource availability.

It is beyond the scope of this book to discuss all theoretical and methodological aspects in mathematical programming. We shall focus on optimality conditions of (2.1) in which f and all g_j and h_i are twice continuously differentiable with respect to $\mathbf{x}$. We review, without formally proving, the following relations and definitions in vector calculus and matrix algebra.

The *gradient* at $\mathbf{x}^0$ of a scalar function f defined on a subset of R^N, is the row vector $(\partial f(\mathbf{x}^0)/\partial x_1, \ldots, \partial f(\mathbf{x}^0)/\partial x_N)$, which is denoted $\nabla f(\mathbf{x}^0)$. Furthermore, we use $\nabla^2 f(\mathbf{x}^0)$ to denote the *Hessian matrix* of f at $\mathbf{x}^0$, i.e.,

$$\nabla^2 f(\mathbf{x}^0) \triangleq \begin{bmatrix} \dfrac{\partial^2 f(\mathbf{x}^0)}{\partial x_1^2} & \dfrac{\partial^2 f(\mathbf{x}^0)}{\partial x_1 \partial x_2} & \cdots & \dfrac{\partial^2 f(\mathbf{x}^0)}{\partial x_1 \partial x_N} \\ \dfrac{\partial^2 f(\mathbf{x}^0)}{\partial x_2 \partial x_1} & \dfrac{\partial^2 f(\mathbf{x}^0)}{\partial x_2^2} & \cdots & \dfrac{\partial^2 f(\mathbf{x}^0)}{\partial x_2 \partial x_N} \\ \vdots & \vdots & & \vdots \\ \dfrac{\partial^2 f(\mathbf{x}^0)}{\partial x_N \partial x_1} & \dfrac{\partial^2 f(\mathbf{x}^0)}{\partial x_N \partial x_2} & \cdots & \dfrac{\partial^2 f(\mathbf{x}^0)}{\partial x_N^2} \end{bmatrix}.$$

[10] See, e.g., Lasdon [1970, p. 69] or Luenberger [1973, p. 119].

For any vector-valued function $\mathbf{g}(\mathbf{x})=[g_1(\mathbf{x}),\ldots,g_m(\mathbf{x})]^{\mathrm{T}}$, the *Jacobian matrix* of $\mathbf{g}(\ )$ at $\mathbf{x}^0$ is written as the following $m \times n$ matrix:

$$\begin{bmatrix} \dfrac{\partial g_1(\mathbf{x}^0)}{\partial x_1} & \dfrac{\partial g_1(\mathbf{x}^0)}{\partial x_2} & \cdots & \dfrac{\partial g_1(\mathbf{x}^0)}{\partial x_N} \\ \vdots & \vdots & & \vdots \\ \dfrac{\partial g_m(\mathbf{x}^0)}{\partial x_1} & \dfrac{\partial g_m(\mathbf{x}^0)}{\partial x_2} & \cdots & \dfrac{\partial g_m(\mathbf{x}^0)}{\partial x_N} \end{bmatrix}.$$

An $m \times n$ matrix P, where $m \leqslant n$, is said to have a *rank* $r \leqslant m$ if there are at most r rows of P that are linearly independent. An $m \times m$ square matrix Q is *real symmetric* if each element of Q is real and the matrix is identical to its transpose. A real symmetric matrix Q is *positive semidefinite*, *positive definite*, *negative semidefinite*, or *negative definite* if for all $\mathbf{y} \in R^m$ the quadratic form $\mathbf{y}^{\mathrm{T}} Q \mathbf{y} \geqslant 0$, >0, $\leqslant 0$, and <0, respectively. Finally Q is said to be *indefinite* if $\mathbf{y}^{\mathrm{T}} Q \mathbf{y} > 0$ for some $\mathbf{y} \in R^m$ and $\mathbf{y}^{\mathrm{T}} Q \mathbf{y} < 0$ for some $\mathbf{y} \in R^m$.

2.3.1 Unconstrained Optimization

When $X = R^N$, (2.1) becomes an unconstrained minimization problem of the form

$$\min_{\mathbf{x} \in R^N} \quad f(\mathbf{x}). \tag{2.4}$$

To solve (2.4), assuming twice continuous differentiability of f, compare the procedure for finding maxima and minima in elementary calculus. To find a local minimum x^* of $f(x)$ in a univariate case, where $x \in R$ (set of real numbers),

$$\frac{df(x^*)}{dx} = 0 \tag{2.5}$$

must be satisfied. Moreover, x^* must also satisfy

$$\frac{d^2 f(x^*)}{dx^2} \geqslant 0. \tag{2.6}$$

Finally, to ensure that x^* is truly a local minimum of f, strict inequality must hold in (2.6). This corresponds to the second-order sufficiency conditions for univariate problems.

Generalization to the multivariate case follows.

Necessary Conditions for Optimality of the Unconstrained Case.[11] *For* $\mathbf{x}^*$ *to be a local minimum of* (2.4), *the following conditions are necessary*:

$$\nabla f(\mathbf{x}^*) = 0; \qquad i.e., \quad \frac{\partial f(\mathbf{x}^*)}{\partial x_i} = 0 \quad \textit{for all } i = 1,\ldots,N. \tag{2.7}$$

---

[11] For a detailed proof of these results see, e.g., Luenberger [1973], Hadley [1964], Zangwill [1969], or Bazaraa and Shelty [1979]. See also Haimes [1977].

$$\nabla^2 f(\mathbf{x}^*) \quad \textit{is a positive semidefinite matrix.} \tag{2.8}$$

Sufficient Conditions for Optimality of the Unconstrained Case. *A point* $\mathbf{x}^*$ *will be a local minimum of* (2.4) *if*

$$\nabla f(\mathbf{x}^*) = 0, \tag{2.9}$$

$$\nabla^2 f(\mathbf{x}^*) \quad \textit{is a positive definite matrix.} \tag{2.10}$$

It can be shown that f is (strictly) convex on a convex set X if and only if $\nabla^2 f(\mathbf{x})$ is positive (definite) semidefinite for all $\mathbf{x} \in X$ (Luenberger [1973, p. 118]).

2.3.2 Equality-Constrained Optimization

The simplest extension of an unconstrained optimization problem is an optimization problem with equality constraints of the form

$$\begin{aligned} &\min \quad f(\mathbf{x}) \\ &\text{subject to} \qquad h_i(\mathbf{x}) = 0, \quad i = 1, \ldots, l. \end{aligned} \tag{2.11}$$

To solve (2.10), assume that there exist Lagrange multipliers $\lambda_1, \ldots, \lambda_l$, or, for short $\boldsymbol{\lambda} = (\lambda_1, \ldots, \lambda_l)^{\mathrm{T}} \in R^l$, which permit the conversion of the constrained problem in (2.11) to an unconstrained problem. This is done by formulating the Lagrangian function $L(\mathbf{x}, \boldsymbol{\lambda})$ of (2.11), where

$$L(\mathbf{x}, \boldsymbol{\lambda}) = f(\mathbf{x}) + \sum_{i=1}^{l} \lambda_i h_i(\mathbf{x}),$$

and solving

$$\begin{aligned} &\min \quad L(\mathbf{x}, \boldsymbol{\lambda}) \\ &\text{subject to} \qquad \mathbf{x} \in R^N \quad \text{and} \quad \boldsymbol{\lambda} \in R^l. \end{aligned} \tag{2.12}$$

Solving (2.12) will also yield a solution to (2.11), as can be easily shown by observing that for any $\mathbf{x}$ satisfying $h_i(\mathbf{x}) = 0$, $i = 1, \ldots, m$, we have

$$\sum_{i=1}^{l} \lambda_i^* h_i(\mathbf{x}^*) = \sum_{i=1}^{l} \lambda_i^* h_i(\mathbf{x}) = 0, \tag{2.13}$$

where $(\mathbf{x}^*, \boldsymbol{\lambda}^*)$ solves (2.12). Since $(\mathbf{x}^*, \boldsymbol{\lambda}^*)$ solves (2.12), we have, for all $\mathbf{x}$ satisfying $h_i(\mathbf{x}) = 0$, $i = 1, \ldots, m$:

$$f(\mathbf{x}^*) + \sum_{i=1}^{l} \lambda_i^* h_i(x^*) \leqslant f(\mathbf{x}) + \sum_{i=1}^{l} \lambda_i^* h_i(\mathbf{x}).$$

Applying (2.13) yields $f(\mathbf{x}^*) \leqslant f(\mathbf{x})$ for all $\mathbf{x}$ satisfying $h_i(\mathbf{x}) = 0$, $i = 1, \ldots, m$, which indicates that $\mathbf{x}^*$ solves (2.11).

Thus, if the assumption concerning the existence of optimal Lagrange multipliers holds true, the necessary and sufficient conditions for equality constraints can easily be derived from those in the unconstrained case. The assumption still cannot be directly verified. We seek, therefore, a more operational assumption, one that is verifiable in practice. A *constraint qualification* is a set of verifiable assumptions about the constraint set that permits the verification of the assumption concerning the existence of multipliers in constrained optimization problems.

There are several types of constraint qualifications, such as Kuhn–Tucker's, Karlin's, Fritz John's, and Slater's. Mangasarian [1969] and Bazaraa and Shelty [1979] give an excellent discussion on different types of constraint qualifications. Differing constraint qualifications usually lead to different sets of necessary and sufficient conditions for optimality in constrained optimization problems. In this section we shall concentrate on the familiar Kuhn–Tucker constraint qualification (KTCQ). A formal statement of KTCQ follows:

Definition. The constraints $\mathbf{h}(\mathbf{x})=(h_1(\mathbf{x}),\ldots,h_l(\mathbf{x}))^{\mathrm{T}}$ are said to satisfy the *Kuhn–Tucker constraint qualification* at the point $\mathbf{x}^*$ if for any $\mathbf{y}\in R^N$ satisfying $\nabla h_i(\mathbf{x}^*)\mathbf{y}=0$ for all $i=1,\ldots,l$ there is a vector-valued function ω defined on $[0,1]$ (i.e., $\omega\colon[0,1]\to R^N$) such that $\omega(0)=\mathbf{x}^*$; $\omega(t)\in\{\mathbf{x}\,|\,h_i(\mathbf{x})=0,\ i=1,\ldots,l\}$ for all $t\in[0,1]$; and $d\omega(0)/dt=\mathbf{y}$.

Simply put, the KTCQ states that for each smooth curve that lies on the constraint surface defined by $\mathbf{h}(\mathbf{x})=0$ and passes through $\mathbf{x}^*$, its tangent to the curve at $\mathbf{x}^*$ is also a tangent to the constraint surface. This permits a useful representation of the tangent plane T to the constraint surface [defined by $\mathbf{h}(\mathbf{x})=0$] at $\mathbf{x}^*$ in terms of the gradient vectors of $h_i(\mathbf{x}^*)$ as

$$T=\{\mathbf{y}\,|\,\mathbf{y}\in R^N,\ \nabla h_i(\mathbf{x}^*)\mathbf{y}=0,\ i=1,\ldots,l\}.$$

An equivalent but more operational condition of KTCQ is that of a regular point.

Definition. A point $\mathbf{x}^*$ is said to be a *regular point* of the constraint $\mathbf{h}(\mathbf{x})=\mathbf{0}$ if $\mathbf{h}(\mathbf{x}^*)=\mathbf{0}$ and $\nabla h_l(\mathbf{x}^*),\ldots,\nabla h_l(\mathbf{x}^*)$ are linearly independent.

It can be shown that the KTCQ and the regularity condition as defined here are in fact equivalent.[12]

Upon assuming the KTCQ or the regularity condition, the following results can be established.

[12] See, e.g., Luenberger [1973, p. 223].

Necessary Conditions for Optimality for Equality Constraints. *Assume that* $\mathbf{x}^*$ *is a regular point of the constraint* $\mathbf{h}(\mathbf{x})=\mathbf{0}$. *For* $\mathbf{x}^*$ *to be a local minimum of* f *subject to* $\mathbf{h}(\mathbf{x})=\mathbf{0}$, *there must exist a set of multipliers* $\boldsymbol{\lambda}=(\lambda_1,\dots,\lambda_l)^{\mathrm{T}}\in R^l$ *such that*

$$\nabla f(\mathbf{x}^*)+\sum_{j=l}^{l}\lambda_j\nabla h_j(\mathbf{x}^*)=0; \tag{2.14}$$

$$\nabla^2 f(\mathbf{x}^*)+\sum_{j=1}^{l}\lambda_j\nabla^2 h_j(\mathbf{x}^*)$$

is a positive semidefinite matrix on

$$T\triangleq\left\{\mathbf{y}|\nabla h_i(\mathbf{x}^*)\mathbf{y}=0,\,i=1,\dots,m,\,\mathbf{y}\in R^N\right\};$$

i.e., for all $\mathbf{y}\neq\mathbf{0}$ *in* T,

$$\mathbf{y}^{\mathrm{T}}\left[\nabla^2 f(\mathbf{x}^*)+\sum_{i=1}^{l}\lambda_i\nabla^2 h_i(\mathbf{x}^*)\right]\mathbf{y}\geqslant 0. \tag{2.15}$$

Sufficient Conditions for Optimality for Equality Constraints. *Assume that* $\mathbf{x}^*$ *is a point of regularity of the constraints* $\mathbf{h}(\mathbf{x})=\mathbf{0}$. *If there exists* $\boldsymbol{\lambda}=(\lambda_1,\dots,\lambda_l)^{\mathrm{T}}\in R^l$ *such that*

$$\nabla f(\mathbf{x}^*)+\sum_{i=1}^{l}\lambda_i\nabla h_i(\mathbf{x}^*)=0; \tag{2.16}$$

$$\nabla^2 f(\mathbf{x}^*)+\sum_{i=1}^{l}\lambda_i\nabla^2 h_i(\mathbf{x}^*)$$

is a positive definite matrix on T, *i.e., for all* $\mathbf{y}\neq\mathbf{0}$ *in* T,

$$\mathbf{y}^{\mathrm{T}}\left(\nabla^2 f(\mathbf{x}^*)+\sum_{i=1}^{l}\lambda_i\nabla^2 h_i(\mathbf{x}^*)\right)\mathbf{y}>0, \tag{2.17}$$

then $\mathbf{x}^*$ *is a local minimum of* (2.11).

The proofs of the above results are involved and will be omitted here.[13] A few comments are in order, however. Upon assuming the regularity condition, which ensures the existence of Lagrange multipliers, the optimality conditions stated in (2.14)–(2.17) can be viewed as applying the optimality conditions for unconstrained problems (2.7)–(2.10) to the Lagrangian function $L(\mathbf{x},\boldsymbol{\lambda})$. However, we require that the Hessian matrix of $L(\mathbf{x},\boldsymbol{\lambda})$ be either positive semidefinite (for necessary conditions) or positive definite (for sufficient conditions) on a subspace of R^N, namely, the tangent plane to

[13] For a detailed proof see, e.g., Luenberger [1973], or Bazaraa and Shelty [1979].

the constraint surface at $\mathbf{x}^*$ (rather than the whole space R^N). The following simple example will illustrate this point.

Example 1: Consider the problem

$$\begin{aligned} &\min \quad f(x_1, x_2) = x_1^2 - x_1 x_2 - x_2^2 \\ &\text{subject to} \qquad h(x_1, x_2) = x_1 - x_2 = 1. \end{aligned} \tag{2.18}$$

Applying the first-order necessary condition (2.14) yields

$$\begin{aligned} 2x_1 - \ x_2 + \lambda &= 0, \\ -x_1 + 2x_2 - \lambda &= 0, \\ x_1 - \ x_2 \qquad &= 1, \end{aligned} \tag{2.19}$$

whose solution is $x_1^* = \frac{1}{2}$, $x_2^* = -\frac{1}{2}$, and $\lambda^* = -1$. Furthermore, the Hessian matrix of the Lagrangian function $L(x_1, x_2, \lambda)$ at $(x_1^*, x_2^*, \lambda^*)$ is

$$\begin{bmatrix} 2 & -1 \\ -1 & 2 \end{bmatrix},$$

which is clearly indefinite in R^2. However, in the tangent plane

$$T = \left\{ (y_1, y_2)^{\mathrm{T}} \middle| y_1 - y_2 = 0,\ y_1 \neq 0 \right\}$$

touching the constraint surface defined by $x_1 - x_2 = 1$ at $(x_1^*, x_2^*) = (\frac{1}{2}, -\frac{1}{2})$, the matrix is clearly positive definite in T since for any $(y_1, y_2)^{\mathrm{T}} \in T$, i.e., $y_1 - y_2 = 0$ with $y_1 \neq 0$, we have

$$(y_1 \quad y_1) \begin{bmatrix} 2 & -1 \\ -1 & 2 \end{bmatrix} \begin{pmatrix} y_1 \\ y_1 \end{pmatrix} = 2y_1^2 > 0.$$

From the sufficiency conditions (2.16) and (2.17), (x_1^*, x_2^*) is at least a local solution of (2.18).

The following example illustrates that positive semidefiniteness of the Hessian of $L(\mathbf{x}, \lambda)$ is not sufficient to guarantee local optimality.

Example 2: Consider the problem

$$\begin{aligned} &\min \quad f(x_1, x_2) = (x_2 - x_1)^3 + 2(x_1 + x_2) \\ &\text{subject to} \qquad h(x_1, x_2) = x_1 + x_2 = 2. \end{aligned} \tag{2.20}$$

First we observe from Figure 2.5 that (2.20) has an unbounded solution. To see this, we substitute $x_2 = 2 - x_1$ for any $x_1 \in R$ in $f(x_1, x_2)$, yielding, $f(x_1, x_2) = 2(1 - x_1)^3 + 4$, which decreases indefinitely as x_1 increases (indefinitely). However, application of the first-order necessary conditions yields

$$\begin{aligned} -3(-x_1 + x_2)^2 + 2 + \lambda &= 0, \\ 3(-x_1 + x_2)^2 + 2 + \lambda &= 0, \\ x_1 + x_2 \qquad\qquad &= 2, \end{aligned} \tag{2.21}$$

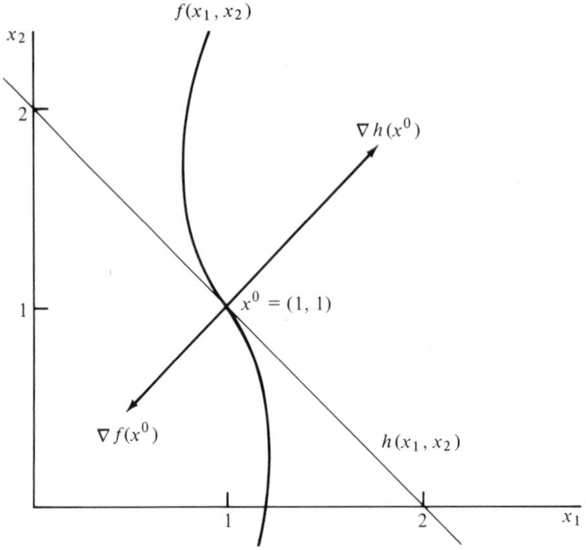

Figure 2.5 Graphical illustration of Example 2.

whose solution is $x_1^0 = 1$, $x_2^0 = 1$, and $\lambda^0 = -2$. The corresponding Hessian matrix of $L(x_1, x_2, \lambda)$ at $(x_1^0, x_2^0, \lambda^0)$ is a zero matrix that is clearly positive semidefinite everywhere in R^N and, hence, in the tangent plant T at $(x_1^0, x_2^0, \lambda^0)$. Although this positive semidefinitiveness condition is satisfied, the point $(x_1^0, x_2^0, \lambda^0)$ is not an optimal solution of (2.20).

Finally, we give an example which will illustrate the significance of the regularity condition in guaranteeing the existence of the Lagrange multipliers satisfying the first-order necessary conditions at the optimal point.

Example 3: Consider the problem

$$\begin{aligned} \min \quad & f(x_1, x_2) = (x_1 - 2)^2 + (x_2 - 1)^2 \\ \text{subject to} \quad & h_1(x_1, x_2) = \quad x_2 = 0, \\ & h_2(x_1, x_2) = x_1^3 - x_2 = 0. \end{aligned} \tag{2.22}$$

Since the feasible region defined by $h_1(x_1, x_2)$ and $h_2(x_1, x_2)$ contains only one point $\mathbf{x}^* = (0,0)^T$, $\mathbf{x}^*$ must be the optimal solution of (2.22). Yet although $\mathbf{x}^*$ is the global solution of (2.22), the necessary condition stated in (2.14) and (2.15) are not satisfied, since there exist no real λ_1 and λ_2 such that

$$\nabla f(\mathbf{x}^*) + \lambda_1 \nabla h_1(\mathbf{x}^*) + \lambda_2 \nabla h_2(\mathbf{x}^*) = 0,$$

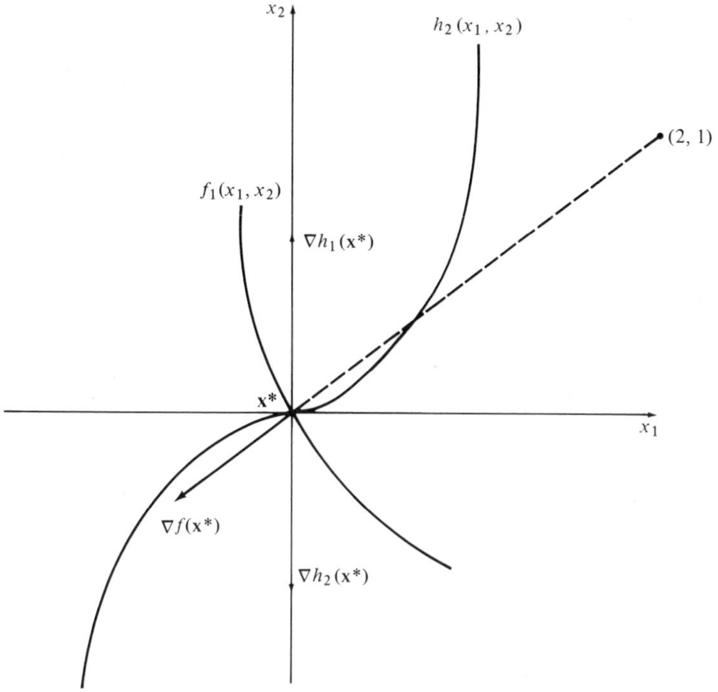

Figure 2.6 Graphical illustration of Example 3.

as is evident from Figure 2.6. This failure to satisfy the necessary conditions for optimality is because at $\mathbf{x}^*$, $\nabla h_1(\mathbf{x}^*) = (0, 1)$ and $\nabla h_2(\mathbf{x}^*) = (0, -1)$ are not linearly independent, indicating that $\mathbf{x}^*$ is not a regular point of the constraints $h_1(x_1, x_2)$ and $h_2(x_1, x_2)$.

2.3.3 Inequality-Constrained Optimization

In general, a constrained optimization problem is of the form given in (2.1), which will be repeated here for convenience:

$$\begin{aligned} \min \quad & f(\mathbf{x}) \\ \text{subject to} \quad & h_i(\mathbf{x}) = 0, \quad i = 1, \ldots, l, \\ & g_j(\mathbf{x}) \leq 0, \quad j = 1, \ldots, m. \end{aligned} \tag{2.23}$$

Extending the foregoing results to this general case is routine if we modify the regularity condition to accommodate inequality constraints. As one may expect, the idea is to disregard all constraints that are not binding at $\mathbf{x}^*$.

Definition. A point $\mathbf{x}^*$ satisfying $\mathbf{h}(\mathbf{x}^*)=\mathbf{0}$ and $\mathbf{g}(\mathbf{x}^*)\leqslant\mathbf{0}$ is said to be a *regular point* of the above constraints if the gradient vectors $\nabla h_j(\mathbf{x}^*)$ and $\nabla g_j(\mathbf{x}^*)$ for all j such that $g_j(\mathbf{x}^*)=0$ are linearly independent.

The following first-order necessary condition for optimality for a general optimization problem, put forth by Kuhn and Tucker [1951], is of historical importance. It is also the basis for many of the existing numerical optimization algorithms.

Kuhn–Tucker Necessary Conditions for Optimality. *Let* $\mathbf{x}^*$ *be a regular point of the constraints in* (2.23). *For* $\mathbf{x}^*$ *to be a local minimum of* (2.23), *there must exist a set of Kuhn-Tucker multipliers*[14] $\boldsymbol{\lambda}^*\in R^l$ *and* $\boldsymbol{\mu}^*\in R^m$ *with* $\boldsymbol{\mu}^*\geqslant\mathbf{0}$ *such that*

$$\nabla f(\mathbf{x}^*)+\sum_{i=1}^{l}\lambda_i^*\nabla h_i(\mathbf{x}^*)+\sum_{j=1}\mu_j^*\nabla g_j(\mathbf{x}^*)=0, \tag{2.24}$$

$$\sum_{j=1}^{m}\mu_j^* g_j(\mathbf{x}^*)=0. \tag{2.25}$$

Formal proof of this well-known result can be found in Kuhn and Tucker [1951] or any standard text in nonlinear programming, such as Luenberger [1973] or Hadley [1964].

It is perhaps fruitful at this point to make a geometrical interpretation of the Kuhn–Tucker conditions. From (2.24), it is clear that

$$-\nabla f(\mathbf{x}^*)=\sum_{i=1}^{l}\lambda_i^*\nabla h_i(\mathbf{x}^*)+\sum_{j=1}^{m}\mu_j^*\nabla g_j(\mathbf{x}^*). \tag{2.26}$$

Geometrically, (2.26) states that for $\mathbf{x}^*$ to be a local minimum of (2.23), the negative gradients of the objective function at $\mathbf{x}^*$ must lie in the positive cone formed by the gradients of binding constraints $g_j(\mathbf{x}^*)=0$ and the cone formed by the gradients $\nabla h_i(\mathbf{x}^*)$, $i=1,\ldots,l$.

To illustrate this point consider an optimization problem.

$$\begin{aligned} &\min \quad f(x_1,x_2)=(x_1-3)^2+(x_2-2)^2\\ &\text{subject to} \quad g_1(x_1,x_2)=x_1+x_2\leqslant 2,\\ &\qquad\qquad\quad g_2(x_1,x_2)=x_1^2+(x_2-1)^2\leqslant 1. \end{aligned} \tag{2.27}$$

From Figure 2.7, it is clear that $\mathbf{x}^*=(1,1)$ is the optimal (minimal) solution

[14] We shall reserve the term "Lagrange multipliers" for those multipliers used in association with the Lagrangian function. Kuhn–Tucker multipliers, sometimes known as generalized Lagrange multipliers, on the other hand, are used in association with the Kuhn–Tucker conditions.

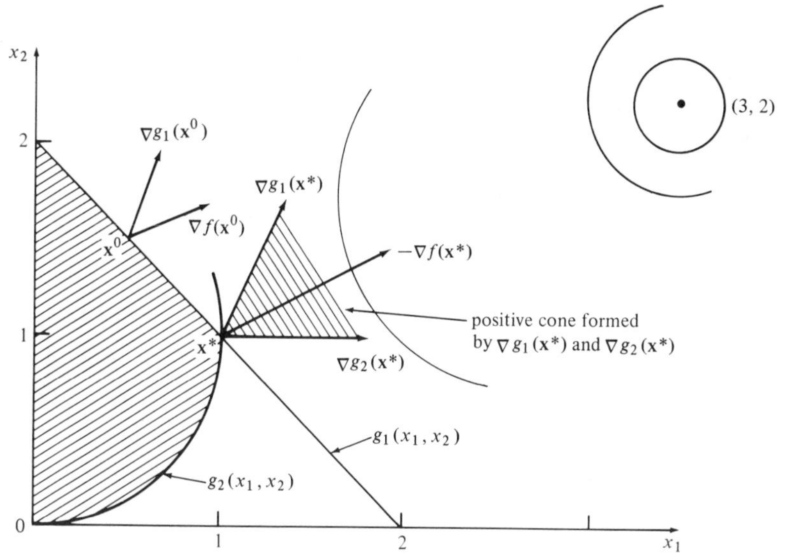

Figure 2.7 Graphical illustration of (2.27).

of (2.27) and that $\mathbf{x}^*$ is a regular point of the constraints in (2.27), since $\nabla g_1(\mathbf{x}^*) = (1,1)$ and $\nabla g_2(\mathbf{x}^*) = (2,0)$ are clearly linearly independent. Moreover, $-\nabla f(\mathbf{x}^*) = (4,1)$ lies in the positive cone formed by $\nabla g_1(\mathbf{x}^*)$ and $\nabla g_2(\mathbf{x}^*)$. In fact

$$-\nabla f(\mathbf{x}^*) = 1\,\nabla g_1(\mathbf{x}^*) + \tfrac{3}{2}\nabla g_2(\mathbf{x}^*).$$

Now consider the point $\mathbf{x}^0 = (\frac{1}{2}, \frac{3}{2})$. Again $\mathbf{x}^0$ is a regular point of the constraint of (2.27) since g_1 is the only binding constraint at $\mathbf{x}^0$. The positive cone formed by $\nabla g_1(\mathbf{x}^0)$ is any vector from $\mathbf{x}^0$ in the same direction as $\nabla g_1(\mathbf{x}^0)$. Clearly, $-\nabla f(\mathbf{x}^0)$ does not lie in such cone, indicating that $\mathbf{x}^0$ can not be a (local) minimum of (2.27), which is evident from the diagram. To put it in terms of (2.24), there exists no $\mu \in R$ such that

$$-\nabla f(\mathbf{x}^0) + \mu \nabla g_1(\mathbf{x}^0) = 0.$$

To state second-order optimality conditions for problem (2.23), we require not only that the Hessian matrix of $L(\mathbf{x}, \boldsymbol{\lambda}, \boldsymbol{\mu})$, where

$$L(\mathbf{x}, \boldsymbol{\lambda}, \boldsymbol{\mu}) = f(\mathbf{x}) + \sum_{i=1}^{l} \lambda_i h_i(\mathbf{x}) + \sum_{j=1}^{m} \mu_j g_j(\mathbf{x}),$$

be positive, semidefinite, or positive definite on the tangent plane formed by the gradient vectors of the binding constraints, but also that the binding constraints forming the subspace of interest be nondegenerate. A binding constraint is said to be *nondegenerate* if the corresponding Kuhn–Tucker multiplier for that binding constraint is strictly positive.

Second-Order Necessary Conditions for Optimality (General Case). *Assume that* $\mathbf{x}^*$, *satisfying the constraints of* (2.23), *is a regular point of such constraints. For* $\mathbf{x}^*$ *to be a local minimum of* (2.23), *there must exist a set of Kuhn-Tucker multipliers* $\boldsymbol{\lambda}^* \in R^l$ *and* $\boldsymbol{\mu}^* \in R^m$ *with* $\boldsymbol{\mu}^* \geqslant \mathbf{0}$ *such that* (2.24) *and* (2.25) *hold and the matrix*

$$\nabla^2 f(\mathbf{x}^*) + \sum_{i=1}^{l} \lambda_i^* \nabla^2 h_i(\mathbf{x}^*) + \sum_{j=1}^{m} \mu_j^* \nabla^2 g_j(\mathbf{x}^*)$$

is positive semidefinite in the subspace $\hat{T}$ *of* R^N, *where*

$$\hat{T} = \{ y \mid \nabla h_i(\mathbf{x}^*)\mathbf{y} = 0, i = 1,\ldots,l, \ \nabla g_j(\mathbf{x}^*)\mathbf{y} = 0 \text{ for all } j \text{ with } \mu_j > 0 \}. \tag{2.28}$$

Second-Order Sufficiency Conditions for Optimality (General Case). *Let* $\mathbf{x}^*$ *be a regular point of the constraints of* (2.23). *Assume that there exist Kuhn–Tucker multipliers* $\boldsymbol{\lambda}^* \in R^l$ *and* $\boldsymbol{\mu}^* \in R^m$ *with* $\boldsymbol{\mu}^* \geqslant \mathbf{0}$ *such that* (2.24) *and* (2.25) *hold and*

$$\nabla^2 f(\mathbf{x}^*) + \sum_{i=1}^{l} \lambda_i^* \nabla^2 h_i(\mathbf{x}^*) + \sum_{j=1}^{m} \mu_j^* \nabla^2 g_j(\mathbf{x}^*)$$

is a positive definite matrix on $\hat{T}$, *where* $\hat{T}$ *is as defined in* (2.28). *Then* $\mathbf{x}^*$ *is a local minimum of* (2.23).

Finally, there is a useful theorem which permits the sensitivity or "shadow-price" interpretation of the Kuhn–Tucker multipliers of (2.23).

Sensitivity Theorem. *Let* f, h_i, *and* g_j *be twice continuously differentiable. In a problem*

$$\begin{aligned} &\min \quad f(\mathbf{x}) \\ &\text{subject to} \quad h_i(\mathbf{x}) = c_i, \quad i = 1,\ldots,l, \\ &\qquad\qquad\quad g_j(\mathbf{x}) \leqslant d_j, \quad j = 1,\ldots,m, \end{aligned} \tag{2.29}$$

let $\mathbf{x}^*$ *be a local solution of* (2.29) *when* $c_i = 0$, $i = 1,\ldots,l$, *and* $d_j = 0$, $j = 1,\ldots,m$, *and let* $\mathbf{x}^*$ *satisfy the following conditions*:

1. $\mathbf{x}^*$ *is a regular point of the constraints of* (2.29).
2. *Second-order sufficiency conditions are satisfied at* $\mathbf{x}^*$.
3. *There is no degenerate binding constraint at* $\mathbf{x}^*$.

Then there is a continuously differentiable vector-valued function $\mathbf{x}(\ )$ *defined on a neighborhood of* $(\mathbf{0},\mathbf{0})$ *in* $R^l \times R^m$ *such that* $\mathbf{x}(\mathbf{0},\mathbf{0}) = \mathbf{x}^*$ *and such that for every* $(\mathbf{c},\mathbf{d})$ *in a vicinity of* $(\mathbf{0},\mathbf{0})$, $\mathbf{x}(\mathbf{c},\mathbf{d})$ *is a strict local solution* *of* (2.29). *Moreover*

$$\partial f[\mathbf{x}(\mathbf{0},\mathbf{0})]/\partial c_i = -\lambda_i, \qquad i=1,\dots,l, \tag{2.30}$$

$$\partial f[\mathbf{x}(\mathbf{0},\mathbf{0})]/\partial d_j = -\mu_j, \qquad j=1,\dots,m. \tag{2.31}$$

This result will be quite useful when we develop trade-off rates in multiobjective optimization problems. Its proof, which is based mainly on the implicit-function theorem, can be found in Luenberger [1973].

2.3.4 Necessary and Sufficient Conditions Without Derivatives

The necessary and sufficient conditions and other results stated thus far require the differentiability assumptions on both the objective function and constraint functions. It is possible to state similar conditions without such assumptions. A concept that makes this possible is the saddle point, which is defined in terms of the Lagrangian function associated with (2.23). The following presentation is based on Lasdon [1970].

For convenience, let us restate (2.23) in a more general form:

$$\begin{aligned} &\min \quad f(\mathbf{x}) \\ &\text{subject to} \qquad g_i(\mathbf{x}) \leqslant 0, \quad i=1,\dots,m, \quad \mathbf{x}\in S, \end{aligned} \tag{2.32}$$

where S includes any other forms of constraints.

We define the Lagrangian function for (2.32) as

$$L(\mathbf{x},\boldsymbol{\mu}) = f(\mathbf{x}) + \sum_{j=1}^{m} \mu_j g_j(\mathbf{x}), \qquad \mu_j \geqslant 0. \tag{2.33}$$

Definition. A point $(\mathbf{x}^0,\boldsymbol{\mu}^0)$ with $\boldsymbol{\mu}^0 \geqslant \mathbf{0}$ and $\mathbf{x}^0 \in S$ is said to be a *saddle point* of $L(\mathbf{x},\boldsymbol{\mu})$ if

$$L(\mathbf{x}^0,\boldsymbol{\mu}) \leqslant L(\mathbf{x}^0,\boldsymbol{\mu}^0) \leqslant L(\mathbf{x},\boldsymbol{\mu}^0) \tag{2.34}$$

for all $\mathbf{x}\in S$ and $\boldsymbol{\mu} \geqslant \mathbf{0}$.

Based on this definition, it is simple to prove the following result:

Necessary and Sufficient Conditions for a Saddle Point of $L(\mathbf{x},\boldsymbol{\mu})$. *A point* $(\mathbf{x}^0,\boldsymbol{\mu}^0)$ *with* $\boldsymbol{\mu}^0 \geqslant 0$ *and* $\mathbf{x}^0 \in S$ *is a saddle point of* $\mathbf{L}(\mathbf{x},\boldsymbol{\mu})$ *if and only if*

$$\mathbf{x}^0 \textit{ minimizes } L(\mathbf{x},\boldsymbol{\mu}^0) \qquad \textit{over } S, \tag{2.35}$$

$$g_j(\mathbf{x}^0) \leqslant 0, \qquad j=1,\dots,m, \tag{2.36}$$

$$\mu_j^0 g_j(x^0) = 0, \qquad j=1,\dots,m. \tag{2.37}$$

Note the similarity of the conditions (2.35)–(2.37) to the Kuhn–Tucker conditions (2.24) and (2.25). Condition (2.35) replaces (2.24), the condition that $L(\mathbf{x}, \boldsymbol{\mu})$ be stationary, while (2.36) is nothing more than the constraint equations. Condition (2.37) is equivalent to (2.25).

With this result it is easy to show that the existence of a saddle point of $L(\mathbf{x}, \boldsymbol{\mu})$ is sufficient to guarantee global optimality at that (saddle) point. We summarize as follows:

Saddle Point Sufficiency Conditions for Optimality. *If* $(\mathbf{x}^0, \boldsymbol{\mu}^0)$ *with* $\mathbf{x}^0 \in S$ *and* $\boldsymbol{\mu}^0 \geqslant \mathbf{0}$ *is a saddle point of* $L(\mathbf{x}, \boldsymbol{\mu})$, *then* $\mathbf{x}^0$ *is a global minimum of* (2.32).

To state necessary conditions for optimality of (2.32) in terms of a saddle point, we need to impose a constraint qualification on the constraints of (2.32) to ensure the existence of Lagrange multipliers $\boldsymbol{\mu}^0$, which together with $\mathbf{x}^0$ form a saddle point of $L(\mathbf{x}, \boldsymbol{\mu})$. Karlin [1959] provides the following constraint qualification, which guarantees the existence of a saddle point of $L(\mathbf{x}, \boldsymbol{\mu})$:

Definition. The constraints of (2.32) are said to satisfy Karlin's constraint qualification if S is a convex subset of R^N; $g_j, j=1,\ldots,m$, are all convex functions defined on S; and there exists $\mathbf{x} \in S$ such that $g_j(\mathbf{x}) \leqslant 0$ for all $j=1,\ldots,m$.

The following result was put forth by Karlin [1959] based on the so-called separation theorem.

Saddle Point Necessary Conditions for Optimality. *Assume that the constraints of* (2.32) *satisfy Karlin's constraint qualification and that* f *is a convex function on* S. *If* $\mathbf{x}^*$ *solves* (2.32), *then there exists* $\boldsymbol{\mu}^* \in R^m$ *with* $\boldsymbol{\mu} \geqslant \mathbf{0}$ *such that* $(\mathbf{x}^*, \boldsymbol{\mu}^*)$ *is a saddle point of* $L(\mathbf{x}, \boldsymbol{\mu})$.

References

Scales of Measurement

Campbell, N. R. (1938). *Symposium: Measurement and Its Importance for Philosophy*, Aristotelian Society, Suppl. Vol. 17, Harrison, London, p. 126.

Luce, R. D., and Suppes, P. (1965). Preferences, utility, and subjective probability, in *Handbook of Mathematical Psychology*, Wiley, New York.

Marchack, J. L. (1960). Binary-choice constraints and random utility indicators, in *Mathematical Methods in Social Sciences*, Stanford University, Stanford University Press, pp. 312–329.

Russell, B. (1938). *The Principle of Mathematics*, Norton, New York.

Stevens, S. S. (1951). Mathematics, measurement, and psychophysics, in *Handbook of Experimental Psychology* (S. S. Stevens, ed.), Wiley, New York.

Stevens, S. S. (1959). Measurement, psychophysics, and utility, in *Measurement Definitions and Theories* (C. West Churchman and P. Ratoosh, eds.), Wiley, New York, pp. 18–63.

Torgerson, W. S. (1958). *Theory and Methods of Scaling*, Wiley, New York.

Decision Analysis

Anderson, J. R., Dillion, J. L., and Hardaker, J. Brian (1977). *Agricultural Decision Analysis*, Iowa State University Press, Ames.

Chen, K., and Patton, G. (1970). Branch and bound approach for decision-tree analysis, *Operations Research Society of America Meeting Record*, October.

Hall, A. D. (1962). *A Methodology for Systems Engineering*, Princeton University Press, Princeton, New Jersey.

Moore, P. G., and Thomas, H. (1976). *The Anatomy of Decisions*, Penguin, Harmondsworth, Middlesex.

Luce, R. D., and Raiffa, H. (1957). *Games and Decisions: Introduction and Critical Survey*, Wiley, New York.

Raiffa, H. (1968). *Decision Analysis: Introductory Lectures on Choice Under Uncertainty*, Addison–Wesley, Reading, Massachusetts.

Sage, A. P. (1977). *Methodology for Large Scale Systems*, McGraw-Hill, New York.

Schlaifer, R. (1969). *Analysis of Decisions Under Uncertainty*, McGraw-Hill, New York.

Optimality Conditions in Mathematical Programming

Bazaraa, M. S., and Shelty, C. M. (1979). *Nonlinear Programming: Theory and Algorithms*, Wiley, New York.

Hadley, G. (1964). *Nonlinear and Dynamic Programming*, Addison-Wesley, Reading, Massachusetts.

Haimes, Y. Y. (1977). *Hierarchical Analyses of Water Resources Systems*, McGraw-Hill, New York.

Karlin, S. (1959). *Mathematical Methods and Theory in Games, Programming, and Economics*, Addison-Wesley, Reading, Massachusetts, Vol. 1.

Kuhn, H. W., and Tucker, A. W. (1951). Nonlinear programming, in *Proceedings of the Second Berkeley Symposium on Mathematical Statistics and Probability* (J. Neyman, ed.), University of California Press, Berkeley, pp. 481–492.

Lasdon, L. S. (1970). *Optimization for Large Systems*, Macmillan, New York.

Luenberger, D. G. (1973). *Introduction to Linear and Nonlinear Programming*, Addison-Wesley, Reading, Massachusetts.

Mangasarian, O. L. (1969). *Nonlinear Programming*, McGraw-Hill, New York.

Zangwill, W. I. (1969). *Nonlinear Programming: A Unified Approach*, Prentice-Hall, Englewood Cliffs, New Jersey.

Chapter 3

Utility Theory

3.1 Introduction

Implicit in any decision-making process is the need to construct, either directly or indirectly, the preference order, so that alternatives can be ranked and the final choice can be selected. For some decision-making problems, this may easily be accomplished. For example, it may be appropriate to make a decision based on a cost-minimization rule (choose an alternative with the lowest cost) wherein the preference order is adequately represented by the natural order of real numbers ($\leqslant$ or $\geqslant$). In this case, application of suitable optimization techniques should yield the final solution and the preference order need not be constructed explicitly.

In some situations, however, it may be desirable to explore the decision maker's preference structure in some direct fashion and to attempt to construct some sort of preference order directly. An important class of decision-making techniques that attempts to construct the preference order by directly eliciting the decision maker's preference is predicated on what is known as utility theory. This, in turn, is based on the premise that the decision maker's preference structure can be represented by a real-valued function called a utility function. Once such a function is constructed the selection of the final alternative should be relatively simple. In the absence of uncertainty, an alternative with the highest possible values of the utility function would represent the most preferred solution. For the uncertainty case, however, an appropriate final choice would correspond to that which attains the highest expected utility.

In this chapter some basic background material on the utility theory will be presented. We do not pretend to be exhaustive or completely rigorous in our treatment. We merely want to highlight some of the basic concepts involved in establishing the existence of the utility function in some of the more important cases. From a practical viewpoint, we shall also consider results characterizing various operational forms of utility functions.

First, we extend the discussion of the concepts of ordering relation (Chapter 2) and put the concept of preference order—the backbone of utility theory—into perspective. Next, we follow a standard strategy in our presentation of the main body of utility theory by dividing the discussion of the theory into two classes, deterministic utility theory or value theory and probabilistic utility theory. In each of these classes, we shall attempt to furnish at least some answers to the following two questions. First, under what conditions, be it the single or multiattribute case, can we assume the existence of utility functions? Second, if such functions exist, what are some practical means of constructing them? The first question is relevant since many multiobjective decision-making techniques, to be discussed in Part II of this book, rely on the assumption of the existence of utility functions. These techniques make no attempt, however, to construct such functions explicitly. The second question is also quite relevant since the most commonly used assessment technique discussed in Chapter 5 relies on explicit construction of utility functions.

3.2 The Preference Order

To develop the utility theory, we must first discuss the primitive concepts involved and an appropriate set of axioms. For the utility theory, the preference order is an ordering relation that can be used to rank alternatives in a way that truly reflects the decision maker's preference. Analogous to the ordering relation defined in Section 2.1.3—the preference order—is a binary relation. Throughout this chapter we shall use the symbol $\succ$ to denote the strict preference order "is preferred to" and the symbol $\sim$ to denote the indifferent order "is indifferent to" and finally the symbol $\succcurlyeq$ to represent the preference–indifference order "is at least as preferable as." Although these different types of preference orders occur naturally in decision-making problems, we can more compactly define one of the preference orders as primitive and the remainder as derivatives. For example, we can begin by using the preference–indifference order $\succcurlyeq$ as primitive and then define indifference $\sim$ and strict preference $\succ$ as follows:

1. A is *indifferent* to B if and only if A is at least as preferable as B and B is at least as preferable as A:

$$A \sim B \quad \Leftrightarrow \quad A \succcurlyeq B \quad \text{and} \quad B \succcurlyeq A; \tag{3.1}$$

2. A is *preferred* to B if and only if A is at least as preferable as B and B is not at least as preferable as A:

$$A \succ B \quad \Leftrightarrow \quad A \succcurlyeq B \quad \text{and not} \quad B \succcurlyeq A. \tag{3.2}$$

Alternatively, Fishburn [1970] begins with the strict preference $\succ$ and defines the other two preference orders accordingly. Since it suffices to treat

$\succsim$ as a primitive notion and to view $\sim$ and $\succ$ as derivatives as given by (3.1) and (3.2), we shall primarily use $\succsim$ in the subsequent development of this chapter and to refer to $\sim$ and $\succ$ only if necessary or convenient to do so.

In any decision-making problem, it is reasonable to assume that $\succsim$ (and hence $\sim$ and $\succ$), which characterizes the underlying preference structure of the decision problem, exists. But whether or not we can assume its existence depends on our ability to find ways to construct $\succsim$ either directly or indirectly.

This is a measurement problem, namely, measurement of preference. In some cases, it may be justifiable to use some easily measurable attribute, such as cost, as a proxy measure of preference. The task of measuring preference then becomes as simple as computing the value of such an attribute (e.g., cost) for each alternative, after which the task of decision making reduces to comparing those values and choosing an optimal alternative (e.g., minimum cost). In more general cases, where it is not clear what proxy measures are to be used, we may begin by investigating properties of the preference order and then decide upon an appropriate scale of measurement. A suitable method and unit of measurement may then be devised. When no other convenient proxy unit is available, preference may be measured in terms of utility.

The existence of the preference order guarantees that preference can at least be measured in an ordinal scale. As described in Section 2.1, there are several levels of such a scale, depending on the properties of the ordering relation defining the scale. Since the properties of the preference order play a major role in determining the choice of scale and method of measurement, we state different possible sets of properties that may be imposed on $\succsim$.

3.3 The Ordering Relation

In a decision-making problem, let X denote the set of all feasible alternatives and let a, b, and c be any alternatives in X. If R is a binary relation, we say that

P1. R is transitive if aRb and bRc imply aRc;

P2. R is *reflexive* if aRa;

P3. R is *irreflexive* if not aRa;

P4. R is *symmetric* if aRb implies bRa;

P5. R is *asymmetric* if aRb implies not bRa;

P6. R is *antisymmetric* if aRb and bRa implies $a=b$ (i.e., a and b are identical); and

P7. R is *connected* (or complete) if aRb and/or bRa for all $a \in X$ and $b \in X$.

For any binary relation to qualify as an ordering relation it must at least be transitive. By adding further properties, different types of ordering relations with varying degrees of ordering "strength"[1] can be constructed. Some of the most important ordering relations have already been described in Section 2.1.3.[2] For convenient reference, we summarize below various properties associated with some familiar ordering relations.

A transitive relation R is called

1. a *quasi-order* (or preorder) if it is also reflexive;
2. a *weak order* if it is also reflexive and connected;
3. a (reflexive) *partial order* if it is also antisymmetric and reflexive;
4. a *linear* (or total or simple) *order* if it is antisymmetric, reflexive, and connected;
5. a *strict partial order* if it is also irreflexive; and
6. *strict* (or strong) order if it is also irreflexive and connected.

A (reflexive) partial order is an antisymmetric quasi-order, while a weak order is a connected quasi-order and a strict order is a connected strict partial order. Moreover, a linear order can be viewed as either a connected partial order or an antisymmetric weak order. The weak order, strict order, and linear order require the connected (or completeness or totality) property, which ensures comparability of each pair of alternatives in X by R. Consequently, each of these orders can also be classified as a *complete* order (as opposed to a *partial* order). Figure 3.1 displays the interrelationships of different types of orders as well as their relative ordering "strength."

What kind of order the preference order $\succcurlyeq$ should be depends on the problem at hand. To qualify as an ordering relation, $\succcurlyeq$ must at least be transitive. If a is at least as preferable as b and b is at least as preferable as c, then a should be at least as preferable as c. This seems at first glance to be a reasonable assumption. There are, however, situations where transitivity is not a valid assumption, for example, in rating three tennis players A, B, and C who have different styles of playing. When A is paired with B, A may be preferred to B; and when B is paired with C, B may be preferred to C. When A is paired with C, however, C may very well be preferred to A owing to their particular styles of playing. Another situation where intransivity of preference often occurs is when the decision maker is asked to make a choice from a set of incomparable alternatives.

---

[1] The term "ordering strength" is used loosely here in the sense that the higher the ordering strength of a relationship R, the greater its power to discriminate and rank elements in X.

[2] In Chapter 2, weak order, strict order, and partial order were treated in a slightly different fashion from what is given here. The local basis for the two can, nonetheless, be shown to be the same.

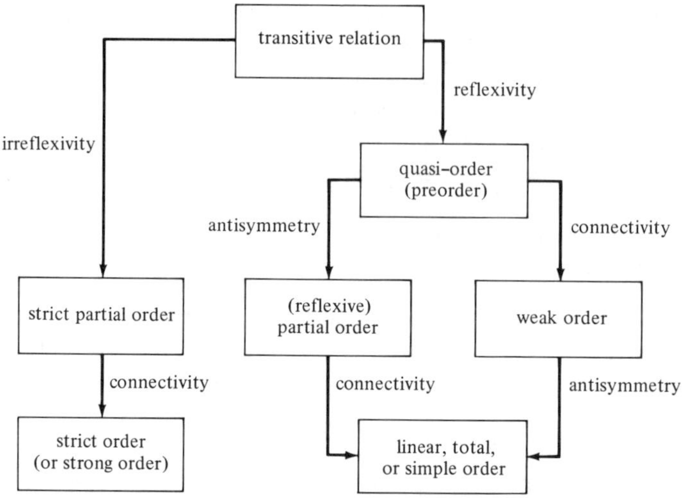

Figure 3.1 Hierarchy of ordering relations.

Connectedness is another property that cannot be assumed to hold without careful verification. The connectedness property entails that for any pair of alternatives (a, b), either a is preferred to b, or b is preferred to a, or they are indifferent. However, the human mind cannot always discriminate between alternatives. If we extend the definition of indifference to include not only genuine indifference but also indecisiveness, connectedness may of course reasonably be assumed.

Finally, irreflexivity and antisymmetry depend on the definition of $\succcurlyeq$ but normally not on the consistency and rationality of the value judgements. They do not therefore pose serious operational problems.

From the point of view of the preference measurement, to guarantee the existence of a real-valued function which preserves the ordering property of $\succcurlyeq$ in some meaningful sense, $\succcurlyeq$ must be at least a weak order (i.e., transitive, reflexive, and connected) or otherwise $\succ$ must be at least a strict partial order, as the following sections will show.

3.4 Deterministic Utility Theory

Utility theory where no uncertainties are involved is particularly relevant in making the utility theory for multiple-objective decision-making problems operational.

3.4.1 The Existence of Value Functions

If $\succcurlyeq$ is a weak order and the set of alternatives X can be partitioned into a countable (i.e., either finite or countably infinite) number of indifference classes, we say that alternatives a and b are in the same indifference class if and only if $a \succcurlyeq b$ and $b \succcurlyeq a$ (i.e., a is indifferent to b). By assuming $\succcurlyeq$ to be a weak order, the corresponding indifference relation $\sim$ is clearly reflexive, symmetric, and transitive, thereby ensuring that an indifference class defined above is indeed an equivalence class.

If χ represents the set of indifference classes induced by $\succcurlyeq$ on X, the above *countability* condition requires that the elements of χ can be put into one-to-one correspondence with the set of natural numbers. Consequently, we can label elements of χ as $X_1, X_2, X_3, \ldots$, where X_i is the ith indifference class. Recalling the symbols $\sim$ and $\succ$, which are derived from $\succcurlyeq$ as given by (3.1) and (3.2), respectively, if alternative $a \in X_i$ and alternative $b \in X_j$, then either

1. $a \sim b$ if $i = j$ (by definition of X_i); or
2. $a \succ b$ or $b \succ a$ if $i \neq j$ (by connectedness of $\succcurlyeq$ on X).

Clearly if $\succcurlyeq$ is a weak order on X, then $\succ$ is a strict order on χ in the sense given by alternative 2.[3]

Theorem 3.1. *If $\succcurlyeq$ is a weak order on X and χ, and the set of indifference classes of X is countable, then there exists a real-valued function called the value function,*[4] *to be denoted v, defined on X such that for any a and b in X*

$$a \succcurlyeq b \quad \text{if and only if} \quad v(a) \geqslant v(b); \tag{3.3}$$

or, more precisely,

$$a \succ b \quad \text{if and only if} \quad v(a) > v(b) \tag{3.4a}$$

and

$$a \sim b \quad \text{if and only if} \quad v(a) = v(b). \tag{3.4b}$$

A proof of this theorem is obtained by construction, as shown by Fishburn [1970]. We demonstrate such a construction process by the following example.

Example: Let X be the set of all points in the first quadrant of the two-dimensional plane R^2 and let $\succcurlyeq$ be defined on X in the following

---

[3] To be more precise, we should define a new ordering relation, say ${}_{\mathrm{I}}\succ$ on χ in terms of $\succ$ and then show that ${}_{\mathrm{I}}\succ$ so defined is a strict order on χ (see a similar treatment, for example, in Fishburn [1970, p. 13]). We feel, however, that if we extend the definition of $\succ$ to be an ordering relation on χ as well as on X, it is not necessary to add a new symbol.

[4] Following Keeney and Raiffa [1976], we use *value function* to represent an order-preserving real-valued function in the deterministic case while *utility function*, which may be defined either on X itself or on the range of $v(\ )$, will be later used in association with the uncertainty case.

manner. For any $\mathbf{a}=(a_1, a_2)\in X$ and $\mathbf{b}=(b_1, b_2)\in X$,

$$\mathbf{a}\succcurlyeq\mathbf{b} \quad \text{if and only if} \quad [a_1]>[b_1] \quad \text{or}$$
$$[a_1]=[b_1] \quad \text{and} \quad [a_2]\geqslant[b_2], \tag{3.5}$$

where $[a_1]$ is defined as the largest integer less than or equal to a_1.[5] The preference order $\succcurlyeq$ as defined by (3.5) is transitive and connected on X and hence a weak order on X. The set of indifference classes on X induced by $\succcurlyeq$ is the set of unit square cells whose four corners have nonnegative integer coordinates. Each cell, which contains all points on the left and bottom edges, but excludes all points on the right and top edges, can be conveniently identified by the coordinates of its lower left corner point. This is because any point $\mathbf{a}=(a_1, a_2)$ in the cell as described above with the point (i, j) as its lower-left corner will always have $[a_1]=i$ and $[a_2]=j$. Figure 3.2 shows typical members of χ. Clearly χ is a countable set and Figure 3.2 shows how members of χ can be numbered. More precisely, if X_k is the kth element of χ whose lower left corner is (i, j), then k can be computed from i and j using the formula

$$k=\tfrac{1}{2}(i+j)(i+j+1)+i+1, \qquad i=0,1,2,\ldots, \quad j=0,1,2,\ldots. \tag{3.6}$$

For example, a cell whose lower left corner is situated at $(1,3)$ is X_{12} since $12=\frac{1}{2}(1+3)(1+3+1)+1+1$. Once we have labeled members of χ in this manner we can construct iteratively the value function v on X corresponding to $\succcurlyeq$. In the following construction, we assign an appropriate value of v to each member of χ. After we have assigned values of v to i members of χ, these members are ordered accordingly. The corresponding list of these i ordered members will be denoted $L(i)$.

1. Let $v(X_1)=0$ and also let $L(1)=\{1\}$.
2. Since $X_2\succ X_1$, let $v(X_2)=1$ and let $L(2)=\{2,1\}$.
3. Also since $X_3\succ X_2\succ X_1$, let $v(X_3)=2$ and $L(3)=\{3,2,1\}$.
4. Next we observe that $X_3\succ X_4\succ X_2$; hence, let
$$v(X_4)=\tfrac{1}{2}\left[v(X_3)+v(X_2)\right]=\tfrac{3}{2}$$
and let $L(4)=\{3,4,2,1\}$.
5. Similarly, we observe that $X_5\succ X_3\succ\cdots$; we then set $v(X_5)=4$ and set $L(5)=\{5,3,4,2,1\}$, and so forth.

Uniqueness of Value Functions Note that in the preceding process of construction the values assigned to the $v(X_i)$ are not unique. In fact the following theorem, whose proof is rather trivial, will show that any strictly increasing monotone transformation (ordinal scales) of $v(\ )$ can also serve as

[5]For example, $[1.011]=1$, $[-2.5]=-3$, and $[3.99]=3$.

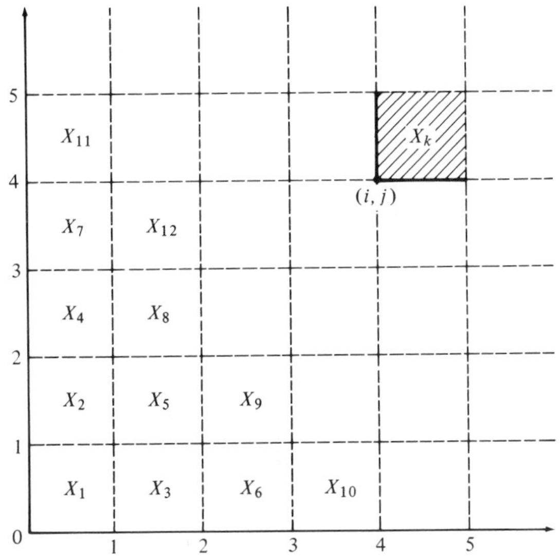

Figure 3.2 Members of χ in the example of Section 3.4.1.

an order-preserving value function in the sense of (3.3). An important implication of this theorem is that order-preserving value functions as guaranteed by Theorem 3.1 are measurable in ordinal or higher scales.

Theorem 3.2. *Let v be a value function induced by $\succsim$ on X satisfying* (3.4a) *and* (3.4b) *and let V be a strictly increasing, monotone, real-valued transformation of v on $v(X)$ (range of v) in the sense that*

$$\begin{aligned} V(v_1) > V(v_2) \quad &\textit{if and only if} \quad v_1 > v_2, \\ V(v_1) = V(v_2) \quad &\textit{if and only if} \quad v_1 = v_2 \end{aligned} \tag{3.7}$$

throughout the range of v over X. Then for any $a, b \in X$

$$a \succsim b \quad \textit{if and only if} \quad V^*(a) \geq V^*(b), \tag{3.8}$$

where $V^*(a) = V[v(a)]$.

More General Existence Theorems In Theorem 3.1, two conditions were used to establish the existence of a real-valued function representing a preference structure characterized by $\succsim$. While the first condition, the weak ordering property of $\succsim$, is the property associated with the preference order itself, the latter condition, namely countability of the set of indifference class χ, is associated with the set of alternatives X (as well as $\succsim$). As natural extensions of Theorem 3.1, either (or both) of these two conditions may be replaced by weaker conditions.

One possibility is to weaken the countability condition on χ. While the set of indifference classes χ is allowed to be uncountable, it must, however, contain a countable subset which is "order dense" with respect to the strict preference relation $\succ$ in χ.

Theorem 3.3. *Let $\succcurlyeq$ be a weak order on X and let B be a subset of χ (the set of indifference classes of X) with the following properties:*

1. *B is countable;*
2. *for any $X_1, X_2 \in \chi$ such that $X_1 \succ X_2$ there exists some $Y \in B$ such that $X_1 \succ Y \succ X_2$ (i.e., B is order dense in χ with respect to $\succ$).*

Then there exists a real-valued function $v: X \to R$ such that for every $a, b \in X$

$$a \succ b \quad \text{if and only if} \quad v(a) > v(b) \tag{3.9a}$$

and

$$a \sim b \quad \text{if and only if} \quad v(a) = v(b). \tag{3.9b}$$

Conversely if (3.9a) *and* (3.9b) *are true, then $\succcurlyeq$ must be a weak order on X and there must exist a subset of χ with Properties* 1 *and* 2 *above.*

The proof is involved; the interested reader may consult Fishburn [1970] or Debreu [1954]. We illustrate an application of this theorem. Let X be the set of points on R^2 and $\succcurlyeq$ be given as follows: For any $\mathbf{a}, \mathbf{b} \in X$,

$$\mathbf{a} \succcurlyeq \mathbf{b} \quad \text{if and only if} \quad 0.4a_1 + 0.6a_2 \geqslant 0.4b_1 + 0.6b_2.$$

It can be shown that $\succcurlyeq$ is a weak order on χ. Also, in this case a typical indifference class associated with $x \in R$ is

$$X_x = \{\mathbf{a} | \mathbf{a} \in R^2, 0.4a_1 + 0.6a_2 = x\}$$

and hence $\chi = \{X_x | x \in R\}$.

Clearly χ is uncountable. Let B be a subset of χ such that

$$B = \{X_{r_1}, X_{r_2}, \ldots, X_{r_n}, \ldots\},$$

where $r_1, r_2, \ldots, r_n$ are rational numbers. Since the set of rational numbers is countable, B is clearly countable. For any two distinct real numbers x and y there always exists a rational number r between x and y. Hence, for any X_x and X_y in χ such that $X_x \succ X_y$, there always exists $X_r \in B$ such that $X_x \succ X_r \succ X_y$. Consequently, the set B satisfies conditions (1) and (2) of Theorem 3.3, thereby ensuring the existence of a real-valued function v defined on X satisfying (3.9a) and (3.9b). Unfortunately, the theorem and its proof do not indicate how such a function may be constructed. Construction of v, therefore, must be done by some other means. In this example, it is rather trivial, since we can simply use

$$v(\mathbf{a}) = 0.4a_1 + 0.6a_2 \qquad \text{for any} \quad \mathbf{a} \in X$$

as our required function.

So far the theory has been stated for any general set X. A special case which is particularly interesting is when X is a subset of the n-dimensional space R^n. An alternative $\mathbf{x} \in X$ is naturally characterized by multiple components $x_1, \ldots, x_n$ each of which can be viewed as an attribute (see Section 1.2.5) used in making decisions. The utility theory developed for this case is therefore quite germane to the theory of multiobjective decision making. The following utility theorem developed for this purpose can be viewed as a special case of Theorem 3.3, where the rather abstract order-denseness condition is replaced by a more practical *continuity* condition.[6]

Theorem 3.4. *Let X be a subset of R^n and let $\succcurlyeq$ be a weak order on X. Moreover, assume*[7]

1. $\mathbf{x} \geqslant \mathbf{y}$ *implies* $\mathbf{x} \succ \mathbf{y}$ *for any* $\mathbf{x}, \mathbf{y} \in X$; *and*
2. *for any* $\mathbf{x}, \mathbf{y}, \mathbf{z} \in X$ *such that* $\mathbf{x} \succ \mathbf{y} \succ \mathbf{z}$, *there exists exactly one* $\lambda \in (0,1)$ *such that* $\mathbf{y} \sim \lambda\mathbf{x} + (1-\lambda)\mathbf{z}$.

Then there exists a real-valued function v defined on X satisfying (3.9a) *and* (3.9b).

This theorem can be proved by using assumptions 1 and 2 to construct a countable subset of χ satisfying conditions 1 and 2 of Theorem 3.3 (see Fishburn [1970, pp. 32–34]). Luce and Suppes [1965] give a much easier proof, which suggests a possible method of constructing the function v as well.

Condition (1) of Theorem 3.4 is generally known as monotonicity (or as dominance or nonsatiety), which stipulates that as the value of at least one attribute increases while there is no decrease in values of any other attributes, preference also increases. This is believed to be reasonable if there is a finite bound on the set of alternatives X itself. Condition (2) is known as the continuity (or Archimedean) condition in the preference space, which is essential in establishing the existence of the function v. This condition asserts that if $\mathbf{y}$ lies between $\mathbf{x}$ and $\mathbf{z}$ in terms of strict preference $\succ$, then there must be some (convex) combination of $\mathbf{x}$ and $\mathbf{z}$ which is indifferent to $\mathbf{y}$. Luce and Suppes [1965, p. 261] give a classic counterexample in which $\succcurlyeq$ is a lexicographic order—a weak order that does not satisfy the continuity condition.

Closing Remarks Similar utility theorems can also be stated even if the weak ordering property of $\succcurlyeq$ is replaced by a strict partial ordering of $\succ$, as can be seen from Fishburn [1970, pp. 18, 29–31, 34]. One notable difference between these two sets of results is that in the latter case, the condition

---

[6] The *continuity* condition, however, implies the *order-denseness* condition.
[7] $\mathbf{x} \geqslant \mathbf{y}$ if and only if $x_i \geqslant y_i$ for all $i = 1, \ldots, n$ with strict inequality for at least one i.

$v(\mathbf{a}) \geqslant v(\mathbf{b})$ for any $\mathbf{a}, \mathbf{b} \in X$ is no longer necessarily sufficient to guarantee the ordering $\mathbf{a} \succcurlyeq \mathbf{b}$ as in the former case,[8] for otherwise $\succcurlyeq$ must necessarily be a weak order.

3.4.2 *Additive Value Functions*

The existence theorems in the preceding subsection are applicable to both single-objective and multiobjective decision problems. However, if the theory is to serve directly as a basis for making decisions in the latter case, the corresponding value function v (which is a multivariate function) should be constructed. One difficulty that is likely to arise when attempting to construct such a function is the amount of work (especially in the process of questioning the decision maker to elicit necessary information) arising from the multidimensionality of the problem. An obvious and effective way of alleviating this difficulty is to reduce the dimensionality if possible. This involves grouping multiple attributes into smaller subgroups, each of which can be considered independently of the others. In an ideal case a value function for each attribute can be constructed, one at a time, after which the corresponding results are combined in some additive fashion. When this happens, we say that the underlying preference structure is *additive*. In this section conditions under which this type of additive utility theory is applicable are discussed. We consider a setting conforming to a more general multiobjective decision-making problem than that stipulated in Theorem 3.4. Let $X_1, X_2, \ldots, X_n$ be the names and the sets of possible values of n attributes (Section 1.2.5), and let the set of alternatives X be the corresponding Cartesian product set, i.e., $X = X_1 \times X_2 \times \cdots \times X_n$. A particular alternative $\mathbf{x} \in X$ is thus given by $\mathbf{x} = (x_1, x_2, \ldots, x_n)$, where $x_1, x_2, \ldots, x_n$ are the corresponding values of $X_1, X_2, \ldots, X_n$, respectively. In terms of this notation, if a preference structure can be represented by some value functions, it will be additive if and only if one such function $v(\mathbf{x})$ can be written

$$v(\mathbf{x}) = v_1(x_1) + v_2(x_2) + \cdots + v_n(x_n) \tag{3.10a}$$

or, alternatively,

$$v(\mathbf{x}) = \lambda_1 v_1(x_1) + \lambda_2 v_2(x_2) + \cdots + \lambda_n v_n(x_n), \tag{3.10b}$$

where, for each $1 \leqslant i \leqslant n$, v_i is the corresponding value function for the ith attribute; $\lambda_i > 0$ is a scaling constant; and $\sum_{i=1}^{n} \lambda_i = 1$. Intuitively we would expect that (3.10) would be true if each x_i is independent of the remaining

[8] That is, the "if and only if" in (3.3) of Theorem 3.1 and in (3.9) of Theorem 3.3 must be replaced by "only if" or $\Rightarrow$ in stating the corresponding results for the case, where $\succ$ is a strict partial order on X.

attributes. The theorems to be stated subsequently in fact give this kind of result under the so-called *preferential independence* condition.

Independence and Other Conditions Let $\Omega=\{X_1, X_2,\ldots,X_n\}$ be a set of attributes, Θ a nonempty proper subset of Ω, and $\bar{\Theta}$ its complement. The set of alternatives will again be described by $X=X_1\times X_2\times\cdots\times X_n$. Let X_Θ and $X_{\bar{\Theta}}$ be the Cartesian product sets of attributes in Θ and $\bar{\Theta}$, respectively. For any alternative $\mathbf{x}\in X$, let the corresponding value of those components of $\mathbf{x}$ in X_Θ and $X_{\bar{\Theta}}$ be $\mathbf{x}_\Theta$ and $\mathbf{x}_{\bar{\Theta}}$, respectively. Consequently an alternative $\mathbf{x}$ can equivalently (neglecting the order of arrangement) be represented by $(\mathbf{x}_\Theta,\mathbf{x}_{\bar{\Theta}})$.

Definition. The subset of attributes Θ is said to be *preferentially independent* of its complement $\bar{\Theta}$ if and only if for a particular feasible value $\mathbf{x}^0_{\bar{\Theta}}$, $(\mathbf{x}'_\Theta,\mathbf{x}^0_{\bar{\Theta}})\succcurlyeq(\mathbf{x}''_\Theta,\mathbf{x}^0_{\bar{\Theta}})$ implies $(\mathbf{x}'_\Theta,\mathbf{x}_{\bar{\Theta}})\succcurlyeq(\mathbf{x}''_\Theta,\mathbf{x}_{\bar{\Theta}})$ for all values of $\mathbf{x}_{\bar{\Theta}}\in X_\Theta$, where $\mathbf{x}'_\Theta$ and $\mathbf{x}''_\Theta$ are arbitrary alternatives.

For example, in a two-attribute decision-making problem where $\Omega=\{X_1, X_2\}$, a possible subset Θ of Ω is either $\{X_1\}$ or $\{X_2\}$ and the corresponding complement $\bar{\Theta}$ is either $\{X_2\}$ or $\{X_1\}$, respectively.

If for some fixed value x_2^0 of the second attribute X_2, an alternative (x_1^0, x_2^0) is at least as preferable as (x_1^1, x_2^0), i.e.,

$$(x_1^0, x_2^0)\succcurlyeq(x_1^1, x_2^0), \tag{3.11a}$$

and if X_1 is preferentially independent of X_2, then

$$(x_1^0, x_2)\succcurlyeq(x_1^1, x_2) \tag{3.11b}$$

for all feasible values of x_2. Conversely, if (3.11a) implies (3.11b) for all feasible values of x_2, we then conclude that X_1 is preferentially independent of X_2. We observe that if X_1 is preferentially independent of X_2, then X_2 is not necessarily preferentially independent of X_1. This is true in general. That is, if Θ is preferentially independent of $\bar{\Theta}$, then $\bar{\Theta}$ is not necessarily independent of Θ. A stronger condition is needed before an additive utility function can be established:

Definition. The set of attributes Ω is said to be *mutually preferentially independent* if every nonempty proper subset Θ of Ω is preferentially independent of its complement $\bar{\Theta}$.

For example, for the two-attribute case, $\Omega=\{X_1, X_2\}$ is mutually preferentially independent if $\{X_1\}$ is preferentially independent of $\{X_2\}$ and $\{X_2\}$ is preferentially independent of $\{X_1\}$. For the three-attribute case, $\Omega=\{X_1, X_2, X_3\}$ is mutually preferentially independent if $\{X_1, X_2\}$ is preferentially independent of $\{X_3\}$, $\{X_2, X_3\}$ is preferentially independent of $\{X_1\}$,

$\{X_1, X_3\}$ is preferentially independent of $\{X_2\}$, and each X_i, $i=1,2,3$, is preferentially independent of its complement.

It can be easily shown that mutually preferential independence is indeed a necessary condition for the existence of the additive preference structure.

On the other hand, mutually preferential independence is, in most cases, also a sufficient condition. In fact, as Theorem 3.7 will show, in a multiobjective decision-making problem with three or more attributes, mutually preferential independence is a sufficient condition to ensure that if a preference structure is describable by a set of numerical functions, then at least one function is additive in the sense of (3.10). Unfortunately, in the two-attribute case we can easily construct counterexamples to show that the independence condition is not sufficient; counterexamples have been given by Adams and Fagot [1959] and Fishburn [1970, p. 43].

Additive Theorems for the Two-Attribute Case For the two-attribute case, we therefore require additional conditions to ensure the existence of additive value functions. One such condition may be derived from the so-called cancellation condition.

Definition. The preference order $\succsim$ in two-attribute decision-making problems is said to satisfy the *cancellation* condition if for any $x_1, y_1, a_1 \in X_1$ and $x_2, y_2, a_2 \in X_2$, $(x_1, a_2) \succsim (a_1, y_2)$ and $(a_1, x_2) \succsim (y_1, a_2)$ together imply $(x_1, x_2) \succsim (y_1, y_2)$.

It can be easily shown that the cancellation condition is also a necessary condition of an additive preference structure.

The cancellation condition is very strong. Once it is known that a value function representing a two-attribute preference structure exists, the cancellation condition is strong enough to imply mutually preferential independence and to guarantee additive structure of the preference. Although this cancellation condition is often difficult to verify, it is nonetheless fruitful to formally state the above statements for further reference.

Theorem 3.5. *Let a real-valued function $v(x_1, x_2)$ represent the preference structure characterized by $\succsim$ of a two-attribute decision-making problem in the sense that*

$$(x_1', x_2') \succsim (x_1'', x_2'') \quad \Leftrightarrow \quad v(x_1', x_2') \geq v(x_1'', x_2''). \tag{3.12}$$

Then

1. *$\succsim$ is mutually preferentially independent if the cancellation condition is satisfied, and*
2. *there exists v_1 and v_2 on X_1 and X_2, respectively, such that*

$$\mathbf{x} \succsim \mathbf{y} \quad \Leftrightarrow \quad v_1(x_1) + v_2(x_2) \geq v_1(y_1) + v_2(y_2) \tag{3.13}$$

for any $\mathbf{x}=(x_1, x_2)$ *and* $\mathbf{y}=(y_1, y_2)$ *in* $X \stackrel{\triangle}{=} X_1 \times X_2$ *if and only if the cancellation condition is satisfied.*

For a detailed proof, the reader is referred to Luce and Tukey [1964]. It should be noted that the proof of sufficiency begins by using the existence of $v(x_1, x_2)$ in (3.12) to show that $\succcurlyeq$ is a weak order (which is quite obvious) and that given any three of x_1, x_2, y_1, and y_2, we can always find the fourth such that

$$(x_1, x_2) \sim (y_1, y_2). \tag{3.14}$$

This last condition is the *solvability* condition. For our case, it easily follows from the fact that (3.14) is equivalent to the simple algebraic equation

$$v(x_1, x_2) = v(y_1, y_2). \tag{3.15}$$

Given any three of the four variables, (3.15) can always be used to solve for the fourth.

A weaker condition than the cancellation condition is obtained when $\succcurlyeq$ in the above definition is replaced by $\sim$. This weaker condition is normally called the Thomsen condition:

Definition. The preference order $\succcurlyeq$ in a two-attribute decision-making problem is said to satisfy the *Thomsen condition* if, for any $x_1, y_1, a_1 \in X_1$ and $x_2, y_2, a_2 \in X_2$, $(x_1, a_2) \sim (a_1, y_2)$ and $(a_1, x_2) \sim (y_1, a_2)$ imply $(x_1, x_2) \sim (y_1, y_2)$.

Clearly, since the cancellation condition implies the Thomsen condition, the latter must also be a necessary condition for additive preference structure as is the former. If X_1 and X_2 are subsets of the real-number set R, then the Thomsen condition can be illustrated graphically as shown in Figure 3.3.

The Thomsen condition can be viewed from an operational standpoint as a trade-off or marginal rate of substitution. Starting at H, if one is willing to give up X_1 by the amount Δx_1^0 to receive an increase in X_2 by the amount Δx_2^0 (the indifference between G and H) and likewise if one begins at F and is willing to give up X_1, by the amount of Δx_1^1 to receive an increase in X_2 of Δx_2^1, then the Thomsen condition requires that one should also be indifferent in trading off X_1 by the amount $\Delta x_1^0 + \Delta x_1^1$ $(=DC)$ to receive an increase of X_2 of $\Delta x_2^0 + \Delta x_2^1$ $(=DA)$.

Because of its close relationship with a trade-off and the marginal rate of substitution, the Thomsen condition is easier to verify and, hence, has more practical implications than the cancellation condition. In fact as an alternative to Theorem 3.5b for the two-attribute case, the Thomsen condition can be used in conjunction with mutually preferential independence to provide somewhat more operational sufficient conditions for additive preference structure than the cancellation condition itself. It should be observed that if Theorem 3.5b is true, so is the following theorem.

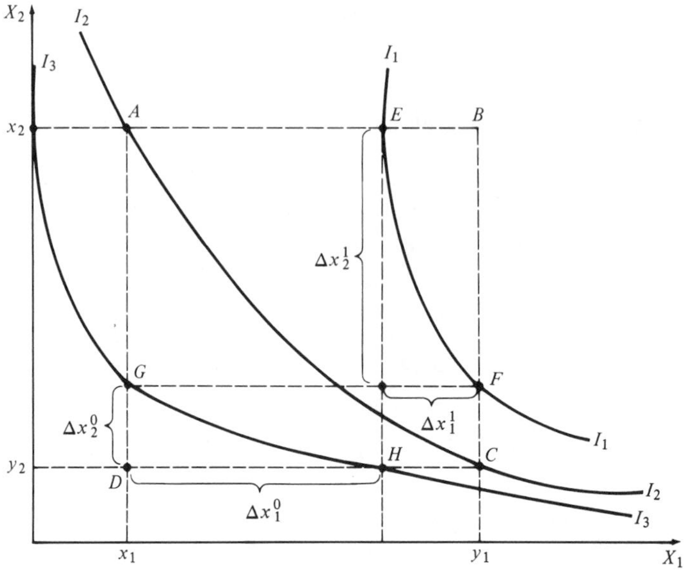

Figure 3.3 The Thomsen condition.

Theorem 3.6. *Let there be a representation of a real-valued function*, $v(x_1, x_2)$ *of the preference structure characterized by* $\succcurlyeq$ *of a two-attribute decision-making problem in the sense of* (3.12). *Then there exists* v_1 *and* v_2 *on* X_1 *and* X_2, *respectively, such that* (3.13) *is satisfied if and only if* $\{X_1, X_2\}$ *is mutually preferentially independent and the Thomsen condition is satisfied.*

The necessity part is obvious from earlier remarks. As in Theorem 3.5, the existence of $v(x_1, x_2)$ and (3.12) ensure that $\succcurlyeq$ is a weak order and that the solvability condition (3.14) is satisfied. Again the proof of sufficiency from this point onward is quite complicated. Krantz et al. [1971] provide a formal proof of essentially the same result. With slight modifications the proof of Luce and Tukey [1964] (of Theorem 3.5b) can also be made to prove this part of Theorem 3.6. We shall not present a formal proof, observing only that one might check the Thomsen condition and construct v_1 and v_2, if they are known to exist, by constructing sequences of points described by $\{(x_i, y_i)\}$, $i=0, \pm 1, \pm 2, \ldots$, where $x_i \in X_1$ and $y_i \in X_2$ and x_i and y_i have the property[9]

$$(x_j, y_k) = (x_m, y_n) \qquad \text{if and only if} \qquad j+k=m+n. \qquad (3.16)$$

The hypotheses of Theorems 3.5 and 3.6 make this construction possible for any given point (x_0, y_0) and x_1 (or y_1). Since the construction process is

[9]A double sequence with Property (3.16) is normally called, in measurement theory, a *dual-standard sequence*.

also of practical importance, it is illustrated graphically in Figure 3.4. Given the point $P_0=(x_0, y_0)$ and x_1, then $P_1=(x_1, y_0)$ can be immediately located. Next, the hypothetical indifference curve I_1 is drawn through P_1, and the point $Q_1=(x_0, y_1)$ of intersection between I_1 and the line $x=x_0$ is identified, thereby giving y_1 and the point $P_2=(x_1, y_1)$. Another indifference curve I_2 is then drawn through P_2 intersecting the line $y=y_0$ at the point $Q_2=(x_2, y_0)$. This determines x_2, from which $P_3=(x_2, y_1)$ can be located. The process can be repeated to generate successive points in the sequence (as indicated by the heavy directed lines) as Q_1, P_2, Q_2, and P_3 were generated. The sequence of points $P_0=(x_0, y_0)$, $P_2=(x_1, y_1)$, $P_4=(x_2, y_2)$, $P_6=(x_3, y_3)$, ... constitutes the "positive half" (i.e., $i>0$) of the required sequence. The "negative half" ($i<0$) can be constructed in a similar manner, as illustrated in Figure 3.4b.

It remains to be shown that condition (3.16) is satisfied by the sequence of points generated. This is equivalent to showing that points A, P_2, and Q_2 lie on I_2; points B, Q_3, P_3, and C lie on I_3; and so on. This is where the Thomsen condition plays an important role. For example, to show that A lies on the same indifference curve as P_2 and Q_2, we note that

$$(x_0, y_1)\sim(x_1, y_0) \qquad (Q_1 \text{ and } P_1 \text{ are on } I_1),$$

$$(x_1, y_2)\sim(x_2, y_1) \qquad (Q_3 \text{ and } P_3 \text{ are on } I_3).$$

Hence, by the Thomsen condition we have $(x_0, y_2)\sim(x_2, y_0)$, indicating that A lies on I_2. Similarly, since

$$(x_1, y_1)\sim(x_2, y_0) \qquad (P_2 \text{ and } Q_2 \text{ are on } I_2),$$

$$(x_2, y_2)\sim(x_3, y_1) \qquad (P_4 \text{ and } Q_4 \text{ are on } I_4).$$

This implies

$$(x_1, y_2)\sim(x_3, y_0) \qquad (\text{by the Thomsen condition}),$$

which ensures that C lies on I_3. Likewise we can use the fact that A and Q_2 lie on the same indifference curve I_2 and that Q_5 and P_5 lie on the same indifference curve I_5 together with the Thomsen condition to show that $B=(x_0, y_3)$ is on the same indifference curve as Q_3, P_3, and C.

The fact that this type of sequence of points can be constructed for any given "initial" point (x_0, y_0) and x_1 (or y_1) has both theoretical and practical implications. First, from the theoretical viewpoint, many properties of the sequence are useful in theoretically defining v_1 and v_2 that satisfy (3.13), thereby proving Theorem 3.5b or Theorem 3.6.[10] Second, from the practical viewpoint, the construction process just demonstrated provides an operational way of constructing the functions v_1 and v_2 empirically, as well as a way of verifying the Thomsen conditions. Two distinct sets of points are generated: the Ps and Qs. While the points labeled P can readily be

[10] See, for example, Luce and Tukey [1964] and Fishburn [1970, pp. 65–71].

determined, the generation of those labeled Q depends on knowledge of indifference curves. In practice the exact form of these indifference curves is usually not known, and the construction of the points requires eliciting information from the decision maker. For example, to construct Q_1, knowing x_0, y_0, and x_1, we ask the decision maker to give the value of y_1 such that $(x_1, y_0) \sim (x_0, y_1)$. Since we indirectly assume the solvability condition, the existence of y_1 is ensured. The points $Q_2, Q_3, Q_6, \ldots$ can be constructed in a similar manner. Once points P and Q have been generated, $A, B, C, D, E, \ldots$ can be located graphically. Checking with the decision maker whether these points lie on the corresponding indifference curves provides a convenient way of verifying the Thomsen condition. If v_1 and v_2 are known to exist, information contained in Figure 3.4 is useful in their construction.

A slightly different treatment of the additive value function for the two-attribute case is given by Keeney and Raiffa [1976]. To begin with, instead of mutually preferential independence and the Thomsen condition, they use a *corresponding trade-offs condition* as a necessary and sufficient condition to guarantee the additive structure in Theorem 3.6. This condition can be viewed as the second-order Thomsen condition or the indifference version of the "double-cancellation" condition. More specifically, we say that $\{X_1, X_2\}$ satisfies the corresponding trade-offs condition if for any $x_1, y_1, a_1, b_1 \in X_1$ and $x_2, y_2, a_2, b_2 \in X_2$,

$$(x_1, a_2) \sim (y_1, b_2), \qquad (b_1, b_2) \sim (a_1, a_2), \qquad (a_1, x_2) \sim (b_1, y_2)$$

imply $(x_1, x_2) \sim (y_1, y_2)$. For detailed construction of v_1 and v_2 using this condition, see Keeney and Raiffa [1976].

An Additive Theorem for the n-Attribute Case As remarked earlier mutually preferential independence is strong enough to guarantee additive preference structure for the n-attribute case under the same hypotheses as those of Theorem 3.6. In fact, it has been shown in general (see Krantz et al. [1971, pp. 306–307]) that if there are three or more attributes,[11] under appropriate assumptions the mutually preferential independence condition implies the "pairwise" cancellation condition and hence the "pairwise" Thomsen condition. Hence, for the case of more than two attributes, we can simply state the following:

Theorem 3.7. *For an n-attribute decision-making problem, where* $n \geq 3$, *let there be a value function* $v(\mathbf{x}) = v(x_1, \ldots, x_n)$ *defined on* X *such that for*

[11]More precisely we say, "if there are three or more 'essential' attributes. . . ." In an n-attribute problem where $X = X_1 \times X_2 \times \cdots \times X_n$, X_1 is essential if there are some values $x_2^0, \ldots, x_n^0$ such that not all $(x_1, x_2^0, \ldots, x_n^0)$, $x_1 \in X_1$, are indifferent.

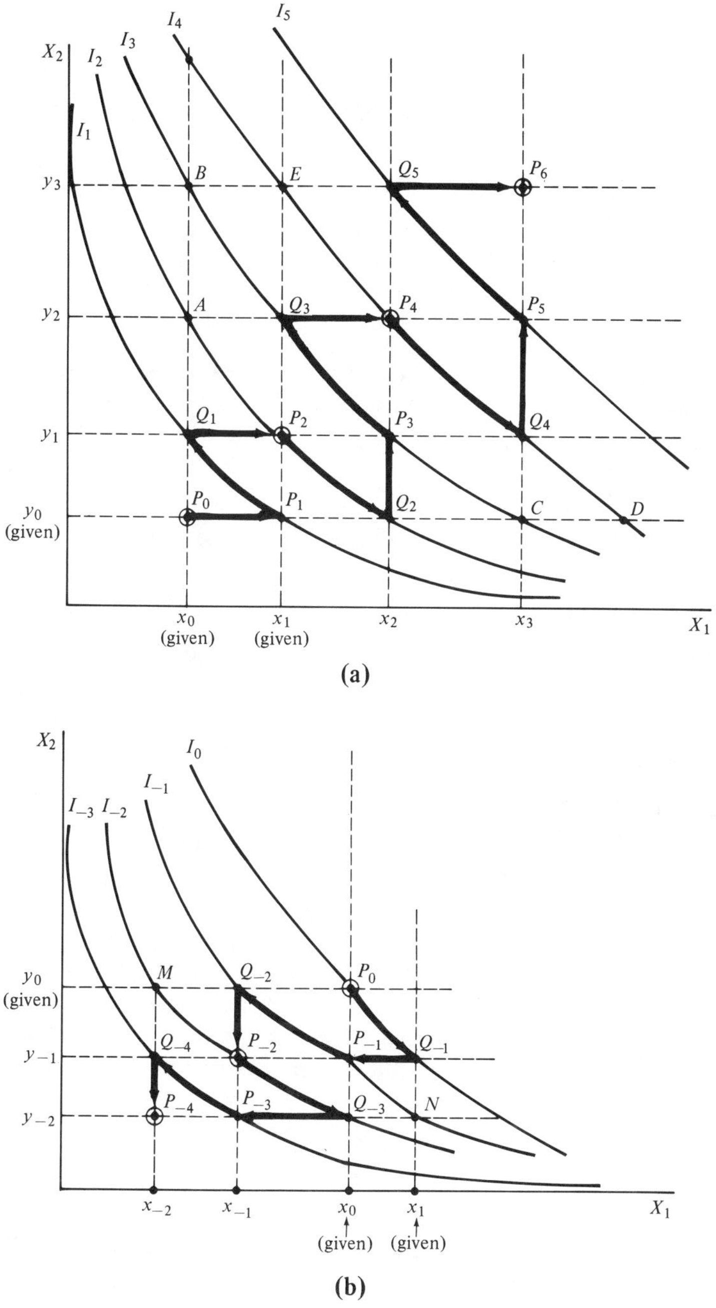

Figure 3.4 A conjoint measurement procedure.

any $\mathbf{x}',\mathbf{x}''\in X$

$$\mathbf{x}'\succsim\mathbf{x}'' \quad \textit{if and only if} \quad v(\mathbf{x}')\geqslant v(\mathbf{x}''). \tag{3.17}$$

Then, there exist real-valued functions $v_1,\ldots,v_n$ *defined on* $X_1,\ldots,X_n$, *respectively, such that*

$$\mathbf{x}'\succsim\mathbf{x}''$$

and

$$v_1(x_1')+\cdots+v_n(x_n')\geqslant v_1(x_1'')+\cdots+v_n(x_n'') \tag{3.18}$$

if and only if the mutually preferential independence condition holds.

Once (3.17) has been used to show that $\succsim$ is a weak order and that the solvability condition holds, Debreu's proof [1960], based on topological results, or algebraic arguments such as those used by Luce [1966] or Krantz et al. [1971, pp. 307–308] can be used to prove the remaining part of the theorem. If it is known that $v_1,\ldots,v_n$ exist with the required properties, it is possible to construct each of them numerically. We shall discuss this *construction* in some detail in Chapter 5.

Closing Remarks In practice, in applying Theorem 3.7 in the present form the task of verifying the mutually preferentially independent conditions when n is large would be truly prohibitive. Fortunately, based on a theorem in Gorman[12] [1968, Theorem 1, pp. 369–371] it can be shown that if each of the n attributes is strictly essential,[13] then in order to use Theorem 3.7 it suffices to verify that every pair of attributes is preferentially independent of its complement.

Second, once the existence of the additive value function has been established by virtue of the results stated in this section, there still remains the question of uniqueness. If an additive value function characterizing a particular preference structure exists, are there others? It is not difficult to show that if $v_1,\ldots,v_n$ are, respectively, the corresponding value functions on $X_1,\ldots,X_n$ satisfying the additive property (3.18) and $V_1,\ldots,V_n$ are, respectively, real-valued functions defined on $X_1,\ldots,X_n$ such that for each $1\leqslant i\leqslant n$,

$$V_i(x_i)=\alpha v_i(x_i)+\beta_i, \tag{3.19}$$

where α, β_i are real constants with $\alpha>0$, then for any $\mathbf{x}'$ and $\mathbf{x}''\in X$

$$\mathbf{x}'\succsim\mathbf{x}''$$

if and only if

$$V_1(x_1')+\cdots+V_n(x_n')\geqslant V_1(x_1'')+\cdots+V_n(x_n''). \tag{3.20}$$

---

[12]Also in Keeney and Raiffa [1976], pp. 112–114. See also Theorem 3.11 in Section 3.4.3 for an analogous result.

[13]X_1 is strictly essential if there are x_1' and x_1'' in X_1 such that $(x_1', x_2,\ldots,x_n)$ is not indifferent to $(x_1'', x_2,\ldots,x_n)$ for all $x_2\in X_2,\ldots,x_n\in X_n$, and $x_1'\neq x_1''$.

That is, any positive linear transformation of the form (3.20) of the original additive value function is also an additive value function characterizing the given preference structure. The converse is also true. More precisely, under the hypotheses of Theorems 3.5–3.7, if $v_1,\dots,v_n$ and $V_1,\dots,V_n$ are two sets of additive value functions on $X_1,\dots,X_n$ satisfying (3.18) then there exist real constants $\alpha, \beta_1,\dots,\beta_n$ such that (3.20) is true for each $1 \leqslant i \leqslant n$.

We conclude the section by remarking on the implications of Theorem 3.2. Because additive value functions, if they exist, are unique up to a linear transformation, such functions (i.e., $v_1,\dots,v_n$) must be measured at least in interval scales (Section 2.1.4).

3.4.3 *Other Decomposition Forms of Value Functions*

Although we would like for practical reasons to have our preference structure be additive, a number of decision problems are better served by other models. A possible alternative is that of decomposable structure. A preference structure with n attributes is *decomposable* if there exist real-valued functions $v_1,\dots,v_n$ defined on $X_1,\dots,X_n$ and v defined on X,[14] such that for any $\mathbf{x}'$ and $\mathbf{x}'' \in X$

$$\mathbf{x}' \succcurlyeq \mathbf{x}'' \quad \text{if and only if} \quad v[v_1(x_1'),\dots,v_n(x_n')] \geqslant v[v_1(x_1''),\dots,v_n(x_n'')]. \tag{3.21}$$

It is clear that an additive model is just a special form of the decomposable model. Necessary and sufficient conditions for decomposable structure are thus less restrictive than those of the additive structure. In fact Krantz et al. [1971, pp. 318–321] show that with the same hypothesis as in Theorem 3.7, the condition that each attribute must be preferentially independent of its complement can be used to replace mutually preferential independence as a necessary and sufficient condition for decomposable preference structure. In addition to additive models, examples of a decomposable utility model include

$$v[v_1(x_1),\dots,v_n(x_n)] = kv_1(x_1)v_2(x)\cdots v_n(x_n) \qquad \text{(multiplicative);}$$

and

$$= kx_1^{\alpha_1}\cdots x_n^{\alpha_n}, \quad \alpha_i \text{ nonnegative integers} \qquad \text{(polynomial);}$$

and

$$= [k_1v_1(x_1) + \cdots + k_{n-2}v_{n-2}(x_{n-2})]\, v_{n-1}(x_{n-1})v_n(x_n) \qquad \text{(partial additive);}$$

and so on.

---

[14] More precisely, v is defined on $v_1(X)\times v_2(X)\times\cdots\times v_n(X)$, where $v_i(X)$ is the image of X under v_i.

The last example also exemplifies the case of partial additivity. We would expect that if Θ is a subset of the set of attributes Ω and if Θ itself satisfies the mutually preferential independence condition, then the corresponding decision problem will have additive preference structure, at least with respect to all attributes in Θ. This is proved by Gorman [1968].

Some additional results used to characterize the preference structure in quasi-additive or multiplicative form were first suggested by Dyer and Sarin [1979], who in turn built upon the familiar works in the uncertainty case (to be discussed in Section 3.5). In order to develop these results, a few more concepts need to be introduced. The first concept has to do with extending the value function to that of a measurable value function.

Definition. A value function v on X is said to be *measurable* if and only if v faithfully reflects 1) the order of elements in X, and 2) the order of differences of elements in X.

More precisely, using the notation introduced in Chapter 2, let the binary operation $\circ$ denote the difference of elements in X, and let $\succcurlyeq^*$ denote the corresponding preference order in $X \times X$ such that for any $\mathbf{w},\mathbf{x},\mathbf{y},\mathbf{z} \in X$, the difference $\mathbf{w} \circ \mathbf{x}$ is preferred to the difference $\mathbf{y} \circ \mathbf{z}$ if and only if $\mathbf{w} \circ \mathbf{x} \succcurlyeq^* \mathbf{y} \circ \mathbf{z}$. Thus v is a measurable value function if for any $\mathbf{w},\mathbf{x},\mathbf{y},\mathbf{z}$ in X,

$$\mathbf{w} \circ \mathbf{x} \succcurlyeq^* \mathbf{y} \circ \mathbf{z} \qquad \text{if and only if} \qquad v(\mathbf{w}) - v(\mathbf{x}) \geqslant v(\mathbf{y}) - v(\mathbf{z}). \tag{3.22}$$

Here we shall not be concerned with the existence of measurable value functions apart from mentioning that a number of axiom systems exist to guarantee such existence (e.g., those of Scott and Suppes [1958], Luce and Suppes [1965, Theorem 7], and Krantz et al. [1970, Theorems 4.1, 4.2]). Rather we shall address the following question: If a measurable value function describing a certain preference structure exists, when would it be possible to write such a function in some decomposable form?

In the preceding section, mutually preferential independence was used as a basis to ensure "simple" additive structure. Krantz et al. [1970] added *difference independence* to guarantee an additive form for an existing measurable function. Dyer and Sarin [1977] added yet another condition, *difference consistency*,[15] to ensure the existence of additive measurable value functions without assuming the existence of a value function in the first place. We shall now focus on a particular axiom system, as proposed by Dyer and Sarin [1979], which leads to a multiplicative measurable value function. The quasi-additive (multilinear) form will also be derived. To do this we need the following.

[15] We say $\Theta \subseteq \Omega$ is difference independent of $\overline{\Theta}$ if for any $\mathbf{x}_\Theta, \mathbf{y}_\Theta \in X_\Theta$ such that $(\mathbf{x}_\Theta, \mathbf{x}^0_{\overline{\Theta}}) \succcurlyeq (\mathbf{y}_\Theta, \mathbf{x}^0_{\overline{\Theta}})$ for some $\mathbf{x}^0_{\overline{\Theta}} \in X_{\overline{\Theta}}$, then $(\mathbf{x}_\Theta, \mathbf{x}^0_{\overline{\Theta}}) \circ (\mathbf{y}_\Theta, \mathbf{x}^0_{\overline{\Theta}}) \succcurlyeq^* (\mathbf{x}_\Theta, \mathbf{x}_{\overline{\Theta}}) \circ (\mathbf{y}_\Theta, \mathbf{x}_{\overline{\Theta}})$ for all $\mathbf{x}_{\overline{\Theta}} \in X_{\overline{\Theta}}$. See Dyer and Sarin [1979] for a definition of difference consistency.

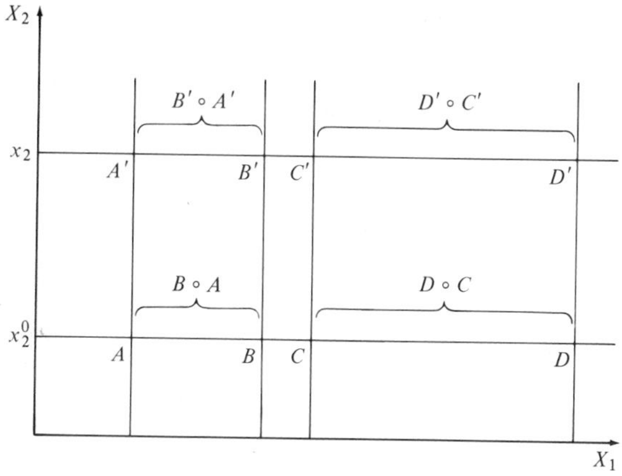

Figure 3.5 Weak-difference independence.

Definition. The subset of attributes Θ is said to be *weak-difference independent* of its complement $\overline{\Theta}$ if for any $\mathbf{w}_\Theta, \mathbf{x}_\Theta, \mathbf{y}_\Theta, \mathbf{z}_\Theta \in X_\Theta$ such that

$$\left(\mathbf{w}_\Theta, \mathbf{w}_{\overline{\Theta}}^0\right) \circ \left(\mathbf{x}_\Theta, w_{\overline{\Theta}}^0\right) \succcurlyeq^* \left(\mathbf{y}_\Theta, \mathbf{w}_{\overline{\Theta}}^0\right) \circ \left(\mathbf{z}_\Theta, \mathbf{w}_{\overline{\Theta}}^0\right) \qquad \text{for some} \quad \mathbf{w}_{\overline{\Theta}} \in X_{\overline{\Theta}}, \tag{3.23}$$

then

$$(\mathbf{w}_\Theta, \mathbf{w}_{\overline{\Theta}}) \circ (\mathbf{x}_\Theta, \mathbf{w}_{\overline{\Theta}}) \succcurlyeq^* (\mathbf{y}_\Theta, \mathbf{w}_{\overline{\Theta}}) \circ (\mathbf{z}_\Theta, \mathbf{w}_{\overline{\Theta}}) \qquad \text{for all} \quad \mathbf{w}_{\overline{\Theta}} \in X_{\overline{\Theta}}. \tag{3.24}$$

In a two-dimensional problem with the two attributes X_1 and X_2 being measured in real-valued units, if the binary operation $\circ$ is ordinary subtraction and if the preference $\succcurlyeq^*$ is directly proportional to "length," then weak-difference independence can be demonstrated graphically as shown in Figure 3.5. Since DC is longer than BA at x_2^0, $D \circ C \succcurlyeq^* B \circ A$ at x_2^0. Clearly $D'C'$ is always longer than $B'A'$ irrespective of the value of x_2, implying that $D' \circ C' \succcurlyeq^* B' \circ A'$ for all $x_2 \in X_2$. Hence X_1 is weak-difference independent of X_2.

Weak-difference independence is a strong condition. For example, it can be easily verified that weak-difference independence implies preferential independence.

The following key result is due to Dyer and Sarin [1979].

Theorem 3.8. *If v is a measurable value function on X, the subset of attribute Θ is weak-difference independent of $\overline{\Theta}$ if and only if functions p and q exist, defined on $X_{\overline{\Theta}}$ with $q > 0$,*[16] *such that for all $\mathbf{x}_\Theta \in X_\Theta$ and $\mathbf{x}_{\overline{\Theta}}, \hat{\mathbf{x}}_{\overline{\Theta}} \in X_{\overline{\Theta}}$:*

$$v(\mathbf{x}_\Theta, \mathbf{x}_{\overline{\Theta}}) = p(\mathbf{x}_{\overline{\Theta}}) + q(\mathbf{x}_{\overline{\Theta}})\, v(\mathbf{x}_\Theta, \hat{\mathbf{x}}_{\overline{\Theta}}), \tag{3.25}$$

where the forms of p and q depend also on the value of $\hat{\mathbf{x}}_{\overline{\Theta}}$.

[16] Here positive difference structure is assumed; see Krantz et al. [1971].

Quasi-Additive Form Dyer and Sarin [1979] called (3.25) *conditional cardinality* and observed that its key roles are similar to the "conditional utility function" used by Keeney [1974] and Keeney and Raiffa [1976] in developing multiplicative and quasi-additive utility functions for the uncertainty case.

Theorem 3.9 (quasi-additive theorem). *Suppose there exists a measurable value function v on X, where $X = X_1 \times \cdots \times X_n$. Assume without loss of generality that v is normalized, i.e., there exist the least element $\mathbf{x}^0$ and the most preferred element $\mathbf{x}^*$ in X, respectively, such that $v(\mathbf{x}^0)=0$ and $v(\mathbf{x}^*)=1$. If attribute X_i is weak-difference independent of its complement set of attributes X_i^- for every $i=1,\ldots,n$, then there exist functions v_i (called conditional value functions) defined on X_i, $i=1,\ldots,n$, such that for any $\mathbf{x}\in X$,*

$$\begin{aligned} v(\mathbf{x}) = {} & \sum_{i=1}^{n} \lambda_i v_i(x_i) + \sum_{i=1}^{n} \sum_{j>i}^{n} \lambda_{ij} v_i(x_i) v_j(x_j) \\ & + \sum_{i=1}^{n} \sum_{j>i}^{n} \sum_{k>j}^{n} \lambda_{ijk} v_i(x_i) v_j(x_j) v_k(x_k) \\ & + \cdots + \lambda_{12\ldots n} v_1(x_1) \cdots v_n(x_n), \end{aligned} \tag{3.26}$$

where $v_i(x_i^*)=1$ and $v_i(x_i^0)=0$ for each $i=1,\ldots,n$.

Multiplicative–Additive Form Clearly the quasi-additive form (3.26) reduces to an additive form if all $\lambda_{ij}, \lambda_{ijk},\ldots$ vanish. On the other hand, if $\lambda_{ij} = \mu\lambda_i\lambda_j$, $\lambda_{ijk} = \mu^2\lambda_i\lambda_j\lambda_k \cdots$, and $\sum_{i=1}^{k}\lambda_i \neq 1$, the quasi-additive form (3.26) reduces to

$$\begin{aligned} v(\mathbf{x}) = {} & \sum_{i=1}^{n} \lambda_i v_i(x_i) + \mu \sum_{i=1}^{n} \sum_{j>i}^{n} \lambda_i \lambda_j v_i(x_i) v_j(x_j) \\ & + \mu^2 \sum_{i=1}^{n} \sum_{j>i}^{n} \sum_{k>j}^{n} \lambda_i \lambda_j \lambda_k v_i(x_i) v_j(x_j) v_k(x_k) \\ & + \mu^{n-1} \lambda_1 \lambda_2 \cdots \lambda_n v_1(x_1) \cdots v_n(x_n). \end{aligned} \tag{3.27}$$

Multiplying by μ and then adding 1 to both sides yields after factoring

$$1 + \mu v(\mathbf{x}) = [1 + \mu\lambda_1 v_1(x_1)][1 + \mu\lambda_2 v_2(x_2)] \cdots [1 + \mu\lambda_n v_n(x_n)]. \tag{3.28}$$

Since $v(\mathbf{x})$ and all $v_i(x_i)$ are normalized, the relationship between μ and the λ_is takes the following form after substituting $\mathbf{x}=\mathbf{x}^*$ in (3.28):

$$1+\mu=(1+\mu\lambda_1)(1+\mu\lambda_2)\cdots(1+\mu\lambda_n). \tag{3.29}$$

We observe further that (3.27) degenerates to an additive form if $\Sigma_{i=1}^{n}\lambda_i=1$. This can be easily verified by substituting $\mathbf{x}=\mathbf{x}^*$ in (3.27). On the other hand, if $\Sigma_{i=1}^{n}\lambda_i\neq 1$, we see that (3.27) is equivalent to a multiplicative form as is evident in (3.28).

Since the multiplicative measurable value function as expressed in (3.27) is a special form of the quasi-additive form (3.26), we must tighten the conditions in Theorem 3.9 to guarantee the former.

Definition. The set of attributes $\Omega=\{X_1,\ldots,X_n\}$ is *mutually weak-difference independent* if every subset Θ of Ω is weak-difference independent of its complement $\overline{\Theta}$.

As it turns out, mutually weak-difference independence is sufficient to ensure multiplicative or additive structure, as the following theorem will indicate [Dyer and Sarin, 1979].

Theorem 3.10 (multiplicative–additive theorem). *Suppose there exists a normalized measurable value function v on X. If the set of attributes Ω is mutually weak-difference independent, then v can be written in the multiplicative–additive form* (3.27) *with* $1>\lambda_i>0$ *for each* $i=1,\ldots,n$ *and* $\mu>-1$.

As remarked earlier, $v(\mathbf{x})$ written in the form (3.27) can be either additive or multiplicative, depending on whether $\Sigma_{i=1}^{n}\lambda_i=1$. In order to find out the applicable form in a particular situation, the following simple check can be carried out. Assume that all hypotheses in Theorem 3.10 hold. Take any two attributes, say X_p and X_q, and set the remaining attributes $X_{\overline{pq}}$ at some fixed values[17] $\hat{\mathbf{x}}^*_{\overline{pq}}$. Next for each attribute X_i, $i=p,q$, choose two levels x_i^1, x_i^2 such that $(x_i^1,\mathbf{x}_{\bar{i}})$ and $(x_i^2,\mathbf{x}_{\bar{i}})$ are not indifferent for some value of $\mathbf{x}_{\bar{i}}\in X_{\bar{i}}$. Now if we ask the decision maker to compare the differences $(x_p^1, x_q^1,\hat{\mathbf{x}}_{\overline{pq}})\circ(x_p^1, x_q^2,\hat{\mathbf{x}}_{\overline{pq}})$ and $(x_p^2, x_q^1,\hat{\mathbf{x}}_{\overline{pq}})\circ(x_p^2, x_q^2,\hat{\mathbf{x}}_{\overline{pq}})$ and if one is strictly preferred to the other, then (3.27) takes a multiplicative form; otherwise, it is an additive form.

Weakening the Sufficiency Conditions As observed by Dewispelare and Sage [1979], to use Theorem 3.10 directly when n is large usually involves a

[17]Since weak-difference independence implies preferential independence, the subsequent testing procedure is valid for any value of $\mathbf{x}_{\overline{pq}}\in X_{\overline{pq}}$.

prohibitive task in verifying the mutually weak-difference independence. Fortunately, we can prove the following results, analogous to Gorman's theorem [1968],[18] which permit development of a number of conditions weaker than mutually weak-difference independence.

Theorem 3.11. *Assume there exists a normalized measurable value function v on X. If Y and Z are two overlapping subsets of the set of attributes Ω and if both are weak-difference independent of their respective complements, then the following sets of attributes are also weak-difference independent of their respective complements:*

a. $Y \cap Z$;
b. $Y \cup Z$;
c. $(Y \cap \bar{Z}) \cup (\bar{Y} \cap Z)$; *and*
d. $Y \cap \bar{Z}$ *and* $\bar{Y} \cap Z$.

A general proof can easily be patterned after that of Keeney and Raiffa [1976, Theorem 6.7].

As remarked earlier, Theorem 3.11 quite powerfully develops conditions equivalent to that required in Theorem 3.10 but much easier to verify in practice. For example, it can be shown that each Θ_i, $i=1,\ldots,n$, is weak-difference independent of $\bar{\Theta}_i$, where Θ_i is either

1. $\Theta_i = X_i^-$;
2. $\Theta_1 = \{X_1,\ldots,X_{n-1}\}$, $\Theta_i = \{X_i, X_{i+1},\ldots,X_n\}$, $i=2,\ldots,n$; or
3. $\Theta_i = \{X_i, X_{i+1}\}$, $i=1,\ldots,n-1$, $n \geqslant 3$,

if and only if Ω is mutually weak-difference independent. We observe that the sufficiency part is trivial. To show the necessity part we simply write X_i as some appropriate combination of intersections, unions, differences, and symmetric differences of the Θ_is.[19] According to Theorem 3.11, each X_i is then weak-difference independent of X_i^-. By Theorem 3.11b, all possible unions of X_is are then weak-difference independent of their respective complements, hence ensuring mutually weak-difference independence of Ω.

Although the task of verifying any of the above three conditions is very much reduced, it still requires checking a number of weak-difference independence assumptions, which is often harder than checking those involving only preferential independence. It is natural, therefore, to seek a set of sufficient conditions wherein weak-difference independence assumptions are replaced by preferentially independent ones as much as possible. To do this,

[18] If weak-preference independence in Theorem 3.11 is replaced by preferential independence, the result is known as Gorman's theorem.

[19] For example, 1) $X_i = \bar{\Theta}_i \cap \Theta_j$, $j \neq i$; 2) $X_1 = \Theta_1 \cap \bar{\Theta}_2$, $X_n = \bar{\Theta}_1 \cap \Theta_2$ and $X_i = \Theta_i \cap \bar{\Theta}_{i+1}$ for $i=2,\ldots,n-1$; or 3) $X_i = \Theta_i \cap \bar{\Theta}_{i+1}$, $i=1,\ldots,n-1$ and $X_n = \Theta_{n-1} \cap \bar{\Theta}_{n-2}$.

we need to develop some kind of relationship between the two "independence" conditions. Dewispelare and Sage [1979] provide a proof analogous to that used by Keeney [1974, Appendix A] (see also Keeney and Raiffa [1976, Theorem 6.6] for the uncertainty case). We provide a somewhat simpler proof.

Theorem 3.12. *Let $\Omega=\{X_1, X_2, X_3\}$. Assume there exists a measureable value function v on X. If $\{X_1\}$ is weak-difference independent of $\{X_2, X_3\}$, and $\{X_1, X_2\}$ is weak-difference independent of $\{X_3\}$, then $\{X_1, X_2\}$ is weak-difference independent of $\{X_3\}$.*

PROOF: By Theorem 3.8, we can write, for all $x_i \in X_i$, $i=1,2,3$,

$$v(x_1, x_2, x_3)=p(x_2, x_3)+q(x_2, x_3)v(x_1, x_2^0, x_3^0). \tag{3.30}$$

Now consider $(x_1^1, x_2^1, \hat{x}_3)$, $(x_1^2, x_2^2, \hat{x}_3)$, $(x_1^3, x_2^3, \hat{x}_3)$, and $(x_1^4, x_2^4, \hat{x}_3)$ in X such that

$$v(x_1^1, x_2^1, \hat{x}_3)-v(x_1^2, x_2^2, \hat{x}_3)\geqslant v(x_1^3, x_2^3, \hat{x}_3)-v(x_1^4, x_2^4, \hat{x}_3). \tag{3.31}$$

To prove Theorem 3.12 we must show that (3.31) is true for all values of x_3 in X_3. To do this we simply use the solvability condition, i.e., $\hat{x}_1^k$ can be found in X_1 such that for each $k=1,\ldots,4$ and for a fixed $\hat{x}_2$ in X_2

$$v(x_1^1, x_2^1, \hat{x}_3)=v(\hat{x}_1^k, \hat{x}_2, \hat{x}_3). \tag{3.32}$$

Hence from (3.31) and (3.32),

$$v(\hat{x}_1^1, \hat{x}_2, \hat{x}_3)-v(\hat{x}_1^2, \hat{x}_2, \hat{x}_3)\geqslant v(\hat{x}_1^3, \hat{x}_2, \hat{x}_3)-v(\hat{x}_1^4, \hat{x}_2, \hat{x}_3).$$

Applying (3.30) and observing that $q(\hat{x}_2, \hat{x}_3)>0$, we have

$$v(\hat{x}_1^1, x_2^0, x_3^0)-v(\hat{x}_1^2, x_2^0, x_3^0)\geqslant v(\hat{x}_1^3, x_2^0, x_3^0)-v(\hat{x}_1^4, x_2^0, x_3^0). \tag{3.33}$$

For any $x_3 \in X_3$, multiplying $q(\hat{x}_2, x_3)>0$ and adding $p(\hat{x}_2, x_3)-p(\hat{x}_2, x_3)$ to both sides of (3.33) and using (3.30) yields

$$v(\hat{x}_1^1, \hat{x}_2, x_3)-v(\hat{x}_1^2, \hat{x}_2, x_3)\geqslant v(\hat{x}_1^3, \hat{x}_2, x_3)-v(\hat{x}_1^4, \hat{x}_2, x_3). \tag{3.34}$$

By the preferential-independence hypothesis, (3.32) is true for all values of x_3 in X_3; i.e., for each $k=1,\ldots,4$,

$$v(x_1^1, x_2^1, x_3)=v(\hat{x}_1^k, \hat{x}_2, x_3) \qquad \text{for all} \quad x_3 \in X_3.$$

Hence (3.34) becomes

$$v(x_1^1, x_2^1, x_3)-v(x_1^2, x_2^2, x_3)\geqslant v(x_1^3, x_2^3, x_3)-v(x_1^4, x_2^4, x_3)$$

for all x_3 in X_3. ■

Based on Theorem 3.12, still weaker sufficient conditions can be put forward. Dyer and Sarin [1979] and Dewispelare and Sage [1979] respectively, suggest

4. Ω is mutually preferentially independent and X_1 is weak-difference independent of its complement;
5. X_1 is weak-difference independent of its complement and $\{X_1, X_i\}$, $i=2,\ldots,n$, is preferentially independent of its complement.

Clearly Condition 5 is less demanding than Condition 4 since Condition 4 implies Condition 5 but not vice versa. Thus, proving Condition 5 also proves Condition 4. To prove Condition 5, we simply note from Theorem 3.12 that $\{X_1, X_i\}$, $i=2,\ldots,n$, is weak-difference independent of its complement and that $X_i=\{X_1, X_i\}\cap \bar{X_1}$ for each $i=2,\ldots,n$. Hence, by Theorem 3.11, all X_is, $i=1,\ldots,n$, and any of their possible unions are weak-difference independent of their respective complements, indicating that Condition 5 is equivalent to mutually weak-difference independence.

3.5 Utility Theory Under Uncertainty: Expected Utility Theory

In the preceding section, a given alternative action was assumed to have a single consequence (outcome or payoff) in the sense that once an alternative is chosen, the corresponding outcome is known precisely and with certainty. The value or preference for a particular alternative can thus be assigned purely on its own merits and the occurrence of any outcome is well within the control of the decision maker simply through his act of choice. In most decision-making problems, however, the outcome is determined not only by the choice of alternatives but also by the state of nature, which is beyond the control of the decision maker. Since it is not known a priori which state of nature will actually prevail, decision making in this type of situation is made under uncertainty. A typical decision problem under uncertainty with finite numbers of alternatives and states of nature is demonstrated in Section 2.2. We again investigate conditions under which we can represent by a numerical function a preference order on a set of alternatives whose outcomes depend on chance. The format of presentation will be the same as in Section 3.4. After introducing necessary terminology, existence theorems concerning utility functions will be presented, applicable irrespective of the dimension of space from which the set of alternatives is drawn. Then focusing on the multiple-objective case, we discuss multiattribute utility theory. Our primary concern will be to investigate those representations of utility functions that will bear on the assessment process for constructing such functions.

3.5.1 The Problem Setting

In keeping with the terminology introduced in Chapter 1 (see especially Figure 1.1), we shall consider a decision-making problem with the decision situation having the following elements:

1. *A set A of acts (or alternatives)*. An *act a* is a course of action available to the decision maker to do a certain job. For the decision problem to be well posed, the set of acts A must be exhaustive and mutually exclusive. The set A can be finite, countable, or uncountable. Clearly one may view A as a set of "controllable" variables in the sense that we can choose any element of A to do the job.
2. A set S of *states* or *states of nature*. A *state s* represents a possible state of environment which affects the outcome of a given act but over which we have no control. In decision problems under uncertainty, we assume that we have no prior knowledge as to what state will prevail. It is under this type of uncertainty that we must choose our act and then accept any consequence of the act under whatever state that actually prevails.
3. A set X of *consequences* (outcomes or payoff). If the state s occurs, the given act a results in a consequence $\mathbf{x}$ or $\mathbf{x}(a, s)$. The latter notation signifies that a consequence $\mathbf{x}$ is a function of not only the act a but also of the state s (i.e., $\mathbf{x}: A \times S \to X$).
4. A consequence $\mathbf{x}$ is characterized by N attributes $X_1, X_2, \ldots, X_N$, where $n \geqslant 1$ in the sense that to completely describe the level of $\mathbf{x}$, we specify the values $x_1, \ldots, x_N$ of attributes $X_1, \ldots, X_N$, respectively. We shall also use $X_1, \ldots, X_N$ to denote the set of possible values of those attributes. Thus the set of consequences X can also be viewed as the product set $X = X_1 \times X_2 \times \cdots \times X_n$, and the consequence is symbolically given by $\mathbf{x} = (x_1, \ldots, x_n) \in X$. Thus, to be consistent with the symbolism used earlier, we shall use a boldface letter to represent a consequence in X when we specifically discuss the multiobjective case (i.e., $n > 1$).

In its most general form, the decision problem which is of concern here is to select an act which yields the greatest satisfaction according to some prespecified decision rule. Some possible decision rules (such as maximizing expected utility, maximin, maximax, Hurwitz, etc.) were discussed in Section 2.2.4. The choice of what decision rule should be used depends not only on the decision maker's attitude toward risk but also on how much we know about the states of nature so as to predict future states. This latter aspect plays an important role in classifying decision problems according to the degree of uncertainty involved. At one extreme, if it is possible to determine with certainty what states of nature will occur, the corresponding decision problems are said to be under certainty and the related utility theory for this class of problems was discussed in the previous section. Moving up the scale in terms of the degree of uncertainty, if sufficient information about the states of nature is known so that probability distributions of their occurrence can be computed either objectively or subjectively, risk analysis can thus be explicitly incorporated in the decision problem. This class of decision problems is therefore known as *decision under risk*. Finally, at the other extreme, when it is impossible or impractical to determine probability distributions of the states of nature by any practical means or when such probability distributions are not meaningful, the corresponding decision problems are said to be under uncertainty, wherein appropriate decision rules such as those described in Section 2.2.4 may be used.

For the remainder of this chapter, we shall be concerned with utility theory for the second class of decision problems discussed above, namely, decision under risk. To be specific, we shall assume that it is possible to determine the probability distributions of the states of nature and that there is a preference order $\succcurlyeq$ on the set of acts A. We shall then ask when it would be possible to represent such preference order by a numerical function U defined on the set of acts A so that for any acts a_1 and a_2 in A

$$a_1 \succcurlyeq a_2 \quad \text{if and only if} \quad U(a_1) \geqslant U(a_2). \tag{3.35}$$

3.5.2 Existence Theorems on Expected Utility: Bernoulli's Principle

As an underlying premise, the utility theory developed for decision problems under risk is inspired by a basic principle originally proposed by Daniel Bernoulli almost two and one-half centuries ago (1738). This principle roughly postulates the following:

Bernoulli's principle. If an individual is confronted with a decision problem in which he has to make a choice from a given set of acts (risky prospects) A, knowing full well that the outcome of a given act depends on the occurrence of the future state of nature whose probability (of occurrence) is known or can be estimated, he should then choose an act which will yield the highest expectation in terms of his preference over the possible consequences.

Implicit in the above statement is the assumption that there is a numerical function u representing the preference structure on the set of consequences.[20] This function will be called throughout this book the *utility function*. To put

[20] Observe the difference between the two functions $U: A \to R$ and $u: X \to R$. In the literature it is common to find that the two functions are denoted identically and are both called utility functions. We prefer to distinguish them here not only because they are mathematically different but also because we feel it gives additional insight to do so. In practice, u is constructed first by some assessment process. The function U is then constructed from u by means of (3.37) according to Bernoulli's principle. Throughout this chapter we shall call u the *utility function* and U the *expected utility function*.

this principle in a more operational form, let $p(s)$ be the probability distribution of $s \in S$, if s is discrete; otherwise, let it be the probability density function of $s \in S$ if s is continuous and real. For convenience we shall use synonymously the symbols $u(\mathbf{x})$ and $u(a, s)$, where $\mathbf{x} \in X$, $a \in A$, and $s \in S$, since $\mathbf{x}$ is a function of a and s. Clearly, since s is a random variable, so is u. Bernoulli's principle then asserts that if $p(s)$ can be estimated, one should choose an act a^* which maximizes the expectation of $u(a, s)$, i.e.,

$$E(a^*) = \max_{a \in A} \sum_{s \in S} p(s) u(a, s) \tag{3.36a}$$

for discrete s, and

$$E(a^*) = \max_{a \in A} \int_{s \in S} p(s) u(a, s)\, ds \tag{3.36b}$$

for real and continuous s. Consequently we can define $U(a)$, which represents the *expected utility* of an act a, as

$$U(a) \equiv \begin{cases} \sum_{s \in S} p(s) u(a, s) & \text{for discrete } s, \quad (3.37a) \\ \int_{s \in S} p(s) u(a, s)\, ds & \text{for real and continuous } s. \quad (3.37b) \end{cases}$$

To use Bernoulli's principle, two functions need to be constructed, namely, the probability distribution of s, $p(s)$, and the utility function [$u(\mathbf{x})$ or $u(a, s)$]. It was not until the 1940s that the full potential of the expected utility hypothesis was recognized through the works of von Neumann and Morgenstern. After assuming the existence of numerical measures of the probability distribution of s, they showed that Bernoulli's principle can be logically deduced from a set of axioms imposed upon the preference order $\succcurlyeq$ on A and the probability distribution itself.

von Neumann–Morgenstern Utility Theorem To make precise the von Neumann–Morgenstern utility theorem [1980], we need to introduce the following terminology. If $\alpha \in [0, 1]$ and x, y are any two possible consequences in X, we shall call a chance mechanism $(\alpha x, (1-\alpha) y)$ a probability mixture (lottery or gamble) of x and y. More generally, if $x^1, \ldots, x^n$ are n possible consequences in X and $\alpha_i \in [0, 1]$ for each $i = 1, \ldots, n$ with $\sum_{i=1}^{n} \alpha_i = 1$, then we shall call $(\alpha_1 x^1, \ldots, \alpha_n x^n)$ a probability mixture (lottery or gamble) of $x^1, \ldots, x^n$.[21] An alternative act (not necessarily in A) with the possibility

[21] This definition of a probability mixture can be extended to infinite or uncountable number of xs in an obvious way. For example, we can write a probability mixture as $\{(x, p(x)) | x \in X\}$ where $p(x)$ is an appropriate probability distribution (or density function) of x. For a more precise treatment, see Fishburn [1970, Chs. 8, 10].

of yielding x^i with probability α_i is called a *risky prospect*. While one represents the chance mechanism and the other represents an act, we shall nonetheless view both the probability mixture and the risky prospect as being the same entity. Also for convenience, a probability mixture $(0x^1,\ldots,1x^i,\ldots,0x^n)$, which represents a *sure prospect* of obtaining x^i with certainty, will also be denoted simply x^i.[22] Finally we shall use $\tilde{X}$ (here viewed simply as a mathematical construct) to denote the mixture set (or the set of prospects), which is the set of all possible probability mixtures of elements in X. An example illustrating this terminology will be given later in this section.

For any consequence $x \in X$ there is always a sure prospect $x \in \tilde{X}$. Observe also that the set of acts A can be viewed as a subset of $\tilde{X}$, since a given act $a \in A$ is a risky prospect. For example, if s is discrete and S has a finite number of elements, say m, then an act a is a probability mixture $(\alpha_1 x^1,\ldots,\alpha_m x^m)$, where $\alpha_i = P(s_i)$ and $x^i = x(a, s_i)$. If we extend the definition of the preference order $\succcurlyeq$ on A to apply also in $\tilde{X}$, and if we can also establish the expected utility function U on $\tilde{X}$, which is capable of rank ordering risky prospects in $\tilde{X}$, such a function will serve the same purpose in A. This is precisely the basic idea in the landmark utility theory of von Neumann–Morgenstern.

Theorem 3.13 (von Neumann–Morgenstern). *Let $\tilde{X}$ be a set of prospects (generated from X) and $\succcurlyeq$ be a preference order on $\tilde{X}$. Then $\succcurlyeq$ satisfies the following system of axioms for any $\tilde{x}$, $\tilde{y}$, $\tilde{z} \in \tilde{X}$:*

NM-A1. *$\succcurlyeq$ is a weak order on $\tilde{X}$;*

NM-A2. *if $\tilde{x} \succ \tilde{y}$, then $\tilde{x} \succ (\alpha\tilde{x},(1-\alpha)\tilde{y}) \succ \tilde{y}$ for all $\alpha \in (0,1)$;*

NM-A3. *if $\tilde{x} \succ \tilde{y} \succ \tilde{z}$, then there exist α_1 and α_2 in $(0,1)$ such that*

$$(\alpha_1\tilde{x},(1-\alpha_1)\tilde{z}) \succ \tilde{y} \succ (\alpha_2\tilde{x},(1-\alpha_2)\tilde{z});$$

NM-A4. $(\alpha\tilde{x},(1-\alpha)\tilde{y}) = ((1-\alpha)\tilde{y},\alpha\tilde{x})$ *for any* $\alpha \in [0,1]$; *and*

NM-A5. *if $\tilde{w} = (\alpha\tilde{x},(1-\alpha)\tilde{y})$, then*

$$(\beta\tilde{w},(1-\beta)\tilde{y}) = (\alpha\beta\tilde{x},(1-\alpha\beta)\tilde{y})$$

if and only if a real-valued function U defined on $\tilde{X}$ exists such that for any $\tilde{x}$, $\tilde{y} \in \tilde{X}$

$$\tilde{x} \succcurlyeq \tilde{y} \quad \text{if and only if} \quad U(\tilde{x}) \geq U(\tilde{y}) \tag{3.38}$$

and

$$U(\alpha\tilde{x},(1-\alpha)\tilde{y}) = \alpha U(\tilde{x}) + (1-\alpha)U(\tilde{y}) \qquad \text{for any} \quad \alpha \in (0,1). \tag{3.39}$$

[22] To avoid confusion over the use of the same notation x^i, we shall always write "a sure prospect x^i" or "a consequence x^i" to make the difference explicit.

Moreover, if U' is another real-valued function on $\tilde{X}, U'$ will satisfy (3.38) *and* (3.39) *if and only if*

$$U'(\tilde{x}) = \lambda U(\tilde{x}) + \mu, \qquad \lambda, \mu \in R, \ \ \lambda > 0. \tag{3.40}$$

Next, we note some important implications of the theorem. Having obtained the numerical function U on $\tilde{X}$ with properties (3.38) to (3.40), it is then easy to construct the utility function u on X and the expected utility function U on A from such a function. The ordering of A in the same spirit as (3.35) is then provided by (3.38) and the expected-utility character as in (3.36) is furnished by (3.37). That the functions U and u, if they exist, are unique up to a postitive linear transformation, as in (3.40), requires the measurement of U to be carried out in an interval or higher scale.

In the above theorem, the first axiom assumes the weak ordering properties of $\succcurlyeq$, which is essential for (3.38) to be possible, as discussed earlier. The second and third axioms, which have often been thought of as the core of von Neumann–Morgenstern expected utility theory, assert certain requirements on the ordering of probability mixtures. In particular, the second axiom postulates that if a prospect $\tilde{x}$ is preferred to another prospect $\tilde{y}$, then any risky prospect $(\alpha\tilde{x},(1-\alpha)\tilde{y})$, where $\alpha \in (0,1)$, should be less preferred to $\tilde{x}$ and strictly preferred to $\tilde{y}$. This seems to be a reasonable assumption if there is no complementarity relationship between $\tilde{x}$ and $\tilde{y}$. For example, if $\tilde{x}$ is a risky prospect of winning \$100 with probability 0.2 and losing \$10 with probability 0.8 and $\tilde{y}$ is a sure prospect of losing \$10, clearly $\tilde{x}$ would be preferred to $\tilde{y}$. Moreover, a risky prospect of winning \$100 with probability 0.2α, $\alpha \in (0,1)$, and losing with probability $1-0.2\alpha$ would also be preferred to $\tilde{y}$ and less preferred than $\tilde{x}$. However, if complementarity between choices exists, the axiom may not hold.

For example, a senior college student has 12 days to prepare for final examinations of the final two courses. He is certain that 1) if he spends at least 10 days on any one course he will pass that course with certainty; 2) if he spends about 6 days on any one course, he will have about 50% chance of passing that course; and finally 3) if he spends less than 3 days on any one course, he will absolutely have no chance of passing that course. Also between passing course I and failing course II for certain (x) and passing course II and failing course I for certain (y), he prefers the former (x) to the latter (y). Yet if passing both courses is a must for graduation, he may very well choose to spend 6 days for each course and take a 50% chance of passing both course I and another 50% chance of passing course II. This violates the axiom, since now we have $(0.5x, 0.5y) \succ x$.

The third axiom postulates one form of what is generally known as the *continuity* (or *Archimedean*) *condition*.[23] If a prospect $\tilde{y}$ lies between pro-

[23]Another common form goes like this. For any $\tilde{x}, \tilde{y}, \tilde{z} \in X$ with $\tilde{x} \succ \tilde{y} \succ \tilde{z}$, there exists $\alpha \in (0,1)$ such that $(\alpha\tilde{x},(1-\alpha)\tilde{z}) \sim \tilde{y}$.

spects $\tilde{x}$ and $\tilde{z}$ in terms of preference, according to this axiom, there exists a probability α_1 other than 0 and 1 such that a risky prospect yielding $\tilde{x}$ with probability α_1 and $\tilde{z}$ with probability $1-\alpha_1$ is preferred to $\tilde{y}$. Also there exists yet another $\alpha_2 \in (0,1)$ such that $\tilde{y}$ is preferred to a risk prospect $(\alpha_2\tilde{x},(1-\alpha_2)\tilde{z})$. This, in effect, asserts that no matter how favorable $\tilde{x}$ is or how unfavorable $\tilde{z}$ is, the effect of either of them on the preference is negligible if its respective chance of occurrence is small enough. This is in most cases a plausible assumption. It may, however, suffer some operational difficulties especially when the choice has to be made from disparate alternatives with extremely polarized outcomes. Such situations occur when the unfavorable outcome $\tilde{z}$ is extremely unfavorable and $\tilde{x}$, although it is preferred to $\tilde{y}$, is not much preferred to $\tilde{y}$.

For example, a person confronted with the choices x, a sure prospect of earning \$101; y, a sure prospect of earning \$100; and z, a sure prospect of being jailed for life (or being executed), will most likely rank them as $x \succ y \succ z$. Yet suppose the following are the choices in a game where a fair die is tossed n times:

$\tilde{a}_1$, being jailed for life if 1 turns up at least once; otherwise receive \$101, i.e., $\tilde{a}_1=((1-\alpha)x,\alpha z)$ where $\alpha=1/6^n$;

a_2, receiving \$100 regardless of the results of the tosses, i.e., $a_2=y$.

It is not uncommon to find that an individual in this and many other cases chooses a_2 (or y) regardless of the number of tosses n. This is because y is almost as good as x and the difference between them is not large enough to warrant taking a risk of receiving an extremely bad outcome z no matter how small that risk is. Thrall [1954, pp. 184–185] gives a few more examples in which the continuity condition may fail to hold.

The fourth (and quite reasonable) axiom simply states that the order in which prospects are combined to form a probability mixture or lottery is irrelevant.

Finally, the fifth axiom, which asserts a reduction rule adhering to the laws of probability, can be viewed pragmatically as "no fun in gambling" behavior. To illustrate such behavior, consider the following two risky prospects. The first is a simple lottery in which a ball is drawn from an urn containing three white balls and one black ball. The decision maker will either win \$10 or lose \$100, depending on whether the ball is white or black, respectively. The second risky prospect is a compound lottery generated by the following game. A ball is drawn from an urn containing one white and one black ball. If the ball is white, the decision maker wins \$10, and the game ends. If the ball is black, it is returned to the urn and another ball is drawn. This time the decision maker will win \$10 if the ball is white or lose \$100 if it is black. Despite the two different mechanisms by which the two risky prospects are generated, the chances of winning \$10 or losing \$100 for both risky prospects are exactly the same, 75% and 25%, respectively.

According to axiom NM-A5, the decision maker should be indifferent between the two risky prospects. However, the thrill or excitement of being able to gamble twice in the second lottery may tempt a risk-taking (or risk-prone) decision maker to prefer the second risky prospect to the first. This is obviously in violation of the axiom.

The following simple example will demonstrate various concepts discussed thus far in this section, as well as a main idea in the proof, which often inspires a method of constructing U itself.

Example: Consider a decision problem in which a farmer must decide which of the three crops a_1, a_2, and a_3 to plant on a particular piece of land in the coming season. His two main concerns are the net return per hectare X_1 and the number of weeks X_2 before the crop can be harvested. The values of X_1 and X_2, of course, depend on the type of season (weather and market conditions, etc.), which can roughly be classified as poor, fair, and good.

Suppose that from past data the information in Table 3.1 can be obtained. The first component of $\mathbf{c}$ represents the corresponding value of X_1 in dollars per hectare, while the second component represents the corresponding value of X_2 in weeks. To use the notations defined earlier, we have

a set of alternative acts $A=\{a_1, a_2, a_3\}$,

a set of states $S=\{s_1, s_2, s_3\}$,

a set of consequences $X=\{c_1, c_2, c_3, c_4, c_5, c_6, c_7, c_8, c_9\}$, and

two attributes X_1, the net return per hectare, and X_2, the number of weeks before harvest, and finally,

the mixture set (set of prospects)

$$\tilde{X}=\left\{(\alpha_1 c_1,\ldots,\alpha_9 c_9)\,|\,\alpha_i \in R \text{ and } \sum_{i=1}^{9} \alpha_i = 1\right\}.$$

Clearly each act $a \in A$ is an element of $\tilde{X}$. For example, act a_1 represents a risky prospect $(\frac{1}{4}c_1, 0c_2, 0c_3, \frac{1}{2}c_4, 0c_5, 0c_6, \frac{1}{4}c_7, 0c_8, 0c_9)$. As remarked earlier, we shall also use the symbol c_i to represent the sure prospect $(0c_1, \ldots, 1c_i, \ldots, 0c_9)$.

Table 3.1 Data for the Example

Type of season	Probability	Crop a_1	a_2	a_3
poor s_1	$\frac{1}{4}$	$c_1=(-400,16)$	$c_2=(10,20)$	$c_3=(-100,10)$
fair s_2	$\frac{1}{2}$	$c_4=(80,14)$	$c_5=(20,18)$	$c_6=(0,8)$
good s_3	$\frac{1}{4}$	$c_7=(200,12)$	$c_8=(50,16)$	$c_9=(100,8)$

To demonstrate how Theorem 3.13 may be used, let us suppose that, given only sure prospects $c_1,\ldots,c_9$, our farmer is able to rank them according to his preference. Suppose he indicates that among the nine sure prospects, he likes c_1 the least and c_9 the most. Further suppose the following:

1. certainty equivalence—for any sure prospect c_i in X, we can always present the farmer with a risky prospect $\tilde{c}_i=((1-\beta_i)c_1,\beta_i c_9)$ (i.e., an act not necessarily in A yielding outcomes c_1 with probability $1-\beta_i$ and c_9 with probability β_i) to which he will be indifferent, i.e.,

$$c_i \sim ((1-\beta_i)c_1, \beta_i c_9) \equiv \tilde{c}_i. \tag{3.41}$$

When this is true we sometimes refer to c_i as the *certainty equivalent* of the mixture or lottery $((1-\beta_i)c_1, \beta_i c_9)$.

2. substitution—if presented with the two risky prospects $(\alpha_1 c_1, \ldots, \alpha_i c_i, \ldots, \alpha_9 c_9)$ and $(\alpha_1 c_1,\ldots,\alpha_i\tilde{c}_i,\ldots,\alpha_9 c_9)$, where the latter is obtained by replacing the sure prospect c_i in the ith component of the former by a risky prospect $\tilde{c}_i$ defined in (3.41), the farmer will be indifferent to which one occurs. More generally, if the above assumption is true, then the farmer will also be indifferent to which of the risky prospects $(\alpha_1 c_1,\ldots,\alpha_i c_i,\ldots,\alpha_9 c_9)$ and $(\alpha_1\tilde{c}_1,\ldots,\alpha_i\tilde{c}_i,\ldots,\alpha_9\tilde{c}_9)$ occurs:

$$(\alpha_1 c_1,\ldots,\alpha_i c_i,\ldots,\alpha_9 c_9) \sim (\alpha_1\tilde{c}_1,\ldots,\alpha_i\tilde{c}_i,\ldots,\alpha_9\tilde{c}_9). \tag{3.42}$$

3. reduction—the farmer has "no fun in gambling" in the sense that his preference toward a particular risky prospect $\tilde{x}\in\tilde{X}$ will always be the same no matter how such prospect is derived. For example, he should be indifferent between risky prospects $\tilde{a}_1$ represented by Figure 3.6a and $(\frac{1}{4}c_1, \frac{3}{4}\tilde{w})$, where $\tilde{w}$ is the risky prospect $(\frac{2}{3}c_4, \frac{1}{3}c_7)$ represented by Figure 3.6b.

This assumption allows reduction of complex compound lotteries to simple ones without affecting the preference. The reduction is carried out by using the familiar laws of probability.

As an important consequence of Assumptions (1)–(3), any risky prospect $\tilde{x}=(\alpha_1 c_1,\ldots,\alpha_9 c_9)\in\tilde{X}$ is always indifferent to some risky prospect involving only c_1 and c_9; i.e., there exists $\alpha\in[0,1]$ such that

$$\tilde{\mathbf{x}} \sim ((1-\alpha)c_1, \alpha c_9). \tag{3.43}$$

4. When comparing two risky prospects $\tilde{x}$ and $\tilde{y}$ in $\tilde{X}$, where $\tilde{x}\sim((1-\alpha_1)c_1,\alpha_1 c_0)$ and $\tilde{y}\sim((1-\alpha_2)c_1,\alpha_2 c_9)$, the farmer always prefers $\tilde{x}$ to $\tilde{y}$ if and only if $\alpha_1>\alpha_2$. He is always indifferent between $\tilde{x}$ and $\tilde{y}$ if and only if $\alpha_1=\alpha_2$. In short,

$$\tilde{x} \succcurlyeq \tilde{y} \qquad \text{if and only if} \qquad \alpha_1 \geqslant \alpha_2. \tag{3.44}$$

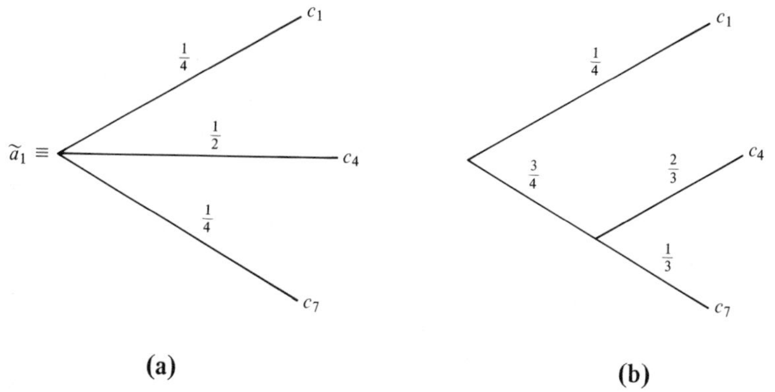

Figure 3.6 "No fun in gambling." (**a**) Risky prospect $\tilde{a}_1$; (**b**) compound lottery equivalent to $\tilde{a}_1$.

Note that α_1 and α_2 always exist for any $\tilde{x}$ and $\tilde{y}$ in $\tilde{X}$ because of the preceding assumptions.

Within these assumptions we now show 1) that the von Neumann–Morgenstern system of axioms in Theorem 3.13 is satisfied so that the expected utility function U on A exists; 2) how such a function might be constructed.

The weak ordering property of the farmer's preference is implicit from (3.43) and (3.44). The fourth axiom is trivial while the fifth follows directly from Assumption 3. It now remains to show that the second and third axioms hold. Let $\tilde{x}$, $\tilde{y}$ be any two risky prospects in $\tilde{X}$ such that $\tilde{x} \succ \tilde{y}$. From (3.43) we can find α_1, α_2 in $(0,1)$ such that

$$\tilde{x} = ((1-\alpha_1)c_1, \alpha_1, c_9) \qquad \text{and} \qquad \tilde{y} = ((1-\alpha_2)c_1, \alpha_2 c_9).$$

From (3.44) and the assumptions we have $\alpha_1 > \alpha_2$. Now for any α in $(0,1)$, by Assumption 3,

$$(\alpha\tilde{x}, (1-\alpha)\tilde{y}) = ([1-\alpha_2-\alpha(\alpha_1-\alpha_2)]c_1, \alpha_2+\alpha(\alpha_1-\alpha_2)c_9). \quad (3.45)$$

Since $\alpha_1 > \alpha_2 + \alpha(\alpha_1 - \alpha_2) > \alpha_2$, we have from (3.44)

$$\tilde{x} \succ (\alpha\tilde{x}, (1-\alpha)\tilde{y}) \succ \tilde{y},$$

indicating that the second axiom is satisfied. To show the validity of the third axiom, let $\tilde{z}$ be another risky prospect with $\tilde{x} \succ \tilde{y} \succ \tilde{z}$. Again from (3.43) there is α_3 in $(0,1)$ such that

$$\tilde{z} = ((1-\alpha_3)c_1, \alpha_3 c_9) \qquad \text{and} \qquad \alpha_1 > \alpha_2 > \alpha_3.$$

Also for any $\alpha \in (0,1)$,

$$(\alpha\tilde{x}, (1-\alpha)\tilde{z}) = ([1-\alpha_3-\alpha(\alpha_1-\alpha_3)]c_1, \alpha_3+\alpha(\alpha_1-\alpha_3)c_9).$$

Thus if α is chosen such that $0<\alpha<(\alpha_2-\alpha_3)/(\alpha_1-\alpha_3)<1$, the risky prospect $(\alpha\tilde{x},(1-\alpha)\tilde{z})$ is less preferred than $\tilde{y}$ according to (3.44). On the other hand if $1>\alpha>(\alpha_2-\alpha_3)/(\alpha_1-\alpha_3)>0$, then from $(\alpha\tilde{x},(1-\alpha)\tilde{z})$ is preferred to $\tilde{y}$, again by virtue of (3.44), showing that the third axiom is satisfied.

Having shown that the system of von Neumann–Morgenstern axioms is satisfied, we now proceed to show the existence of the expected utility function U by means of construction. First, we construct the utility function u on X. Since for any outcome c_i in X, there corresponds the sure prospect c_i in $\tilde{X}$, then from Assumption 1 we can always find β_i such that (3.41) is true. Hence we can define $u: X \to R$ as

$$u(c_i)=\beta_i, \qquad i=1,\ldots,9. \tag{3.46}$$

Likewise for any $\tilde{x}\in\tilde{X}$, we can define U: $\tilde{X}\to R$ as

$$U(\tilde{x})=\alpha, \tag{3.47}$$

where α is obtained from (3.43). Consequently, the expected utility function U: $A\to R$ is defined as (3.47), but the domain is now restricted to A instead of $\tilde{X}$. It now remains to show that the expected utility function U so defined indeed satisfies both (3.38) and (3.39). The first property (3.38) trivially follows from (3.44) and (3.47). To show (3.39), we note from (3.45) and (3.47) that

$$\begin{aligned} U(\alpha\tilde{x},(1-\alpha)\tilde{y}) &= U([1-\alpha_2-\alpha(\alpha_1-\alpha_2)]c_1,\alpha_2+\alpha(\alpha_1-\alpha_2)c_9) \\ &= \alpha_2+\alpha(\alpha_1-\alpha_2)=\alpha\alpha_1+(1-\alpha)\alpha_2 \\ &= \alpha U(\tilde{x})+(1-\alpha)U(\tilde{y}), \end{aligned} \tag{3.48}$$

as required. Also from (3.46) and (3.48), it is not difficult to show that for any $\tilde{x}=(\alpha_1c_1,\ldots,\alpha_9c_9)\in\tilde{X}$,

$$U(\tilde{x})=\sum_{i=1}^{9}\alpha_iU(c_i)=\sum_{i=1}^{9}\alpha_iu(c_i). \tag{3.49}$$

Thus the expected utility function U: $A\to R$ also satisfies Bernoulli's principle (3.37).

For example, suppose we ask the farmer to give some estimate of the probability β_i that he will be indifferent between the sure prospect c_i and the lottery $((1-\beta_i)c_1,\beta_ic_9)$ for each $i=2,\ldots,8$[24] and obtain the answers shown in Table 3.2. The corresponding expected utility function U: $A\to R$, as

[24]This is often difficult to do. In practice we normally provide the decision maker with a lottery and ask him to estimate the certainty equivalent of that lottery, which is much easier to accomplish in the single-attribute case. Practical methods of assessing the utility function will be discussed in Chapter 5.

Table 3.2 Numerical Utility Function for the Example

	Outcome								
	c_1	c_2	c_3	c_4	c_5	c_6	c_7	c_8	c_9
β_i	0	0.2	0.1	0.8	0.3	0.5	0.9	0.6	1
$U(c_i)=\beta_i$	0	0.2	0.1	0.8	0.3	0.5	0.9	0.6	1

computed from (3.49) and the data, is therefore

$$U(a_i)=\begin{cases}0.625 & \text{if } i=1,\\ 0.350 & \text{if } i=2,\\ 0.525 & \text{if } i=3.\end{cases}$$

Hence, according to Bernoulli's principle, the farmer should select crop a_1.

Another aspect as demonstrated by this example is that Theorem 3.13 is applicable to the multiattribute case as well as the single-attribute case.

Other Existence Theorems It has often been observed that some of the von Neumann–Morgenstern axioms are difficult to verify. Fishburn [1970] replaced the second axiom by the *independence condition*, which asserts that for any $\tilde{x}$, $\tilde{y}$ in $\tilde{X}$, $0<\alpha<1$,

$$\tilde{x}\succ\tilde{y} \quad\Rightarrow\quad (\alpha\tilde{x},(1-\alpha)\tilde{z})\succ(\alpha\tilde{y},(1-\alpha)\tilde{z}) \quad \text{for all } \tilde{z}\in X. \tag{3.50}$$

The subsequent results, which can be deduced from this modified set of axioms, are the same as Theorem 3.13. Hausner [1954] also used the independence condition (3.50) instead of NM-A2 and replaces axiom NM-A3 by the *cancellation condition*, which states that for all $\tilde{z}\in\tilde{X}$

$$(\alpha\tilde{x},(1-\alpha)\tilde{z})\succcurlyeq(\alpha\tilde{y},(1-\alpha)\tilde{z}) \quad \text{for some } 0<\alpha<1 \quad\Rightarrow\quad \tilde{x}\succcurlyeq\tilde{y}. \tag{3.51}$$

He showed for the n-attribute case that a function U mapping $\tilde{X}$ into a lexicographically ordered n-dimensional vector space V exists such that the ordering of $\tilde{X}$ by $\succcurlyeq$ is equivalent to the ordering of the range of $\tilde{X}$ in V under U by a lexicographic order. Aumann [1962], on the other hand, relaxes one of the most demanding conditions, namely, the connectedness of the preference order $\succcurlyeq$. After replacing the second axiom by the independence condition (3.50) and substituting for the third axiom

$$(\alpha\tilde{x},(1-\alpha)\tilde{y})\succ\tilde{z} \quad \text{for all } \alpha>0 \quad\Rightarrow\quad \text{not } \tilde{z}\succ\tilde{y}, \tag{3.52}$$

he showed that the expected utility function U on $\tilde{X}$ exists such that for any $\tilde{x}, \tilde{y} \in \tilde{X}$

$$\tilde{x} \succcurlyeq \tilde{y} \quad \Rightarrow \quad U(\tilde{x}) \geqslant U(\tilde{y}), \tag{3.53}$$

where the inverse implication is not necessarily true. Herstein and Milnor [1953], in searching for a system of axioms that would allow more concise and elegant treatment of the expected utility theorem, postulated the following in place of NM-A2 and NM-A3, respectively. For any $\tilde{x}, \tilde{y}, \tilde{z} \in \tilde{X}$,

HM-A2. $\tilde{x} \sim \tilde{y}$ implies $(\frac{1}{2}\tilde{x}, \frac{1}{2}\tilde{z}) > (\frac{1}{2}\tilde{y}, \frac{1}{2}\tilde{z})$;

HM-A3. the sets $\{\alpha | (\alpha\tilde{x}, (1-\alpha)\tilde{y}) \succcurlyeq \tilde{z}\}$ and $\{\alpha | \tilde{z} \succcurlyeq (\alpha\tilde{x}, (1-\alpha)\tilde{y})\}$ are closed.

Herstein and Milnor [1953] showed that the topological axiom HM-A3 implies a certain continuity condition of the following form: $\tilde{x} \succ \tilde{y} \succ \tilde{z}$ implies there exists $0 < \alpha < 1$ such that

$$\tilde{y} \sim (\alpha\tilde{x}, (1-\alpha)\tilde{z}). \tag{3.54}$$

Furthermore, they show that their system of axioms implies the independence condition (3.50). This is sufficient to guarantee the existence of an expected utility function with properties as in Theorem 3.13.

Perhaps the most appealing alternatives of the von Neumann–Morgenstern utility theory are those pursued by Ramsey [1931] and Savage [1954]. In the results stated thus far, it has been assumed that "complete" information about the states of nature is known so that quantitative measure of the probability of their occurrences can be computed objectively. Various systems of axioms were then formulated in order to guarantee the existence of the expected utility function. It has often been argued that in certain decision problems such "complete" information is unlikely to be available. In these cases, however, partial information may be obtainable: The decision maker may have some qualitative feeling about the probability of states. The probability measure obtained through the decision maker's qualitative evaluation is known as *subjective probability*. On this basis it is then natural to try to formulate the systems of axioms that allow both the probability measure and the utility function to be determined. Ramsey [1931] developed a procedure by which the utility function is measured first and from this the corresponding subjective probability measure is then constructed. Savage [1954] on the other hand, builds on de Finetti's ideas by developing a system of axioms whereby the subjective probability is first measured and the utility function is obtained next. The details of these interesting results are beyond the scope of this book. The interested reader is encouraged to read Ramsey [1931], Davidson and Suppes [1956], Suppes and Winet [1955], and Luce and Suppes [1965] for Ramsey's approach, and Savage [1954], Luce and Suppes [1965], and Fishburn [1970] for the second approach.

3.5.3 Additive Utility Functions

The additive form is the simplest (from the practical standpoint) but most restricted (from the theoretical standpoint) form of decomposition. Consider a set of acts A and a set of consequences X. The latter is taken to be a Cartesian product of n attributes $X_1, \ldots, X_n$ so that a consequence in X can be written $\mathbf{x} = (x_1, \ldots, x_n)$, where $x_i \in X_i$, $i = 1, \ldots, n$. Associated with X, there exists a set of prospects (or probability mixtures or lotteries) $\tilde{X}$ which is the set of all probability mixtures of elements in X. For convenience, we may write a member $\tilde{\mathbf{x}}$ of $\tilde{X}$ as $\tilde{\mathbf{x}} = \{(\mathbf{x}, p(\mathbf{x})) | \mathbf{x} \in X\}$, where $p(\mathbf{x})$ is the probability distribution on X satisfying $\Sigma_{\mathbf{x} \in X} p(\mathbf{x}) = 1$ if $\mathbf{x}$ is discrete or $\int_{\mathbf{x} \in X} p(\mathbf{x})\, d\mathbf{x} = 1$ if $\mathbf{x}$ is continuous. An element $\tilde{\mathbf{x}} \in \tilde{X}$ can thus be viewed as a prospect of obtaining consequence $\mathbf{x} \in X$ with probability $p(\mathbf{x})$ when $\mathbf{x}$ is discrete, or a prospect of obtaining a consequence between $\mathbf{x}$ and $\mathbf{x} + \delta\mathbf{x}$ with probability $\int^{\mathbf{x}+\delta\mathbf{x}} p(\mathbf{s})\, d\mathbf{s}$, when $\mathbf{x}$ is continuous. Since for any fixed X, any element of $\tilde{X}$ is characterized only by the probability distribution $p(\ )$ (p for short), there is a one-to-one correspondence between $\tilde{X}$ and the set of all possible probability distributions p on X. It is convenient, therefore, to write an element $\tilde{\mathbf{x}} \in \tilde{X}$ associated with the probability distribution $p(\mathbf{x})$ as $\tilde{\mathbf{x}}(p)$. Observe that any consequence $\mathbf{x} \in X$ is characterized by multiple attributes $(x_1, \ldots, x_n)$, each of which can be treated as a random variable with its own marginal probability distribution. Denote the marginal probability distribution of the value of the ith attribute X_i by $p_i(x_i)$ (p_i for short), $i = 1, \ldots, n$. If $\Omega = \{X_1, \ldots X_n\}$ and Θ is any proper subset of Ω, the marginal probability distribution of $\mathbf{x}_\Theta$, denoted p_Θ, is given by

$$p_\Theta(\mathbf{x}_\Theta) = \sum_{\mathbf{x}_{\bar{\Theta}} \in X_{\bar{\Theta}}} p(\mathbf{x}_\Theta, \mathbf{x}_{\bar{\Theta}}) \tag{3.55a}$$

when $\mathbf{x}$ is discrete, or

$$p_\Theta(\mathbf{x}_\Theta) = \int_{\mathbf{x}_{\bar{\Theta}} \in X_{\bar{\Theta}}} p(\mathbf{x}_\Theta, \mathbf{x}_{\bar{\Theta}})\, d\mathbf{x}_{\bar{\Theta}}, \tag{3.55b}$$

when $\mathbf{x}$ is continuous.

We can now define the set $\tilde{X}_i$ as the set of prospects generated from X_i. That is, a typical element of $\tilde{X}_i$ is $\tilde{x}_i(p_i) = \{(x_i, p_i(x_i) | x_i \in X_i\}$. Finally, we recall that utility function on X and the expected utility function on $\tilde{X}$ are denoted, respectively, u and U, while the conditional utility function on X_i and expected utility function on $\tilde{X}_i$ are to be denoted u_i and U_i, respectively. For convenience, we shall write for any $\tilde{\mathbf{x}}(p)$ in $\tilde{X}$ and $\tilde{x}_i(p_i)$ in $\tilde{X}_i$

$$U(\tilde{\mathbf{x}}(p)) \equiv E_p(u(\mathbf{x})) \tag{3.56}$$

and

$$U_i(x_i(p_i)) \equiv E_{p_i}(u_i(x_i)) \tag{3.57}$$

where $E_p(\ )$ is the mathematical expectation with respect to the probability distribution p.[25]

The following independence condition, essential in deriving additive forms of utility functions, is due to Fishburn [1970].[26] Let $\Theta_1,\ldots,\Theta_m$ be proper subsets of Ω such that their union $\Theta_1 \cup \Theta_2 \cup \cdots \cup \Theta_m = \Omega$. The independence condition introduced by Fishburn for the purpose of deriving additive utility functions is called value independence (marginal independence or additive independence).

Definition. $\Theta_1,\ldots,\Theta_m$ are said to be *value independent* if and only if, for any prospects $\tilde{\mathbf{x}}(p)$ and $\tilde{\mathbf{x}}(q)$ in $\tilde{X}$ whose corresponding (joint) probability distributions are p and q, respectively, we say

$$\tilde{\mathbf{x}}(p) \sim \tilde{\mathbf{x}}(q) \qquad \text{whenever} \qquad p_{\Theta_i} = q_{\Theta_i}, \quad i=1,\ldots,m. \tag{3.58}$$

An important characteristic of value independence is that, unlike other independence conditions, it is symmetric in the sense that if Θ is value independent of $\bar{\Theta}$, so is the reverse.

With the value independence condition, Fishburn [1970] proves the following key results for additive utility functions.

Theorem 3.14 (additive theorem). *Suppose there exists a utility function u defined on X such that for any $\tilde{\mathbf{x}}(p)$ and $\tilde{\mathbf{x}}(q)$ in $\tilde{X}$*

$$\tilde{\mathbf{x}}(p) \succcurlyeq \tilde{\mathbf{x}}(q) \qquad \textit{if and only if} \qquad E_p(u(\mathbf{x})) \geqslant E_q(u(\mathbf{x})). \tag{3.59}$$

Then there exist functions u_i defined on X_i, $i=1,\ldots,n$, such that each u_i is unique up to a positive linear transformation; and

$$u(\mathbf{x}) = u_1(x_1) + u_2(x_2) + \cdots + u_n(x_3), \tag{3.60}$$

or, equivalently,

$$\tilde{\mathbf{x}}(p) \succcurlyeq \tilde{\mathbf{x}}(q) \qquad \textit{if and only if} \qquad \sum_{i=1}^{n} E_{p_i}(u_i(x_i) \geqslant E_{q_i}(u_i(x_i)) \tag{3.61}$$

if and only if $X_1,\ldots,X_n$ are value independent.

---

[25] We assume the normal definition of mathematical expectation, i.e.,

$$E_p(u(\mathbf{x})) = \begin{cases} \sum_{\mathbf{x}\in X} p(\mathbf{x})u(\mathbf{x}) & \text{if } \mathbf{x} \text{ is discrete;} \\ \int_{x\in X} p(\mathbf{x})u(\mathbf{x})\,d\mathbf{x} & \text{if } \mathbf{x} \text{ is continuous.} \end{cases}$$

[26] Additive utility functions have been extensively studied by Fishburn. Apart from the above references, see also Fishburn [1965a, 1965b, 1966a, 1966b, 1967a, 1971, 1972].

Although the additive utility function of the form (3.60) is the easiest to implement in practice, the value independence condition required to ensure it is quite restrictive and often difficult to verify. It involves checking marginal probability distribution of every attribute. The value independence condition in Theorem 3.14 does not allow any form of interaction of preference among attributes. A natural generalization of the above theorem is, therefore, to allow for some interaction. For this result, see Fishburn [1970]. Also, some other additive results can be found in, for example, Pollak [1967].

3.5.4 *Quasi-Additive and Multiplicative Utility Functions*

Two other decomposition forms of multiattribute utility functions are less restrictive and often easier to implement than the additive forms. The results presented are the work of Keeney [1968, 1971, 1972a, 1972b, 1973a, 1973b, 1973c, and especially 1974] and Keeney and Raiffa [1976], although multiplicative and quasi-additive utility functions have also been studied by Pollak [1967], Raiffa [1969], Meyer [1970], Fishburn and Keeney [1974], and Fishburn [1976]. We begin by rewriting preferential independence in the risky setting and then extend it to establish quasi-additive and multiplicative utility functions.

Definition. The subset of attributes Θ is said to be *preferentially independent* of its complement $\overline{\Theta}$ if preference between sure prospects or consequences $(\mathbf{x}_\Theta^1, \mathbf{x}_{\overline{\Theta}})$ and $(\mathbf{x}_\Theta^2, \mathbf{x}_{\overline{\Theta}})$ does not depend on the level $\mathbf{x}_{\overline{\Theta}}$ in $X_{\overline{\Theta}}$ for any $\mathbf{x}_\Theta^1$ and $\mathbf{x}_\Theta^2$ in X_Θ.

More precisely, Θ is preferentially independent of $\overline{\Theta}$ if for some $\hat{\mathbf{x}}_\Theta$ in $X_{\overline{\Theta}}$

$$(\mathbf{x}_\Theta^1, \hat{\mathbf{x}}_{\overline{\Theta}}) \succcurlyeq (\mathbf{x}_\Theta^2, \hat{\mathbf{x}}_{\overline{\Theta}}) \quad \Rightarrow \quad (\mathbf{x}_\Theta^1, \mathbf{x}_{\overline{\Theta}}) \succcurlyeq (\mathbf{x}_\Theta^2, \mathbf{x}_{\overline{\Theta}}) \qquad \text{for all} \quad \mathbf{x}_{\overline{\Theta}} \in X_{\overline{\Theta}}. \tag{3.62}$$

Utility independence can be viewed as lying somewhere between preferential independence and value independence.

Definition. The subset of attributes Θ is *utility independent* of $\overline{\Theta}$ if, for any fixed lotteries $\tilde{\mathbf{x}}_\Theta^1(p_\Theta)$ and $\tilde{\mathbf{x}}_\Theta^2(p_\Theta)$ in $\tilde{X}_\Theta$, the preference between two lotteries $(\tilde{\mathbf{x}}_\Theta^1(p_\Theta), \mathbf{x}_{\overline{\Theta}})$ and $(\tilde{\mathbf{x}}_\Theta^2(p_\Theta), \mathbf{x}_{\overline{\Theta}})$ does not depend on the sure prospect or consequence $\mathbf{x}_{\overline{\Theta}}$ in $X_{\overline{\Theta}}$. More precisely, for some consequence $\mathbf{x}_{\overline{\Theta}}$ in $X_{\overline{\Theta}}$,

$$(\tilde{\mathbf{x}}_\Theta^1(p_\Theta), \hat{\mathbf{x}}_{\overline{\Theta}}) \succcurlyeq (\tilde{\mathbf{x}}_\Theta^2(p_\Theta), \mathbf{x}_{\overline{\Theta}}) \quad \Rightarrow \quad (\tilde{\mathbf{x}}_\Theta^1(p_\Theta), \mathbf{x}_{\overline{\Theta}}) \succcurlyeq (\tilde{\mathbf{x}}_\Theta^2(p_\Theta), \mathbf{x}_{\overline{\Theta}}) \tag{3.63}$$

for all $\mathbf{x}_{\overline{\Theta}} \in X_{\overline{\Theta}}$.

Utility independence implies preferential independence but not the converse. The key result, which is so powerful for developing the subsequent results in this section, is obtained when the utility independence condition is converted into a utility function equivalence.

Theorem 3.15. *Suppose there exists a utility function u defined on X satisfying* (3.59). *The subset of attributes* Θ *is utility independent of* $\bar{\Theta}$ *if and only if*

$$u(\mathbf{x}_\Theta,\mathbf{x}_{\bar{\Theta}})=g(\mathbf{x}_{\bar{\Theta}})+h(\mathbf{x}_{\bar{\Theta}})u(\mathbf{x}_\Theta,\hat{\mathbf{x}}_{\bar{\Theta}}), \tag{3.64}$$

with $h(\ )>0$ *for all* $\mathbf{x}_\Theta\in X_\Theta$, $\mathbf{x}_{\bar{\Theta}}\in X_{\bar{\Theta}}$ *and some* $\hat{\mathbf{x}}_{\bar{\Theta}}$ *in* $X_{\bar{\Theta}}$.

Because of the striking similarity between (3.25) in Theorem 3.8 and (3.64) as well as the analogous roles they play, we state without proof the following results due to Keeney [1974], which are analogous to those in the certainty case (Section 3.4.3). The first result establishes the quasi-additive form of the utility function.

Theorem 3.16. *Assume there exists a normalized utility function u on X satisfying* (3.59) *with* $u(\mathbf{x}^*)=1$ *and* $u(\mathbf{x}^0)=0$. *There exist functions* u_i *defined on* X_i, $i=1,\ldots,n$, *such that for any* $\mathbf{x}\in X$,

$$\begin{aligned}u(\mathbf{x})=&\sum_{i=1}^{n}\lambda_i u_i(x_i)+\sum_{i=1}^{n}\sum_{j>i}^{n}\lambda_{ij}u_i(x_i)u_j(x_j)+\cdots\\&+\sum_{i=1}^{n}\sum_{j>i}^{n}\sum_{k>j}^{n}\lambda_{ijk}u_i(x_i)u_j(x_j)u_k(x_k)+\cdots\\&+\lambda_{12\ldots n}u_1(x_1)\cdots u_n(x_n),\end{aligned}\tag{3.65}$$

where $u_i(x_i^*)=1$ *and* $u_i(x_i)=0$ *for all* $i=1,\ldots,n$ *if* X_i *is utility independent of* $X_{\bar{i}}$ *for each* $i=1,\ldots,n$.

We again remark that the quasi-additive form (3.65) reduces to an additive form if $\lambda_{ij}=\lambda_{ijk}=\cdots=0$ and to a multiplicative form

$$\begin{aligned}u(\mathbf{x})=&\sum_{i=1}^{n}\lambda_i u_i(x_i)+\mu\sum_{i=1}^{n}\sum_{j>i}^{n}\lambda_i\lambda_j u_i(x_i)u_j(x_j)\\&+\mu^2\sum_{i=1}^{n}\sum_{j>i}^{n}\sum_{k>j}^{n}u_i(x_i)u_j(x_j)u_k(x_k)+\cdots\\&+\mu^{n-1}\lambda_1\lambda_2\cdots\lambda_n u_1(x_1)\ldots u_n(x_n)\end{aligned}\tag{3.66}$$

or

$$1+\mu u(\mathbf{x})=[1+\mu\lambda_1(u_1(x_1)][1+\mu\lambda_2u_2(x_2)]\cdots[1+\mu\lambda_n u_n(x_n)], \tag{3.67}$$

if

$$\lambda_{ij}=\mu\lambda_i\lambda_j,\quad \lambda_{ijk}=\mu^2\lambda_i\lambda_j\lambda_k,\quad \ldots,\qquad \sum_{i=1}^{n}\lambda_i\neq 1.$$

To reduce the quasi-additive form (3.65) to the multiplicative form (3.66) or (3.67), we need further to restrict the independence conditions to mutual utility independence.

Definition. The set of attributes Ω is said to be *mutually utility independent* if every subset Θ of Ω is utility independent of its complement $\overline{\Theta}$.

Theorem 3.17. *Assume there exists a normalized utility function u on X satisfying* (3.59). *Then u can be written in the additive–multiplicative form* (3.66) *or* (3.67) *with* $0<\lambda_i<1$ *for each* $i=1,\ldots,n$ *and* $\mu>-1$ *if* Ω *is mutually utility independent.*

The relationship between μ and $(\lambda_1,\ldots,\lambda_n)$ can also be derived from (3.67). After substituting $\mathbf{x}=\mathbf{x}^*$, we have

$$1+\mu=(1+\mu\lambda_1)(1+\mu\lambda_2)\cdots(1+\mu\lambda_n). \qquad (3.68)$$

Again, if $\sum_{i=1}^{n}\lambda_i=1$, $\mu=0$ from (3.68). Hence (3.66) reduces to an additive form. On the other hand if $\sum_{i=1}^{n}\lambda_i\neq 1$, (3.66) is in the true multiplicative form, as reflected by (3.67). Hence to determine precisely whether (3.66) is additive or multiplicative, the following simple check similar to that described in Section 3.4.3 (following Theorem 3.10) can be used.

Assume all the hypotheses of Theorem 3.17. Take any two attributes, say X_q and X_r and set the remaining attributes $X_{\overline{qr}}$ at some fixed level $\hat{\mathbf{x}}_{\overline{qr}}$. For each X_i, $i=q,r$, choose two levels x_i^1 and x_i^2 such that $(x_i^1,\mathbf{x}_{\bar{i}})$ and $(x_i^2,\mathbf{x}_{\bar{i}})$ are not indifferent for some value of $\mathbf{x}_{\bar{i}}$ in $X_{\bar{i}}$. Now ask the decision maker to compare the prospect of obtaining consequences $(x_q^1, x_r^1, \hat{\mathbf{x}}_{\overline{qr}})$ and $(x_q^2, x_r^2, \hat{\mathbf{x}}_{\overline{qr}})$ with equal probability and the prospect of obtaining consequences $(x_q^1, x_r^2, \hat{\mathbf{x}}_{\overline{qr}})$ and $(x_q^2, x_r^1, \hat{\mathbf{x}}_{\overline{qr}})$ with equal probability. If the decision maker prefers one or the other of the two proposed prospects, then (3.66) is multiplicative. Otherwise, the additive form prevails. Comparing Theorem 3.14 and the above discussion, it is obvious that value independence is indeed equivalent to mutual utility independence together with the indifference of the two lotteries.

Just as mutually weak-difference independence is often difficult to verify to establish additive–multiplicative measurable value functions, mutual utility independence is also difficult to validate, particularly when n is large. We thus seek alternative sets of sufficient conditions that are less difficult to verify in practice. To generate such sets, we turn to the utility independence version of Gorman's theorem, as proposed by Keeney and Raiffa [1976].

If Y and Z are two overlapping subsets of the set of attributes Ω and if both are utility independent of their respective complements, then the union, intersection, symmetric difference, and difference of Y and Z are also utility independent of their respective complements.

Again several sets of useful sufficient conditions can be derived from this result. For example, it can be shown that if Θ_i, $i=1,\ldots,n$, is given by any one of the following:

1. $\Theta_i = X_{\bar{i}}$;
2. $\Theta_1 = \{X_1,\ldots,X_{n-1}\}$, $\Theta_i = \{X_1, X_{i+1},\ldots,X_n\}$, $i=2,\ldots,n$; or
3. $\Theta_i = \{X_i, X_{i+1}\}$, $i=1,\ldots,n-1$, $n \geqslant 3$,

then Ω is mutually utility independent if and only if each Θ_i is utility independent of its complement.

Utility independence is harder to verify than preferential independence. Thus if as many as possible utility independence assumptions were replaced by preferential independence assumptions, the verification task would be much simpler. Such replacement is possible through a result proved by Keeney [1976] and is analogous to Theorem 3.12.

Theorem 3.18. *Assume there exists a utility function u on X satisfying* (3.59). *If $\Omega = \{X_1, X_2, X_3\}$ and $\{X_1\}$ is utility independent of $\{X_2, X_3\}$ and $\{X_1, X_2\}$ is preferentially independent of $\{X_3\}$, then $\{X_1, X_2\}$ is utility independent of $\{X_3\}$.*

A general proof of this theorem can be found in Keeney [1974] or Keeney and Raiffa [1976]. Similar arguments to those used in the proof of Theorem 3.12 can be used here.

By relying on a relationship between utility independence and preferential independence we can formulate even simpler forms of sufficiency conditions for the additive–multiplicative utility function. For example it can be easily shown that Ω is mutually utility independent if and only if, for some $1 \leqslant i \leqslant n$, X_i is utility independent of $X_{\bar{i}}$ and $\{X_i, X_j\}$ is preferentially independent of $X_{\overline{ij}}$ for each $j=1,\ldots,n$ and $j \neq i$. This set of sufficiency conditions is obviously much easier to verify than those described earlier.

3.5.5 Other Decomposition Forms

Fishburn [1974] and Fishburn and Keeney [1975] generalized the utility independence concept to allow complete reversal of preferences as well as complete indifference. An important consequence of *generalized utility independence* is that Θ is generalized utility independent of $\overline{\Theta}$ if and only if

$$u(\mathbf{x}_\Theta, \mathbf{x}_{\overline{\Theta}}) = g(\mathbf{x}_{\overline{\Theta}}) + h(\mathbf{x}_{\overline{\Theta}})u(\mathbf{x}_\Theta, \hat{\mathbf{x}}_{\overline{\Theta}}) \tag{3.69}$$

for all $\mathbf{x}_\Theta$ in X_Θ and $\mathbf{x}_{\overline{\Theta}}$ in $X_{\overline{\Theta}}$. Observe that, in addition to the usual case with $h>0$, h in (3.69) can also be strictly negative, corresponding to the complete reversal case; or h can be identically zero, corresponding to the complete indifference case.

Another concept related to utility independence is *conditional utility independence*. Several useful results have been derived when conditional utility independence conditions are imposed. See, for example, Bell [1974], Fishburn [1973], and Keeney and Raiffa [1976]. If utility independence fails to hold, Kirkwood [1976] introduces the concept of *parametrical dependence* which is in a sense an approximation of utility independence.

There are many real-life risky choice problems that cannot be described by value independence or utility independence, or the above related concepts. For example, given two elements $\mathbf{x}'_{\bar{\Theta}}$ and $\mathbf{x}''_{\bar{\Theta}}$ in $X_{\bar{\Theta}}$ and for any $\tilde{\mathbf{x}}_{\Theta}(p_{\Theta})$ and $\tilde{\mathbf{x}}_{\Theta}(q_{\Theta})$ in $\tilde{X}_{\Theta}$, the 50–50 lottery between lotteries $(\tilde{\mathbf{x}}_{\Theta}(p_{\Theta}),\mathbf{x}'_{\Theta})$ and $(\tilde{\mathbf{x}}_{\Theta}(q_{\Theta}),\mathbf{x}''_{\bar{\Theta}})$ may be strictly preferred to the 50–50 lottery between lotteries $(\tilde{\mathbf{x}}_{\Theta}(p_{\Theta}),\mathbf{x}''_{\Theta})$ and $(\tilde{\mathbf{x}}_{\Theta}(q_{\Theta}),\mathbf{x}_{\bar{\Theta}})$. In such a case, the value independence condition (3.58) is not satisfied since value independence requires that the two 50–50 gambles above be indifferent. Consequently, additive utility models do not apply here. To overcome this difficulty, Fishburn [1973, 1974] introduces the concept of *bilateral independence* which is an extension of both value and utility independence. In the same way as was utility independence, bilateral independence can also be generalized to *generalized bilateral independence*, which allows complete reversal of preference or complete indifference. Like value independence, bilateral and generalized bilateral independence are symmetric. Based on this concept, Fishburn [1974] was able to derive another decomposition of the multiattribute utility function of the form

$$
\begin{aligned}
u(\mathbf{x}) = {} & \sum_{i=1}^{n} \lambda_i u_i(x_i) + \sum_{i=1}^{n} \sum_{j>i}^{n} \lambda_{ij} f_i(x_i) f_j(x_j) \\
& + \sum_{i=1}^{n} \sum_{j>1}^{n} \sum_{k>j}^{n} \lambda_{ijk} f_i(x_i) f_j(x_j) f_k(x_k) + \cdots \\
& + \lambda_{12\ldots n} f_1(x_1) \cdots f_n(x_n),
\end{aligned}
\tag{3.70}
$$

where, for each $i=1,\ldots,n$, $u_i(x_i)$ is the normalized conditional utility function on X_i and $f_i(x_i)$ are the normalized differences between $u(x_i,\mathbf{x}_{\bar{i}}^*)$ and $u(x_i,\mathbf{x}_{\bar{i}}^0)$. (Note that $\mathbf{x}_i^*$ and $\mathbf{x}_i^0$ represent the best and worst outcomes, respectively.)

Finally, we observe the pattern of generalizations. While value independence and utility independence are defined in terms of *one* fixed element in $X_{\bar{\Theta}}$, bilateral independence is defined in terms of *two* fixed elements in $X_{\bar{\Theta}}$. It is natural, therefore, to make further generalizations to multilateral independence conditions, which are defined in terms of n fixed elements in $X_{\bar{\Theta}}$, where $n \geqslant 3$. Farquhar [1975] developed a framework based on a geometrical concept called the *fractional hypercube*, which facilitates a systematic scheme for generating the above generalizations. In addition, this *fractional independence* concept also provides a framework by which all independence concepts discussed in this section can be unified. (For further details, see Farquhar [1975, 1976, 1977, and 1978].)

Note that as the independence assumptions become more general, and hence less restrictive from the theoretical viewpoint, the resulting utility models become more realistic in capturing the true preference structure in a wider range of decision problems. The price we have to pay may, however, be immense. The more general the independence assumptions become, the more difficult they are to verify and the larger the number of conditional utility functions and constants to be assessed.

Another independence condition, whose special cases include most of the better-known independence conditions discussed thus far, is known as interpolation independence and is proposed by Bell [1978, 1979a, 1979b]. The subset of attributes Θ is said to be *interpolation independent* of $\bar{\Theta}$ if and only if for any fixed $\hat{\mathbf{x}}_{\bar{\Theta}}$ in $X_{\bar{\Theta}}$, the conditional utility function $u(\mathbf{x}_{\Theta},\hat{\mathbf{x}}_{\bar{\Theta}})$ is given by

$$u(\mathbf{x}_{\Theta},\hat{\mathbf{x}}_{\bar{\Theta}})=\mu(\hat{\mathbf{x}}_{\Theta},\mathbf{x}^{*}_{\bar{\Theta}})+\left[1-\mu(\hat{\mathbf{x}}_{\bar{\Theta}})\right]u\left(\mathbf{x}_{\Theta},\mathbf{x}^{0}_{\bar{\Theta}}\right). \tag{3.71}$$

As Bell [1977] pointed out, interpolation independence is symmetric if and only if $\mu(\hat{\mathbf{x}}_{\bar{\Theta}})$ has a special form. In addition to deriving appropriate utility decomposition models, based on (3.71), Bell [1978, 1979a, 1979b] also showed that value independence, utility independence, and bilateral independence leading to bilateral utility models are special cases of interpolation independence. Further generalization of the interpolation independence concept and further advances on multiattribute utility theory have been given by Tamura and Nakamura [1978] and Farquhar [1979].

3.6 Summary

We have presented the basic constructs of multiattribute utility theory, highlighting two fundamental issues: the existence of a real-valued functional representation of the underlying preference structure and, given such a representation exists, decomposition models that are both realistic and easy to construct. Both the certainty and uncertainty cases were described. We focused on weak ordering, a necessary property for the existence of a real-valued function that will *faithfully* preserve the ordering of $\succsim$ itself.

In riskless decision problems, the real-valued functional representation of preference structure was called the value function to distinguish it from its counterpart in the risky case (the utility function). In the general case, the existence of value functions under various conditions was discussed. For the class of problems where each attribute is measured in any real-valued unit (but may still be in an ordinal scale), it was shown that the abstract order denseness property could be replaced by more practical nonsatiety and continuity or Archimedean conditions. It was emphasized that if a value function exists, it is unique up to a monotone increasing transformation.

To find appropriate decomposition forms, we focused on additive, quasi-additive, and multiplicative value functions. For problems with three or more attributes, mutually preferential independence was found to be sufficient to ensure additive value functions. For two-attribute problems, however, the Thomsen condition was needed; otherwise the cancellation condition alone was found to be adequate. Additive value functions were shown to be unique up to a positive linear transformation. As for quasi-additive and multiplicative value functions, weak-difference independence was used as the fundamental instrument in establishing their existence. Particularly useful results, which might be used in deriving equivalent but less demanding sets of sufficiency conditions, were also established.

For the case of uncertainty, the theory is one of risky choice problems, meaning that the uncertainty aspect of the problem is assumed to be adequately modeled by numerical probability distributions derivable either objectively (including empirically) or subjectively. Second, it is a theory that is based on Bernoulli's principle of maximizing expected utility, whence the name "expected utility theory." On the question of existence of a utility function, we discussed mainly the landmark theorem of von Neumann–Morgenstern. The form and practical implications of the von Neumann–Morgenstern system of axioms, which are both necessary and sufficient for the establishment of expected utility functions, were discussed and illustrated. Other equivalent systems of axioms, as well as some possible generalizations, were briefly discussed. Unlike value functions, utility functions, if they exist, are unique up to a positive linear transformation, indicating that each attribute must be measured in at least an interval scale.

Finally, various possible decompositions of multiattribute utility functions were discussed. Again we emphasized additive, quasi-additive, and multiplicative forms, mainly because of their potential practical applications. Value independence was found to be instrumental in establishing additive utility functions. Interdependent additive utility models, where some interactions among attributes are possible, were derived from utility independence and some forms of value independence shown to be unique up to a positive linear transformation.

References

Adams, E. W., and Fagot, R. F. (1959). A model of riskless choice, *Behavioral Sciences* 4, 1–10.

Aumann, R. J. (1962). Utility theory without the completeness axiom, *Econometrica* 30, 445–462.

Bell, D. E. (1974). Evaluating time streams of income, *Omega* 2, 691–699.

Bell, D. E. (1978). Interpolation independence, in *Multiple-Criteria Problem Solving: Buffalo, New York, 1977* (S. Zionts, ed.), Springer, Berlin, pp. 1–7.

Bell, D. E. (1979a). Multiattribute utility functions: decompositions using interpolation, *Management Sciences* 25, 744–753.

Bell, D. E. (1979b). Consistent assessment procedures using conditional utility functions, *Operations Research* 27, 1054–1064.

Davidson, D., and Suppes, P. (1956). A finitistic axiomization of subjective probability and utility, *Econometrica* 24, 264–275.

Debreu, G. (1954). Representation of a preference ordering by a numerical function, in *Decision Processes* (R. M. Thrall, C. H. Coombs, and R. L. Davis, eds.), Wiley, New York, pp. 159–166.

Debreu, G. (1960). Topological methods in cardinal utility theory, in *Mathematical Methods in the Social Sciences* (K. J. Arrow, S. Karlin, and P. Suppes, eds.), Stanford University Press, Stanford, pp. 16–26.

Dewispelare, A. R., and Sage, A. P. (1979). On weakened sufficiency requirements for the multiplicative form of value function, *IEEE Transactions Systems, Man Cybernetics* SMC-9, 442–445.

Dyer, J., and Sarin, R. K. (1977). An axiomatization of cardinal additive conjoint measurement theory, Working Paper No. 265. Western Management Science Institute, UCLA, February.

Dyer, J., and Sarin, R. K. (1979). Measurable multiattribute value functions, *Operations Research* 27, 810–822.

Farquhar, P. H. (1975). A fractional hypercube decomposition theorem for multiattribute utility functions, *Operations Research* 23, 941–967.

Farquhar, P. H. (1976). A pyramid and semicube decompositions of multiattribute utility functions, *Operations Research* 24, 256–271.

Farquhar, P. H. (1977). A survey of multiattribute utility theory and applications, *TIMS Studies in the Management Sciences 6*, North Holland, Amsterdam, pp. 59–89.

Farquhar, P. H. (1978). Interdependence criteria in utility analysis, in *Multiple-Criteria Problem Solving: Buffalo, New York, 1977* (S. Zionts, ed.), Springer, Berlin, pp. 131–180.

Farquhar, P. H. (1979). Advances in multiattribute utility theory, Working Paper HBS 79-56, Graduate School of Business Administration, Harvard, July.

Fishburn, P. C. (1965a). Independence in utility theory with whole product sets, *Operations Research* 13, 28–45.

Fishburn, P. C. (1965b). Markovian dependence in utility theory with whole product sets, *Operations Research* 13, 238–257.

Fishburn, P. C. (1966a). Additivity in utility theory with denumerable product sets, *Econometrica* 34, 500–503.

Fishburn, P. C. (1966b). A note on recent developments in additive utility theories for multiple-factor situations, *Operations Research* 14, 1143–1148.

Fishburn, P. C. (1967a). Additive utilities with incomplete product: Applications to priorities and assignments, *Operations Research* 15, 537–542.

Fishburn, P. C. (1967b). Interdependence and additivity in multivariate, unidimensional expected utility theory, *International Economics Review* 8, 335–342.

Fishburn, P. C. (1970). *Utility Theory for Decision Making*, Wiley, New York.

Fishburn, P. C. (1971). Additive representations of real-valued functions on subsets of product sets, *Journal of Mathematical Psychology* 8, 382–388.

Fishburn, P. C. (1972). Interdependent preferences on finite sets, *Journal of Mathematical Psychology* 9, 225–236.

Fishburn, P. C. (1973). Bernoullian utilities for multiple-factor situations, in *Multiple Criteria Decision Making* (J. L. Cochrane and M. Zeleney, eds.), University of South Carolina Press, South Carolina.

Fishburn, P. C. (1974). von Neumann–Morgenstern utility functions on two attributes, *Operations Research* 22, 35–45.

Fishburn, P. C. (1976). Utility independence on subsets of product sets, *Operations Research* 24, 245–255.

Fishburn, P. C. (1977). Multiattribute utilities in expected utility theory, in *Conflicting Objectives in Decision* (D. E. Bell, R. L. Keeney, and H. Raiffa, eds.), Wiley, Chichester, Great Britain.

Fishburn, P. C., and Keeney, R. L. (1974). Seven independence concepts and continuous multiattribute utility functions, *Journal of Mathematical Psychology* 11, pp. 294–327.

Fishburn, P. C., and Keeney, R. L. (1975). Generalized utility independence and some implications, *Operations Research* 23, 928–940.

Gorman, W. M. (1968). The structure of utility functions, *Review of Economic Studies* 35, 367–390.

Hausner, M. (1954). Multidimensional utilities, in *Decision Processes* (R. M. Thrall, C. H. Coombs, and R. L. Davis, eds.), Wiley, New York.

Herstein, I. N., and Milnor, J. (1953). An axiomatic approach to measurable utility, *Econometrica* 21, 291–297.

Keeney, R. L. (1968). Quasi-separable utility functions, *Naval Research Logistics Quarterly* 15, 551–565.

Keeney, R. L. (1971). Utility independence and preferences for multiattributed consequences, *Operations Research* 19, 875–893.

Keeney, R. L. (1972a). Utility functions for multiattribute consequences, *Management Science* 18, 276–287.

Keeney, R. L. (1972b). An illustrated procedure for assessing multiattributed utility functions, *Sloan Management Review*, Fall, 38–50.

Keeney, R. L. (1973a). Risk independence and multiattributed utility functions, *Econometrica* 41, 27–34.

Keeney, R. L. (1973b). A decision analysis with multiple objectives: the Mexico City airport, *Bell Journal of Economics and Management Science* 4, 101–117.

Keeney, R. L. (1973c). Concepts of independence in multiattribute utility theory, in *Multiple-Criteria Decision Making* (J. L. Cochrane and M. Zeleny, eds.), University of South Carolina Press, pp. 62–71.

Keeney, R. L. (1974). Multiplicative utility functions, *Operations Research* 22, 22–34.

Keeney, R. L., and Raiffa, H. (1976). *Decisions with Multiple Objectives*, Wiley, New York.

Kirkwood, C. W. (1976). Parametrically dependent preferences for multiattributed consequences, *Operations Research* 24, 92–103.

Krantz, D. H., Luce, R. D., Suppes, P., and Tversky, A. (1971). *Foundations of Measurement*, Academic, New York, Vol. 1.

Luce, R. D. (1966). Two extensions of conjoint measurement, *Journal of Mathematical Psychology* 3, 348–370.

Luce, R. D., and Suppes, P. (1965). Preference, utility, and subjective probability, in *Handbook of Mathematical Psychology*, Vol. II (R. D. Luce, R. R. Bush, and E. Galanter, eds.), Wiley, New York, pp. 249–410.

Luce, R. D., and Tukey, J. W. (1964). Simultaneous conjoint measurement: a new type of fundamental measurement, *Journal of Mathematical Psychology* 1, 1–27.

Meyer, R. F. (1970). On the relationship among the utility of assets, the utility of consumption, and investment strategy in an uncertain, but time-invariant, world, in OR-69 *Proceedings of the Fifth International Conference on Operations Research — Venice, 1969* (J. Lawrence ed.), Tavistock, New York.

Pollak, R. A. (1967). Additive von Neumann–Morgenstern utility functions, *Econometrica* 35, 485–494.

Raiffa, H. (1969). Preferences for multiattributed alternatives, RM-5868-DOT/RC, Rand Corporation, Santa Monica, April.

Ramsey, F. P. (1931). Truth and probability, in *The Foundations of Mathematics and Other Logical Essays* (F. P. Ramsey ed.), Harcourt Brace, New York, pp. 156–198.

Savage, L. J. (1954). *The Foundations of Statistics*, Wiley, New York.

Scott, D., and Suppes, P. (1958). Foundational aspects of theories of measurement, *Journal of Symbolic Logic* 23, pp. 113–128.

Suppes, P., and Winet, M. (1955). An axiomatization of utility based on the notion of utility differences, *Management Sciences* 1, 259–270.

Tamura, H., and Nakamura, Y. (1978). Decompositions of multiattribute utility functions based on a new concept of convex dependence, in *Proceedings of International Conference on Cybernetics and Society*, IEEE Systems, Man and Cybernetics Society, Tokyo.

Thrall, R. M. (1954). Applications of multidimensional utility theory, in *Decision Processes* (R. M. Thrall, C. M. Coombs, and R. L. Davis, eds.,), Wiley, New York, pp. 181–186.

von Neumann, J., and Morgenstern, O. (1980). *Theory of Games and Economic Behavior*, 4th ed., Princeton University Press, Princeton (first published 1944).

Chapter 4
Vector Optimization Theory

4.1 Introduction

An important class of multiobjective decision problems (MDP) is the vector optimization (VOP) or multiobjective optimization problems (MOP). From a methodological viewpoint, these are mathematical programming problems with a vector-valued objective function. From the decision-making viewpoint, this class of MDP arises when the decision rule implies that each attribute (or objective function) is to be kept as extreme (i.e., as high or as low) as possible.[1]

The solutions of a vector optimization problem are referred to in the literature variously as noninferior, efficient, Pareto-optimal, and nondominated solutions. In the remainder of this book we shall follow Zadeh [1963] in referring to a solution of a vector optimization problem as *noninferior*.

The concept of noninferior solution was introduced at the turn of the century [1896] by Pareto, a prominent economist, but it is only since 1951, when Kuhn and Tucker published necessary and sufficient conditions for (proper) noninferiority, that considerable effort has been devoted to developing procedures for generating noninferior solutions to a VOP. To characterize noninferior solutions is, loosely speaking, to relate them to something that we already know and can apply. Since a VOP is in a sense an extension of scalar optimization, whose solution techniques are well known, it is natural to characterize noninferior solutions of the former in terms of optimal solutions of the latter. Indeed, upon satisfying certain conditions, a

[1] This class of MDPs corresponds to Example 3 in Section 1.3.

solution of an appropriate scalar optimization problem will qualify as a noninferior solution of the corresponding vector optimization.

4.2 Notions of Noninferior Solution

Let $\mathbf{x}$ be an N-dimensional (column) vector of decision variables. For $i=1,\ldots,m$, we reserve the symbol $g_i(\mathbf{x})$ to denote the real-valued function defined on R^n that represents the ith system constraint. We shall include *any* other form of constraint (i.e., those which cannot be expressed as a g function) in the set $S \subseteq R^n$. The *decision space* or the *feasible region* of the system will be characterized by the set

$$X=\{\mathbf{x}|\, g_i(\mathbf{x}) \leqslant 0,\, i=1,\ldots,m \text{ and } \mathbf{x}\in S\}. \tag{4.1}$$

Note that $X \in R^N$. Likewise for each $j=1,\ldots,n$ we shall reserve the symbol $f_j(\mathbf{x})$ to denote the real-valued function defined on X that represents the jth attribute (or objective function or decision criterion). For compact notation, the *multiobjective function* (or vector-valued criterion) will be denoted by $\mathbf{f}(\mathbf{x})=(f_1(\mathbf{x}),\ldots,f_n(\mathbf{x}))$, i.e., $f\colon X \to R^n$ for $X \subseteq R^N$. Correspondingly, the *objective space* (or criterion space) refers to the set $F=\{\mathbf{f}(\mathbf{x})|\mathbf{x}\in X\}$. Thus $F \subseteq \mathrm{R}^n$. In summary, the decision space belongs to R^N and the functional space belongs to R^n. A VOP is then formulated as

$$\min_{\mathbf{x}\in X} \quad [f_1(\mathbf{x}),\ldots,f_n(\mathbf{x})]. \tag{4.2}$$

Solving a VOP entails finding its set of noninferior solutions.[2] Conceptually, a noninferior solution is one which is not dominated by any other feasible solution. Precisely what we mean by "one solution dominates the other" depends on the type of analysis being used (which, in turn, depends on the manner in which the decision maker interacts with the model). Yu [1974] introduced a generalized concept of nondominated (or noninferior) solutions, which is based on the so-called domination structure. Intuitively, the domination structure of a multiobjective decision problem is a structure related to the decision maker's preference, which determines how one alternative dominates another alternative. We say $\mathbf{x}^1$ *dominates* $\mathbf{x}^2$, or

$$\mathbf{x}^1 \geqslant \mathbf{x}^2 \qquad \text{if and only if} \qquad v(\mathbf{f}(\mathbf{x}^1)) \geqslant v(\mathbf{f}(\mathbf{x}^2)), \tag{4.3}$$

where v is the value function. We can say that (4.3) defines the domination structure for this decision problem. In general, Yu [1974] uses the so-called domination cone, which is a convex cone $D(\mathbf{f})$ in R^n, to define the domination structure. For $\mathbf{x}^1, \mathbf{x}^2$ in X, alternative $\mathbf{x}^1$ dominates alternative $\mathbf{x}^2$ if and

---

[2] Naturally, we distinguish between a VOP and a MDP. Solving the former, i.e., findings its noninferior solutions, is to be viewed as a first step in solving the latter.

only if

$$\mathbf{f}^2-\mathbf{f}^1 \in D(\mathbf{f}^1), \tag{4.4}$$

where $\mathbf{f}^1=\mathbf{f}(\mathbf{x}^1)$, $\mathbf{f}^2=\mathbf{f}(\mathbf{x}^2)$, and $D(\mathbf{f})$ is the domination (convex) cone at $\mathbf{f}$. Consequently, we say $\mathbf{x}$ is nondominated if it is not dominated by any $\mathbf{x}$ in X. Bergstresser et al. [1976] later generalized the concept and used a convex set $D(\mathbf{f})$, rather than a convex cone, to represent the domination structure. They call $D(\mathbf{f})$ the set of domination factors at $\mathbf{f}$. In terms of this definition and (4.4), the domination structure reflected by (4.3) can be represented by the convex set $D(\mathbf{f})$, where, for each $\mathbf{f}\in F$,

$$D(\mathbf{f}) \triangleq \{\mathbf{d} \mid v(\mathbf{f}) > v(\mathbf{f}+\mathbf{d})\}. \tag{4.5}$$

The use of the generalized domination structure to define the concept of nondominated solution opens up opportunities to develop theoretical results that are applicable to more than one type of preference structure. In addition to the above references, some of these results may also be found in Naccache [1978], Tanino and Sawaragi [1979], and Tamura and Miura [1979]. We shall focus on the specific class of domination problems of (4.2). The implicit preference structure, which underlies this formulation, is in tune with *monotonicity* of preference. It states that, for each objective function f_j, $j=1,\ldots,n$, an alternative having a smaller value of f_j is always preferred to an alternative having a larger value of f_j, with all other objective functions being equal. The corresponding domination structure for VOP in (4.2) is thus represented by a constant convex cone of the form[3]

$$D \triangleq \{\mathbf{d} \mid \mathbf{d}\in R^n, \mathbf{d} \geqslant \mathbf{0}\}. \tag{4.6}$$

The general nondominated (or noninferior) solution defined by (4.4) and (4.6) then becomes the familiar Pareto-optimal solution as introduced by Pareto [1896].

Definition. $\mathbf{x}^*$ is said to be a *noninferior solution* of VOP if there exists no other feasible $\mathbf{x}$ (i.e., $\mathbf{x}\in X$) such that $\mathbf{f}(\mathbf{x}) \leqslant \mathbf{f}(\mathbf{x}^*)$, meaning that $f_j(\mathbf{x}) \leqslant f_j(\mathbf{x}^*)$ for all $j=1,\ldots,n$ with strict inequality for at least one j.

For convenience of notation, we shall denote the set of all noninferior solutions of VOP by X^*, and the noninferior set $\{\mathbf{f}(\mathbf{x}) \mid \mathbf{x}\in X^*)$ by F^*.

Intuitively the alternative $\mathbf{x}^*$ in X is noninferior if and only if we cannot find any other alternative $\mathbf{x}$ in X such that some objective functions at $\mathbf{x}$

[3] Throughout this and the remaining chapters, we shall use standard notation for the ordering of vector-valued variables. More specifically, for $\mathbf{y}$ and $\mathbf{z}\in R^n$, i) $\mathbf{y}\geqq\mathbf{z}$ if and only if $y_i \geqq z_i$ for each $i=1,\ldots,n$; ii) $\mathbf{y}>\mathbf{z}$ if and only if $y_i \geqq z_i$ for each $i=1,\ldots,n$ with strict inequality for at least one $1\leqslant i\leqslant n$; and iii) $\mathbf{y}=\mathbf{z}$ if and only if $y_i=z_i$ for each $i=1,\ldots,n$.

improve (i.e., decrease) from those at $\mathbf{x}^*$ without degrading at least one of the other objective functions.

To illustrate the concept of noninferiority, consider a simple VOP.

$$\begin{aligned} \min \quad & [f_1(x), f_2(x)] \\ \text{subject to} \quad & x \geq 0, \quad x \in R, \end{aligned} \tag{4.7}$$

where $f_1(x) = x - 1$, $f_2(x) = (x-3)^2 + 1$.

Figure 4.1 illustrates the set of noninferior solutions X^* and the noninferior set F^* of (4.7) in the decision space and the objective space, respectively. Clearly, any point x between 1 and 3 inclusive is a noninferior solution of the simple VOP since in this interval, whenever $f_1(x)$ decreases, $f_2(x)$ increases and vice versa. Thus, $X^* = \{x | x \in R,\ 1 \leq x \leq 3\}$ and $F^* = \{\mathbf{f} | \mathbf{f} = (f_1, f_2), f_2 = (f_1 - 2)^2 + 1,\ 0 \leq f_1 \leq 2\}$. Likewise, any point $y \notin X^*$ is an inferior solution, since we can always improve both objective functions f_1 and f_2 by selecting an appropriate point in X^*. For the two-objective problem, the noninferior set F^* is the left portion (minimization problem) of the boundary of the feasible region in the objective space F, which has negative slope. In fact, it can be shown that F^* traces a curve $f_2 = f_2(f_1)$, where $f_2(\ )$ is a strictly decreasing function of f_1. $df_2(f_1)/df_1$ must be negative at every point in F^* because in F^*, a decrease in one objective can be achieved only at the expense of an increase in the other objective. The quantity $df_2(f_1)/df_1$ reflects the *trade-off rate*, which will be defined and discussed in Section 4.9. For problems with more than two attributes, F^* will be a hypersurface forming a left portion of the boundary of F with the properties that $\partial f_k / \partial f_j < 0$ for at least one pair $1 \leq j \neq k \leq n$.

Figure 4.1 Noninferior solution set of a simple VOP (**a**) in decision space and (**b**) in objective space.

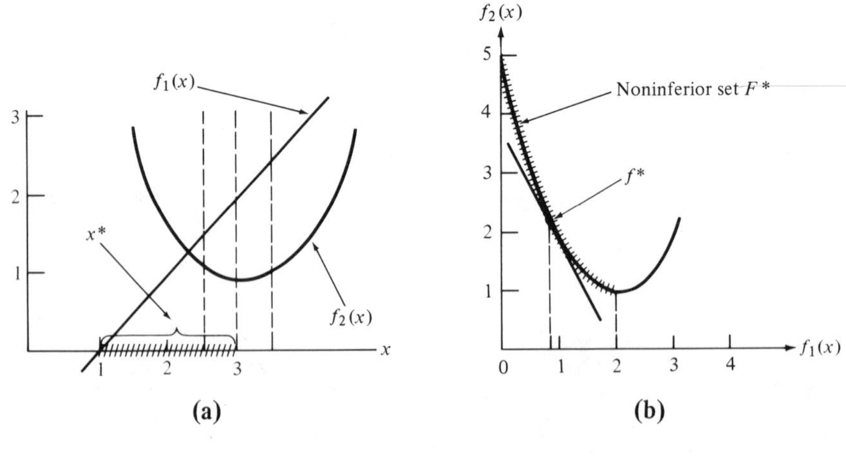

4.3 Three Common Approaches to Characterizing Noninferior Solutions

In order to operationalize the concept of noninferior solutions, we should relate it to a familiar concept. The most common strategy is to characterize noninferior solutions in terms of optimal solutions of appropriate scalar optimization problems (SOP). Among the many possible ways of obtaining a scalar problem from a VOP, the following are common.

1. *The weighting problem*: Let $W=\{\mathbf{w}|\mathbf{w}\in R^n,\ w_j\geq 0 \text{ and } \sum_{j=1}^n w_j=1\}$ be the set of nonnegative weights. The weighting problem is defined for some $\mathbf{w}\in W$ as $P(\mathbf{w})$:

$$\min_{\mathbf{x}\in X} \sum_{j=1}^{n} w_j f_j(\mathbf{x}). \tag{4.8}$$

2. *The kth-objective Lagrangian problem*[4] $P_k(\mathbf{u})$:

$$\min_{\mathbf{x}\in X} f_k(\mathbf{x})+\sum_{j\neq k} u_j f_j(\mathbf{x}), \tag{4.9}$$

where $\mathbf{u}=U_k \triangleq \{(u_1,\ldots,u_{k-1},u_{k+1},\ldots,u_n)^{\mathrm{T}}\,|\,u_j\geq 0 \text{ for each } j\neq k\}$.

3. *The kth-objective ε-constraint problem* $P_k(\boldsymbol{\varepsilon})$:

$$\min_{\mathbf{x}\in X} f_k(\mathbf{x}) \tag{4.10}$$

$$\text{subject to} \quad f_j(\mathbf{x})\leq \varepsilon_j, \quad j=1,\ldots,n, \quad j\neq k, \tag{4.11}$$

where $\boldsymbol{\varepsilon}=(\varepsilon_1,\ldots,\varepsilon_{k-1},\varepsilon_{k+1},\ldots,\varepsilon_n)^{\mathrm{T}}$. For a given point $\mathbf{x}^*$, we shall use the symbol $P_k(\boldsymbol{\varepsilon}^*)$ to represent the problem $P_k(\boldsymbol{\varepsilon})$, where $\varepsilon_j=\varepsilon_j^*=f_j(\mathbf{x}^*)$, $j\neq k$ [Haimes et al., 1971; Haimes and Hall, 1974].

Other forms of "scalarization" of a VOP also exist. For example, Lin [1976a, b] characterizes noninferior solutions of a VOP in terms of solutions of a *proper equality constraint* (PEC) problem. This is exactly the same as the ε-constraint problem stated in (4.10) and (4.11) except that strict equality holds in (4.11). Wendell and Lee [1977] and Corley [1980] propose yet another form of scalarization, which combines the weighting approach and the constraint approach. A generalized version of the weighting problem, called the weighted norm problem, is also a possible form of scalarizing VOP. The *weighted norm* problem is formulated as

$$\min_{\mathbf{x}\in X} \sum_{j=1}^{n} w_j |f_j(\mathbf{x})-\hat{f}_j|^p, \tag{4.12}$$

[4] Although from the computational viewpoint there is very little difference between the Lagrangian and the weighting problems, the two problems will be treated separately here to emphasize that the former touches upon two important concepts, *saddle point* and *stability*, whereas the usual direct treatment of the latter goes a different route.

where $|\ |$ is absolute value, $1 \leq p < \infty$, and $\hat{f}_j = \min_{\mathbf{x} \in X} f_j(\mathbf{x})$. Observe that when $p=1$ (4.12) reduces to (4.8). All these characterizations will be discussed in detail in Section 4.6.

Note that the symbols $P(\mathbf{w})$, $P_k(\mathbf{u})$, and $P_k(\boldsymbol{\varepsilon})$ will generally be used to represent, for brevity, the weighting problem, the Lagrangian problem, and the constraint problem, respectively. However, when the occasion arises and confusion is minimal, they will also be used to represent appropriate extremum functions [e.g., $P(\mathbf{w}) = \min_{\mathbf{x} \in X} \sum_{j=1}^{n} w_j f_j(\mathbf{x})$].

In this section, we treat fundamental relationships among the three scalar optimization problems, $P_k(\boldsymbol{\varepsilon})$, $P_k(\mathbf{u})$, and $P(\mathbf{w})$. Then we describe fundamental results concerning the characterization of a noninferior solution of VOP in terms of solutions of the three SOPs above. In the subsequent two sections, precise statements of the necessary and sufficient conditions for noninferiority, which are based on the Kuhn–Tucker conditions for optimality, will be established, and various types of necessary and sufficient conditions for proper noninferiority will be discussed.

To emphasize how closely these results are related, the presentation of these three sections will be based entirely on the *implication* diagram (Figure 4.2). Not only does the diagram summarize all relevant results, it also promptly displays connections among them.

The following symbols, conventions, and assumptions are used in the implication diagram.

Assumptions

- CA, the convexity assumption: X is a convex set and f_j, $j=1,\ldots,n$, are convex functions defined on X.
- FC, the faithfully convex assumption: All functions f_j, $j=1,\ldots,m$, are either linear or nonlinear and contain no straight-line segment in their graphs.
- RA, the regularity assumption: $\mathbf{x}^*$ is a regular point of the constraint of the interested problem.
- KQ, Karlin's constraint qualification: X has nonempty interior.
- S1, stability assumption 1: $P_k(\boldsymbol{\varepsilon}^*)$, defined in association with the given point $\mathbf{x}^*$, is stable.
- S2, stability assumption 2: $P_k(\boldsymbol{\varepsilon}^*)$ is stable for every $k=1,\ldots,n$.
- DA, differentiability assumption: All functions are continuously differentiable.
- KTC, Kuhn–Tucker condition for optimality (see Section 2.3 for a definition).
- KTCN, Kuhn-Tucker conditions for noninferiority (see the definition in Section 4.4).

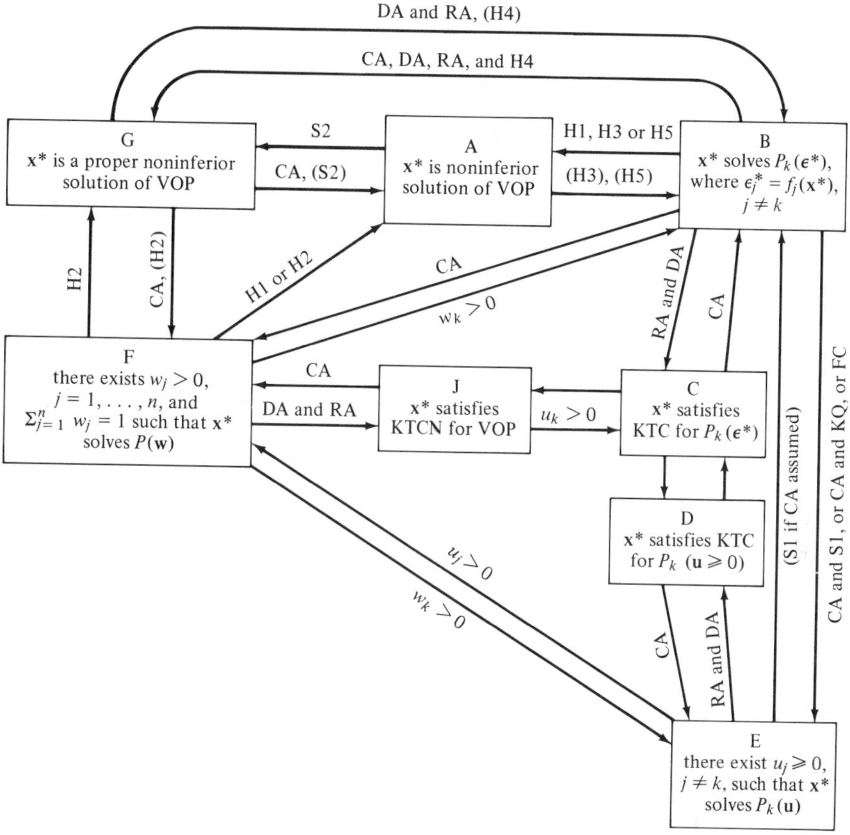

Figure 4.2 The implication diagram.

Hypotheses

H1: The concerned SOP problem has a unique solution.

H2: All the weights of the weighting problem concerned are strictly positive.

H3: The implying statement or the implied statement (whichever is appropriate) is true for every $k = 1, \ldots, n$.

H4: All Kuhn–Tucker multipliers[5] (if they exist) associated with the constraint $f_j(\mathbf{x}) \leq \varepsilon_j^*$, $j \neq k$, of $P_k(\boldsymbol{\varepsilon}^*)$ are strictly positive.

H5: Lin's conditions (see Theorem 4.3).

[5] Kuhn–Tucker multipliers are those that, together with the optimal solution, satisfy the Kuhn–Tucker conditions for optimality.

Conventions

$$\boxed{\text{A}} \overset{\alpha}{\rightarrow} \boxed{\text{B}}$$

is read, on applying the assumptions (or hypotheses) α, A implies B.

$$\boxed{\text{A}} \xrightarrow{\alpha \text{ or } \beta} \boxed{\text{B}}$$

is read, on applying either assumption α or assumption β, A implies B.

$$\boxed{\text{A}} \overset{(\alpha)}{\rightarrow} \boxed{\text{B}}$$

is read, A implies both α and B.

$$\boxed{\text{A}} \xrightarrow{\alpha,\,(\beta)} \boxed{\text{B}}$$

is read, on applying assumption α, A implies both β and B. Finally, all implications are transitive.

To illustrate the utility of the implication diagram, assume we want to know whether the sufficient conditions for a solution of a weighting problem are also sufficient for a noninferior solution of a VOP. We begin with box F (which represents the statement that $\mathbf{x}^*$ is an optimal solution of $P(\mathbf{w})$ for some given nonnegative weights $\mathbf{w}$), and seek a connected path having all arrows pointed toward A. Several paths exist. Each of these paths represents a required sufficient condition, although different paths do not necessarily represent different sufficient conditions. For example, one of the paths from box F to box A is

$$\boxed{\text{F}} \xrightarrow{\text{H1 or H2}} \boxed{\text{A}},$$

which implies that for an optimal solution of $P(\mathbf{w})$ to be a noninferior solution, one of the following two sufficient conditions should be satisfied. That is, either i) the optimal solution of $P(\mathbf{w})$ is unique (H1), or ii) all the weights of $P(\mathbf{w})$ are strictly positive (H2).

Another path from F to A is

$$\boxed{\text{F}} \xrightarrow{w_K > 0} \boxed{\text{B}} \xrightarrow{\text{H1 or H3 or H5}} \boxed{\text{A}}.$$

Careful examination reveals that the condition $w_k > 0$ and hypothesis H3 together represent the same sufficient condition as stated in Condition (ii). Furthermore, the condition $w_k > 0$ and hypothesis H1 together clearly constitute a more restricted sufficient condition than stated in Condition (i). Thus, the sufficient conditions implied by the latter path are either the same or more restricted than those implied by the former path. Nevertheless, the second path allows the relationships between $P(\mathbf{w})$ and $P_k(\boldsymbol{\varepsilon})$ (box F and box B) and $P_k(\boldsymbol{\varepsilon})$ and VOP (box B and box A) to be displayed.

As another illustrative example, suppose we want to know the necessary conditions, expressed in terms of an optimal solution of $P_k(\boldsymbol{\varepsilon})$, for a point $\mathbf{x}^*$ to be noninferior. Reading a direct path from A to B,

$$\boxed{\text{A}} \xrightarrow{\text{(H3)(H5)}} \boxed{\text{B}}$$

will give these required conditions. That is, for a point $\mathbf{x}^*$ to be a noninferior solution of VOP, it must solve $P_k(\boldsymbol{\varepsilon}^*)$, where $\varepsilon_j^* = f_j(\mathbf{x}^*)$, $j=1,\ldots,n$, $j \neq k$, for each $k=1,\ldots,n$.

4.3.1 Relationships Among the Three Forms of Scalarization

Most results, except in Section 4.3.2, rely heavily on a convexity assumption. It is convenient, therefore, to refer to the convexity assumption as meaning that X is a convex set, and the f_j, $j=1,\ldots,n$, are convex functions defined on X.

Lemma 4.1

$$\boxed{\text{B}} \xrightarrow{\text{CA}} \boxed{\text{F}}.$$

Assume the convexity assumption. If for any given k, $\mathbf{x}^*$ solves $P_k(\boldsymbol{\varepsilon}^*)$, then there exists $\mathbf{w} \in W$ such that $\mathbf{x}^*$ also solves $P(\mathbf{w})$.

NOTE: The proof of this result relies on the *generalized Gordon theorem*, which is (roughly speaking) a nonlinear version of Farkas's lemma. For a more detailed discussion of these topics, see Mangasarian [1969].

PROOF: Since $\mathbf{x}^*$ solves $P_k(\boldsymbol{\varepsilon}^*)$, the system of inequalities

$$f_k(\mathbf{x}) < f_k(\mathbf{x}^*), \qquad f_j(\mathbf{x}) \leqslant f_j(\mathbf{x}^*), \quad j=1,\ldots,n, \quad j \neq k, \tag{4.13}$$

has no solution in X.

Upon imposing the convexity assumption and applying the generalized Gordon theorem [Mangasarian 1969], there exists $\mathbf{p} \in R^n$ with $\mathbf{p} \geqslant \mathbf{0}$ such that $\sum_{j=1}^n p_j[f_j(\mathbf{x}) - f_j(\mathbf{x}^*)] \geqslant 0$ for all $\mathbf{x} \in X$. By choosing $w_j = p_j / \sum_{j=1}^n p_j$ (possible since $\sum_{j=1}^n p_j > 0$), we have $\mathbf{w} \geqslant \mathbf{0}$ and $\sum_{j=1}^n w_j = 1$. With this choice of $\mathbf{w}$, we have, for all $\mathbf{x} \in X$

$$\sum_{j=1}^n w_j\big[f_j(\mathbf{x}) - f_j(\mathbf{x}^*)\big] \geqslant 0 \qquad \Rightarrow \qquad \sum_{j=1}^n w_j f_j(\mathbf{x}) \geqslant \sum_{j=1}^n w_j f_j(\mathbf{x}^*). \tag{4.14}$$

Hence $\mathbf{x}^*$ solves $P(\mathbf{w})$. ■

Now let

$$Y_k \triangleq \{\boldsymbol{\varepsilon} | \{\mathbf{x} | f_j(\mathbf{x}) \leqslant \varepsilon_j, j \neq k, \mathbf{x} \in X\} \neq \varnothing\}. \tag{4.15}$$

That is, Y_k is the set of all $\boldsymbol{\varepsilon}$ such that $P_k(\boldsymbol{\varepsilon})$ is feasible.

$$X^k(\hat{\boldsymbol{\varepsilon}}) \triangleq \{\mathbf{x} | \mathbf{x} \text{ solves } P_k(\hat{\boldsymbol{\varepsilon}})\}; \tag{4.16a}$$

$$X^k(\boldsymbol{\varepsilon}) \triangleq \{\mathbf{x} | \mathbf{x} \text{ solves } P_k(\boldsymbol{\varepsilon}) \text{ for some } \boldsymbol{\varepsilon} \in Y_k\}; \tag{4.16b}$$

$$X_w \triangleq \{\mathbf{x} | \mathbf{x} \text{ solves } P(\mathbf{w}) \text{ for some } \mathbf{w} \in W\}. \tag{4.16c}$$

Using these notations and the above lemma, we state:

Corollary. *Assume the convexity assumption. Then for any given* $\hat{\boldsymbol{\varepsilon}} \in Y_k$,

$$X^k(\hat{\boldsymbol{\varepsilon}}) \subseteq X_w; \tag{4.17a}$$

$$X^k(\boldsymbol{\varepsilon}) \subseteq X_w. \tag{4.17b}$$

PROOF: For any given $\hat{\boldsymbol{\varepsilon}}$ if $X^k(\hat{\boldsymbol{\varepsilon}}) = \phi$, (4.17a) is trivial. Assume that $X^k(\hat{\boldsymbol{\varepsilon}}) \neq \phi$ [i.e., $\hat{\boldsymbol{\varepsilon}} \in Y_k$ and $P_k(\hat{\boldsymbol{\varepsilon}})$ has an optimal solution]. Consider $\mathbf{x}^* \in X^k(\hat{\boldsymbol{\varepsilon}})$. Clearly $\mathbf{x}^* \in X^k(\boldsymbol{\varepsilon}^*)$, since $\varepsilon_j^* \leqslant \hat{\varepsilon}_j$ for all $j \neq k$ and $\mathbf{x}^*$ is a feasible point of $P_k(\boldsymbol{\varepsilon}^*)$. From Lemma 4.1 it follows that $\mathbf{x}^* \in X_w$. Thus $X^k(\hat{\boldsymbol{\varepsilon}}) \subseteq X_w$ and (4.17a) is proved. The proof of (4.17b) follows easily by observing that

$$X^k(\boldsymbol{\varepsilon}) \subseteq \bigcup_{\boldsymbol{\varepsilon} \in Y_k} X^k(\hat{\boldsymbol{\varepsilon}}) \subseteq X_w, \tag{4.18}$$

where the second inclusion is furnished by (4.17a). ■

This result simply states that, under the convexity assumption, any optimal solution of an ε-constraint problem can also be found by means of the weighting problems. The converse of the above result, i.e., transferring from $P(\mathbf{w})$ to $P_k(\boldsymbol{\varepsilon})$, does not require the convexity assumption. However, it does require another condition:

Lemma 4.2

$$\boxed{\text{F}} \xrightarrow{w_k > 0} \boxed{\text{B}}.$$

If there exists $\mathbf{w} \in W$ *such that* $\mathbf{x}^*$ *solves* $P(\mathbf{w})$, *then either*

1. *if* $w_k > 0$, $\mathbf{x}^*$ *also solves* $P_k(\boldsymbol{\varepsilon}^*)$; *or*
2. *if* $\mathbf{x}^*$ *is the unique minimizer of* $P(\mathbf{w})$, *then* $\mathbf{x}^*$ *solves* $P_k(\boldsymbol{\varepsilon})^*$ *for all* k.

PROOF: Let $\mathbf{x}^*$ solve $P(\mathbf{w})$ for some $\mathbf{w} \in W$. Then

$$\sum_{j=1}^{n} w_j\left[f_j(\mathbf{x}) - f_j(\mathbf{x}^*)\right] \geqslant 0 \qquad \text{for all} \quad \mathbf{x} \in X. \tag{4.19}$$

(1) Assume that $\mathbf{x}^*$ does not solve $P_k(\boldsymbol{\varepsilon}^*)$, then there exists $\mathbf{x}^0 \in X$ such that $f_k(\mathbf{x}^0) < f_k(\mathbf{x}^*)$ and $f_j(\mathbf{x}^0) \leqslant f_j(\mathbf{x}^*), j \neq k$. Since by the hypothesis $w_k > 0$ and $w_j \geqslant 0$ for all $j \neq k$, we have

$$w_k\left[f_k(\mathbf{x}^0) - f_k(\mathbf{x}^*)\right] + \sum_{j \neq k} w_j\left[f_j(\mathbf{x}^0) - f_j(\mathbf{x}^*)\right] < 0,$$

which contradicts (4.19). Hence $\mathbf{x}^*$ solves $P_k(\boldsymbol{\varepsilon}^*)$.

(2) If $\mathbf{x}^*$ is the unique minimizer of $P(\mathbf{w})$, then from (4.19)

$$\sum_{j=1}^{n} w_j\left[f_j(\mathbf{x}) - f_j(\mathbf{x}^*)\right] > 0 \qquad \text{for all} \quad \mathbf{x} \in X. \tag{4.20}$$

Now if there is a k such that $\mathbf{x}^*$ does not solve $P_k(\boldsymbol{\varepsilon})$, this means we can find $\mathbf{x}^0 \in X$ such that $f_k(\mathbf{x}^0) < f_k(\mathbf{x}^*)$ and $f_j(\mathbf{x}^0) \leqslant f_j(\mathbf{x}^*), j \neq k$. So for any $\mathbf{w} \geqslant \mathbf{0}$, $\sum_{j=1}^{n} w_j[f_j(x^0) - f_j(\mathbf{x}^*)] \leqslant 0$, which contradicts (4.20). Thus $\mathbf{x}^*$ solves $P_k(\boldsymbol{\varepsilon}^*)$ for all k. ■

Using notation defined in (4.16) and

$$X_w^k \triangleq \{\mathbf{x} | \mathbf{x} \text{ solves } P(\mathbf{w}) \text{ for some } \mathbf{w} \in W \text{ with } w_k > 0\}, \tag{4.21}$$

$$\tilde{X}_w \triangleq \{\mathbf{x} | \mathbf{x} \text{ uniquely solves } P(\mathbf{w}) \text{ for some } \mathbf{w} \in W\}, \tag{4.22}$$

we can rewrite Lemma 4.2:

Corollary

1. *For each* k, $X_w^k \subseteq X^k(\boldsymbol{\varepsilon})$
2. $\tilde{X}_w \subseteq X^k(\boldsymbol{\varepsilon})$ *for all* k.

Observe that Lemma 4.2 provides two alternative sufficiency conditions guaranteeing the legitimacy of transferring from $P(\mathbf{w})$ to $P_k(\boldsymbol{\varepsilon})$.

In the foregoing results, we have seen how convexity and uniqueness of an optimal solution play the role of restricting the freedom to transfer between $P_k(\boldsymbol{\varepsilon})$ and $P(\mathbf{w})$. Now we shall see that either stability or saddle point concepts can be used to perform the same function in the case of transferring from $P_k(\boldsymbol{\varepsilon})$ to $P_k(\mathbf{u})$. There is no restriction on the reverse transformation.

The concept of stability for problems of forms like $P_k(\boldsymbol{\varepsilon})$ helps establish the relationship between primal and dual optimization problems. Thus, it furnishes a possible link between $P_k(\boldsymbol{\varepsilon})$ and $P_k(\mathbf{u})$.

The *sensitivity function* $w_k(\mathbf{y})$ of $P_k(\boldsymbol{\varepsilon})$, where $w_k\colon R^{n-1} \to R$, is defined as

$$w_k(\mathbf{y}) \triangleq \inf_{\mathbf{x} \in X} \{ f_k(\mathbf{x}) | f_j(\mathbf{x}) - \varepsilon_j \leqslant y_i, j \neq k \}. \tag{4.23}$$

The sensitivity function is sometimes called the perturbation function [Benson and Morin, 1977]. Observe that $w_k(\mathbf{0})$ is the optimal value of $P_k(\boldsymbol{\varepsilon})$.

Definition. $P_k(\boldsymbol{\varepsilon})$ is said to be *stable* if $w_k(\mathbf{0})$ is finite and there exists $M > 0$ such that for all $\mathbf{y} \neq \mathbf{0}$,

$$[w_k(\mathbf{0}) - w_k(\mathbf{y})] / \|\mathbf{y}\| < M,$$

where $\| \ \|$ is any norm of interest [Geoffrion, 1971].

Lemma 4.3

$$\boxed{\text{B}} \xrightarrow{\text{CA and S1}} \boxed{\text{E}}.$$

If i) $\mathbf{x}^*$ *solves* $P_k(\boldsymbol{\varepsilon}^*)$, *ii)* $P_k(\boldsymbol{\varepsilon}^*)$ *is stable, and iii) the convexity assumption holds, then there exist* $u_j \geqslant 0$ *for all* $j \neq k$ *such that* $\mathbf{x}^*$ *solves* $P_k(\mathbf{u})$.

PROOF: From the hypotheses and by Geoffrion's strong duality theorem [1971, Theorem 3], the dual of $P_k(\boldsymbol{\varepsilon}^*)$, written

$$\sup_{\mathbf{u} \geqslant \mathbf{0}} \left(\inf_{\mathbf{x} \in X} \left\{ f_k(\mathbf{x}) + \sum_{j \neq k} u_j [f_j(\mathbf{x}) - f_j(\mathbf{x}^*)] \right\} \right), \tag{4.24}$$

has an optimal solution, and its optimal value is equal to the optimal value of the primal $P_k(\boldsymbol{\varepsilon}^*)$. This means that there exist $u_j^0 \geqslant 0$ for all $j \neq k$ such that

$$f_k(\mathbf{x}^*) = \min_{\mathbf{x} \in X} \left\{ f_k(\mathbf{x}) + \sum_{j=1} u_j^0 [f_j(\mathbf{x}) - f_j(\mathbf{x}^*)] \right\}. \tag{4.25}$$

This implies

$$f_k(\mathbf{x}^*) \leqslant f_k(\mathbf{x}) + \sum_{j \neq k} u_j^0 [f_j(\mathbf{x}) - f_j(\mathbf{x}^*)]$$

for all $\mathbf{x} \in X$, which is equivalent to

$$f_k(\mathbf{x}^*) + \sum_{j \neq k} u_j^0 f_j(\mathbf{x}^*) \leqslant f_k(\mathbf{x}) + \sum_{j \neq k} u_j^0 f_j(\mathbf{x})$$

for all $\mathbf{x} \in X$. Hence $\mathbf{x}^*$ solves $P_k(\mathbf{u}^0)$. ■

Let

$$U_k \triangleq \{ \mathbf{u} | \mathbf{u} \in R^{n-1}, u_j \geqslant 0 \text{ for all } j \neq k \}, \tag{4.26}$$

$$X_u^k \triangleq \{ \mathbf{x} | \mathbf{x} \text{ solves } P_k(\mathbf{u}) \text{ for some } \mathbf{u} \in U_k \}. \tag{4.27}$$

Corollary. *If the convexity assumption holds and $P_k(\boldsymbol{\varepsilon})$ is stable for all $\boldsymbol{\varepsilon} \in Y_k$, then $X^k(\boldsymbol{\varepsilon}) \subseteq X_u^k$.*

PROOF: Consider any $\mathbf{x}^* \in X^k(\boldsymbol{\varepsilon})$. Then by definition there exists $\hat{\boldsymbol{\varepsilon}} \in Y_k$ such that $\mathbf{x}^*$ solves $P_k(\hat{\boldsymbol{\varepsilon}})$. But since $\varepsilon_j^* \leqslant \hat{\varepsilon}_j$ for all $j \neq k$ [recalling that $\varepsilon_j^* = f_j(\mathbf{x}^*)$], $\mathbf{x}^*$ must also solve $P_k(\boldsymbol{\varepsilon}^*)$. Since the given hypothesis implies stability of $P_k(\boldsymbol{\varepsilon}^*)$, it then follows from Lemma 4.3 that $\mathbf{x}^* \in X_u^k$. Hence $X^k(\boldsymbol{\varepsilon}) \subseteq X_u^k$ as required. ■

As an alternative to the stability condition in Lemma 4.3, other conditions that guarantee the absence of a duality gap between the primal and dual problems can also be used (cf. Figure 4.4). Two of these will be discussed here. One is the combination of *faithful convexity*[6] and *feasibility* (or consistency) of $P_k(\boldsymbol{\varepsilon}^*)$, and the other is the saddle point condition. The following result relies on a duality result due to Rockafellar [1971] and the so-called weak duality theory for nonlinear programming (see Geoffrion [1971, Theorem 2, p. 9]).

Lemma 4.4

$$\boxed{\mathrm{B}} \overset{\mathrm{FC}}{\rightarrow} \boxed{\mathrm{E}}.$$

Assume i) all f_j, $j=1,\ldots,n$, and g_i, $i=1,\ldots,m$, are faithfully convex; ii) X is given by (4.1) *when $S=\varnothing$; and iii) $\mathbf{x}^*$ solves $P_k(\boldsymbol{\varepsilon}^*)$. Then there exists $u_j \geqslant 0$ for all $j \neq k$ such that $\mathbf{x}^*$ solves $P_k(\mathbf{u})$.*

To prove this lemma, we need to consider two types of duals of $P_k(\boldsymbol{\varepsilon}^*)$: One is given in (4.24),

$$d_1(\mathbf{x}^*) \triangleq \sup_{\mathbf{u} \geqslant \mathbf{0}} \left(\inf_{\mathbf{x} \in X} \left\{ f_k(\mathbf{x}) + \sum_{j \neq k} u_j \big[f_j(\mathbf{x}) - f_j(\mathbf{x}^*) \big] \right\} \right); \tag{4.28}$$

the other is given by

$$d_2(\mathbf{x}^*) \triangleq \sup_{\substack{\mathbf{u} \geqslant \mathbf{0} \\ \boldsymbol{\mu} \geqslant \mathbf{0}}} \left(\inf_{\mathbf{x} \in R^n} \left\{ f_k(\mathbf{x}) + \sum_{j \neq k} u_j \big[f_j(\mathbf{x}) - f_j(\mathbf{x}^*) \big] + \sum_{i=1} \mu_i g_i(\mathbf{x}) \right\} \right). \tag{4.29}$$

The strategy is to show that $f_k(\mathbf{x}^*) = d_1(\mathbf{x}^*)$ by applying the weak duality theorem to the dual in (4.28) and Rockafellar's result to the dual in (4.29).

[6]A real-valued function f is said to be *faithfully convex* if and only if it is either linear, or nonlinear containing no straight-line segment in its graph.

PROOF: By the weak duality theorem, for some $\mathbf{u}^0 \in R^{n-1}$ with $\mathbf{u}^0 \geqslant \mathbf{0}$

$$f_k(\mathbf{x}^*) \geqslant d_1(\mathbf{x}^*) = \min_{\mathbf{x} \in X} \left\{ f_k(\mathbf{x}) + \sum_{j \neq k} u_j^0 \left[f_j(\mathbf{x}) - f_j(\mathbf{x}^*) \right] \right\}. \tag{4.30}$$

We observe from (iii) that $P_k(\boldsymbol{\varepsilon}^*)$ is feasible. Also from Assumptions (i)–(iii) in Lemma 4.4, we have, upon applying Rockafellar's result [1971, p. 145] to (4.29),

$$f_k(\mathbf{x}^*) = d_2(\mathbf{x}^*) \leqslant \sup_{\substack{\mathbf{u} \geqslant \mathbf{0} \\ \boldsymbol{\mu} \geqslant \mathbf{0}}} \left(\inf_{\mathbf{x} \in X} \left\{ f_k(\mathbf{x}) + \sum_{j \neq k} u_j \left[f_j(\mathbf{x}) - f_j(\mathbf{x}^*) \right] + \boldsymbol{\mu} \cdot \mathbf{g}(\mathbf{x}) \right\} \right). \tag{4.31}$$

The inequality in (4.31) is due to the fact that the infimum in (4.31) is taken over X, which is a subset of R^n. Furthermore, since the argument of the infimum in (4.31) is always less than or equal to

$$f_k(\mathbf{x}) + \sum_{j \neq k} u_j \left[f_j(\mathbf{x}) - f_j(\mathbf{x}^*) \right],$$

we thus have

$$f_k(\mathbf{x}^*) \leqslant \sup_{\mathbf{u} \geqslant \mathbf{0}} \left[\inf_{\mathbf{x} \in X} \left\{ f_k(\mathbf{x}) + \sum_{j \neq k} u_j \left[f_j(\mathbf{x}) - f_j(\mathbf{x}^*) \right] \right\} \right]. \tag{4.32}$$

Consequently from (4.28), (4.30), and (4.32) we have

$$f_k(\mathbf{x}^*) = d_1(\mathbf{x}^*) = \min_{\mathbf{x} \in X} \left\{ f_k(\mathbf{x}) + \sum_{j \neq k} u_j^0 \left[f_j(\mathbf{x}) - f_j(\mathbf{x}^*) \right] \right\}. \tag{4.33}$$

This implies

$$f_k(\mathbf{x}^*) \leqslant f_k(\mathbf{x}) + \sum_{j \neq k} u_j^0 \left[f_j(\mathbf{x}) - f_j(\mathbf{x}^*) \right]$$

for all $\mathbf{x} \in X$ or

$$f_k(\mathbf{x}^*) + \sum_{j \neq k} u_j^0 f_j(\mathbf{x}^*) \leqslant f_k(\mathbf{x}) + \sum_{j \neq k} u_j^0 f_j(\mathbf{x})$$

for all $\mathbf{x} \in X$. Thus $\mathbf{x}^*$ solves $P_k(\mathbf{u}^0)$. ■

As mentioned earlier, conditions that guarantee the existence of the saddle point of the Lagrangian of $P_k(\boldsymbol{\varepsilon}^*)$ at $\mathbf{x}^*$ can also be used to establish the link between $P_k(\boldsymbol{\varepsilon}^*)$ and $P_k(\mathbf{u})$. This is a direct result of Karlin's theorem [1959] (or see Lasdon [1970, p. 87]).

Lemma 4.5. *Assume i) the convexity assumption and ii) the constraints of $P_k(\boldsymbol{\varepsilon}^*)$ satisfy Karlin's constraint qualification (see definition in Section 2.3). Then if $\mathbf{x}^*$ solves $P_k(\boldsymbol{\varepsilon}^*)$, there exists $u_j \geqslant 0, j \neq k$, such that $\mathbf{x}^*$ solves $P_k(\mathbf{u})$.*

PROOF: By Assumptions (i) and (ii), we can apply Karlin's theorem to $P_k(\boldsymbol{\varepsilon}^*)$; i.e., there exists $u_j^0 \geqslant 0$ for all $j \neq k$ such that $(\mathbf{x}^*, \mathbf{u}^0)$ is a saddle point of $L(\mathbf{x}, \mathbf{u}) = f_k(\mathbf{x}) + \sum_{j \neq k} u_j[f_j(\mathbf{x}) - f_j(\mathbf{x}^*)]$. Hence by definition of the saddle point, we have for all $\mathbf{x} \in X$,

$$f_k(\mathbf{x}^*) = L(\mathbf{x}^*, \mathbf{u}^0) \leqslant L(\mathbf{x}, \mathbf{u}^0) = f_k(\mathbf{x}) + \sum_{j \neq k} u_j^0\left[f_j(\mathbf{x}) - f_j(\mathbf{x}^*)\right],$$

which immediately implies

$$f_k(\mathbf{x}^*) + \sum_{j \neq k} u_j^0 f_j(\mathbf{x}^*) \leqslant f_k(\mathbf{x}) + \sum_{j \neq k} u_j^0 f_j(\mathbf{x}).$$

Hence $\mathbf{x}^*$ solves $P_k(\mathbf{u}^0)$. ■

Corollary. *Assume i) the convexity assumption and ii) the constraints of $P_k(\boldsymbol{\varepsilon})$ satisfy Karlin's constraint qualification for all $\boldsymbol{\varepsilon} \in Y_k$. Then $X^k \subseteq X_u^k$.*

The proof of this corollary follows very much in the same fashion as the corollary of Lemma 4.3 and will, therefore, be omitted.

As we observe from Figure 4.2, there is yet another alternative link from $P_k(\boldsymbol{\varepsilon})$ to $P_k(\mathbf{u})$ (as displayed by the link from B to E via C and D). Here, instead of Karlin's constraint qualification (which is essential in establishing the saddle point optimality condition), use the Kuhn–Tucker constraint qualification.

Lemma 4.6. *Assume that i) the convexity assumption and ii) the constraint $P_k(\boldsymbol{\varepsilon}^*)$ satisfy the regularity assumption at $\mathbf{x}^*$ [i.e., $\mathbf{x}^*$ is a regular point of the constraints of $P_k(\boldsymbol{\varepsilon}^*)$]. Then if $\mathbf{x}^*$ solves $P_k(\boldsymbol{\varepsilon}^*)$, there exist $u_j \geqslant 0, j \neq k$, such that $\mathbf{x}^*$ solves $P_k(\mathbf{u})$.*

This lemma automatically requires the differentiability assumption as demanded by Assumption (ii).

PROOF: The proof, as suggested by Figure 4.2, is immediate. The regularity assumption and the fact that $\mathbf{x}^*$ solves $P_k(\boldsymbol{\varepsilon}^*)$ guarantee the existence of $u_j \geqslant 0$, $j \neq k$, such that Kuhn–Tucker conditions for optimality for $P_k(\boldsymbol{\varepsilon}^*)$ are satisfied (see Section 2.3). This is equivalent to the Kuhn–Tucker conditions for optimality for $P_k(\mathbf{u})$, with $u_k = 1$ and $u_j > 0$, $j \neq k$, being satisfied. This, together with the fact that all f_j and X are convex, guarantees that $\mathbf{x}^*$ solves $P_k(\mathbf{u})$ [Mangasarian, 1979, Theorem 5, p. 92]. ■

Corollary. *Assume i) the convexity assumption and ii) the constraints of $P_k(\boldsymbol{\varepsilon}^*)$ satisfy the regularity assumption at all points in X. Then $X^k(\boldsymbol{\varepsilon}) \subseteq X_u^k$.*

The converse relation [from $P_k(\mathbf{u})$ to $P_k(\boldsymbol{\varepsilon})$] is simple and is due to Everett [1963].

Lemma 4.7

$$\boxed{\text{E}} \xrightarrow{\text{(S1, if CA assumed)}} \boxed{\text{B}}.$$

If $\mathbf{x}^*$ *solves* $P_k(\mathbf{u})$ *for some* $\mathbf{u} \in U_k$, *then* $\mathbf{x}^*$ *also solves* $P_k(\boldsymbol{\varepsilon}^*)$. *Moreover* $P_k(\boldsymbol{\varepsilon}^*)$ *is stable if the convexity assumption is assumed.*

PROOF: Since $\mathbf{x}^*$ solves $P_k(\mathbf{u})$ for some $\mathbf{u} \in U_k$, then for all $\mathbf{x} \in X$

$$f_k(\mathbf{x}) + \sum_{j \neq k} u_j f_j(\mathbf{x}) \geqslant f_k(\mathbf{x}^*) + \sum_{j \neq k} u_j f_j(\mathbf{x}^*);$$

$$f_k(\mathbf{x}) - f_k(\mathbf{x}^*) \geqslant \sum_{j \neq k} u_j\left[f_j(\mathbf{x}^*) - f_j(\mathbf{x})\right] \qquad \text{for all} \quad \mathbf{x} \in X.$$

The right-hand side is always nonegative in the feasible region of $P_k(\boldsymbol{\varepsilon}^*)$. Hence the conclusion follows. ■

The stability result is given by Geoffrion [1971, Theorem 1, p. 7].

Corollary. $X_u^k \subseteq X^k(\boldsymbol{\varepsilon})$.

4.3.2 Characterizing Noninferior Solutions in Terms of the Solutions of Constraint Problems

The idea of using the constraint problem of the $P_k(\boldsymbol{\varepsilon})$ form as a means for obtaining noninferior solutions of a VOP is common. In fact, this has become a basic component in many well-established algorithms. The surrogate worth trade-off method [Haimes and Hall, 1974], for example, uses this as one of its key components. A distinct advantage, apart from its key function in transforming a VOP to a scalar optimization problem, is that it generates (as a byproduct) Kuhn–Tucker multipliers associated with the ε constraints, whose interpretation as *local* trade-offs (see Section 4.8) has made them quite valuable for further analysis. Because of this significant role of the constraint problem, we identify precisely the theoretical foundations of noninferior solutions of VOP in terms of solutions of $P_k(\boldsymbol{\varepsilon})$. These are displayed in Figure 4.2 by the links (both direct and indirect) between blocks A and B.

Haimes et al. [1971] established the theoretical equivalence between the VOP and $P_k(\boldsymbol{\varepsilon})$ problems. Theorems 4.1 and 4.2 are extensions of their result.

Theorem 4.1

$$\boxed{\text{A}} \underset{\text{H3}}{\leftrightarrows} \boxed{\text{B}}.$$

$\mathbf{x}^*$ *is a noninferior solution of* VOP *if and only if* $\mathbf{x}^*$ *solves* $P_k(\boldsymbol{\varepsilon}^*)$ *for every* $k = 1, \ldots, n$.

PROOF: Necessity—assume that $\mathbf{x}^*$ does not solve $P_k(\boldsymbol{\varepsilon}^*)$ for some k; then there exists $\mathbf{x} \in X$ such that $f_k(\mathbf{x}) < f_k(\mathbf{x}^*)$ and $f_k(\mathbf{x}) \leqslant f_k(\mathbf{x}^*)$, implying that $\mathbf{x}^* \notin X^*$. Thus the conclusion follows.

Sufficiency—since $\mathbf{x}^*$ solves $P_k(\boldsymbol{\varepsilon}^*)$ for every $k = 1,\dots,n$, then there exists no other $\mathbf{x} \in X$ such that $f_j(\mathbf{x}) \leqslant f_j(\mathbf{x}^*)$, $j = 1,\dots,n$, with strict inequality holding for at least one j. This implies by definition that $\mathbf{x}^* \in X^*$. ■

Using the notation in (4.16), the following corollary follows from the above theorem.

Corollary

$$\bigcap_{k=1}^{n} X^k(\boldsymbol{\varepsilon}) \subseteq X^* \subseteq X^k(\boldsymbol{\varepsilon}) \tag{4.34}$$

for each $k = 1,\dots,n$, *where* $X^k(\boldsymbol{\varepsilon}) = \{\mathbf{x} | \mathbf{x}$ *solves* $P_k(\boldsymbol{\varepsilon})$ *for some* $\boldsymbol{\varepsilon}$ *in* $Y_k\}$.

The implications of this theorem and its corollary are that in searching for noninferior solutions of VOP, one need only search among optimal solutions of $P_k(\boldsymbol{\varepsilon})$ for any k. Given an $\boldsymbol{\varepsilon} \in Y_k$, not all optimal solutions of $P_k(\boldsymbol{\varepsilon})$ for one particular $1 \leqslant k \leqslant n$ are noninferior except for those that solve $P_k(\boldsymbol{\varepsilon})$ for every k from 1 to n. The theorem is, however, not very practical as a basis for testing noninferiority of a given point $\mathbf{x}^*$ since it requires $P_k(\boldsymbol{\varepsilon})$ to be solved for all k before a conclusion can be drawn.

An alternative sufficiency condition for noninferiority as evident from Figure 4.2 is given below.

Theorem 4.2

$$\boxed{\text{B}} \overset{\text{H1}}{\rightarrow} \boxed{\text{A}}.$$

If $\mathbf{x}^*$ *solves* $P_k(\boldsymbol{\varepsilon}^*)$ *for some* k *and if the solution is unique, then* $\mathbf{x}^*$ *is a noninferior solution of* VOP.

PROOF: Follows directly from definition. Since $\mathbf{x}^*$ uniquely minimizes $P_k(\boldsymbol{\varepsilon}^*)$ for some k, then for all $\mathbf{x}$ satisfying $f_j(\mathbf{x}) \leqslant f_j(\mathbf{x}^*)$, $j \neq k$, $f_k(\mathbf{x}) > f_k(\mathbf{x}^*)$. Hence none of the f_j, $j \neq k$, can be decreased without increasing f_k. Therefore $\mathbf{x}^*$ must be noninferior. ■

Observe that without uniqueness of solution (or the sufficiency condition in Theorem 4.1), B does not necessarily imply A. This is because there may exist some $\mathbf{x} \in X$ such that $f_k(\hat{\mathbf{x}}) = f_k(\mathbf{x}^*)$ and $f_j(\hat{\mathbf{x}}) \leqslant f_j(\mathbf{x}^*)$, $j \neq k$, where strict inequality holds for at least one $j \neq k$, which implies that $\mathbf{x}^*$ is inferior to that particular $\hat{\mathbf{x}}$. The following corollary, which follows trivially from Theorem 4.2, is useful for generating noninferior solutions.

Corollary. *For any given* $\boldsymbol{\varepsilon} \in Y_k$, *an optimal solution of* $P_k(\boldsymbol{\varepsilon})$ *is noninferior if it is the unique solution.*

There is yet another set of necessary and sufficient conditions for noninferiority expressible in terms of optimal solutions of the constraint problem $P_k(\boldsymbol{\varepsilon})$. This result is due to Lin [1976b, 1977]. First we define the following:

$$\phi_k(\boldsymbol{\varepsilon}) = \inf\{ f_k(\mathbf{x}) | \mathbf{x} \in X, f_j(\mathbf{x}) \leqslant \varepsilon_j \text{ for each } j \neq k \}; \qquad (4.35\text{a})$$

and

$$\hat{Y}_k = \{ \boldsymbol{\varepsilon} | \boldsymbol{\varepsilon} \in Y_k, \phi_k(\boldsymbol{\varepsilon}) > -\infty, \text{ and there exists an } \mathbf{x}^* \in X \text{ such that } f_k(\mathbf{x}^*) = \phi_k(\boldsymbol{\varepsilon}) \}. \qquad (4.35\text{b})$$

Observe that for any given $\boldsymbol{\varepsilon}$, if $P_k(\boldsymbol{\varepsilon})$ has an optimal solution, say at $\mathbf{x}^*$, then the infimum in (4.35a) becomes a minimum and $\phi_k(\boldsymbol{\varepsilon}) = f_k(\mathbf{x}^*)$, which is the optimal value of $P_k(\boldsymbol{\varepsilon})$. Note also that Y_k is the set of all $\boldsymbol{\varepsilon}$ such that $P_k(\boldsymbol{\varepsilon})$ has an optimal solution with finite optimal value. With this terminology, Lin [1976, 1977] derives the following result, whose proof is simple.

Theorem 4.3. *Let* $\mathbf{x}^*$ *solve* $P_k(\boldsymbol{\varepsilon}^*)$ *with* $\varepsilon_j^* = f_j(\mathbf{x}^*)$, $j \neq k$. *Then* $\mathbf{x}^*$ *is a noninferior solution of* VOP *if and only if* $\phi_k(\boldsymbol{\varepsilon}) > \phi_k(\boldsymbol{\varepsilon}^*)$ *for all* $\boldsymbol{\varepsilon} \in \hat{Y}_k$ *such that* $\boldsymbol{\varepsilon} \leqslant \boldsymbol{\varepsilon}^*$.

From the practical viewpoint, it is useful to summarize the sufficient conditions of noninferiority put forth in Theorems 4.1–4.3 in the form of the following corollary.

Corollary 4.1. *Given an* $\boldsymbol{\varepsilon}$ *in* Y_k, *let* $\mathbf{x}^*$ *be an optimal solution of* $P_k(\boldsymbol{\varepsilon})$. *Then* $\mathbf{x}^*$ *is a noninferior solution of VOP if*

i. $\mathbf{x}^*$ *solves* $P_k(\boldsymbol{\varepsilon})$ *for every* $k = 1, \ldots, n$;
ii. $\mathbf{x}^*$ *is the unique solution of* $P_k(\boldsymbol{\varepsilon})$; *or*
iii. *the optimal value of* $P_k(\boldsymbol{\varepsilon}^0)$ *is strictly greater than* $f_k(\mathbf{x}^*)$ *for any* $\boldsymbol{\varepsilon}^0 \leqslant \boldsymbol{\varepsilon}^*$.

If $f_k(\boldsymbol{\varepsilon}^*)$ is finite in (iii), so is the optimal value of $P_k(\boldsymbol{\varepsilon}^0)$, since $\phi_k(\boldsymbol{\varepsilon}^0) \geqslant \phi_k(\boldsymbol{\varepsilon}^*)$ whenever $\boldsymbol{\varepsilon}^0 \leqslant \boldsymbol{\varepsilon}^*$. Observe also that (i) and (iii) are also necessary conditions for noninferiority.

The above results can be utilized in two ways. First, they allow noninferior solutions to be generated by solving $P_k(\boldsymbol{\varepsilon})$ for some $\boldsymbol{\varepsilon}$ and k. Second, they can be used at least as a partial test of noninferiority of a given point $\mathbf{x}^*$.

To generate noninferior solutions using the results in Corollary 4.1, we simply select a value of $\boldsymbol{\varepsilon}$, solve $P_k(\boldsymbol{\varepsilon})$ and test whether any of the sufficiency conditions (i)–(iii) are satisfied. By systematically varying $\boldsymbol{\varepsilon}$ in Y_k, a subset of noninferior solutions of the VOP can be obtained. Computationally, any method based on (i) of Corollary 4.1 will not be too practical since it requires $P_k(\boldsymbol{\varepsilon})$ to be solved for all k to generate each noninferior solution. Condition (iii) is generally not easy to check numerically, although Lin [1977] develops a procedure for doing so. To use Condition (ii), only one $P_k(\boldsymbol{\varepsilon})$ need be solved, but sometimes uniqueness of solution is also difficult to check. Even for a convex problem, only the use of a strictly convex objective function as the primary objective guarantees uniqueness without further checking. For a differentiable convex problem, if the objective function of $P_k(\boldsymbol{\varepsilon})$ is only known to be convex (but not strictly convex), after a solution of $P_k(\boldsymbol{\varepsilon})$ is found and before claiming it to be a noninferior solution of VOP, second-order sufficiency conditions should be checked.

The testing of second-order sufficiency conditions, apart from being used to determine whether or not a solution of $P_k(\boldsymbol{\varepsilon})$ is unique (so that Theorem 4.2 can be used), serves a second purpose. The satisfaction of those conditions, together with the regularity assumption, permits one to interpret Kuhn–Tucker multipliers associated with certain active constraints of $P_k(\bar{\boldsymbol{\varepsilon}})$ as local trade-offs between a pair of objectives in VOP. This information on local trade-offs is useful as an interactive link between the decision maker and the model so that the final choice can be effectively chosen among the set of noninferior choices of the system. This will be discussed in some detail in later sections of this chapter.

To illustrate the use of $P_k(\boldsymbol{\varepsilon})$ and condition (ii) as a means for generating noninferior solutions, consider the following vector optimization example problem:

Example:

$$\text{VOP}_1: \qquad \min_{\mathbf{x}\in X}\left[f_1(\mathbf{x}), f_2(\mathbf{x}), f_3(\mathbf{x})\right], \tag{4.36}$$

where

$$f_1(\mathbf{x})=(x_1-3)^2+(x_2-2)^2, \qquad f_2(\mathbf{x})=x_1+x_2, \qquad f_3(\mathbf{x})=x_1+2x_2$$

and

$$X=\left\{\mathbf{x}|\mathbf{x}\in R^2, g_1(\mathbf{x})=-x_1\leqslant 0, g_2(\mathbf{x})=-x_2\leqslant 0\right\}.$$

Taking f_1 as the primary objective, the ε-constraint problem $P_1(\boldsymbol{\varepsilon})$, which will be used to generate noninferior solutions of VOP_1 is $P_1(\varepsilon_2, \varepsilon_3)$:

$$\min \quad f_1(\mathbf{x})=(x_1-3)^2+(x_2-2)^2 \tag{4.37a}$$

$$\text{subject to} \quad f_2(\mathbf{x})= x_1+ x_2\leqslant \varepsilon_2; \tag{4.37b}$$

$$f_3(\mathbf{x})= x_1+2x_2\leqslant \varepsilon_3; \tag{4.37c}$$

$$g_1(\mathbf{x})=-x_1 \leqslant 0; \tag{4.37d}$$

$$g_2(\mathbf{x})= -x_2\leqslant 0. \tag{4.37e}$$

To illustrate the salient features of the results, we shall solve $P_1(\varepsilon_2, \varepsilon_3)$ graphically. The formal solution of $P_1(\varepsilon_2, \varepsilon_3)$ using this and other techniques is shown in full in Example 8 of Chapter 6. We first observe that for any given positive ε_2^0 and ε_3^0, the feasible region of $P_1(\varepsilon_2^0, \varepsilon_3^0)$ is as illustrated in Figure 4.3. Since $f_1(\mathbf{x})$ is a circle centered at the point (3,2), solving $P_1(\varepsilon_2, \varepsilon_3)$ is equivalent to finding a point in the feasible region of $P_1(\varepsilon_2, \varepsilon_3)$ closest to P. Thus for $P_1(\varepsilon_2^0, \varepsilon_3^0)$ as shown in Figure 4.3, $\mathbf{x}^0$ is its unique optimal solution, implying that $\mathbf{x}^0$ is a noninferior solution of VOP_1 by Corollary 4.1(ii). Also, for $P_1(\varepsilon_2^0, \varepsilon_3^1)$ $\mathbf{x}^1$ is its unique optimal solution and hence a noninferior solution of VOP. In fact, by the same reasoning, we can conclude by inspection that those and only those points that lie within and on the boundary of the triangle PAB as well as those points along the line OA are noninferior solutions of VOP_1. We shall return to this example later in this chapter and also in Chapter 6.

Let us now return to the second use of the result stated in this section. Given a feasible solution $\mathbf{x}^*$, we want to know whether it is noninferior based on the constraint characterization. To do this, we simply formulate $P_k(\boldsymbol{\varepsilon}^*)$ and solve it. One of three things can happen:

1. $\mathbf{x}^*$ solves $P_k(\boldsymbol{\varepsilon}^*)$ and at least one of the conditions in Corollary 4.1 is satisfied, in which case we conclude that $\mathbf{x}^*$ is noninferior;
2. $\mathbf{x}^*$ solves $P_k(\boldsymbol{\varepsilon}^*)$, but (i) or (iii) or both in Corollary 4.1 are not satisfied, in which case we conclude that $\mathbf{x}^*$ is inferior, since they are both necessary conditions; or
3. $\mathbf{x}^*$ does not solve $P_k(\boldsymbol{\varepsilon}^*)$, in which case we again conclude that $\mathbf{x}^*$ is inferior since Condition (i) in Corollary 4.1 is violated.

Figure 4.3 Graphical solution of $P_1(\varepsilon_2, \varepsilon_3)$ and noninferior solutions.

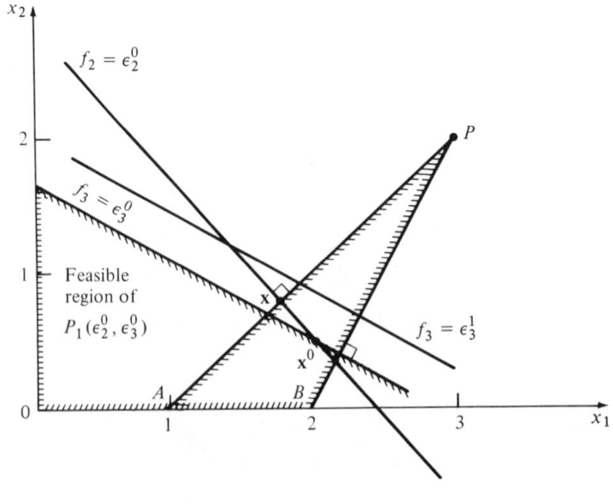

The last case is interesting and warrants further investigation because additional information can be obtained. If $P_k(\boldsymbol{\varepsilon}^*)$ has an optimal solution that satisfies any one of the conditions in Corollary 4.1, such optimal solution of $P_k(\boldsymbol{\varepsilon}^*)$ can, then, serve as a noninferior solution. If $P_k(\boldsymbol{\varepsilon}^*)$ has no optimal solution in the sense that $\phi_k(\boldsymbol{\varepsilon}^*)$ is finite but there is no $\mathbf{x}$ in X such that $f_k(\mathbf{x})=\phi_k(\boldsymbol{\varepsilon}^*)$, no conclusion can be derived. If, on the other hand, $P_k(\boldsymbol{\varepsilon}^*)$ has no bounded solution in the sense that $\phi_k(\boldsymbol{\varepsilon}^*)=-\infty$, then it may be indicative that no noninferior solutions of VOP exist. A result derived in the same spirit as those of Wendell and Lee [1977] and Benson [1978] may be useful to check out this possibility:

Theorem 4.4. *Assume that either of the following holds:*

a. *$P_k(\boldsymbol{\varepsilon}^*)$ is stable, X is a convex set, and f_j, $j=1,\ldots,n$, are convex throughout R^n; or*
b. *all f_j, $j=1,\ldots,n$, and g_i, $i=1,\ldots,m$, are faithfully convex throughout R^n and $X=\{\mathbf{x}\in R^N \mid g_i(\mathbf{x})\leqslant 0,\ i=1,\ldots,m\}$.*

Then X^* of VOP *is empty if $\phi_k(\boldsymbol{\varepsilon}^*)=-\infty$.*

PROOF: Since $\phi_k(\boldsymbol{\varepsilon}^*)=-\infty$, the weak duality theorem requires that the dual of $P_k(\boldsymbol{\varepsilon}^*)$ given in (4.28) also be $-\infty$. That is,

$$\sup_{\mathbf{u}\geqslant\mathbf{0}}\left\{\inf_{\mathbf{x}\in X}\left\{f_k(\mathbf{x})+\sum_{j\neq k}u_j\left[f_j(\mathbf{x})-f_j(\mathbf{x}^*)\right]\right\}\right\}=-\infty.$$

Consequently, for any bounded $\mathbf{x}^1\in X$

$$\sup_{\mathbf{u}\geqslant\mathbf{0}}\left(\inf_{\mathbf{x}\in X}\left\{f_k(\mathbf{x})+\sum_{j\neq k}u_j\left[f_j(\mathbf{x})-f_j(\mathbf{x}^1)\right]\right\}\right)=-\infty. \tag{4.38}$$

Suppose, on the contrary, that there exists a noninferior solution, say $\mathbf{x}^0$, of VOP. From Theorem 4.1, $\mathbf{x}^0$ solves $P_k(\boldsymbol{\varepsilon}^0)$, where $f_j(\mathbf{x}^0)=\varepsilon_j^0$, $j\neq k$. If Assumption (a) prevails, apply Geoffrion's strong duality theorem, and if Assumption (b) prevails, apply (4.33). In any case, we have

$$-\infty< f(\mathbf{x}^0)=\sup_{\mathbf{u}\geqslant\mathbf{0}}\left\{\inf_{\mathbf{x}\in X}\left[f_k(\mathbf{x})+\sum_{j\neq k}u_j\left[f_j(\mathbf{x})-f_j(\mathbf{x}^0)\right]\right]\right\},$$

which contradicts (4.35). Thus X^* must be empty, which completes the proof. ■

4.3.3 Characterizing Noninferior Solutions in Terms of the Solutions of Weighting Problems

An equally common way of characterizing noninferior solutions of VOP is in terms of the solutions of associated weighting problems. The parametric method (see Gass and Saaty [1955] and Zadeh [1963]) of solving VOP is a classic example of this type.

Similar to the results presented in the last section, we now establish relationships between noninferior solutions of a VOP and solutions of $P(\mathbf{w})$. These results are represented in Figure 4.2 by links between A and F.

Theorem 4.5

$$\boxed{\mathrm{A}} \xrightarrow{\mathrm{CA}} \boxed{\mathrm{F}}\,.$$

Assume convexity. If $\mathbf{x}^* \in X^*$, *then there exists* $\mathbf{w} \in W$ *such that* $\mathbf{x}^*$ *solves* $P(\mathbf{w})$, *i.e.*, $X^* \subseteq X_{\mathbf{w}}$.

PROOF: As evident from the diagram: $\mathrm{A} \to \mathrm{B} \overset{\mathrm{CA}}{\to} \mathrm{F}$. By the corollary of Theorem 4.1, $X^* \subseteq X^k(\boldsymbol{\varepsilon})$ for each k. With the convexity assumption, the corollary of Lemma 4.1 applies such that for any k $X^k(\boldsymbol{\varepsilon}) \subseteq X_w$. ■

This result is well known. DaCunha and Polak [1967] obtained a similar result requiring two additional imposing conditions. Arrow et al. [1953] also proved a similar result, but instead of requiring the convexity assumption, they used the convexity of the set $\{\mathbf{f}(\mathbf{x}) | \mathbf{x} \in X\}$. See also Yu [1974b].

In order to state the converse of the previous theorem, it should be observed that there are two alternative (opposing) conditions along the direct link from F to A. Accordingly,

Theorem 4.6

$$\boxed{\mathrm{F}} \xrightarrow{\mathrm{H1\ or\ H2}} \boxed{\mathrm{A}}\,.$$

$\mathbf{x}^*$ *is a noninferior solution of* VOP *if there exists* $\mathbf{w} \in W$ *such that* $\mathbf{x}^*$ *solves* $P(\mathbf{w})$ *and if either one of the following two conditions holds*:

i. $w_j > 0$ *for all* $j = 1, \ldots, n$ (*Geoffrion* [1968], *Kuhn and Tucker* [1951], *or Yu* [1974]); *or*
ii. $\mathbf{x}^*$ *is the unique solution of* $P(\mathbf{w})$ (*Zadeh* [1963] *and Yu* [1974*b*]).

PROOF: Let $\mathbf{x}^*$ solve $P(\mathbf{w})$ for some $\mathbf{w} \in W$. Thus

$$\sum_{j=1}^{n} w_j \big[f_j(\mathbf{x}) - f_j(\mathbf{x}^*) \big] \geq 0 \qquad \text{for all} \quad \mathbf{x} \in X. \tag{4.39}$$

Suppose $\mathbf{x}^* \notin X^*$. Then there exists $\hat{\mathbf{x}} \in X$ such that $f(\hat{\mathbf{x}}) \leq f(\mathbf{x}^*)$. This supposition together with (i) implies that

$$\sum_{j=1}^{n} w_j \big[f_j(\hat{\mathbf{x}}) - f_j(\mathbf{x}^*) \big] < 0,$$

which contradicts (4.39).

If (ii) holds, then (4.39) becomes

$$\sum_{j=1}^{n} w_j\left[f_j(\mathbf{x})-f_j(\mathbf{x}^*)\right]>0$$

for all $\mathbf{x}\in X$, while the supposition implies the existence of $\mathbf{x}\in X$ such that

$$\sum_{j=1}^{n} w_j\left[f_j(\hat{\mathbf{x}})-f_j(\mathbf{x}^*)\right]\leqslant 0,$$

which contradict one another. Hence, if either (i) or (ii) holds and in addition $\mathbf{x}^*$ solves $P(\mathbf{w})$ for some $\mathbf{w}\in W$, then $\mathbf{x}^*\in X^*$. ■

The results of the last two theorems can be conveniently summarized as follows:

Corollary. *Assume convexity. Then*

$$X'_{\mathbf{w}}\subseteq X^*\subseteq X_{\mathbf{w}} \tag{4.40}$$

where $X'_{\mathbf{w}}=\{\mathbf{x}|\mathbf{x}$ *solves* $P(\mathbf{w})$ *for some* $\mathbf{w}\in W$ *and* $w_j>0, j=1,\ldots,n\}$; *and*

$$X''_{\mathbf{w}}\subseteq X^*\subseteq X_{\mathbf{w}} \tag{4.41}$$

where $X''_{\mathbf{w}}=\{\mathbf{x}|\mathbf{x}$ *uniquely minimizes* $P(\mathbf{w})$ *for some* $\mathbf{w}\in W\}$.

One is reminded that the first inclusion of either (4.40) or (4.41) does not require the convexity assumption.

Again Theorems 4.5 and 4.6 provide the bases for generating noninferior solutions of VOP by solving $P(\mathbf{w})$ for some $\mathbf{w}\in W$. By systematically varying $\mathbf{w}$ (the parametric method), Theorem 4.5 guarantees that if all f_j and g_i are convex, the entire X^* could theoretically be generated by such a procedure. From the computational standpoint, Theorem 4.6 says that one can proceed from any arbitrary $\mathbf{w}\in W$ as long as either Condition (i) or (ii) in Theorem 4.6 is satisfied afterward. Examples illustrating how these results may be used are given in Section 6.2.

It is important to note that, without the convexity assumption, X^* is not necessarily included in X_w. It is known from duality theory that this means that some noninferior solutions may never be discovered by this procedure (whereas all solutions are discovered by the ε-constraint approach). For nonconvex problems, the nonexistence of $\mathbf{w}\in W$ such that $\mathbf{x}^*$ solves $P(\mathbf{w})$ is equivalent to the nonexistence of a supporting hyperplane to the feasible region in the objective space $F\triangleq\{\mathbf{f}(\mathbf{x})|\mathbf{x}\in X\}$ of $P(\mathbf{w})$ at $\mathbf{x}^*$.

This is illustrated in the two-dimensional case in Figure 4.4. F^*, which coincides with the curve $AEBCGD$, is not convex. Any point on the convex portions (e.g., AEB and CGD) can be discovered by $P(\mathbf{w})$ by selecting appropriate $\mathbf{w}$. For example, E and G can be generated by solving $P(\mathbf{w}^1)$ and $P(\mathbf{w}^2)$, respectively. On the other hand, we can never find $\mathbf{w}$ such that

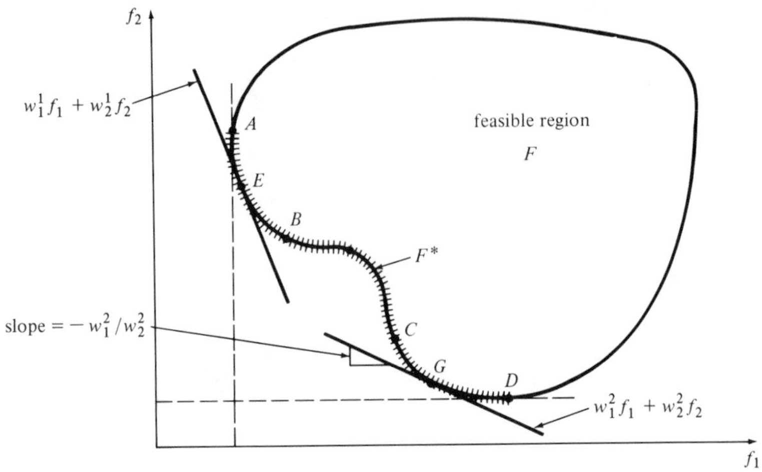

Figure 4.4 Duality gaps in nonconvex problems.

the line $w_1 f_1 + w_2 f_2$ will be a tangent (supporting line) to F^* at any point on the nonconvex part, i.e., between B and C. Thus any point on this part can never be discovered by solving $P(\mathbf{w})$. We call this phenomenon on the nonconvex part of F^* the *duality gap*. For more examples of duality gaps see Gembicki [1974] and Gembicki and Haimes [1975].

4.3.4 Characterizing Noninferior Solutions in Terms of Solutions of Lagrangian Problems

Although according to its form $P_k(\mathbf{u})$ may be viewed as a special class of $P(\mathbf{w})$, the former is created mainly for use in studying the dual of $P_k(\boldsymbol{\varepsilon})$. It is precisely in this context that $P_k(\mathbf{u})$ warrants a distinct identity and, hence, a separate discussion.

Through relationships with $P_k(\boldsymbol{\varepsilon})$ (Section 4.3.1), the following necessary conditions for noninferiority expressed in terms of solutions of $P_k(\mathbf{u})$ can be established:

Theorem 4.7

$$\boxed{\text{A}} \xrightarrow{\textit{appropriate conditions}} \boxed{\text{E}}.$$

Assuming convexity, if $\mathbf{x}^* \in X^*$ *and, for any given* k,

i. $P_k(\boldsymbol{\varepsilon}^*)$ *is stable;*
ii. *all* f_j, $j=1,\ldots,n$, *and* g_i, $i=1,\ldots,m$, *are faithfully convex with* $X=\{\mathbf{x}\in R^n \mid g_i(\mathbf{x})\leq 0,\ i=1,\ldots,m\}$;

iii. *the constraint of* $P_k(\boldsymbol{\varepsilon}^*)$ *satisfies Karlin's constraint qualification; or*
iv. *the constraint on* $P_k(\boldsymbol{\varepsilon}^*)$ *satisfies the regularity assumption of* $\mathbf{x}^*$;

then there exists $\mathbf{u} \in U_k$ *such that* $\mathbf{x}^*$ *solves* $P_k(\mathbf{u})$.

PROOF:

$$\boxed{\text{A}} \rightarrow \boxed{\text{B}} \rightarrow \boxed{\text{E}}.$$

By Theorem 4.1, if $\mathbf{x}^* \in X^*$, then $\mathbf{x}^*$ solves $P_k(\boldsymbol{\varepsilon}^*)$. By Lemmas 4.3–4.6, depending on (i)–(iv), respectively, $\mathbf{x}^* \in X_u^k$. ■

Let $X_u = \{\mathbf{x} | \mathbf{x} \text{ solves } P_k(\mathbf{u}) \text{ for some } k \text{ and some } \mathbf{u} \in U_k\}$, i.e.,

$$X_u = \bigcup_{k=1}^{n} X_u^k. \tag{4.42}$$

Corollary. $X^* \subseteq X_u^k \subseteq X_u$ *if any of conditions* (*i*)–(*iv*) *holds for all* $\boldsymbol{\varepsilon} \in Y_k$ *and for all* $k = 1, \ldots, n$.

As for sufficient conditions, they virtually coincide with those in Theorem 4.6.

Theorem 4.8

$$\boxed{\text{E}} \xrightarrow{\text{H1 or H2}} \boxed{\text{A}}.$$

$\mathbf{x}^*$ *is a noninferior solution of* VOP *if for some* k *there exists* $\mathbf{u} \in U_k$ *such that* $\mathbf{x}^*$ *solves* $P_k(\mathbf{u})$, *and if either*

i. $u_j > 0$ *for all* $j \neq k$, *or*
ii. $\mathbf{x}^*$ *is the unique minimizer of* $P_k(\mathbf{u})$.

The proof of this theorem is much like that of Theorem 4.6 and will therefore be omitted.

Observe that, like the case of $P(\mathbf{w})$, not all noninferior solutions of a VOP are optimal solutions of $P_k(\mathbf{u})$ for some $\mathbf{u} \geqslant \mathbf{0}$ or vice versa. Imposed conditions that allow this to be true are somewhat more complicated.

4.4 The Kuhn–Tucker Necessary and Sufficient Conditions for Noninferiority

Necessary and sufficient conditions for noninferiority due to Kuhn and Tucker are analogous to the classic Kuhn–Tucker conditions for optimality of a scalar optimization problem. In their well-known paper of 1951, they were interested only in proper noninferiority, which is the concept to be discussed in the next section.

The Kuhn–Tucker conditions for noninferiority (KTCN) will be defined in the same spirit as in Cohon and Marks [1975] or Cohon [1978].

Definition. A feasible solution $\mathbf{x}^*$ is said to satisfy KTCN for VOP if

i. all f_j and g_i are differentiable and $S=\varnothing$; and
ii. there exists $\lambda_j \geqslant 0, j=1,\ldots,n$, with strict inequality holding for at least one j and $\mu_i \geqslant 0$, $i=1,\ldots,m$, such that

$$g_i(x^*) \leqslant 0, \quad \mu_i g_i(x^*)=0 \qquad (i=1,\ldots,m); \tag{4.43}$$

and

$$\sum_{j=1}^{n} \lambda_j \nabla f_j(x^*) + \sum_{i=1}^{m} \mu_i \nabla g_i(x^*) = 0. \tag{4.44}$$

On close examination this definition of KTCN is seen to be almost equivalent to the Kuhn–Tucker conditions for optimality for $P_k(\boldsymbol{\varepsilon}^*)$ or $P_k(\mathbf{u})$. In fact, the latter imply the former, and the converse is also true if $\lambda_k > 0$ or $\mu_k > 0$. Note also that the noninferiority condition is by no means exclusive. Just as a different set of assumptions and constraint qualifications gives rise to a different set of optimality conditions, different sets of necessary and sufficient conditions for noninferiority resulting from different sets of optimality conditions should be anticipated. For example, it may be possible to derive a noninferiority condition from the saddle point optimality condition which does not require differentiability but depends on Karlin's constraint qualification (see Lasdon [1970] or Mangasarian [1969]). Other examples can also be found in Ben-Tal [1980] and Jahn [1980].

Unlike most of the previous results, the following theorems, represented in the diagram by the links (direct and indirect) between blocks A and J, are not valid without the differentiability and regularity assumptions.

Theorem 4.9

$$\boxed{\text{A}} \xrightarrow{\text{DA and RA}} \boxed{\text{J}}\,.$$

Assume that all f_j and g_i are differentiable and that $\mathbf{x}^*$ is a regular point of $P_k(\boldsymbol{\varepsilon}^*)$ for at least one k. Then $\mathbf{x}^* \in X^*$ implies that $\mathbf{x}^*$ satisfies the KTCN.

PROOF:

$$\boxed{\text{A}} \rightarrow \boxed{\text{B}} \xrightarrow{\text{DA, RA}} \boxed{\text{C}} \rightarrow \boxed{\text{J}}\,.$$

Let $\mathbf{x}^* \in X^*$. By Theorem 4.1 $\mathbf{x}^*$ solves $P_k(\boldsymbol{\varepsilon}^*)$ for all $k=1,\ldots,n$. By the hypotheses, there exists $\hat{k}$ such that $\mathbf{x}^*$ is a regular point of $P_{\hat{k}}(\boldsymbol{\varepsilon}^*)$. This, with differentiability and the Kuhn–Tucker theorem (see Section 2.3), implies that $\mathbf{x}^*$ satisfies the Kuhn–Tucker conditions for optimality and, in turn, implies that $\mathbf{x}^*$ satisfies the KTCN. ■

Theorem 4.10

$$\boxed{\text{J}} \xrightarrow{\text{DA and CA and H1}} \boxed{\text{A}}.$$

Assume that all f_j and g_i are differentiable and that the convexity assumption holds with all f_j, $j=1,\ldots,n$, being strictly convex. Then $\mathbf{x}^* \in X^*$ if $\mathbf{x}^*$ satisfies the KTCN.

PROOF:

$$\boxed{\text{J}} \overset{u_k>0}{\rightarrow} \boxed{\text{C}} \overset{\text{CA}}{\rightarrow} \boxed{\text{B}} \overset{\text{H1}}{\rightarrow} \boxed{\text{A}}.$$

Let $\mathbf{x}^*$ satisfy the KTCN. From the hypothesis of the KTCN, we can select k such that $\lambda_k > 0$. It is then trivial to show that $\mathbf{x}^*$ satisfies the Kuhn–Tucker condition for optimality for $P_k(\boldsymbol{\varepsilon}^*)$. Now since all f_j, $j=1,\ldots,n$, are strictly convex, so is f_k. This, with the convexity assumption, implies that $\mathbf{x}^*$ is the unique global solution of $P_k(\boldsymbol{\varepsilon}^*)$. Thus, by applying Theorem 4.2, it follows that $\mathbf{x}^* \in X^*$. ■

It should be noted that the strict convexity assumption could be weakened somewhat, since the only f_j that needs to be strictly convex is one such that $\lambda_j > 0$ in the KTCN. However, the mere convexity of all objective functions is not sufficient to guarantee the implication of A from J as asserted by Cohon and Marks [1975]. Strict convexity of at least one appropriate objective function is needed. Consider a simple example as follows: min $[f_1(x), f_2(x)]$ such that $g(x) = -x < 0$, $x \in R$, where $f_1(x)$ and $f_2(x)$ are shown in Figure 4.5.

We see that both f_1 and f_2 are convex, and at any point $x^0 \in (1,2)$, KTCN is always satisfied; i.e., there always exists $\boldsymbol{\lambda} = (\lambda_1, \lambda_2)^{\mathrm{T}} \geqslant 0$ (with $\boldsymbol{\lambda} \neq 0$) and $\mu \geqslant 0$ such that $g(x) \leqslant 0$, $\mu g(x) = 0$ and

$$\lambda_1 \frac{df_1}{dx}(x^0) + \lambda_2 \frac{df_2(x^0)}{dx} - \mu = 0. \tag{4.45}$$

One particular choice that always furnishes the required μ and $\boldsymbol{\lambda}$ whenever $x^0 \in (1,2)$ is $\lambda_2 = 0$, $\mu = 0$, and $\lambda_1 > 0$. Yet each $x^0 \in (1,2)$ is inferior to the point $x = 2$. The difficulty lies in the fact that in the interval $(1,2)$ $(df_1/dx)(x^0)$ vanishes, which allows arbitrary selection of λ_1 to satisfy (4.45) and, hence, KTCN. Had $f_1(x)$ been strictly convex, as is $f_2(x)$, this difficulty would not have been encountered.

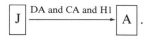

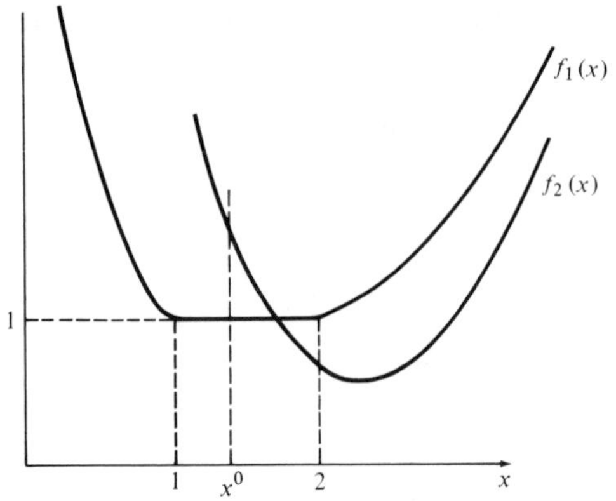

Figure 4.5 The need for strict convexity in KTCN.

An alternative to the preceding sufficient condition can be stated using an alternative path from B to A, as set out in Theorem 4.1. This alternative path suggests that the condition that $\mathbf{x}^*$ solve $P_k(\boldsymbol{\varepsilon}^*)$ for every $k=1,\ldots,n$ can be used to replace the uniqueness of solution and, hence, the strict convexity condition.

4.5 Necessary and Sufficient Conditions for Proper Noninferiority

Kuhn and Tucker [1951] first noted that even certain noninferior solutions possessed some undesirable properties concerning the ratio of the rate of gain in one attribute over the corresponding rate of loss in another attribute. In order to distinguish those noninferior solutions that should not be considered in the final screening process from those that should be considered, they introduced the concept of proper noninferior solutions and derived necessary and sufficient conditions for proper noninferiority in the same paper in which they presented conditions for optimality for a scalar optimization problem. Geoffrion [1968] modified the concept and defined a proper noninferior solution as follows:

Definition. A noninferior solution of VOP, $\mathbf{x}^*$ is said to be a *proper noninferior solution* of VOP if there exists a scalar $M>0$ such that for each i, $i=1,\ldots,n$, and each $\mathbf{x}\in X$ satisfying $f_i(\mathbf{x})<f_i(\mathbf{x}^*)$, there exists at least one $j\neq i$ with $f_j(\mathbf{x})>f_j(\mathbf{x}^*)$ and $[f_i(\mathbf{x})-f_i(\mathbf{x}^*)]/[f_j(\mathbf{x}^*)-f_j(\mathbf{x})]\leq M$. A noninferior solution which is not proper is an *improper noninferior solution*.

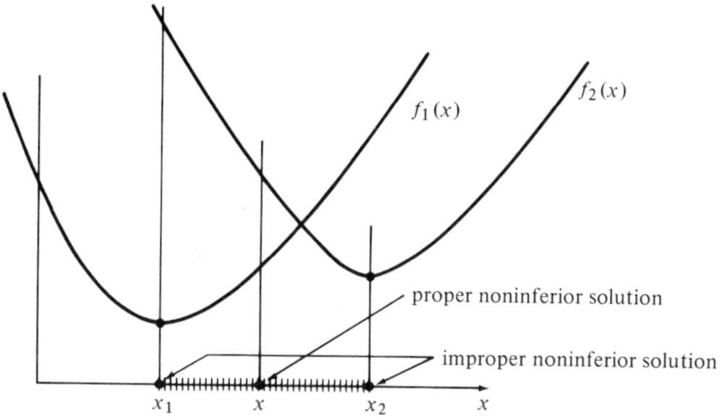

Figure 4.6 Proper and improper noninferior solutions.

A simple example illustrating proper and improper noninferior solutions is shown in Figure 4.6, which corresponds to VOP_1:

$$\begin{aligned} &\min \quad [f_1(x), f_2(x)] \\ &\text{subject to} \quad x \geqslant 0, \quad x \in R. \end{aligned} \tag{4.46}$$

It is clear from Figure 4.6 that any point in the interval $[x_1, x_2]$ inclusive is a noninferior solution of VOP_1 (i.e., $X^* = \{x | x \in R,\ x_1 \leqslant x \leqslant x_2\}$). Moreover, the point x_1 is an improper noninferior solution, since for any $x = x_1 + h$, $h > 0$, $f_2(x) < f_2(x_1)$, but the ratio

$$\frac{f_2(x) - f_2(x_1)}{f_1(x) - f_1(x_1)} \to \infty \qquad \text{as} \quad h \to 0^+.$$

Likewise, x_2 is also an improper noninferior solution, while all points in the interval (x_1, x_2) can be shown to be proper noninferior.

Geoffrion [1968] (see also Kuhn and Tucker [1951]) derives necessary and sufficient conditions that enable some (or all, if the convexity assumption is imposed) of the proper noninferior solutions to be generated. These conditions are expressed in terms of solutions of $P(\mathbf{w})$:

Theorem 4.11

$$\boxed{F} \xrightarrow{\text{H2}} \boxed{G}, \qquad \boxed{F} \xleftrightarrow{\text{CA, (H2)}} \boxed{G}.$$

a. *If* $\mathbf{x}^*$ *solves* $P(\mathbf{w})$ *for some* $\mathbf{w} > \mathbf{0}$, *then* $\mathbf{x}^*$ *is a proper noninferior solution of VOP.* [*This is in fact a more precise statement than Theorem* 4.6(*i*).]
b. *Assume the convexity assumption. If* $\mathbf{x}^*$ *is a proper noninferior solution of VOP, then* $\mathbf{x}^*$ *solves* $P(\mathbf{w})$ *for some* $\mathbf{w} > \mathbf{0}$.

The proof of this theorem is rather involved. The reader should refer to Geoffrion [1968] for a detailed proof. Benson and Morin [1974, 1977], through the study of $P_k(\mathbf{u})$ and $P_k(\boldsymbol{\varepsilon})$, derived the following necessary and sufficient conditions expressed in terms of $P_k(\boldsymbol{\varepsilon})$:

Theorem 4.12

$$\boxed{\text{A}} \xrightarrow{\text{CA, S2}} \boxed{\text{G}}, \qquad \boxed{\text{A}} \xleftarrow{\text{CA, S2}} \boxed{\text{G}}.$$

Assume the convexity assumption. A necessary and sufficient condition for a noninferior solution $\mathbf{x}^*$ *to be a proper noninferior solution is that* $P_k(\boldsymbol{\varepsilon}^*)$ *be stable for all* k.

Close examination of the diagram will reveal a proof of this theorem if one traces out the path G–F–E–B. For example, a proof of the necessity part easily follows from Theorem 4.11b,

$$\boxed{\text{G}} \xrightarrow{\text{CA, (H2)}} \boxed{\text{F}},$$

and Lemma 4.7,

$$\boxed{\text{E}} \xrightarrow{\text{(S1 if CA assumed)}} \boxed{\text{B}}.$$

As for the sufficiency part, we apply Lemma 4.3 to $P_k(\boldsymbol{\varepsilon}^*)$ n times for each $k=1,\ldots,n$, after which it can easily be shown that there exist $u_j>0, j\neq k$, such that $\mathbf{x}^*$ solves $P_k(\mathbf{u})$. From here application of Theorem 4.11(a) will give the required result.

In working with the ε-constraint problem, and from the algorithmic viewpoint, the stability of $P_k(\boldsymbol{\varepsilon}^*)$ for *all* k is quite difficult to check in general. We offer the following alternative necessary and sufficient noninferiority conditions as a means for checking whether or not a solution of $P_k(\boldsymbol{\varepsilon})$ is a proper noninferior solution:

Theorem 4.13

$$\boxed{\text{B}} \xleftarrow{\text{DA and RA, (H4)}} \boxed{\text{G}}, \qquad \boxed{\text{B}} \xrightarrow{\text{CA and RA and DA and H4}} \boxed{\text{G}}.$$

Let $\mathbf{x}^*$ *be a regular point of the constraints of* $P_k(\boldsymbol{\varepsilon}^*)$, *and assume that all functions are continuously differentiable.*

a. *If* $\mathbf{x}^*$ *is a proper noninferior solution of VOP, then* $\mathbf{x}^*$ *solves* $P_k(\boldsymbol{\varepsilon}^*)$ *with all the Kuhn–Tucker multipliers associated with the constraints* $f_j(\mathbf{x})\leqslant\varepsilon_j$, $j\neq k$ *(which will be denoted* $\lambda^*_{kj}, j\neq k$*) being strictly positive.*
b. *Assume the convexity assumption. Then,* $\mathbf{x}^*$ *is a proper noninferior solution of VOP if* $\mathbf{x}^*$ *solves* $P_k(\boldsymbol{\varepsilon}^*)$ *with* $\lambda^*_{kj}>0$ *for all* $j\neq k$.

PROOF: (a) $\mathbf{x}^*$, being a proper noninferior solution of VOP, must also be noninferior. Hence by Theorem 4.1 $\mathbf{x}^*$ solves $P_k(\boldsymbol{\varepsilon}^*)$. This, together with the fact that $\mathbf{x}^*$ is a regular point of the constraint of $P_k(\boldsymbol{\varepsilon}^*)$, guarantees the existence of the *unique* set of Kuhn–Tucker multipliers $\lambda_{kj}^* \geqslant 0$ for all $j \neq k$ and $\mu_i^* \geqslant 0$ for all $i=1,\ldots,m$, such that the Kuhn–Tucker conditions for optimality for $P_k(\boldsymbol{\varepsilon}^*)$ are satisfied. All we need to show now is that λ_{kj}^* must necessarily be strictly positive for all $j \neq k$. To show this, we invoke Geoffrion's [1968] comprehensive theorem. Because of the proper noninferiority and the regularity properties of $\mathbf{x}^*$, there exist $\lambda_j^0 > 0$, $j=1,\ldots,n$, and $\mu_j^0 \geqslant 0$, $i=1,\ldots,m$, such that

$$\sum_{j=1}^{n} \lambda_j^0 \nabla f_j(\mathbf{x}^*) + \sum_{i=1}^{m} \mu_i^0 \nabla g_i(\mathbf{x}^*) = 0, \tag{4.47a}$$

$$\mu_i^0 g_i(\mathbf{x}^*) = 0, \qquad i=1,\ldots,m; \tag{4.47b}$$

or

$$\nabla f_k(\mathbf{x}^*) + \sum_{j \neq k} (\lambda_j^0/\lambda_k^0) \nabla f_j(\mathbf{x}^*) + \sum_{i=1}^{m} (\mu_i^0/\lambda_k^0) \nabla g_i(\mathbf{x}^*) = 0, \tag{4.48a}$$

$$(\mu_i^0/\lambda_k^0) g_i(\mathbf{x}^*) = 0, \qquad i=1,\ldots,m. \tag{4.48b}$$

Given $\mathbf{x}^*$, (4.47) possesses a unique solution in terms of λ_j^0/λ_k^0, $j \neq k$, and μ_i^0/λ_k^0, $i=1,\ldots,m$ [since $\nabla f_j(\mathbf{x}^*)$, $j \neq k$ and the binding constraints $\nabla g_i(\mathbf{x}^*)$ are linearly independent]. Furthermore, (4.48a) and (4.48b) are just the Kuhn–Tucker conditions for optimality for $P_k(\boldsymbol{\varepsilon}^*)$, which must also be satisfied by λ_{kj}^*, $j \neq k$, and μ_i^*, $i=1,\ldots,m$. Therefore, $\lambda_{kj}^* = \lambda_j^0/\lambda_k^0 > 0$ for all $j \neq k$ as required.

(b) The proper in this part is suggested by the implication diagram

$$\boxed{\mathrm{B}} \xrightarrow{\text{RA and DA}} \boxed{\mathrm{C}} \rightarrow \boxed{\mathrm{D}} \overset{\text{CA}}{\rightarrow} \boxed{\mathrm{E}} \rightarrow \boxed{\mathrm{F}} \overset{\text{H2}}{\rightarrow} \boxed{\mathrm{G}}.$$

The first three implications (i.e., from B to E) are established in Lemma 4.6, while the implication $\mathrm{E} \rightarrow \mathrm{F}$ is trivial. Finally, Theorem 4.11 gives the last implication, in which the required condition H2 is guaranteed by the positivity of λ_{kj}^* for all $j \neq k$. ■

Theorem 4.13 is computationally convenient in conjunction with the ε-constraint problem. We must observe, however, that, unlike the case of the weighting problem, where a strictly positive weight can be preselected to guarantee proper noninferiority of the generated point, the positivity of all relevant Kuhn–Tucker multipliers (and, hence, the proper noninferiority of the generated solution) can at best be achieved only through trial and error.

This is because we can only control ε, not the multipliers, in using the ε-constraint problem. Haimes et al. [1975] present guidelines as to how to choose those εs to ensure the strict positivity required of all relevant Kuhn–Tucker multipliers.

4.6 Other Characterizations of Noninferior Solutions

4.6.1 The Weighted-Norm Approach

Consider scalarizing a VOP by the following weighted norm problem, $P(\mathbf{w}, p)$:

$$\min_{\mathbf{x}\in X} \quad \sum_{j=1}^{n} w_j |f_j(\mathbf{x}) - f_j^*|^p, \tag{4.49}$$

where $1 \leqslant p < \infty$, $f_j^* = \min_{\mathbf{x}\in X} f_j(\mathbf{x})$, and the w_js are nonnegative weights satisfying $w_j \geqslant 0$ for all $j = 1,\ldots,n$ and $\sum_{j=1}^{n} w_j = 1$. Observe that when $p = 1$, $P(\mathbf{w}, p)$ reduces to the ordinary weighting problem. It is easy to show that a unique solution of $P(\mathbf{w}, p)$ for any $1 \leqslant p < \infty$ is a noninferior solution of VOP. It can also be shown that any solution $P(\mathbf{w}, p)$ with $w_j > 0$ for all $j = 1,\ldots,m$ for any $1 \leqslant p < \infty$ is also a noninferior solution of VOP. The following theorem summarizes these results:

Theorem 4.14. *Let $\mathbf{x}^*$ solve $P(\mathbf{w}, p)$ for any $1 \leqslant p < \infty$ when either*

i. *$\mathbf{x}^*$ is a unique solution of $P(\mathbf{w}, p)$, or*
ii. *$w_j > 0$ for all $j = 1,\ldots,n$*

holds. Then $\mathbf{x}^*$ is a noninferior solution of VOP.

PROOF: Let $\mathbf{x}^*$ solve $P(\mathbf{w}, p)$ for any $1 \leqslant p < \infty$ and for some $\mathbf{w} \in W$. Thus

$$\sum_{j=1}^{n} w_j \left(|f_j(\mathbf{x}) - f_j^*|^p - |f_j(\mathbf{x}^*) - f_j^*|^p \right) \geqslant 0 \qquad \text{for all} \quad \mathbf{x} \in X. \tag{4.50}$$

Suppose $\mathbf{x}^* \notin X^*$. Then there exists an $\hat{\mathbf{x}} \in X$ such that $f_j(\hat{\mathbf{x}}) \leqslant f_j(\mathbf{x}^*)$ where strict inequality holds for at least one $j = 1,\ldots,n$, since by definition $f_j^* \leqslant f_j(\mathbf{x})$ for all $\mathbf{x} \in X$. Hence, for any $1 \leqslant p < \infty$, $|f_j(\hat{\mathbf{x}}) - f_j^*|^p \leqslant |f_j(\mathbf{x}^*) - f_j^*|^p$, with strict inequality holding for at least one $j = 1,\ldots,n$.

Taking the nonnegativity w_j into account, it follows from the last inequality that

$$\sum_{j=1}^{n} w_j \left(|f_j(\hat{\mathbf{x}}) - f_j^*|^p - |f_j(\mathbf{x}^*) - f_j^*|^p \right) \leqslant 0. \tag{4.51}$$

Now, if (i) holds, strict inequality prevails in (4.50), which contradicts (4.51). Or, if (ii) holds, strict inequality prevails in (4.51), which again contradicts (4.50). Hence, if either (i) or (ii) holds, $\mathbf{x}^*$ must be a noninferior solution of VOP. ■

The theorem does not necessarily hold for $p=\infty$, nor is $P(\mathbf{w}, p)$ defined in this case. To use l_∞ norm, the corresponding weighted-norm problem may be written as $P(\mathbf{w}, \infty)$:

$$\min_{\mathbf{x}\in X} \left\{ \max_{1\leq j\leq n} w_j\left[f_j(\mathbf{x}) - f_j^* \right] \right\}. \tag{4.52}$$

However, it can be demonstrated through a counterexample that a solution of $P(\mathbf{w}, \infty)$ is not necessarily a noninferior solution. Consider a VOP (adapted from Yu [1973]), $\max_{x\in X}[f_1(x), f_2(x)]$, where $X=\{x|x\in R, 0\leq f_1(x)\leq 2, 0\leq f_2(x)\leq 2, \max[f_1(x), f_2(x)]\geq 1$, and $\min[f_1(x), f_2(x)]\leq 1\}$. An equivalent VOP in the objective space is

$$\max_{f_1, f_2} \quad (f_1, f_2)$$

$$\text{subject to} \quad (f_1, f_2)\in F,$$

where

$$F=\{(f_1, f_2)| f_1 = f_1(x), f_2 = f_2(x), x\in X\}.$$

From Figure 4.7 it is evident that the noninferior set F^* consists of two points, namely, (1,2) and (2,1).

Consider now the corresponding weighted-norm problem with $w_1 = w_2 = \frac{1}{2}$ and $p=\infty$ as given by (see Figure 4.7) $P(\mathbf{w}, \infty)$:

$$\min_{(f_1, f_2)\in F} \{\max\ [(2-f_1), (2-f_2)]\}.$$

Figure 4.7 A counterexample for the case $p=\infty$. The feasible region F is shaded and the solution set of $P(\mathbf{w}, \infty)$ is indicated by hatched line segments.

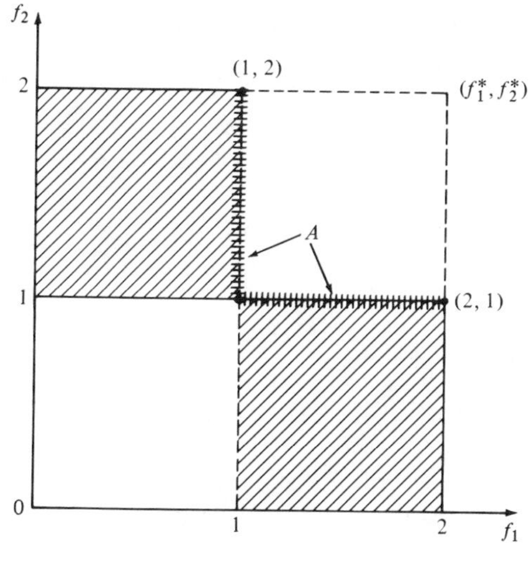

From Figure 4.7, any point in the set A, where

$$A=\{(f_1,f_2)\,|\,f_1=1,\ 1\leqslant f_2\leqslant 2 \text{ or } f_2=1,\ 1\leqslant f_1\leqslant 2\}$$

is a solution of $P(\mathbf{w},\infty)$. Except for $(1,1)$ and $(2,1)$, however, none of the points in A are noninferior solutions of the VOP example. Yu [1973] shows, however, that at least one optimal solution of $P(\mathbf{w},\infty)$ is noninferior.

The point $\mathbf{f}^*=(f_1^*,f_2^*,\ldots,f_n^*)$ is normally called the *utopia* or *ideal point*. This utopia point is normally infeasible in most VOPs with conflicting objectives. When it is feasible, it is obviously the best point available and no further search is required. The weighted-norm approach can be interpreted as an attempt to minimize deviation from the ideal point. The solution so obtained $\mathbf{x}_w^p$ for any $\mathbf{w}\geqslant\mathbf{0}$ and $1\leqslant p<\infty$ is called *a compromise solution* (Yu [1973], Zeleny [1973]). Further properties of a compromise solution will be discussed in Chapter 7.

A well-known variation of the weighted-norm problem is obtained if the utopia vector $\mathbf{f}^*$ is replaced by a goal vector $\hat{\mathbf{f}}=(\hat{f}_1,\ldots,\hat{f}_n)$, whose value is prespecified by the decision maker. The resulting problem becomes a generalized version of the so-called goal programming GP:

$$\min_{\mathbf{x}\in X}\ \sum w_j|f_j(\mathbf{x})-\hat{f}_j|^p. \tag{4.53}$$

Unfortunately, if $\hat{f}_j$ is not properly set, a solution of GP is not necessarily noninferior even if condition (i) or (ii) of Theorem 4.14 is satisfied.

In the preceding example, for $\hat{f}_1=\hat{f}_2=1$, and irrespective of the values of $1\leqslant p<\infty$ and $\mathbf{w}\geqslant\mathbf{0}$, the point $(1,1)$ will always be the (unique) solution of the corresponding GP. It is not, however, a noninferior solution. The reader should be able to construct other more common examples to confirm this point.

When the problem is linear, i.e., when all f_j are linear and X is a convex polyhedral formed by linear constraints, Hasenauer [1976] developed a set of necessary and sufficient conditions for a solution of GP to be noninferior. Goal programming will be discussed from the algorithmic viewpoint in Chapter 7.

4.6.2 The Proper Equality Constraint Approach

Another form of characterization of noninferior solutions is due to Lin [1976a]. Instead of using inequality in the ε-constraint approach $P_k(\boldsymbol{\varepsilon})$, he characterizes a VOP by an equality constraint problem of the form $E_k(\boldsymbol{\varepsilon})$:

$$\min_{\mathbf{x}\in X}\ f_k(\mathbf{x}) \tag{4.54}$$

$$\text{subject to}\qquad f_j(\mathbf{x})=\varepsilon_j,\qquad j\neq k. \tag{4.55}$$

If $\boldsymbol{\varepsilon}$ is chosen properly, then a solution of $E_k(\boldsymbol{\varepsilon})$ which satisfies additional conditions is a noninferior solution of the corresponding VOP. This result will now be stated formally (see Lin [1976a]).

Theorem 4.15. *For some given $\boldsymbol{\varepsilon}^*$ for which $E_k(\boldsymbol{\varepsilon}^*)$ is feasible, let $\mathbf{x}^*$ be an optimum solution of $E_k(\boldsymbol{\varepsilon}^*)$ and let $f_k(\mathbf{x}^*)$ be finite. Then $\mathbf{x}^*$ is a noninferior solution if and only if*

i. $\phi(\boldsymbol{\varepsilon}) \geqslant \phi(\boldsymbol{\varepsilon}^*)$ *for all* $\boldsymbol{\varepsilon}$ *in* A_k *satisfying* $\varepsilon_j \leqslant \varepsilon_j^*$, *for all* $j \neq k$; *and*
ii. $\phi(\boldsymbol{\varepsilon}) > \phi(\boldsymbol{\varepsilon}^*)$ *for all* $\boldsymbol{\varepsilon}$ *in* B_k *satisfying* $\varepsilon_j \leqslant \varepsilon_j^*$ *for all* $j \neq k$, *with strict inequality holding for at least one* $j \neq k$;

where

$$\phi(\boldsymbol{\varepsilon}) \triangleq \inf\left[f_k(\mathbf{x}) | \mathbf{x} \in X, f_j(\mathbf{x}) = \varepsilon_j, j \neq k \right],$$

$$A_k \triangleq \left\{ \boldsymbol{\varepsilon} | \boldsymbol{\varepsilon} \in R^{n-1}, E_k(\boldsymbol{\varepsilon}) \text{ is feasible} \right\},$$

$$B_k \triangleq \left\{ \boldsymbol{\varepsilon} | \boldsymbol{\varepsilon} \in A, \phi(\boldsymbol{\varepsilon}) > -\infty, \text{and } \phi(\boldsymbol{\varepsilon}) = f_k(\hat{\mathbf{x}}) \text{ for some feasible } \hat{\mathbf{x}} \text{ of } E_k(\boldsymbol{\varepsilon}) \right\}.$$

To illustrate how this theorem can be used, consider the following VOP:

$$\begin{aligned} &\min \quad \left(x_1 x_2, x_1^2 + x_2^2 \right) \\ &\text{subject to} \quad x_1 + x_2 = 1, \qquad x_1 \geqslant 0, \quad x_2 \geqslant 0. \end{aligned} \tag{4.56}$$

The corresponding $E_k(\boldsymbol{\varepsilon})$, with f_1 as the primary objective is $E_1(\varepsilon_2)$:

$$\min \quad \left\{ f_1(\mathbf{x}) \triangleq x_1 x_2 \right\} \tag{4.57}$$

$$\text{subject to} \quad f_2(\mathbf{x}) = x_1^2 + x_2^2 = \varepsilon_2, \tag{4.58}$$

$$g_1(\mathbf{x}) = x_1 + x_2 = 1, \tag{4.59}$$

$$g_2(\mathbf{x}) = -x_1 \leqslant 0, \tag{4.60}$$

$$g_3(\mathbf{x}) = -x_2 \leqslant 0. \tag{4.61}$$

Applying the Kuhn–Tucker necessary conditions (2.24)–(2.25) in Chapter 2 to $E_1(\varepsilon_2)$ yields

$$x_2 + 2\lambda_1 x_1 + \mu_1 - \mu_2 = 0, \tag{4.62}$$

$$x_1 + 2\lambda_1 x_2 + \mu_1 - \mu_3 = 0, \tag{4.63}$$

$$x_1^2 + x_2^2 = \varepsilon_2, \tag{4.64a}$$

$$x_1 + x_2 = 1, \tag{4.64b}$$

$$\mu_2 x_1 = 0, \tag{4.64c}$$

$$\mu_3 x_2 = 0, \tag{4.64d}$$

with $\mu_2, \mu_3, x_1, x_2 \geqslant 0$. From (4.64a) and (4.64b), and taking the nonnegativity of x_1, x_2 into account, we find that

$$x_1 = 1 - \sqrt{\varepsilon_2 - 1}, \qquad x_2 = \sqrt{\varepsilon_2 - 1}$$

or

$$x_1=\sqrt{\varepsilon_2-1}, \qquad x_2=1-\sqrt{\varepsilon_2-1}, \tag{4.65}$$

$1\leqslant\varepsilon_2\leqslant 2$. Upon further substitution we find that x_1 and x_2 as given by (4.65) are the unique solution of the system (4.62)–(4.64) for any given ε_2 between 1 and 2. Since f_1 is convex for all $x_1\geqslant 0$, $x_2\geqslant 0$, (4.62)–(4.64) must also be a sufficient condition for optimality of $E_1(\varepsilon_2)$. For any value of ε_2 outside this range, (4.62)–(4.64) have no real solution, and hence $E_1(\varepsilon_2)$ has no solution. We therefore have $A_1=\{\varepsilon_2\in R|1\leqslant\varepsilon_2\leqslant 2\}$. In fact, since $E_1(\varepsilon_2)$ always has a finite solution within this range, we have $B_1=A_1$. To check which part of B_1 yields noninferior solutions, we observe that for any $\varepsilon_2\in B_1$, the optimal value of $E_1(\varepsilon_2)$ is given by

$$\hat{f}_1(\varepsilon_2)=f(\mathbf{x})=\left(1-\sqrt{\varepsilon_2-1}\right)\left(\sqrt{\varepsilon_2-1}\right)=\sqrt{\varepsilon_2-1}-(\varepsilon_2-1). \tag{4.66}$$

Hence the gradient of $f_1(\varepsilon_2)$ with respect to ε_2 at every point in B_1 except $\varepsilon_2=1$ is

$$d\hat{f}_1(\varepsilon_2)/d\varepsilon_2=1/2\sqrt{\varepsilon_2-1}-1. \tag{4.67}$$

We find that $\hat{f}_1(\varepsilon_2)$ increases whenever ε_2 decreases if and only if $df_1(\varepsilon_2)/d\varepsilon_2<0$ implying that $\frac{5}{4}<\varepsilon_2\leqslant 2$. Hence the set of noninferior solutions of (4.54)–(4.56) is given by $X^*=\{(x_1,x_2)|x_1=1-\sqrt{\varepsilon_2-1},$ $x_2=\sqrt{\varepsilon_2-1}$ or $x_1=\sqrt{\varepsilon_2-1}$, $x_2=1-\sqrt{\varepsilon_2-1}$, $\frac{5}{4}<\varepsilon_2\leqslant 2\}$, or simply $X^*=\{(x_1,x_2)|x_1+x_2=1, 0\leqslant x_1\leqslant 1\}$ and $F^*=\{(f_1,f_2)|f_1+2f_2=1, \frac{1}{2}\leqslant f_1\leqslant 1\}$. Figure 4.8 illustrates the noninferior solutions in ε_2, $\mathbf{x}$, and $\mathbf{f}$ spaces.

More examples on the use of this result will be given in Section 6.3. Conditions (i) and (ii) in Theorem 4.15 are usually not simple to verify numerically. Lin [1976, 1979] provides slightly more operational conditions based on the concept of Lagrange multipliers similar to the use of (4.67) above for checking these conditions. The interested reader should consult the above references.

4.6.3 *The Hybrid Approach: Weighting and Constraint*

Let us now turn to another form of characterization which was studied by Wendell and Lee [1977] and Corley [1980]. This form combines the characteristics of both the weighting and constraint characterizations. Accordingly, it will be called the *hybrid* characterization. Here noninferior solutions of VOP in (6.3) are characterized in terms of optimal solutions of the following problem $P(\mathbf{w},\boldsymbol{\varepsilon})$:

$$\min \quad \mathbf{w}^{\mathrm{T}}\mathbf{f}(\mathbf{x}) \tag{4.68}$$

$$\text{subject to} \quad f_j(\mathbf{x})\leqslant\varepsilon_j, \quad j=1,\ldots,n, \tag{4.69a}$$

$$\mathbf{x}\in X, \tag{4.69b}$$

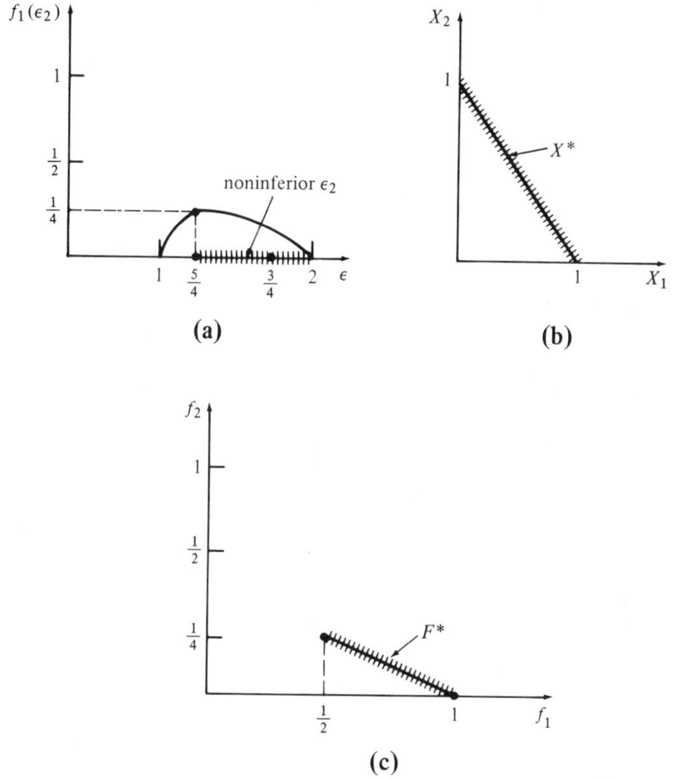

Figure 4.8 Noninferior solutions for the sample problem of Section 4.6.2 in (**a**) ε_2-space, (**b**) decision space, and (**c**) objective space.

where $\mathbf{w} > \mathbf{0}$. Wendell and Lee [1977] use $\mathbf{w} = \mathbf{e}$ in their development, and Corley [1980] suggests the above form with $\mathbf{w}$ being any strictly positive vector in R^n. The following result is useful and is easy to prove.

Theorem 4.16. $\mathbf{x}^*$ *is a noninferior solution of VOP if and only if* $\mathbf{x}^*$ *is an optimal solution of* $P(\mathbf{w}^0, \boldsymbol{\varepsilon})$ *for any given* $\mathbf{w}^0 > \mathbf{0}$ *and for some* $\boldsymbol{\varepsilon} \in R^n$ *for which* $P(\mathbf{w}^0, \boldsymbol{\varepsilon})$ *is feasible.*

PROOF: Necessity—assume that, for any given $\mathbf{w}^0 > \mathbf{0}$, $\mathbf{x}^*$ does not solve $P(\mathbf{w}^0, \boldsymbol{\varepsilon})$ for any $\boldsymbol{\varepsilon}$ including $P(\mathbf{w}^0, \boldsymbol{\varepsilon}^*)$, where $\boldsymbol{\varepsilon}^* = \mathbf{f}(\mathbf{x}^*)$. Let $\mathbf{x}^0$ be an optimal solution of $P(\mathbf{w}^0, \boldsymbol{\varepsilon}^*)$. Hence we have

$$(\mathbf{w}^0)^{\mathrm{T}}\mathbf{f}(\mathbf{x}^0) < (\mathbf{w}^0)^{\mathrm{T}}\mathbf{f}(\mathbf{x}^*) \tag{4.70}$$

and

$$\mathbf{f}(\mathbf{x}^0) \leqslant \mathbf{f}(\mathbf{x}^*). \tag{4.71}$$

Since $\mathbf{w}^0 > \mathbf{0}$, (4.70)–(4.71) imply $\mathbf{f}(\mathbf{x}^0) \leq \mathbf{f}(\mathbf{x}^*)$. Hence $\mathbf{x}^*$ is not noninferior, proving necessity.

Sufficiency—suppose $\mathbf{x}^*$ solves $P(\mathbf{w}^0, \boldsymbol{\varepsilon})$ for some $\boldsymbol{\varepsilon} \in R^n$. It must also solve $P(\mathbf{w}^0, \boldsymbol{\varepsilon}^*)$, where $\boldsymbol{\varepsilon}^* = \mathbf{f}(\mathbf{x}^*)$. Suppose $\mathbf{x}^*$ is not noninferior implying the existence of an $\mathbf{x}^0 \in X$ such that $\mathbf{f}(\mathbf{x}^0) \leq \mathbf{f}(\mathbf{x}^*)$. Hence for any $\mathbf{w}^0 > \mathbf{0}$, $(\mathbf{w}^0)^T\mathbf{f}(\mathbf{x}^0) < (\mathbf{w}^0)^T\mathbf{f}(\mathbf{x}^*)$. This clearly contradicts the fact that $\mathbf{x}^*$ solves $P(\mathbf{w}^0, \boldsymbol{\varepsilon}^*)$, since $\mathbf{x}^0$ is a feasible point of $P(\mathbf{w}^0, \boldsymbol{\varepsilon}^*)$. Thus $\mathbf{x}^*$ must be noninferior. ■

From a computational standpoint, Theorem 4.16 is quite powerful since it allows noninferior solutions to be generated without the necessity of performing a test of noninferiority, regardless of the problem we are working with. As Corley [1980] points out, it combines the advantages of both the weighting approach (using $\mathbf{w} > \mathbf{0}$ to ensure noninferiority) and the constraint approach (handling duality gaps).

The hybrid problem can also be used to test the noninferiority of a given point $\mathbf{x}^*$. We simply choose some convenient $\mathbf{w}^0 > \mathbf{0}$ and formulate and solve $P(\mathbf{w}^0, \boldsymbol{\varepsilon}^*)$. Either $\mathbf{x}^*$ solves $P(\mathbf{w}^0, \boldsymbol{\varepsilon}^*)$, implying that $\mathbf{x}^*$ is noninferior by Theorem 4.16, or else we conclude that $\mathbf{x}^*$ is not noninferior. Again, further investigation of the last case may yield additional useful information about X^*. Suppose $P(\mathbf{w}^0, \boldsymbol{\varepsilon}^*)$ has an optimal solution $\mathbf{x}^0$; we can then use $\mathbf{x}^0$ as our noninferior solution. If $P(\mathbf{w}^0, \boldsymbol{\varepsilon}^*)$ does not have an optimal solution in the sense that $\phi(\boldsymbol{\varepsilon}^*) \triangleq \inf\{(\mathbf{w}^0)^T\mathbf{f}(\mathbf{x}) | \mathbf{f}(\mathbf{x}) \leq \boldsymbol{\varepsilon}^*, \mathbf{x} \in X\}$ is finite, but there exists no $\mathbf{x}^0$ in X such that $(\mathbf{w}^0)^T\mathbf{f}(\mathbf{x}^0) = \phi(\boldsymbol{\varepsilon}^*)$, then no conclusion can be drawn. If, however, $\phi(\boldsymbol{\varepsilon}^*) = -\infty$ and $P(\mathbf{w}^0, \boldsymbol{\varepsilon}^*)$ has an unbounded solution, the set of noninferior solutions of VOP is empty if the same hypotheses as in Theorem 4.4 hold. The following results, which summarize these statements, can be proved in a similar fashion to Theorem 4.4.

Theorem 4.17. *Assume that one of the following holds:*

a. $P(\mathbf{w}^0, \boldsymbol{\varepsilon})$ *is stable, X is a convex set, and f_j, $j = 1, \ldots, n$, are convex throughout R^n; or*
b. *all f_j, $j = 1, \ldots, n$, and g_i, $i = 1, \ldots, m$, are faithfully convex throughout R^n and $X = \{\mathbf{x} \in R^N | \mathbf{g}(\mathbf{x}) \leq 0\}$ [Wendell and Lee, 1977];*

then X^* of VOP $= \not{f}$ *if* $\phi(\boldsymbol{\varepsilon}^*) = -\infty$.

4.6.4 Characterization and Noninferiority Test

Finally, yet another formulation of the corresponding scalar optimization problem, somewhat related to $P(\mathbf{w}, \boldsymbol{\varepsilon})$, is often used as a method of testing the noninferiority of a given point, rather than an arbitrarily selected $\boldsymbol{\varepsilon}$. Given any point $\mathbf{x}^* \in X$, we select a convenient $\boldsymbol{\alpha} > 0$, $\boldsymbol{\alpha} \in R^n$, and formulate P^*:

$$\delta^* = \max \boldsymbol{\alpha}^{\mathrm{T}}\boldsymbol{\varepsilon} \tag{4.72}$$

$$\text{subject to} \qquad \mathbf{f}(\mathbf{x}) + \boldsymbol{\varepsilon} = \mathbf{f}(\mathbf{x}^*), \tag{4.73a}$$

$$\mathbf{x} \in X, \quad \boldsymbol{\varepsilon} \geqslant \mathbf{0}. \tag{4.73b}$$

One of three cases can arise:

1. P^* has a bounded optimal solution with $\delta^* = 0$;
2. P^* has a bounded optimal solution with finite optimal value $\delta^* > -\infty$; or
3. P^* has an unbounded optimal solution with unbounded optimal value $\delta^* = -\infty$, in which case the maximum problem in (4.72) becomes the supremum problem.

As the following results will indicate, a prevalence of case 1 implies the noninferiority of $\mathbf{x}^*$. Case 2 on the other hand implies the inferiority of $\mathbf{x}^*$ and noninferiority of an optimal solution of P^*. Imposing convexity assumptions, Benson [1978] case 3 implies the emptiness of the set of proper noninferior solutions of VOP, which leads to the emptiness of X^* if a further condition is imposed. Theorem 4.18(a) and 4.18(b), whose proof we shall sketch, generalize well-known results originally developed for linear problems (see, for example, Charnes and Cooper [1961] and Ecker and Kouada [1975]). Parts (c) and (d), dealing with case 3 above, are due to Benson [1978] and stated without proof. Later the utility of these results will become evident.

Theorem 4.18. *For any given $\boldsymbol{\alpha} > \mathbf{0}$ in R^n and $\mathbf{x}^*$ in X, let δ^* denote the optimal value (or supremum) of P^* in* (4.72) *and* (4.73):

a. $\mathbf{x}^*$ *is noninferior if and only if* $\delta^* = 0$;
b. *an optimal solution of P^* is noninferior if* $0 < \delta^* < -\infty$;
c. *if P^* has an unbounded solution with $\delta^* = -\infty$ and if X is a convex set and f_j, $j = 1,\ldots,n$, are convex functions, then,* VOP *has no proper noninferior solutions*;
d. *if in addition to the conditions in (c), the set* $\{\tilde{\mathbf{f}} \mid \tilde{\mathbf{f}} \leqslant \mathbf{f}(\mathbf{x})$ *for some* $\mathbf{x} \in X\}$ *is closed, then* $X^* = \varnothing$.

PROOF:

(a) Since $\mathbf{x}^*$ is a feasible point of P^* with $\boldsymbol{\varepsilon} = \mathbf{0}$, P^* is feasible and $\delta^* \geqslant 0$. Now, if $\delta^* = 0$, the nonnegativity of $\boldsymbol{\varepsilon}$ implies that $\boldsymbol{\varepsilon} = \mathbf{0}$. Consequently there is no $\mathbf{x} \in X$ with $\mathbf{f}(\mathbf{x}) \leqslant \mathbf{f}(\mathbf{x}^*)$, which implies noninferiority of $\mathbf{x}^*$. This completes the proof of the sufficiency part. For the necessity part we assume that $\delta^* > 0$ at the optimal solution $\mathbf{x}^0$ of P^*. Clearly we must have $\varepsilon_i > 0$ in this case for at least one $1 \leqslant i \leqslant n$, where all other $\varepsilon_i \geqslant 0$. Hence we have $\mathbf{x}^0 \in X$ such that $\mathbf{f}(\mathbf{x}^0) \leqslant \mathbf{f}(\mathbf{x}^*)$, which implies the inferiority of $\mathbf{x}^*$. The necessity half of (a) follows from a contrapositive argument.

(b) Let $(\mathbf{x}^0, \boldsymbol{\varepsilon}^0)$ be an optimal solution of P^* with $0 < \delta^* = \boldsymbol{\alpha}^T \cdot \boldsymbol{\varepsilon}^0 < +\infty$. Suppose $\mathbf{x}^0$ is not noninferior, implying the existence of an $\hat{\mathbf{x}}$ in X such that $\mathbf{f}(\hat{\mathbf{x}}) \leqslant \mathbf{f}(\mathbf{x}^0)$. Let $\hat{\boldsymbol{\varepsilon}} \triangleq \mathbf{f}(\mathbf{x}^*) - \mathbf{f}(\hat{\mathbf{x}})$. Hence $\hat{\boldsymbol{\varepsilon}} \geqslant \mathbf{f}(\mathbf{x}^*) - \mathbf{f}(\mathbf{x}^0) \triangleq \boldsymbol{\varepsilon}^0$. Consequently, for $\boldsymbol{\alpha} > \mathbf{0}$ with $\delta^* = \boldsymbol{\alpha}^T \cdot \boldsymbol{\varepsilon} < +\infty$, we must have $\boldsymbol{\alpha}^T \cdot \hat{\boldsymbol{\varepsilon}} > \boldsymbol{\alpha}^T \cdot \boldsymbol{\varepsilon}^0$, leading to a contradiction since $(\mathbf{x}^0, \boldsymbol{\varepsilon}^0)$ solves P^*. ∎

4.7 Local Noninferior Solutions

In practice, without convexity assumptions available scalar optimization techniques guarantee only *local* optimal solutions. Therefore any method for generating noninferior solutions based on solutions of scalar optimization problems can be expected to guarantee only local noninferior solutions, unless appropriate convexity assumptions are imposed. It is useful, therefore, to characterize local noninferior solutions in terms of local optimal solutions of some scalar problems. Although one can easily establish "local" counterparts of all the results stated earlier in this chapter, only those related to the constraint problem will be discussed in this section.

In addition to the notation defined earlier, we denote a feasible neighborhood of a feasible alternative $\mathbf{x}$ by $X \cap N(\mathbf{x})$ and a δ neighborhood of $\mathbf{x}$ by $N(\mathbf{x}, \delta)$, where $N(\mathbf{x}, \delta) \triangleq \{\mathbf{y} | \mathbf{y} \in R^N, \|\mathbf{x} - \mathbf{y}\| < \delta\}$ and $\| \ \|$ is any norm of interest. Finally, the set of local noninferior solutions will be denoted $\bar{X}^*$.

Definition. $\mathbf{x}^*$ is said to be a local noninferior solution of a VOP (i.e., $\mathbf{x}^* \in \bar{\mathbf{X}}^*$) if there exists $\delta > 0$ such that x^* is noninferior in $X \cap N(\mathbf{x}^*, \delta)$ [i.e., there exists no other $\mathbf{x} \in X \cap N(\mathbf{x}^*, \delta)$ such that $f(\mathbf{x}) \leqslant f(\mathbf{x}^*)$].

The following two theorems are "local" counterparts of Theorems 4.1 and 4.2.

Theorem 4.19. $\mathbf{x}^*$ *is a local noninferior solution of a VOP if and only if* $\mathbf{x}^*$ *is a local solution of* $P_k(\boldsymbol{\varepsilon}^*)$ *for all* $k = 1, \ldots, n$.

PROOF: Necessity is proved by a contrapositive argument. If there is a k for which $\mathbf{x}^*$ is not a local solution of $P_k(\boldsymbol{\varepsilon}^*)$, then for all $\delta > 0$, there exists $\mathbf{x}(\delta) \in X \cap N(\mathbf{x}^*, \delta)$ such that $f_k(\mathbf{x}(\delta)) < f_k(\mathbf{x}^*)$ and $f_j(\mathbf{x}(\delta)) \leqslant f_j(\mathbf{x}^*)$ for all $j \neq k$. Hence, $\mathbf{x}^* \notin \bar{X}^*$.

For the converse, if $\mathbf{x}^*$ is a local solution of $P_k(\boldsymbol{\varepsilon}^*)$ for all $k = 1, \ldots, n$, then for each k there exists $\delta_k > 0$ such that $\mathbf{x}^*$ is a minimizer of $P_k(\boldsymbol{\varepsilon}^*)$ within $X \cap N(\mathbf{x}^*, \delta_k)$. Setting $\delta = \min\{\delta_1, \ldots, \delta_n\} > 0$ makes x^* a minimizer of $P_k(\boldsymbol{\varepsilon}^*)$ in $X \cap N(\mathbf{x}^*, \delta)$ for all $k = 1, \ldots, n$. Hence there is no $\mathbf{x} \in X \cap N(\mathbf{x}^*, \delta)$ such that $f(\mathbf{x}) \leqslant f(\mathbf{x}^*)$, implying that $\mathbf{x}^* \in \bar{X}^*$. ∎

Theorem 4.20. $\mathbf{x}^*$ *is a local noninferior solution of a VOP if* x^* *is a strict solution of* $P_k(\boldsymbol{\varepsilon}^*)$ *for some* k.

PROOF: Let $\mathbf{x}^*$ be a local solution of $P_k(\boldsymbol{\varepsilon}^*)$ for some k. Then there exists $\delta > 0$ such that for all $\mathbf{x} \in X \cap N(\mathbf{x}^*, \delta)$ satisfying $f_j(\mathbf{x}) \leq f_j(\mathbf{x}^*)$ for all $j \neq k$, $f_k(\mathbf{x}) > f_k(\mathbf{x}^*)$. Hence there is no $\mathbf{x} \in X \cap N(\mathbf{x}^*, \delta)$ such that $f(\mathbf{x}) \leq f(\mathbf{x}^*)$, implying that $\mathbf{x}^* \in \bar{X}^*$. ∎

Corollary. *If* $\mathbf{x}^*$ *solves* $P_k(\boldsymbol{\varepsilon}^*)$ *with second-order sufficiency conditions being satisfied for some* k, *then* $\mathbf{x}^*$ *is a local noninferior solution of VOP.*

Upon imposing appropriate convexity assumptions, as in the case of a scalar optimization problem, a local noninferior solution becomes a *global* noninferior solution, as the following theorem indicates:

Theorem 4.21. *If* X *is a convex set and all* f_j *are convex functions on* X, *then any local noninferior solution of VOP is also a global noninferior solution.*

PROOF: Let $\mathbf{x}^*$ be a local noninferior solution of VOP. By Theorem 4.19, $\mathbf{x}^*$ is a local solution of $P_k(\boldsymbol{\varepsilon}^*)$ for all $k = 1, \ldots, n$. By convexity and Theorem 4.1, the result immediately follows. ∎

4.8 Special Results for Linear Problems

Linear multiobjective decision problems have attracted considerable attention both from a practical and a theoretical viewpoint. They have broad application, and their special structure allows theoretical and algorithmic developments that would not be possible for general nonlinear problems alone.

Although the results discussed thus far in this chapter are applicable to linear as well as to general nonlinear decision problems, we now turn our attention to a number of interesting results applicable specifically to linear problems. We shall discuss in this section only those results which describe the general characteristics of noninferior solutions of linear problems. In Chapter 6 special results derived from some specific algorithmic procedures such as the simplex method will be obtained as the need arises. Since linear problems are convex, it suffices, therefore (see Section 4.3.3), to use only the weighting approach to characterize the entire set of noninferior solutions of linear problems.

Let us first rewrite a VOP as a linear vector optimization problem LVOP of the form

$$\min \quad C\mathbf{x} \tag{4.74}$$

$$\text{subject to} \quad A\mathbf{x} = \mathbf{b}, \quad \mathbf{x} \geq \mathbf{0}, \tag{4.75}$$

where

C is an $n \times N$ objective functions matrix with $f_i = \mathbf{c}_i \cdot \mathbf{x}$, $i = 1, \ldots, n$, and $\mathbf{c}_i$ is the ith row of C;

A is an $m \times N$ coefficient matrix with rank m;

$\mathbf{b}$ is an $m \times 1$ constant vector; and

$\mathbf{x}$ is an $N \times 1$ vector of decision variables, which may include slack variables.

Also let

$$X \triangleq \{\mathbf{x} \in R^N \,|\, A\mathbf{x} = \mathbf{b},\ \mathbf{x} \geqslant \mathbf{0}\}. \tag{4.76}$$

The corresponding weighting problem of LVOP is $P(\mathbf{w})$:

$$\min \quad \mathbf{w}^{\mathrm{T}} C \mathbf{x} \tag{4.77}$$

$$\text{subject to} \qquad \mathbf{x} \in X, \tag{4.78}$$

where

$$\mathbf{w} \in W \triangleq \left\{ \mathbf{w} \in R^n \,|\, \mathbf{w} \geqslant \mathbf{0},\ \sum_{i=1}^{n} w_i = 1 \right\}. \tag{4.79}$$

Also define the interior of W,

$$W^\circ \triangleq \left\{ \mathbf{w} \in R^n \,|\, \mathbf{w} > \mathbf{0},\ \sum_{i=1}^{n} w_i = 1 \right\}. \tag{4.80}$$

We begin with a remarkable result which will form the basis of most of this section, as well as the algorithmic development to be described in Section 6.2.3.

Theorem 4.22. $\mathbf{x}^* \in X$ *is a noninferior solution of LVOP if and only if there exists* $\mathbf{w}^\circ \in W^\circ$ *(i.e.,* $\mathbf{w}^\circ > \mathbf{0}$*) such that* $\mathbf{x}^*$ *solves* $P(\mathbf{w}^\circ)$.

Sufficiency follows trivially from Theorem 4.6(i), which applies irrespective of the type of VOP. For necessity, which applies specifically to linear problems, a number of proofs exist (see, for example, Zeleny [1976], Yu and Zeleny [1975], and Isermann [1976]).

As an immediate consequence of this theorem and Geoffrion's result [Theorem 4.11(a)], we can conclude that any noninferior solution of LVOP is also a proper noninferior solution:

Corollary. $\mathbf{x}^*$ *in* X *is a noninferior solution of LVOP if and only if it is a proper noninferior solution of LVOP.*

Given a set of points $Q=\{\mathbf{x}^1,\ldots,\mathbf{x}^q\}$, $q\geq 2$, we define the convex hull of Q, denoted

$$H(Q)=\left\{\mathbf{x}|\mathbf{x}=\sum_{i=1}^{q}\lambda_i\mathbf{x}^i,\lambda_i\geq 0, i=1,\ldots,q, \sum_{i=1}^{q}\lambda_i=1\right\}. \tag{4.81}$$

The relative interior of a convex hull $H(Q)$, is defined as

$$H^\circ(Q)=\left\{\mathbf{x}|\mathbf{x}=\sum_{i=1}^{q}\lambda_i\mathbf{x}^i,\lambda_i> 0, i=1,\ldots,q, \sum_{i=1}^{q}\lambda_i=1\right\}. \tag{4.82}$$

Observe that both $H(Q)$ and $H^\circ(Q)$ are always convex.

The following results can now be obtained:[7]

Theorem 4.23. *Given $Q=\{\mathbf{x}^1,\ldots,\mathbf{x}^q\}$, $q\geq 2$, if any point $\mathbf{x}^\circ\in H^\circ(Q)$ is a noninferior solution of LVOP, then the entire convex hull $H(Q)$ is noninferior.*

Corollary

a. *If $\mathbf{x}\in H^\circ(Q)$ is inferior, then the entire $H^\circ(Q)$ is inferior.*
b. *If each $\mathbf{x}^i$, $i=1,\ldots,q$, is inferior then $H(Q)$ is inferior.*
c. *If some $\mathbf{x}^i$, $1\leq i\leq q$, is inferior then $H(Q)-\{\mathbf{x}^i\}$ is inferior.*

To verify the corollary we merely observe that if any point in $H^\circ(Q)$ is noninferior, then the entire $H(Q)$ is noninferior, in which case there can be no inferior point in $H^\circ(Q)$ or in Q.

The following result is due to Gal [1976].

Theorem 4.24. *Given $Q=\{\mathbf{x}^1,\ldots,\mathbf{x}^q\}$, $q\geq 2$, the entire $H(Q)$ is noninferior if and only if there exists $\mathbf{w}^\circ\in W^\circ$ such that every $\mathbf{x}$ in $H(Q)$ solves $P(\mathbf{w}^\circ)$.*

Theorems 4.23 and 4.24 are easily shown to be applicable to an unbounded polyhedron as well as a bounded convex hull, because one can always find a convex hull as a subset of such a polyhedron which encloses any finite member of relative interior points of the polyhedron. We therefore state the following result.

Theorem 4.25. *Let Q be the set of r extreme points, $\mathbf{x}^1,\ldots,\mathbf{x}^r$, and $q-r$ extreme rays, $\mathbf{x}^{r+1},\ldots,\mathbf{x}^q$, and consider the polyhedron generated by Q,*

$$P(Q)=\left\{\mathbf{x}|\mathbf{x}=\sum_{i=1}^{r}\lambda_i\mathbf{x}^i+\sum_{i=r+1}^{q}\mu_i\mathbf{x}^i, \sum_{i=1}^{r}\lambda_i=1,\lambda_i,\mu_i\geq 0\right\}. \tag{4.83}$$

---

[7]For an alternative development of this result and its corollaries, see, for example, Zeleny [1974] and Yu and Zeleny [1976].

Let $P°(Q)$ *denote the relative interior of* $P(Q)$ *defined as in* (4.83), *but with* $\lambda_i > 0$, $\mu_i > 0$. *Then if a point* $\mathbf{x}° \in P°(Q)$ *is noninferior, so is every point in* $P(Q)$. *Moreover there exists a* $\mathbf{w}° \in W°$ *such that every* $\mathbf{x} \in P(Q)$ *solves* $P(\mathbf{w}°)$.

PROOF: We proceed by contradiction. Suppose there exists an $\hat{\mathbf{x}} \in P(Q)$ such that $\hat{\mathbf{x}}$ is not noninferior. We can always find a point on extreme rays $\hat{\mathbf{x}}^{r+1}, \ldots, \hat{\mathbf{x}}^q$ such that the set $\hat{Q} = \{\mathbf{x}^1, \ldots, \mathbf{x}^r, \hat{\mathbf{x}}^{r+1}, \ldots, \hat{\mathbf{x}}^q\}$ forms a convex hull enclosing both $\mathbf{x}°$ and $\hat{\mathbf{x}}$ with $\mathbf{x}° \in H°(\hat{Q}) \subseteq H(\hat{Q}) \subseteq P(Q)$. By Theorem 4.23, $H(\hat{Q}) \subseteq X^*$, contradicting the assumption that $\hat{\mathbf{x}} \in H(Q)$ is inferior. Hence we conclude that the entire $P(Q)$ is noninferior. By the same contradiction argument and Theorem 4.24, there can be no point $\hat{\mathbf{x}} \in P(Q)$ which does not solve $P(\mathbf{w}°)$ whose optimal solution is $\mathbf{x}°$. ■

To state the next result, we observe that the feasible region of a linear problem X is a convex polyhedron completely characterized by its sets of extreme points and extreme rays and that its outer surface is formed by a finite number of faces. Let $E(X)$ be the set of M extreme points and extreme rays of X and let $S \subset E(X)$. We call $\mathcal{F}$ a *face* of X if and only if i) $\mathcal{F}$ is a convex hull or a convex polyhedron generated by a subset of $E(X)$, and ii) there is a supporting hyperplane to X that contains $\mathcal{F}$. Note that not every subset of $E(X)$ generates a face. With these observations, we can state the following useful result.

Theorem 4.26. *In the LVOP in* (4.76)–(4.75), *if there exists a* $\mathbf{w}° \in W°$ *such that* $(\mathbf{w}°)^{\mathrm{T}} C\mathbf{x} \equiv \text{const}$, *then* $X^* = X$. *Otherwise* $X^* \subseteq \bigcup_{t=1}^{T} \mathcal{F}_t$, *where* $\mathcal{F}_t$ *is face t of X and T is the number of faces of X.*

PROOF: Clearly if there is a $\mathbf{w}° \in W°$ such that $(\mathbf{w}°)^{\mathrm{T}} C\mathbf{x}$ is identical to a constant, the objective function of $P(\mathbf{w}°)$ is just a constant. Hence any $\mathbf{x} \in X$ solves $P(\mathbf{w}°)$. By virtue of Theorem 4.22, $X \subseteq X^*$, which implies $X = X^*$. On the other hand, if for all $\mathbf{w}° \in W$, $(\mathbf{w}°)^{\mathrm{T}} C\mathbf{x}$, the objective function of $P(\mathbf{w}°)$, is always a nonconstant hyperplane in the decision space, then the solution of $P(\mathbf{w}°)$, which is just an ordinary linear programming problem, will always occur at the surface or a face of X for all $\mathbf{w}°$. This together with Theorem 4.22 ensures that

$$X^* \subseteq \bigcup_{t=1}^{T} \mathcal{F}_t \tag{4.84}$$

as required. ■

The result is quite useful, for it tells us that either the whole feasible region is noninferior or else all noninferior solutions lie on its surface. The former case requires no further work to generate noninferior solutions but is of little practical interest. Throughout the remainder of this chapter and in Chapter 6, we shall therefore deal exclusively with the latter case.

We call a face $\mathcal{F}$ a *noninferior face* if every point in $\mathcal{F}$ is noninferior. We also call $\mathcal{F}$ a *maximal noninferior face* if it is a noninferior face not contained in any other noninferior face. In other words, if $\mathcal{F}$ is a maximal noninferior face generated by $S \subseteq E(X)$, then there is no $S' \subseteq E(X)$ such that $S \subset S'$ and a face generated by S' is a noninferior face.

Theorem 4.27. *A face $\mathcal{F}$ of X is a noninferior face if and only if there exists a $\mathbf{w}^\circ \in W^\circ$ such that every $\mathbf{x} \in \mathcal{F}$ solves $P(\mathbf{w}^\circ)$.*

Since $\mathcal{F}$ is either a convex hull or a convex polyhedron, Theorem 4.27 follows from either Theorem 4.23 or 4.25, respectively.

Let us now investigate the relationships between the weighting characterization and the noninferior extreme points of X. To do this, let $E(X^*)$ be the set of noninferior extreme points or extreme rays of X^*. For any $\mathbf{x}^i \in E(X^*)$, let $W(\mathbf{x}^i)$ be

$$W(\mathbf{x}^i) \triangleq \{\mathbf{w} | \mathbf{w} \in W^\circ,\ \mathbf{x}^i \text{ solves } P(\mathbf{w})\}. \tag{4.85}$$

Clearly $W(\mathbf{x}^i)$ cannot be empty for each $\mathbf{x}^i$ in $E(X^*)$, for otherwise it cannot be noninferior. In fact, it can be shown that

$$\bigcup_{\mathbf{x}^i \in E(X^*)} W(\mathbf{x}^i) = W^\circ. \tag{4.86}$$

That the left-hand side of (4.86) is included in W° is obvious. We only need to show the reverse. Let $\mathbf{w}^\circ \in W^\circ$. We know from the elementary theory of linear programming that an optimal solution of $P(\mathbf{w}^\circ)$ must be an extreme point of X. In fact such an extreme point, being noninferior, must lie in $E(X^*)$. Consequently $\mathbf{w}^\circ \in \bigcup_{\mathbf{x}^i \in E(X^*)} W(\mathbf{x}^i)$, and (4.86) follows. In view of these observations, the following useful result is a corollary of Theorem 4.27.

Theorem 4.28. *Let a face $\mathcal{F}$ be generated by $S \subseteq E(X^*)$. Then $\mathcal{F}$ is a noninferior face if and only if*

$$\bigcap_{\mathbf{x}^i \in S} W(\mathbf{x}^i) \neq \varnothing. \tag{4.87}$$

We observe further that by definition and from (4.87) *the $\mathcal{F}$ generated by $S \subseteq E(X^*)$ is a maximal noninferior face if and only if*

$$\bigcap_{\mathbf{x}^i \in S} W(\mathbf{x}^i) \neq \varnothing; \tag{4.88a}$$

and

$$\bigcap_{\mathbf{x}^i \in S'} W(\mathbf{x}^i) = \varnothing \qquad \text{for all} \quad S \subset S' \subseteq E(X^*). \tag{4.88b}$$

Consequently if $\hat{\mathbf{x}}$ is a relative interior point of a maximal noninferior face $\mathcal{F}$ generated by $S \subseteq E(X^*)$, then $\hat{\mathbf{x}}$ solves $P(\mathbf{w})$ if and only if $\mathbf{w} \in \bigcap_{\mathbf{x}^i \in S} W(\mathbf{x}^i)$.

This simply means that two maximal noninferior faces cannot have a common characterizing weight vector.

The final result to be stated in this section will have a significant impact on the algorithmic development for linear problems, which we shall discuss in Section 6.2.3. In order to ensure that all noninferior solutions can be identified using some simplex-based procedure, we need to be sure that every noninferior extreme point in $E(X^*)$ can be reached through a series of noninferior extreme edges or noninferior extreme rays. Loosely speaking, if $E(X^*)$ has the above property, we say $E(X^*)$ is *connected*. Since an extreme edge is a line joining two adjacent extreme points, it is a face. By virtue of Theorem 4.28, an extreme edge joining two noninferior extreme points $\mathbf{x}^i$ and $\mathbf{x}^{i+1}$ is noninferior if and only if $W(\mathbf{x}^i)\cap W(\mathbf{x}^{i+1})\neq\varnothing$. Consequently $E(X^*)$ is *connected* in the above sense if and only if for every pair of noninferior extreme points $\mathbf{x}^\circ,\mathbf{x}^*$ in $E(X^*)$, there is a finite sequence of noninferior extreme points in $E(X^*)$, $\mathbf{x}^1,\ldots,\mathbf{x}^{q*}$, such that $\mathbf{x}^\circ=\mathbf{x}^1$, $\mathbf{x}^*=\mathbf{x}^{q*}$, and

$$W(\mathbf{x}^i)\cap W(\mathbf{x}^{i+1})\neq\varnothing \qquad \text{for all} \quad i=1,\ldots,q_*-1. \tag{4.89}$$

From a well-known topological result, if the sets A and B are not connected in the sense that $A\cap B=\varnothing$, then a portion of a line joining any point in A with any point in B will lie neither in A nor in B, as illustrated in Figure 4.9. We may therefore note that $E(X^*)$ is connected, for otherwise there would exist a pair $\{\mathbf{x}^\circ,\mathbf{x}^*\in E(X^*)\}$ and a pair $\{w^\circ\in W(\mathbf{x}^\circ),\ \mathbf{w}^*\in W(\mathbf{x}^*)\}$, with a portion of the line joining $\mathbf{w}^\circ$ and $\mathbf{w}^*$ not being covered by any one of the set $W(\mathbf{x}^i)$, where $x^i\in E(X^*)$. But this is impossible since every $\mathbf{w}$ of the form $\mathbf{w}=\lambda\mathbf{w}^\circ+(1-\lambda)\mathbf{w}^*$, $0\leqslant\lambda\leqslant 1$, is in W°, and thus lies in one of the $W(\mathbf{x}^i)$, $\mathbf{x}^i\in E(X^*)$, by virtue of (4.89). We summarize the above statement in the form of a theorem, which is also proved in Zeleny [1976] and Yu and Zeleny [1976].

Theorem 4.29. *The set $E(X^*)$ is connected in the sense given by* (4.89).

Figure 4.9 Two nonconnected sets.

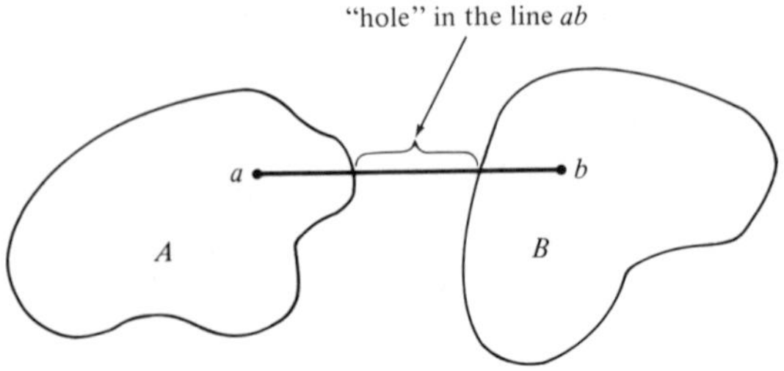

In Chapter 6 the significance and implications of the results stated in this section, particularly from the point of view of developing algorithms, will become evident. We briefly summarize them here. Theorem 4.26 indicates that, barring those problems that are usually of no practical interest, one need only search the surface or faces of the feasible region X in order to find the entire set of noninferior surfaces X^* for linear problems. Moreover, one need only look for maximal noninferior surfaces of X. Theorems 4.27 and 4.28 not only suggest the possibility of using appropriate weight vectors as identification parameters for maximal noninferior faces; they also imply that a maximal noninferior face can be conveniently found by identifying all noninferior extreme points or extreme rays characterized by a common weight vector. Finally, as remarked earlier, Theorem 4.29 guarantees that all noninferior extreme points will be discovered by a procedure that moves from one noninferior extreme point to the next along noninferior edges. This makes the application of a method such as the simplex algorithm not only feasible but also convenient.

4.9 Trade-offs on the (Local) Noninferior Surface[8]

Generating noninferior solutions serves only as an initial screening process in a multiobjective decision-making analysis. The next step is to select the "best" among noninferior alternatives. This task is not routine; it means finding some way of ordering those (noninferior) solutions in a *complete* order. The natural ordering relation $\geqslant$ in an n-dimensional Euclidean space is only a partial order, and hence inadequate for this purpose. By definition, two noninferior solutions are incomparable by the natural order $\geqslant$. Thus, to order the noninferior set completely we must call upon a new ordering relation, a *preference relation*, which reflects the preference structure of the decision maker.

Much of the effort behind theoretical and methodological developments in multiobjective decision making has been devoted, directly or indirectly, to the construction of the preference relation. Since considerable subjectivity and value judgement are involved, inaccuracy and inconsistency in the preference assessment process are commonly encountered.

The availability of additional information about the noninferior set would make the selection of the best alternative solution more accurate, consistent, and perhaps easier to perform. We shall describe the gradient, or tangent, of the noninferior surface, which in turn will yield information on the trade-off rates (among attributes) within the noninferior set.

---

[8] The material presented here is based on Haimes and Chankong [1979].

4.9.1 Trade-offs and Kuhn–Tucker Multipliers

First, recall that we use $P_k(\boldsymbol{\varepsilon})$ to denote the constraint problem of the form

$$\begin{aligned} &\min \quad f_k(\mathbf{x}) \\ &\text{subject to} \quad f_j(\mathbf{x}) \leqslant \varepsilon_j, \quad j=1,\ldots,n, \quad j \neq k, \\ &\qquad\qquad \mathbf{x} \in X, \end{aligned} \tag{4.90}$$

where $X=\{\mathbf{x}|\mathbf{x}\in R^N,\ g_i(x)\leqslant 0,\ i=1,\ldots,m\}$. The set of $\boldsymbol{\varepsilon}\in R^{n-1}$ for which $P_k(\boldsymbol{\varepsilon})$ is feasible is denoted Y_k. If $\mathbf{x}^*$ solves $P_k(\boldsymbol{\varepsilon})$ for some $\boldsymbol{\varepsilon}\in Y_k$, we shall use λ^*_{kj}, $j=1,\ldots,n$ and $j\neq k$, and μ^*_i, $i=1,\ldots,m$, to denote the Kuhn–Tucker multipliers associated with the f_j and g_i constraints, respectively. That is, we say that λ^*_{kj} and μ^*_i are the Kuhn–Tucker multipliers of $P_k(\boldsymbol{\varepsilon})$ at $\mathbf{x}^*$ if $(\mathbf{x}^*, \lambda^*_{k1},\ldots,\lambda^*_{kk-1}, \lambda^*_{kk+1},\ldots,\lambda^*_{kn},\ \mu^*_1,\ldots,\mu^*_m)$ satisfies the Kuhn–Tucker optimality conditions for $P_k(\boldsymbol{\varepsilon})$. We now restate a result of Section 2.3.3 in a form suitable to the present discussion.

Sensitivity Theorem. *Given $\boldsymbol{\varepsilon}^0\in Y_k$, let $\mathbf{x}^*$ solve $P_k(\boldsymbol{\varepsilon}^0)$ with $\lambda^*_{kj}, j\neq k$, being the corresponding Kuhn–Tucker multipliers associated with the constraints $f_j(\mathbf{x})\leqslant\varepsilon^0_j, j\neq k$. If*

i. *$\mathbf{x}^*$ is a regular point of the constraint of $P_k(\boldsymbol{\varepsilon}^0)$;*
ii. *the second-order sufficiency conditions are satisfied at $\mathbf{x}^*$; and*
iii. *there are no degenerate constraints at $\mathbf{x}^*$,*

then $\lambda^*_{kj} = -\partial f_k(\mathbf{x}^*)/\partial\varepsilon_j$ for all $j\neq k$.

Corollary 1. *If $\mathbf{x}^*$ solves $P_k(\boldsymbol{\varepsilon}^0)$ and satisfies* (i)–(iii), *then there exists a neighborhood $N(\boldsymbol{\varepsilon}^0)$ of $\boldsymbol{\varepsilon}^0$ such that, for all $\boldsymbol{\varepsilon}\in N(\boldsymbol{\varepsilon}^0)$, $\mathbf{x}(\boldsymbol{\varepsilon})$ which uniquely solves $P_k(\boldsymbol{\varepsilon})$ locally exists and is a continuously differentiable function of $\boldsymbol{\varepsilon}$ with $\mathbf{x}(\boldsymbol{\varepsilon}^0)=\mathbf{x}^*$.*

Corollary 2. *With all the hypotheses of the sensitivity theorem satisfied, there exists a neighborhood $N(\boldsymbol{\varepsilon}^0)$ of $\boldsymbol{\varepsilon}^0$ such that for each j such that $\lambda^*_{kj}>0$, $f_j(\mathbf{x}(\boldsymbol{\varepsilon}))=\varepsilon_j$ for all $\boldsymbol{\varepsilon}\in N(\boldsymbol{\varepsilon}^0)$.*

Corollaries 1 and 2 arise naturally from the sensitivity theorem, which relies heavily on the implicit function theorem.[9] It should be stressed here that Conditions (i), (ii), and (iii), required for the sensitivity interpretation of Kuhn–Tucker multipliers above, are merely sufficient conditions. In Section 4.9.2 we shall investigate another set of sufficient conditions applicable to the linear case. Also, as required by (ii), we shall assume throughout

[9] For a detailed proof of Corollary 1, see Chankong [1977].

the remainder of this chapter that all f_j and g_i are twice continuously differentiable.

For notational convenience in presenting the following results and without loss of generality, we shall use $P_n(\boldsymbol{\varepsilon})$ as a means of generating noninferior solutions.

Theorem 4.30. *Let* $\mathbf{x}^*$ *solve* $P_n(\boldsymbol{\varepsilon}^0)$ *(for some given* $\boldsymbol{\varepsilon}^0 \in Y_n$*) with*

i. $\mathbf{x}^*$ *a regular point of the constraint of* $P_k(\boldsymbol{\varepsilon}^0)$,
ii. *the second-order sufficiency conditions satisfied at* $\mathbf{x}^*$, *and*
iii. *all binding constraints at* $\mathbf{x}^*$ *nondegenerate.*

Let λ_{nj}^* *denote the optimal Kuhn–Tucker multipliers corresponding to the constraint* $f_j(x) \leqslant \varepsilon_j$. *Also assume without loss of generality that the first* p, $1 \leqslant p \leqslant n-1$, *of these multipliers are strictly positive and the remaining* $n-1-p$ *multipliers are zero (i.e.,* $\lambda_{kj}^* > 0$ *for all* $j = 1,\ldots,p$ *and* $\lambda_{kj}^* = 0$ *for all* $j = p+1,\ldots,n-1$).

a. *If* $\varepsilon_j^0 = f_j(\mathbf{x}^*)$ *for all* $j = 1,\ldots,n-1$ *(i.e.,* $p = n-1$*), there exists a neighborhood* $N(\mathbf{x}^*)$ *of* $\mathbf{x}^*$ *and a continuously differentiable vector-valued function* $\mathbf{x}(\ )$ *defined on some neighborhood* $N(\boldsymbol{\varepsilon}^0)$ *of* $\boldsymbol{\varepsilon}^0$ *such that*

$$X^* \cap N(\mathbf{x}^*) \subseteq \mathbf{x}\big(N(\boldsymbol{\varepsilon}^0)\big) \subseteq X^*, \tag{4.91}$$

where $\mathbf{x}(N(\boldsymbol{\varepsilon}^0))$ *is the image of* $N(\boldsymbol{\varepsilon}^0)$ *under the function* $\mathbf{x}(\ )$;

b. *Again, if* $p = n-1$ *and* $N(\mathbf{x}^*)$ *is obtained as in (a), let* $F^* \triangleq \{(f_1,\ldots,f_n) \mid f_j = f_j(\mathbf{x}),\ j = 1,\ldots,n,\ \mathbf{x} \in X^* \cap N(\mathbf{x}^*)\}$ *and let* $F_n^* \triangleq \{(f_1,\ldots,f_{n-1}) \mid f_j = f_j(\mathbf{x}),\ j = 1,\ldots,n-1,\ \mathbf{x} \in X^* \cap N(\mathbf{x}^*)\}$. *There exists a continuously differentiable function* $\bar{f}_n$ *defined on* F_n^* *such that for each* $(f_1,\ldots,f_n) \in F^*$, $f_n = \bar{f}_n(f_1,\ldots,f_{n-1})$. *Moreover for each* $1 \leqslant j \leqslant n-1$, $(\partial \bar{f}_n / \partial f_j)(f_1^*,\ldots,f_{n-1}^*) = -\lambda_{nj}^*$, *where* $f_j^* = f_j(\mathbf{x}^*)$.

c. *If* $1 \leqslant p < n-1$ *[i.e.,* $\varepsilon_j^0 > f_j(\mathbf{x}^*)$ *for some* $1 \leqslant j \leqslant n-1$*], let* $F_\varepsilon^* = \{(f_1,\ldots,f_n) \mid f_j = f_j(\mathbf{x}),\ j = 1,\ldots,n,\ \mathbf{x} \in \mathbf{x}[N(\boldsymbol{\varepsilon}^0)]\}$. *There exist continuously differentiable functions* $\bar{f}_n(\ ), \bar{f}_{p+1}(\ ),\ldots,\bar{f}_{n-1}(\ )$ *defined on* $N(\boldsymbol{\varepsilon}^0)$ *such that, for each* $(f_1,\ldots,f_n) \in F_\varepsilon^*$,

$$f_j = \bar{f}_j\big(f_1,\ldots,f_p,\varepsilon_{p+1}^0,\ldots,\varepsilon_{n-1}^0\big) \qquad \text{for all} \quad j = p+1,\ldots,n.$$

Moreover, for each $1 \leqslant l \leqslant p$,

$$\left.\frac{\partial \bar{f}_n}{\partial f_l}\right|_{\boldsymbol{\varepsilon}=\boldsymbol{\varepsilon}^0} = -\lambda_{nl}^* = \frac{[\nabla f_n(\mathbf{x}^*)\cdot \mathbf{d}_l^*]}{[\nabla f_l(\mathbf{x}^*)\cdot \mathbf{d}_l^*]},$$

where $\mathbf{d}^*$ *is the direction of* $\partial \mathbf{x}(\boldsymbol{\varepsilon}^0)/\partial \varepsilon_l$. *Also, for each* $p+1 \leqslant j \leqslant n-1$,

$$\left.\frac{\partial \bar{f}_j}{\partial f_l}\right|_{\boldsymbol{\varepsilon}=\boldsymbol{\varepsilon}^0} = \nabla f_j(\mathbf{x}^*)\cdot \frac{\partial \mathbf{x}(\boldsymbol{\varepsilon}^0)}{\partial \varepsilon_l}. \tag{4.92}$$

Before we prove the theorem it is appropriate to discuss its practical implications. In general, Theorem 4.30 enables one to make a comprehensive study of local properties of the local noninferior set, both in the decision and objective spaces. Part (a) indicates that, under the specified conditions and hypotheses, the locally noninferior surface in the neighborhood of $\mathbf{x}^*$ can be completely specified parametrically in terms of the $\boldsymbol{\varepsilon}$s. That is, there is a one-to-one correspondence between every local noninferior solution in the neighborhood of $\mathbf{x}^*$ and $\boldsymbol{\varepsilon}$ in the neighborhood $N(\boldsymbol{\varepsilon}^0)$ of $\boldsymbol{\varepsilon}^0$. Although the explicit form of such a parametric description is not generally known, the knowledge that it exists can be very useful in some theoretical or algorithmic developments. For example, suppose we want to find a local noninferior solution which maximizes a utility function $U(f_1,\ldots,f_n)$. On the locally noninferior surface in a neighborhood of $\mathbf{x}^*$, since all f_j are functions of $\mathbf{x}$, which is in turn a function of $\boldsymbol{\varepsilon}$, $U(\ )$ is an (implicit) function of $\boldsymbol{\varepsilon}$. Hence, instead of searching over $X^* \cap N(\mathbf{x}^*)$, we need only to search over $N(\boldsymbol{\varepsilon}^0)$, over which we have complete control.

Part (b) gives similar results but in the objective space. It states that, under the specified conditions and hypotheses, there are exactly $n-1$ degrees of freedom in specifying a point on the locally noninferior surface in a neighborhood of $f(\mathbf{x}^*)$, in the objective space. In fact, one can choose any values of $f_1,\ldots,f_{n-1}$ from $N(\boldsymbol{\varepsilon}^0)$ and compute f_n from $\bar{f}_n(f_1,\ldots,f_{n-1})$; the resulting point $(f_1,\ldots,f_n)$ will lie on the locally noninferior surface in the objective space. Most importantly, since $-\lambda^*_{nj} = (\partial \bar{f}_n/\partial f_j)(f^*_1,\ldots,f^*_{n-1})$ (for any $1 \leqslant j \leqslant n-1$), which represents the rate of change of f_n per unit change in f_j when all other objectives remain unchanged, $-\lambda^*_{nj}$ represents the *partial trade-off rate* between f_n and f_j and $\mathbf{x}^*$. This concept will be discussed in Chapter 7 (see also Haimes and Chankong [1979]).

Finally, part (c) extends somewhat the result in part (b) by relaxing one assumption. Among others, one of the assumptions required in (b) is that all constraints $f_j(\mathbf{x}) \leqslant \varepsilon^0_j$, $j=1,\ldots,n-1$, are binding at $\mathbf{x}^*$ (and nondegenerate) or $\lambda^*_{nj} > 0$ for all $j=1,\ldots,n-1$. If this assumption is violated, i.e., if there are only p nondegenerate binding constraints, where $1 \leqslant p < n-1$, then the degrees of freedom to specify a locally noninferior point in a neighborhood of $f(\mathbf{x}^*)$ in the objective space are exactly the number of nondegenerate binding constraints (p in this case). In particular, one can choose any values of $f_1,\ldots,f_p$ [in some neighborhood of $f_1(\mathbf{x}^*),\ldots,f_p(\mathbf{x}^*)$], then determine $f_{p+1},\ldots,f_{n-1}$ by some specific rules (to be denoted by $A_{p+1},\ldots,A_{n-1}$) defined in terms of $f_1,\ldots,f_p$, and finally compute f_n from a specified function of $f_1,\ldots,f_{n-1}$. The resulting point $(f_1,\ldots,f_n)$ will be a local noninferior solution in the objective space. These specific rules $A_{p+1},\ldots,A_{n-1}$ are generally point-to-set mappings defined on $N(\boldsymbol{\varepsilon}^0)$, and each f_j, $p+1 \leqslant j \leqslant n-1$, is chosen from $A_j(\ )$; i.e., $f_j \in A_j(f_1,\ldots,f_p, \varepsilon^0_{p+1},\ldots,\varepsilon^0_{n-1})$. Further investigation will show that A_j takes one of the following three forms: i) the set of points [on the real line in a neighborhood of $f_j(\mathbf{x}^*)$] less than or equal to $\bar{f}_j(f_1,\ldots,f_p,\ \varepsilon^0_{p+1},\ldots,\varepsilon^0_{n-1})$; ii) the single point $\bar{f}_j(f_1,\ldots,f_p,\ \varepsilon^0_{p+1},\ldots,\varepsilon^0_{n-1})$; or iii) the set of points (in a neighborhood of $f_j(\mathbf{x}^*)$) greater than or equal to $\bar{f}_j(f_1,\ldots,f_p,\ \varepsilon^0_{p+1},\ldots,\varepsilon^0_{n-1})$. (See the example in Section 4.9.2.) The criterion for deciding which of these forms A_j should take is complicated.

In part (c) we consider only those local noninferior solutions which correspond to the case $A_j \equiv \bar{f}_j$ and $f_n = \bar{f}_n(f_1,\ldots,f_{n-1})$. To remain within this special subset of local noninferior solutions, a small change ∂f_l in the level of the binding objective f_l $(l=1,\ldots,p)$, with all other *binding* objectives remaining unchanged, will induce the (approximate) change in f_n by $-\lambda^*_{nl}\,\partial f_l$ as well as approximate change in each f_j, $p+1 \leqslant j \leqslant n-1$, by $\nabla f_j(\mathbf{x}^*)\cdot(\partial \mathbf{x}(\boldsymbol{\varepsilon}^*)/\partial \varepsilon_l)\,\delta f_l$. In this case, $-\lambda^*_{nl}$ represents the *total trade-off rate* between f_n and f_l at $\mathbf{x}^*$ in the direction of $\partial \mathbf{x}(\boldsymbol{\varepsilon}^*)/\partial \varepsilon_l$ (see Chapter 7).

From a practical point of view parts (b) and (c) provide a convenient way of estimating "objective" trade-off information necessary for continuing into the analyst–DM interactive phase of the objective trade-off analysis. To see how this information may be used, suppose we have generated a noninferior solution $\mathbf{x}^0$ by solving $P_n(\boldsymbol{\varepsilon}^0)$ and with it have obtained $-\lambda^0_{nj}$ for all $j=1,\ldots,n-1$. If case (b) applies, then for each and every $j=1,\ldots,$ $n-1$, we may ask the DM the question: Given the current levels of objectives (i.e., $f_j = f_j(\mathbf{x}^0)$ for all $j=1,\ldots,n$), would you like to decrease f_n by λ^0_{nj} units per unit increase in f_j, all other objective levels remaining unchanged?

Or, when case (c) applies (i.e., $\lambda^0_{nj}>0$, $j=1,\ldots,p$, and $\lambda^0_{nj}=0$, $j=p+1,\ldots,n-1$), then for each and every $j=1,\ldots,p$ we may ask the DM the question, Given the current levels of objectives, would you like to decrease f_n by λ^0_{nj} units and change each f_j, $j=p+1,\ldots,n-1$, by $\nabla f_j(\mathbf{x}^0)\cdot[\partial \mathbf{x}(\boldsymbol{\varepsilon}^0)/\partial \varepsilon_l]$ units per unit increase in f_l, all other objective levels f_k, $k=1,\ldots,p$ and $k \neq l$, remaining unchanged?

The DM should respond by expressing his preference on the prescribed trade-off in some given ordinal scale. Although there are p questions [$p=n-1$ if (b) applies] to be asked, the DM will need to consider only one question at a time.

How to process the DM's response to arrive at the final solution is treated elsewhere. The *interactive surrogate worth trade-off method*, to be discussed in Chapter 8, utilizes the results developed in this section to complete the multiobjective decision-making process with an efficient analyst–DM interactive scheme.

PROOF OF THEOREM 4.30:

(a) From Corollary 1 of the sensitivity theorem, there exists a neighborhood $N(\boldsymbol{\varepsilon}^0)$ of $\boldsymbol{\varepsilon}^0$ such that for each $\boldsymbol{\varepsilon} \in N(\boldsymbol{\varepsilon}^0)$, $P_n(\boldsymbol{\varepsilon})$ has a strict local solution $\mathbf{x}(\boldsymbol{\varepsilon})$ and $\mathbf{x}(\boldsymbol{\varepsilon})$ is a continuously differentiable function of $\boldsymbol{\varepsilon}$ defined on $N(\boldsymbol{\varepsilon}^0)$. Thus, $\mathbf{x}(N(\boldsymbol{\varepsilon}^0)) \subseteq X^*$ easily follows from Theorem 4.20. To show the first part of (a) is to show that there exists a neighborhood $N(\mathbf{x}^*)$ of $\mathbf{x}^*$ such that for each $\hat{\mathbf{x}} \in X^* \cap N(\mathbf{x}^*)$, there exists $\boldsymbol{\varepsilon} \in N(\boldsymbol{\varepsilon}^0)$ such that $\hat{\mathbf{x}} = \mathbf{x}(\boldsymbol{\varepsilon})$.

We can construct such $N(x^*)$ in the following manner. Let $N(\boldsymbol{\varepsilon}^0) \triangleq \{\boldsymbol{\varepsilon} | \boldsymbol{\varepsilon} \in R^{n-1}, \|\boldsymbol{\varepsilon} - \boldsymbol{\varepsilon}^0\|_{\boldsymbol{\varepsilon}} < \delta_{\boldsymbol{\varepsilon}}\}$, where $\delta_{\boldsymbol{\varepsilon}} > 0$ and $\| \ \|_{\boldsymbol{\varepsilon}}$ is the l_p norm, $1 \leq p \leq \infty$, in R^{n-1}. By the continuity of f_j for each $1 \leq j \leq n-1$ in $\mathbf{x}$ there exists $\delta_j > 0$ such that

$$\|\mathbf{x} - \mathbf{x}^*\|_x < \delta_j \qquad \Rightarrow \qquad |f_j(\mathbf{x}) - f_j(\mathbf{x}^*)| < \delta_{\boldsymbol{\varepsilon}}/(n-1)^{1/p}.$$

Let $\delta \triangleq \min_{1 \leq j \leq n-1} \delta_j$. The set $N(\mathbf{x}^*) \triangleq \{\mathbf{x} | \mathbf{x} \in R^N, \|\mathbf{x} - \mathbf{x}^*\|_x < \delta\}$ is therefore the required neighborhood of $\mathbf{x}^*$.

Now, to complete the proof consider any $\hat{\mathbf{x}} \in X^* \cap N(\mathbf{x}^*)$. Define $\hat{\varepsilon}_j = f_j(\mathbf{x})$ for all $j = 1, \ldots, n-1$. Since $\hat{\mathbf{x}} \in N(\mathbf{x}^*)$ and $\varepsilon_j^0 = f_j(\mathbf{x}^*)$ for all $j = 1, \ldots, n-1$, it follows that $\hat{\boldsymbol{\varepsilon}} \in N(\boldsymbol{\varepsilon}^0)$. Hence, by definition of $N(\varepsilon^0)$, $P_n(\hat{\boldsymbol{\varepsilon}})$ has the unique local solution $\mathbf{x}(\hat{\boldsymbol{\varepsilon}})$. Also, since $\hat{\mathbf{x}} \in X^*$ by Theorem 4.19 $\hat{\mathbf{x}}$ is also a local solution of $P_n(\boldsymbol{\varepsilon})$. It immediately follows that $\hat{\mathbf{x}} = \mathbf{x}(\hat{\boldsymbol{\varepsilon}})$, which completes the proof of part (a).

(b) From (a), for any $\hat{\mathbf{x}} \in X^* \cap N(\mathbf{x}^*)$, there exists $\hat{\boldsymbol{\varepsilon}} \in N(\boldsymbol{\varepsilon}^0)$ so that $\hat{\mathbf{x}} = \mathbf{x}(\hat{\boldsymbol{\varepsilon}})$. Hence for all $\hat{\mathbf{x}} \in X^* \cap N(\mathbf{x}^*)$, $f_n(\hat{\mathbf{x}}) = f_n(\mathbf{x}(\hat{\boldsymbol{\varepsilon}})) \triangleq \bar{f}_n(\hat{\boldsymbol{\varepsilon}})$, where $\bar{f}_n(\ )$ is a function of $\boldsymbol{\varepsilon}$ defined on $N(\boldsymbol{\varepsilon}^0)$. The continuous differentiability of $\bar{f}_n(\ )$ follows from those of $f_n(\ )$ and $\mathbf{x}(\ )$. Also by Corollary 2 of the sensitivity theorem and by the definition of $\mathbf{x}(\ )$, we have for each $\hat{\mathbf{x}} \in X^* \cap N(\mathbf{x}^*)$, $f_j(\mathbf{x}) = \hat{\varepsilon}_j$ for all $j = 1, \ldots, n-1$. Hence, $f_n(\hat{\mathbf{x}}) = \bar{f}_n(f_1(\hat{\mathbf{x}}), \ldots, f_{n-1}(\hat{\mathbf{x}}))$ for each $\hat{\mathbf{x}} \in X^* \cap N(\mathbf{x}^*)$. Consequently for each $(f_1, \ldots, f_n) \in F^*$, $f_n = \bar{f}_n(f_1, \ldots, f_{n-1})$ as required.

Moreover, for each $j = 1, \ldots, n-1$

$$\frac{\partial \bar{f}_n}{\partial f_j}(f_1^*, \ldots, f_{n-1}^*) \equiv \frac{\partial \bar{f}_n(\boldsymbol{\varepsilon}^0)}{\partial \varepsilon_j} = -\lambda_{nj}^*, \tag{4.93}$$

where the equality is given by the sensitivity theorem.

(c) We again construct the required functions. By definition of $\mathbf{x}(\ )$ and $\mathbf{x}(N(\boldsymbol{\varepsilon}^0))$, for each $\hat{\mathbf{x}} \in \mathbf{x}(N(\boldsymbol{\varepsilon}^0))$ there exists $\hat{\boldsymbol{\varepsilon}} \in N(\boldsymbol{\varepsilon}^0)$ for which $\hat{\mathbf{x}} = x(\hat{\boldsymbol{\varepsilon}})$. Hence $f_j(\hat{\mathbf{x}}) = f_j(\mathbf{x}(\hat{\boldsymbol{\varepsilon}})) \equiv \bar{f}_j(\hat{\boldsymbol{\varepsilon}})$ for all $j = p+1, \ldots, n-1, n$. Further, by Corollary 2 of the sensitivity theorem, $f_l(\hat{\mathbf{x}}) = \hat{\varepsilon}_l$ for all $l = 1, \ldots, p$. Hence for each $j = p+1, \ldots, n$, $f_j(\hat{\mathbf{x}}) = \bar{f}_j(f_1(\hat{\mathbf{x}}), \ldots, f_p(\hat{\mathbf{x}}), \hat{\varepsilon}_{p+1}, \ldots, \hat{\varepsilon}_{n-1})$ for all $\hat{\mathbf{x}} \in \mathbf{x}(N(\hat{\boldsymbol{\varepsilon}}))$, which shows that $\bar{f}_j(\ )$, $j = p+1, \ldots, n$, are the required functions.

It is now simple to prove (c). First observe that for any $1 \leq l \leq p$

$$\left.\frac{\partial \bar{f}_n}{\partial f_l}\right|_{\boldsymbol{\varepsilon} = \boldsymbol{\varepsilon}^0} \equiv \left.\frac{\partial \bar{f}_n}{\partial \varepsilon_l}\right|_{\boldsymbol{\varepsilon} = \boldsymbol{\varepsilon}^0} = -\lambda_{nl}^*, \tag{4.94}$$

where again the equality is given by the sensitivity theorem.

Moreover, since for each $1 \leqslant l \leqslant p$, $f_l(\mathbf{x}(\boldsymbol{\varepsilon})) = \varepsilon_l$ for all $\boldsymbol{\varepsilon} \in N(\boldsymbol{\varepsilon}^0)$, by the chain rule

$$1 = \left.\frac{\partial \bar{f}_l}{\partial \varepsilon_l}\right|_{\boldsymbol{\varepsilon} = \boldsymbol{\varepsilon}^0} = \nabla f_l(\mathbf{x}^*) \cdot \frac{\partial \mathbf{x}(\boldsymbol{\varepsilon}^0)}{\partial \varepsilon_l}. \tag{4.95}$$

Also

$$\left.\frac{\partial \bar{f}_n}{\partial \varepsilon_l}\right|_{\boldsymbol{\varepsilon} = \boldsymbol{\varepsilon}^0} = \nabla f_n(\mathbf{x}^*) \cdot \frac{\partial \mathbf{x}(\boldsymbol{\varepsilon}^0)}{\partial \varepsilon_l}.$$

Hence

$$-\lambda^*_{nl} = \frac{\nabla f_n(\mathbf{x}^*) \cdot \partial \mathbf{x}(\boldsymbol{\varepsilon}^0)/\partial \varepsilon_l}{\nabla f_l(\mathbf{x}^*) \cdot \partial \mathbf{x}(\boldsymbol{\varepsilon}^0)/\partial \varepsilon_l} = \frac{\nabla f_n(\mathbf{x}^*) \cdot \mathbf{d}^*_l}{\nabla f_l(\mathbf{x}^*) \cdot \mathbf{d}^*_l}. \tag{4.96}$$

Finally, for each $1 \leqslant l \leqslant p$ and $p+1 \leqslant j \leqslant n-1$, by the chain rule,

$$\left.\frac{\partial \bar{f}_j}{\partial f_l}\right|_{\boldsymbol{\varepsilon} = \boldsymbol{\varepsilon}^0} \equiv \left.\frac{\partial \bar{f}_j}{\partial \varepsilon_l}\right|_{\boldsymbol{\varepsilon} = \boldsymbol{\varepsilon}^0} = \nabla f_j(\mathbf{x}^*) \cdot \frac{\partial \mathbf{x}(\boldsymbol{\varepsilon}^0)}{\partial \varepsilon_l}. \quad \blacksquare \tag{4.97}$$

When addressing minimax functions, where the differentiability assumption no longer prevails, trade-off relationships similar to (4.105) and (4.108) can still be derived, as developed in the Appendix.

4.9.2 *Trade-offs and Simplex Multipliers in Linear Problems*

So far we have insisted on using the regularity, second-order sufficiency, and nondegeneracy conditions as the underlying assumptions on which our results have been developed. It has been pointed out, however, that those conditions are merely sufficient, not necessary. For example, for a linear case the second-order sufficiency condition[10] is never satisfied, since the Hessian matrix of a linear Lagrangian is always a zero matrix. Yet similar *shadow price* interpretations of Lagrange multipliers for LP problems have long been known [Dantzig, 1963].

---

[10] The second-order sufficiency condition requires that the Hessian of the Lagrangian function of $P_k(\boldsymbol{\varepsilon})$,

$$L_k(\mathbf{x}, \boldsymbol{\lambda}, \boldsymbol{\mu}) = f_k(\mathbf{x}) + \sum_{j \neq k}^{n} \lambda_j [f_j(\mathbf{x}) - \varepsilon_j] + \sum_{i=1}^{n} \mu_i g_i(\mathbf{x}),$$

be positive definite on the subspace corresponding to the supporting hyperplane to the nondegenerate binding constraints surface.

In solving linear $P_k(\boldsymbol{\varepsilon}^0)$ a special technique, such as the simplex method (or any of its variants), is normally used. As a result, the simplex multipliers

$$\boldsymbol{\pi}^0 = \left(-\lambda_{k1}^0, \ldots, -\lambda_{k,k-1}^0, -\lambda_{k,k+1}^0, \ldots, -\lambda_{kn}^0, -\mu_1^0, \ldots, -\mu_m^0\right) \tag{4.98}$$

are also generated. Suppose $\mathbf{x}^0$ solves a linear $P_k(\boldsymbol{\varepsilon}^0)$, having $\mathbf{x}_B^0$ as the optimal basic variables and $\boldsymbol{\pi}^0$ as the corresponding simplex multipliers. Let $B(\boldsymbol{\varepsilon}^0)$ be the coefficient matrix of the optimal basic variables and $\mathbf{c}_{B(\boldsymbol{\varepsilon}^0)}$ be the cost coefficients of the optimal basic variables. It is known (see Dantzig [1963], for example) that $B(\boldsymbol{\varepsilon}^0)$ is nonsingular and $\boldsymbol{\pi}^0 = \mathbf{c}_{B(\boldsymbol{\varepsilon}^0)} B(\boldsymbol{\varepsilon}^0)^{-1}$. Furthermore, if

$$\mathbf{b}(\boldsymbol{\varepsilon}^0) = \left(\varepsilon_1^0, \ldots, \varepsilon_{k-1}^0, \varepsilon_{k+1}^0, \ldots, \varepsilon_n^0, 0, \ldots, 0\right)^{\mathrm{T}}, \tag{4.99}$$

then

$$\mathbf{x}_B^0 = B(\boldsymbol{\varepsilon}^0)^{-1}\mathbf{b}(\boldsymbol{\varepsilon}^0) \tag{4.100}$$

and

$$f_k(\mathbf{x}^0) = \mathbf{c}_{B(\boldsymbol{\varepsilon}^0)} \cdot \mathbf{x}_B^0 = \mathbf{c}_{B(\boldsymbol{\varepsilon}^0)} B(\boldsymbol{\varepsilon}^0)^{-1}\mathbf{b}(\boldsymbol{\varepsilon}^0) = \boldsymbol{\pi}^0 \cdot \mathbf{b}(\boldsymbol{\varepsilon}^0). \tag{4.101}$$

Moreover, if each component of $\mathbf{x}_B^0$ is positive (or nonzero) (the nondegenerate case), then there exists a neighborhood of $\boldsymbol{\varepsilon}^0, N(\boldsymbol{\varepsilon}^0)$, such that for all $\boldsymbol{\varepsilon} \in N(\boldsymbol{\varepsilon}^0)$, the optimal set of basic variables of $P_k(\boldsymbol{\varepsilon})$ does not change; i.e., $B(\boldsymbol{\varepsilon}) = B(\boldsymbol{\varepsilon}^0)$ and $\mathbf{c}_{B(\boldsymbol{\varepsilon})} = \mathbf{c}_{B(\boldsymbol{\varepsilon}^0)}$. Hence, $\boldsymbol{\pi}(\boldsymbol{\varepsilon}) = \boldsymbol{\pi}(\boldsymbol{\varepsilon}^0) \triangleq \boldsymbol{\pi}^0$ for all $\boldsymbol{\varepsilon} \in N(\boldsymbol{\varepsilon}^0)$. Also, $\mathbf{x}_B(\boldsymbol{\varepsilon}) = B(\boldsymbol{\varepsilon}^0)^{-1}\mathbf{b}(\boldsymbol{\varepsilon})$, which is a continuously differentiable (linear) function of $\boldsymbol{\varepsilon}$. From this, two conclusions follow: i) Since $f_k(\mathbf{x}(\boldsymbol{\varepsilon})) = \boldsymbol{\pi}^0\mathbf{b}(\boldsymbol{\varepsilon})$ for all $\boldsymbol{\varepsilon} \in N(\boldsymbol{\varepsilon}^0)$, then $-\lambda_{kj}^0 = \partial f_k(\mathbf{x}^0)/\partial \varepsilon_j$ for all $j \neq k$; and ii) since the set of optimal basic variables does not change with $\boldsymbol{\varepsilon}$ in $N(\boldsymbol{\varepsilon}^0)$, we conclude that any constraints that are binding at $\mathbf{x}^0$ will also be binding at $\mathbf{x}(\boldsymbol{\varepsilon})$; i.e., $f_j(\mathbf{x}(\boldsymbol{\varepsilon})) = \varepsilon_j$ for all j so that $\lambda_{kj}^0 > 0$ and for all $\boldsymbol{\varepsilon} \in N(\boldsymbol{\varepsilon}^0)$.

We have established equivalent statements of the sensitivity theorem and its two corollaries using the existence of $B(\boldsymbol{\varepsilon}^0)^{-1}$ and nondegeneracy as underlying assumptions. From here we can proceed as before, arriving at the same relationships between trade-offs and Lagrange multipliers (or simplex multipliers) as in nonlinear cases.

We summarize these results in a theorem:

Theorem 4.31 (linear case). *Let f_j, $j = 1, \ldots, n$, and g_i, $i = 1, \ldots, m$, be linear. For some given $\boldsymbol{\varepsilon}^0 \in R^{n-1}$, let $\mathbf{x}^*$ be a nondegenerate solution of $P_k(\boldsymbol{\varepsilon}^0)$ and let $-\lambda_{kj}^*$ denote the optimal simplex multipliers corresponding to the constraint $f_j(\mathbf{x}) \leq \varepsilon_j$, $j \neq k$. Then Theorem* 4.30 *holds at $\mathbf{x}^*$ for the linear case.*

4.9.3 Example

We end this chapter with a simple numerical example. Consider again a convex vector optimization problem (see Section 4.3.2) VOP_1:

$$\min_{\mathbf{x}\in X} \quad [f_1(\mathbf{x}), f_2(\mathbf{x}), f_3(\mathbf{x})], \tag{4.102}$$

where $f_1(\mathbf{x})=(x_1-3)^2+(x_2-2)^2$, $f_2(\mathbf{x})=x_1+x_2$, $f_3(\mathbf{x})=x_1+2x_2$, and $X=\{\mathbf{x}|\mathbf{x}\in R^2,\ g_1(\mathbf{x})=-x_1\leqslant 0$ and $g_2(\mathbf{x})=-x_2\leqslant 0\}$.

Taking f_1 as the primary objective, the corresponding ε-constraint problem is $P_1(\varepsilon_2, \varepsilon_3)$:

$$\min \quad f_1(\mathbf{x}) \tag{4.103}$$

$$\text{subject to} \quad f_2(\mathbf{x}) = x_1 + x_2 \leqslant \varepsilon_2, \tag{4.104a}$$

$$f_3(\mathbf{x}) = x_1 + 2x_2 \leqslant \varepsilon_3, \tag{4.104b}$$

$$g_1(\mathbf{x}) \quad -x_1 \leqslant 0, \tag{4.104c}$$

$$g_2(\mathbf{x}) \quad -x_2 \leqslant 0. \tag{4.104d}$$

As we have shown in Section 4.3.2, those and only those points that lie i) on the line OA and ii) within and on the boundary of the triangle PAB in Figure 4.10 are noninferior solutions of VOP_1. By applying Theorems 4.21 and 4.13 we can determine that each point in the interior of PAB is a proper noninferior solution of VOP_1, whereas each point on the lines PA and PB is improperly noninferior.

Figure 4.10 Graphical solution of $P_1(2.5, 3)$.

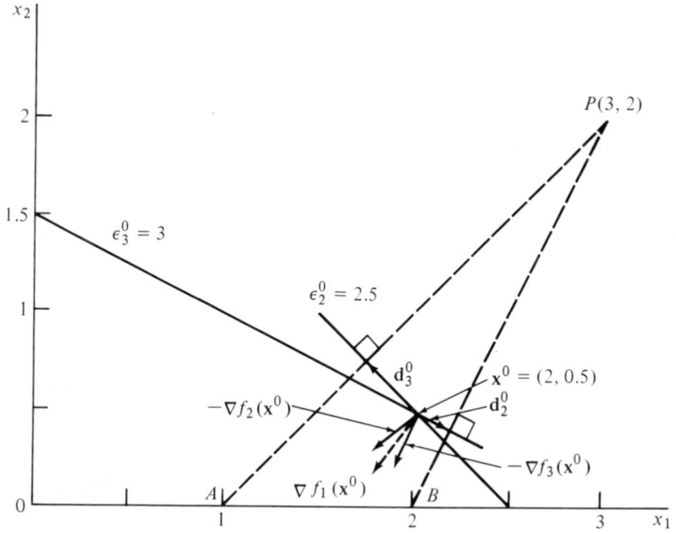

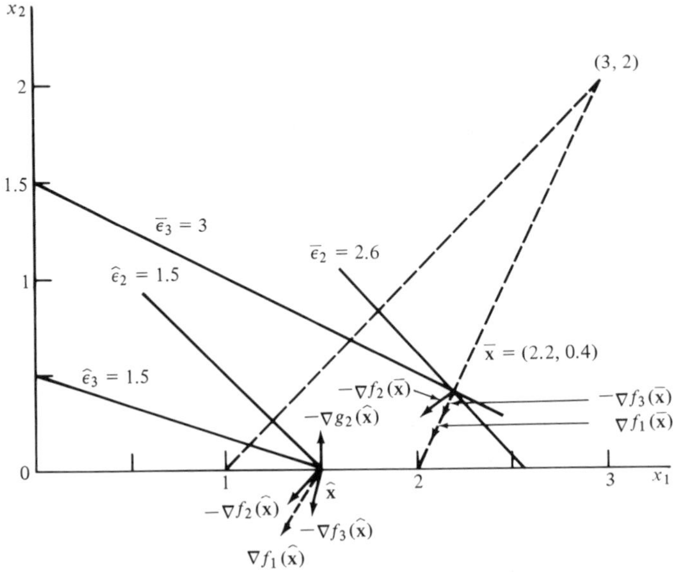

Figure 4.11 Graphical solution of $P_1(2.6, 3)$.

The only portion of PAB that has not been accounted for is the line AB. Along this line, Theorem 4.13 fails to apply either way, owing to failure of the regularity assumption. Consider, for example, the point $\hat{\mathbf{x}} = (1.5, 0)$ and the corresponding ε-constraint problem $P_1(\hat{\varepsilon}_2, \hat{\varepsilon}_3)$, where $(\hat{\varepsilon}_2, \hat{\varepsilon}_3) = (f_2(\hat{\mathbf{x}}), f_3(\hat{\mathbf{x}})) = (1.5, 1.5)$. Although $\hat{\mathbf{x}}$ solves (uniquely) $P_1(\hat{\varepsilon}_2, \hat{\varepsilon}_3)$, it is not a regular point since there are three binding constraints at that point (see Figure 4.11) and there is no way three vectors can be linearly independent in a two-dimensional plane. It can, however, be shown, with the aid of Geoffrion's theorem 4.11a, that each point along the line AB (excluding A and B) is properly noninferior.

Note that—irrespective of $\mathbf{x}$, λ_{12}, λ_{13}, μ_1, and μ_2—the Hessian matrix $H(\mathbf{x}, \lambda_{12}, \lambda_{13}, \mu_1, \mu_2)$ of the Lagrangian function of VOP_1 is $2I$, where I is the 2×2 identity matrix. Thus, irrespective of its argument, $H(\ )$ is positive definite in R^2 or any of its subsets (including X and any subsets of X). We have, therefore, justified that the second-order sufficiency conditions for strict optimality always prevail.

Now, we consider the point $\mathbf{x}^0 = (2, 0.5)$ and the corresponding problem $P_1(\varepsilon_2^0, \varepsilon_3^0)$, where $(\varepsilon_2^0, \varepsilon_3^0) = (2.5, 3)$ (see Figure 4.10). At this point we have $\nabla f_1(\mathbf{x}^0) = (-2, -3)^T$, $\nabla f_2(\mathbf{x}^0) = (1, 1)^T$, and $\nabla f_3(\mathbf{x}^0) = (1, 2)^T$. Since $\mathbf{x}^0$ is the (unique) solution of $P_1(\varepsilon_2^0, \varepsilon_3^0)$ as well as a regular point and since the gradients of binding constraints $\nabla f_2(\mathbf{x}^0)$ and $\nabla f_3(\mathbf{x}^0)$ are linearly independent, the Kuhn–Tucker conditions must be satisfied. In particular, we must have

$$\nabla f_1(\mathbf{x}^0)+\lambda_{12}^0\nabla f_2(\mathbf{x}^0)+\lambda_{13}^0\nabla f_3(\mathbf{x}^0)=0, \tag{4.105}$$

which implies $\lambda_{12}^0=1$ and $\lambda_{13}^0=1$.

Also, because of the simplicity of the problem, we can obtain several quantities and expressions. First, we have $N(\boldsymbol{\varepsilon}^0)$, a neighborhood of $\boldsymbol{\varepsilon}^0$ such that there exists a continuously differentiable function $\mathbf{x}$: $N(\boldsymbol{\varepsilon}^0)\to R^n$ defined by the following rule: For each $\boldsymbol{\varepsilon}\in N(\boldsymbol{\varepsilon}^0)$, $\mathbf{x}(\boldsymbol{\varepsilon})$ solves $P_1(\boldsymbol{\varepsilon})$.

There are many such neighborhoods, including

$$N_1(\boldsymbol{\varepsilon}^0)=\{(\varepsilon_2,\varepsilon_3)|\varepsilon_2=2.5,\ \tfrac{17}{6}<\varepsilon_3<\tfrac{13}{4}\},$$

$$N_2(\boldsymbol{\varepsilon}^0)=\{(\varepsilon_2,\varepsilon_3)|\tfrac{7}{3}<\varepsilon_2<\tfrac{13}{5},\ \varepsilon_3=3\},$$

$$N_3(\boldsymbol{\varepsilon}^0)=\{(\varepsilon_2,\varepsilon_3)|2.417<\varepsilon_2<2.552,\ 2.92<\varepsilon_3<3.125\}.$$

Second, we compute $\mathbf{x}(\boldsymbol{\varepsilon})$, $\partial\mathbf{x}(\boldsymbol{\varepsilon}^0)/\partial\varepsilon_2$, and $\partial\mathbf{x}(\boldsymbol{\varepsilon}^0)/\partial\varepsilon_3$, taking $N(\boldsymbol{\varepsilon}^0)=N_3(\boldsymbol{\varepsilon}^0)$.

The simplicity of the problem permits us to find an analytical expression for $\mathbf{x}(\boldsymbol{\varepsilon})$ (defined above). For any $\boldsymbol{\varepsilon}\in N(\boldsymbol{\varepsilon}^0)$, the unique solution of $P_1(\boldsymbol{\varepsilon})$ is always the point of intersection of the two constraints, $f_2(\mathbf{x})\leqslant\varepsilon_2$ and $f_3(\mathbf{x})\leqslant\varepsilon_3$ (see Figure 4.10). Thus for any $\boldsymbol{\varepsilon}\in N(\boldsymbol{\varepsilon}^0)$, $\mathbf{x}(\boldsymbol{\varepsilon})$, the solution of $P_1(\boldsymbol{\varepsilon})$, is given by

$$f_2(\mathbf{x})=x_1+x_2=\varepsilon_2, \tag{4.106a}$$

$$f_3(\mathbf{x})=x_1+2x_2=\varepsilon_3. \tag{4.106b}$$

Thus

$$\mathbf{x}(\boldsymbol{\varepsilon})=\begin{pmatrix}x_1(\boldsymbol{\varepsilon})\\ x_2(\boldsymbol{\varepsilon})\end{pmatrix}=\begin{pmatrix}2\varepsilon_2-\varepsilon_3\\ \varepsilon_3-\varepsilon_2\end{pmatrix}. \tag{4.106c}$$

Hence,

$$\mathbf{d}_2^0\triangleq\left.\frac{\partial\mathbf{x}(\boldsymbol{\varepsilon})}{\partial\varepsilon_2}\right|_{\boldsymbol{\varepsilon}=\boldsymbol{\varepsilon}^0}=\begin{pmatrix}2\\-1\end{pmatrix}\quad\text{and}\quad\mathbf{d}_3^0\triangleq\left.\frac{\partial\mathbf{x}(\boldsymbol{\varepsilon})}{\partial\varepsilon_3}\right|_{\boldsymbol{\varepsilon}=\boldsymbol{\varepsilon}^0}=\begin{pmatrix}-1\\1\end{pmatrix}.$$

The directions of $\mathbf{d}_2^0$ and $\mathbf{d}_3^0$ are shown in Figure 4.10.

Next examine $f_1(f_2,f_3)$. Observe that for all $\boldsymbol{\varepsilon}\in N(\boldsymbol{\varepsilon}^0)$ the constraints $f_2(\mathbf{x})\leqslant\varepsilon_2$ and $f_3(\mathbf{x})\leqslant\varepsilon_3$ are always binding at the optimal solution $\mathbf{x}(\boldsymbol{\varepsilon})$ of $P_1(\boldsymbol{\varepsilon})$, i.e., $f_2(\mathbf{x}(\boldsymbol{\varepsilon}))=\varepsilon_2$ and $f_3(\mathbf{x}(\boldsymbol{\varepsilon}))=\varepsilon_3$. Clearly, for each $\boldsymbol{\varepsilon}\in N(\boldsymbol{\varepsilon}^0)$,

$$f_1(\mathbf{x}(\boldsymbol{\varepsilon}))=[(2\varepsilon_2-\varepsilon_3)-3]^2+[(\varepsilon_3-\varepsilon_2)-2]^2,$$

$$f_1(f_2,f_3)=(2f_2-f_3-3)^2+(f_3-f_2-2)^2. \tag{4.107}$$

Hence $\partial f_1(\mathbf{x}^0)/\partial f_2=-1=-\lambda_{12}^0$ and $\partial f_1(\mathbf{x}^0)/\partial f_3=-1=-\lambda_{13}^0$.

An operational meaning of these results is that the DM may want to find a new alternative (rather than stay with $\mathbf{x}^0$). For example, it might be best to let the level of f_3 be *at most* as high as before and to let the level of f_2

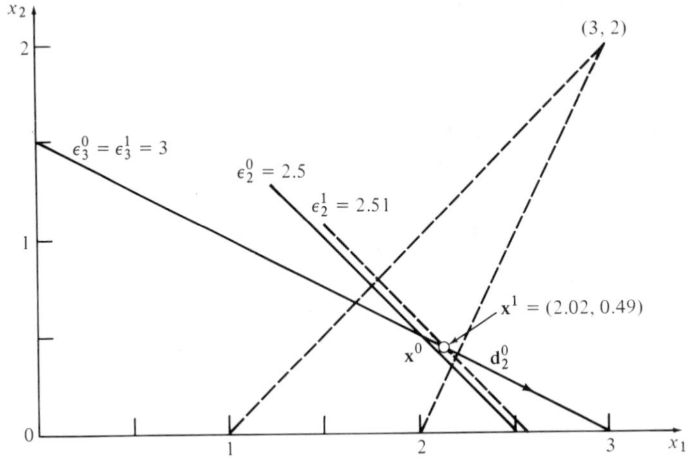

Figure 4.12 Graphical solution of $P_1(2.51,3)$.

increase by at most $\delta\varepsilon_2$, where $0<\delta\varepsilon_2\leqslant 1$. Then, according to this resolution, there is no better alternative than $\mathbf{x}^1=\mathbf{x}(\varepsilon_2+\delta\varepsilon_2,\varepsilon_3)$, at which $f_2(\mathbf{x}^1)=\varepsilon_2^0+\delta\varepsilon_2$, $f_3(\mathbf{x}^1)=\varepsilon_3^0$, and $f_1(\mathbf{x}^1)=[2f_2(\mathbf{x}^1)-f_3(\mathbf{x}^1)-3]^2+[f_3(\mathbf{x}^1)-f_2(\mathbf{x}^1)-2]^2$, or approximately $f_1(\mathbf{x}^1)$ given by $f_1(\mathbf{x}^0)+\lambda_{12}^0\,\delta\varepsilon_2$. Moreover, in moving from $\mathbf{x}^0$ to $\mathbf{x}^1$, we have moved in the direction $\mathbf{d}_2^0$ in the (x_1,x_2) decision space. For example, if $\delta\varepsilon_2=0.01$, the new noninferior alternative $\mathbf{x}^1$, as shown in Figure 4.12, is (2.02,0.49), at which $f_2(\mathbf{x}^1)=2.51$, $f_3(\mathbf{x}^1)=3$, and $f_1(\mathbf{x}^1)=3.2405$ (exactly). Thus, the change in f_1, which is exactly -0.0095 units, is approximately given by $-\lambda_{12}^0\,\delta\varepsilon_2(=-0.01$ units), thereby justifying the use of $-\lambda_{12}^0$ as an approximation of the noninferior partial trade-off rate at $\mathbf{x}^0$. Similar examples involving λ_{13}^0 can be constructed.

Next, we consider the nondegeneracy and nonbinding cases. Suppose we set $\varepsilon_3=3$ and ε_2 to be 2.6 or greater (see Figure 4.13). The unique solution of $P_1(\varepsilon_2,3)$ is always $\bar{\mathbf{x}}=(2.2,0.4)$. In particular, when $\varepsilon_2 \geq 2.6$, the constraint $f_2(x)\leqslant\varepsilon_2$ will always be nonbinding (and hence $\bar{\lambda}_{12}=0$). If we attempt to make this binding by setting $\varepsilon_2=2.6$, we run into another problem; the constraint $f_2(\mathbf{x})\leqslant 2.6$, although binding, is now degenerate since the corresponding optimal Kuhn–Tucker multiplier $\bar{\lambda}_{12}$ is still zero. It can be shown that there exists no neighborhood $N(\bar{\boldsymbol{\varepsilon}})$, where $\bar{\boldsymbol{\varepsilon}}=(2.6,3)$ on which a continuously differentiable function $\mathbf{x}$ could be defined such that $\mathbf{x}(\boldsymbol{\varepsilon})$ solves $P_1(\boldsymbol{\varepsilon})$ for each $\varepsilon\in N(\bar{\boldsymbol{\varepsilon}})$.

Here $\bar{\lambda}_{12}$ (which is equal to 1.6) represents the total trade-off rate (at $\bar{\mathbf{x}}$) between f_1 and f_2 along $\bar{\mathbf{d}}$, as indicated in Figure 4.9. However, $\bar{\lambda}_{13}=0$ does not represent a trade-off rate (at $\bar{\mathbf{x}}$) between f_1 and f_3.

To illustrate the result in Theorem 4.30(c), suppose that $\bar{\mathbf{x}}$ and $\bar{\lambda}_{12}$ are obtained by solving $P_1(\varepsilon_2,3)$, where $\varepsilon_2>2.6$ (i.e., the nonbinding constraint

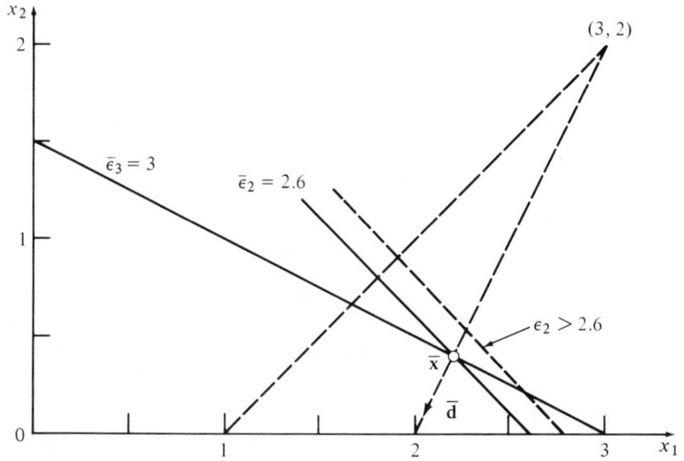

Figure 4.13 Graphical solution of $P_1(\varepsilon_2, 3)$, $\varepsilon_2 \geqslant 2.6$.

case). Now there exists a neighborhood $N(\varepsilon_2, 3)$ around $(\varepsilon_2, 3)$ such that for every $\boldsymbol{\varepsilon} \in N(\varepsilon_2, 3)$, there exists $\mathbf{x}(\boldsymbol{\varepsilon})$ that solves $P_1(\boldsymbol{\varepsilon})$, so that $\mathbf{x}(\boldsymbol{\varepsilon})$ is a continuously differentiable function of $\boldsymbol{\varepsilon}$. In fact, $\mathbf{x}(\boldsymbol{\varepsilon})$ will move along the line OB. Observe that we deliberately make the constraint $f_2(\mathbf{x}) \leqslant \varepsilon_2$ nonbinding throughout so that it will not have an active and direct role in determining the optimal solution of $P_1(\boldsymbol{\varepsilon})$. Observe also that each time there is a change in the optimal solution from $\bar{\mathbf{x}}$ to $\mathbf{x}(\varepsilon)$ due to a change in ε_3, the levels of f_1 and f_2 also change. In particular, if f_3 changes by $\delta\varepsilon_3$ and ε_2 remains constant, then the change in f_1 is approximately $-\bar{\lambda}_{12}\,\delta\varepsilon_3$ and the change in f_2 is about $\nabla f_3(\varepsilon_2, \varepsilon_3) \cdot [\partial \mathbf{x}(\varepsilon_2, \varepsilon_3)/\partial \varepsilon_3]\,\boldsymbol{\delta}\varepsilon_3 = \frac{1}{3}\boldsymbol{\delta}\varepsilon_3$.

Figure 4.14 Graphical solution of $P_1(\varepsilon_2, 1.5)$, $\varepsilon_2 > 1.5$.

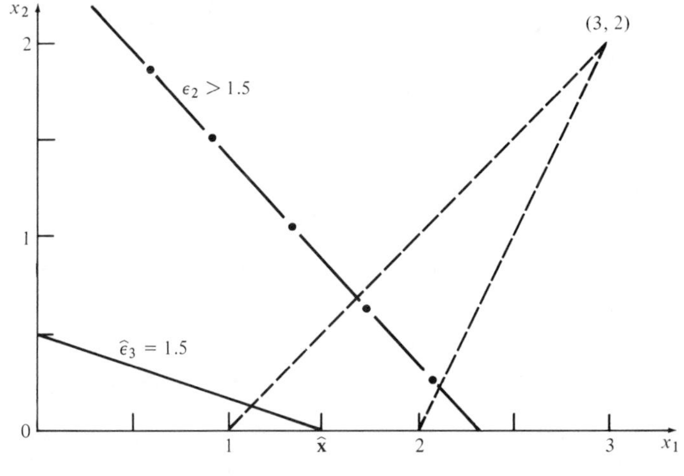

4.10 Summary

There is a class of multiobjective decision problems in which generating noninferior solutions is a suitable initial screening process. Theoretical machinery for carrying out such a task has been developed in this chapter. Various ways of scalarizing a vector optimization problem, leading to various ways of characterizing noninferior solutions in terms of optimal solutions of appropriate scalar optimization problems, have been described. Results for the three common methods of characterization—the ε-constraint approach, the weighting approach, and the Lagrangian approach—were discussed and their interrelationships summarized. Convexity, stability, regularity, and other constraint qualifications were found to play important roles in these characterizations. Other forms of scalarizations, and hence characterizations; also treated were the weighted-norm approach, Lin's proper equality constraint approach, the hybrid (weighting-constraint) approach, and an approach used for testing noninferiority of a given point. A number of special results which describe the general properties of the set of noninferior solutions for linear problems were also discussed. These results form the underlying basis of many of the methodologies to follow in Part II.

The concepts of local noninferior solution, proper noninferior solution, and special results for linear cases were introduced, and various necessary and sufficient conditions for each were developed. Finally, through the solution of the ε-constraint problem and through the sensitivity interpretation of the Kuhn–Tucker multipliers associated with this solution, some local properties of the noninferior surface of a VOP, both in the decision and objective spaces, were investigated. It was noted that the gradient of the noninferior surface at a given point $\mathbf{x}^*$ (on the surface) can be determined from the values of the corresponding Kuhn–Tucker multipliers associated with the ε-constraint problem to which $\mathbf{x}^*$ is the strict local solution. This leads to the trade-off intepretation of such multipliers, thereby providing a convenient way of obtaining necessary information for continuing into the analyst–decision maker interactive mode of the multiobjective decision-making process.

References

Arrow, K. J., Barankin, E. W., and Blackwell, D. (1953). Admissible points of convex sets, in *Contributions to the Theory of Games* (H. W. Kuhn and A. W. Tucker, eds.), Princeton University Press, Princeton, New Jersey, pp. 87–91.

Benayoun, R., de Montgolfier, J., Tergny, J., and Larichev, O. I. (1971). Linear programming with multiple objective functions: STEP method (STEM), *Mathematical Programming* 1, 366–375.

Benson, H. P. (1978). Existence of efficient solutions for vector maximization problems, *Journal of Optimization Theory and Applications* 26, 569–580.

Benson, H. P., and Morin, T. L. (1974). The vector maximization problem: proper efficiency and stability, working paper No. 117, The Technological Institute, Northwestern University, Evanston.

Benson, H. P., and Morin, T. L. (1977). The vector maximization problem: proper efficiency and stability, *SIAM Journal on Applied Mathematics* 32, 64–72.

Ben-Tal, A. (1980). Characterization of Pareto and lexicographic optimal solutions, in *Multiple Criteria Decision Making and Applications* (G. Fandel and T. Gal, eds.), Springer, Berlin, pp. 1–11.

Bergstresser, K., Charnes, A., and Yu, P. L. (1976). Generalization of domination structures and nondominated solutions in multicriteria decision making, *Journal of Optimization Theory and Applications* 18, 3–13.

Chankong, V. (1977). Multiobjective decision making analysis: the interactive surrogate worth trade-off method (Ph.D. dissertation), Systems Engineering Department, Case Western Reserve, Cleveland.

Chankong, V., and Haimes, Y. Y. (1981). On characterization of noninferior solutions of a vector optimization problem, in *Proceedings of the 8th IFAC Triennial World Congress, Kyoto, Japan*, Part B, Vols. 9–16.

Charnes, A., and Cooper, W. (1961). *Management Models and Industrial Applications of Linear Programming*, Wiley, New York, Vol. 1.

Cohon, J. L. (1978). *Multiobjective Programming and Planning*, Academic, New York.

Cohon, J. L., and Marks, D. H. (1975). A review and evaluation of multiobjective programming techniques, *Water Resource Research* 2, 208–220.

Corley, H. W. (1980). A new scalar equivalence for Pareto optimization, *IEEE Transactions on Automatic Control* AC-25, 829–830.

DaCunha, N. D., and Polak, E. (1967). Constraint minimization under vector-valued optimization, *Journal of Mathematical Analysis and Applications* 19, 103–124.

Dantzig, G. (1963). *Linear Programming and Extensions*, Princeton University Press, Princeton, New Jersey.

Ecker, J. G., and Kouada, I. A. (1975). Finding efficient points for linear multiple objective programs, *Mathematical Programming* 8, 375–377.

Everett, H. (1963). Generalized Lagrange multiplier method for solving problem of optimum allocation of resources, *Operations Research* 11, 399–417.

Gal, T. (1976). A general method for determining the set of all efficient solutions to a linear vector maximum problem, Report No. 76/12, Institut für Wirtschaftswissenschaften, Aachen, Germany.

Gass, S., and Saaty, T. (1955). The computational algorithm for the parametric objective functions, *Naval Research Logistic Quarterly* 2, No. 39.

Gembicki, F. W. (1974). Performance and sensitivity optimization: a vector index approach (Ph.D. dissertation), Systems Engineering Department, Case Western Reserve, Cleveland.

Gembicki, F., and Haimes, Y. Y. (1975). Approach to performance and multiobjective sensitivity optimization: the goal attainment method, *IEEE Transactions on Automatic Control* AC-20, 769–771.

Geoffrion, A. M. (1967). Solving bicriterion mathematical programs, *Operations Research* 15, 39–54.

Geoffrion, A. M. (1968). Proper efficiency and theory of vector maximization, *Journal of Mathematical Analysis and Applications* 22, 618–630.

Geoffrion, A. M. (1971). Duality in nonlinear programming: a simplified applications-oriented development, *SIAM Review* 13, 1–37.

Haimes, Y. Y. (1970). The integration of system identification and system optimization, School of Engineering and Applied Sciences, University of California, Los Angeles, Report No. UCLA-ENG-7029.

Haimes, Y. Y., and Chankong, V. (1979). Kuhn–Tucker multipliers as trade-offs in multi-objective decision making analysis, *Automatica* 15, 59–72.

Haimes, Y. Y., and Hall, W. A. (1974). Multiobjectives in water resource analysis: the surrogate worth trade-off method, *Water Resources Research* 10, 615–624.

Haimes, Y. Y., Hall, W., and Freedman, H. T. (1975). *Multiobjective Optimization in Water Resources Systems: The Surrogate Worth Trade-off Method*, Elsevier, Amsterdam.

Haimes, Y. Y., Lasdon, L., and Wismer, D. (1971). On a bicriterion formulation of the problems of integrated system identification and system optimization, *IEEE Transactions on Systems, Man, and Cybernetics* SMC-1, 296–297.

Hasenauer, R. (1976). Theoretical analysis and empirical application of goal programming with preemptive priority structures, in *Multiple Criteria Decision Making, Jouy-en-Josas, France, 1975* (H. Thiriez and S. Zionts, eds.), Springer, Berlin, pp. 120–135.

Isermann, M. (1976). Proper efficiency and linear vector maximum problems, *Operations Research* 22, 189–191.

Jahn, J. (1980). The Haar condition in vector optimization, in *Multiple Criteria Decision Making: Theory and Applications* (G. Fandel and T. Gal, eds.), Springer, Berlin, pp. 128–134.

Karlin, S. (1959). *Mathematical Methods and Theory in Games, Programming, and Economics*, Addison-Wesley, Reading, Massachusetts, Vol. 1.

Kuhn, H. W., and Tucker, A. W. (1951). Nonlinear programming, in *Proceedings of the Second Berkeley Symposium on Mathematics, Statistics, and Probability*, University of California Press, Berkeley, pp. 481–492.

Lasdon, L. S. (1970). *Optimization Theory for Large Systems*, Macmillan, New York.

Lin, J. G. (1976a). Multiple-objective problems: Pareto-optimal solutions by the method of proper equality constraints, *IEEE Transactions on Automatic Control* AC-21, 641–650.

Lin, J. G. (1976b). Three methods for determining Pareto-optimal solutions of multiobjective problems, in *Directions in Large-Scale Systems: Many-Person Optimization and Decentralized Control* (Y. C. Ho and S. K. Milter, eds.), Plenum, New York, pp. 117–138.

Lin, J. G. (1976c). Proper equality constraints and maximization of index vectors, *Journal of Optimization Theory and Applications* 20, 215–244.

Lin, J. G. (1977). Proper inequality constraints and maximization of index vectors, *Journal of Optimization Theory and Applications* 21, 505–521.

Lin, J. G. (1979). Multiple-objective optimization by a multiplier method of proper equality contraints—Part I: Theory, *IEEE Transactions on Automatic Control* AC-24, 567–573.

Luenberger, D. G. (1973). *Introduction to Linear and Nonlinear Programming*, Addison-Wesley, Reading, Massachusetts.

Mangasarian, O. L. (1969). *Nonlinear Programming*, McGraw-Hill, New York.

Naccache, P. H. (1978). Connectedness of the set of nondominated outcomes in multicriteria optimization, *Journal of Optimization Theory and Applications* 25, 459–467.

Pareto, V. (1896). *Cours d'Economie Politique*, Rouge, Lausanne, Switzerland.

Rockafellar, R. T. (1971). Ordinary convex programs without a duality gap, *Journal of Optimization Theory and Applications* 7, 143–148.

Roy, B. (1971). Problems and methods with multiple objective functions, *Mathematical Programming* 1, 239–266.

Tamura, K., and Miura, S. (1979). Necessary and sufficient conditions for local and global nondominated solutions in decision problems with multiobjectives, *Journal of Optimization Theory and Applications* 28, 501–523.

Tanino, T., and Sawaragi, Y. (1979). Duality theory in multiobjective programming, *Journal of Optimization Theory and Applications* 27, 509–529.

Wendell, R. E., and Lee, D. N. (1977). Efficiency in multiple objective optimization problems, *Mathematical Programming* 12, 406–414.

Yu, P. L. (1974a). A class of solutions of group decision problems, *Management Sciences* 19, 936–946.

Yu, P. L. (1974b). Cone convexity, cone extreme points, and nondominated solutions in decision problems with multiobjectives, *Journal of Optimization Theory and Applications* 14, 319–377.

Yu, P. L., and Zeleny, M. (1975). The set of all nondominated solutions in linear cases and a multicriteria simplex method, *Journal of Mathematical Analysis and Applications* 49, 430–468.

Zadeh, L. A. (1963). Optimality and nonscalar-valued performance criteria, *IEEE Transactions on Automatic Control* AC-8, 59–60.

Zeleny, M. (1974). *Linear Multiobjective Programming, Lecture Notes in Economics and Mathematical Systems Series*, Springer, New York.

PART II
METHODOLOGY

Chapter 5
Assessment Methodologies

5.1 Introduction

Our discussion of methodological aspects of multiobjective problem solving focuses mainly on the process of assessing the decision maker's preference. The structure of the system, that is, the complex of means–end relationships, can often be deemphasized in the actual assessment process. The techniques that result are most suitable for, although not limited to, problems typified by the following characteristics:

First, the means–end (attribute–objective) relationships are in simplest form, in the sense that the attributes typically serve as both decision variables and objectives.

Second, the set of alternatives can be made explicit. That is, once the set of constraints on possible values of the attributes is given, the value of each attribute can be picked *independently* from this set without raising concerns about infeasibility.

Third, the final outcome (the "best compromise" solution) can be obtained if a reasonably accurate preference measurement can be made.

By virtue of the third characteristic, methods in this class treat decision making as an act rather than a process. The process of measuring preference is merely a means of modeling the decision maker's preference structure; we shall therefore be able to substitute some prespecified decision rule for the action of the decision maker. The decision maker has, therefore, limited control over the decision-making process. These methods can be described as *product oriented* or *outcome oriented* [Starr and Zeleny, 1977] rather than *process oriented*. Examples 1.1 and 1.2 exemplify the type of problems best served by these methods.

MacCrimmon [1973] has identified three main categories in which the process of assessing preference can be conducted in the multiobjective setting. These are direct assessment, sequential elimination, and spatial proximity. These three categories reflect different ways in which the decision maker is involved, the kind of information being given to and elicited from the decision maker, and the way in which information about preference is processed.

5.2 The Direct Assessment Approach: The Multiattribute Utility Function

The most prominent direct assessment method is based on the premise that the decision maker's preference can be quantified, measured, and represented in the form of a real-valued function called the multiattribute value function or utility function. The formal basis for the existence of such a function is described in Chapter 3. Once a multiattribute value or utility function is constructed to represent the "global" preference structure pertinent to the corresponding decision problem, the decision-making process is reduced to a routine evaluation and search procedure. The main efforts in this approach center around the construction of the multiattribute value function.

After identifying the set of attributes and the set of alternatives, five basic steps must be carried out:

1. Verify the existence of a multiattribute value function or utility function (depending on whether or not there is uncertainty).
2. Select a suitable form of the function.
3. Construct appropriate component functions (single or other reduced dimension) for use in Step 2.
4. Determine appropriate scaling constants.
5. Check consistency and perform final analysis.

We now describe each of the above steps.

5.2.1 Verifying the Existence of the Multiattribute Utility Function

A utility function that accurately represents the preference structure of the decision problem must exist for this approach to be valid. Unfortunately, available sets of criteria for the existence of appropriate preference functions (i.e., Theorems 3.1, 3.3, and 3.4 for value functions and Theorem 3.13, or its equivalent, for utility functions) are rather abstract. Some of the criteria even lack intuitive interpretation, and thus are not easy to verify empirically.

In practice, the existence of appropriate preference functions is usually taken for granted. Nonetheless there are a few areas in which it is possible to verify the existence of appropriate functions empirically, as discussed in Chapter 3.

Utility functions are generally used as a prescriptive tool in decision making, and their existence normally is assumed. The primary concern is constructing and using utility functions in the final analysis of alternatives. However, the existence question remains a major concern, particularly from the behavioral viewpoint. Several counterexamples exist showing that the utility theory as a whole may fail as a descriptive tool to describe human choice behavior. One of these is commonly known as Allais's [1953] paradox.

To a person owning absolutely nothing, the sure prospect of obtaining \$1 million would most likely be preferred to the risky prospects of obtaining \$2 million with probability 0.09, \$1 million with probability 0.9, or nothing with probability 0.01: When one starts from nothing, the sure gain of \$1 million is quite staggering, so why would one risk ending up with nothing, even if the risk is small and there is a chance to double the "pot"? However, presented with a choice between the risky prospect of obtaining \$2 million with probability 0.09 (or nothing with probability 0.91) and the risky prospect of obtaining \$1 million with the probability 0.1 (or nothing with probability 0.9), the same person would most likely prefer the former, for the chance of gaining \$2 million in the former risky prospect is not much lower (10%) than the chance of gaining \$1 million in the latter. Since each choice involves nearly the same amount of risk, but in one the "pot" is twice as large, why not take just a slightly greater risk with a chance of gaining twice as much? This type of choice behavior is common, yet it can easily be shown that it defies the basic principle of utility theory.

Let us assume that a utility function conforming to the above choice behavior exists, and let it be denoted u. Clearly, from the principle of *expected utility*, the first choice problem implies that $u(\$1 \text{ million}) > 0.09u(\$2 \text{ million}) + 0.9u(\$1 \text{ million}) + 0.01u(\$0)$ or, equivalently,

$$0.1u(\$1 \text{ million}) > 0.09u(\$2 \text{ million}) + 0.01u(\$0). \tag{5.1}$$

The second choice problem, on the other hand, implies that $0.09u(\$2 \text{ million}) + 0.91u(\$0) > 0.1u(\$1 \text{ million}) + 0.9u(\$0)$, or, equivalently,

$$0.09u(\$2 \text{ million}) + 0.01u(\$0) > 0.1u(\$1 \text{ million}). \tag{5.2}$$

The obvious contradiction between (5.1) and (5.2) implies that the utility function u cannot exist. Bell [1981], who discusses these issues in more detail, attributes this type of inconsistency to the failure of utility theory to treat such behavior as "decision regret."

5.2.2 *Selecting Suitable Forms of the Multiattribute Utility Function*

After ascertaining the existence of appropriate preference functions, whether by assumption or by verification, we must select a suitable functional form. We check which set of independence conditions discussed in Chapter 3 holds for the decision problem under consideration and choose the functional form accordingly. The basic strategy will now be summarized.

The Certainty Case If one has no notion of what the underlying preference structure should be, one may follow the strategy summarized in the flow diagram of Figure 5.1. This strategy is based on the premise that the simplest possible form (i.e., in decreasing order of simplicity, additive, multiplicative, or quasi-additive) should be identified and used first.

In using this strategy, however, much effort is spent on validating various independent conditions. An alternative strategy may be to begin with box E. If the test is unsuccessful, follow boxes F and H or I as before. But if the test in box E is successful, use the simple test discussed earlier to identify whether Equation (3.27) is additive or multiplicative, completing the process.

The Uncertainty Case In risky choice problems, the most common forms of the utility function are additive, quasi-additive, and multiplicative. Which of these forms, if any, best represents the underlying preference structure is determined by verifying the following conditions: value (or additive) independence, preferential independence, and utility independence.

To select a suitable form for the utility function in the two-attribute uncertainty case, we begin by testing the value independence condition directly. If the test fails, then we try verifying other independence conditions. For the case of three or more attributes, it may be easier to begin by checking the appropriate preference and utility independence conditions. The flow diagram depicted in Figure 5.2 suggests a strategy for selecting a suitable form of the utility function.

5.2.3 Constructing Component Preference Functions

After it has been determined that one of the decomposition forms (additive, quasi-additive, or multiplicative) is applicable to a particular decision problem, the major remaining tasks are the construction of appropriate component preference (value or utility) functions and the estimation of scaling constants. Sections 5.2.4–5.2.6 discuss methods for assessing component preference functions, and Section 5.2.7 addresses estimating the scaling constants.

5.2.4 Assessing One-Dimensional Value Functions

Most notable among the techniques which can be used to assess one-dimensional value functions are the direct rating method and the midpoint method, which will be described here. Other methods can be found in Fishburn [1967] and the references cited therein. We do not distinguish

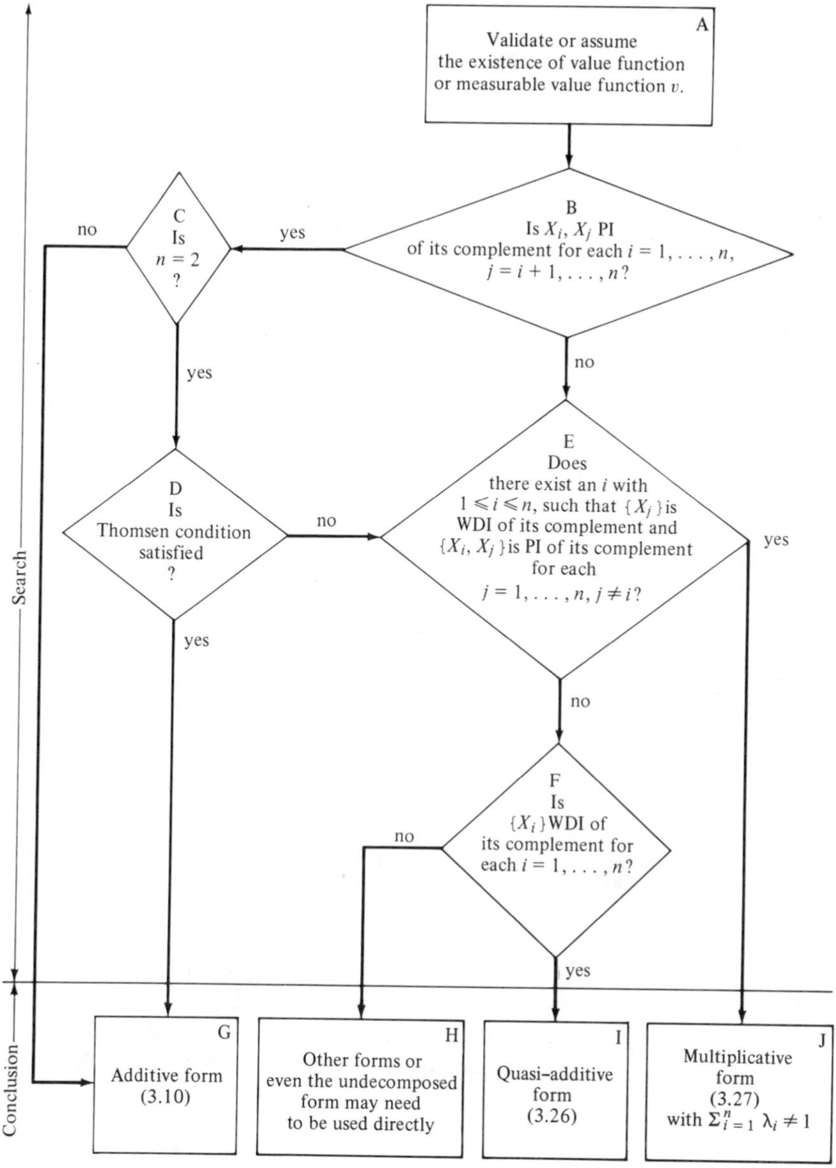

Figure 5.1 A strategy for finding a suitable form of value function. (PI: preferentially independent; WDI: weak difference independent.)

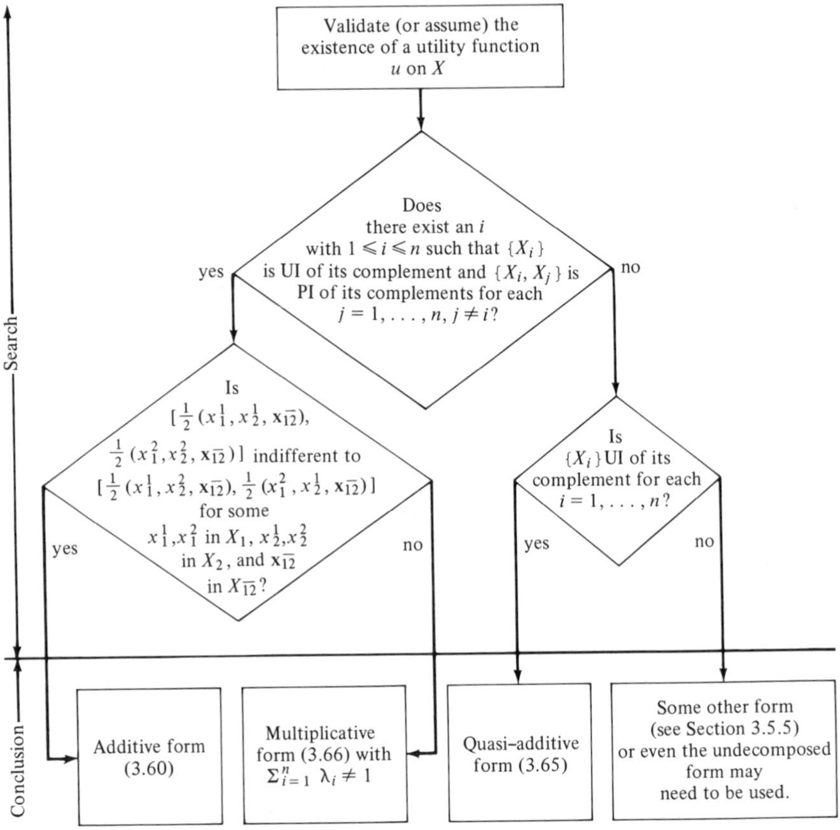

Figure 5.2 A strategy for finding a suitable form of utility function. (UI: utility independent; PI: preferentially independent.)

nonmeasurable and measurable component value functions since the methods to be described are applicable to either.

Once it has been ascertained that the value function can be expressed in additive, quasi-additive, or multiplicative form, each component value function $v_i(x_i)$ can be constructed independently, by setting all other attributes at some fixed value x_i^0. It can easily be shown that the resulting value function v will always give the same ordering of elements in X, irrespective of these fixed values of other attributes.

Direct Rating Method Certainly, one of the simplest ways of obtaining a one-dimensional value function $v_i(x_i)$ is to ask the decision maker to assess directly the value of $v_i(x_i)$ for each value of x_i. This is particularly suitable if X_i is discrete and has a small (finite) number of members. For example, X_1 may represent the type of power generator that a regional power

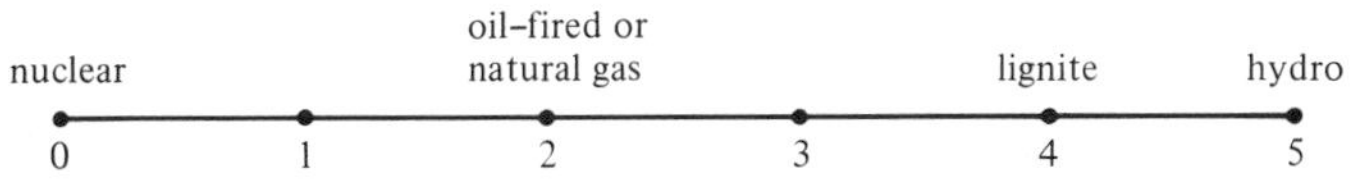

Figure 5.3 The direct rating method (discrete).

authority must select for an expansion program. Clearly X_1 is measured in a nominal scale and may have the following values: hydro, oil fired, coal (lignite), natural gas, or nuclear. In the direct rating method, the decision maker is asked to rate these five possible power units on the scale of, say, 0–5, with 0 representing the least desirable unit and 5 representing the most desirable. A typical response is shown in Figure 5.3.

In this case we can write

$$v_1(x_1) = \begin{cases} 5 & \text{if} \quad x_1 = \text{hydro}, \\ 4 & \text{if} \quad x_1 = \text{lignite}, \\ 2 & \text{if} \quad x_1 = \text{oil-fired or natural gas}, \\ 0 & \text{if} \quad x_1 = \text{nuclear}. \end{cases}$$

For the case where X_i is continuous, Edwards [1977] suggests the following:

i. Identify the physical bounds of the value of attribute X_i. Let these be a_i and b_i. Fix all other attributes at $X_{\bar{i}}^0$.
ii. Ask the decision maker to estimate his preference of a_i and b_i on a scale of 0–100, with 0 representing the least preferred and 100 the most preferred; if normalized $v_i(x_i)$ is required, a scale from 0 to 1 may be used instead.
iii. Draw a straight line between these two points to obtain an approximation of $v_i(x_i)$.

A natural modification of Step iii is to obtain the values of $v_i(x_i)$ for a few additional points between a_i and b_i and to fit an appropriate curve to these points. Edwards argues for the straight-line method because it is simpler and produces results similar to those of more complicated methods. This is especially true if $v_i(\ )$ can be assumed monotonic in x_i.[1] In a situation where the law of diminishing returns prevails, however, the straight-line approach, which ignores that law, must be carefully scrutinized before it can be used.

As an example of the direct rating approach in the continuous case, consider another attribute, cost X_2, in the power generating capacity expansion program. Suppose it can be estimated from preliminary analysis that

[1]That is, the larger (or smaller) the value of x_i, the larger the value of $v_i(x_i)$.

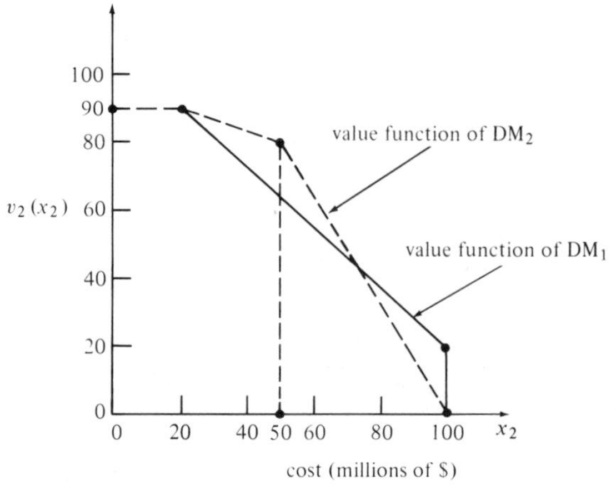

Figure 5.4 The direct rating method (continuous).

the plausible range of cost of all possible expansion programs is from $20 million to $100 million. An official in the regional power authority may be moderately happy about this range and accordingly assign the values of, say, 90 and 60 to $20 million and $100 million, respectively. He may also indicate that his preference decreases proportionally with cost. A straight line can thus be drawn between these two points to reflect his preference structure on cost as shown in Figure 5.4. Another official, also expressing strong preference for the lower end of the cost may show very little difference in terms of preference if the cost lies below $50 million. His preference may begin to decrease very rapidly as the cost goes beyond $50 million. A possible value function representing his preference structure is also shown in Figure 5.4.

Midpoint Method The midpoint method is probably the one most commonly used for continuous attributes since it is simple to apply for any number of attributes and for any decomposition form chosen. It also gives the normalized form of component functions. The basic idea is to find, through questioning the decision maker, the "midpoint" between two given values of X_i. Informally,[2] the point $\hat{x}_i$ is said to be the *midpoint* between x_i'

[2]A more standard definition of the midpoint or midvalue point is given in terms of trade-offs between X_i and one other attribute. More precisely $\hat{x}_i$ is said to be the midpoint of the interval $[x_i', x_i'']$ if, in going from x_i' to $\hat{x}_i$, one has to give up the same amount of some other attribute, say x_j, as going from $\hat{x}_i$ to x_i'. By assuming additive structure, this definition implies (5.3). In the case of measurable value functions, what is normally called the equal-difference point [Kirkwood and Sarin, 1980] also corresponds to the midpoint defined by (5.3).

and x_i'' of the attribute X_i if

$$v_i(\hat{x}_i) = \tfrac{1}{2}\left[v_i(x_i') + v_i(x_i'')\right] \tag{5.3a}$$

or

$$v_i(x_i') - v_i(\hat{x}_i) = v_i(\hat{x}_i) - v_i(x_i''). \tag{5.3b}$$

Equation (5.3b) suggests that for the midpoint of an interval to exist the decision maker must offer no preference between certain *differences* in attribute level. In practice, it is often difficult for the decision maker to provide a midpoint value directly. Instead, a series of questions may be asked that require judging between such differences, thus "zeroing in" on a midpoint.

Let us consider the method in detail:

1. Fix all other attributes at their least desirable values $X_{\bar{i}}^0$, and identify the lower and upper bounds of values of x_i, denoted a_i and b_i, respectively. Then set

$$v_i(a_i) = 0 \qquad \text{and} \qquad v_i(b_i) = 1$$

(or vice versa if the situation is reversed, i.e., if an increase in X_i causes a decrease in preference).

2. To find the midpoint $x_i^{0.5}$ between a_i and b_i, pick a point x_i' between a_i and b_i and ask the decision maker to compare exchanging a_i for x_i' with exchanging x_i' for b_i. If the decision maker is indifferent between the two exchanges, set $x_i^{0.5} = x_i'$. If, on the other hand, the decision maker prefers one or the other, select x_1'' from the interval with higher preference (e.g., choose x_i'' between a_i and x_i' if the former trade-off is preferred to the latter) and repeat the above process with x_i'' replacing x_i'. Repeat the process until the midpoint $x_i^{0.5}$ is found. Clearly from (5.3a)

$$v(x_i^{0.5}) = \tfrac{1}{2}\left[v_i(a_i) + v_i(b_i)\right] = 0.5. \tag{5.4}$$

(This is why the midpoint between a_i and b_i is denoted $x_i^{0.5}$.)

3. Repeat Step 2 to find the midpoint between a_i and $x_i^{0.5}$, denoted $x_i^{0.25}$, and the midpoint between $x_i^{0.5}$ and b_i, denoted $x_i^{0.75}$.
4. To ensure consistency check whether $x_i^{0.5}$ is the midpoint between $x_i^{0.25}$ and $x_i^{0.75}$ in the sense given by Condition (5.3).
5. Steps 2–4 can be repeated to find midpoints between points that have already been generated, until enough points have been obtained for curve fitting.

While the direct rating method asks the decision maker to furnish the value of $v_i(x_i)$ at specified points x_i, the midpoint method asks the decision maker to provide values of X_i at which his preference is reflected by specified values of $v_i(x_i)$.

As an example, consider again the power expansion problem. Suppose we want to construct the value function v_2 as a function of cost X_2 by means of the midpoint method. The lower and upper bounds on X_2 are \$20 million and \$100 million, respectively. We set v_2(\$20 million)$=1$ and v_2(\$100 million)$=0$. Next, to find the midpoint level between \$20 million and \$100 million, pick $x_2^1=$\$60 million and ask the decision maker the following question:

"With the values of all other attributes fixed at, say, $X_{\bar{2}}^0$, suppose you are given two situations: a) You estimate the cost of a program to be \$60 million. Later you are told that you made a mistake—the cost should be \$20 million. b) You estimate the cost to be \$100 million. Later you discover that it should be \$60 million. Would you be more delighted in your discovery in the first situation or the second, or would you feel equally delighted in both cases?"

If the decision maker shows greater preference for the second situation, pick x_2'' to be, say, \$70 million and repeat the question with \$70 million replacing \$60 million. If the decision maker is less delighted to go from \$100 million to \$70 million, than to go from \$70 million to \$20 million, pick yet another point, say \$65 million, and repeat the process. If the decision maker is exactly as delighted to go from \$100 to \$65 million as to go from \$65 million to \$20 million, the midpoint between \$20 million and \$100 million is $x_2^{0.5}=$\$65 million. Suppose that by continuing this process we find that $x_2^{0.25}=$\$85 million and $x_2^{0.75}=$\$40 million. To check for consistency, we ask the decision maker to verify whether he would be equally delighted to go from \$85 million to \$65 million and to go from \$65 million to \$40 million. (If the answer is negative, $x_2^{0.5}$ is adjusted accordingly and $x_2^{0.25}$ and $x_2^{0.75}$ are checked again.) Suppose the answer to the above question is affirmative so that the values of $x_2^{0.25}$, $x_2^{0.5}$, and $x_2^{0.75}$ are consistent. These points can be plotted and the appropriate curve fitted through these points to obtain $v_2(x_2)$, as shown in Figure 5.5. Once the curve $v_2(x_2)$ is drawn, its shape should be discussed with the decision maker to confirm its validity.

A Special Method In relation to the midpoint approach, Kirkwood and Sarin [1980] proposed verifying further properties of the preference structure. If either of such properties is satisfied, then the corresponding one-dimensional value function $v_i(x_i)$ can be assumed to have special analytical forms, simplifying the assessment task considerably. The two related properties proposed by Kirkwood and Sarin [1980] are the delta property and the proportional delta property. The attribute X_i is said to satisfy *the delta property* if for any δ, $\hat{x}_i+\delta$ is the midpoint between $x_i'+\delta$ and $x_i''+\delta$, whenever $\hat{x}_i$ is the midpoint between x_i' and x_i''. It is said to satisfy the *proportional delta property* with respect to x_i^1 if for any δ, $x_i^1+\delta(\hat{x}_i-x_i^1)$ is the midpoint between $x_i^1+\delta(x_i'-x_i^1)$ and $x_i^1+\delta(x_i''-x_i^1)$, whenever $\hat{x}_i$ is the midpoint of x_i' and x_i''. The following theorem is due to Kirkwood and Sarin [1980].

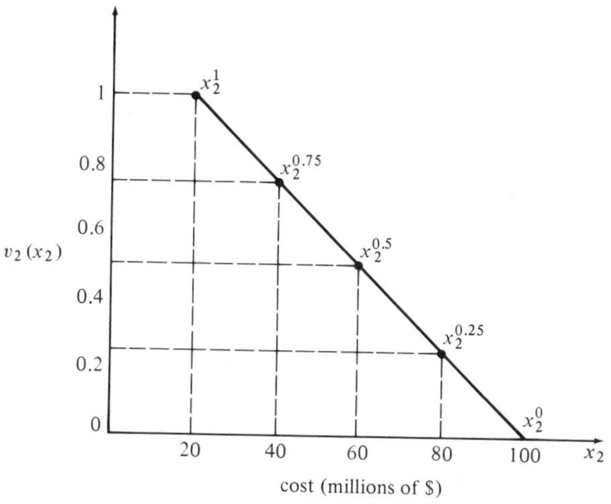

Figure 5.5 The midpoint method.

Theorem 5.1. *If a value function v on X exists and if it can be written in additive (measurable and nonmeasurable), quasi-additive (measurable), or multiplicative (measurable) form, then the component value function $v_i(x_i)$ may be written in one of the following forms:*

a. *either*

$$v_i(x_i) = \alpha_i + \beta_i x_i \tag{5.5a}$$

or

$$v_i(x_i) = \alpha_i + \beta_i e^{k_i x_i}, \tag{5.5b}$$

where α_i, β_i, and k_i are constants, if and only if the delta property is satisfied;

b. *either*

$$v_i(x_i) = \alpha_i + \beta_i \ln(x_i, x_i^1) \tag{5.6a}$$

or

$$v_i(x_i) = \alpha_i + \beta_i (x_i - x_i^1)^{k_i}, \tag{5.6b}$$

where α_i, β_i, and k_i are constants, if and only if the proportional delta property is satisfied.

5.2.5 Assessing One-Dimensional Utility Functions

A utility function describes the corresponding preference structure under risky situations. Assessing component utility functions therefore involves eliciting risk behavior from the decision maker. This assessment of $u_i(x_i)$ can be carried out by 1) using standard gamble questions or 2) directly

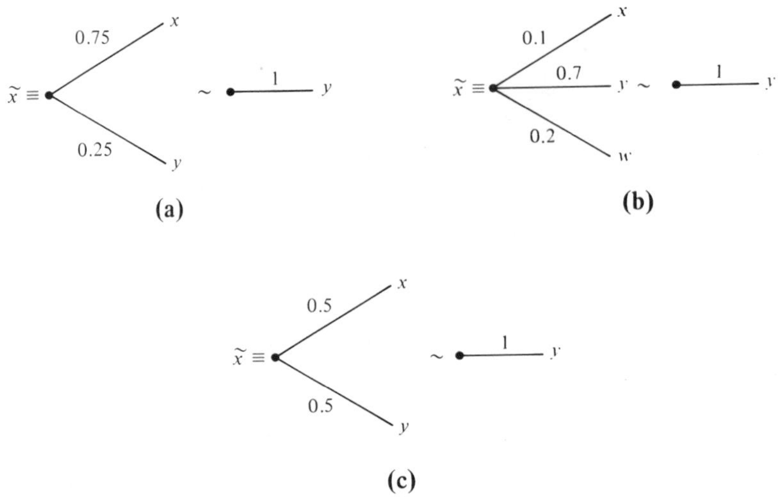

Figure 5.6 Certainty equivalent.

observing the risk behavior of the decision maker. We begin by describing two standard gamble assessment approaches.[3]

Certainty Equivalent Approach For the continuous attribute X_i, the most common form of assessment through standard gamble questions involves the concept of certainty equivalent. Given a risky prospect $\tilde{x}$, we say y is a *certainty equivalent* of $\tilde{x}$ if i) y is a consequence or a sure prospect (i.e., y will certainly be obtained) and ii) the decision maker is indifferent between $\tilde{x}$ and y. Conceptually it may be possible to find a certainty equivalent for any type of risk prospect $\tilde{x}$ as illustrated in Figure 5.6. The concept of certainty equivalent plays a dominant role in the assessment of one-dimensional utility functions, because it is often easier and more accurate to elicit such information from the decision maker. There are three variations of the certainty equivalent approach. These are demonstrated in Figures 5.7–5.9.

Example: To illustrate the basic steps involved in these procedures, consider yet another attribute X_3, representing an index of environmental quality, in the problem of expanding power-generating capacity discussed earlier. The value of X_3 ranges from 0 to 100 with 0 being the most desirable and 100 being the least desirable. The index of environmental quality depends not only on the type of project chosen but also on the states of nature and

---

[3]Additional assessment methods can be found in, for example, Fishburn [1970], Sarin [1977], and Sage [1977].

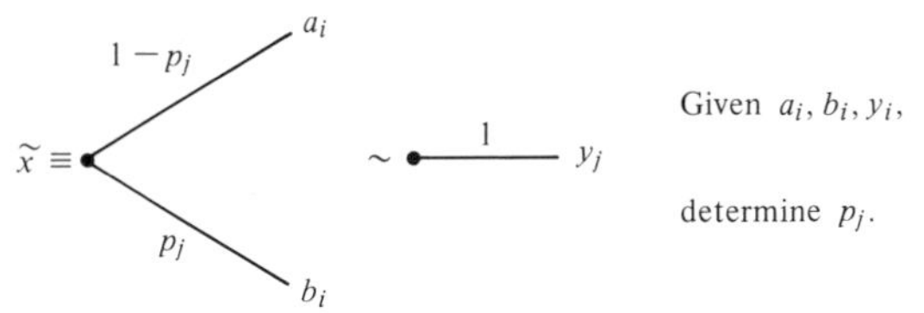

Figure 5.7 The first variant of the certainty equivalent approach.

various technologies being developed. All these involve uncertain events. The one-dimensional preference function required for X_3 must therefore be a utility function. To assess $u_3(x_3)$ using the first variant of the certainty equivalent approach, we first set $u_3(0)=1$ and $u_3(100)=0$. Next we estimate $u_3(25)$ by asking the decision maker to compare the risky prospect of obtaining $X_3=0$ with probability p and $X_3=100$ with probability $1-p$ and the prospect of obtaining $X_3=25$ for certain. The value of p is varied until the decision maker is indifferent between the two choices. Let this value be $p=0.96$. Hence we have $u_3(25)=0.96$. Now $u_3(50)$ and $u_3(75)$ can be estimated in much the same way. Suppose after going through the above procedure we find that $u_3(50)=0.86$ and $u_3(75)=0.70$. We now have five points, which are sufficient to obtain $u_3(x_3)$ by curve fitting, as shown in Figure 5.10.

In the second variant the decision maker is asked to compare the risky prospect of obtaining $X_3=0$ with probability 0.25 and $X_3=100$ with probability 0.75 and the prospect of obtaining $X_3=y$ for certain. The value of y is then varied until the decision maker shows indifference between the two given prospects. If the resulting $X_3=95$, then $u_3(95)=0.25$. For consistency, if we find that $u_3(88)=0.5$ and $u_3(65)=0.75$, then the decision maker should show indifference between the risky prospect of obtaining either $X_3=65$ or $X_3=95$ with equal probability and the sure prospect of obtaining $X_3=88$. A smooth curve is then fitted through these five points,

Figure 5.8 The second variant of the certainty equivalent approach.

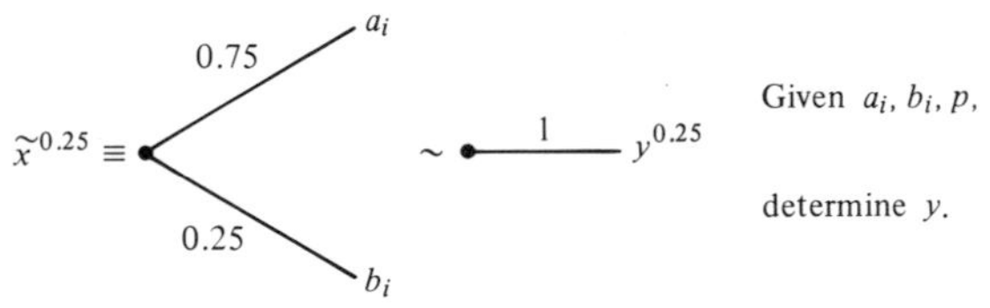

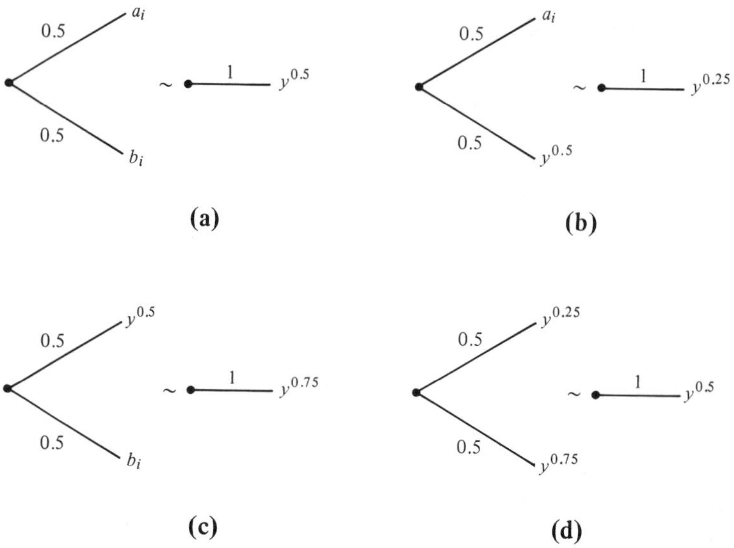

Figure 5.9 The third variant of the certainty equivalent approach.

Figure 5.10 Utility function of the environmental quality index, constructed by the certainty equivalent approach. (Circles: points generated in the first variant; squares: points generated in the second and third variants.)

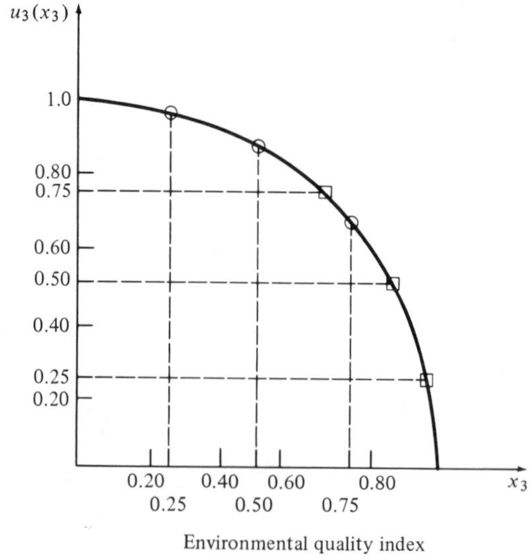

which should yield results similar to those in Figure 5.10. All the steps in the third variant are the same as second, except for the values of X_3 at which $u_3 = 0.25, 0.5, 0.75$ are obtained through different gamble questions. First the certainty equivalence of the equally likely risky prospect of obtaining either the worst ($X_3 = 100$) or the best ($X_3 = 0$) environmental quality indices is elicited from the decision maker. Suppose this gives $X_3 = 88$. Next the certainty equivalents of the equally likely risky prospect of obtaining either the worst index or the index $X_3 = 88$ and of the equally likely risky prospect of obtaining either the best index or the index $X_3 = 88$ are elicited to yield the required points.

Lottery Equivalent Approach In the previous approach, the decision maker has to compare a risky prospect with a sure prospect in a particular gamble question. This may lead to seriously biased judgments, particularly if the decision maker is strongly adverse to gambling. An alternative approach, based on "lottery equivalence," is to ask the decision maker to compare a risky prospect with a risky prospect. Although this approach does not have the same drawback as the certainty equivalent approach, the associated questioning procedure may be more complicated. The decision maker may also face another type of difficulty, having to conceptualize and make judgments solely on the more abstract entity of risky prospects. Nevertheless, it is a viable approach if only equally likely risky prospects are used in gamble questions.

Relationship Between a One-Dimensional Utility Function and Risk Behavior As mentioned earlier, there is a close relationship between the shape of one-dimensional utility functions and the risk behavior of the decision maker. Knowledge of these relationships is sometimes quite useful in the construction and consistency checking of one-dimensional utility functions, since the decision maker's attitude towards risk is often directly observable.

Risk behavior is associated with how the decision maker values the attribute X_i in the face of uncertainty. If a decision maker judges the actual values of X_i in situations under uncertainty in the same way as under certainty, we would describe such a decision maker as a risk-neutral individual who does not care about risk one way or the other. In this case, if preference increases as X_i increases, we can use x_i (the value of X_i) itself or any positive linear transformation of x_i of the form $\lambda x_i + \mu$, $\lambda > 0$, such as $u_i^0(x_i)$ shown in Figure 5.11, to represent the utility function of X_i. If preference increases as x_i decreases, any linear transformation of x_i with $\lambda < 0$ can be used as a utility function of X_i.

For example, a risk-neutral decision maker is willing to enter an unbiased situation where he has an equal probability of winning or losing \$10,000. If we assume Bernoulli's principle, this decision maker will assign \$0 as the certainty equivalent of the above gamble, which is equal to the expected

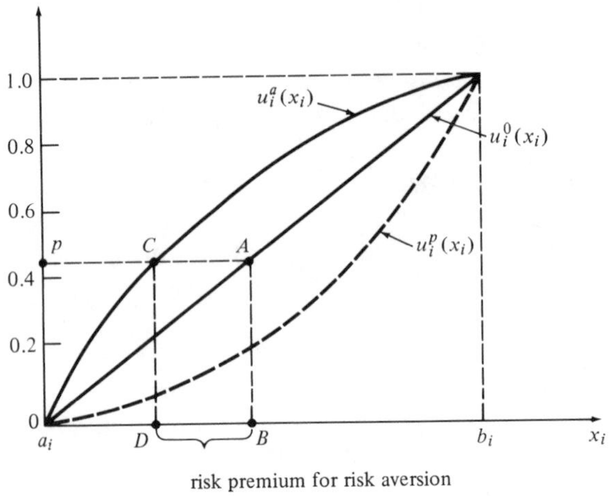

Figure 5.11 Risk behavior and utility functions.

monetary value EMV. In general, for a risk-neutral decision maker, the certainty equivalent of any lottery will be just the expected value of all the values of X_i contained in that lottery. For this reason, we can formally define risk-neutral behavior in the following manner.

Let $\text{CE}(\tilde{x}_i)$ denote the certainty equivalent of the risk prospect (lottery) $\tilde{x}_i$ involving consequences in X_i and let $E(\tilde{x}_i)$ denote the expected value of $\tilde{x}_i$. Then we say that a decision maker is *risk neutral* in X_i if and only if

$$\text{CE}(\tilde{x}_i) = E(\tilde{x}_i). \tag{5.7}$$

From the discussion it is clear that (5.7) is true (i.e., the decision maker is risk neutral) if and only if the corresponding utility function is a straight line.

Let us now consider another type of decision maker—one who tends to assign an *apparent* worth to a unit of X_i in gambling situations different from its face value. Consider the case in which preference increases as X_i increases. In a win–loss gambling situation, these decision makers may value a unit of X_i that could be won less than the same unit of X_i that there is risk of losing. When asked to give the certainty equivalent of the risky prospect of winning or losing \$10,000 with equal probability, the possible loss of \$10,000 figures more prominently in their judgment. Consequently, despite the fact that the probability and the amount of winning are exactly the same as those of losing, their certainty equivalent to the above risky prospect would be negative, rather than \$0 as in the risk-neutral case. Decision makers who tend to be more cautious in gambling situations than the risk-neutral type are said to be risk averse. More formally, if more X_i is preferred to less X_i (i.e., the utility function is an increasing function of X_i), a decision maker is said to be *risk averse* in X_i if and only if his certainty equivalent $\mathrm{CE}(\tilde{x}_i)$ of any risky prospect $\tilde{x}_i$ involving consequences in X_i is strictly less than $E(\tilde{x}_i)$, the expected value of $\tilde{x}_i$;

$$\mathrm{CE}(\tilde{x}_i) < E(\tilde{x}_i). \tag{5.8}$$

On the other hand, if the utility function is a decreasing function of X_i, we say the decision maker is *risk averse* in X_i if and only if the inequality in (5.8) is reversed;

$$\mathrm{CE}(\tilde{x}_i) > E(\tilde{x}_i) \qquad \text{(for a decreasing utility function)}. \tag{5.9}$$

In any case, the quantity $E(\tilde{x}_i) - \mathrm{CE}(\tilde{x}_i)$ is known as the *risk premium* and is a prime determinant of the *degree* of risk aversion. Intuitively, the larger the (absolute value of the) risk premium, the higher the decision maker's aversion to risk.[4]

It can be shown that a decision maker is risk averse if and only if the corresponding utility function is strictly concave,[5] as depicted in Figure 5.11 by $u_i^{\mathrm{a}}(x_i)$.

Other decision makers value a prospective gain of \$10,000 more than the equally possible loss of the same amount. Their certainty equivalents to the risky prospect of winning \$10,000 or losing \$10,000 with equal probability will thus be positive rather than \$0 or negative, as it is in the risk-neutral or risk-averse case, respectively. These decision makers will be more apt or willing to take risks than those in other categories. We accordingly call this type of risk behavior risk prone. More formally, we say that a decision maker is *risk prone* in X_i if and only if his certainty equivalent $\mathrm{CE}(\tilde{x}_i)$ of any risky prospect $\tilde{x}_i$ involving consequences in X_i, and the expected value $E(\tilde{x}_i)$ of $\tilde{x}_i$ are related in the following manner:

$$\mathrm{CE}(\tilde{x}_i) > E(\tilde{x}_i) \tag{5.10a}$$

if the utility function is an increasing function or

$$\mathrm{CE}(\tilde{x}_i) < E(\tilde{x}_i) \tag{5.10b}$$

if the utility function is a decreasing function.

Again it can be shown that risk-prone behavior is equivalent to a strictly convex utility function, such as that represented in Figure 5.11 by $u_i^{\mathrm{p}}(x_i)$.

The following definition summarizes the above discussion.

---

[4]See Pratt [1964] and Keeney and Raiffa [1976] for a more detailed treatment of this issue.

[5]A real-valued function $f(y)$ is strictly concave in the interval $[y_*, y^*]$ if and only if for any $y_1, y_2 \in [y_*, y^*]$ and $0 < \lambda < 1$,

$$f[\lambda y_1 + (1-\lambda) y_2] > \lambda f(y_1) + (1-\lambda) f(y_2).$$

If the strict inequality is reversed, we say that $f(y)$ is strictly convex.

Definition. Assuming that a one-dimensional utility function $u_i(x_i)$ for the attribute X_i exists, a decision maker is said to be

i. risk neutral if and only if $u_i(x_i)$ is a linear function of x_i,
ii. risk averse if and only if $u_i(x_i)$ is a strictly concave function of x_i, and
iii. risk prone if and only if $u_i(x_i)$ is a strictly convex function of x_i.

Observe that the criteria of the definition are irrespective of whether $u_i(x_i)$ is an increasing or a decreasing function. The definition can help narrow down the classes of functions to be used in curve fitting in the actual construction of $u_i(x_i)$. For example, after an adequate number of points has been obtained by the assessment methods described earlier and after the decision maker is observed to be risk averse, a utility function of the form $u_i(x_i)=\lambda e^{-\alpha x_i}+\mu$ with $\lambda<0$, $\alpha>0$, which is strictly concave, might be tried. If the decision maker is observed to exhibit risk-prone behavior, the same form with $\lambda>0$, which is strictly convex, might be used in the curve-fitting process.

5.2.6 Closing Remarks on Component Preference Functions

Assessing utility functions involves gambling questions which may present conceptual problems to decision makers. It may thus be easier first to assess appropriate value functions, which can then be translated into appropriate multiattribute utility functions, provided that some necessary and sufficient conditions are satisfied. For this approach to be viable, some forms of relationships between value functions and utility functions are needed. Some of these results are already available. See, for example, Keeney and Raiffa [1976], Sarin [1980], and Dyer and Sarin [1979].

5.2.7 Estimating Scaling Constants

Suppose that a specific form of numerical function representing the decision maker's preference structure, whether additive, quasi-additive, or multiplicative, has already been established and that the corresponding component functions have already been assessed. What remain to be determined are the scaling constants. The basic strategy is to use preference information elicited from the decision maker to set up a system of independent equations, with as many equations as there are scaling constants to be determined.[6] Theoretically, there are a number of ways for obtaining the desired equations. The following have often been suggested.

[6]For example, the numbers of scaling constants to be determined are n, $n+1$, and 2^n-1 for additive, multiplicative, and quasi-additive forms, respectively.

First assume that for each attribute X_i, $i=1,\ldots,n$, there are a worst level a_i and a best level b_i. Assume, without loss of generality, that for each $i=1,\ldots,n$ preference increases as X_i increases. Hence, for a typical value x_i of X_i, $a_i \leqslant x_i \leqslant b_i$.

Perhaps the most general way (but not necessarily the simplest) of setting up the required set of equations is to find at least L pairs of values of $\mathbf{x}$, say, $(\mathbf{x}^1,\mathbf{y}^1),\ldots,(\mathbf{x}^L,\mathbf{y}^L)$, where L is the number of constants to be determined such that for each $l=1,\ldots,L$, $\mathbf{a} \leqslant \mathbf{x}^l \leqslant \mathbf{b}$, $\mathbf{a} \leqslant \mathbf{y}^l \leqslant \mathbf{b}$, and $\mathbf{x}^l \sim \mathbf{y}^l$. We can produce a set of equations

$$v(\mathbf{x}^l)=v(\mathbf{y}^l) \tag{5.11a}$$

for deterministic cases and

$$u(\mathbf{x}^l)=u(\mathbf{y}^l) \tag{5.11b}$$

for risky cases for $l=1,\ldots,L$.

If these L equations are independent (i.e., there are no redundant equations), then they can be solved to determine the required L constants. A practical way of obtaining the indifference pairs $(\mathbf{x}^1,\mathbf{y}^1)$ is to select a suitable $\mathbf{x}^1$ and suitable levels of y_1, y_2^1, $y_3^1,\ldots,y_n^1$, making sure, of course, that $x_i^1 > y_i^1$ for some i and $x_j^1 < y_j^1$ for some j; then the decision maker is asked to compare two consequences, $\mathbf{x}^1$ and $(y_1, y_2^1,\ldots,y_n^1)$. The value of y_1 is varied until indifference is achieved, and the corresponding value of y_1 is then set at y_1^1. We thus obtain $\mathbf{y}^1$ indifferent to $\mathbf{x}^1$. Other indifference pairs can be determined in similar manner, remembering that the component to be varied is not necessarily restricted to the first.

Alternatively, the normalized properties of $v(\;)$ and $v_i(\;)$ may be used to develop a system of independent equations. Equations produced this way are easier to solve, and sometimes they may be solved by mere inspection.

Observe that if we can find a level x_i^j of X_i and a level x_j' of X_j, $j \neq i$, such that

$$(a_1,\ldots,a_{i-1},x_i^j,a_{i+1},\ldots,a_n) \sim (a_1,\ldots,a_{j-1},x_j',a_{j+1},\ldots,a_n), \tag{5.12}$$

then from (3.26) or (3.65)

$$\lambda_i v_i(x_i^j)=\lambda_j v_j(x_j') \tag{5.13a}$$

for the deterministic case and

$$\lambda_i u_i(x_i^j)=\lambda_j u_j(x_j') \tag{5.13b}$$

for the risky case. Obviously, if x_j' is set at b_j, (5.13) simplifies further.

By fixing i, say $i=1$, the above procedure can be used to obtain simple equations similar to (5.13) for every $j=2,\ldots,n$. This technique only produces at most $n-1$ independent equations of the form (5.13). The nth independent equation, which together with the previously determined $n-1$ equations yield n scaling constants $\lambda_1,\ldots,\lambda_n$, must be determined by some other means. If the additive form is used, the nth equation is furnished by the fact that the sum of all scaling constants must equal unity, i.e.,

$$\lambda_1+\lambda_2+\cdots+\lambda_n=1. \tag{5.14}$$

For the multiplicative or quasi-additive form,[7] the equation must be established by eliciting preferences. Following Dyer and Sarin [1979] in the deterministic case, the decision maker may be asked how many times better he considers the trade-offs, from the least desirable levels **a** to the most desirable levels **b** than the trade-offs from **a** to $(x_1', a_2,\ldots,a_n)$, where x_1' is a selected level of X_1 and $a_1<x_1'\leq b_1$.[8] Suppose the decision maker considers the former trade-offs to be r times better than the latter; then from (3.26), we have

$$r\lambda_1 v_1(x_1')=1$$

or

$$\lambda_1=1/rv_1(x_1'). \tag{5.15}$$

This obviously yields the required nth independent equation. All $\lambda_1,\ldots,\lambda_n$ can now be determined. The remaining scaling constants for either the multiplicative or quasi-additive form must now be estimated.

In the multiplicative case, μ is the only constant remaining to be determined, and this is easily accomplished by using (3.28). For the quasi-additive case, an additional question to elicit preference is required for each additional constant. For example, to estimate λ_{12}, we again ask the decision maker to compare the consequence $(x_1, b_2, a_3,\ldots,a_n)$ and the consequence $(b_1, x_2'', a_3,\ldots,a_n)$, where x_1 and x_2'' are selected values of X_1 and X_2, respectively. The value of x_1 is varied until the decision maker is indifferent between the two consequences; let that value of x_1 be x_1''. Hence from (3.26) we have

$$\lambda_1 v_1(x_1'')+\lambda_2+\lambda_{12}v_1(x_1'')=\lambda_1+\lambda_2 v_2(x_2'')+\lambda_{12}v_2(x_2''). \tag{5.16}$$

Knowing $\lambda_1, \lambda_2, v_1(x_1'')$, and $v_2(x_2'')$, λ_{12} can obviously be determined from (5.16) as long as $v_1(x_1'')\neq v_2(x_2'')$. Other constants of the form λ_{ij} can be estimated in a similar manner. Finally, the constant $\lambda_{12\ldots n}$ can easily be found by solving the equation

$$1=\sum_{i=1}^{n}\lambda_i+\sum_{i=1}^{n}\sum_{j>i}^{n}\lambda_{ij}+\sum_{i=1}^{n}\sum_{j>1}^{n}\sum_{k>j}^{n}\lambda_{ijk}+\cdots+\lambda_{12\ldots n}, \tag{5.17}$$

which is obtained by substituting $\mathbf{x}=\mathbf{b}$ in (3.26).

---

[7] Recall that for multiplicative and quasi-additive forms, we have to work with measurable value functions for which the concept of preference difference is viable. See Section 3.4.3 for more detail.

[8] See an alternative approach for the multiplicative case in Dyer and Sarin [1979, p. 820], and also in the example to be given subsequently.

To obtain the nth independent equation for the multiplicative and quasi-additive cases in risky problems, we may employ certainty equivalence gamble questions. This is the only basic difference between the technique used for value functions in the preceding paragraphs and the technique used for utility functions now being described. Through a proper questioning procedure described earlier, we may elicit from the decision maker the value of p_1 with $0<p_1<1$ for which the decision maker is indifferent between the risky prospect yielding either the most desirable consequence **b** with probability p_1 or the least desirable consequence **a** with probability $1-p_1$, and the consequence (sure prospect) $(a_1, a_2,\ldots,a_n)$. Thus, by Bernoulli's principle, we must have

$$\lambda_1 = p_1, \tag{5.18}$$

which serves as our nth independent equation as required. The procedures for obtaining the remaining constants are exactly the same as for the case of value functions, although some gamble questions similar to the above can be used to replace some of the "indifference to consequences" questions, if it is so desired.

5.2.8 Consistency Checks and Final Analysis

Since value functions or utility functions are models, or abstractions, of decision makers' preference structures that will be used in the final analysis, it is critical that they be carefully validated before implementation. There are two complementary basic strategies in validating prescriptive models:

1. to compare the model's performance with something known or well established (such as existing theoretical or experimental results), and
2. to compare the model's predictive capability with observed data.

Techniques for validating value or utility functions may thus proceed as follows.

First, check for internal consistency whenever possible. For example, in assessing the component value or utility functions, it should be possible to perform several consistency checks in the manner already described. For the case under uncertainty, after a component utility function for a particular attribute X_i has been assessed, check also that the shape of the function truly reflects the decision maker's risk behavior. In the process of estimating scaling constants, a number of consistency checks can also be administered. For example, in setting up and solving for an appropriate system of equations, particularly in the multiplicative and quasi-additive cases, there is no guarantee that the scaling constants obtained will satisfy the properties they are supposed to, namely, $0<\lambda_i<1$ for each $i=1,\ldots,n$ and $\mu>-1$. Clearly, if at least one of these conditions is violated, the existing preference information should be reexamined and the sources of inconsistency identified. After proper modifications have been made and any possible inconsistencies rectified, we may perform yet another check. Since there is more than one way to set up the system of equations to be solved for the required scaling constants, if one method is actually used for the above purpose, others may be used for consistency checking.

The second and final test is of the predictive or simulating capability of the value or utility function just obtained. To carry out this test, we first choose a reasonable number of representative consequences (sure prospects) and risky prospects, including both trivial and nontrivial choices. Through proper questioning techniques, we ask the decision maker to rank order these consequences and risky prospects as a whole or in pairwise comparison. If the value function or utility function is to truly reflect the decision maker's preference structure, its application should yield the same rank order.

5.3 The Lexicographic Method

The lexicographic method, which first received significant attention in the early fifties by Debreu [1954] and Geogescu-Roegen [1954], can be classified as a sequential elimination method. The basic idea is quite simple. The decision maker is first asked to rank order the attributes (or criteria) $X_1,\ldots,X_n$ in terms of their importance. The most important attribute, say X_1, is then used in the first screening step, in which alternatives yielding the most preferred value of X_1 are kept, the others discarded. From this modified set of alternatives, one selects only those yielding the most preferred value of the second most important attribute, say X_2. The process continues until either the modified set of alternatives contains only a unique element, which is then used as the best alternative, or until every attribute is screened once. In the latter case, if the final set of alternatives contains more than one element, some other means of selecting the final alternative (e.g., introducing additional attributes) may have to be devised. We shall later formalize this idea along with some of its variations and give explicit solution techniques. This approach is appealing from the practical viewpoint, since it closely corresponds to the way individuals actually make decisions. One tends to try to satisfy one's most important criteria before taking less important criteria into consideration. Russ [1971], for example, found that housewives used the lexicographic process in choosing among electrical appliances. Its second appeal is that it may be a practical alternative to the multiattribute utility function approach that works under much less demanding conditions.

To be more explicit, we consider a decision problem having a set A of alternatives (acts) and the n attributes $X_1,\ldots,X_n$. For convenience, we shall use $x_i=X_i(a)$, $i=1,\ldots,n$, to denote the value of attribute (consequence) X_i

corresponding to an alternative a in A. Hence, a particular consequence $\mathbf{x}$ in $X = X_1 \times X_2 \times \cdots \times X_n$ associated with alternative a is characterized by $\mathbf{x} = (x_1, \ldots, x_n) = (X_1(a), \ldots, X_n(a))$. Finally, let $w_i(x_i)$ be the appropriate component preference function for the attribute X_i. Clearly, $w_i(x_i)$ is the component value function $v_i(x_i)$ for riskless (certainty) decision problems and it is the component expected utility function $U_i(x_i)$ for risky (uncertainty) decision problems.

The basic steps of the lexicographic method are as follows:

i. The decision maker is asked to rank order the importance of (or to give priority to) all n attributes. Assume without loss of generality that the decision maker ranks the attributes in decreasing order of importance, $X_1, X_2, \ldots, X_n$.

ii. As the need arises, appropriate component preference functions $w_1(x_1), \ldots, w_n(x_n)$ are assessed using appropriate assessment techniques as described in Section 5.2.3.

iii. Start the sequential elimination process by solving the following sequence of problems consecutively:

$$P_1: \quad \max_{a \in A} \quad w_1[X_1(ab)],$$

$$P_2: \quad \max_{a \in A_1} \quad w_2[X_2(a)],$$

$$\vdots$$

$$P_i: \quad \max_{a \in A_{i-1}} \quad w_i[X_i(a)], \qquad A_{i-1} = \{a \mid a \text{ solves } P_{i-1}\},$$

$$i = 2, \ldots, n+1,$$

$$\vdots$$

until either a) we reach the ith problem $1 \leqslant i < n$, which has a unique solution (A_i has a single element); or b) the nth problem P_n is solved.

iv. If in Step iii, (a) prevails, then the unique solution of P_i is chosen as the best alternative. If, on the other hand, (b) prevails, the decision maker examines A_n and chooses the final alternatives based on other criteria.

In the uncertainty case, it is evident that although we do not require the existence, and therefore the construction, of a multiattribute utility function $u(\mathbf{x})$, we do need the existence and the construction of the component utility function $u_i(x_i)$. Consequently, we require that each conditional preference order for each attribute X_i satisfy the von Neumann–Morgenstern system of axioms (or its equivalent) in Theorem 3.13. The construction of $u_i(x_i)$ can be carried out by methods described in Section 5.2.3. The function $w_i(x_i)$ is then computed from $u_i(x_i)$ using Bernoulli's principle, yielding

$$w_i(X_i(a)) = E(u_i(x_i)). \tag{5.19}$$

As an example, consider a risky decision problem with three attributes X_1, X_2, X_3, four alternatives $A = \{a_1, a_2, a_3, a_4\}$, and two states of nature $S = \{s_1, s_2\}$. The corresponding consequences of an alternative a_i for any particular state of nature are

		a_1	a_2	a_3	a_4
$P(s_i) = \frac{1}{3}$	s_1	(40,4,250)	(30,5,500)	(20,8,300)	(45,6,300)
$P(s_i) = \frac{2}{3}$	s_2	(20,5,400)	(40,7,600)	(45,1,500)	(30,8,600)

Note that a typical entry is $\mathbf{x}(a_j, s_l) = (x_1^{jl}, x_2^{jl}, x_3^{jl})]$. Suppose it has been determined that the lexicographic method is appropriate for this problem. We may proceed as follows:

i. The decision maker is asked to rank the importance of X_1, X_2, X_3. Suppose the answer obtained is that X_1 has top priority, then X_2, and then X_3.

ii. Suppose also that the assessment process in Section 5.2.3 is used and the corresponding component utility functions are as shown in Figure 5.12.

Using (5.19) we can compute w_i for $i = 1, \ldots, n$ for each a_j from the formula

$$w_i(a_j) = \tfrac{1}{3}u_i(x_i^{j1}) + \tfrac{2}{3}u_i(x_i^{j2}). \tag{5.20}$$

Using Figure 5.12, the results of the computation are

	a_1	a_2	a_3	a_4
w_1	0.42	0.67	0.67	0.63
w_2	0.47	0.63	0.33	0.73
w_3	0.57	0.14	0.36	0.28.

iii. We solve P_1: $\max_{a \in A} w_1(a)$ by searching the first row above; we find that w_1 is at maximum when $a = a_2$ and $a = a_3$. Hence we have $A_1 = \{a_2, a_3\}$ and the pertinent data for P_2 is reduced to

	a_2	a_3
w_2	0.63	0.33
w_3	0.14	0.36.

Next we solve P_2: $\max_{a \in A_1} w_2(a)$ by examining the first row above. We find that w_2 is maximum when $a = a_2$. Consequently, $A_2 = \{a_2\}$, which has only one element. Hence a_2 is taken to be the best alternative.

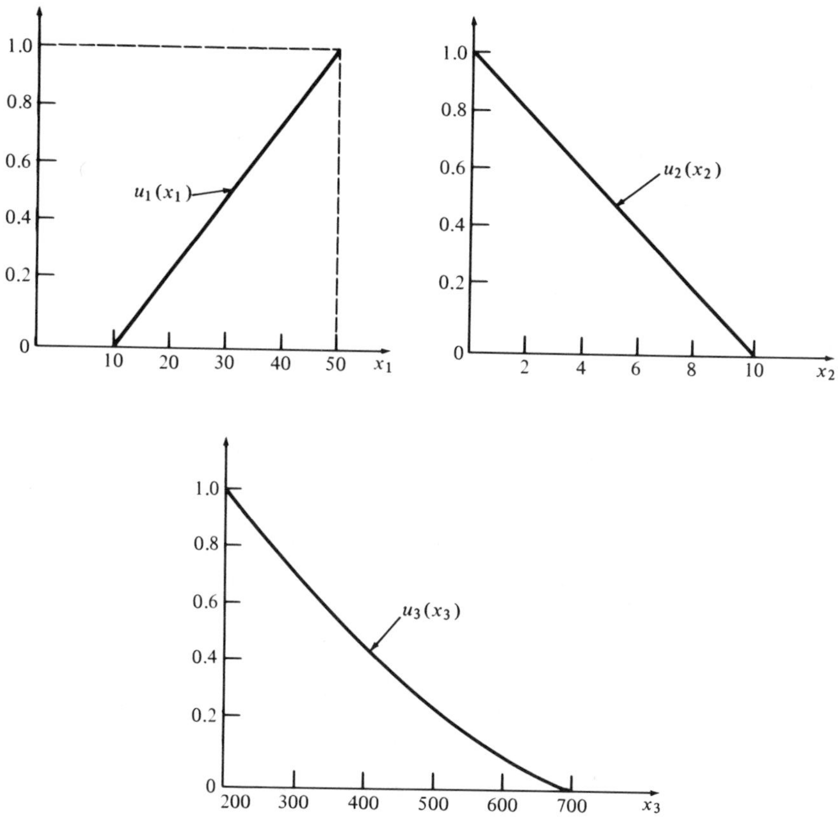

Figure 5.12 Component utility function for the problem of Section 5.2.3.

Observe that the attribute X_3 did not play any part in the decision-making process in this example. This is perhaps one of the main drawbacks of the method. Considering how poorly a_2 does on w_3, the decision maker may need to reassess his priority structure before using a_2 as suggested by the lexicographic method.

We now return to the component preference structure in the case of certainty. In risk-free decision problems, more often than not the most preferred value of X_i is either its maximum value (if preference increases as X_i increases) or its minimum value (if preference increases as X_i decreases). By the very nature of the lexicographic process, which works only with the most preferred value of X_i as reflected by Step iii, the component value functions need not be constructed and their existence is not even required; hence the method is relieved of many restrictive assumptions.

For risk-free decision problems, the lexicographic method can be simplified accordingly. Steps i and iv remain unchanged while Step ii is eliminated. Assuming for each $i=1,\ldots,n$ the preference increases as X_i decreases, then the sequence of problems to be solved consecutively in the original Step iii (which is now Step ii) is simply

$$\left\{\hat{P}_1: \min_{a\in A} X_1(a)\right\}, \quad \left\{\hat{P}_2: \min_{a\in A_1} X_2(a)\right\}, \quad \ldots, \quad \left\{\hat{P}_i: \min_{a\in A_{i-1}} X_i(a)\right\}, \quad \ldots,$$

where, as before, $A_{i-1}=\{a|a \text{ solves } \hat{P}_{i-1}\}$, $i=2,\ldots,n+1$. Equivalently, and sometimes more operationally, we can write, for each $i=2,\ldots,n+1$,

$$A_{i-1}=\left\{a|a\in A, X_j(a)=X_j(a^j), \ j=1,\ldots,i-1\right\},$$

where

$$X_j(a^j)\triangleq \min_{a\in A_{j-1}} X_j(a), \quad j=1,\ldots,i-1.$$

By the monotonicity assumption on preferences above, solutions of $\hat{P}_i$ are clearly also solutions of P_i and vice versa. The two procedures must therefore produce the same results.

As an example illustrating the use of lexicographic technique in risk-free decision problems, consider a continuous decision problem having three attributes X_1, X_2, X_3 with the set of alternatives A given implicitly in terms of decision variables y_1, y_2, y_3 by

$$A=\left\{\mathbf{y}|\mathbf{y}\in R^3, y_1^2+2y_2\geqslant 1, y_2\geqslant 0, y_3\geqslant 2\right\}.$$

The relationships among X_1, X_2, X_3 and $\mathbf{y}$ are as follows:

$$X_1(\mathbf{y})=-y_1^2-2y_2+y_1^2y_3+2y_2y_3,$$
$$X_2(\mathbf{y})=y_1^2y_3+3y_2y_3,$$
$$X_3(\mathbf{y})=-y_1y_3+3y_1^3y_2.$$

Suppose it is appropriate to solve this risk-free problem by the lexicographic method and the decision maker ranks X_1, X_2, X_3 in that order of decreasing priority. We next solve $\hat{P}_1$:

$$\begin{aligned} \min \quad & X_1(\mathbf{y})=(y_1^2+2y_2)(y_3-1) \\ \text{subject to} \quad & y_1^2+2y_2\geqslant 1, \\ & y_2\geqslant 0, \\ & y_3\geqslant 2. \end{aligned}$$

Clearly the solution is of the form $\mathbf{y}^*=(y_1, y_2, 2)$, where $y_1+2y_2=1$ at which point $X_1(\mathbf{y})=1$. That is,

$$A_1=\left\{\mathbf{y}|\mathbf{y}\in R^3, y_1+2y_2=1, y_3=2\right\}.$$

Next we solve $\hat{P}_2$:

$$\begin{aligned} \min \quad & X_2(\mathbf{y})=(y_1^2+2y_2)y_3+y_2y_3 \\ \text{subject to} \quad & \mathbf{y}\in A_1, \end{aligned}$$

or

$$X_1(\mathbf{y}) = (y_1^2 + 2y_2)(y_3 - 1) = 1,$$
$$y_1^2 + 2y_2 \geq 1,$$
$$y_2 \geq 0,$$
$$y_3 \geq 2.$$

By inspection we see that the solution of P_2 is $y_1 = -1$ or 1, $y_2 = 0$, $y_3 = 2$; or $A_2 = \{\mathbf{y} | \mathbf{y} \in R^3, y_1 = -1 \text{ or } 1, y_2 = 0, y_3 = 2\}$. Finally, P_3 is solved via $\hat{P}_3$:

$$\min \quad X_3(\mathbf{y}) = -y_1 y_3 + 3y_1^2 y_2$$
$$\text{subject to} \quad \mathbf{y} \in A_2,$$

which yields the unique solution $\mathbf{y}^* = (1, 0, 2)$. Clearly $\mathbf{y}^*$ is the best alternative for this problem lexicographically.

The basic shortcoming of the lexicographic method is that the decision maker must determine the priorities of the attributes before much information about the system is available. The problem is quite critical when it is not clear which criterion is most important, in which case it is difficult to assign priorities. Solution by the lexicographic method is quite sensitive to these priorities. In the example given for the uncertainty case, if X_2 is the top priority instead of X_1, the method will produce a_4 as the best alternative. If, on the other hand, X_3 is the highest priority, a_1 will become the best alternative. In order to reduce the sensitivity of the lexicographic method to priorities, Waltz [1967] suggested that A_i, the feasible region of problem P_{i+1}, $i = 1, \ldots, n-1$, be slightly enlarged by allowing $X_i(a)$ to be within some small percentage of its best value rather than insisting on keeping it at its best value. More specifically, the subproblem to be solved according to Waltz at the $(i+1)$th iteration is of the form $\hat{P}_{i+1}$:

$$\min \quad X_{i+1}(a)$$
$$\text{subject to} \qquad a \in A, \quad X_j(a) \geq X_j(a^j)(1+\delta), \quad j = 1, \ldots, i,$$

where δ is a small positive number, and a^j solves $\hat{P}_j$. For more details see Waltz [1967] or Hwang and Masud [1979].

5.4 The ELECTRE Method

The ELECTRE method, which is designed for multiobjective decision problems under certainty with a relatively small (finite) set of alternatives, can be described as a sequential elimination method. It was first introduced in 1968 by Bernard Roy, although there have been a number of subsequent modifications and applications.[9] Given a *finite* set of alternatives, the

---

[9] See, for example, Roy [1971, 1972, 1973, 1977], Roy and Bertier [1973], David and Duckstein [1975], and Nijkamp and Vos [1977].

ELECTRE method can be used to i) make the final selection, ii) classify alternatives into "reject" or "nonreject" classes, or iii) classify alternatives into indifference classes and rank order these classes. From a theoretical point of view, the method was developed as a procedure that is free from the restrictive assumption of completeness. We recall from Section 3.3 that to satisfy the completeness (connectedness) assumption, which is so often assumed (e.g., in the multiattribute utility function approach), any pair of alternatives a_1 and a_2 in the set of alternatives A must always be comparable by the preference order $\succcurlyeq$, i.e., $a_1 \succcurlyeq a_2$, or $a_2 \succcurlyeq a_1$, or $a_1 \sim a_2$. There are a number of real-world situations in which the decision maker cannot easily discriminate between a pair of alternatives because of cognitive strain or because of lack of sufficient information. This fact makes the completeness assumption indeed restrictive. From the practical viewpoint in relation to the above observation, there is also a need for a procedure that allows the decision maker to express *conditional* preference on a given pair of alternatives based on current information and to modify the preference should new information become available. To fulfill these needs, a new and weaker preference relation can be constructed. This is called the *outranking relation* and denoted by S. It may be thought of in terms of the risk of admitting the hypothesis $a' \succcurlyeq a''$. More formally, we can define the outranking relation as follows:

Definition. Given the set of alternatives A, for any a', a'' in A, we say $a'S_A a''$, which is read "a' outranks or is indifferent to a''" if and only if, given the decision maker's preference ordering $\succcurlyeq$, and given information on the values of the attributes $X_1(a)$, $X_2(a), \ldots, X_n(a)$, we have reason to believe that $a' \succcurlyeq a''$. We also say not $a'S_A a''$ if and only if with knowledge of $\succcurlyeq$ and the available information, particularly on the values of $X_1, \ldots, X_n$, we have no good reason to believe that $a' \succcurlyeq a''$.

Implicit in the above definition is that the outranking relation is normally dependent on the particular A (in particular, on its structure). If this is known not to be the case, the subscript A can be dropped and we are left with S, which Roy calls the *intrinsic* outranking relation.

Associated with the outranking relation S_A is the indifference (symmetric) outranking relation, denoted $\tilde{S}_A$, which may be defined as follows:

Definition. Given A, and a' and a'' in A, we say $a'\tilde{S}_A a''$ if and only if there exist alternatives $b_1, \ldots, b_j$ and $c_1, \ldots, c_k$ all in A, where $j \geqslant 1$ and $k \geqslant 1$ such that either $a'S_A a''$ or else $a'S_A b_1, b_1 S_A b_2, \ldots, b_j S_a a''$ occur simultaneously, with either $a''S_A a'$ or $a''S_A c_1, c_1 S_A c_2, \ldots, c_k S_A a'$.

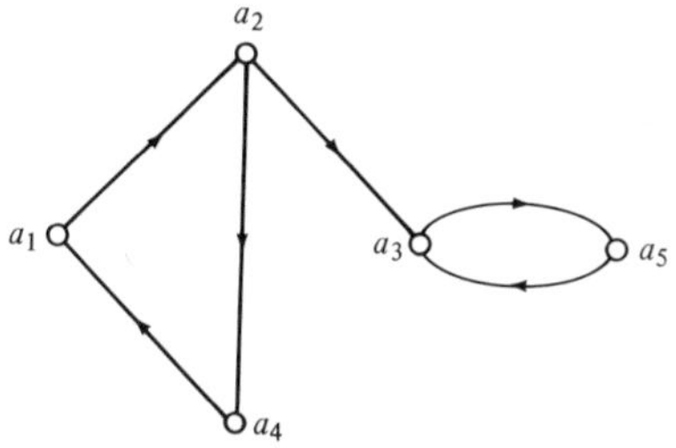

Figure 5.13 Graph of the outranking relation.

A graphic aid that is often useful in working with the ELECTRE method is a representation of the outranking relation S_A by a directed graph of the form

$$a'S_Aa'' \equiv \overset{a'}{\circ}\longrightarrow\overset{a''}{\circ}$$

For example, if $A=\{a_1,a_2,a_3,a_4,a_5\}$ and if $a_1S_Aa_2$, $a_2S_Aa_3$, $a_2S_Aa_4$, $a_3S_Aa_5$, $a_4S_Aa_1$, and $a_5S_Aa_3$, the graph in Figure 5.13 displays this outranking relation in A.

Clearly, $a'\tilde{S}_Aa''$ if and only if there is a closed directed path (or a circuit) on which both a' and a'' lie. For example, we see from Figure 5.13 that $a_1\tilde{S}_Aa_2$, $a_2\tilde{S}_Aa_4$, $a_1\tilde{S}_Aa_4$, and $a_3\tilde{S}_Aa_5$; a_1, a_2, a_4 are therefore in the same indifference class and likewise a_3 and a_5.

If an appropriate outranking relation can be constructed, the finite feasible set of alternatives A may be reduced to a smaller set A_1 by methods to be described. If A_1 already contains a single element (or a small number of elements), then the process is terminated because the element in A_1 outranks all other alternatives based on current information. But if A_1 still contains too many elements, we may try to construct yet another outranking relation, with more discriminating power (but also with greater risk) to reduce the set A_1 even further. This sequential elimination process continues until the remaining set of alternatives contains a single element or few enough elements for the decision maker to be comfortable making the final selection. To make the idea operational, we must i) construct S_A for a particular multiobjective decision problem and ii) use such a relation to reduce the set of alternatives. We first list some fundamental properties of S_A.

5.4.1 Properties of the Outranking Relation

We again use $x_1=X_1(a),\ldots,x_n=X_n(a)$ to represent the values of attributes $X_1,\ldots,X_n$ corresponding to alternative a and $\mathbf{x}(a)=(x_1,\ldots,x_n)=(X_1(a),\ldots,X_n(a))$.

The fundamental axiom states that for any a', a^0, and a'' in A,

$$a'S_Aa^0 \quad \text{and} \quad \mathbf{x}(a^0) \geqslant \mathbf{x}(a'') \quad \Rightarrow \quad a'S_Aa'', \tag{5.21a}$$

$$\mathbf{x}(a') \geqslant \mathbf{x}(a^0) \quad \text{and} \quad a^0S_Aa'' \quad \Rightarrow \quad a'S_Aa''. \tag{5.21b}$$

This is a reasonable assumption. If we have good reason to believe that a' is preferred or indifferent to a^0, which in turn dominates a'' [i.e., $\mathbf{x}(a^0) \geqslant \mathbf{x}(a'')$], we should have good reason to believe that a' is preferred or indifferent to a''. Roy calls this property *weak transitivity*. Since the outranking relation S_A is defined in terms of acceptable risk in admitting the hypothesis that something is at least as preferable as the other, such a relation is not necessarily transitive. For example, we may define S_A as $a'S_Aa''$ if and only if the probability of $a' \succcurlyeq a''$ is at least 0.95. Suppose the probabilities of $a' \succcurlyeq a^0$ and of $a^0 \succcurlyeq a''$ are each 0.96. Then by the above definition, we can write $a'S_Aa^0$ and a^0S_Aa''. Yet it is not true that $a'S_Aa''$, since the probability of $a' \succcurlyeq a''$ is 0.92, which is less than the threshold value 0.95 for accepting the hypothesis.

It is also reasonable to assume that S_A is reflexive:

$$aS_Aa \qquad \text{for all} \quad a \in A, \tag{5.22}$$

since we expect a to be indifferent to itself.

Using (5.21) and (5.22), and substituting $a^0 = a'$ in (5.21a), we have the following property:

$$\mathbf{x}(a') \geqslant \mathbf{x}(a'') \quad \Rightarrow \quad a'S_Aa'', \tag{5.23}$$

which we might expect. Clearly, the knowledge that a' dominates a'' should be reason enough to think that a' is at least as preferable as a''.

From the definition, it is easy to deduce that $\tilde{S}_A$ is reflexive, symmetric, and transitive. This should be easily observable from the illustration in Figure 5.13.

Observe that we do not assume the connectedness property of S_A in A. We allow incomparability as shown in Figure 5.13 by any pair of nodes that are not connected by either a direct arc or a closed (directed) path. For example, a_1 and a_3 are not comparable, nor are the pairs (a_1, a_5), (a_2, a_5), (a_3, a_4), and (a_4, a_5). This is despite the fact that there is a path $a_1 - a_2 - a_3$ joining a_1 and a_3. But since S_A is not necessarily transitive, such a path does not lead to any conclusion about comparability between a_1 and a_3.

If $a_3S_Aa_4$, then there would be a closed path joining a_1 and a_3, making them comparable. In fact, in such a case we would have $a_1\tilde{S}_Aa_3$, since $\tilde{S}_A$ is transitive. Later we shall show how incomparable alternatives are handled by this method. We can formalize incomparability and other "grades" of outranking, namely indifference, strict preference, and large preference [Roy, 1977] by associating a parameter $d(a', a)$ with the outranking relation S_A. Such parameters, whose values range from 0 to 1 inclusive, are used to reflect the *degree of outranking* or *degree of credibility* of using S_A, which in turn reflects the "fuzzy" nature of value judgment used in constructing S_A. The outranking relation so defined is called the *fuzzy outranking relation*. For a more detailed treatment of this interesting concept see Roy [1977].

5.4.2 Construction of the Outranking Relation

As Roy [1977] pointed out, the outranking relation is used as a surrogate model for the value function discussed in Chapter 3 and Section 5.2. The outranking relation is less formal and weaker in terms of *ordering strength* than the value function. It is, however, less restrictive and often easier to construct. The assessment process requires information that is normally less taxing to obtain from the decision maker. There are a number of ways for constructing the outranking relation for any particular decision problem; we shall describe what seems to be conceptually the simplest construction method. For other methods see, for example, Roy [1973, 1977] and Nijkamp and Vos [1977].

The values of attributes $X_1(a),\dots,X_n(a)$ for each a in A are assumed to be available. It is also assumed without loss of generality that for each $i=1,\dots,n$, the greater the values of X_i, the better (more preferred).

The method, due to Roy [1968, 1973], is based on the so-called concordance and discordance concepts and consists of two tests. The first is called the concordance test:

1. The decision maker is asked to indicate the relative importance of $X_1,\dots,X_n$. (Observe that whereas the lexicographic method requires only the order of importance, this method also requires the relative *magnitudes* of importance in order to give relative weights $w_1,\dots,w_n$.)
2. For each pair of alternatives a_j and a_k in A, construct the following index sets:

$$I^+(a_j,a_k)=\{i\,|\,1\leqslant i\leqslant n,\ X_i(a_j)>X_i(a_k)\},$$

$$I^=(a_j,a_k)=\{i\,|\,1\leqslant i\leqslant n,\ X_i(a_j)=X_i(a_k)\},$$

$$I^-(a_j,a_k)=\{i\,|\,1\leqslant i\leqslant n,\ X_i(a_j)<X_i(a_k)\}.$$

3. Construct the concordance indices I_{jk} and $\hat{I}_{jk}$, where

$$I_{jk}=\Bigg(\sum_{i\in I^+(a_j,a_k)} w_i+\sum_{i\in I^=(a_j,a_k)} w_i\Bigg)\Bigg/\Bigg(\sum_{i=1}^{n} w_i\Bigg) \tag{5.24}$$

and

$$\hat{I}_{jk}=\Bigg(\sum_{i\in I^+(a_j,a_k)} w_i\Bigg)\Bigg/\Bigg(\sum_{i\in I^-(a_j,a_k)} w_i\Bigg). \tag{5.25}$$

4. Choose a suitable value of the parameter α, which is called the minimum level of concordance. (This may be done by the analyst, in

consultation with the decision maker.) The concordance test is said to pass if

$$I_{ij} \geqslant \alpha \quad \text{and} \quad \hat{I}_{jk} \geqslant 1. \tag{5.26}$$

An assumption implicit in the concordance test is that compensations or trade-offs between attributes are always acceptable regardless of the magnitudes of compensations that have to be made.

The second test mitigates the limitation of the concordance test by working with *nondiscordance*. It is accordingly called the nondiscordance test:

1. Obtain the weights $w_1, \ldots, w_n$ as in the concordance test. Also construct $I^-(a_j, a_k)$ as before.
2. For each $i = 1, \ldots, n$, construct the discordance set D_i, which intuitively is the set of all possible pairs of values of X_i whose difference is not *compensable* by other attributes. For example, it may be possible to choose the level of discrepancy $d_i > 0$ for attribute X_i beyond which compensation by any other attributes is not acceptable, i.e.,

$$D_i = \{(x_i, y_i) | x_i, y_i \in X_i, (y_i - x_i) \geqslant d_i\}. \tag{5.27}$$

   That is, for any two alternatives a_j and a_k, if $X_i(a_k) - X_i(a_j) \geqslant d_i$, we cannot admit the hypothesis $a_j S_A a_k$, regardless of the values of the other attributes. Thus d_i can be viewed as a limit within which compensation is allowed.
3. The discordance test for a given pair a_j and a_k is said to be satisfied if

$$(X_i(a_j), X_i(a_k)) \notin D_i \quad \text{for all} \quad i \in I^-(a_j, a_k). \tag{5.28}$$

   Therefore, using only the concordance test,

$$a_j S_A a_k \quad \text{if and only if} \quad (5.26) \text{ holds}, \tag{5.29}$$

   or, alternatively, using both tests,

$$a_j S_A a_k \quad \text{if and only if} \quad (5.26) \text{ and } (5.28) \text{ hold}. \tag{5.30}$$

   It should be emphasized here that the construction method based on the concordance and discordance concepts just described is in no way unique. Several other methods can be devised, such as that proposed by Nijkamp and Vos [1977].

5.4.3 How to Use the Outranking Relation

Once the construction procedure summarized by either (5.29) or (5.30) is carried out for every pair of alternatives in A, the outranking relation constructed can be used to eliminate those alternatives which are outranked with respect to S_A. To carry out this elimination process, it is often helpful to construct a graphic representation of this outranking relation, as shown in Figure 5.13. Clearly, if any given node (representing an alternative) is situated at the tip of at least one arrow (directed arc) that does not form a part of a closed (directed) path, that node is definitely outranked (with respect to S_A) by at least one other alternative in A.

If we carefully eliminate some or all such alternatives, together with at least one alternative for each circuit, what remains is called by Roy the *minimal dominating subset* A_1 of A with respect to S_A. More formally, we define a *minimal dominating subset* A_1 as the smallest subset of A with the following property: for each $a' \in \bar{A}_1$,

$$a^* S_A a' \qquad \text{for some} \quad a^* \in A_1, \tag{5.31}$$

where $\bar{A}_1$ is the complement set of A_1. The minimal dominating subset A_1 is not necessarily unique. For example, in Figure 5.13 both $\{a_1, a_2, a_5\}$ and $\{a_2, a_4, a_5\}$ are the minimal dominating subsets of A with respect to the outranking relation shown. Despite this nonuniqueness characteristic, it suffices to pick any minimal dominating subset and proceed to the next step, which will be described later. There is one special class of minimal dominating subsets that is of special interest. If no two alternatives in a minimal dominating subset A_1 are comparable by S_A (i.e., no direct arc connecting any pair of members of A_1 exists), such a minimal dominating subset is called a *kernel* of A. If a kernel exists, it should be used in the next step, since it is a smallest subset of A with the minimal dominating property (5.31), containing only incomparable alternatives. Unfortunately, while there is always a minimal dominating subset corresponding to any given S_A, the kernel does not necessarily exist. For example, in Figure 5.13, no kernel exists. Had the direct arc between a_1 and a_2 been removed, as shown in Figure 5.14, the set $\{a_1, a_2, a_5\}$ would be both a minimal dominating subset and the (unique) kernel of A with respect to the modified outranking relation illustrated in Figure 5.14. Observe that although $(a_2, a_4, a_5\}$ is still another minimal dominating subset of A, it is not a kernel since there is a direct arc joining a_2 and a_4.

Having obtained a minimal dominating subset (or a kernel) A_1, we may terminate the process if the number of elements in A_1 is small enough for

Figure 5.14 Modified outranking relation.

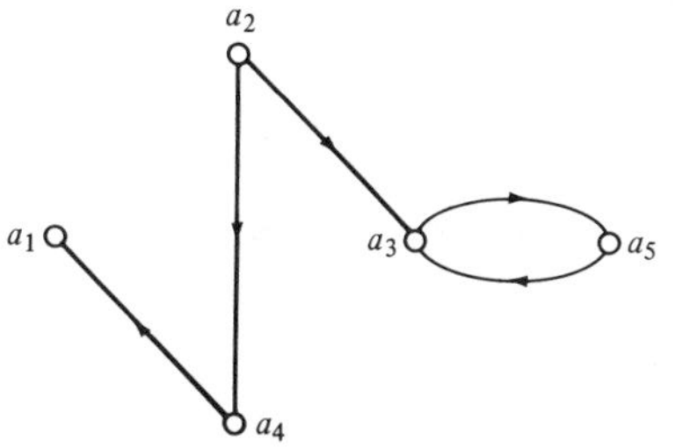

the decision maker to use value judgments to comfortably select the final solution. Otherwise, a stronger (but often riskier) outranking relation is constructed to further eliminate outranked alternatives from A_1. This may be done, for example, by reducing the minimum level of concordance α (5.26) or adjusting the values of d_i in (5.27).

5.4.4 Summary of the Algorithm

The steps for the ELECTRE method may now be summarized:

1. Obtain the values of attribute $X_1(a),\ldots,X_n(a)$ for every alternative in $A=\{a_1,\ldots,a_m\}$ and display the values in a matrix:

	a_1	a_2	$\cdots$	a_m
X_1	x_{11}	x_{12}	$\cdots$	x_{1m}
X_2	x_{21}	x_{22}	$\cdots$	x_{2m}
$\vdots$	$\vdots$	$\vdots$		$\vdots$
X_n	x_{n1}	x_{n2}	$\cdots$	x_{nm}.

2. Construct the outranking relation S_A by concordance–discordance or some other appropriate method and construct a graph representing such outranking relation.
3. Obtain a minimum dominating subset A_1 of A. If a kernel exists, choose such kernel as A_1.
4. If A_1 has a single element or is small enough to apply value judgment to select the final decision(s)—STOP. Otherwise, repeat Steps 2–4.

Example: Consider a four-attribute decision problem in which $A=\{a_1,a_2,a_3,a_4,a_5,a_6\}$. Suppose for each $i=1,\ldots,4$, the preference increases as X_i increases. Suppose also that the payoff matrix for this problem is

	a_1	a_2	a_3	a_4	a_5	a_6
X_1	20	13	15	30	5	40
X_2	0.3	0.5	0.1	0.7	0.9	0
X_3	1.3×10^6	4.0×10^6	2.2×10^6	1.0×10^6	4.0×10^6	1.0×10^6
X_4	3	3	5	2	7	1

To construct the outranking relation S_A by the concordance–discordance method, assume the decision maker determined that

a. the relative weights of X_1, X_2, X_3, X_4 are 0.3, 0.2, 0.4, 0.1, implying that $\Sigma_{i=1}^4 w_i=1$;
b. the minimum level of concordance $\alpha=0.70$;

c. no compensation is allowed if the difference in X_1, namely d_1, is at least 15 units or the difference in X_3, namely d_3, is at least 2.0×10^6 units.

Consequently,

$$D_1=\{(x_1,y_1)|x_1,y_1\in X_1 \text{ and } (y_1-x_1)\geqslant 15\},$$

and

$$D_3=\{(x_3,y_3)|x_3,y_3\in X_3 \text{ and } (y_3-x_3)\geqslant 2.0\times 10^6\}.$$

We illustrate how S_A is constructed using both the concordance and nondiscordance tests. To compare a_1 and a_2, observe that $X_3(a_2)-X_3(a_1)>2.0\times 10^6$, so that $a_1 S_A a_2$ is not true, irrespective of the values of other attributes. To check whether the reverse, i.e., $a_2 S_A a_1$, is true, we observe that the nondiscordance test is satisfied. For the concordance test we construct

$$I^+(a_2,a_1)=\{2,3\},\qquad I^=(a_2,a_1)=\{4\},\qquad \text{and}\qquad I^-(a_2,a_1)=\{1\}.$$

Hence, $I_{21}=[(0.2+0.4)+0.1]/1=0.7$, and $\hat{I}_{21}=(0.2+0.4)/0.3=2.0$. Since both indices meet requirements (5.26) for the concordance test, $a_2 S_A a_1$.

By continuing the same procedure for each other pair of alternatives in A, we find that $a_4 S_A a_6$, $a_5 S_A a_2$, and $a_5 S_A a_3$. The corresponding graph of this outranking relation is shown in Figure 5.15.

Clearly, $\{a_1,a_4,a_5\}$ and $\{a_2,a_5,a_6\}$ are two minimal dominating subsets of A, the former being the (unique) kernel of A. We thus choose $A_1=\{a_1,a_4,a_5\}$. If we want to reduce A_1 even further, a new outranking relation S_A^1 may be constructed by, for example, relaxing the minimum level of concordance α from 0.7 to, say, 0.5. In this case we find $a_1 S_A^1 a_4$ and $a_4 S_A^1 a_1$, whose corresponding graph is shown in Figure 5.16.

Furthermore, $A_2=\{a_1,a_5\}$ is a minimum dominating subset and a kernel (not unique) of A_1 with respect to S_A^1. If we want to reduce A_2 even further, a new outranking relation S_A^2 can be constructed by relaxing the restriction d_1 from 15 to 20 units. In this case, we conclude $a_5 S_A a_1$. This yields a_5 as the unique alternative resulting from the above sequential elimination process.

Figure 5.15 The outranking relation graph.

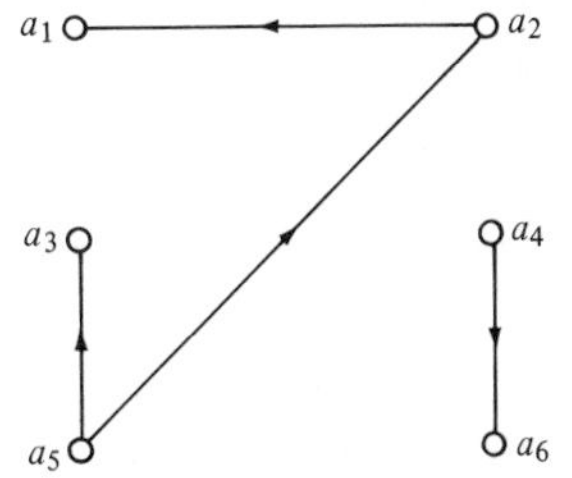

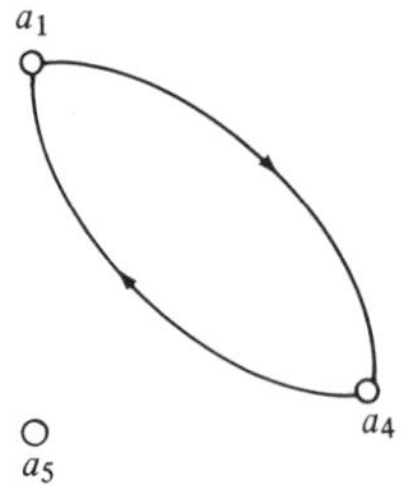

Figure 5.16 Graph of S_A^1.

Application of the final outranking relation, such as S_A^2 in the example, to the original set A does not necessarily produce the same final minimal dominating subset (and consequently, not the same final result). The sequential elimination procedure is recommended mainly because it furnishes opportunities to gain greater understanding and appreciation of what is being done, and more importantly, what levels of risk are involved when eliminating certain alternatives. Also, construction of the outranking relation using the concordance–discordance method normally involves tedious pairwise comparisons. Some bookkeeping tools, such as the concordance dominance matrix, the discordance dominance matrix, and the total dominance matrix described in Nijkamp and Vos [1977], are often useful for this purpose.

5.5 The Indifference Curves (Surfaces) Method

Given a reference point (x_1^0, x_2^0) in a two-attribute decision problem, if an indifference curve passing through the reference point can be constructed as illustrated in Figure 5.17, the set of alternatives can then be divided into three parts. Those alternatives which lie on the same indifference curve I_1 are indifferent to the reference point, and hence, to one another. If a simple test shows that A is preferred to (x_1^0, x_2^0) and the latter is, in turn, preferred to B, then those alternatives in the unshaded area are less preferred then (x_1^0, x_2^0) (and all alternatives lying on I_1). They should, therefore, be eliminated from further consideration. Finally, all those alternatives in the shaded area are preferred to (x_1^0, x_2^0) and all other alternatives. Further exploration to find the best alternative should thus be carried out on this subset of alternatives. Such exploration may involve the construction of another indifference curve (say I_2) and an elimination procedure similar to the one just described. The principal task of this approach, to which we shall later return, is the construction of indifference curves (or surfaces).

The type of problem for which the method is viable has the following characteristics. First, because of the need for geometrical representation and analysis, only two (or at most three) attributes can be handled at a time. For

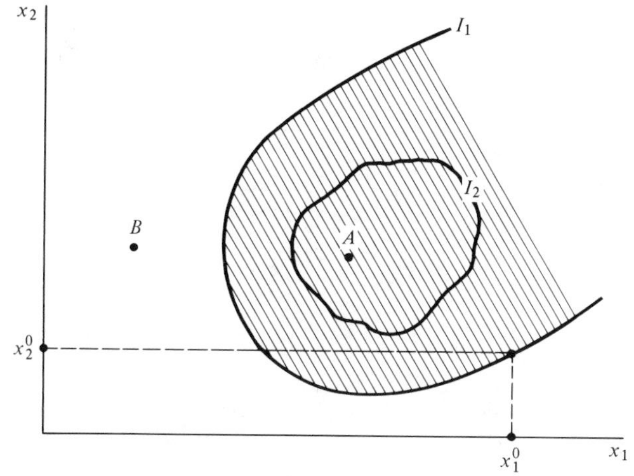

Figure 5.17 The indifference curve method.

problems with more than three attributes, some form of dimensionality reduction is needed. Second, the method is designed mainly for deterministic problems with numerically scaled (interval or ratio scales) attributes. Third, necessary conditions guaranteeing the existence of indifference curves must be satisfied.

Because of the last two characteristics, there is a closed relationship between this and the multiattribute value function methods described earlier in this chapter. Clearly if, for an n-attribute decision problem, a multiattribute value function $v(\mathbf{x})$ exists, a family of indifference surfaces also exists and is given by

$$v(\mathbf{x}) = \text{const.} \tag{5.32}$$

The converse is, however, not necessarily true. Some forms of integrability conditions [Samuelson, 1950] are required to established $v(\mathbf{x})$ from a family of indifference surfaces. The indifference-curve approach is thus less restrictive but, at the same time, less prescriptive than the multiattribute value function approach.

We now return to the question of how to construct indifference curves. For any two points on the same indifferent curve, there is always a trade-off involving a certain amount of degradation of one attribute the decision maker is willing to tolerate in exchange for a certain amount of improvement of the other attribute while preferences for the two points remain the same. This may be called *indifference trade-off* or *marginal rate of substitution* (see Chapter 7) and is illustrated in Figure 5.18.

In going from alternative $A(x_1^0, x_2^0)$ to alternative $B(x_1^1, x_2^1)$, we have to give up (decrease) Δx_1 units of X_1 in exchange for an increase of Δx_2 units of X_2. Hence, the indifference trade-off associated with this exchange is Δx_2

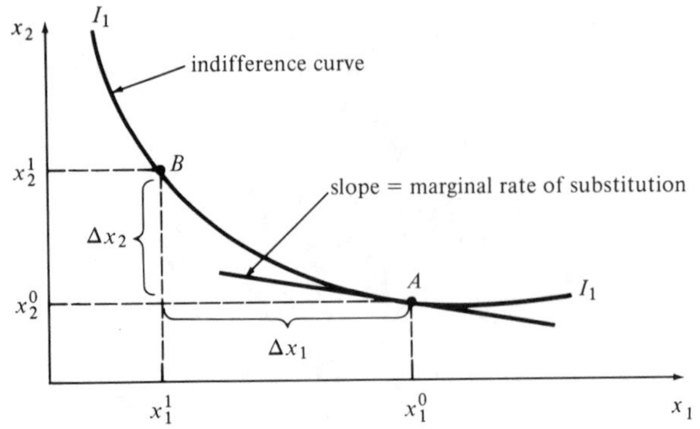

Figure 5.18 Indifference trade-offs.

units of $X_2/\Delta x_1$ units of X_1. The determination of an indifference curve passing through a reference point (x_1^0, x_2^0) is therefore equivalent to finding all points having indifference trade-offs with (x_1^0, x_2^0). Furthermore, we may solve (5.32) for some fixed constant to obtain X_2 as a function of X_1 whose graph is typically represented in Figure 5.18 by the indifference curve I_1. The slope of the tangent to the curve at (x_1^0, x_2^0), which is given by $-dX_2/dX_1|_{x_1^0, x_2^0}$, is called the marginal rate of substitution between X_2 and X_1.

For two-attribute decision problems, MacCrimmon and Wehrung [1977] describe three methods for constructing indifference curves which they call the line procedure, the square procedure, and the diamond or circle procedure. All these procedures involve preference-indifference judgments. The line procedure asks the decision maker to compare two alternatives, one being the reference point (x_1^0, x_2^0) and the other being of the form (x_1^1, x_2) or (x_1, x_2^1). The value of x_1 (or x_2) is fixed at some convenient value while x_2 (or x_1) is varied until indifference is achieved. This is illustrated in Figure 5.19. For example, suppose we select $X_2 = y_1$ and ask the decision maker to compare (x_1^0, x_2^0) and (x_1^1, y_1); if the decision maker indicates the former is preferred to the latter, we increase (i.e., assume that more of it is preferred) X_2 from y_1 to y_2 and offer the choice (x_1^0, x_2^0) and (x_1^1, y_2) to the decision maker. If this time the decision maker prefers the latter to the former, y_2 is decreased to y_3 and the process is repeated. Suppose the decision maker is indifferent between (x_1^0, x_2^0) and (x_1^1, y_4); then (x_1^1, x_2^1), where $x_2^1 = y_4$, is one point on the indifference curve passing through (x_1^0, x_2^0) that we are seeking. After repeating the procedure for various values of x_1 (say, $x_1^1, x_1^2, x_1^3, x_1^4, x_1^5$) until a sufficient number of points is generated, a smooth curve can be fitted to generate the required indifference curve.

For details of the other two approaches, see MacCrimmon and Wehrung [1977], who also discuss methods for constructing the so-called preferred

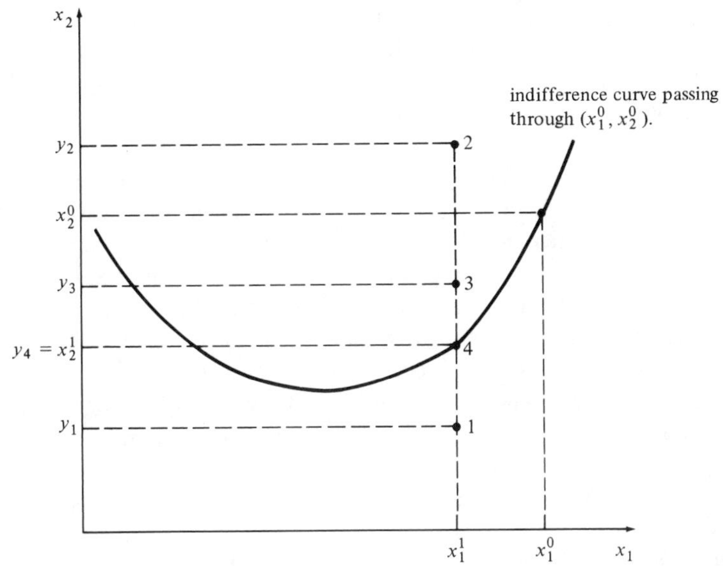

Figure 5.19 The line procedure.

proportion curves and methods for constructing indifference surfaces in three dimensions.

It is possible to extend the approach to n-attribute $(n>3)$ decision problems as suggested by MacCrimmon and Wehrung [1977]. One alternative is to combine this approach with the lexicographic method by performing indifference trade-off analysis between the two most important attributes. Another alternative is to use information about pairwise trade-offs successively to form composite attributes whose number become smaller as we increase the hierarchical level. The highest level should consist of two composite attributes for which indifference trade-off analysis can be performed.

5.6 Summary

A number of outcome-oriented techniques for handling multiple objective decision problems have been described in this chapter. Each of these techniques is designed primarily to measure with varying degrees of intensity and sophistication the decision maker's preference.

Among them, the multiattribute utility function method is a direct assessment approach. It aims at obtaining a global representation of the preference structure in terms of a numerical function both for certainty and uncertainty. Based on the theoretical developments in Chapter 3, the method proceeds in five steps. First, necessary conditions are verified to ensure the existence of multiattribute utility functions. Second, appropriate independent conditions are checked to see which decomposition form is applicable. Third, component preference functions are assessed. Fourth, appropriate scaling constants are estimated. Finally, consistency checks are carried out.

Two of the sequential elimination methods were also described. In the lexicographic method, preference is assessed in terms of the rank order or priorities of attributes and the component utility or value functions. In the deterministic case, however, the value of attributes themselves may be used as surrogate models for component value functions, if monotonicity of preference for each attribute can be assumed. In the ELECTRE method, which is applicable to deterministic, discrete, and finite decision problems, measurement of preference is accomplished by means of the construction of outranking relations. Finally, the indifference curve method, which exemplifies the spatial proximity approach, was also described.

References

Allais, M. (1953). Le comportement de l'homme rational—devant le risque: critique des postulates et axiomes de l'école americaine, *Econometrica* 21, 503–546.

Bell, D. E. (1981). Decision regret: a component of risk aversion? paper presented at the *The Multiple Criteria Decision Making Conference* at University of Delaware, Newark, 10–15 August 1980, and to appear in the Proceedings (J. N. Morse, ed.), Springer, Berlin.

Ben-Tal, A. (1980). Characterization of Pareto and lexicographic optimal solutions, in *Multiple Criteria Decision Making: Theory and Application — Proceedings, Hagen / Königswinter, West Germany*, 1979 (G. Fandel and T. Gal, eds.), Springer, Berlin, pp. 1–11.

David, L., and Duckstein, L. (1975). Long range planning of water resources: A multiobjective approach, *UNDP/UN Interregional Seminar on River Basin and Interbasin Development, Budapest, Hungary*, Center for Natural Resources, Energy and Transport, U.N., New York, pp. 16–26.

Debreu, G. (1954). Representation of a preference ordering by a numerical function, in *Decision Processes* (R. M. Thrall, C. H. Coombs, and R. L. Davis, eds.), Wiley, New York, pp. 159–166.

Dyer, J., and Sarin, R. K. (1979). Measurable multiattribute value functions, *Operations Research* 27, 810–822.

Edwards, W. (1977). How to use multiattribute utility measurement for social decision making, *IEEE Transactions on Systems, Man, and Cybernetics* SMC-7, 326–340; also in *Conflicting Objectives in Decisions* (D. E. Bell, R. L. Keeney, and H. Raiffa, eds.), Wiley, Chichester, Great Britain, pp. 247–276.

Fishburn, P. C. (1967). Methods of estimating additive utilities, *Management Science* 13, 435–453.

Fishburn, P. C. (1970). *Utility Theory for Decision Making*, Wiley, New York.

Fishburn, P. C. (1976). Lexicographic orders, utilities, and decision rules: a survey, *Management Science* 20, 1442–1471.

Geogescu-Roegen, N. (1954). Choice, expectations, and measurability, *Quarterly Journal of Economics* 68, 503–534.

Gorman, W. M. (1968). The structure of utility functions, *Review of Economic Studies* 35, 367–390.

Harvey, C. M. (1979). *Operations Research: An Introduction to Linear Optimization and Decision Analysis*, North-Holland, New York.

Hwang, C. L., and Masud, A. S. M. (1979). *Multiple Objective Decision Making—Methods and Applications*, Lecture Notes in Economics and Mathematical Systems No. 164, Springer, Berlin.

Keeney, R. L., and Raiffa, H. (1976). *Decisions with Multiple Objectives*, Wiley, New York.

Kirkwood, C. W., and Sarin, R. K. (1980). Preference conditions for multiattribute value functions, *Operations Research* 28, 225–231.

Luce, R. D., and Suppes, P. (1965). Preference, utility, and subjective probability, in *Handbook of Mathematical Psychology* (R. D. Luce, R. R. Bush, and E. Galanter, eds.), Wiley, New York, Vol. 2, pp. 249–410.

MacCrimmon, K. R. (1973). An overview of multiple objective decision making, in *Multiple Criteria Decision Making* (J. Cochrane and M. Zeleny, eds.), University of South Carolina Press, Columbia, pp. 18–44.

MacCrimmon, K. R., and Wehrung, D. A. (1977). Trade-off analysis: the indifference and preferred proportions approaches, in *Conflicting Objectives in Decisions* (D. E. Bell, R. L. Keeney, and H. Raiffa, eds.), Wiley, Chichester, Great Britain, pp. 123–147.

Nijkamp, P., and Vos, J. B. (1977). A multicriteria analysis for water resource and land use development, *Water Resources Research* 13, pp. 513–518.

Pratt, J. W. (1964). Risk aversion in the small and in the large, *Econometrica* 32, 122–136.

Roy, B. (1968). Classement et choix en présence de critères multiples, *RIRO*, No. 8, pp. 57–75.

Roy, B. (1971). Problems and methods with multiple objective functions, *Mathematical Programming* 1(2).

Roy, B. (1972). Décision avec critères multiples: problèmes et methodes, *Revue METRA* 11, 121–151.

Roy, B. (1973). How outranking relation helps multiple criteria decision making, in *Multiple Criteria Decision Making* (J. Cochrane and M. Zeleny, eds.), University of South Carolina Press, Columbia, pp. 179–201.

Roy, B. (1977). Partial preference analysis and decision-aid: the fuzzy outranking relation concept, in *Conflicting Objectives in Decisions* (D. E. Bell, R. L. Keeney, and H. Raiffa, eds.), Wiley, Chichester, Great Britain, pp. 40–75.

Roy, B., and Bertier, P. (1972). La méthode ELECTRE II: une application au media-planning, in *VIIème Conférence Internationale de Recherche Operationnelle, Dublin* (M. Ross, ed.), OR72, North-Holland, Amsterdam, pp. 291–302.

Russ, F. (1971). Consumer evaluation of alternative product models (Ph.D. dissertation), Carnegie-Mellon University.

Sage, A. P. (1977). *Methodology for Large-Scale Systems*, McGraw-Hill, New York.

Samuelson, P. (1950). The problem of integrability in utility theory, *Economica* 17, 355–385.

Sarin, R. K. (1977). Interactive evaluation and bound procedure for selecting multi-attributed alternatives, in *Multiple Criteria Decision Making—TIMS Studies in Management Sciences* (M. K. Starr and M. Zeleny, eds.), North-Holland, Amsterdam, pp. 211–224.

Sarin, R. K. (1980). Ranking of multiattribute alternatives with an application to coal power plant siting, in *Multiple Criteria Decision Making: Theory and Application — Proceedings, Hagen/Königswinter, West Germany, 1979* (G. Fandel and T. Gal, eds.), Springer, Berlin, pp. 405–429.

Starr, M. K., and Zeleny, M. (1977). MCDM—state and future of the arts in *Multiple Criteria Decision Making—TIMS Studies in Management Sciences* (M. K. Starr and M. Zeleny, eds.), North-Holland, Amsterdam, pp. 5–30.

Thrall, R. M. (1954). Applications of multidimensional utility theory, in *Decision Processes* (R. M. Thrall, C. M. Coombs, and R. L. Davis, eds.), Wiley, New York, pp. 181–186.

von Neumann, J., and Morgenstern, O. *Theory of Games and Economic Behavior*, Princeton University, Princeton, 1944.

Waltz, F. M. (1967). An engineering approach: hierarchical optimization criteria, *IEEE Transactions on Automatic Control* AC-12, 179–180.

Chapter 6

Methods for Generating Noninferior Solutions

6.1 Introduction

Chapters 6–8 will be exclusively concerned with the computational aspects of decision problems with the following characteristics:

1. The set of alternatives, to be denoted by X, is implicitly defined in terms of the decision variables $(x_1,\ldots,x_N)$, rather than being given explicitly as a list of alternatives.
2. The criteria upon which decisions are based are given in terms of multiple objective functions $f_1,\ldots,f_n$, which are functions of decision variables.

Whereas in the foregoing chapter attributes were used as both decision variables and decision criteria (objective functions), in the present chapter we make a distinction between these two types of variables to allow simultaneous consideration of a large number of decision variables and to accommodate explicit consideration of causal relationships characterizing the system's structure. This is particularly relevant in large and complex decision problems where not only is the number of decision variables very large, but there is also a complex of means–ends relationships that needs to be considered in the solution process. These decision problems arise naturally in such problems as engineering design, planning for resource management, and regional development or production. In these situations, the system's responses to alternative actions are complex and not easily perceived. A preference structure, needed for decision making, should not, therefore, be constructed based on hypothetical responses and without knowing the actual responses of the system. If, without overwhelming him, information about the system's actual behavior can be presented to the decision maker, then he can judge his preferences more accurately. It is therefore important to consider the complexity of causal relations in the solution process, and thus active interplay between the systems analysis and preference assessment may be not only prudent but necessary. Solution techniques that take into account complex causal relations treat decision making not as an act, but as a process. Accordingly, we shall call these techniques *process oriented.*

Using the notation and terminology introduced in Chapter 4, we let a set of alternatives be represented by X and characterized by N decision variables of the form

$$X=\{\mathbf{x}|\mathbf{x}\in R^N,\ g_i(\mathbf{x})\leqslant 0,\ i=1,\ldots,m,\ \mathbf{x}\in S\}, \tag{6.1}$$

where $g_i(\mathbf{x})$ is a real-valued function representing a system constraint or a causal relationship; $S\subseteq R^N$ is any other form of system constraint (e.g., $\{0,1\}$). Also let the n objective functions $f_1(\mathbf{x}),\ldots,f_n(\mathbf{x})$ be real-valued functions defined on X. Each of these functions represents a decision criterion upon which the decision is based. Normally, the number of decision variables N will be much larger than the number of objective functions n. The multiobjective decision problem MDP we are interested in can be stated in the most general term as follows: *Based on the decision criteria* $f(\mathbf{x})=(f_1(\mathbf{x}),\ldots,f_n(\mathbf{x}))$, *choose the best alternatives* $\mathbf{x}$ *from* X.

Implicit in our definition of the multiobjective decision problem is the existence and prominent role of a preference structure. What the best alternative is depends on the underlying preference structure, which in turn determines the final decision rule, as discussed in Chapter 1. One particular preference structure, which will interest us in this chapter and the major part of the remainder of this book, is characterized in part by the following monotonicity property:

Monotonicity Assumption. A preference is a monotone function of the value of each objective function. More specifically, without loss of generality, we say that for each $i=1,\ldots,n$, when all f_j except $j=i$ are held fixed at any of their feasible values, a preference does not decrease as f_i decreases, and indifference prevails if f_i remains constant.

If we again let $\succcurlyeq$ represent the preference order (see Chapter 3 for formal definition) characterizing our preference structure, then, from the monotonicity property, we can say that

$$\mathbf{f}(\mathbf{x}^1)\leqslant\mathbf{f}(\mathbf{x}^2) \quad\Rightarrow\quad \mathbf{x}^1\succcurlyeq\mathbf{x}^2 \tag{6.2a}$$

and

$$\mathbf{f}(\mathbf{x}^1)=\mathbf{f}(\mathbf{x}^2) \quad\Rightarrow\quad \mathbf{x}^1\sim\mathbf{x}^2 \tag{6.2b}$$

for any $\mathbf{x}^1$ and $\mathbf{x}^2$ in X. Since $\succcurlyeq$ is normally a partial order, due to the potential incompleteness[1] of the set $F \triangleq \{\mathbf{f}(\mathbf{x}) | \mathbf{x} \in X\}$, the converse of (6.2) is not necessarily true. For this reason, other properties of the preference structure usually must be exploited before the best alternative can be determined. Nevertheless, it is useful to know whether the preference structure is monotonic, since that provides an initial screening process: The monotonicity of the preference structure can be used to partition X into two mutually exclusive subsets X^* and $\bar{X}^*$, with $X^* \cap \bar{X}^* = \varnothing$ and $X^* \cup \bar{X}^* = X$ having the following properties (for a vector minimization problem):

i. For any $\mathbf{x}^* \in X^*$, there exists no $\mathbf{x} \in X$ such that $\mathbf{f}(\mathbf{x}) \leqslant \mathbf{f}(\mathbf{x}^*)$;
ii. for any $\mathbf{x}^1$ in $\bar{X}^*$, there exists an $\mathbf{x}^*$ in X^* such that $\mathbf{f}(\mathbf{x}^*) \leqslant \mathbf{f}(\mathbf{x}^1)$; hence $\mathbf{x}^* \succcurlyeq \mathbf{x}^1$ by (6.2a).

As in Chapter 4, we call X^* the set of noninferior solutions, whose typical element $\mathbf{x}^*$ is called a noninferior solution. Likewise, $\bar{X}^*$ is called the inferior solution set. By virtue of the monotonicity of the preference structure, we should explore the best alternative from among noninferior ones. It is in this context that the concept of noninferior solution prevails; the first phase of the MDP is traditionally transformed into the so-called *vector optimization problem* (VOP) of the form

$$\min_{\mathbf{x} \in X} \quad \{\mathbf{f}(\mathbf{x}) = (f_1(\mathbf{x}), \ldots, f_n(\mathbf{x}))\}. \tag{6.3}$$

We may explore the preference structure to define a complete order and use it to rank order elements in X, hence identifying the best alternative. This strategy is used in methods discussed previously. If the preference structure is known to be monotonic, then as a check of consistency, we may test the best alternative for noninferiority. If, however, our primary objective is merely to find the best alternative, we need consider only noninferior solutions. Then we need apply preference ordering only to the noninferior sets to be sure that the final decision is noninferior. Most methods described in this and in the next two chapters follow the second strategy, which has two substrategies: one incorporates preference as a basis for generating only needed noninferior solutions; the other generates, in the absence of preference, all or *representative* subsets of noninferior solutions upon which the decision maker can later act. In this chapter, we follow the latter substrategy and describe computational methods for generating all or representative subsets of noninferior solutions.

---

[1] This is because there may be elements of $\mathbf{f}(\mathbf{x}^1)$ and $\mathbf{f}(\mathbf{x}^2)$ in F which are not comparable in the sense that neither $\mathbf{f}(\mathbf{x}^1) \leqslant \mathbf{f}(\mathbf{x}^2)$ nor $\mathbf{f}(\mathbf{x}^1) \geqslant \mathbf{f}(\mathbf{x}^2)$.

6.2 Methods Based on a Weighting Characterization

As we have seen in Chapter 4, a common method for finding noninferior solutions of a VOP is to convert it into a scalar problem using the weighting (or Lagrangian[2]) formulation of the form $P(\mathbf{w})$:

$$\min_{\mathbf{x}\in X} \quad \sum_{i=1}^{n} w_i f_i(\mathbf{x}) = \mathbf{w}^{\mathrm{T}}\cdot\mathbf{f}(\mathbf{x}), \tag{6.4}$$

where the row weight vector

$$\mathbf{w}\in W \triangleq \left\{\mathbf{w}|\mathbf{w}\in R^n,\ w_j \geqslant 0 \text{ for each } j=1,\ldots,n \text{ and } \sum_{j=1}^{n} w_j = 1\right\}. \tag{6.5}$$

The fundamental properties of this technique (see Sections 4.3.3 and 4.3.4) can be summarized as follows:

a. Given a weight vector $\mathbf{w}^0$, if we solve $P(\mathbf{w}^0)$ and obtain an optimal solution $\mathbf{x}^0$, we can claim that $\mathbf{x}^0$ is a noninferior solution of VOP if $\mathbf{x}^0$ is the unique solution of $P(\mathbf{w}^0)$ or if each w_j is strictly positive, i.e., $\mathbf{w} > 0$ (Theorem 4.6). This implies that at least some noninferior solutions can be generated by solving $P(\mathbf{w})$ for some properly chosen $\mathbf{w}$, whether or not the objective functions and X are convex.
b. If the convexity assumptions on $\mathbf{f}$ and X are assumed, then for any given noninferior solution $\mathbf{x}^*$, we can always find a weight vector $\mathbf{w}$ such that $\mathbf{x}^*$ is a solution of $P(\mathbf{w})$ (Theorem 4.5). That is to say that under the convexity assumption *all* noninferior solutions can be found by solving the weighting problem $P(\mathbf{w})$.

The need for the convexity assumption is demonstrated in the example following Theorem 4.6. For any given noninferior solution $\mathbf{x}^*$, the weight vector $\mathbf{w}$ yielding $\mathbf{x}^*$ is not necessarily unique. Clearly, there may be more than one way (weight) of producing a noninferior solution $\mathbf{x}^*$. This is true particularly in linear problems, as will be discussed. In short, if $X'_w = \{\mathbf{x}|\mathbf{x}$ solves $P(\mathbf{w})$ for some $\mathbf{w} > \mathbf{0}$ in $W\}$, $X''_w = \{\mathbf{x}|\mathbf{x}$ is a unique minimizer of $P(\mathbf{w})$ for some $\mathbf{w}\in W\}$, and $X_w = \{\mathbf{x}|\mathbf{x}$ solves $P(\mathbf{w})$ for some $\mathbf{w}\in W\}$, then properties (a) and (b) imply

$$X'_w \subseteq X^* \tag{6.6a}$$

and

$$X''_w \subseteq X^*; \tag{6.6b}$$

---

[2] For the purpose of the discussion in this section, note that the Lagrangian formulation is also one form of the weighting formulation. Most of the subsequent discussions are therefore applicable to the Lagrangian formulation as well.

and under the convexity assumptions,

$$X^* \subseteq X_w. \tag{6.7}$$

Because of property (b), we shall not consider nonconvex problems in this section. In particular, we assume that the set X and all functions $f_1(\mathbf{x}),\ldots,f_n(\mathbf{x})$ are convex, so that we can make use of both (6.6) and (6.7). If we assume further that at least one of the objective functions, say $f_k(\mathbf{x})$, is strictly convex, then the optimal solution of $P(\mathbf{w})$ must necessarily be unique for any weight $\mathbf{w}$ with $w_k > 0$. Consequently if each $f_i(\mathbf{x})$ is strictly convex, we have from (6.6) and (6.7) that

$$X^* = X_w'' = X_w'. \tag{6.8}$$

Even with these assumptions, the question of how to choose and vary the weights $w_1,\ldots,w_n$ to scan through the entire or a representative part of the noninferior solutions set X^* remains.

6.2.1 *The Analytical Approach*

For some relatively simple problems, one may solve analytically for the set of noninferior solutions X^* and the required set of weights.

Formulate the weighting problem $P(\mathbf{w})$ as in (6.4) without assigning specific values to the weights. Next apply appropriate necessary and sufficient conditions to $P(\mathbf{w})$ for optimality, such as those discussed in Section 2.3. This should yield a set of equations and inequalities which can be analyzed for the required X^*. The following examples will demonstrate the procedure.

Example 1: Consider a VOP

$$\min \quad (f_1(\mathbf{x}), f_2(\mathbf{x}), f_3(\mathbf{x})) \tag{6.9}$$

$$\text{subject to} \quad g_1(\mathbf{x}):\ x_1 + 2x_2 \leqslant 10, \tag{6.10a}$$

$$g_2(\mathbf{x}):\quad x_2 \leqslant 4, \tag{6.10b}$$

$$g_3(\mathbf{x}):\ -x_1 \leqslant 0, \tag{6.10c}$$

$$g_4(\mathbf{x}):\ -x_2 \leqslant 0, \tag{6.10d}$$

where

$$f_1(\mathbf{x}) = (x_1-1)^2 + (x_2-1)^2,$$
$$f_2(\mathbf{x}) = (x_1-2)^2 + (x_2-3)^2,$$

and

$$f_3(\mathbf{x}) = (x_1-4)^2 + (x_2-2)^2.$$

The weighting problem corresponding to (6.9)–(6.10) is $P(\mathbf{w})$:

$$\min \quad w_1 f_1(\mathbf{x}) + w_2 f_2(\mathbf{x}) + w_3 f_3(\mathbf{x})$$

$$\text{subject to} \quad (6.10),$$

where $w_i \geqslant 0$ for each $i=1,2,3$ and $w_1+w_2+w_3=1$.

Applying the Kuhn–Tucker necessary conditions (2.24)–(2.25) yields

$$2x_1 - 2(w_1 + 2w_2 + 4w_3) + \mu_1 - \mu_3 = 0, \tag{6.11a}$$

$$2x_2 - 2(w_1 + 3w_2 + 2w_3) + \mu_1 + \mu_2 - \mu_4 = 0, \tag{6.11b}$$

$$\mu_1(x_1 + 2x_2 - 10) = 0, \tag{6.11c}$$

$$\mu_2(x_2 - 4) = 0, \tag{6.11d}$$

$$\mu_3 x_1 = 0, \tag{6.11e}$$

$$\mu_4 x_2 = 0, \tag{6.11f}$$

and $x_1 + 2x_2 - 10 \leqslant 0$, $x_2 - 4 \leqslant 0$, $x_1 \geqslant 0$, $x_2 \geqslant 0$, where $\mu_j \geqslant 0$ for each $j=1,2,3,4$ is the Kuhn–Tucker multiplier associated with the jth constraint.

For this specific problem, none of the constraints in (6.10) can be binding at the optimal point, since otherwise the corresponding solution of (6.11) satisfying all the nonnegativity requirements for w_is and μ_js and $w_1 + w_2 + w_3 = 1$ will not exist. For example, if both $x_1 = 0$ and $x_2 = 0$, then from (6.11c) and (6.11d), $\mu_1 = \mu_2 = 0$. Consequently, (6.11a) and (6.11b) become

$$-2(w_1 + 2w_2 + 4w_3) - \mu_3 = 0,$$

$$-2(w_1 + 3w_2 + 2w_3) - \mu_4 = 0,$$

which clearly have no nonnegative solutions with $w_1 + w_2 + w_3 = 1$. A more complicated case, when (6.10a) and (6.10d) are binding, implies that $x_2 = 0$ and $x_1 = 10$, which implies from (6.11d) and (6.11e) that $\mu_2 = \mu_3 = 0$. Substituting these values in (6.11a) and (6.11b) and subtracting (6.11a) from (6.11b) yields

$$-20 - 2w_2 + 4w_3 - \mu_4 = 0$$

or

$$w_3 = \tfrac{1}{4}(20 + 2w_2 + \mu_4) \geqslant 5,$$

which clearly violates the requirement $0 \leqslant w_3 \leqslant 1$. By performing similar analyses we can conclude that the only possible solution to (6.11) is $\mu_i = 0$ for all $i = 1,2,3,4$ and

$$x_1^* = w_1 + 2w_2 + 4w_3, \tag{6.12a}$$

$$x_2^* = w_1 + 3w_2 + 2w_3; \tag{6.12b}$$

or, if we define

$$\mathbf{x}^1 = \begin{pmatrix} 1 \\ 1 \end{pmatrix}, \quad \mathbf{x}^2 = \begin{pmatrix} 2 \\ 3 \end{pmatrix}, \quad \mathbf{x}^3 = \begin{pmatrix} 4 \\ 2 \end{pmatrix},$$

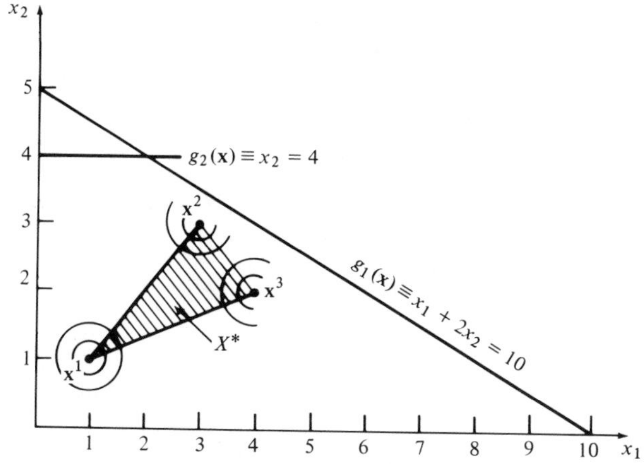

Figure 6.1 Noninferior solution set of Example 1.

then

$$\mathbf{x}^* = \begin{pmatrix} x_1^* \\ x_2^* \end{pmatrix} = w_1\mathbf{x}^1 + w_2\mathbf{x}^2 + w_3\mathbf{x}^3. \tag{6.13}$$

Since each $f_i(\mathbf{x})$ is convex and $\mathbf{x}$ defined in (6.13) is a unique solution of (6.11), $\mathbf{x}$ is also a unique solution of $P(\mathbf{w})$ for a given $\mathbf{w} \in W$. [One can also apply the second-order sufficiency in Section 2.3 to verify that $\mathbf{x}$ in (6.13) is indeed a unique solution of $P(\mathbf{w})$.] Consequently $\mathbf{x}$ defined in (6.13) is a noninferior solution of (6.9)–(6.10), or we can say that the set of noninferior solutions X^* of (6.9)–(6.10) is the convex hull represented by (6.13); i.e.,

$$X^* = \{\mathbf{x}^* | \mathbf{x}^* \in R^2,\ \mathbf{x} = w_1\mathbf{x}^1 + w_2\mathbf{x}^2 + w_3\mathbf{x}^3,\ w_i \geq 0,$$
$$i = 1, 2, 3, \text{ and } w_1 + w_2 + w_3 = 1\}. \tag{6.14}$$

This set is illustrated in Figure 6.1.

Example 2: Consider an example used in Chapter 4:

$$\min \quad (f_1(\mathbf{x}), f_2(\mathbf{x}), f_3(\mathbf{x})) \tag{6.15}$$

$$\text{subject to } g_1(\mathbf{x}): \quad -x_1 \leq 0, \tag{6.16a}$$

$$g_2(\mathbf{x}): \quad -x_2 \leq 0, \tag{6.16b}$$

where

$$f_1(\mathbf{x}) = (x_1 - 3)^2 + (x_2 - 2)^2,$$
$$f_2(\mathbf{x}) = x_1 + x_2,$$
$$f_3(\mathbf{x}) = x_1 + 2x_2.$$

To apply the weighting method to find the set of all noninferior solutions, we first formulate the corresponding weighting problem of the form $P(\mathbf{w})$:

$$\begin{aligned} &\min \quad w_1 f_1(\mathbf{x}) + w_2 f_2(\mathbf{x}) + w_3 f_3(\mathbf{x}) \\ &\text{subject to} \quad (6.16) \end{aligned} \tag{6.17}$$

where $w_i \geqslant 0$, $i=1,2,3$, and $w_1+w_2+w_3=1$. Applying the Kuhn–Tucker necessary condition (2.24)–(2.25) to $P(\mathbf{w})$ yields

$$2(x_1-3)w_1 + w_2 + w_3 - \mu_1 = 0, \tag{6.18a}$$

$$2(x_2-2)w_1 + w_2 + 2w_3 - \mu_2 = 0, \tag{6.18b}$$

$$\mu_1 x_1 = 0, \tag{6.18c}$$

$$\mu_2 x_2 = 0, \tag{6.18d}$$

and $x_1 \geqslant 0$, $x_2 \geqslant 0$, $\mu_1 \geqslant 0$, and $\mu_2 \geqslant 0$.

Note that since $f_1(\mathbf{x})$ is strictly convex, any solution of (6.18) with $w_1>0$ (which is precisely the case, as we shall see shortly) is a unique solution of $P(\mathbf{w})$. By (6.6) such a solution must be a noninferior solution of (6.15)–(6.16). From (6.18a) and (6.18b) and the fact that $w_1+w_2+w_3=1$ we have

$$x_1 = (7w_1 - 1 + \mu_1)/2w_1, \tag{6.19a}$$

$$x_2 = (5w_1 - w_3 - 1 + \mu_2)/2w_1. \tag{6.19b}$$

If $x_2>0$, then from (6.18d) $\mu_2=0$. Hence from (6.19b), $5w_1-1>w_3$. Consequently $7w_1-1+\mu_1>2w_1+w_3+\mu_1\geqslant 0$, implying from (6.19a) that $x_1>0$ and from (6.18c) that $\mu_1=0$. Hence we cannot have $x_2>0$ and $x_1=0$. But the following is possible:

$$x_1 = (7w_1-1)/2w_1, \qquad w_1 > \tfrac{1}{7}, \tag{6.20a}$$

and

$$x_2 = (5w_1 - w_3 - 1)/2w_1, \qquad 5w_1 > 1 + w_3. \tag{6.20b}$$

Now if $w_2=0$, we can have either $x_1=0$ or $x_1>0$. If $x_1>0$, (6.20a) still prevails. We also see from (6.19b) that if $w_1 \leqslant \frac{1}{5}$, we have $0 \leqslant x_2 \leqslant (-w_3 + \mu_2)/2w_1$, implying that $\mu_2 \geqslant w_3$. Hence, from (6.18d), $x_2=0$. Also when $w_1>\frac{1}{3}$, we must have $w_3<\frac{2}{3}$. From (6.19b) and (6.18d) it follows that $x_2>0$. From the above analysis we conclude that a set of weights that generates the set of all noninferior solutions of (6.15)–(6.16) has the properties

$$W' \equiv \{(w_1, w_2, w_3) | \mathbf{w} \in W,\ \tfrac{1}{7} \leqslant w_1 \leqslant \tfrac{1}{5} \text{ or else } \tfrac{1}{5} \leqslant w_1 \leqslant 1,\ 5w_1 \geqslant 1 + w_3\};$$

and the full set of noninferior solutions X^* can be described as

i. $0 \leqslant x_1^* \leqslant 1$, $x_2^* = 0$, corresponding to $\frac{1}{7} \leqslant w_1 \leqslant \frac{1}{5}$ (this corresponds to the line $0A$ in Figure 6.2);

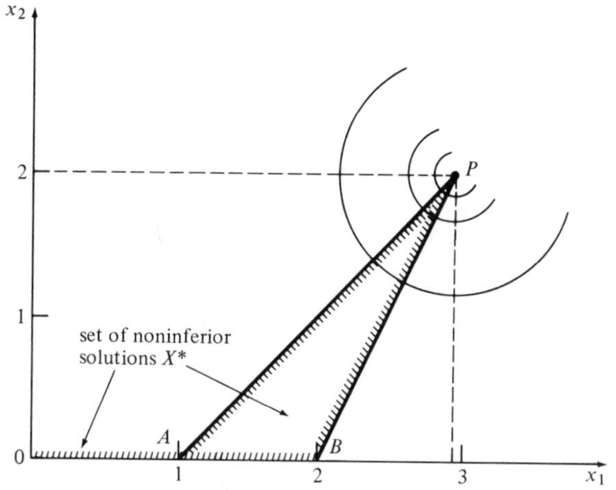

Figure 6.2 Noninferior solution set of Example 2.

ii. when $5w_1 \geq 1 + w_3$ (which implies $\frac{1}{5} \leq w_1 \leq 1$), we have

$$x_1^* = (7w_1 - 1)/2w_1 \quad \text{and} \quad x_2^* = (5w_1 - w_3 - 1)/2w_1,$$

or, if we let

$$\mathbf{x}^1 = \begin{pmatrix} 1 \\ 0 \end{pmatrix}, \qquad \mathbf{x}^2 = \begin{pmatrix} 2 \\ 0 \end{pmatrix}, \qquad \mathbf{x}^3 = \begin{pmatrix} 3 \\ 2 \end{pmatrix},$$

we have

$$\mathbf{x}^* = \begin{pmatrix} x_1^* \\ x_2^* \end{pmatrix} = \lambda_1 \mathbf{x}^1 + \lambda_2 \mathbf{x}^2 + \lambda_3 \mathbf{x}^3, \tag{6.21}$$

where

$$\lambda_1 = \frac{w_2}{4w_1}, \qquad \lambda_2 = \frac{w_3}{2w_1}, \qquad \lambda_3 = \frac{5w_1 - w_3 - 1}{4w_1}.$$

Observe that when w_1 and w_3 are selected with the properties above, then $0 \leq \lambda_i \leq 1$, $i = 1,2,3$, and $\lambda_1 + \lambda_2 + \lambda_3 = 1$. Hence the set of noninferior solutions represented by $\mathbf{x}^*$ in (6.21) is the convex hull formed by $\mathbf{x}^1$, $\mathbf{x}^2$, and $\mathbf{x}^3$. This is demonstrated in Figure 6.2 by the triangle PAB.

The whole set of noninferior solutions becomes

$$X^* = \{(x_1, x_2) | \text{either } 0 \leq x_1 \leq 1, x_2 = 0, \text{ or } \mathbf{x}^* = \lambda_1 \mathbf{x}^1 + \lambda_2 \mathbf{x}^2 + \lambda_3 \mathbf{x}^3,$$
$$\lambda_1 + \lambda_2 + \lambda_3 = 1, \lambda_i \geq 0 \text{ for each } i = 1,2,3\}.$$

Example 3: Consider a simple linear multiobjective optimization problem of the form

$$\min \quad (f_1(\mathbf{x}), f_2(\mathbf{x})) \tag{6.22}$$

$$\text{subject to} \quad g_1(\mathbf{x}): \quad x_2 \leqslant 5, \tag{6.23a}$$

$$g_2(\mathbf{x}): \quad x_1 + x_2 \leqslant 6, \tag{6.23b}$$

$$g_3(\mathbf{x}): \quad 2x_1 + x_2 \leqslant 9, \tag{6.23c}$$

$$g_4(\mathbf{x}): \quad x_1 \leqslant 4, \tag{6.23d}$$

$$g_5(\mathbf{x}): \quad -x_1 \leqslant 0, \tag{6.23e}$$

$$g_6(\mathbf{x}): \quad -x_2 \leqslant 0, \tag{6.23f}$$

where

$$f_1(\mathbf{x}) = -x_1 - 2x_2 \quad \text{and} \quad f_2(\mathbf{x}) = -3x_1 - x_2.$$

Applying the Kuhn–Tucker necessary conditions (2.24)–(2.25) to the weighting problem $P(\mathbf{w})$,

$$\min \quad f(\mathbf{x}) = w_1 f_1(\mathbf{x}) + w_2 f_2(\mathbf{x})$$

$$\text{subject to} \quad (6.23)$$

yields

$$-w_1 - 3w_2 + \lambda_2 + 2\lambda_3 + \lambda_4 - \mu_1 = 0, \tag{6.24a}$$

$$-2w_1 - w_2 + \lambda_1 + \lambda_2 + \lambda_3 - \mu_2 = 0, \tag{6.24b}$$

$$\lambda_1(x_2 - 5) = 0, \tag{6.24c}$$

$$\lambda_2(x_1 + x_2 - 6) = 0, \tag{6.24d}$$

$$\lambda_3(2x_1 + x_2 - 9) = 0, \tag{6.24e}$$

$$\lambda_4(x_1 - 4) = 0, \tag{6.24f}$$

$$\mu_1 x_1 = 0, \tag{6.24g}$$

$$\mu_2 x_2 = 0, \tag{6.24h}$$

with (6.23) being satisfied and $\lambda_i \geqslant 0$, $i = 1, 2, 3, 4$, and $\mu_1, \mu_2 \geqslant 0$. Since both f_1 and f_2 are linear, any solution of (6.24) is necessarily a solution of $P(\mathbf{w})$. Moreover for any given w_1, w_2, the unique solution of (6.24), if it exists, is also the unique solution of $P(\mathbf{w})$, hence, a noninferior solution of (6.22)–(6.23). However, as we shall see later, there exist some weights w_1, w_2 for which $P(\mathbf{w})$ does not have a unique solution. We shall deal with such cases in the course of the discussion.

In order to analyze the constraints in (6.24), we must consider three cases: i) none of the constraints (6.24) are binding; ii) one and only one constraint is binding; and iii) exactly two constraints are binding. It is highly unlikely in problems with two decision variables that three or more constraints will be binding. In problems of higher-dimension, such cases must obviously be considered. Since $P(\mathbf{w})$ is a linear, single-objective optimization problem, case (i) is impossible. Also since $\hat{f}(\mathbf{x}) = (-w_1 - 3w_2)x_1 + (-2w_1 - w_2)x_2$, the coefficients of x_1 and x_2 can never be zero for any positive weights w_1 and w_2. Consequently $f(\mathbf{x})$ can never be parallel to either the x_1 axis or x_2 axis. We can thus eliminate the possibility that $g_1(\mathbf{x})$, $g_4(\mathbf{x})$, $g_5(\mathbf{x})$, or $g_6(\mathbf{x})$ alone will be binding at the optimal solution. So we need only consider $g_2(\mathbf{x})$ and $g_3(\mathbf{x})$ in order to analyze case (ii). Consider the case where $g_2(\mathbf{x})$ is the only binding constraint. From (6.24c) and (6.24e)–(6.24h), $\lambda_1 = \lambda_3 = \lambda_4 = \mu_1 = \mu_2 = 0$. Hence from (6.24a) and (6.24b) and the fact that $w_1 + w_2 = 1$, we have

$$w_1 = \tfrac{2}{3}, \qquad w_2 = \tfrac{1}{3}, \qquad \text{and} \qquad \lambda_2 = \tfrac{5}{3}. \tag{6.25}$$

In other words, if we let $w_1' = \frac{2}{3}$ and $w_2' = \frac{1}{3}$ in $P(\mathbf{w})$, the optimal solutions of $P(\mathbf{w})$ will be any point between points A and B in Figure 6.3. This is to be expected since with such weights $f(\mathbf{x})$ is parallel to the constraint $g_2(\mathbf{x})$. Solutions of $P(\mathbf{w})$ are not unique; however, because both $w_1 > 0$ and $w_2 > 0$, any point along the line AB is a noninferior solution of (6.22)–(6.23) by virtue of (6.6a). By a similar analysis, we find that any point along the line BC is also a noninferior solution of (6.22)–(6.23) obtainable from $P(\mathbf{w})$ with $w_1'' = \frac{1}{4}$ and $w_2'' = \frac{3}{4}$.

We observe that points A, B, and C correspond to the case where exactly two constraints are binding. Since each of them can be obtained as a solution of $P(\mathbf{w})$ using one of the above two sets of weights, each of those

Figure 6.3 Example 3. Note that $\hat{f}(\mathbf{x}) = w_1 f_1(\mathbf{x}) + w_2 f_2(\mathbf{x})$, where $\frac{1}{4} \leq w_1 \leq \frac{2}{3}$, $\frac{1}{3} \leq w_2 \leq \frac{3}{4}$, and $w_1 + w_2 = 1$.

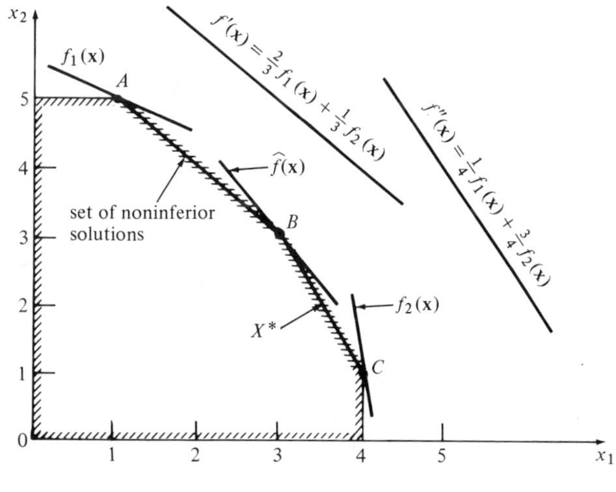

three points is also a noninferior solution of (6.22)–(6.23). Since no other point satisfies (6.24), we conclude that the set of noninferior solutions to (6.22)–(6.23) consists of every point along the lines AB and BC in Figure 6.3 inclusive.

Points A, B, and C are both noninferior solutions and the extreme points of the problem (6.22)–(6.23). More than one set of weights can be used to obtain each of these points by solving $P(\mathbf{w})$. By analyzing (6.24), the entire set of weights corresponding to each of these noninferior extreme points can be derived algebraically. For example, point A is the point where both $g_1(\mathbf{x})$ and $g_2(\mathbf{x})$ are binding. Hence, from (6.24), λ_3, λ_4, μ_1, and μ_2 will vanish. This together with (6.24a), (6.24b), and the fact that $w_1+w_2=1$ yields

$$w_1=\tfrac{1}{3}(2+\lambda_1),\quad w_2=\tfrac{1}{3}(1-\lambda_1),\qquad \text{where}\quad 0\leqslant\lambda_1\leqslant 1.$$

This is to say that any weights $\mathbf{w}=(w_1,w_2)$ selected from the set $W_A=\{(w_1,w_2)|\frac{2}{3}\leqslant w_1\leqslant 1,\ w_1+w_2=1\ (\text{hence } 0\leqslant w_2\leqslant\frac{1}{3})\}$ will yield the noninferior extreme point A. By similar argument it can be shown that

$$W_B=\{(w_1,w_2)|\tfrac{2}{3}\leqslant w_1\leqslant 1,\ w_1+w_2=1\ (\text{hence } \tfrac{1}{3}\leqslant w_2\leqslant\tfrac{3}{4})\}$$

and

$$W_C=\{(w_1,w_2)|0\leqslant w_1\leqslant\tfrac{1}{4},\ w_1+w_2=1\ (\text{hence } \tfrac{3}{4}\leqslant w_2\leqslant 1)\}.$$

Being able to describe these sets of weights for each noninferior extreme point in a linear multiobjective optimization problem may be useful for developing algorithms, as we shall see later.

Example 4: Reid and Vermuri [1971] and Vermuri [1974] consider the following multiobjective geometric programming problem:

$$\min\quad (f_1(\mathbf{x}),\ldots,f_n(\mathbf{x})) \tag{6.26}$$

$$\text{subject to}\qquad \mathbf{x}>\mathbf{0},\quad \mathbf{x}\in R^N, \tag{6.27}$$

where each f_j is a posynomial of the form

$$f_j(\mathbf{x})=\prod_{i=1}^{N} x_i^{a_{ji}}.$$

We assume that $a_{ji}\leqslant 0$ or $a_{ji}\geqslant 1$ for each $i=1,\ldots,N$ and $j=1,\ldots,n$. It can be easily shown that under such assumptions $f_j(\mathbf{x})$ is a convex function for each $j=1,\ldots,N$. The corresponding weighting problem for (6.26)–(6.27) for $\mathbf{w}\in W$ is $P(\mathbf{w})$:

$$\min\quad \sum_{j=1}^{n} w_j f_j(\mathbf{x}) \tag{6.28}$$

$$\text{subject to}\quad \mathbf{x}>\mathbf{0}. \tag{6.29}$$

Applying the Kuhn–Tucker necessary conditions to $P(\mathbf{w})$, we get

$$\sum_{j=1}^{n} w_j a_{jk} x^{a_{jk}-1} \prod_{i \neq k} x^{a_{ji}} = 0, \qquad k=1,\ldots,N$$

or

$$\sum_{j=1}^{n} w_j a_{jk} f_j(\mathbf{x}) = 0, \qquad k=1,\ldots,N. \tag{6.30}$$

Note that by (6.30), for any given $\mathbf{w}$ we have N equations and n unknowns, $f_1(\mathbf{x}),\ldots,f_n(\mathbf{x})$, which may not have a solution, particularly when $N>n$. But if such a solution exists, and if each a_{ji} is negative or $\geqslant 1$, which ensures convexity of each f_j, then that solution of (6.30) is also an optimal solution of (6.26)–(6.27).

Consider the case where $n=N+1$. Since $\Sigma_{j=1}^{n} w_j f_j(\mathbf{x})>0$ for all $\mathbf{x}>\mathbf{0}$, we can define

$$\alpha_j = w_j f_j(\mathbf{x}) \Big/ \sum_{j=1}^{n} w_j f_j(\mathbf{x}), \qquad j=1,\ldots,n. \tag{6.31}$$

Clearly

$$\alpha_j \geqslant 0, \quad j=1,\ldots,n, \qquad \alpha_1+\alpha_2+\cdots+\alpha_n=1. \tag{6.32}$$

Dividing (6.30) by $\Sigma_{j=1}^{n} w_j f_j(\mathbf{x})$ and using (6.31) yields

$$\sum_{j=1}^{n} a_{jk}\alpha_j = 0, \qquad k=1,\ldots,N. \tag{6.33}$$

If the solution to the n equations (6.32)–(6.33) exists and is denoted by $(\alpha_1^*,\ldots,\alpha_n^*)$, it is obviously unique. With these assumptions one can derive the subset of noninferior solutions of (6.26)–(6.27) corresponding to all $\mathbf{w}>\mathbf{0}$ as follows. For consistency with (6.31) and the fact that according to our assumptions $f_i(\mathbf{x})>0$ for all $\mathbf{x}>\mathbf{0}$ and $\mathbf{w}>\mathbf{0}$, α_j^* must be strictly positive for each $j=1,\ldots,n$. From (6.32) we obtain

$$\sum_{j=1}^{n} w_j f_j(\mathbf{x}) = \left[\sum_{j=1}^{n} w_j f_j(\mathbf{x})\right]^{\sum_{j=1}^{n} w_j} = \prod_{j=1}^{n}\left[\sum_{j=1}^{n} w_j f_j(\mathbf{w})\right]^{w_j}. \tag{6.34}$$

Substituting $\Sigma_{j=1}^{n} w_j f_j(\mathbf{x}) = (w_j/\alpha_j^*) f_j(\mathbf{x})$ from (6.31) in both sides of (6.34) and observing that $f_j(\mathbf{x})=\Pi_{i=1}^{N} x_i^{a_{ji}}$, we have for any $1 \leqslant m \leqslant n$

$$\frac{w_m f_m(\mathbf{x})}{\alpha_m^*} = \left[\prod_{j=1}^{n}\left(\frac{w_j}{\alpha_j^*}\right)^{w_j}\left(\prod_{i=1}^{N} x_i^{a_{ij}}\right)^{w_j}\right]$$

$$= \left[\prod_{j=1}^{n}\left(\frac{w_j}{\alpha_j^*}\right)^{w_j}\right]\left(\prod_{i=1}^{N} x_i^{\Sigma_{j=1}^{n} a_{ji} w_j}\right).$$

From (6.33), we have for any $1 \leqslant m \leqslant n$

$$f_m(\mathbf{x}) = (\alpha_m^*/w_m) \prod_{j=1}^{n} (w_j/\alpha_j^*)^{w_j}. \tag{6.35}$$

The entire subset of noninferior solutions in the objective space of (6.26)–(6.27) generated by strictly positive weights $\mathbf{w} > \mathbf{0}$ is given by (6.35).

6.2.2 Ad Hoc Numerical Approach

Using the set of necessary and sufficient conditions as a direct means of solving the weighting problem and producing noninferior solutions is practical in only a rather limited number of problems. Very often a numerical solution procedure is required to solve $P(\mathbf{w})$ for a given $\mathbf{w}$. In this case, the question how should $\mathbf{w}$ be varied so as to generate the whole or a representative subset of noninferior solutions remains. When the objective functions and the constraint set have no special properties (apart from being convex), it seems natural to proceed in an ad hoc manner. First we consider each weight w_i between 0 and 1 as having a reasonable number of discrete values. Then we solve $P(\mathbf{w})$ numerically for each combination of values of $w_1, w_2, \ldots, w_n$.

It is clearly not practical to generate the entire set of noninferior solutions in this manner. The most one can hope for is a representative subset so that a reasonably good, if not the best, final choice can be selected from this subset. This not only makes sense, but is also practical. It may be inhibiting, if not overwhelming, for the decision maker to have to select the best alternative from the entire set of noninferior solutions, if there is no systematic search procedure to help him.

The following numerical test of noninferiority may be useful in the ad hoc numerical approach. If $\mathbf{x}^*$ is an optimal solution of $P(\mathbf{w}')$ for some selected $\mathbf{w}'$, and if none of the sufficiency conditions for noninferiority discussed earlier [see (6.6a) and (6.6b)] are satisfied, then we may perform a numerical test of noninferiority for $\mathbf{x}^*$ by solving the following single-objective optimization problem for any $\boldsymbol{\alpha} = (\alpha_1, \ldots, \alpha_n) > \mathbf{0}$:

$$P^*: \quad \delta \equiv \max \sum_{i=1}^{n} \alpha_i \varepsilon_i \tag{6.36}$$

$$\text{subject to} \quad \mathbf{x} \in X \tag{6.37a}$$

$$f_i(\mathbf{x}) + \varepsilon_i = f_i(\mathbf{x}^*), \quad \varepsilon_i \geqslant 0 \tag{6.37b}$$

for each $i = 1, \ldots, n$. This test is based on the well-known result stated in Theorem 4.18.

Using the result in Theorem (4.18a), we can check whether a given point $\mathbf{x}^*$ is noninferior by solving P^*, say for $\boldsymbol{\alpha} = (1, 1, \ldots, 1)$, and search for the optimal value $\delta_{\max}$. If $\delta_{\max}=0$, we claim that $\mathbf{x}^*$ is noninferior. If on the other hand $\delta_{\max}>0$, $\mathbf{x}^*$ should be disregarded since it is an inferior solution. However, the effort may not be totally wasted, since from Theorem (4.18b) we may use $\mathbf{x}^0$, an optimal solution of P^*, as our noninferior solution, should the corresponding optimal value $\delta_{\max}$ be finite. If P^* has an unbounded solution, and if each $f_j, j>1,\ldots,n$, and the set X are convex, then according to Theorem (4.18c) [Benson, 1978], VOP in (6.3) has no proper noninferior solution. In addition, if we also assume that the set $\{\tilde{\mathbf{f}}|\tilde{\mathbf{f}}=\mathbf{f}(\mathbf{x})$ for some $\mathbf{x}\in X\}$ is a closed set, then by virtue of Theorem 4.18d [Benson, 1978] VOP in (6.3) has no noninferior solution.

This test of noninferiority is powerful and simple to perform. It has been used extensively in developing algorithms for linear multiobjective optimization problems. Another test of noninferiority, based on the hybrid characterization discussed in Sections 4.3 and 4.6, can be used similarly.

To summarize, the ad hoc numerical approach of generating noninferior solutions is based on the weighting characterization and proceeds as follows: First, for each $i=1,\ldots,n$, select suitable discrete values of w_i from 0 to 1, say

$$\hat{W}_i=\{w_i^0, w_i^1,\ldots,w_i^{k_i}\},$$

where $w_i^0=0$ and $w_i^{k_i}=1$. Then form $\hat{W}=\hat{W}_1\times\hat{W}_2\times\cdots\times\hat{W}_n$. Second, for each of the $k_1k_2\cdots k_n$ combinations of $\mathbf{w}$ in $\hat{W}$, solve $P(\mathbf{w})$. Third, check each solution generated for noninferiority. The following strategy may be followed:

a. Check to see whether each $w_i>0$; if YES, the solution is noninferior; otherwise, go to step (b).
b. Use simple strategies (if they are available) to test if the solution is unique. For example, if all objective functions are convex and at least one is strictly convex, check to see whether there is at least one weight w_i for which one of the strictly convex objective functions is strictly positive. If YES, we may conclude that the solution is noninferior; otherwise, go to step (c).
c. Formulate P^* and use the numerical test of noninferiority described above.

The obvious limitation of this approach is the number of computations to be performed. To generate at most $k_1k_2\cdots k_n$ noninferior solutions, $P(\mathbf{w})$ has to be solved $k_1k_2\cdots k_n$ times, and each time P^* may also need to be solved. The number of calculations increases exponentially with the number of objective functions and the number of grid points selected for each weight w_i. We should like a more systematic and efficient way of doing a similar or even better job. For special classes of problems, there are numerical parametric programming algorithms. For example, the parametric method of Gass and Saaty [1955] is designed for two objective linear problems, while the parametric algorithm of Wolfe [1959] is designed for two objective problems with one objective function having linear constraints and the other objective function being a positive semidefinite quadratic function. The strictly concave parametric programming of Geoffrion [1966, 1967] is also designed for two objective problems with a convex constraint set and the two objective functions locally strictly concave. For general linear problems, namely, when the objective functions are linear and the constraint set is convex polyhedral (or simply convex), more efficient techniques for generating noninferior solutions based on the weighting characterization can be developed, as we shall describe.

6.2.3 *Simplex-Based Methods for Linear Problems*

Linear problems constitute an important class of multiobjective decision-making problems both from the practical and theoretical viewpoints. This is evident from the voluminous literature devoted to theoretical and algorithmic developments for linear multiobjective decision problems. In this section we shall be concerned mainly with the algorithmic aspect. In particular, we shall discuss simplex-based procedures for generating the set of (all) noninferior solutions X^*. Although some simplex-based methods exist that do not directly use the weighting characterization (see, for example, the second approach of Zeleny [1974]), we shall focus on those methods for which the weighting characterization is a key element.

Motivation and General Strategy As shown in Chapter 4 (Theorem 4.26), the set of noninferior solutions X^* of a linear vector optimization problem (LVOP) is either the entire set of feasible solutions X or a part, or the entire frontier of X. In particular, if we assume that all objective functions are linearly independent,[3] then X^* will lie only on the frontier of X. Moreover, since X for a linear problem is a convex polyhedron, its frontier consists only of faces characterized by extreme points or extreme rays. It has also been shown that if an interior part of a face or edge (e.g., an interior point) is noninferior, then the entire face (or edge), including its extreme points and edges (lines joining two adjacent extreme points), must also be noninferior (see Theorem 4.23). Finally the entire set of noninferior solutions X^* is connected, meaning that for any two points in X^*, one can travel from one to the other without having to leave X^*. More precisely, the set of extreme points in X^* is connected in the sense that one can traverse from one extreme point to the other without having to leave the edges of X^* (see Theorem 4.29). Figure 6.4 illustrates these points.

---

[3]The least restrictive assumption is that there exist no strictly positive weights $\mathbf{w} > \mathbf{0}$ such that $\mathbf{w}^T \cdot \mathbf{f}(\mathbf{x}) = \text{constant}$, where $\mathbf{f}(\mathbf{x})$ is the vector of objective functions.

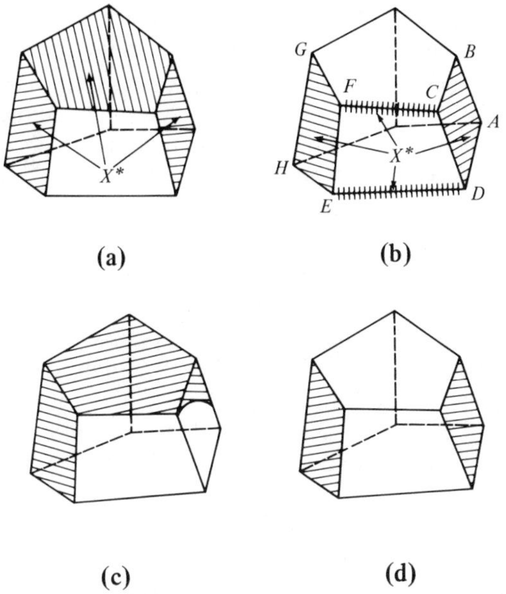

Figure 6.4 Possible [(**a**) and (**b**)] and impossible configurations [(**c**) and (**d**)] of the noninferior solution set X^* on a convex polyhedron X. In (**c**) and (**d**) the shaded areas are invalid configurations for X^*.

The above results suggest an efficient strategy for generating the noninferior solution set X^*: Since all points in a face are completely determined by the extreme points or extreme rays or both characterizing the face and because of Theorem 4.23, it is logical to determine all noninferior extreme points or extreme rays as the first step or as a primary goal. Then because of the "connectedness" of noninferior extreme points through noninferior edges, it is possible to carry out that task iteratively beginning at a noninferior extreme point and proceeding along one of the noninferior edges emanating from it. It is always possible to reach every noninferior extreme point in this manner, although not necessarily in a closed path. For example, in Figure 6.4b, one may begin at the noninferior extreme point A and proceed along the closed path passing through the points B, C, D, E, F, G, H, consecutively. However, if the face $EFGH$ is removed from X^*, so that X^* consists of only the face $ABCD$ and the edges CF and DE (a valid configuration), there is no closed path reaching each of the nodes in X^* without going through at least one node twice. A possible sequence of nodes reached by the method may be A, B, C, D, E, then back to D, C, and then to F.

The strategy of moving from one noninferior extreme point to an adjacent noninferior extreme point is particularly convenient if the simplex algorithm is used to generate extreme points. Indeed, given a noninferior extreme point and its corresponding simplex tableau, one can easily identify all extreme points adjacent to the given extreme point. The simplex tableau also provides a convenient mechanism for moving from one extreme point to one of its adjacent extreme points along the edge connecting them by means of a single pivot operation (assuming there is no degeneracy).

One question that remains is how one can identify the adjacent noninferior extreme points or, more precisely, identify which of the edges emanating from the given noninferior extreme point is noninferior and therefore leads to an adjacent noninferior extreme point. We shall answer this question after we describe a general strategy for algorithmic development.

If we have identified all noninferior extreme points, or at least have a tool for doing so, the next task is to identify the combinations of these noninferior extreme points which form the corresponding noninferior faces or edges. For example, in Figure 6.4b, if we have identified the list of noninferior extreme points to be $\{A, B, C, D, E, F, G, H\}$, we know that the combinations $\{A, B, C, D\}$, $\{C, F\}$, $\{D, E\}$, and $\{E, F, G, H\}$—and only these combinations—form noninferior faces and edges whose union defines X^*. Not all combinations of noninferior extreme points form the faces of the feasible set X, let alone the faces of X^*. Even if a certain combination of noninferior extreme points forms a face (or an edge) of X, such a face (or edge) is not necessarily noninferior. The inferiority of the face $CDEF$ of X in Figure 6.4b illustrates this point. We may address this issue from yet another angle by asking on how many noninferior faces (or edges) a given noninferior extreme point lies. In Figure 6.5, which is Figure 6.4b redrawn for clarity, vertex A lies on the noninferior face $ABCD$, as does vertex B. On the other hand, vertex C lies on two faces, $ABCD$ and CF, while vertex D lies on both $ABCD$ and DE. This suggests that if we can associate a distinct parameter (or a distinct set of parameters) with each of these faces for identification purposes, we can associate an appropriate list of those parameters with each extreme point. The list of parameters will identify the noninferior faces which are incident to the extreme point. To completely identify all noninferior faces, one simply collects all groups of noninferior extreme points such that each group has the largest number of members, where the intersection of the lists in the group is of a single element. This is illustrated in Figure 6.5. Identify the faces $ABCD$, CF, DE, and $EFGH$ by numbers 1, 2, 3, and 4, respectively. Then the lists associated with each noninferior extreme point are $L_A=\{1\}$, $L_B=\{1\}$, $L_C=\{1,2\}$, $L_D=\{1,3\}$, $L_E=\{3,4\}$, $L_F=\{2,4\}$, $L_G=L_H=\{4\}$. Consequently, we collect A, B, C, D in one group defining one noninferior face, since $L_A \cap L_B \cap L_C \cap L_D=\{1\}$, implying that $ABCD$ corresponds to face 1. The same analysis applies to other faces characterized by $\{C, F\}$, $\{D, E\}$, and $\{E, F, G, H\}$.

Thus to follow this strategy of generating all noninferior faces from a given set of all noninferior extreme points, we need i) a suitable identification parameter to be associated with each noninferior face, ii) a method for

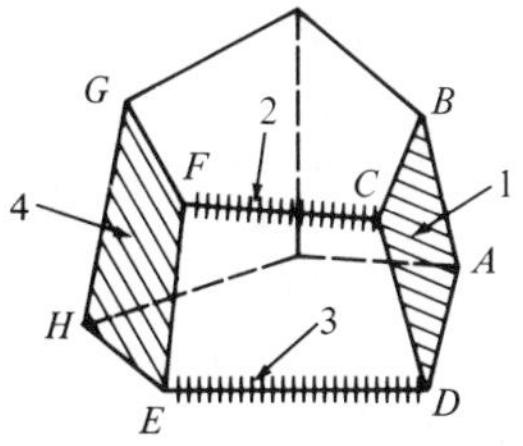

Figure 6.5 Identification mechanism.

identifying those parameters, and iii) a method for associating a list of noninferior faces with each noninferior extreme point. In addition, we also have to establish procedures for initiating the generation process and for terminating it. In the foregoing discussion, we assumed that the process begins at an initial noninferior extreme point: We need to resolve how to obtain such a point. We can easily resolve how to terminate the generating process if we can devise an efficient bookkeeping scheme, and such a scheme is necessary for completeness and efficiency. We want to be sure that every noninferior extreme point is reached, not only so we can explore its adjacent noninferior extreme points but also so we can assign it an appropriate list identifying the associated noninferior faces. We also do not want to cycle endlessly, which may happen if we do not have a mechanism preventing going from one noninferior extreme point to a previously explored one. Lastly, we do not want to repeat the calculation of an identification parameter of a noninferior face that has already been encountered.

An outline of the solution strategy follows:

1. *Initialization.* Find an initial noninferior extreme point.
2. *Exploration and bookkeeping.* At the current noninferior extreme point, find all adjacent noninferior extreme points (or edges). Classify these points as those whose adjacent noninferior extreme points have already been explored and those whose adjacent noninferior extreme points have not been explored. Add these to the lists of a) all noninferior extreme points which have been discovered, b) all noninferior extreme points whose adjacent noninferior extreme points have already been explored, and c) the complement set of (b) in (a).
3. *Identification and bookkeeping.* At the current noninferior extreme point, identify all noninferior faces incident to the noninferior extreme point. Then classify these faces as those which have and have not been previously encountered. Next, determine appropriate identification parameters for all newly discovered noninferior faces, and add them to the list of noninferior faces which have been discovered, as identified by their identification parameters.

4. *Progression.* To move from one noninferior extreme point to the next, move to one of the unexplored adjacent noninferior extreme points (which can be reached by at most a finite number of simplex pivot operations). If none exists, move to an unexplored noninferior extreme point in the list (c) in step 2 above.
5. *Termination.* The process of generating noninferior solutions clearly terminates when list (c) in step 2 is empty. The union of all noninferior faces produced is the set of noninferior solutions X^* sought.

   We shall attempt to answer the following questions.

   i. How do we get an initial noninferior extreme point?
   ii. How do we find all adjacent noninferior extreme points to a given noninferior extreme point?
   iii. What parameter should we use to identify a noninferior face and how can it be identified?
   iv. How do we identify all noninferior faces incident to a given noninferior extreme point?
   v. What kind of bookkeeping scheme should we use?

Basic Definitions We shall be focusing on linear vector optimization problems LVOP of the following form:

$$\min \quad \mathbf{Z} \triangleq C\mathbf{x} \tag{6.38}$$

$$\text{subject to} \qquad A\mathbf{x} = \mathbf{b}, \quad \mathbf{x} \geqslant \mathbf{0}, \tag{6.39}$$

where

A is an $m \times N$ constraint matrix $(m \leqslant N)$,

C is an $n \times N$ cost factor matrix,

$\mathbf{x}$ is an $N \times 1$ decision variable vector (which may include slack variables),

$\mathbf{b}$ is an $m \times 1$ constant vector, and

Z is an $n \times 1$ vector of n objective functions $(\mathbf{Z} = (\mathbf{z}_1, \mathbf{z}_2, \ldots, \mathbf{z}_n)^{\mathrm{T}})$.

Naturally, we assume that if the original problem is of the form $A\mathbf{x} \leqslant \mathbf{b}$ (or $A\mathbf{x} \geqslant \mathbf{b}$), appropriate slack variables have already been introduced to convert it to the form of (6.39).

Assuming that all redundant constraints have been eliminated so that the rank of A is equal to its number of rows m, the following definitions from the elementary theory of linear programming should be familiar.

Definition. A vector $\mathbf{x}$ is called a *basic feasible solution* of the constraint set X defined by (6.39) if and only if i) it is feasible (i.e., satisfying (6.39)) and ii) it contains *at most m* nonzero elements, which are called *basic variables*. The remaining $N - m$ variables whose values are set exactly at zero are called *nonbasic variables*.

Definition. A basic feasible solution $\mathbf{x}$ is said to be *nondegenerate* if it contains *exactly* m positive components.

Definition. A vector $\mathbf{x}$ is said to be an extreme point of the constraint set X if and only if it is a basic feasible solution of X.

We observe that, given the set of extreme points of a bounded convex polyhedron X, then the entire set X is completely determined. If the decision vector $\mathbf{x}$ contains both real decision variable $\mathbf{x}^r$ which has r components and slack decision variable $\mathbf{x}^s$, it is useful to think of two types of convex polyhedra X_r and X. The latter is as exactly defined by (6.39) and is drawn in an N-dimensional space consisting of both real and slack variables. The former, i.e., X_r, is defined by

$$X_r \triangleq \{\mathbf{x}^r | \mathbf{x}^r \in R^r, A_r \mathbf{x}^r \leqslant \mathbf{b}, \mathbf{x}^r \geqslant \mathbf{0}\}, \tag{6.40}$$

where A_r is an $m \times r$ matrix whose r columns are the r columns of A corresponding to real variables $\mathbf{x}^r$. X_r is, of course, a convex polyhedron drawn on the r-dimensional space. The extreme points of X_r and of X are therefore not the same geometrically. The following is a summary of relationships between them and the basic feasible solutions of X:

a. A basic feasible solution of X corresponds to a single extreme point of X and vice versa.
b. If $r < N$, an extreme point of X (and hence a basic feasible solution of X) corresponds to a single extreme point of X_r and vice versa if and only if all basic feasible solutions of X are nondegenerate. (The convex polyhedron in Figure 6.4 drawn in R^3 is an example of this case.)
c. For the degenerate case, while an extreme point of X (and hence, a basic feasible solution of X) corresponds to a single extreme point of X_r, the converse is *not* necessarily true. That is, an extreme point of X_r may correspond to more than one basic feasible solution of X.

In the nondegenerate case, we can speak of a basic feasible solution of X, an extreme point of X, and an extreme point of X_r, synonymously. Only in the degenerate case do we have to distinguish between an extreme point of X_r and a basic feasible solution of X. In generating solutions to LVOP, we shall be interested mostly in extreme points of X_r. For brevity, therefore, we have used and shall use the term "extreme point" to mean "extreme point of X_r" and shall refer to "the extreme point of X" by its full name or as "a basic feasible solution of X."

Definition. Let $\mathbf{x}_1$ and $\mathbf{x}_2$ be two basic feasible solutions of X. We say that $\mathbf{x}^1$ and $\mathbf{x}^2$ are *adjacent basic feasible solutions of* X, and hence *adjacent extreme points of* X, if and only if they have exactly $n-1$ common basic variables.

It should be observed that the above definitions have nothing to do with the objective functions. They are thus applicable to both the single-objective and the multiobjective cases. For the latter case, however, we also need the following definitions:

Definition. A vector $\mathbf{x}$ is called a *noninferior extreme point* of LVOP if and only if i) it is a noninferior solution of LVOP and ii) it is a basic feasible solution of X.

Definition. Two vectors $\mathbf{x}^1$ and $\mathbf{x}^2$ are said to be *adjacent noninferior extreme points* if and only if i) they are an adjacent basic feasible solution of X, ii) they are both noninferior, and iii) any $\mathbf{x} \triangleq \alpha\mathbf{x}^1 + (1-\alpha)\mathbf{x}^2$, $0 \leqslant \alpha \leqslant 1$, is also noninferior.

Observe from the previous definition that for two adjacent basic feasible solutions to be adjacent noninferior extreme points, not only do they both have to be noninferior, but every point on the line joining them has to be noninferior. This definition follows Gal [1976], Gal and Leberling [1977], and Isermann [1977, 1979], and is slightly different from that used by Zeleny [1974, 1982], where the third condition is not required.

Useful Results from Linear Programming In solving a single-objective linear programming problem (i.e., when $n=1$ in LVOP), it is well known that an optimal solution must lie on one of the extreme points of X. The search for an optimal solution reduces therefore to searching over the set of extreme points of X, rather than the entire X. To do that, we need to conveniently identify extreme points of X and to move from one extreme point of X to the next. This is accomplished with the simplex tableau. There is one simplex tableau for every basic feasible solution, and hence for each extreme point of X.

Assume that the vector objective function $\mathbf{Z}$ in (6.38) reduces to a single objective $z = \mathbf{c} \cdot \mathbf{x} = \sum_{j=1}^{N} c_j x_j$, and let

$$A = \begin{pmatrix} a_{11} & a_{12} & \cdots & a_{1N} \\ a_{21} & a_{22} & \cdots & a_{2N} \\ \vdots & \vdots & & \vdots \\ a_{m1} & a_{m2} & \cdots & a_{mN} \end{pmatrix}, \qquad \mathbf{b} = \begin{pmatrix} b_1 \\ b_2 \\ \vdots \\ b_m \end{pmatrix}.$$

A typical single-objective linear programming problem LP can be written

$$\begin{aligned} &\min \quad z \triangleq \mathbf{c} \cdot \mathbf{X} = \sum_{j=1}^{N} c_j x_j \\ &\text{subject to} \quad \mathbf{x} \in X = \left\{ \mathbf{x} \mid \mathbf{x} \in R^N, A\mathbf{x} = \mathbf{b}, \mathbf{x} \geqslant \mathbf{0} \right\}. \end{aligned} \tag{6.41}$$

A typical simplex tableau corresponding to a basic feasible solution of (6.41) is

$$
\begin{array}{cc}
\begin{array}{c}\text{Basic}\\\text{variables}\end{array} & \begin{array}{ccc} \mathbf{x}_B & \mathbf{x}_D & \text{Constants}\end{array}\\
T:\ \begin{cases} x_{\bar 1}\\ x_{\bar 2}\\ \vdots \\ x_{\bar m}\end{cases} &
\left(\begin{array}{cccc|cccc|c}
1 & & & & \bar a_{1,\overline{m+1}} & \bar a_{1,\overline{m+2}} & \cdots & \bar a_{a,\bar N} & \bar b_1\\
 & 1 & & & \bar a_{2,\overline{m+1}} & \bar a_{2,\overline{m+2}} & \cdots & \bar a_{2,\bar N} & \bar b_2\\
 & & \ddots & & \vdots & \vdots & & \vdots & \vdots\\
 & & & 1 & \bar a_{m,\overline{m+1}} & \bar a_{m,\overline{m+2}} & \cdots & \bar a_{m,\bar N} & \bar b_m\\
\hline
0 & 0 & \cdots & 0 & \bar c_{\overline{m+1}} & \bar c_{\overline{m+2}} & \cdots & \bar c_{\bar N} & -\bar z
\end{array}\right).\\
-z &
\end{array}
\tag{6.42}
$$

The basic feasible solution of X corresponding to this tableau is $\mathbf{x}^0 = (\mathbf{x}_B, \mathbf{x}_D)$, where $\mathbf{x}_B = (x_{\bar 1}, x_{\bar 2}, \ldots, x_{\bar m})$ is the vector of basic variables and $\mathbf{x}_D = (x_{\overline{m+1}}, \ldots, x_{\bar N})$ is the vector of nonbasic variables. Note that we use $\bar j$ to denote the jth component of $\mathbf{x}_B$ and $\mathbf{x}_D$, corresponding to the $\bar j$th component of the original vector $\mathbf{x}$. Note also that the jth column in the tableau (6.42) corresponds to the $\bar j$th column of $\mathbf{A}$. By definition, the values of the basic variables in $\mathbf{x}_B$ are obtained by setting all nonbasic variables equal to zero, i.e., $\mathbf{x}_D = \mathbf{0}$. It thus follows from the tableau (6.42) that $\mathbf{x}_B = \bar{\mathbf{b}} = (\bar b_1, \bar b_2, \ldots, \bar b_m)$. Consequently, the basic solution $(\mathbf{x}_B, \mathbf{x}_D)$ is *feasible* if and only if $\bar{\mathbf{b}} \geqslant \mathbf{0}$. Furthermore it is *nondegenerate* if and only if $\bar{\mathbf{b}} > \mathbf{0}$. If some components of $\bar{\mathbf{b}}$ are zero, the basic solution $(\mathbf{x}_B, \mathbf{x}_D)$ is said to be degenerate. It can be seen that an adjacent basic feasible solution of $\mathbf{x}^0$ can easily be obtained from the tableau (6.42) by performing a single pivoting operation around any positive entry of a nonbasic column of the current coefficient matrix.

The value of the objective function z at the current basic feasible solution $\mathbf{x}^0$ is given by

$$z = \bar z + \bar c_{\overline{m+1}} x_{\overline{m+1}} + \cdots + \bar c_{\bar N} x_{\bar N} = \bar z, \tag{6.43}$$

since $\mathbf{x}_D = \mathbf{0}$. The vector $\bar{\mathbf{c}}_D \triangleq (\bar c_{\overline{m+1}}, \ldots, \bar c_{\bar N})$ is normally called the *reduced cost* or the *relative cost* factor.

The following theorem, whose proof may be found in standard texts on linear programming [Dantzig, 1963; Hadley, 1962] summarizes fundamental results in linear programming.

Theorem 6.1. *Given the tableau* (6.42) *representing a basic feasible solution of X,*

a. $\mathbf{x}^0$ *is an optimal solution of LP* (6.41) *if and only if* $\bar c_j \geqslant 0$ *for all nonbasic columns, i.e.,* $\bar{\mathbf{c}} = (\bar c_{\overline{m+1}}, \ldots, \bar c_{\bar N}) \geqslant \mathbf{0}$;

b. $\mathbf{x}^0$ *is the unique optimal solution of LP* (6.41) *if and only if* $\bar{c}_j > 0$ *for all nonbasic columns, i.e.,* $\bar{\mathbf{c}}_{\mathrm{D}} > \mathbf{0}$;

c. *LP* (6.41) *has an unbounded solution, i.e., the value of z has no lower bound, if and only if there exists a nonbasic column* $j \in \{\overline{m+1,\ldots,N}\}$ *such that* $\bar{c}_j > 0$ *and* $\bar{a}_{ij} \leq 0$ *for all* $i = 1,\ldots,m$.

The simplex tableau T can also be written in a matrix form as

$$\begin{array}{c} \\ \mathbf{x}_{\mathrm{B}} \\ -z \end{array} \left(\begin{array}{c|c|c} \mathbf{x}_{\mathrm{B}} & \mathbf{x}_{\mathrm{D}} & \mathbf{b} \\ I_m & \bar{D} & \bar{\mathbf{b}} \\ \hline \mathbf{0} & \bar{\mathbf{c}}_{\mathrm{D}} & -\bar{z} \end{array} \right), \tag{6.44}$$

where

$$\bar{D} = \begin{pmatrix} \bar{a}_{1,\overline{m+1}} & \bar{a}_{1,\overline{m+2}} & \cdots & \bar{a}_{1,\bar{N}} \\ \vdots & \vdots & & \vdots \\ \bar{a}_{m,\overline{m+1}} & a_{m,\overline{m+2}} & \cdots & \bar{a}_{m,\bar{N}} \end{pmatrix}, \tag{6.45}$$

and I_m is the $m \times m$ identity matrix, $\mathbf{0}$ the $1 \times m$ zero vector, $\bar{\mathbf{c}}_{\mathrm{D}} = (\bar{c}_{m+1},\ldots,\bar{c}_{\bar{N}})$, and $\bar{\mathbf{b}} = (\bar{b}_1,\ldots,\bar{b}_m)^{\mathrm{T}}$.

Let B be an $m \times m$ *basic matrix* corresponding to the basic variables $\mathbf{x}_{\mathrm{B}}$ whose jth column is the $\bar{j}$th column of A, and let D be the corresponding nonbasic $m \times (N-m)$ matrix corresponding to the nonbasic variables $\mathbf{x}_D$. Then $A = (B|D)$. We can also partition the cost factors $\mathbf{c}$ into $\mathbf{c} = (\mathbf{c}_{\mathrm{B}}|\mathbf{c}_{\mathrm{D}})$. Thus, comparing (6.42) and (6.43), the following relations hold:

$$\bar{D} = B^{-1}D, \qquad \bar{\mathbf{c}}_{\mathrm{D}} = \mathbf{c}_{\mathrm{D}} - \mathbf{c}_{\mathrm{B}}B^{-1}\mathbf{D}, \qquad \bar{\mathbf{b}} = B^{-1}\mathbf{b}. \tag{6.46}$$

The dual problem DLP of the primal problem LP (6.41) is defined as[4]

$$\begin{array}{ll} \max & \mathbf{b}^{\mathrm{T}}\mathbf{u} \\ \text{subject to} & A^{\mathrm{T}}\mathbf{u} \leq \mathbf{c}^{\mathrm{T}}. \end{array} \tag{6.47}$$

The dual variables in DLP have no sign restriction.

The following duality results are proved in standard texts on linear programming [Dantzig, 1963; Hadley, 1962; Lasdon, 1970; Haimes, 1977].

Theorem 6.2

a. *If* $\mathbf{x}^0$ *and* $\mathbf{u}^0$ *are feasible solutions to primal and dual problems, respectively, then*

$$\mathbf{c} \cdot \mathbf{x}^0 \geq \mathbf{b}^{\mathrm{T}} \cdot \mathbf{u}^0. \tag{6.48}$$

---

[4]In general the dual of the primal $\min \mathbf{c} \cdot \mathbf{x}$ subject to $A\mathbf{x} \geq \mathbf{b}$, $\mathbf{x} \geq \mathbf{0}$ is $\max \mathbf{b}^{\mathrm{T}} \cdot \mathbf{u}$ subject to $A^{\mathrm{T}}\mathbf{u} \leq \mathbf{c}^{\mathrm{T}}$, $\mathbf{u} \geq 0$. Note that this definition is symmetric. One can also derive the dual form in (6.45)–(6.47) from this symmetric form.

b. *If the primal has an optimal solution, so has the dual, and vice versa, and they both have the same optimal values of objective functions.*
c. *If the primal problem has an unbounded solution, the dual is infeasible. Likewise, if the dual has an unbounded solution then the primal is infeasible.*
d. *Complementary slackness. If* $\mathbf{x}^0$ *and* $\mathbf{u}^0$ *are primal and dual feasible, respectively, then* $\mathbf{x}^0$ *and* $\mathbf{u}^0$ *are primal and dual optimal, respectively, if and only if*

$$\left(\mathbf{c}-(\mathbf{u}^0)^{\mathrm{T}}A\right)\cdot\mathbf{x}^0=0. \tag{6.49}$$

The Simplex Tableau for the Multiobjective Case Let us now return to the simplex tableau T in (6.42) or (6.43) and modify it in order to accommodate multiple objective functions $\mathbf{Z}$ in (6.38). As remarked earlier, the presence of multiple objectives should not alter the top part (above the z row) of the simplex tableau in either (6.42) or (6.44), for it is dependent only upon the constraint set X. The z row is used, in the single objective case, only for analyzing the optimality of the problem. One obvious modification is to append to the bottom part of the tableau as many rows as there are additional objective functions. A typical tableau T of this nature is

$$\begin{array}{c}\text{Basic}\\ \text{variables}\end{array} \qquad \mathbf{x}_{\mathrm{B}} \qquad\qquad \mathbf{x}_{\mathrm{D}} \qquad\qquad \text{Constants}$$

$$\begin{array}{c} x_{\bar 1}\\ x_{\bar 2}\\ \vdots\\ x_{\bar m}\\ -z_1\\ -z_2\\ \vdots\\ -z_n \end{array}
\left(\begin{array}{cccccccc|c}
1 & & & & \bar a_{1,\overline{m+1}} & \bar a_{1,\overline{m+2}} & \cdots & \bar a_{1,\bar N} & \bar b_1\\
 & 1 & & & \bar a_{2,\overline{m+1}} & \bar a_{2,\overline{m+2}} & \cdots & \bar a_{2,\bar N} & \bar b_2\\
 & & \ddots & & \vdots & \vdots & & \vdots & \vdots\\
 & & & 1 & \bar a_{m,\overline{m+1}} & \bar a_{m,\overline{m+2}} & \cdots & \bar a_{m,\bar N} & \bar b_m\\
\hline
0 & 0 & \cdots & 0 & \bar c_{1,\overline{m+1}} & \bar c_{1,\overline{m+2}} & \cdots & c_{1,\bar N} & -\bar z_1\\
 & & & & \bar c_{2,\overline{m+1}} & \bar c_{2,\overline{m+2}} & \cdots & \bar c_{2,\bar N} & -\bar z_2\\
\vdots & \vdots & & \vdots & & & & & \\
 & & & & \vdots & \vdots & & \vdots & \vdots\\
0 & 0 & \cdots & 0 & \bar c_{n,\overline{m+1}} & \bar c_{n,\overline{m+2}} & \cdots & \bar c_{n,\bar N} & -\bar z_n
\end{array}\right). \tag{6.50}$$

The calculation in each additional row of objectives is done in exactly the same manner as in the top objective row. In the matrix form, the tableau T can be written as

$$\begin{array}{c}\mathbf{x}_{\mathrm{B}}\\ -\mathbf{Z}\end{array}\left(\begin{array}{c|c|c} I & B^{-1}D & B^{-1}\mathbf{b}\\ \hline 0 & C_{\mathrm{D}}-C_{\mathrm{B}}B^{-1}D & -C_{\mathrm{B}}B^{-1}\mathbf{b}\end{array}\right), \tag{6.51}$$

where we again partition $C=(C_{\mathrm{B}}|C_{\mathrm{D}})$.

The current value of objectives functions are also given by

$$\mathbf{Z}=\overline{\mathbf{Z}}+\left(C_{\mathrm{D}}-C_{\mathrm{B}}B^{-1}D\right)\mathbf{x}_{\mathrm{D}}=\overline{\mathbf{Z}}=+C_{\mathrm{B}}B^{-1}\mathbf{b}. \tag{6.52}$$

Another possible modification is to eliminate the objective function rows completely. The remaining part is used to determine adjacent basic feasible solutions or extreme points, where the analysis of noninferiority can be done on a separate tableau. The utility of both of these modifications will be evident subsequently.

We can now proceed to address the major issues raised earlier in this subsection.

Initial Noninferior Extreme Point There are a number of ways of obtaining an initial noninferior extreme point. We shall describe two here.[5] In the first we simply select a convenient value of a strictly positive weight $\mathbf{w}^0>\mathbf{0}$ and solve the corresponding weighting problem $P(\mathbf{w}^0)$:

$$\begin{aligned}&\min \quad (\mathbf{w}^0)^{\mathrm{T}}\mathbf{Z}=(\mathbf{w}^0)^{\mathrm{T}}C\mathbf{x}\\ &\text{subject to} \qquad A\mathbf{x}=\mathbf{b}, \quad \mathbf{x}\geqslant\mathbf{0}.\end{aligned} \tag{6.53}$$

Note $P(\mathbf{w}^0)$ is a single-objective linear programming problem. If it has a finite optimal solution, say $\mathbf{x}^0$, such a solution will be an extreme point of X. Also since $\mathbf{w}^0>\mathbf{0}$ from Theorem 4.6 or 4.22, $\mathbf{x}^0$ is surely a noninferior solution of LVOP (6.38)–(6.39). This and the fact that it is an extreme point of X ensure that $\mathbf{x}^0$ is a required noninferior extreme point which we can use to start the process. If $P(\mathbf{w}^0)$ has an unbounded solution, then we select another strictly positive weight $\mathbf{w}$ and solve $P(\mathbf{w})$ again until we find a bounded solution. Of course, if the original LVOP has no noninferior solution, we may repeat this process endlessly, but such problems are usually of no interest in practice. Nevertheless, if we want a foolproof method that either generates a noninferior solution or signals that none exists, then the second method [Ecker and Kouada 1975] is recommended. In this method we find a basic feasible solution $\mathbf{x}^0$ of X in the same way as for a single-objective linear programming problem. Then we use a noninferiority test similar to that described in Section 6.2.2 to test whether $\mathbf{x}^0$ is noninferior. More precisely we solve the linear programming problem[6] P^*:

$$\begin{aligned}\delta= \max\,&\mathbf{e}^{\mathrm{T}}\cdot\boldsymbol{\varepsilon}\\ \text{subject to} \qquad &A\mathbf{x}=\mathbf{b},\\ &C\mathbf{x}+I\boldsymbol{\varepsilon}=C\mathbf{x}^0,\\ &\mathbf{x}\geqslant\mathbf{0}, \quad \boldsymbol{\varepsilon}\geqslant\mathbf{0},\end{aligned} \tag{6.54}$$

[5] For other methods see, for example, Evans and Steuer [1973b] and Zeleny [1974].

[6] Philip [1972, 1977] uses a slightly different problem for this purpose formulated from the current simplex tableau.

where $\mathbf{e}^T$ is the unit row vector $(1,1,\ldots,1)$. Theorem 6.3, of which Theorem 4.18 is a generalized version, forms the underlying basis of this test.

Theorem 6.3 (Ecker and Kouada [1975]). *Let* $(\mathbf{x}^*, \boldsymbol{\varepsilon}^*)$ *be an optimal solution of* (6.54). *Then*

a. $\mathbf{x}^0$ *is noninferior if and only if* $\delta(\mathbf{x}^*)=0$,
b. $\mathbf{x}^*$ *is noninferior if* $0<\delta(\mathbf{x}^*)<\infty$,
c. *LVOP* (6.38)–(6.39) *has no noninferior solution if* P^* *in* (6.54) *has an unbounded solution.*

PROOF: Parts (a) and (b) are apparent from Theorem 4.18(a) and (b), respectively. Part (c)[7]—If (6.54) has an unbounded solution, its dual,

$$\min \quad \mathbf{b}^T \cdot \mathbf{u}+(C\mathbf{x}^0)^T \cdot \mathbf{v} \tag{6.55}$$

$$\text{subject to} \quad A^T\mathbf{u}+C^T\mathbf{v} \geqslant \mathbf{0}, \quad \mathbf{v} \geqslant \mathbf{e}, \tag{6.56}$$

is infeasible by the duality theorem (Theorem 6.2). Assume that LVOP (6.38)–(6.39) has a noninferior solution. According to Theorem 4.22, there exists a strictly positive weight $\mathbf{w}^0>\mathbf{0}$ such that weighting problem $P(\mathbf{w}^0)$,

$$\min \quad (\mathbf{w}^0)^T C\mathbf{x} \tag{6.57}$$

$$\text{subject to} \quad A\mathbf{x}=\mathbf{b}, \quad \mathbf{x} \geqslant \mathbf{0}, \tag{6.58}$$

has an optimal solution. By Theorem 6.2, the dual of $P(\mathbf{w}^0)$ must be feasible, implying the existence of $\boldsymbol{\lambda} \in R^m$ such that

$$A^T\boldsymbol{\lambda} \leqslant C^T\mathbf{w}^0. \tag{6.59}$$

Let $\theta>0$ be the smallest component of $\mathbf{w}^0$ and let $\mathbf{w}=\mathbf{w}^0/\theta \geqslant \mathbf{e}$; then (6.59) becomes

$$C^T\mathbf{w}-A^T\boldsymbol{\lambda}/\theta \geqslant 0,$$

implying that $\mathbf{u}=-\boldsymbol{\lambda}/\theta$ and that $\mathbf{v}=\mathbf{w}$ is a feasible point of (6.56), which is clearly a contradiction. ■

Since $\mathbf{x}^0$ is a feasible point of P^* in (6.54) and $\delta(\mathbf{x}^0)=0$, this implies that the optimal value of P^*, δ_{max}, must be nonnegative. If an optimal solution of P^* is at $\mathbf{x}^*$, three cases are possible:

Case 1. If $\delta_{max} \equiv \delta(\mathbf{x}^*)=0$, then by Theorem 6.3a $\mathbf{x}^0$ is the noninferior solution of LVOP of (6.38)–(6.39). Because it is a basic feasible solution, $\mathbf{x}^0$ serves as an initial noninferior extreme point.

Case 2. If $\infty>\delta_{max} \equiv \delta(\mathbf{x}^*)>0$, not only does Theorem 6.3b indicate that $\mathbf{x}^0$ is an inferior point, it also shows that $\mathbf{x}^*$ is a noninferior solution of

[7]Although this result is a special case of Theorem 4.18(c) and a corollary of Theorem 4.22, we sketch a direct proof because if is of conceptual interest.

(6.38)–(6.39). Unfortunately $\mathbf{x}^*$ is not necessarily a basic feasible solution and, thus, not necessarily an extreme point. However, since any noninferior point must lie on a face of the polyhedron X (unless all of X is noninferior, in which case no further work is required), $\mathbf{x}^*$, which is noninferior but not an extreme point, must lie in an interior of at least one face. By Theorem 4.23, the entire face, including the extreme points that characterize it, must be noninferior. One such extreme point can thus be used to initiate the process. To find such an extreme point we perform the appropriate pivot operation on the simplex tableau.

Case 3. If $\delta_{\max}$ is unbounded (from above), as stated in Theorem 6.3c, the LVOP in (6.38)–(6.39) has no noninferior solutions.

Exploring Adjacent Noninferior Extreme Points or Edges If we are at a current noninferior extreme point $\mathbf{x}^0$ whose corresponding simplex tableau $T(\mathbf{x}^0)$ is given by (6.50), our task is to find from the tableau all adjacent noninferior extreme points.

One approach, which is used by Zeleny [1982], Yu and Zeleny [1975], Philip [1972], and Evans and Steuer [1973a, b], relies on checking all extreme points adjacent to $\mathbf{x}^0$ (actually basic feasible solutions adjacent to $\mathbf{x}^0$) for noninferiority. For each adjacent basic feasible solution found, the linear programming problem of the form (6.54) is formulated and solved and the noninferiority test is carried out as described. There are two difficulties associated with this approach. First, since a basic feasible solution may have a large number of adjacent basic feasible solutions, the number of linear programming problems of the form (6.54) that have to be solved may be prohibitively large. Second, the method as described does not indicate whether two noninferior extreme points are adjacent as defined earlier since the noninferiority of the edges joining any two noninferior extreme points has not been ascertained.

To alleviate the first difficulty, Zeleny [1974] (see also Yu and Zeleny [1975]) proposes an easily applied and easily proved simplex-based mechanism to screen out adjacent basic feasible solutions that need not be examined.

Theorem 6.4 (Zeleny [1974] and Yu and Zeleny [1975]). *Given a basic feasible solution* $\mathbf{x}^0$ *and its corresponding simplex tableau* $T(\mathbf{x}^0)$ *shown in* (6.50), *denote*

$$\alpha_j = \min_{1 \leq i \leq m} \{\bar{b}_i / \bar{a}_{ij} : \bar{a}_{ij} > 0\}$$

for any nonbasic column $j \in \{\overline{m+1}, \overline{m+2}, \ldots, \overline{N}\}$.

a. *If a nonbasic column* $j \in \{\overline{m+1}, \overline{m+2}, \ldots, \overline{N}\}$ *exists such that* $\alpha_j > 0$ *and* $\bar{c}_{ij} \leq 0$ *for all* $i = 1, \ldots, m$, *with strict inequality holding for at least one* $1 \leq i \leq m$, *then* $\mathbf{x}^0$ *is inferior.*

b. *The basic feasible solution obtained by introducing the jth column into the basis is inferior if i)* $\bar{c}_{ij} \geqslant 0$ *for all* $i = 1, \ldots, m$ *or ii) there exists another nonbasic column k such that* $\alpha_j \bar{c}_{ij} \leqslant \alpha_k \bar{c}_{ik}$ *for all* $i = 1, \ldots, m$, *with strict inequality for at least one* $1 \leqslant i \leqslant m$.

Part (a) provides a simple check of whether a current basic feasible solution is inferior. Failing to identify $\mathbf{x}^0$ as inferior does not, however, guarantee that it is noninferior. Part (b) provides simple checks for identifying "inferior" nonbasic columns for further consideration. It indicates that only those nonbasic columns that cannot be compared (by partial ordering $\geqslant$ in R^n) either with $\mathbf{0}$ or with each other need be explored further. This method may save considerable time and cost in the process of generating all noninferior extreme points.

A second approach, used by Gal [1976], Ecker and Kouada [1978], and Ecker et al. [1980], makes explicit but indirect use of the weighting characterization and a powerful result embodied in Theorem 4.27. Two vectors $\mathbf{x}^0$ and $\mathbf{x}^1$ are adjacent noninferior extreme points (i.e., they are the extreme points of a noninferior edge) if and only if i) they are adjacent basic feasible solutions and ii) they are both optimal solutions of the same weighting problem $P(\mathbf{w})$ of the form (6.53) for some strictly positive weight $\mathbf{w} > \mathbf{0}$. In terms of the simplex tableau, suppose $\mathbf{x}^0$ is the current noninferior extreme point with the corresponding simplex tableau $T(\mathbf{x}^0)$ given in (6.50). For $\mathbf{x}^1$ to be an adjacent noninferior extreme point to $\mathbf{x}^0$, condition (i) requires that it must be obtainable from the tableau $T(\mathbf{x}^0)$ by introducing one and only one nonbasic column into the basis. Thus, to check the noninferiority of an edge corresponding to the jth nonbasic column, we first check whether the coefficient $\bar{a}_{ij} > 0$ holds for at least one $1 \leqslant i \leqslant m$; otherwise the introduction of the jth nonbasic column would not be possible. This is essentially the same test as Theorem 6.4(a). Condition (ii), on the other hand, implies the existence of a weight vector $\mathbf{w}^0 > \mathbf{0}$ such that $P(\mathbf{w}^0)$ in (6.53) has multiple optima and that $\mathbf{x}^0$ and $\mathbf{x}^1$ are both optimal solutions of $P(\mathbf{w}^0)$. Let us suppose that $\mathbf{x}^1$ is obtained from the optimal simplex tableau $\hat{T}(\mathbf{x}^0)$ of $P(\mathbf{w}^0)$ at $\mathbf{x}^0$ shown in (6.50), by introducing the jth nonbasic column, $j \in \{m+1, \ldots, \bar{N}\}$, into the basis. $\hat{T}(\mathbf{x}^0)$ is then

$$
\begin{array}{c} \text{Basic} \\ \text{variables} \\ x_{\bar{1}} \\ x_{\bar{2}} \\ \vdots \\ x_{\bar{m}} \\ z = \sum_{i=1}^{n} \mathbf{w}_i^0 \mathbf{C}_i \mathbf{x} \end{array}
\begin{array}{c} \\ \\ \left(\begin{array}{cccc|cccc|c}
 & \mathbf{x}_B & & & & \mathbf{x}_D & & & \text{Constants} \\
1 & & & & \bar{a}_{1,\overline{m+1}} & \bar{a}_{1,\overline{m+2}} & \cdots & \bar{a}_{1,\bar{N}} & \bar{b}_1 \\
 & 1 & & & \bar{a}_{2,\overline{m+1}} & \bar{a}_{2,\overline{m+2}} & \cdots & \bar{a}_{2,\bar{N}} & \bar{b}_2 \\
 & & \ddots & & \vdots & \vdots & & \vdots & \vdots \\
 & & & 1 & \bar{a}_{m,\overline{m+1}} & \bar{a}_{m,\overline{m+2}} & \cdots & a_{m,\bar{N}} & \bar{b}_m \\
\hline
0 & 0 & \cdots & 0 & c_{\overline{m+1}} & \bar{c}_{\overline{m+2}} & \cdots & \bar{c}_{\bar{N}} & \bar{z}
\end{array} \right). \end{array}
\tag{6.60}
$$

Note that from (6.45), $\bar{c}_j = \Sigma_{i=1} w_i \bar{c}_{ij}$, where $\bar{c}_{ij} = c_{ij} - \Sigma_{k=1}^{m} c_{ik}\bar{a}_{kj}$, for each $j = \overline{m+1,\ldots,N}$. The values of $\bar{c}_{ij}$ are readily obtainable from the tableau $T(\mathbf{x}^0)$.

By virtue of Theorem 6.1(b), $\mathbf{x}^1$ will be an alternate optimal solution of $P(\mathbf{w}^0)$ if and only if the corresponding *reduced cost* at the jth column, $\bar{c}_j$, is zero. Since $\hat{T}(\mathbf{x}^0)$ is an optimal simplex tableau of $P(\mathbf{w}^0)$, we must by Theorem 6.1(a) have $\bar{c}_k \geqslant 0$ for all other nonbasic columns in $T(\mathbf{x}^0)$. Consequently, it can be shown that $\mathbf{x}^1$ obtained in the above manner is an adjacent noninferior solution to a given noninferior extreme point $\mathbf{x}^0$ if the equations

$$\sum_{i=1}^{n} \bar{c}_{ij} x_i = 0, \tag{6.61}$$

$$\sum_{i=1}^{n} \bar{c}_{ik} w_i \geqslant 0, \qquad k = \overline{m+1,\ldots,N}, \tag{6.62}$$

$$\sum_{i=1}^{n} w_i = 1 \tag{6.63}$$

have a strictly positive solution $\mathbf{w}$ in R^n. This is a necessary condition if $\mathbf{x}^0$ is nondegenerate.

One may attempt to solve (6.61)–(6.63) directly as a means of testing adjacent noninferiority. A more operational alternative as suggested by Gal [1976] is to solve the following linear programming problem with j defined as before:

$$\delta_j \triangleq \min \varepsilon_j \tag{6.64}$$

$$\text{subject to} \qquad -\sum_{i=1}^{n} \bar{c}_{ik} w_i + \varepsilon_k = 0, \quad k = \overline{m+1,\ldots,N}, \tag{6.65}$$

$$\sum_{i=1}^{n} w_i = 1, \tag{6.66}$$

where $w_i \geqslant 0$ for each $i = 1,\ldots,n$ and $\varepsilon_k \geqslant 0$ for each $k = \overline{m+1,\ldots,N}$.

The equivalent of (6.61)–(6.63) and (6.64)–(6.66) is established by the following result.

Theorem 6.5. *Given a noninferior extreme point* $\mathbf{x}^0$, *the system* (6.61)–(6.63) *has a strictly positive solution* $\mathbf{w}$ *in* R^n *if and only if the optimal value of* (6.64)–(6.66) *is equal to zero, i.e.,* $\delta_j = 0$, *and the optimal solution is* $\mathbf{w} > \mathbf{0}$.

PROOF: Since $\mathbf{x}^0$ is an optimal solution of $P(\mathbf{w}^0)$, by Theorem 6.1(a) $\bar{c}_k = \Sigma_{i=1}^{n} \bar{c}_{ik} w_i \geqslant 0$ for all $k = \overline{m+1,\ldots,N}$. Thus (6.64)–(6.66) is feasible and $\delta_j \geqslant 0$. With this observation, both the necessity and sufficiency parts follow immediately. ■

Naturally we can apply the above test to all nonbasic columns in the tableau $T(\mathbf{x}^0)$ that have not been eliminated by simple checks based on Theorem 6.4(b). We now summarize a strategy suggested by Gal [1976] for finding all adjacent noninferior extreme points to a given nondegenerate noninferior extreme point $\mathbf{x}^0$:

i. Based on Theorem 6.4(b), eliminate all inferior nonbasic columns in the tableau $T(\mathbf{x}^0)$. Let $J_{\mathrm{D}} \subseteq \{\overline{m+1}, \overline{m+2}, \ldots, \overline{N}\}$ be the set of all the remaining uncomparable nonbasic columns.
ii. Select a $j \in J_{\mathrm{D}}$ and solve (6.64)–(6.66). If $\delta_j = 0$ and an optimal $\mathbf{w} > \mathbf{0}$, then the adjacent basic solution obtained by introducing the jth column into the basis is a noninferior extreme point adjacent to the edge joining it and $\mathbf{x}^0$ is noninferior. (This conclusion is not necessarily true for degenerate $\mathbf{x}^0$, which case we shall discuss shortly.) This is not the case if there are no $\mathbf{w} > \mathbf{0}$ such that $\delta_j = 0$.
iii. Repeat (ii) for every $j \in J_{\mathrm{D}}$.

In solving (6.64)–(6.66), we may either apply suitable standard linear programming methods or use a special method proposed by Gal [1976].

The above method works even if the constraint set X is unbounded. Degeneracy of $\mathbf{x}^0$ can easily be handled, as the following example demonstrates.

Example 5: Consider an LVOP

$$\min \quad \mathbf{Z} = C\mathbf{x} \tag{6.67}$$

$$\begin{aligned} \text{subject to} \qquad x_1 \qquad + x_3 \qquad + 6x_5 &\leqslant 1, \\ x_2 + x_3 \qquad - 3x_5 &\leqslant 0, \\ -x_1 + 2x_2 + x_3 + x_4 + 3x_5 &\leqslant 4, \end{aligned} \tag{6.68}$$

and $x_i \geqslant 0$ for all $i = 1, 2, 3, 4, 5$, where

$$C = \begin{pmatrix} -1 & -3 & -2 & -1 & -0 \\ +4 & -4 & -2 & +1 & -7 \\ +1 & -3 & 0 & -1 & -2 \end{pmatrix}$$

or

$$\begin{aligned} z_1 &= \ -x_1 - 3x_2 - 2x_3 - x_4 - 8x_5, \\ z_2 &= +4x_1 - 4x_2 - 2x_3 + x_4 - 7x_5, \\ z_3 &= \ +x_1 - 3x_2 \qquad\quad - x_4. \end{aligned}$$

After adding appropriate slack variables x_6, x_7, x_8 and performing a pivoting operation, we find an initial noninferior extreme point $\mathbf{x}^0$ given by the simplex tableau $T(\mathbf{x}^0)$ and shown in (6.69). The basic variables are $\mathbf{x}_{\mathrm{B}}^0 = (x_1, x_3, x_4)^{\mathrm{T}}$, the nonbasic variables are $\mathbf{x}_{\mathrm{D}}^0 = (x_2, x_5, x_6, x_7, x_8)^{\mathrm{T}}$, and the current value of $\mathbf{x}_B^0$ is $(1,0,5)^T$. We now wish to find all adjacent noninferior extreme points of $\mathbf{x}^0$ by the second approach discussed.

Observe, first, that $\mathbf{x}^0$ is degenerate both for the primal ($x_3=0$) and dual (the column corresponding to x_2 in $T(\mathbf{x}^0)$ is identically zero). Moreover, the column corresponding to x_5 is an unbounded edge (extreme ray), since the coefficients $\bar{a}_{i2}<0$ for all $i=1,2,3$. Despite these apparent difficulties, however we can still apply the method. Observe first that in $T(\mathbf{x}^0)$,

$$\begin{array}{c} \text{Basic} \\ \text{variables} \\ x_1 \\ x_3 \\ x_4 \\ -z_1 \\ -z_2 \\ -z_3 \end{array}
\begin{array}{c} \\ \\ \\ \\ \\ \\ \\ \\ \end{array}
\left(\begin{array}{ccc|ccccc|c}
\multicolumn{3}{c}{\mathbf{x}_B^0} & \multicolumn{5}{c}{\mathbf{x}_D^0} & \\
x_1 & x_3 & x_4 & x_2 & x_5 & x_6 & x_7 & x_8 & \mathbf{b} \\
1 & & & -1 & -3 & 1 & -1 & 0 & 1 \\
 & 1 & & 1 & -3 & 0 & 1 & 0 & 0 \\
 & & 1 & 2 & -1 & 1 & 0 & 1 & 5 \\
\hline
 & & & 0 & -1 & 2 & 1 & 1 & +6 \\
 & & & 0 & 2 & -5 & 2 & -1 & -9 \\
 & & & 0 & 1 & 0 & 1 & 2 & +4
\end{array}\right). \tag{6.69}$$

Column x_7 can be eliminated from further consideration by virtue of Theorem 6.4(b), since $\bar{c}_{i,7}\geqslant 0$ for all $i=1,2,3$. Likewise column x_8 can be eliminated since $\alpha_6^-=1$ and $\alpha_8^-=5$, so that by

$$\alpha_6^-\begin{pmatrix} 2 \\ -5 \\ 0 \end{pmatrix} \leqslant \alpha_8^-\begin{pmatrix} 1 \\ -1 \\ 2 \end{pmatrix},$$

column x_8 is dominated by column x_6. Since the remaining columns are noncomparable, we set $J_D=\{2,5,6\}$. To test the adjacent noninferiority of these columns, we solve the following problem, equivalent to (6.64)–(6.66), for each $j\in J_D$:

$$\min \quad \varepsilon_j \tag{6.70}$$

$$\begin{aligned}
\text{subject to} \qquad 0w_1+0w_2+0w_3+\varepsilon_3&=0, && (6.71\text{a})\\
+w_1-2w_2-w_3+\varepsilon_5&=0, && (6.71\text{b})\\
-2w_1+5w_2\qquad +\varepsilon_6&=0, && (6.71\text{c})\\
-w_1-2w_2-w_3+\varepsilon_7&=0, && (6.71\text{d})\\
-w_1+w_2-2w_3+\varepsilon_8&=0, && (6.71\text{e})\\
w_1+w_2+w_3\qquad &=1. && (6.71\text{f})
\end{aligned}$$

Note that (6.71d) is redundant, and it is eliminated for simplicity. Problems (6.70)–(6.71) for all $j\in J_D$ can be solved simultaneously using the same simplex tableau. In fact, after the appropriate pivot operation to get w_1, w_2, w_3 into the basis (a necessary step for making sure that they are all strictly positive), we obtain a simplex tableau:

Basic variables	Basic w_1	w_2	w_3	ε_2	ε_8	Nonbasic ε_5	ε_6	Constants
ε_2	0	0	0	1	0	0	0	0
w_1	1	0	0	0	0	$-\frac{1}{2}$	$-\frac{7}{8}$	$\frac{5}{8}$
w_2	0	1	0	0	0	0	$\frac{1}{4}$	$\frac{1}{4}$
ε_8	0	0	0	0	1	0	$-\frac{1}{2}$	$\frac{1}{2}$
w_3	0	0	1	0	0	$-\frac{3}{8}$	0	$\frac{1}{8}$

(6.72)

Although (6.72) has no objective function row, the solution to (6.70)–(6.71) for each $j \in \{2,5,6\}$ is evident. Since the current basic solution $\mathbf{v} = (w_1, w_2, w_3, \varepsilon_2, \varepsilon_5, \varepsilon_6, \varepsilon_8)^{\mathrm{T}} = (\frac{5}{8}, \frac{1}{4}, \frac{1}{8}, 0, 0, 0, \frac{1}{2})^{\mathrm{T}}$ is feasible for (6.70)–(6.71) for each $j \in J_{\mathrm{D}}$ with $\varepsilon_2 = 0$, $\varepsilon_5 = 0$, and $\varepsilon_6 = 0$, the current value of $\delta_j = 0$ for each $j \in J_{\mathrm{D}}$ must be a minimum. Thus $\mathbf{v}$ is an optimal solution of (6.70)–(6.71) for each $j \in J_{\mathrm{D}}$. Since all weights w_1, w_2, and w_3 are strictly positive, it follows that the basic feasible solution obtained by introducing column x_2, x_5, or x_6 is an adjacent noninferior basic solution to $\mathbf{x}^0$. However, introducing x_2 into the basis, although it produces a different basic feasible solution, yields the same extreme point of $\mathbf{x}^0$ due to degeneracy. Thus the only noninferior extreme points adjacent to $\mathbf{x}^0$ are $\mathbf{x} = (0,0,0,5,0,0,0,0)^{\mathrm{T}}$ and the extreme ray $\mathbf{x}^2 = \mathbf{x}^0 + \alpha \mathbf{e}_5$, where $\alpha > 0$ and $\mathbf{e}_5 = (0,0,0,0,1,0,0,0)^{\mathrm{T}}$. Moreover since the same set of weights $\mathbf{w}_4 = (\frac{5}{8}, \frac{1}{4}, \frac{1}{8})^{\mathrm{T}}$ can be used to characterize all $\mathbf{x}^0$, $\mathbf{x}^1$, and $\mathbf{x}^2$, we can conclude, by virtue of Theorem 4.27, that they must lie on the same noninferior face.

This approach can be viewed from another angle. With every noninferior extreme point $\mathbf{x}^i$ we can associate a set of weights $W(\mathbf{x}^i)$ such that $\mathbf{x}^i$ is an optimal solution of the weighting problem $P(\mathbf{w})$ for all $\mathbf{w} \in W(\mathbf{x}^i)$. Given the simplex tableau corresponding to the noninferior extreme point $\mathbf{x}^i$, $W(\mathbf{x}^i)$ can be readily constructed from a tableau such as

$$W(\mathbf{x}^i) = \left\{ \mathbf{w} \,|\, \mathbf{w} \in R^n,\ \sum_{i=1}^{n} \bar{c}_{ij} w_i \geq 0,\ \sum_{i=1}^{n} w_i = 1, w_i \geq 0 \quad \text{for all } i = 1,\ldots,n \right\}. \tag{6.73}$$

Zeleny [1974] has shown that the union of $W(\mathbf{x}^i)$ for all noninferior extreme points covers exactly the entire interior of W, defined as the set $W^\circ \triangleq \{\mathbf{w} | \mathbf{w} \in R^n, \Sigma_{i=1}{}^n w_i = 1,\ w_i > 0 \text{ for all } i = 1,\ldots,n\}$. The parametric space W° can thus be decomposed into a finite number of subspaces $W(\mathbf{x}^i)$. The underlying premise upon which the second approach is based can be stated in terms of these subspaces: The noninferior extreme points $\mathbf{x}^1$ and $\mathbf{x}^2$ are adjacent to one another if and only if i) $\mathbf{x}^1$ and $\mathbf{x}^2$ are adjacent basic feasible solutions and ii) $W(\mathbf{x}^1) \cap W(\mathbf{x}^2) \neq \varnothing$. Solving problems of the form (6.64)–(6.66) is merely a means of operationalizing these conditions. A slightly different version can be found in Zeleny [1974, pp. 15–62]. At the end of Example 3 in Section 6.2.1, we illustrated some of the concepts discussed here. In Figure 6.3 there are three noninferior extreme points A, B, C with W_A, W_B, and W_C the corresponding sets of weights. The union of these three sets is clearly equal to the entire parametric space W. Moreover since $W_A \cap W_B = (\frac{2}{3}, \frac{1}{3})^{\mathrm{T}}$, $W_B \cap W_C = (\frac{1}{4}, \frac{3}{4})^{\mathrm{T}}$, and $W_A \cap W_C = \varnothing$, we may conclude that A is adjacent to B but not to C, and B is adjacent to both A and C. The noninferior edge between A and B is characterized by the weight vector $\mathbf{w}_{AB} = (\frac{2}{3}, \frac{1}{3})^{\mathrm{T}}$; likewise, the noninferior edge between B and C is characterized by $\mathbf{w}_{BC} = (\frac{1}{4}, \frac{3}{4})^{\mathrm{T}}$. The common weight vector may be used to characterize or identify the noninferior edge, as we shall do in the next section.

A slightly different and more compact version of this approach has been proposed by Ecker and Kouada [1978]. Their development, which is based on explicit consideration of the duals of problems similar to (6.64)–(6.66), is, however, different from the one presented here.

We write (6.65) in the matrix form as

$$-\mathbf{w}^{\mathrm{T}} \overline{C}_{\mathrm{D}}^{\mathrm{T}} + \boldsymbol{\varepsilon} = 0, \tag{6.74}$$

where $\overline{C}_{\mathrm{D}} = C_{\mathrm{D}} - C_{\mathrm{B}} B^{-1} D$ is the matrix of the reduced cost coefficients corresponding to nonbasic columns [see also (6.51)], $\mathbf{w} = (w_1, \ldots, w_n)^{\mathrm{T}}$ and $\boldsymbol{\varepsilon} = (\varepsilon_1, \ldots, \varepsilon_n)^{\mathrm{T}}$. The following result, due to Ecker et al. [1980], enables a more compact test of noninferiority of an edge to be formulated.

Theorem 6.6. *The problem* (6.64)–(6.66) *has an optimal solution* $\mathbf{w} > \mathbf{0}$ *with* $\delta_j = 0, j \in J_D$, *if and only if*

$$\hat{\delta}_j = \min \hat{\varepsilon}_j \tag{6.75}$$

$$\textit{subject to} \qquad -\mathbf{v}^{\mathrm{T}} \overline{C}_{\mathrm{D}}^{\mathrm{T}} + \hat{\boldsymbol{\varepsilon}} = +\mathbf{w}^{\mathrm{T}} \overline{C}_{\mathrm{D}}^{\mathrm{T}}, \quad \mathbf{v} \geqslant \mathbf{0}, \quad \hat{\boldsymbol{\varepsilon}} \geqslant \mathbf{0} \tag{6.76}$$

has an optimal solution with $\hat{\delta}_j = 0$.

This result indicates that one can solve problems (6.75)–(6.76) to test whether the introduction of the jth column into the basis leads to an adjacent noninferior extreme point. This is often easily accomplished by inspecting the initial simplex tableau $t(\mathbf{x}^0)$ of (6.75)–(6.76), which is obtainable from the tableau $T(\mathbf{x}^0)$ in (6.50) or (6.51):

$$\begin{array}{cccc} \text{Basis} & \mathbf{x}_{\mathrm{B}} = \hat{\boldsymbol{\varepsilon}} & \mathbf{x}_{\mathrm{D}} = \mathbf{v} & \text{Constant} \\ \hat{\boldsymbol{\varepsilon}} & \Big(\;\; \mathrm{I} & -\overline{C}_{\mathrm{D}}^{\mathrm{T}} & \mathbf{e}^{\mathrm{T}} \overline{C}_{\mathrm{D}}^{\mathrm{T}} \;\; \Big) \end{array} \tag{6.77a}$$

or

$$
\begin{array}{c|ccc|cccc|c}
 & & \mathbf{x}_{\mathrm{B}} & & & & \mathbf{x}_{\mathrm{D}} & & \\
\text{Basis} & \hat{\varepsilon}_{m1} & \cdots & \hat{\varepsilon}_{\overline{N}} & v_1 & v_2 & \cdots & v_n & \text{Constants} \\
\hline
\hat{\varepsilon}_{\overline{m+1}} & 1 & & & -\bar{c}_{1,\overline{m+1}} & -\bar{c}_{2,\overline{m+1}} & \cdots & -\bar{c}_{n,\overline{m+1}} & \sum_{i=1}^{n} c_{i,\overline{m+1}} \\
\vdots & & \ddots & & \vdots & & & & \\
\hat{\varepsilon}_{\overline{N}} & & & 1 & -\bar{c}_{1,\overline{N}} & -\bar{c}_{2,\overline{N}} & \cdots & -\bar{c}_{n,\overline{N}} & \sum_{i=1}^{n} c_{i,\overline{N}}
\end{array}
\qquad (6.77\text{b})
$$

By inspecting and pivoting the tableau $t(\mathbf{x}^0)$ in (6.77), one can solve (6.75)–(6.76) for all needed values of j without having to look at the objective row at all. We observe that for (6.75)–(6.76) for a particular j to have an optimal solution with $\hat{\delta}_j = \hat{\varepsilon}_j = 0$, there are only two possibilities at the optimal solution. Either i) $\hat{\varepsilon}_j$ is a nonbasic variable or ii) $\hat{\varepsilon}_j$ is a degenerate basic variable. Any basic feasible solution having $\hat{\varepsilon}_j = 0$ is always an optimal solution of (6.75)–(6.76) since $\hat{\delta}_j = \hat{\varepsilon}_j \geqslant 0$. Therefore first check whether $\hat{\varepsilon}_j$ in $t(\mathbf{x}^0)$ is degenerate. If not, pivot $\hat{\varepsilon}_j$ into the nonbasis $\mathbf{x}_{\mathrm{D}}$. If this is possible, then the introduction of the jth column will lead to an adjacent noninferior extreme point. Note the similarity between the optimal tableau (6.72) in Example 5 and a possible optimal tableau of $t(\mathbf{x}^0)$ in (6.77). The use of the tableau $t(\mathbf{x}^0)$ is not only convenient, it is also a powerful tool for identifying noninferior faces, as demonstrated by Ecker et al. [1980].

The problem of degeneracy can be dealt with in the manner described earlier. Often no modification is needed, especially when (6.75)–(6.76) has an optimal solution. Only when (6.75)–(6.76) does not have a solution and there is at least one element in a degenerate row being strictly positive, do we require modification of (6.75)–(6.76) or the tableau $t(\mathbf{x}^0)$ before drawing any conclusions. One such modification is suggested by Ecker and Kouada [1978], to which we urge the reader to refer.

Identification of Noninferior Faces One way of identifying individual noninferior faces and the entire collection of such faces (given a set of noninferior extreme points) is to use information about pairwise adjacency of these extreme points to construct appropriate undirected graphs or binary interaction matrices (see Sage [1977]). Proper analysis of these graphs or interaction matrices will yield noninferior faces. Examples of the uses of this approach can be found in, for example, Zeleny [1974], Yu and Zeleny [1975], and Isermann [1977, 1979].

Another approach is to use weights as a means of identifying noninferior faces, as demonstrated in Example 5 and the discussion following Example 3. This is a powerful approach, particularly when used in conjunction with the tableau $t(\mathbf{x}^0)$ in (6.77).

Theorem 4.28 forms the underlying basis for this approach. The set of feasible points $\mathcal{F}_S \subseteq X$ is a noninferior face if and only if i) every point $\mathbf{x} \in \mathcal{F}_S$ is noninferior and ii) $\mathcal{F}_S$ is completely characterized by some set of noninferior extreme points and extreme rays $S = \{\mathbf{x}^1, \ldots, \mathbf{x}^s\}$. The second condition requires that if all members of S are extreme points, then

$$\mathcal{F}_S = \left\{ \mathbf{x} | \mathbf{x} = \sum_{i=1}^{s} \lambda_i \mathbf{x}^i, \mathbf{x}^i \in S, \lambda_i \geq 0 \text{ for each } i = 1, \ldots, s \text{ and } \sum_{i=1}^{n} \lambda_i = 1 \right\} \tag{6.78a}$$

is a convex hull of S, or if S contains r extreme points $\mathbf{x}^1, \ldots, \mathbf{x}^r$ and $s-r$ extreme rays $\mathbf{x}^{r+1}, \ldots, \mathbf{x}^s$, then

$$\mathcal{F}_S = \left\{ \mathbf{x} | \mathbf{x} = \sum_{i=1}^{r} \lambda_i \mathbf{x}^i + \sum_{i=r+1}^{s} \mu_i \mathbf{x}^2 \text{ for some } \lambda_i \geq 0, i = 1, \ldots, r, \right.$$
$$\left. \sum_{i=1}^{r} \lambda_i = 1 \text{ and } \mu_i \geq 0, i = r+1, \ldots, s \right\}. \tag{6.78b}$$

We say that a face $\mathcal{F}$ is a maximal noninferior face if and only if it is a noninferior face not contained in another noninferior face. More specifically, given the set S of extreme points or extreme rays or both, $\mathcal{F}_S$ defined in (6.78) is a maximal noninferior face if and only if i) $\mathcal{F}_S$ is a noninferior face and ii) there does not exist S' such that $S \subset S'$ and that $\mathcal{F}_{S'}$ is a noninferior face itself. We seek these maximal noninferior faces since their union is precisely the set of all noninferior solutions X^*.

Let E be the set of all noninferior extreme points and extreme rays of X. For each noninferior extreme point or extreme ray $\mathbf{x}^i$ in E, there is a set of strictly positive weights $W(\mathbf{x}^i)$ such that $\mathbf{x}^i$ is an optimal solution of $P(\mathbf{w})$ for all $\mathbf{w} \in W(\mathbf{x}^i)$. Moreover, it can be easily shown that

$$\bigcup_{\mathbf{x}^i \in E} W(\mathbf{x}^i) = W^\circ, \tag{6.79}$$

where

$$W^\circ = \left\{ \mathbf{w} | \mathbf{w} \in R^n, \sum_{i=1}^{n} w_i = 1, w_i > 0 \text{ for each } i = 1, \ldots, n \right\}. \tag{6.80}$$

An explicit expression for $W(\mathbf{x}^i)$ is given in (6.73). From Theorem 4.28, $\mathcal{F}_S$ is a noninferior face generated by $S \subseteq E$ if and only if

$$\bigcap_{\mathbf{x}^i \in S} W(\mathbf{x}^i) \neq \varnothing. \tag{6.81}$$

Moreover, by definition and (6.81), $\mathcal{F}_S$ is a maximal noninferior face if S is the largest subset of E such that

$$\bigcap_{x^i \in S} W(\mathbf{x}^i) \neq \varnothing. \tag{6.82}$$

Equation (6.82) guarantees the existence of a weight vector $\mathbf{w}_S$, which can be used to identify a maximal noninferior face $\mathcal{F}_S$. It also guarantees that no single weight vector can be used to identify two different maximal noninferior faces. Unfortunately, the fact that the set $\bigcap_{\mathbf{x}^i \in S} W(\mathbf{x}^i)$ in (6.82) may not be a singleton indicates that the weight vector that identifies a single maximal noninferior face is not necessarily unique. Nevertheless, the use of weight vectors as an identification parameter of maximal noninferior faces is useful, as we shall show.

Using the weight vector $\mathbf{w}$ as a parameter to identify maximal noninferior faces, our task is to determine the weight vector for each maximal noninferior face. This is easily accomplished by using the tableau $t(\mathbf{x}^0)$ in (6.77).

Given a noninferior extreme point $\mathbf{x}^0$ and a subset S of noninferior extreme points adjacent to $\mathbf{x}^0$, we want to find whether $\mathbf{x}^0$ and all members of S lie on the same maximal noninferior face. A nonbasic column j in the tableau $T(\mathbf{x}^0)$ in (6.50) can be introduced into the basis, leading to an adjacent noninferior extreme point of $\mathbf{x}^0$, if and only if the corresponding variable ε_j in the tableau $t(\mathbf{x}^0)$ in (6.77) is zero either by being a nonbasic variable or a degenerate basic variable. Let J_S^0 be the set of indices of the nonbasic columns in the tableau $T(\mathbf{x}^0)$ in (6.50) that corresponds to S. Then all members of S as well as $\mathbf{x}^0$ will lie on the same maximal noninferior face if and only if all $\varepsilon_j, j \in J_S^0$, are nonbasic variables, or at least some of them are degenerate basic variables (which cannot be brought into the nonbasic set without causing some nonbasic ε_j, $j \in J_S^0$, to become positive basic variables). If such a tableau, say $t^*(\mathbf{x}^0)$, can be obtained, then it is clear that there exists a weight vector

$$\mathbf{w}^* = \mathbf{v}^* + \mathbf{e} > \mathbf{0},$$

where $\mathbf{v}^*$ is the value of $\mathbf{v}$ taken from the tableau $t^*(\mathbf{x}^0)$ such that $\mathbf{x}^0$ and all members of S are optimal solutions of the weighting problem $P(\mathbf{w}^*)$. Consequently $\mathbf{x}^0$ and all members of S must lie on the same maximal noninferior face, determined by the weight vector $\mathbf{w}^*$. On the other hand if a tableau $t^*(\mathbf{x}^0)$ does not exist, we say that $\mathbf{x}^0$ and all members of S do not lie on the same maximal noninferior face.

Given a noninferior extreme point $\mathbf{x}^0$, how do we find out all the maximal noninferior faces incident to this point? First we use the tableau $t(\mathbf{x}^0)$ in (6.77) (or any procedure described in this section) to find the set of all noninferior extreme points adjacent to $\mathbf{x}^0$. Call this set $E(\mathbf{x}^0)$.

Consider $E(\mathbf{x}^0) = \{\mathbf{x}^1, \mathbf{x}^2, \mathbf{x}^3, \mathbf{x}^4\}$. Suppose there is no maximal noninferior face containing both $\mathbf{x}^0$ and all four of its adjacent noninferior extreme points in $E(\mathbf{x}^0)$. We consider all four combinations of three members of $E(\mathbf{x}^0)$, namely $S_3^1 = \{\mathbf{x}^1, \mathbf{x}^2, \mathbf{x}^3\}$, $S_3^2 = \{\mathbf{x}^1, \mathbf{x}^2, \mathbf{x}^4\}$, $S_3^3 = \{\mathbf{x}^1, \mathbf{x}^3, \mathbf{x}^4\}$, and $S_3^4 = \{\mathbf{x}^2, \mathbf{x}^3, \mathbf{x}^4\}$. Suppose we perform the above test and determine that S_3^2 is the only noninferior face containing $\mathbf{x}^0$ and exactly three of its adjacent noninferior extreme points. Denote the face corresponding to S_3^2 and its weight vector $\mathcal{F}_1$ and $\mathbf{w}^1$, respectively. Then consider the following combinations of two members of $E(\mathbf{x}^0)$: $S_2^1=\{\mathbf{x}^1,\mathbf{x}^3\}$, $S_2^2=(\mathbf{x}^2,\mathbf{x}^3\}$, $S_2^3=\{\mathbf{x}^3,\mathbf{x}^4\}$. Note that we do not need to consider the combinations $\{\mathbf{x}^1,\mathbf{x}^2\}$, $\{\mathbf{x}^1,\mathbf{x}^4\}$, and $\{\mathbf{x}^2,\mathbf{x}^4\}$, since each of these combinations is a (proper) subset of S_3^2, implying that the noninferior faces generated by each of those combinations are contained in the maximal noninferior face, which has already been identified. After performing the test, let us suppose that we have identified two new maximal noninferior faces $\mathcal{F}_2$ and $\mathcal{F}_3$, together with their respective weights $\mathbf{w}^2$ and $\mathbf{w}^3$ containing $\{\mathbf{x}^0,\mathbf{x}^1,\mathbf{x}^3\}$ and $\{\mathbf{x}^0,\mathbf{x}^3,\mathbf{x}^4\}$, respectively. We can then conclude that there are three maximal noninferior faces incident to $\mathbf{x}^0$, namely $\mathcal{F}_1,\mathcal{F}_2,\mathcal{F}_3$ as identified by $\mathbf{w}^1$, $\mathbf{w}^2$, and $\mathbf{w}^3$, respectively.

Bookkeeping and a Complete Algorithm We now choose an initial noninferior extreme point and move to all subsequent noninferior extreme points, in the process identifing all maximal noninferior faces of X. If A is our initial noninferior extreme point (see Figure 6.6), then using the procedures discussed earlier, we can identify the set of all noninferior extreme points $E(A)$ adjacent to A, and the set of all maximal noninferior faces $F(A)$ and their respective weight vectors. We should have

$$E(A)=\{B,D\} \qquad \text{and} \qquad F(A)=\{\mathbf{w}^1\},$$

where $\mathbf{w}^1$ is the weight vector corresponding to the face $\mathcal{F}_1$, and we can identify $\mathcal{F}_1$ as a maximal noninferior face incident to B and to D. Any information thus obtained should be recorded in the set $P(\mathcal{F})$ of currently found noninferior extreme points lying on the face $\mathcal{F}$. For our example

$$P(\mathcal{F}_1)=\{A,B,D\}. \tag{6.83}$$

It is useful to keep the list of all maximal noninferior faces encountered. For this purpose, we let F_g to be the set of weight vectors corresponding to all maximal noninferior faces already generated. At this stage of our example we have

$$F_g=\{\mathbf{w}^1\}.$$

Figure 6.6 Maximal noninferior faces (shaded faces or edge).

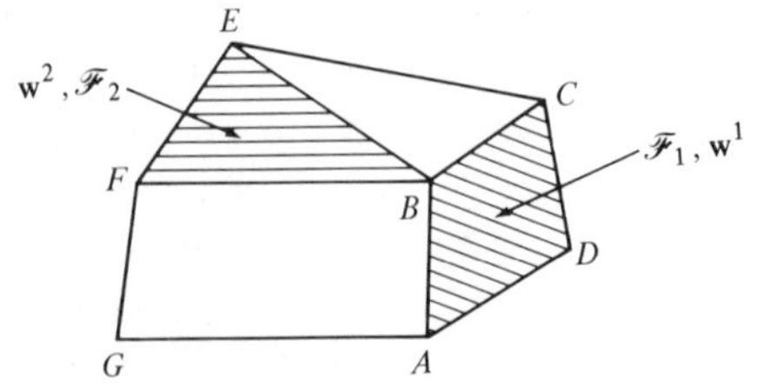

Having completed the exploration of A, we can now move to explore one of its adjacent noninferior extreme points, either B or D. If we choose B, then D is still unexplored and we shall need to come back to it. We must also insure that we never explore A again. For bookkeeping purposes, then, let E_u be the set of all generated or encountered noninferior extreme points which are unexplored and E_e be the set of all explored noninferior extreme points. Before moving to B, we then have

$$E_u = \{B, D\} \qquad \text{and} \qquad E_e = \{A\}. \tag{6.84}$$

We now use the procedures described previously and the information [contained in (6.83)] that B lies on $\mathcal{F}_1$ to identify $E(B)$, the set of all noninferior extreme points adjacent to B, and $F(B)$, the set of weights corresponding to maximal noninferior faces incident to B. After successful completion of this step, we should find that

$$E(B) = \{A, C, E, F\} \qquad \text{and} \qquad F(B) = \{\mathbf{w}^1, \mathbf{w}^2\}, \tag{6.85}$$

where $\mathbf{w}^2$ is the weight vector corresponding to the face $\mathcal{F}_2$. The information about B lying on a previously encountered maximal noninferior face $\mathcal{F}_1$ can be used, among other things, to improve the efficiency of the procedure by avoiding unnecessary tests.

Note the role played by the weight vector $\mathbf{w}^1$ in determining $F(B)$ and updating $P(\mathcal{F}_1)$. Such a weight vector can be used for this purpose in one of the following two ways.

The first, suggested by Gal [1976], is to use the procedures in the preceding subsection to find all maximal noninferior faces together with their respective weight vectors incident to B. By comparing the newly found weight vectors with $\mathbf{w}^1$, we should be able to identify which newly found maximal noninferior face exactly coincides with $\mathcal{F}_1$. For example, in carrying out the usual steps, we should be able to identify that $\{B, C, A\}$ lies on a maximal noninferior face incident to B. If the corresponding weight vector is also found to be $\mathbf{w}^1$, we conclude that the newly found maximal noninferior face is in fact the same as $\mathcal{F}_1$. We can thus update $P(\mathcal{F}_1)$ to include C.

The second approach, suggested by Ecker et al. [1980], is more decisive and hence more efficient. They first updated $P(\mathcal{F}_1)$, using the weight vector $\mathbf{w}^1$ to test which of the adjacent noninferior extreme points to B not currently in $P(\mathcal{F}_1)$ lie on $\mathcal{F}_1$. For example, to test whether C, which is in $E(B)$ but not in the current $P(\mathcal{F}_1)$, lies on $\mathcal{F}_1$, we simply examine the corresponding nonbasic column in the tableau of the form (6.50) associated with the current noninferior extreme point B. Let $\tilde{c}_j$ be the corresponding nonbasic column in the tableau $T(B)$ which leads to C when introduced into the basic variable set. For B and C to lie on $\mathcal{F}_1$, they must be optimal solutions $P(\mathbf{w}^1)$. By Theorem 6.1(b) and the above observation, C lies on $\mathcal{F}_1$

if and only if

$$(\mathbf{w}^1)^{\mathrm{T}}\tilde{c}_j = \sum_{i=1}^{n} w_i^1 \tilde{c}_{ij} = 0. \tag{6.86}$$

Using the above test, more complicated tests may be eliminated in the process of constructing $F(B)$ and updating $P(\mathscr{F}_1)$.

Having explored B, the following sets should be updated for further use:

$$P(\mathscr{F}_2) = \{B, E, F\}, \tag{6.87}$$

$$P(\mathscr{F}_1)_{\text{new}} = \{A, B, C, D\}, \tag{6.88}$$

$$F_{\text{g,new}} = \{\mathbf{w}^1, \mathbf{w}^2\}, \tag{6.89}$$

$$E_{\text{e,new}} = E_{\text{e,current}} \cup B = \{A, B\}, \tag{6.90}$$

$$E_{\text{u,new}} = E_{\text{u,current}} \cup E(B) - E_{\text{e,new}} = \{C, D, E, F\}. \tag{6.91}$$

We can now move on to the next noninferior extreme point. Theoretically we can move to any of the unexplored points in $E_{\text{u,new}}$. From a practical point of view, however, it is more convenient to move to one of those points in E_{u} which is also adjacent to the current noninferior extreme point, because the new simplex tableau of the form (6.50), corresponding to the new point, can easily be obtained from the previous tableau through a single pivot operation. Obviously, if such a point does not exist, we select the next most convenient point, namely one which has all but two basic variables in common with the current point. The new tableau then can be obtained from the current tableau by two pivot operations. The entire process terminates when there is no other noninferior extreme point to move to. The criterion for stopping is thus

$$E_{\text{u, current}} = \varnothing. \tag{6.92}$$

Finally there is the question of convergence and optimality of the algorithm in the sense of guaranteeing the generation of the entire X^*. Since there are a finite number of extreme points and extreme rays on X, only a finite number of noninferior extreme points and extreme rays need to be explored. Since the algorithm guarantees that no noninferior extreme point is explored more than once, the algorithm will always converge in a finite number of steps. That the entire X^* is generated is also guaranteed:

1. The set of noninferior extreme points of X is connected, in the sense that any two noninferior extreme points are always connected by a path of extreme edges (Theorem 4.29). Therefore every noninferior extreme point is reachable by the method, and all noninferior extreme points are guaranteed to be explored.
2. Since every maximal noninferior face will be incident to at least one noninferior extreme point, since at every noninferior extreme point explored all maximal noninferior faces incident to it will be found, and

because of property (1), all maximal noninferior faces of X^* will be found.

3. By Theorem (4.26), X^* consists only of all maximal noninferior faces; otherwise $X^* = X$. Thus the generation of the entire X^* is guaranteed by the algorithm.

For a more rigorous proof of convergence and optimality and a more elaborate scheme (ready to be converted into a computer program) of the algorithm of this nature, see Ecker et al. [1980].

Example 6: We illustrate how the algorithm works by considering the following example:

$$\min \quad \mathbf{Z} = C\mathbf{x} \tag{6.93}$$

$$\text{subject to} \qquad \begin{aligned} x_1 + x_2 \quad &\leqslant 1, \\ + x_2 \quad &\leqslant 2, \\ -x_1 - x_2 + x_3 &\leqslant 4, \end{aligned} \tag{6.94}$$

where $x_i \geqslant 0$ for all $i = 1, 2, 3$, and

$$C = \begin{pmatrix} -1 & -2 & 0 \\ -1 & 0 & +2 \\ 1 & 0 & -1 \end{pmatrix}. \tag{6.95}$$

After adding appropriate slack variables x_4, x_5, x_6 and solving $P(\mathbf{w}^*)$, where $\mathbf{w} = (\frac{1}{4}, \frac{1}{4}, \frac{1}{2})^{\mathrm{T}}$, we get $\mathbf{x}^0 = (3, 2, 1)^{\mathrm{T}}$ as an initial noninferior extreme point and the following initial tableau $T(\mathbf{x}^0)$:

	$\mathbf{x}_B^0$			$\mathbf{x}_D^0$			
Basis	x_1	x_2	x_3	x_4	x_5	x_6	Constants
x_1	1			1	−1	0	3
x_2		1		0	1	0	2
x_3			1	1	0	1	1
$-z_1$				1	1	0	2
$-z_2$				−1	−1	−2	1
$-z_3$				0	1	1	−2

(6.96)

Next we construct J_D^0. Since $\alpha_4 = 3, \alpha_5 = 2, \alpha_6 = 1$, we have $\alpha_5 \bar{c}_{0.5} \geqslant \alpha_6 \bar{c}_{0.6}$. Hence we eliminate column 5 from further consideration in this iteration and we set $J_D^0 = \{4, 6\}$. The corresponding tableau $t(\mathbf{x}^0)$ of the form (6.77) for $\mathbf{x}^0$ is $T(\mathbf{x}^0)$ given by

Basis	ε_4	ε_5	ε_6	v_1	v_2	v_3	Constants
ε_4	1			−1	1	0	0
ε_5		1		−1	1	−1	−1
ε_6			1	0	2	(−1)	−1

(6.97)

Since ε_4 is a degenerate basic variable and ε_6 can be brought into the nonbasic set by the indicated pivot on the third row of $t(\mathbf{x}^0)$, both columns 4 and 6 in $T(\mathbf{x}^0)$ lead to noninferior extreme points $(2,2,0)^{\mathrm{T}}$ and $(3,2,0)^{\mathrm{T}}$ adjacent to $\mathbf{x}^0$. We thus set $J(\mathbf{x}^0)=\{4,6\}$ and $E(\mathbf{x}^0)=\{(2,2,0)^{\mathrm{T}},(3,2,0)^{\mathrm{T}}\}$. Moreover, ε_4 and ε_6 are zero simultaneously through the indicated pivot, leading to the following tableau $t(\mathbf{x}^0)$:

$$\begin{array}{c|cccccc|c} \text{Basis} & \varepsilon_4 & \varepsilon_5 & \varepsilon_6 & v_1 & v_2 & v_3 & \text{Constants} \\ \hline \varepsilon_4 & 1 & & & -1 & 1 & 0 & 0 \\ \varepsilon_5 & & 1 & -1 & -1 & -1 & 0 & 2 \\ v_3 & & & -1 & 0 & -2 & 1 & 1 \end{array} \tag{6.98}$$

The corresponding extreme points $(2,2,0)^{\mathrm{T}}$ and $(3,2,0)^{\mathrm{T}}$ thus lie on the same maximal noninferior face incident to $\mathbf{x}^0$. From the tableau $\hat{t}(\mathbf{x}^0)$, the corresponding weight vector $\mathbf{v}=(0,0,1)$ for this maximal noninferior face $\mathcal{F}_1$ is $\mathbf{w}^1=(\mathbf{v}+\mathbf{e})/\sum_{i=1}^{3}(1+v_i)=(\frac{1}{4},\frac{1}{4},\frac{1}{2})^{\mathrm{T}}$. Moreover, $\mathcal{F}_1$ is the only maximal noninferior face incident to $\mathbf{x}^0$. We summarize:

$$E(\mathbf{x}^0)=\{(2,2,0)^{\mathrm{T}},(3,2,0)^{\mathrm{T}}\},\qquad F(\mathbf{x}^0)=\{\mathbf{w}^1\},\qquad F_{\mathrm{g}}=\{\mathbf{w}^1\},$$

$$E_{\mathrm{e}}=\varnothing\cup\{\mathbf{x}^0\}=\{\mathbf{x}^0\},\qquad E_{\mathrm{u}}=\varnothing\cup E(\mathbf{x}^0)-E_{\mathrm{e}}=\{(2,2,0)^{\mathrm{T}},(3,2,0)^{\mathrm{T}}\},$$

$$P(\mathcal{F}_1)=\{\mathbf{x}^0,(2,2,0)^{\mathrm{T}},(3,2,0)^{\mathrm{T}}\}.$$

Select $\mathbf{x}^1=(2,2,0)^{\mathrm{T}}$ as our new noninferior extreme point to start the next iteration. The corresponding tableau $T(\mathbf{x}^1)$ is obtained from $T(\mathbf{x}^0)$ by pivoting column 4 into the basic set:

$$\begin{array}{c|cccccc|c} \text{Basis} & x_1 & x_2 & x_3 & x_4 & x_5 & x_6 & \text{Constants} \\ \hline x_1 & 1 & & -1 & & -1 & -1 & 2 \\ x_2 & & 1 & 0 & & 1 & 0 & 2 \\ x_4 & & & 1 & 1 & 0 & 1 & 1 \\ \hline -z_1 & & & -1 & & 1 & -1 & 6 \\ -z_2 & & & 1 & & -1 & -1 & 2 \\ -z_3 & & & 0 & & 1 & 1 & -2 \end{array} \tag{6.99}$$

Columns 3, 5, and 6 are nonbasic. Since no column can be eliminated based on Theorem 6.4 alone, we set $J_{\mathrm{D}}^1=\{3,5,6\}$. To find $E(\mathbf{x}^1)$ we observe that pivoting columns 3 or 6 into the basic set of the tableau leads to $\mathbf{x}^0$ or $(3,2,0)^{\mathrm{T}}$, respectively, and $\mathbf{x}^0$, $\mathbf{x}^1$, and $(3,2,0)^{\mathrm{T}}$ lie on the same maximal noninferior face $\mathcal{F}_1$. On the other hand, after performing the necessary analysis, we find that introduction of column x_5 into the basis leads to an inferior extreme point. Consequently, we can conclude that $E(\mathbf{x}^1)=\{\mathbf{x}^0,(3,2,0)^{\mathrm{T}}\}$, $F(\mathbf{x}^1)=\{\mathbf{w}^1\}$, and no new maximal noninferior face is encountered in this iteration. Consequently, we also have

$$F_g = \{\mathbf{w}^1\}, \qquad E_e = \{\mathbf{x}^0\} \cup \{\mathbf{x}^1\} = \{\mathbf{x}^0, \mathbf{x}^1\},$$

$$E_u = \{\mathbf{x}^1, (3,2,0)^T\} \cup E(\mathbf{x}^1) - E_e = \{(3,2,0)^T\},$$

$$P(\mathcal{F}_1) = \{\mathbf{x}^0, \mathbf{x}^1, (3,2,0)^T\}.$$

For the next iteration we choose the only candidate in E_u, i.e., $\mathbf{x}^2 = (3,2,0)^T$. The corresponding tableau $T(\mathbf{x}^2)$ obtained by pivoting column 6 in $T(\mathbf{x}^1)$ into the basic set is

$$\begin{array}{c} \text{Basis} \\ x_1 \\ x_2 \\ x_6 \\ \\ -z_1 \\ -z_2 \\ -z_3 \end{array}
\begin{array}{c} \begin{array}{cccccc|c} x_1 & x_2 & x_3 & x_4 & x_5 & x_6 & \text{Constants} \end{array} \\
\left(\begin{array}{cccccc|c}
1 & & 0 & 1 & -1 & & 3 \\
 & 1 & 0 & 0 & 1 & & 2 \\
 & & 1 & 1 & 0 & 1 & 1 \\ \hline
 & & 0 & 1 & 1 & & 7 \\
 & & 2 & 1 & -1 & & 3 \\
 & & -1 & -1 & 1 & & -3
\end{array}\right)\end{array}. \tag{6.100}$$

Since no columns are *inferior* in the sense of Theorem 6.4(b) we set $J_D^2 = \{3,4,5\}$. To find $E(\mathbf{x}^2)$ and $F(\mathbf{x}^2)$ we construct the tableau $t(\mathbf{x}^2)$,

$$\begin{array}{c} \text{Basis} \\ \varepsilon_3 \\ \varepsilon_4 \\ \varepsilon_5 \end{array}
\begin{array}{c} \begin{array}{cccccc|c} \varepsilon_3 & \varepsilon_4 & \varepsilon_5 & v_1 & v_2 & v_3 & \text{Constants} \end{array} \\
\left(\begin{array}{cccccc|c}
1 & & & 0 & -2 & 1 & 1 \\
 & 1 & & -1 & -1 & \textcircled{1} & 1 \\
 & & 1 & -1 & 1 & -1 & 1
\end{array}\right)\end{array}. \tag{6.101}$$

We note that each ε_3, ε_4, and ε_5 can be pivoted into the nonbasic set, implying that $J(\mathbf{x}^2) = \{3, 4, 5\}$ and the corresponding $E(\mathbf{x}^2) = \{\mathbf{x}^0, \mathbf{x}^1, (5,0,0)^T\}$. We observe also that ε_3 and ε_4 can be made equal to zero simultaneously by the indicated pivot in the second row, yielding $\hat{\mathbf{v}} = (0,0,1)$ or $\hat{\mathbf{w}} = (\frac{1}{4}, \frac{1}{4}, \frac{1}{2})^T$. This is to be expected, since we have found earlier that both $\mathbf{x}^0$ and $\mathbf{x}^1$ (obtained by pivoting columns 3 and 4 in $T(\mathbf{x}^2)$, respectively, into the basic set) lie on $\mathcal{F}_1$, whose weight vector is precisely $\mathbf{w}^1 = \hat{\mathbf{w}}$. Further investigation reveals that neither of the pairs $(\varepsilon_3, \varepsilon_5)$ and $(\varepsilon_4, \varepsilon_5)$ can be made equal to zero simultaneously either as nonbasic variables or as degenerate basic variables. Consequently, we conclude there exists just one other maximal noninferior face incident to $\mathbf{x}^2$, denoted $\mathcal{F}_2$. By pivoting ε_5 into the nonbasic column in $t(\mathbf{x}^2)$ through the indicated pivot on the third row, we have $\mathbf{v} = (0,1,0)^T$. Hence the corresponding weight vector of $\mathcal{F}_2$ is

$$\mathbf{w}^2 = \left[(0,1,0)^T + (1,1,1)^T\right] \Big/ \sum_{i=1}^{3} (1 + v_i) = (\tfrac{1}{4}, \tfrac{1}{2}, \tfrac{1}{4})^T.$$

The extreme point $(5,0,0)^{\mathrm{T}}$ is obtained when column 5 in $T(\mathbf{x}^2)$ is introduced into the basic set. Consequently we have $(5,0,0)^{\mathrm{T}}$ as well as $\mathbf{x}^2$ lying on $\mathcal{F}_2$. We summarize our findings at the end of this iteration:

$$E(\mathbf{x}^2)=\{\mathbf{x}^0,\mathbf{x}^2,(5,0,0)^{\mathrm{T}}\},\qquad F(\mathbf{x}^2)=\{\mathbf{w}^1,\mathbf{w}^2\},\qquad F_{\mathrm{g}}=\{\mathbf{w}^1,\mathbf{w}^2\},$$
$$E_{\mathrm{e}}=\{\mathbf{x}^0,\mathbf{x}^1\}\cup\{\mathbf{x}^2\}=\{\mathbf{x}^0,\mathbf{x}^1,\mathbf{x}^2\},$$
$$E_{\mathrm{u}}=\{\mathbf{x}^2\}\cup E(\mathbf{x}^2)-E_{\mathrm{e}}=\{(5,0,0)^{\mathrm{T}}\}$$
$$P(\mathcal{F}_1)=\{\mathbf{x}^0,\mathbf{x}^1,\mathbf{x}^2\},\qquad P(\mathcal{F}_2)=\{\mathbf{x}^2,(5,0,0)^{\mathrm{T}}\}.$$

Next we move to $\mathbf{x}^3=(5,0,0)^{\mathrm{T}}$, which is again the only member of E_{u}. Continuing the calculation we obtain $T(\mathbf{x}^3)$,

$$\begin{array}{c|cccccc|c}
\text{Basic} & x_1 & x_2 & x_3 & x_4 & x_5 & x_6 & \text{Constants}\\
\hline
x_1 & 1 & 1 & 0 & 1 & & & 5\\
x_5 & & 1 & 0 & 0 & 1 & & 2\\
x_6 & & 0 & 1 & 1 & & 1 & 1\\
\hline
-z_1 & -1 & 0 & 1 & & & & 5\\
-z_2 & 1 & 2 & 1 & & & & 5\\
-z_3 & -1 & -1 & -1 & & & & -5
\end{array} \qquad (6.102)$$

Since column 2 dominates column 3, $J_{\mathrm{D}}^3=\{2,4\}$. Thus $T(\mathbf{x}^3)$ becomes

$$\begin{array}{c|cccccc|c}
\text{Basic} & \varepsilon_2 & \varepsilon_3 & \varepsilon_4 & v_1 & v_2 & v_3 & \text{Constants}\\
\hline
\varepsilon_2 & 1 & & & 1 & -1 & 1 & -1\\
\varepsilon_3 & & 1 & & 0 & -2 & 1 & 1\\
\varepsilon_4 & & & 1 & -1 & -1 & 1 & 1
\end{array} \qquad (6.103)$$

Since only ε_2 can be pivoted into the nonbasic columns, $J(\mathbf{x}^3)=\{2\}$. Also, $E(\mathbf{x}^3)=\{\mathbf{x}^2\}$. Setting $\varepsilon_2=0$ yields the expected conclusion, namely, the edge $\{\mathbf{x}^2,\mathbf{x}^3\}$ lies on $\mathcal{F}_2$. We therefore have

$$E(\mathbf{x}^3)=\{\mathbf{x}^2\},\qquad F(\mathbf{x}^3)=\{\mathbf{w}^2\},\qquad F_{\mathrm{g}}=\{\mathbf{w}^1,\mathbf{w}^2\},$$
$$E_{\mathrm{e}}=\{\mathbf{x}^0,\mathbf{x}^1,\mathbf{x}^2\}\cup\{\mathbf{x}^3\}=\{\mathbf{x}^0,\mathbf{x}^1,\mathbf{x}^2,\mathbf{x}^3\},$$
$$E_{\mathrm{u}}=\{\mathbf{x}^3\}\cup E(\mathbf{x}^3)-E_{\mathrm{e}}=\varnothing,$$
$$P(\mathcal{F}_1)=\{\mathbf{x}^0,\mathbf{x}^1,\mathbf{x}^2\},\qquad \text{and}\qquad P(\mathcal{F}_2)=\{\mathbf{x}^2,\mathbf{x}^3\}.$$

Since $E_{\mathrm{u}}=\varnothing$, the process terminates, and we conclude that X^* consists of two convex hulls, one formed by $\{\mathbf{x}^0,\mathbf{x}^1,\mathbf{x}^2\}$, the other by $(\mathbf{x}^2,\mathbf{x}^3\}$. Had we not kept track of $P(\mathcal{F}_1)$ and $P(\mathcal{F}_2)$, we would have been able to retrieve $\mathcal{F}_1$ and $\mathcal{F}_2$ by recognizing that $F(\mathbf{x}^0)\cap F(\mathbf{x}^1)\cap F(\mathbf{x}^2)=\{\mathbf{w}^1\}$ implies $\{\mathbf{x}^0,\mathbf{x}^1,\mathbf{x}^2\}$ lie on $\mathcal{F}_1$ and that $F(\mathbf{x}^2)\cap F(\mathbf{x}^3)=\{\mathbf{w}^2\}$ implies $\{\mathbf{x}^2,\mathbf{x}^3\}$ lie on $\mathcal{F}_2$.

6.2.4 *Other Methods Applicable to Linear Problems*

In this section we discuss two other interesting methods based on the weighting characterization and designed to generate noninferior solutions for linear problems. The second can also be used to approximate the noninferior set for any two-objective convex problem.

Interval Weights Method The interval weights method, due to Steuer [1976], is predicated on two premises. First, when presented with too many choices or with too much information, one tends to ignore major portions, if not all, of the information in making judgments. This is not because one doubts the credibility of the information, but simply because the information is so overwhelming that one is unable to filter out the information which is relevant to the judgments. The second premise is that human judgment is often fuzzy. When asked to estimate weights that reflect his preference of a set of objectives, the decision maker is often more comfortable giving a range than a single value.

Suppose we want to solve an LVOP linear vector optimization of the form (6.38)–(6.39), or the equivalent weighting problem $P(\mathbf{w})$:

$$\min \quad \mathbf{w}^{\mathrm{T}} C\mathbf{x} \tag{6.104}$$

$$\text{subject to} \quad \mathbf{x} \in X = \{\mathbf{x} | A\mathbf{x} = \mathbf{b}, \mathbf{x} \geqslant 0, \mathbf{x} \in R^N\}, \tag{6.105}$$

$$\mathbf{w} \in \mathbf{W}^\circ = \left\{ \mathbf{w} \,\middle|\, \sum_{i=1}^{n} w_i = 1, 0 < w_i < 1, \mathbf{w} \in R^n \right\}. \tag{6.106}$$

The first premise suggests that, instead of generating the entire set of noninferior solutions, it is sufficient and more practical to generate only the "best" part of X^*. By virtue of the second premise, the availability of the interval weights of the form $0 \leqslant \alpha_i < w_i < \beta_i \leqslant 1$, $i = 1, \ldots, n$, should help determine that "best" part. In other words, we shall be looking for $\hat{X}^* \subseteq X^*$, that is, for those points in X^* which are the solutions of $\hat{P}(\mathbf{w})$:

$$\min \quad \mathbf{w}^{\mathrm{T}} C\mathbf{X} \tag{6.107}$$

$$\text{subject to} \quad \mathbf{x} \in X \tag{6.108}$$

$$\mathbf{w} \in \hat{W}^\circ = \left\{ \mathbf{w} \,\middle|\, \sum_{i=1}^{n} w_i = 1, \alpha_i < w_i < \beta_i, \mathbf{w} \in R^n \right\}. \tag{6.109}$$

The use of interval weights reduces the size of the set of noninferior solutions to be considered from X^* to $\hat{X}^*$. This can be demonstrated by referring to Example 3 and Figure 6.3. While the entire X^* of problem (6.22)–(6.23) consists of the lines AB and AC inclusive, the size of noninferior solutions of interest reduces to just the line AB if the weights are restricted to the intervals $\frac{2}{3} \leqslant w_1 < 1$ and $0 < w_2 \leqslant \frac{1}{3}$. Even more dramatic is the fact that it reduces to the single point B if the interval weights are $\frac{1}{4}<w_1<\frac{2}{3}$ and $\frac{1}{3}<w_2<\frac{3}{4}$.

Having agreed on using $\hat{X}^*$ as a source from which the final choice(s) should be made, it remains to find a way of solving $\hat{P}(\mathbf{w})$ in (6.107)–(6.108) to determine $\hat{X}^*$. Since there exist efficient algorithms for solving problems of the form LVOP in (6.38)–(6.39) or $P(\mathbf{w})$ in (6.104)–(6.106), as described in the preceding subsection, our problem is solved if we can find a way of transforming $\hat{P}(\mathbf{w})$ into the form $P(\mathbf{v})$:

$$\min \mathbf{v}\hat{C}\mathbf{x} \tag{6.110}$$

$$\text{subject to} \quad \mathbf{x}\in X, \tag{6.111}$$

$$\mathbf{v}\in V^{\circ} \tag{6.112}$$

where $\hat{C}$ is an $\hat{n}\times N$ matrix, with $\hat{n}$ to be determined, and

$$V^{\circ}=\left\{\mathbf{v}\,\middle|\,\sum_{i=1}^{n} v_i=1, 0<v_i<1, i=1,2,,\ldots,\hat{n}, \mathbf{v}\in R^{\hat{n}}\right\}.$$

Let

$$\Lambda=\Big\{\boldsymbol{\lambda}=(\lambda_1,\ldots,\lambda_n)^{\mathrm{T}}\,|\,\lambda_{j_i}\in\{\alpha_{j_i},\beta_{j_i}\}, i=1,\ldots,n-1, \alpha_{j_n}\leqslant\lambda_{j_n}\leqslant\beta_{j_n}$$

$$\text{for all possible combinations of } n-1 \text{ elements}$$

$$(j_1,\ldots,j_{n-1}) \text{ from } (1,\ldots,n)\Big\}, \qquad \lambda_{j_n}=1-\sum_{i=1}^{n-1}\lambda_{j_i}. \tag{6.113}$$

Let there be $\hat{n}$ distinct members of Λ, namely,

$$\Lambda=\{\boldsymbol{\lambda}^1,\ldots,\boldsymbol{\lambda}^{\hat{n}}\}. \tag{6.114}$$

Also let $\mathbf{c}_i$ denote the ith row of C, $i=1,\ldots,n$, and let $\hat{\mathbf{c}}_j$ denote the jth row of $\hat{C}$, $j=1,\ldots,\hat{n}$.

Steuer [1976] proves the following results which make the transformation from (6.107)–(6.109) to (6.110)–(6.112) possible.

Theorem 6.7. *The set of solutions of* $\hat{P}(\mathbf{w})$ *in* (6.107)–(6.109) *is precisely the set of solutions of* $\hat{P}(\mathbf{v})$ *in* (6.110)–(6.112) *if*

$$\hat{\mathbf{c}}_j=\sum_{i=1}^{n}\lambda_i^j\mathbf{c}_i \qquad \textit{for each} \quad j=1,\ldots,\hat{n}. \tag{6.115}$$

The following example demonstrates the use of Theorem 6.7.

Example 7: Suppose we want to solve the problem in Example 6, namely,

$$\min \quad \mathbf{Z}=\mathbf{C}\mathbf{x} \tag{6.116}$$

$$\text{subject to} \quad \mathbf{x}\in X=\{\mathbf{x}|\mathbf{x}\in R^3, A\mathbf{x}\leqslant\mathbf{b}, \mathbf{x}\geqslant 0\}, \tag{6.117}$$

where

$$C=\begin{pmatrix} -1 & -3 & 0 \\ -1 & 0 & 2 \\ 1 & 0 & -1 \end{pmatrix},\qquad A=\begin{pmatrix} 1 & 1 & 0 \\ 0 & 1 & 0 \\ -1 & -1 & 1 \end{pmatrix},\qquad \mathbf{b}=\begin{pmatrix} 1 \\ 2 \\ 4 \end{pmatrix},$$

given that the weights w_1, w_2, w_3 must lie in the intervals

$$0 < w_1 < 0.5, \qquad 0.2 < w_2 < 0.6, \qquad \text{and} \qquad 0.4 < w_3 < 0.7.$$

To convert this problem to that of the form (6.110)–(6.112), we first construct Λ. To construct Λ we must test every possible combination of $\lambda_{j_1}, \lambda_{j_2}$ for every permutation (j_1, j_2, j_3), each of which can be either the lower or upper bound of w_{j_1}, w_{j_2}, whether $\lambda_{j_3} = 1 - \lambda_{j_1} - \lambda_{j_2}$ lies within the bounds of w_{j_3}.

$(j_1, j_2) = (1, 2)$ or $(2, 1)$:

$$\begin{aligned}
\lambda_1 = 0.0,\quad \lambda_2 = 0.2 \quad &\Rightarrow \quad \lambda_3 = 0.8 \quad \text{(unusable)},\\
\lambda_1 = 0.0,\quad \lambda_2 = 0.6 \quad &\Rightarrow \quad \lambda_3 = 0.4 \quad \text{(usable)},\\
&\Rightarrow \quad \boldsymbol{\lambda}^1 = (0.0, 0.6, 0.4)^{\mathrm{T}},\\
\lambda_1 = 0.5,\quad \lambda_2 = 0.2 \quad &\Rightarrow \quad \lambda_3 = 0.3 \quad \text{(unusable)},\\
\lambda_1 = 0.5,\quad \lambda_2 = 0.6 \quad &\Rightarrow \quad \lambda_3 = -0.1 \quad \text{(unusable)}.
\end{aligned}$$

$(j_1, j_2) = (1, 3)$ or $(3, 1)$:

$$\begin{aligned}
\lambda_1 = 0.0,\quad \lambda_3 = 0.4 \quad &\Rightarrow \quad \lambda_2 = 0.6 \quad \text{(usable)},\\
&\Rightarrow \quad \boldsymbol{\lambda}^2 = (0.0, 0.4, 0.6)^{\mathrm{T}},\\
\lambda_1 = 0.0,\quad \lambda_3 = 0.7 \quad &\Rightarrow \quad \lambda_2 = 0.3 \quad \text{(usable)},\\
&\Rightarrow \quad \boldsymbol{\lambda}^3 = (0.0, 0.3, 0.7)^{\mathrm{T}},\\
\lambda_1 = 0.5,\quad \lambda_3 = 0.4 \quad &\Rightarrow \quad \lambda_2 = 0.1 \quad \text{(unusable)},\\
\lambda_1 = 0.5,\quad \lambda_3 = 0.7 \quad &\Rightarrow \quad \lambda_2 = -0.2 \quad \text{(unusable)}.
\end{aligned}$$

$(j_1, j_2) = (2, 3)$ or $(3, 2)$:

$$\begin{aligned}
\lambda_2 = 0.2,\quad \lambda_3 = 0.4 \quad &\Rightarrow \quad \lambda_1 = 0.4 \quad \text{(usable)},\\
&\Rightarrow \quad \boldsymbol{\lambda}^4 = (0.4, 0.2, 0.4)^{\mathrm{T}},\\
\lambda_2 = 0.2,\quad \lambda_3 = 0.7 \quad &\Rightarrow \quad \lambda_1 = 0.1 \quad \text{(usable)},\\
&\Rightarrow \quad \boldsymbol{\lambda}^5 = (0.1, 0.2, 0.7)^{\mathrm{T}},\\
\lambda_2 = 0.6,\quad \lambda_3 = 0.4 \quad &\Rightarrow \quad \lambda_1 = 0.0 \quad \text{(usable but the same as } \boldsymbol{\lambda}^1\text{)},\\
\lambda_2 = 0.6,\quad \lambda_3 = 0.7 \quad &\Rightarrow \quad \lambda_1 = -0.3 \quad \text{(unusable)}.
\end{aligned}$$

Therefore $\Lambda = \{\boldsymbol{\lambda}^1, \boldsymbol{\lambda}^2, \boldsymbol{\lambda}^3, \boldsymbol{\lambda}^4, \boldsymbol{\lambda}^5\}$ and $\hat{n}=5$. Hence from (6.115) $\hat{c}_j = \Sigma_{i=1}^{n} \lambda_i^j c_i, j=1,\ldots,5$, which yields

$$\hat{C} = \begin{pmatrix} -0.2 & 0 & 0.8 \\ 0.2 & 0 & 0.2 \\ 0.4 & 0 & -0.1 \\ -0.2 & -1.2 & 0 \\ 0.4 & -0.3 & -0.3 \end{pmatrix}. \tag{6.118}$$

We can use an algorithm from Section 6.2.3 to solve the LVOP of the form

$$\begin{aligned} &\min \quad \hat{C}\mathbf{x} \\ &\text{subject to} \quad \mathbf{x} \in X, \end{aligned}$$

where $\hat{C}$ is given by (6.118) and X is given by (6.117).

The number of rows in $\hat{C}$ is normally larger than the number of rows in C, especially when the latter is large at the outset. For more computational results and further extensions to an interactive version, see Steuer [1976a–c, 1977].

NISE Method Cohon et al. [1979] developed a weighting-based algorithm that is capable of generating the entire set of noninferior solutions for two-objective linear problems (see also Cohen [1978]). It can also be used to approximate such a noninferior set to any degree of accuracy for any two-objective convex problems. In view of the latter application, it is called by its developers the noninferior set estimation method (NISE).

Consider the two-objective vector optimization problem VOP:

$$\begin{aligned} &\min \quad (f_1(\mathbf{x}), f_2(\mathbf{x})) \\ &\text{subject to} \quad \mathbf{x} \in X. \end{aligned} \tag{6.119}$$

We assume that X is a convex set in R^N and f_1 and f_2 are convex functions on X. Again, X^* represents the set of noninferior solutions. Also let $F = \{\mathbf{f} = (f_1(\mathbf{x}), f_2(\mathbf{x})) | \mathbf{x} \in X\}$ and $F^* = \{\mathbf{f} = (f_1(\mathbf{x}), f_2(\mathbf{x})) | \mathbf{x} \in X^*\}$. We call F the feasible region in the objective space and F^* the noninferior set (in the objective space).

Figure 6.7 illustrates several well-known observations. First, if X, f_1, and f_2 are convex, so is the set F. In particular, if X is a convex polyhedron, and f_1, f_2 are linear, F is also a convex polyhedron. To demonstrate, let X be a convex hull generated by the extreme points $\{\mathbf{x}^1, \mathbf{x}^2, \ldots, \mathbf{x}^s\}$. By the linearity of $\mathbf{f}$, the equalities $\Sigma_{i=1}^{s} \alpha_i = 1$, $\mathbf{f}(\mathbf{x}) = \mathbf{f}(\Sigma_{i=1}^{s} \alpha_i x^i) = \Sigma_{i=1}^{s} \alpha_i \mathbf{f}(\mathbf{x}) = \Sigma_{i=1}^{s} \alpha_i \mathbf{f}(\mathbf{x}^i)$ imply that F is a convex hull generated by the extreme points $\{\mathbf{f}(\mathbf{x}^1), \ldots, \mathbf{f}(\mathbf{x}^s)\}$.

Second, it can be shown that the noninferior set F^* is always at the boundary of F. In fact, since F is convex, F^* traces out a convex curve with

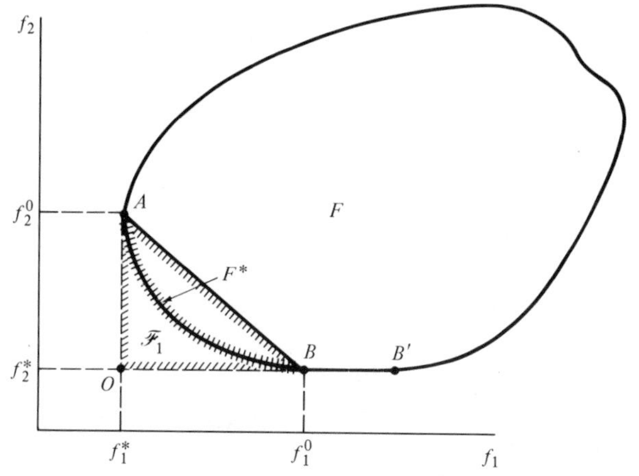

Figure 6.7 Properties of the noninferior set F^* of convex problems.

endpoints

$$A = \left(f_1(\mathbf{x}^1), f_2(\mathbf{x}^1) \right) \triangleq \left(f_1^*, f_2^0 \right), \qquad f_1(\mathbf{x}^1) = f_1^* = \min_{x \in X} f_1(\mathbf{x}), \tag{6.120}$$

$$B = \left(f_1(\mathbf{x}^2), f_2(\mathbf{x}^2) \right) \triangleq \left(f_1^0, f_2^* \right), \qquad f_2(\mathbf{x}^2) = f_2^* = \min_{x \in X} f_2(\mathbf{x}) \tag{6.121}$$

in Figure 6.7. Geometrically, $\mathbf{x}^1$ is the point where f_1 attains its minimum value in X and where f_2 attains the lowest value possible consistent with maintaining f_1 at its minimum.[8] Likewise $\mathbf{x}^2$ is the point where f_2 attains its minimum in X and f_1 attains its lowest possible value while maintaining f_2 at its minimum.

Third, the set F^* must lie wholly within the set $\mathscr{F}_1$, where

$$\mathscr{F}_1 = \{ \mathbf{f} = (f_1, f_2) | f_1 \geqslant f_1^*, f_2 \geqslant f_2^*, \mathbf{f} \leqslant \alpha \mathbf{f}(A) + (1-\alpha)\mathbf{f}(B), 0 \leqslant \alpha \leqslant 1 \} \tag{6.122}$$

and $\mathbf{f}(A)$ and $\mathbf{f}(B)$ are the values of function $\mathbf{f}$ at A and B, respectively. The set $\mathscr{F}_1$ is illustrated as the triangle OAB in Figure 6.7. An implication of this observation is that the set $\mathscr{F}_1$ forms a *bound* within which the noninferior set must lie. The set F^* cannot lie above the line AB because of the convexity of F^*, nor can it lie below OB or to the left of OA because of noninferiority and the minimality of f_1^* and f_2^*.

Fourth, for any two points PQ on the noninferior curve F^*, there always exists a supporting hyperplane (a line in the two-dimensional case) having the same slope (or gradient) as the line joining PQ. This line is tangent to

[8] We see that although f_2 is minimum at any point along BB', only B is noninferior, since at any other point in BB' we can always decrease f_1 without increasing f_2.

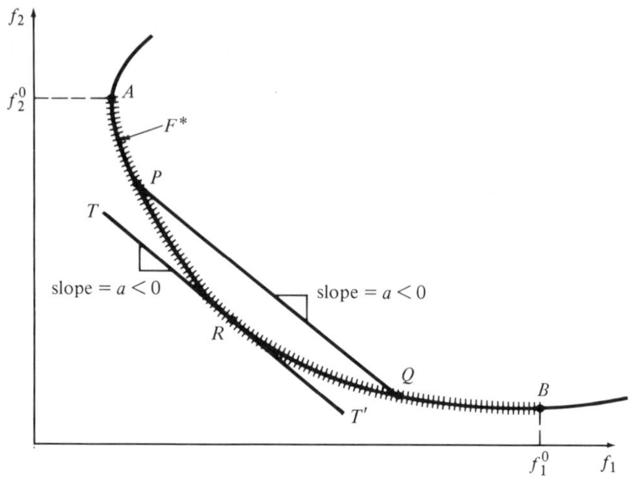

Figure 6.8 Tangent plane of F^* and F. TT' is a supporting hyperplane to F^* at R parallel to PQ.

the curve F^* at a point R lying between P and Q (see Figure 6.8). This point R can be obtained by solving the parametric problem $P(\lambda)$ of finding f to

$$\begin{aligned} &\min \quad \lambda_1 f_1(\mathbf{x}) + \lambda_2 f_2(\mathbf{x}) \\ &\text{subject to} \quad \mathbf{x} \in X \end{aligned} \tag{6.123}$$

where $\lambda_1/\lambda_2 = -a$ (a is the slope of line PQ, which is always negative by the noninferiority of F^*). Observe that when λ_1 and λ_2 are chosen so that $\lambda_1+\lambda_2=1$, $P(\boldsymbol{\lambda})$ becomes the usual weighting problem. As a corollary of this observation, it can be seen that every noninferior point along the curve F^* between A and B can always be generated by solving $P(\boldsymbol{\lambda})$ in (6.123) for some selected $\lambda_1>0$, $\lambda_2>0$. Conversely any solution of (6.123) for some selected $\lambda_1>0$, $\lambda_2>0$ will always correspond to a point between A and B on the noninferior curve F^*. At the extremes, when setting $\lambda_1=1$, $\lambda_2=0$, A is obtained, and when setting $\lambda_1=0$, $\lambda_2=1$, B is obtained.

This fourth observation is the basis for the NISE method. In the context of linear problems it is capable of generating the entire set X^*. Let X be a convex polyhedron and let f_1 and f_2 in (6.119) be linear. By the first observation, F is a convex polyhedron. Consequently F^* must consist of a set of extreme points (or extreme rays) (in the objective space) and the lines joining each pair of adjacent extreme points, as shown in Figure 6.9.

Suppose we select any two noninferior extreme points on F^*, say P and Q in Figure 6.9, and find the slope of the line joining those two points, by (6.124):

$$\text{slope}(PQ) = a = \frac{f_2(P) - f_2(Q)}{f_1(P) - f_1(Q)} < 0. \tag{6.124}$$

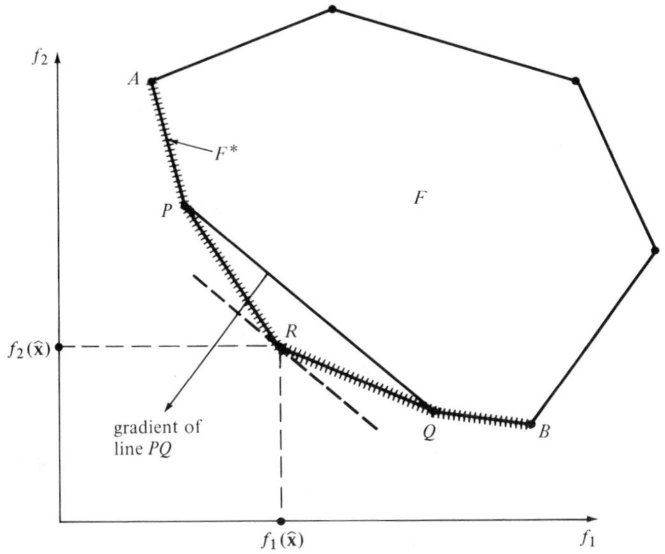

Figure 6.9 Noninferior set in linear problems.

We formulate $P(\boldsymbol{\lambda})$ as in (6.123) with $\lambda_1/\lambda_2 = -a$ and solve. In view of the fourth observation, two cases associated with the optimal solution $\hat{\mathbf{x}}$ of $P(\boldsymbol{\lambda})$ may prevail: either

$$\hat{f} \equiv \lambda_1 f_1(P) + \lambda_2 f_2(P) = \lambda_1 f_1(Q) + \lambda_2 f_2(Q), \tag{6.125}$$

or

$$\hat{f} > \lambda_1 f_1(P) + \lambda_2 f_2(P) = \lambda_1 f_1(Q) + \lambda_2 f_2(Q), \tag{6.126}$$

where $\hat{f} = \lambda_1 f_1(\hat{\mathbf{x}}) + \lambda_2 f_2(\hat{\mathbf{x}})$, and $f_i(P)$, $f_i(Q)$, $i = 1,2$, are values of f_i at points P and Q, respectively. For the case of (6.126) we conclude that since $P(\boldsymbol{\lambda})$ is a simple linear programming problem, the point $R = (f_1(\hat{\mathbf{x}}), f_2(\hat{\mathbf{x}}))$ must be another noninferior extreme point in F^* lying furthest from the line PQ in the direction of the gradient of that line. Consequently, no point on the line PQ, other than P and Q, can lie on F^* (due to the convexity of F^*). This implies the inferiority of the points on PQ. If (6.125) prevails, then we conclude that both P and Q are two of the multiple optima of $P(\boldsymbol{\lambda})$. Moreover, any point along the line PQ of the form $Y = \alpha P + (1-\alpha)Q$, $0 \leqslant \alpha \leqslant 1$, must be an optimal solution of $P(\boldsymbol{\lambda})$ since

$$\begin{aligned}\lambda_1 f_1(Y) + \lambda_2 f_2(Y) &= \lambda_1 f_1[\alpha P + (1-\alpha)Q] + \lambda_2 f_2[\alpha P + (1-\alpha)Q] \\ &= \alpha[\lambda_1 f_1(P) + \lambda_2 f_2(P)] + (1-\alpha)[\lambda_1 f_1(Q) + \lambda_2 f_2(Q)] \\ &= \hat{f}.\end{aligned}$$

Equation (6.6a), the inequality $\lambda > 0$, and the fact that Y is a noninferior solution imply that P and Q are adjacent extreme points joined by a line that is noninferior.

Thus, the NISE procedure can be used to find new extreme points or to check any two given extreme points for adjacency. With an appropriate bookkeeping scheme, all noninferior extreme points lying on F^* and between A and B, and hence the entire X^*, can be found and tested for adjacency. Cohon et al. [1979] suggest that all generated extreme points be ordered and kept in a sequence of decreasing order of their corresponding values of $f_2(\mathbf{x})$, and that the adjacency of any two consecutive points in the sequence be indicated by a binary-valued indicator.

To be more precise, if K extreme points have been generated, they should be recorded in the sequence $\{A = P_1, P_2, \ldots, P_K = B\}$ having the property

$$f_2(P_k) > f_2(P_{k+1}) \qquad \text{for all} \quad k = 1, \ldots, K-1.$$

Moreover, for any two consecutive members in the sequence we record the indicator $L(k, k+1)$ having the value 0 if P_k and P_{k+1} are adjacent (with the line joining them being noninferior) and 1 otherwise. In this way one can always use (6.124) to compute the slope of the line joining any two consecutive P_k, P_{k+1}. With such a record, one need only look for two consecutive points with nonzero $L(k, k+1)$; one can then either find a new extreme point between them or verify that the indicator $L(k, k+1)$ should be zero. The process terminates when all $L(k, k+1) = 0$, indicating that all consecutive pairs in the sequence are adjacent. The entire X^* has then been derived.

We summarize the NISE algorithm for linear problems:

i. Obtain A and B by solving $\min_{x \in X} f_1(\mathbf{x})$ and $\min_{x \in X} f_2(\mathbf{x})$, respectively, and set $K = 2$, $L(1,2) = 1$, $P_1 = A$, $P_2 = B$.

ii. In the current iteration, find a $1 \leqslant k \leqslant K-1$ such that $L(k, k+1) > 0$. If none exists, stop. Otherwise, formulate and solve $P(\boldsymbol{\lambda}^k)$ of the form (6.123) with

$$\lambda_1^k = f_2(P_k) - f_2(P_{k+1}) \qquad \text{and} \qquad \lambda_2^k = f_1(P_k) - f_1(P_{k+1}).$$

iii. Let $\hat{f}^k$ be the optimal value of $P(\boldsymbol{\lambda}^k)$ corresponding to the optimal solution $\hat{\mathbf{x}}$. If $\hat{f}^k = \lambda_1^k f_1(P_k) + \lambda_2^k f_2(P_k)$, let $L(k, k+1) = 0$. If $\hat{f}^k > \lambda_1^k f_1(P_k) + \lambda_2^k f_2(P_k)$, then set

$$P_{j+1} = P_j \qquad \text{for all} \quad j = k+1, \ldots, K,$$

$$P_{k+1} = (f_1(\hat{\mathbf{x}}), f_2(\hat{\mathbf{x}})),$$

$$L(k+1, k+2) = 1,$$

$$L(j, j+1) = L(j-1, j), \qquad j = k+2, \ldots, K,$$

$$K = K+1.$$

In either case, return to step (ii).

To demonstrate the actual mechanism of the algorithm, consider the problem presented in Figure 6.9. We begin with points $P_1 = A$ and $P_2 = B$ and $L(1,2) = 1$. Carrying out step (ii) yields point R as the optimal solution of (6.123) with $\lambda_1^1 = f_2(A) - f_2(B)$ and $\lambda_2^1 = f_1(A) - f_1(B)$. Since $f(R) > \lambda_1^1 f_1(A) + \lambda_2^1 f_2(A)$, we let $P_2 = R$, $P_3 = B$, and $L(2,3) = 1$. We now have the sequence A, R, B with $L(1,2) = 1$, $L(2,3) = 1$. Therefore we can choose any consecutive pair in the sequence for the next iteration. Suppose we choose $\{A, R\}$. The end of three iterations yields $\{P_1, P_2, P_3, P_4\} = \{A, P, R, B\}$ with $L(1,2) = 0$, $L(2,3) = 0$, $L(3,4) = 1$. Choosing the pair $\{R, B\}$ and continuing the process yields $\{A, P, R, Q, B\}$ with all $L(k, k+1) = 0$ for all $k = 1, 2, 3, 4$. This indicates that F^* consists of the extreme points $\{A, P, R, Q, B\}$ and the lines joining each consecutive pair in the sequence.

This method may be extended for approximating the noninferior set of a two-objective convex problem. In such problems, the exact F^* is not generally obtainable by the NISE method in a practical number of steps. To approximate F^* we extend the method based on our earlier observation about the bound enclosing the true F^*. As more points are generated, the bound becomes tighter, and hence a better approximation (less error). Consider a third noninferior point C on F^* between A and B in Figure 6.7, which is redrawn in Figure 6.10 for clarity.

The true curve F^* is bounded from the inside by the lines AC and CB and on the outside by the vertical line AE, the line EF parallel to AB, and the horizontal line FB. Thus, the lengths of EG and FH are measures of the maximum error in using the lines AC and CB as the estimates of the AC and CB portions of F^*, respectively. These measures of maximum error will be reduced as more points are generated. If GE is less than a specified value of maximum allowable error, say $\varepsilon > 0$, we would be content to use AC as the

Figure 6.10 Inner and outer bounds of noninferior sets.

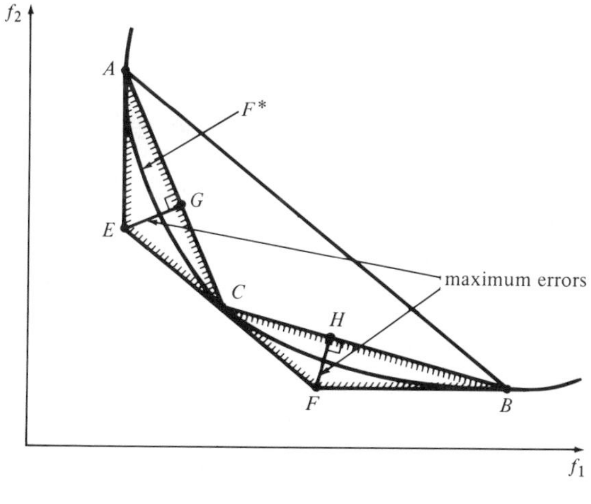

estimate of the AC portion of the true F^*, and likewise for the CB portion of F^*. This suggests that a possible modification of the NISE method would be to set $L(k, k+1)$ equal to the measure of maximum error between P_k and P_{k+1}. If $L(k, k+1) \leq \varepsilon$, we are satisfied with using the line $P_k P_{k+1}$ to approximate the true F^* between P_k and P_{k+1}. Otherwise, we generate a new point between P_k and P_{k+1} as before. For more examples as well as extensions to three or more objective cases, see Cohon [1978] and Cohon et al. [1979].

6.3 Methods Based on ε-Constraint Characterizations

Characterizing noninferior solutions of VOP in (6.3) by solutions of appropriate constraint problems is also common. In fact, as we have seen in Chapter 4, we can generate the entire set of noninferior solutions X^*, at least theoretically, for nonconvex as well as convex problems through this characterization. We now show how the basic results discussed in Chapter 4 can be used computationally to generate X^*.

In the most common type of ε-constraint problem, one primary objective f_k is selected to be minimized, and the other objectives are converted into inequality constraints (Haimes et al. [1971], and Haimes and Hall [1974]). The problem may be denoted $P_k(\boldsymbol{\varepsilon})$:

$$\min \quad f_k(\mathbf{x}) \tag{6.127}$$

$$\text{subject to} \qquad \mathbf{x} \in X, \tag{6.128}$$

$$f_j(\mathbf{x}) \leq \varepsilon_j, \quad j=1,\ldots,n, \quad j \neq k. \tag{6.129}$$

The following results from Sections 4.3.2 and 4.6 are useful, the first two due mainly to Haimes et al. [1971]. First suppose $\boldsymbol{\varepsilon}^0$ is a vector for which $P_k(\boldsymbol{\varepsilon}^0)$ is feasible, and $\mathbf{x}^0$ is the optimal solution of $P_k(\boldsymbol{\varepsilon}^0)$. Then $\mathbf{x}^0$ is a noninferior solution of VOP if $\mathbf{x}^0$ is a unique solution of $P_k(\boldsymbol{\varepsilon}^0)$ for some $1 \leq k \leq n$, or if it solves $P_k(\boldsymbol{\varepsilon}^0)$ for every $k=1,\ldots,n$ (Theorems 4.1 and 4.2). This means that at least some noninferior solutions of VOP can always be discovered by solving $P_k(\boldsymbol{\varepsilon})$ as long as $\boldsymbol{\varepsilon}$ is chosen so that $P_k(\boldsymbol{\varepsilon})$ is feasible.

On the other hand, for any given noninferior solution $\mathbf{x}^*$, we can always find $\boldsymbol{\varepsilon}$ such that $\mathbf{x}^*$ solves $P_k(\boldsymbol{\varepsilon})$ for every $k=1,\ldots,n$. In fact one such $\boldsymbol{\varepsilon}$ is given by $\boldsymbol{\varepsilon}^* = (\varepsilon_1^*, \ldots, \varepsilon_{k-1}^*, \varepsilon_{k+1}^*, \ldots, \varepsilon_n^*)^T$, where $\varepsilon_j^* = f_i(\mathbf{x}^*)$ for all $j=1,\ldots,n$, $j \neq k$ (Theorem 4.1).

Since this second result does not require the convexity assumption, this means that all noninferior solutions can always be discovered by means of solving the constraint problem $P_k(\boldsymbol{\varepsilon})$ for any k. Thus if we let

$Y_k =$ set of all $\boldsymbol{\varepsilon}$ such that $P_k(\boldsymbol{\varepsilon})$ is feasible,
$X_\varepsilon^k = \{\mathbf{x} | \mathbf{x}$ solves $P_k(\boldsymbol{\varepsilon})$ for some $\boldsymbol{\varepsilon}$ in $Y_k\}$, and
$\hat{X}_\varepsilon^k = \{\mathbf{x} | \mathbf{x}$ is a unique minimizer of $P_k(\boldsymbol{\varepsilon})$ for some $\boldsymbol{\varepsilon}$ in $Y_k\}$,

then we have

$$\hat{X}_\varepsilon^k \subseteq X^* \subseteq X_\varepsilon^k \tag{6.130}$$

and

$$\bigcap_{k=1}^{n} X_\varepsilon^k \subseteq X^* \subseteq X_\varepsilon^k. \tag{6.131}$$

Theorem 4.3, which is due to Lin [1976b, 1977], provides alternative necessary and sufficient conditions for noninferiority, again expressed in terms of solutions of $P_k(\boldsymbol{\varepsilon})$. For any given $\boldsymbol{\varepsilon}^*$ in Y_k, a solution $\mathbf{x}^*$ of $P_k(\boldsymbol{\varepsilon}^*)$ is a noninferior solution of VOP if and only if for all $\boldsymbol{\varepsilon} \in Y_k$ such that

$$\phi_k(\boldsymbol{\varepsilon}) \triangleq \min\{ f_k(\mathbf{x}) | \mathbf{x} \in X, f_j(\mathbf{x}) \leqslant \varepsilon_j, j \neq k \} \tag{6.132}$$

exists and is finite, we have

$$\phi_k(\boldsymbol{\varepsilon}) > \phi_k(\boldsymbol{\varepsilon}^*) \triangleq f_k(\mathbf{x}^*) \qquad \text{for all} \quad \boldsymbol{\varepsilon} \leqslant \boldsymbol{\varepsilon}^*. \tag{6.133}$$

Similar necessary and sufficient conditions expressed in terms of solutions of the following equality constraint problem $E_k(\boldsymbol{\varepsilon})$ have also been established by Lin [1976a, 1976b]:

$$\min \quad f_k(\boldsymbol{\varepsilon}) \tag{6.134a}$$

$$\text{subject to} \qquad \mathbf{x} \in X, \quad f_j(\mathbf{x}) = \varepsilon_j, \quad j = 1, \ldots, n, \quad j \neq k. \tag{6.134b}$$

According to Theorem 4.15, for any given $\boldsymbol{\varepsilon}^*$, we conclude that a solution $\mathbf{x}^*$ of $E_k(\boldsymbol{\varepsilon}^*)$ is a noninferior solution of VOP if and only if

$$\inf\{ f_k(\mathbf{x}) | \mathbf{x} \in X, f_j(\mathbf{x}) = \varepsilon_j, j \neq k \} \geqslant f_k(\mathbf{x}^*) \qquad \text{for all} \quad \boldsymbol{\varepsilon} \leqslant \boldsymbol{\varepsilon}^* \text{ in } Y_k \tag{6.135}$$

and

$$\phi_k(\boldsymbol{\varepsilon}) > f_k(\mathbf{x}^*) \qquad \text{for all} \quad \boldsymbol{\varepsilon} \leqslant \boldsymbol{\varepsilon}^* \tag{6.136}$$

such that

$$\phi_k(\boldsymbol{\varepsilon}) \triangleq \min\{ f_k(\mathbf{x}) | \mathbf{x} \in X, f_j(\mathbf{x}) = \varepsilon_j, j \neq k \} \tag{6.137}$$

exists and is finite.

Finally, we can have a mixed characterization of noninferior solutions in the sense of a hybrid problem $P(\mathbf{w}, \boldsymbol{\varepsilon})$:

$$\min \quad \mathbf{w}^{\mathrm{T}} \cdot \mathbf{f}(\mathbf{x}) \tag{6.138}$$

$$\text{subject to} \qquad \mathbf{x} \in X, \quad \mathbf{f}(x) \leqslant \boldsymbol{\varepsilon}, \tag{6.139}$$

where

$$\mathbf{w} \in W^0 \triangleq \{ \mathbf{w} | \mathbf{w} \in R^n, \Sigma_{i=1}^n w_i = 1, w_i > 0, i = 1, \ldots, n \} \tag{6.140}$$

and

$$\boldsymbol{\varepsilon} \in Y \triangleq \{\boldsymbol{\varepsilon} | \boldsymbol{\varepsilon} \in R^n, \{\mathbf{x} | \mathbf{x} \in X, \mathbf{f}(\mathbf{x}) \leqslant \boldsymbol{\varepsilon}\} \neq \phi\}. \tag{6.141}$$

According to Theorem 4.16 developed by Wendel and Lee [1977] and Corley [1980], given any $\boldsymbol{\varepsilon}^*$ in Y and $\mathbf{w}^*$ in W^0, an optimal solution $\mathbf{x}^*$ of $P(\mathbf{w}^*, \boldsymbol{\varepsilon}^*)$ is a noninferior solution of VOP. Conversely given any $\mathbf{w}^0 \in W^0$, a noninferior solution $\mathbf{x}^*$ must solve $P(\mathbf{x}^0, \boldsymbol{\varepsilon}^*)$, where $\boldsymbol{\varepsilon}^* = \mathbf{f}(\mathbf{x}^*)$. In short if, for any given $\mathbf{w} \in W^0$,

$$X_{\varepsilon}^{w} \triangleq \{\mathbf{x} | \mathbf{x} \text{ solves } P(\mathbf{w}, \boldsymbol{\varepsilon}) \text{ for some } \boldsymbol{\varepsilon} \in Y\}, \tag{6.142}$$

then

$$X_{\varepsilon}^{w} = X^*. \tag{6.143}$$

This is a powerful result. Not only does it guarantee the entire set X^* regardless of whether the problem is convex, it also needs no qualifications such as uniqueness or those stated by Lin in order to claim the noninferiority of an optimal solution of $P(\mathbf{w}, \boldsymbol{\varepsilon})$. All solutions of $P(\mathbf{w}, \boldsymbol{\varepsilon})$, for any given $\mathbf{w}, \boldsymbol{\varepsilon}$, are noninferior. To use this result, one need only select $\mathbf{w}$ in W^0 and vary only $\boldsymbol{\varepsilon}$.

In using these results, the practical question remains of how to vary the $\boldsymbol{\varepsilon}$s so that the entire X^*, or a representative subset of it, can be generated. We now consider the computational problem.

6.3.1 Analytical Approach

Like the weighting characterization in the last section, the constraint characterizations can be used as a means for generating the entire X^* analytically. After an appropriate constraint problem is formulated, necessary and sufficient conditions for optimality, such as the Kuhn–Tucker conditions (Section 2.3), are applied. The resulting set of equations and inequalities is analyzed and, if necessary, appropriate sufficiency conditions for noninferiority are checked.

Example 8: Consider the problem (6.15)–(6.16) posed in Example 2. We solved it graphically, by the constraint method, in Chapter 4 and analytically, by the weighting method, in Example 2. Let us now solve it analytically by the constraint method and its variants.

First let us try applying the ε-constraint approach and noninferiority observations of Haimes et al. [1971]. The equivalent constraint problem $P_1(\boldsymbol{\varepsilon})$, taking f_1 as the primary objective, is given by

$$\min \quad f_1(\mathbf{x}) = (x_1 - 3)^2 + (x_2 - 2)^2 \tag{6.144}$$

$$\text{subject to} \quad f_2(\mathbf{x}) = x_1 + \ x_2 \leqslant \varepsilon_2, \tag{6.145a}$$

$$f_3(\mathbf{x}) = x_1 + 2x_2 \leqslant \varepsilon_3, \tag{6.145b}$$

$$g_1(\mathbf{x}) = -x_1 \leqslant 0, \tag{6.145c}$$

$$g_2(\mathbf{x}) = -x_2 \leqslant 0. \tag{6.145d}$$

Applying the Kuhn–Tucker necessary conditions (which are also sufficient for this problem) to $P_1(\boldsymbol{\varepsilon})$, we have

$$2(x_1-3)+\lambda_1+\lambda_2-\mu_1=0, \tag{6.146a}$$

$$2(x_2-2)+\lambda_1+2\lambda_2-\mu_2=0, \tag{6.146b}$$

$$\lambda_1(x_1+x_2-\varepsilon_2)=0, \tag{6.146c}$$

$$\lambda_2(x_1+2x_2-\varepsilon_3)=0, \tag{6.146d}$$

$$\mu_1 x_1=0, \tag{6.146e}$$

$$\mu_2 x_2=0, \tag{6.146f}$$

with

$$x_1+x_2-\varepsilon_2\leqslant 0, \qquad x_1+2x_2-\varepsilon_3\leqslant 0,$$
$$x_1\geqslant 0, \qquad x_2\geqslant 0, \qquad \lambda_1,\lambda_2,\mu_1,\mu_2\geqslant 0.$$

Since f_1 is strictly convex, any solution of (6.146) will also be a unique solution of $P_1(\boldsymbol{\varepsilon})$, hence a noninferior solution of (6.15)–(6.16). To analyze (6.146), we consider various combinations of from zero to four binding constraints. For example, suppose (6.145c) is binding, which means that $x_1=0$. This also implies that if $\varepsilon_2, \varepsilon_3>0$, the constraint (6.145c) cannot be binding. Therefore we need only consider binding constraints from (6.145a), (6.145b), and (6.145d). This procedure yields the solution of the system (6.146) in terms of $\boldsymbol{\varepsilon}$:

1. If $\boldsymbol{\varepsilon}$ is chosen from Y_1, where

$$Y_1=\{(\varepsilon_2,\varepsilon_3)|\,\varepsilon_2=\varepsilon_3,\ 0\leqslant\varepsilon_2\leqslant 1 \text{ or } 3\varepsilon_2-2\varepsilon_3\geqslant 1,\ 5\varepsilon_2-3\varepsilon_3\leqslant 4,\ 1\leqslant\varepsilon_2\leqslant 5,\ 1\leqslant\varepsilon_3\leqslant 7\}, \tag{6.147}$$

then

$$\mathbf{x}(\varepsilon)=\begin{pmatrix}2\varepsilon_2-\varepsilon_3\\ \varepsilon_3-\varepsilon_2\end{pmatrix}. \tag{6.148}$$

2. If $\boldsymbol{\varepsilon}$ is chosen from Y_2, where

$$Y_2\triangleq\{(\varepsilon_2,\varepsilon_3)|1\leqslant\varepsilon_2\leqslant 5,\ 3\varepsilon_2-2\varepsilon_3\leqslant 1 \text{ or } \varepsilon_3\geqslant\varepsilon_2,\ 0\leqslant\varepsilon_2\leqslant 1\}, \tag{6.149}$$

then

$$\mathbf{x}(\boldsymbol{\varepsilon}) = \begin{cases} \begin{pmatrix} \frac{1}{2}(\varepsilon_2+1) \\ \frac{1}{2}(\varepsilon_2-1) \end{pmatrix} & \text{if } 1 \leqslant \varepsilon_2 \leqslant 5, \\ \begin{pmatrix} \varepsilon_2 \\ 0 \end{pmatrix} & \text{if } 0 \leqslant \varepsilon_2 \leqslant 1. \end{cases} \tag{6.150}$$

3. If $\boldsymbol{\varepsilon}$ is chosen from Y_3, where

$$Y_3 \triangleq \{(\varepsilon_2, \varepsilon_3) | 0 \leqslant \varepsilon_2 \leqslant 1, \varepsilon_2 \geqslant \varepsilon_3 \text{ or } 5\varepsilon_2 - 3\varepsilon_3 \geqslant 4, 1 \leqslant \varepsilon_2 \leqslant 5\}, \tag{6.151a}$$

then

$$\mathbf{x}(\boldsymbol{\varepsilon}) = \begin{cases} \begin{pmatrix} \frac{1}{5}(\varepsilon_3+8) \\ \frac{1}{5}(2\varepsilon_3-4) \end{pmatrix} & \text{if } 2 \leqslant \varepsilon_3 \leqslant 7, \\ \begin{pmatrix} \varepsilon_3 \\ 0 \end{pmatrix} & \text{if } 0 \leqslant \varepsilon_3 \leqslant 2. \end{cases} \tag{6.151b}$$

4. If $\boldsymbol{\varepsilon}$ is chosen from Y_4, where

$$Y_4 \triangleq \{(\varepsilon_2, \varepsilon_3) | \varepsilon_3 \geqslant 7, \varepsilon_2 \geqslant 5\}, \tag{6.152}$$

then

$$\mathbf{x}(\boldsymbol{\varepsilon}) = \begin{pmatrix} 3 \\ 2 \end{pmatrix}.$$

Although these four different regions give rise to four different formulas for $\mathbf{x}(\boldsymbol{\varepsilon})$, we find that the images of Y_2, Y_3, Y_4 under $\mathbf{x}(\ )$ are all contained in the image of Y_1 under $\mathbf{x}(\ )$. It suffices therefore to describe the entire set of noninferior solutions X^* by

$$X^* \left\{ \mathbf{x} | \mathbf{x} = \begin{pmatrix} 2\varepsilon_2 - \varepsilon_3 \\ \varepsilon_3 - \varepsilon_2 \end{pmatrix}, \boldsymbol{\varepsilon} \in Y_1 \right\}. \tag{6.153}$$

The set of noninferior solutions is illustrated in Figure 6.2. Figure 6.11 demonstrates in the $\varepsilon_2 - \varepsilon_3$ plane the four regions of $\boldsymbol{\varepsilon}$—Y_1, Y_2, Y_3, and Y_4—which give rise to different formulas for the noninferior solution set.

Lin's results concerning proper inequality constraints (6.131)–(6.132) could also be used here. All steps up to analyzing the system (6.146) are the same. But instead of relying on the uniqueness of the solution $P_1(\boldsymbol{\varepsilon})$ to ensure the noninferiority of the solution of the system (6.146) as given by (6.148), (6.150), (6.151), or (6.152), condition (6.133) is used. To use such a condition, $\phi_1(\boldsymbol{\varepsilon})$ as defined in (6.131) must be constructed. We observe that f_2 is always bounded below by zero and that the right-hand side of (6.131)

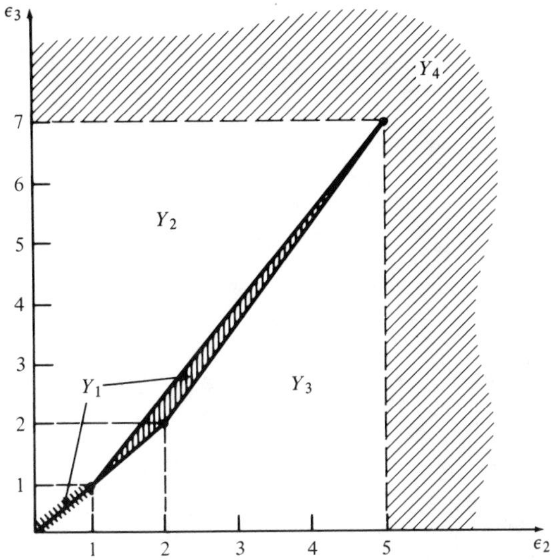

Figure 6.11 Ranges of selections of **ε** for Example 8.

always exists as long as $\varepsilon_2, \varepsilon_3 \geqslant 0$. Therefore, $\phi_1(\boldsymbol{\varepsilon})$ is simply

$$\phi_1(\boldsymbol{\varepsilon}) = f_1(x(\boldsymbol{\varepsilon})), \tag{6.154}$$

where $\mathbf{x}(\varepsilon)$ is given by (6.148), (6.150), (6.151), or (6.152) depending on how ε is chosen. It is then routine to check condition (6.133) to ensure the noninferiority of a given solution of (6.146). When uniqueness of the solution of $P_k(\boldsymbol{\varepsilon})$ is easily ascertained, it is not necessary to test condition (6.133), but when it is difficult to verify, condition (6.133) may be useful.

The preceding analysis of the system (6.146) is complicated by the number of combinations of binding constraints to be considered. It is in this context of solving a VOP analytically that Lin's proper equality constraint approach appears more efficient. Formulating $E_1(\boldsymbol{\varepsilon})$ as in (6.134)–(6.135) by changing (6.145a) and (6.145b) into equalities and then applying the Kuhn–Tucker conditions yields exactly the same set of equations and inequalities as (6.146). However, the constraints (6.145a) and (6.145b) are now strictly binding, implying no sign restriction on λ_1 and λ_2, and the solution of the system (6.146) is always given by

$$\mathbf{x}(\varepsilon) = \begin{pmatrix} 2\varepsilon_2 - \varepsilon_3 \\ \varepsilon_3 - \varepsilon_2 \end{pmatrix} \tag{6.155}$$

as long as $\boldsymbol{\varepsilon}$ is in $\hat{Y} \triangleq \{(\varepsilon_2, \varepsilon_3) | 2\varepsilon_2 - \varepsilon_3 \geqslant 0 \text{ and } \varepsilon_3 - \varepsilon_2 \geqslant 0\}$ shown in Figure 6.12. Note that if $\boldsymbol{\varepsilon} \notin \hat{Y}$, $E_1(\boldsymbol{\varepsilon})$ will be infeasible. Note also that Y_1 is included in $\hat{Y}$ and that $\mathbf{x}(\boldsymbol{\varepsilon})$ given by (6.155) is not necessarily noninferior for every $\boldsymbol{\varepsilon}$ in $\hat{Y}$. To screen out those which are noninferior, conditions

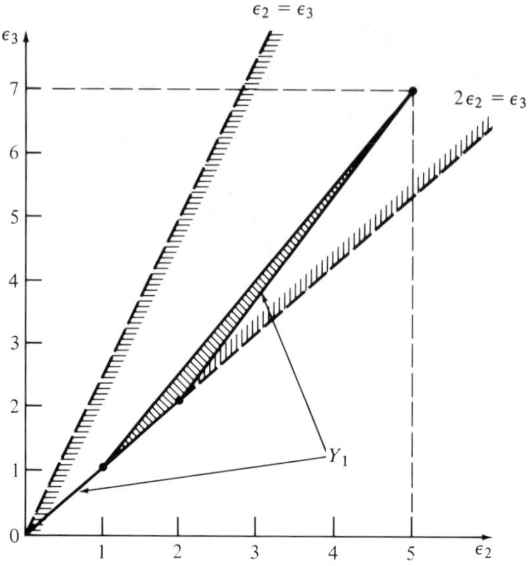

Figure 6.12 Feasible region of $E_1(\boldsymbol{\varepsilon})$ in the $\boldsymbol{\varepsilon}$ plane: The region $\hat{Y}$ lies between the lines $2\varepsilon_2 = \varepsilon_3$ and $\varepsilon_2 = \varepsilon_3$.

(6.135) and (6.136) must now be checked. By the same reasoning as before $\phi_1(\boldsymbol{\varepsilon})$ as defined in (6.133) always exists. Also the infimum on the left-hand side of (6.132) is exactly $\phi_1(\boldsymbol{\varepsilon})$ and is given by

$$\phi_1(\boldsymbol{\varepsilon}) = f_1(\mathbf{x}(\varepsilon)) = [(2\varepsilon_2 - \varepsilon_3) - 3]^2 + [(\varepsilon_3 - \varepsilon_2) - 2]^2. \qquad (6.156)$$

Since, in this case, (6.136) implies (6.135), we shall check only (6.136). The gradient of $\phi_1(\boldsymbol{\varepsilon})$ is given by

$$\nabla_\varepsilon f_1(\mathbf{x}\ (\boldsymbol{\varepsilon}\ )) = \nabla\phi_1(\boldsymbol{\varepsilon}) \triangleq \begin{pmatrix} \partial\phi_1(\boldsymbol{\varepsilon})/\partial\varepsilon_1 \\ \partial\phi_2(\boldsymbol{\varepsilon})/\partial\varepsilon_2 \end{pmatrix} = 2\begin{pmatrix} 5\varepsilon_2 - 3\varepsilon_3 - 4 \\ -3\varepsilon_2 + 2\varepsilon_3 + 1 \end{pmatrix}. \qquad (6.157)$$

Consider

$$\begin{pmatrix} \varepsilon_1 \\ \varepsilon_2 \end{pmatrix} = \begin{pmatrix} \varepsilon_1^* - \delta\varepsilon_1 \\ \varepsilon_2^* - \delta\varepsilon_2 \end{pmatrix},$$

where $\delta\varepsilon_1 \geqslant 0$, $\delta\varepsilon_2 \geqslant 0$, with at least one $\delta\varepsilon_i > 0$. By convexity

$$f(\boldsymbol{\varepsilon}) \geqslant f(\boldsymbol{\varepsilon}^*) + \nabla\phi_1(\boldsymbol{\varepsilon}^*) \cdot \delta\boldsymbol{\varepsilon} \qquad \text{for all} \quad \delta\boldsymbol{\varepsilon}. \qquad (6.158)$$

For $\mathbf{x}(\boldsymbol{\varepsilon}^*)$ to be noninferior, according to (6.136), we must have $f(\boldsymbol{\varepsilon}) > f(\boldsymbol{\varepsilon}^*)$

for all $\delta\boldsymbol{\varepsilon} \geqslant \mathbf{0}$. It follows from (6.158) that $\mathbf{x}(\boldsymbol{\varepsilon}^*)$ is noninferior if and only if[9]

$$\nabla\phi_1(\boldsymbol{\varepsilon}^*) = 2\begin{pmatrix} 5\varepsilon_2^* - 3\varepsilon_3^* - 4 \\ -3\varepsilon_2^* - 2\varepsilon_3^* + 1 \end{pmatrix} \leqslant \mathbf{0}, \tag{6.159}$$

which means that $\boldsymbol{\varepsilon}^*$ lies in Y_1 and only in Y_1. Hence the noninferior solution set X^* is precisely the image of Y_1 under $\mathbf{x}(\ )$ given by (6.155), as we have found before.

Example 9: This example demonstrates how nonconvexity or a duality gap is handled by the constraint approach.

Consider a VOP

$$\begin{aligned} &\min \quad (f_1(x), f_2(x)) \\ &\text{subject to} \qquad x \geqslant 0, \quad x \in R, \end{aligned} \tag{6.160}$$

where

$$f_1(x) = \sqrt{x^2+1},$$

$$f_2(x) = \begin{cases} -x^2+16 & \text{for} \quad 0 \leqslant x \leqslant \sqrt{15}, \\ 1 & \text{for} \quad x > \sqrt{15}. \end{cases}$$

This is indeed a nonconvex problem and the set of noninferior solutions X^* is also nonconvex, as demonstrated in Figure 6.13.

First observe that apart from A and B, no weights $\mathbf{w} \in W$ can be chosen to obtain a noninferior point between A and B because of the nonconvex (or duality gap) nature of the noninferior set. In fact, for all $\mathbf{w} \in W$, a solution of $P(\mathbf{w})$ will either yield A or B. Let us now try to solve this problem by the constraint problem $P_2(\varepsilon)$ for any $\varepsilon \geqslant 1$:

$$\min \quad f_2(x) \tag{6.161}$$

$$\text{subject to} \qquad f_1(x) = \sqrt{x^2+1} \leqslant \varepsilon, \quad x \geqslant 0. \tag{6.162}$$

Observe that the constraint (6.162) carves out a certain portion of the feasible set as shown in Figure 6.13. The objective function in the objective

---

[9]Note that if

$$\nabla\phi_1(\boldsymbol{\varepsilon}^*) = \begin{pmatrix} 0 \\ -3\varepsilon_2^* + 2\varepsilon_3^* + 1 \end{pmatrix} \quad \text{or} \quad \begin{pmatrix} 5\varepsilon_2^* - 3\varepsilon_3^* - 4 \\ 0 \end{pmatrix}$$

and $\delta\boldsymbol{\varepsilon} \geqslant 0$, then we must have $\delta\boldsymbol{\varepsilon} > 0$. For example, if $5\varepsilon_2^* - 3\varepsilon_3^* - 4 = 0$ or $5\varepsilon_2^* = 3\varepsilon_3^* + 4$, any positive variation in ε_2 implies a positive variation in ε_3 and vice versa.

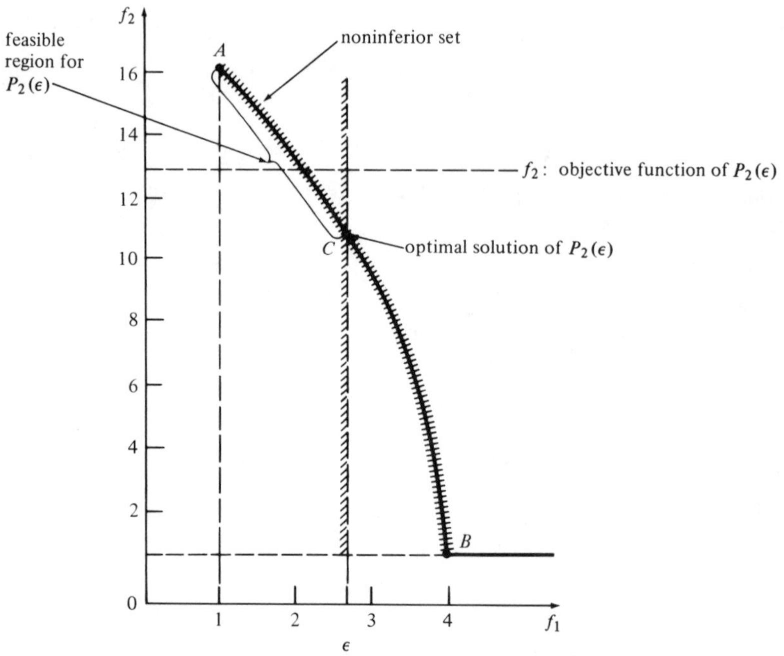

Figure 6.13 Nonconvex inferior set of Example 9.

space is simply the horizontal line. Thus, graphically, $P_2(\varepsilon)$ is equivalent to finding the lowest point (lowest value of f_2) on the curve AB that lies within the feasible region of $P_2(\varepsilon)$. For a nonconvex noninferior set such as in this problem, the optimal solution normally occurs at some intersection of the noninferior set and a plane defined by at least one of the ε-constraints as in (6.162). Thus by tightening or loosening the ε-constraints, all noninferior solutions can always be reached and discovered.

We solve analytically, applying the Kuhn–Tucker necessary conditions to $P_2(\varepsilon)$, giving two cases. For $1 \leqslant \varepsilon \leqslant 4$

$$-2x + \lambda x\sqrt{x^2+1} - \mu = 0, \tag{6.163}$$

$$\lambda\left(\sqrt{x^2+1} - \varepsilon\right) = 0, \tag{6.164}$$

$$\mu x = 0, \tag{6.165}$$

with

$$\sqrt{x^2+1} - \varepsilon \leqslant 0 \tag{6.166}$$

and

$$\lambda, \mu, x \geqslant 0. \tag{6.167}$$

For $\varepsilon > 4$

$$\lambda x\sqrt{x^2+1} - \mu = 0 \tag{6.168}$$

and (6.164)–(6.166) hold.

For the first case we find that there are two possible solutions to the system (6.163)–(6.166), namely, $x=0$ and $x=\sqrt{\varepsilon^2-1}$. By checking the sufficiency condition, we verify that $x=\sqrt{\varepsilon^2-1}$ is the only minimum point. Hence the set of noninferior solutions for $1 \leqslant \varepsilon \leqslant 4$ is given by

$$\left\{x \mid x=\sqrt{\varepsilon^2-1}\,,\ 1 \leqslant \varepsilon \leqslant 4\right\}. \tag{6.169}$$

The second case clearly implies $\lambda = 0$ (since $x > 0$ no other terms can be zero) and x can be any value from $\sqrt{15}$ to $+\sqrt{\varepsilon^2-1}$. Hence, this case has multiple solutions. Since not all of these solutions are noninferior, we have to screen out only the noninferior ones. To do this we may simply reverse the role of f_1 and f_2 in $P_2(\boldsymbol{\varepsilon})$ by solving

$$\min \quad f_1(x) \tag{6.170}$$

$$\text{subject to} \qquad f_2(x) \leqslant 1, \quad x \geqslant 0. \tag{6.171}$$

Note that the constraint (6.171) is now set at the value of f_2, where the multiple optima occur. This should yield point B, hence completing the noninferior solution set,

$$X^* = \left\{x \mid x=\sqrt{\varepsilon^2-1}\,,\ 1 \leqslant \varepsilon \leqslant 4\right\}.$$

Note that this problem can also be conveniently solved by the hybrid approach (6.138)–(6.139). No difficulty concerning multiple optima will be encountered, since the objective function of $P(\mathbf{w}, \boldsymbol{\varepsilon})$ for any $\mathbf{w} > \mathbf{0}$ is now a line with a negative slope and not a horizontal line as before. Figure 6.14 demonstrates this approach.

6.3.2 Numerical Methods

Very often we must rely on numerical algorithms to solve the optimization problems needed to generate noninferior solutions. Although in Example 8 we found the equality constraint approach to be more efficient for finding the set of noninferior solutions analytically, the traditional ε-constraint approach $P_k(\boldsymbol{\varepsilon})$ of (6.127)–(6.129) and the hybrid approach $P(\mathbf{w}, \boldsymbol{\varepsilon})$ of (6.138)–(6.139) are more suitable for numerical applications. Since efficient numerical algorithms are available to solve single-objective optimization problems, the difficulty in solving directly the set of equations and inequalities resulting from application of necessary and sufficient conditions is removed.

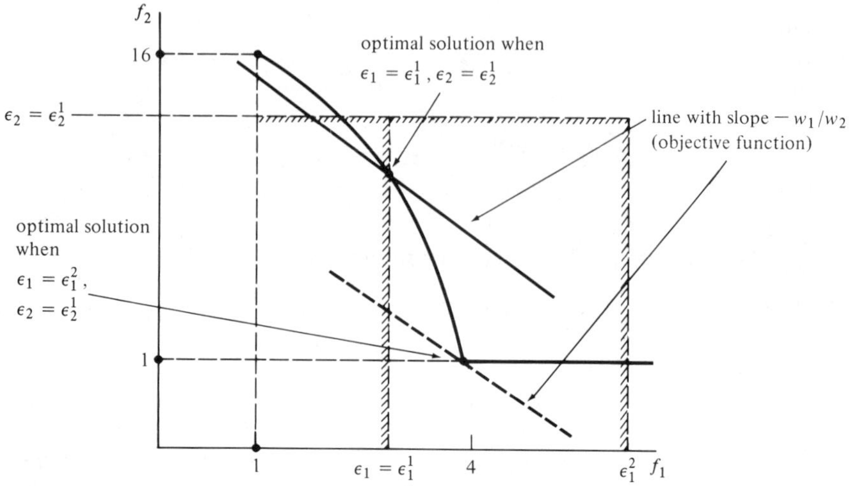

Figure 6.14 The hybrid method.

As we have seen in Example 8, unlike in the inequality constraint or hybrid approach the choice of $\boldsymbol{\varepsilon}$ that yields noninferior solutions as an optimal solution of $E_k(\boldsymbol{\varepsilon})$ is rather limited (Figures 6.11 and 6.12). If $\boldsymbol{\varepsilon}$ is chosen outside $\hat{Y}$, $E_k(\boldsymbol{\varepsilon})$ will be infeasible. Moreover, if $\boldsymbol{\varepsilon}$ is chosen outside Y_1, any solution of $E_k(\boldsymbol{\varepsilon})$ will be inferior. Several trials and errors may be needed before a point in Y_1 is selected. This is not the case if $P_k(\boldsymbol{\varepsilon})$ or $P(\mathbf{w}, \boldsymbol{\varepsilon})$ is used, where any selection in the first quadrant of the $\varepsilon_2 - \varepsilon_3$ plane will always yield a noninferior solution. Furthermore, as of now, there is no numerically general way of checking the noninferiority conditions posed by (6.135)–(6.136), whereas this difficulty is not encountered when using the ε-constraint or the hybrid approach.

We recommend $P(\mathbf{w}, \boldsymbol{\varepsilon})$ over $P_k(\boldsymbol{\varepsilon})$ to generate noninferior solutions in general problems, because it needs no test of noninferiority. However, whenever further information about the behavior of the system is required for the latter phase of decision making, the traditional ε-constraint approach $P_k(\boldsymbol{\varepsilon})$ should be considered since it generates as a by-product trade-off information that reflects the local behavior of the system (Haimes and Hall [1974]). In Example 8, using the $P_k(\boldsymbol{\varepsilon})$ approach, it was always possible to compute the optimal Kuhn–Tucker multipliers λ_1, λ_2 associated with each noninferior solution, which can be interpreted as trade-offs between f_1, f_2 and f_1, f_3, respectively. This facet of computation was discussed in Section 4.9.3.

In using $P_k(\boldsymbol{\varepsilon})$, some test for noninferiority may need to be performed. If the uniqueness of the solutions of $P_k(\boldsymbol{\varepsilon})$ cannot easily be ascertained, the simple numerical test of noninferiority posed by (6.36)–(6.37), which is used in the weighting case, can also be used here. A possible ad hoc strategy for using $P_k(\boldsymbol{\varepsilon})$ to generate a representative subset or an approximation of the whole set of noninferior solutions is as follows (Haimes et al. [1975]):

i. Choose an appropriate f_k as the primary objective. For convenience, let it be f_1. Then formulate $P_1(\boldsymbol{\varepsilon})$ as in (6.127)–(6.129).
ii. For each $j=2,\ldots,n$, find $f_j^* = \min_{\mathbf{x}\in X} f_j(x)$. Then select a suitable increment $\Delta\varepsilon_j > 0$ and a number k_j such that the discrete values $\varepsilon_j^k = f_j^* + k\,\Delta\varepsilon_j$, $k=0,\ldots,k_j$ will cover the entire range of interest of the value of f_j.
iii. Solve $P_k(\boldsymbol{\varepsilon})$ for each possible combination of discrete values of $\varepsilon_2, \varepsilon_3, \ldots, \varepsilon_n$ selected.
iv. Check each solution generated for noninferiority, by examining whether the solution is unique (e.g., is f_1 strictly convex?) or by formulating (6.36)–(6.37) and checking whether its optimal value is zero. If yes, we conclude by Theorem 4.18 that the point generated is noninferior. Otherwise we disregard such a point.
v. If a representative subset of X^* has been generated, we may stop or we may attempt curve fitting to find $\mathbf{x}^*$ as a function of $\boldsymbol{\varepsilon}$ and approximate the entire X^*.

Again the obvious limitation of this ad hoc strategy is the exponentially increasing number of computations required as the number of grid points selected for each ε_j increases. Its efficiency is greatly enhanced if a more systematic procedure is available for selecting grid points. Giesy [1978] developed an approximation algorithm that incorporates a threshold of acceptability on $\boldsymbol{\varepsilon}$ specified by the decision maker. Tabac et al. [1979] apply the algorithm to an aircraft control system design problem.

One possible method for two-objective problems is due to Payne et al. [1975] (see also Polak [1976]). They view the optimal value of $P_k(\boldsymbol{\varepsilon})$ as a sensitivity function $w_k(\boldsymbol{\varepsilon})$, which is a real-valued function of $\boldsymbol{\varepsilon}$ defined on the set Y_k, the set of all $\boldsymbol{\varepsilon}$ such that $P_k(\boldsymbol{\varepsilon})$ is feasible. The noninferior set $F^* = \{\mathbf{f} | \mathbf{f}(x),\ \mathbf{x}\in X^*\}$ is a nonhorizontal portion of the graph $\Gamma \triangleq \{(\boldsymbol{\varepsilon}, w_k(\boldsymbol{\varepsilon})) | \boldsymbol{\varepsilon}\in Y_k \text{ and } w_k(\boldsymbol{\varepsilon})\in\{f_k(\mathbf{x})|\mathbf{x} \text{ solves } P_k(\boldsymbol{\varepsilon})\}\}$. Based on this result and with the help of the Hermite interpolating cubic, Payne et al. [1975] develop an algorithm that approximates F^* to any degree of the interpolation error for two-objective problems. A key step is solving $P_k(\boldsymbol{\varepsilon})$ for its associated Lagrange multipliers. Like the NISE method, this algorithm generates a string of noninferior points [by solving $P_k(\boldsymbol{\varepsilon})$] and arranges them in the order in which they should appear on the graph Γ. This is accomplished by checking the monotonicity of the Hermite interpolation between two consecutive points in the string. If the monotonicity test fails or when it is found that the Hermite interpolation between the two consecutive points deviates from the true Γ between those two points more than a specified threshold, a noninferior point is inserted between those two points.

6.4 Related Problems

Problems in which some or all of decision variables are discrete have not been dealt with explicitly in this chapter. It should be observed, however, that the theoretical results summarized at the beginning of Sections 6.2 and 6.3 do not specify whether the variables have to be continuous or discrete. In other words, for discrete variable problems, we can find noninferior solutions by formulating appropriate scalar optimization problems, solving these problems, and checking the necessary and sufficient conditions for noninferiority, as stated. The only difference is that necessary and sufficient conditions for optimality (such as the Kuhn–Tucker conditions), which are based on differentiability, and hence continuity, cannot be used. Neither can they be solved numerically by optimization algorithms designed for continuous variables, such as the simplex method. In this case, one need only apply proper implicit or explicit enumeration algorithms (such as branch and bound designed for discrete scalar optimization problems) to generate noninferior solutions for discrete multiobjective problems. For a more rigorous development, we recommend the works of Bitran [1977, 1979] and Bitran and Rivera [1980]. Pasternack and Passy [1973], Zionts and Wallenius [1980], and Zionts [1976, 1977] also deal with this class of problems both from the theoretical and algorithmic aspects.

A second special class of problems not dealt with explicitly in this chapter is related to multiobjective linear fractional programming. This relatively new area has been pioneered by Kornbluth and Steuer [1980] and Kornbluth [1980].

6.5 Summary

In this chapter we focused on a class of multiobjective decision problems in which decision criteria and decision variables are distinguished, the set of alternatives is given implicitly as a complex of causal relationships relating decision variables, and an intrinsic monotonic preference structure is assumed. Because of the monotonic preference structure, it is desirable or necessary for an alternative to be *noninferior* before it can even be considered as a final choice. In view of these characteristics, it is appropriate to formulate the problems in this class as vector optimization or multiobjective programming problems.

In problems of this class it is necessary to identify noninferior alternatives, which is often done early in the solution process. The methods discussed in this chapter are designed exclusively for this purpose.

We classified these methods based on the type of scalar optimization problem associated with noninferior solutions: the weighting problem, including the Lagrangian problem, or the ε-constraint problem. For the former class of methods we described how weighting characterizations can be used directly, both analytically and numerically, by explicit formulation of the weighting problems. Solutions were obtained both analytically and parametrically. Special simplex-based methods for generating the entire set of noninferior solutions of linear problems were also discussed in some detail. Of the many variations, we followed strategies proposed by Gal [1976], Ecker and Kouada [1975, 1978], and Ecker et al. [1980], as well as Steuer's interval weights method for generating the desired subset of noninferior solutions in linear problems. The NISE method, developed by Cohon et al. [1979] for generating the noninferior set in two-objective linear problems or for approximating the noninferior set in two-objective convex problems was also described. This method involves solving a series of weighting problems with the weights systematically selected.

Generating methods based on the ε-constraint characterization were described next. There are three principal variations of the ε-constraint method: the inequality constraint approach, the equality constraint approach, and the hybrid (weighting-constraint) approach. The second variation seems to be more efficient for solving small problems analytically, but the first and the third are more amenable to numerical treatment. The hybrid approach does not require noninferiority tests; it is therefore more efficient when we are merely interested in generating noninferior solutions numerically. The ε-constraint approach, on the other hand, appears best suited to integration with the subsequent interactive phases of multiobjective decision making because, in addition to generating noninferior solutions, it also furnishes trade-off information at each noninferior solution generated.

References

Benson, H. P. (1978). Existence of efficient solutions for vector maximization problems, *Journal of Optimization Theory and Application* 26, 569–580.

Bitran, G. R. (1977). Linear multiple objective programs with zero–one variables, *Mathematical Programming* 13, 121–139.

Bitran, G. R. (1979). Theory and algorithms for linear multiple objective programs with zero–one variables, *Mathematical Programming* 17, 362–390.

Bitran, G. R., and Rivera, J. M. (1980). An efficient point-utility theory approach to solve binary multicriteria problems, *Technical Report No. 181, Operations Research Center*, Massachusetts Institute of Technology.

Charnes, A., and Cooper, W. (1961). *Management Models and Industrial Applications of Linear Programming*, Wiley, New York, Vol. 1.

Cohon, J. L. (1978). *Multiobjective Programming and Planning*, Academic, New York.

Cohon, J. L., Church, R., and Sheer, D. (1979). Generating multiobjective trade-offs: an algorithm for bicriterion problems, *Water Resources Research* 15, 1001–1010.

Corley, N. W. (1980). A new scalar equivalent for Pareto optimization, *IEEE Transactions on Automatic Control* AC-25, 829–830.

Dantzig, G. (1963). *Linear Programming and Extensions*, Princeton University Press, Princeton, N.J.

Ecker, J. G., Hegner, N. S., and Kouada, I. A. (1980). Generating all maximal efficient faces for multiple objective linear programs, *Journal of Optimization Theory and Application* 30, 353–381.

Ecker, J. G., and Kouada, I. A., (1975). Finding efficient points for linear multiple objective programs, *Mathematical Programming* 8, 375–377.

Ecker, J. G., and Kouada, I. A. (1978). Finding all efficient extreme points for linear multiple objective programs, *Mathematical Programming* 14, 249–261.

Evans, J. P., and Steuer, R. E. (1973a). Generating efficient extreme points in linear multiobjective programming: two algorithms and computing experiences, in *Multiple Criteria Decision Making* (J. L. Cochrane and M. Zeleny, eds.), University of South Carolina Press, Columbia, pp. 349–365.

Evans, J. P., and Steuer, R. E. (1973b). A revised simplex method for linear multiple objective programs, *Mathematical Programming* 5, 54–72.

Gal, T. (1976). A general method for determining the set of all efficient solutions to a linear vector maximum problem, *Report No. 76/12*, Institut für Wirtschaftswissenschaften, Aachen, Germany.

Gal, T., and Leberling, H. (1977). Redundant objective functions in linear vector maximum problems and their determination, *European Journal of Operational Research* 1, 176–184.

Gass, S., and Saaty, T. (1955). The computational algorithm for the parametric objective function, *Naval Research Logistic Quarterly*, 2, 39–45.

Geoffrion, A. M. (1966). Strictly concave parametric programming, Part I—basic theory, *Management Science* 13, 244–253.

Geoffrion, A. M. (1967). Strictly concave parametric programming, Part II—additional theory and computational consideration, *Management Science* 13, 359–370.

Giesy, D. P. (1978). Calculation of Pareto-optimal solutions to multiple-objective problems using threshold-of-acceptability constraints, *IEEE Transactions on Automatic Control* AC-23, 1114–1115.

Hadley, G. (1962). *Linear Programming*, Addison-Wesley, Reading, Mass.

Haimes, Y. Y. (1977). *Hierarchical Analyses of Water Resources Systems*, McGraw-Hill, New York.

Haimes, Y. Y., and Hall, W. A. (1974). Multiobjectives in water resources systems analysis: the surrogate worth trade-off (SWT) method, *Water Resources Research* 10, 615–624.

Haimes, Y. Y., Hall, W. A., and Freedman, H. T. (1975). *Multiobjective Optimization in Water Resources Systems: The Surrogate Worth Trade-off (SWT) Method*, Elsevier, Amsterdam.

Haimes, Y. Y., Wismer, D. A., and Lasdon, L. S. (1971). On bicriterion formulation of the integrated systems identification and system optimization, *IEEE Transactions on Systems, Man, and Cybernetics* SMC-1, 296–297.

Isermann, M. (1977). The enumeration of the set of all efficient solutions for a linear multiple objective program, *Operational Research Quarterly* 28, 711–725.

Isermann, M. (1979). The enumeration of all efficient solutions for a linear multiple-objective transportation problem, *Naval Research Logistics Quarterly* 26, 123–139.

Kornbluth, J. S. H. (1980). Computational experience with multiple objective linear fractional programming algorithms, presented at the multiple-criteria decision-making conference, University of Delaware, Newark.

Kornbluth, J. S. H., and Steuer, R. E. (1980). On computing the set of all weakly efficient vertices in multiple objective linear fractional programming, in *Multiple Criteria Decision Making: Theory and Application — Hagen / Königswinter, West Germany, 1979* (G. Fandel and T. Gal, eds.), Springer, Berlin-Heidelberg, pp. 189–202.

Lasdon, L. S. (1970). *Optimization Theory for Large Systems*, Macmillan, New York.

Lin, J. G. (1967a). Multiple-objective problems: Pareto-optimal solutions by method of proper equality constraints, *IEEE Transactions on Automatic Control* AC-21, 641–650.

Lin, J. G. (1976b). Three methods for determining Pareto-optimal solutions of multiple objective optimization problems, in *Directions in Large-Scale Systems: Decentralized Control and Many-Person Optimization* (Y. C. H. and S. K. Mitter, eds.), Plenum, New York.

Lin, J. G. (1977). Proper inequality constraints and maximization of index vectors, *Journal of Optimization Theory and Applications* 21, 505–521.

Pasternack, M., and Passy, V. (1973). Bicriterion mathematical programs with Boolean variables, in *Multiple Criteria Decision Making* (J. L. Cochrane and M. Zeleny, eds.), University of South Carolina Press, Columbia, pp. 327–348.

Payne, M., Polak, E., Collins, D. C., and Miesel, W. S. (1975). An algorithm for bicriteria optimization based on the sensitivity function, *IEEE Transactions on Automatic Control* AC-20, 546–548.

Philip, J. (1972). Algorithm for the vector maximization problem, *Mathematical Programming* 2, 207–209.

Philip, J. (1977). Vector maximization at a degenerate vertix, *Mathematical Programming* 13, 357–359.

Polak, E. (1976). On the approximation of solutions to multiple criteria decision making problems, in *Multiple Criterion Decision Making — Kyoto, 1975* (M. Zeleny, Ed.), Springer, Berlin-Heidelberg.

Reid, R. W., and Vermuri, V. (1971). On the noninferior index approach to large-scale multi-criteria systems, *Journal of the Franklin Institute* 291, 241–254.

Sage, A. P. (1977). *Methodology for Large-Scale Systems*, McGraw-Hill, New York.

Steuer, R. E. (1976a). ADBASE: an adjacent efficient basis algorithm for solving vector-maximum and interval weighted sums linear programming problems in FORTRAN, College of Business and Economics, University of Kentucky.

Steuer, R. E. (1976b). ADEX: an adjacent efficient extreme point algorithm for solving vector-maximum and interval weighted sums linear programming problems in FORTRAN, SHARE Program Library, Distribution Code 360D-15.2.

Steuer, R. E. (1976c). Multiple objective linear programming with interval criterion weights, *Management Science* 23, 305–316.

Steuer, R. E. (1977). An interactive multiple objective linear programming procedure, *TIMS Studies in the Management Sciences* (M. K. Starr and M. Zeleny, eds.), North-Holland, Amsterdam, Vol. 6, pp. 225–239.

Tabak, D., Schy, A. A., Giesy, D. P., and Johnson, K. G. (1979). Application of multiobjective optimization in aircraft control systems design, *Automatica* 15, 595–600.

Vermuri, V. (1974). Multiple-objective optimization in water resource systems, *Water Resources Research* 10, 44–48.

Wendel, R. E., and Lee, D. N. (1977). Efficiency in multiobjective optimization problems, *Mathematical Programming* 12, 406–515.

Wolfe, P. (1959). The simplex method for quadratic programming, *Econometrica* 27, 382–398.

Yu, P. L., and Zeleny, M. (1975). The set of all nondominated solutions in linear cases and a multicriteria simplex method, *Journal of Mathematical Analysis and Applications* 49, 430–468.

Zeleny, M. (1974). *Linear Multiobjective Programming*, Springer, Berlin/Heidelberg.

Zeleny, M. (1982). *Multiple Criteria Decision Making*, McGraw-Hill, New York.

Zionts, S. (1976). An interactive method for evaluating discrete alternatives involving multiple criteria, *Working Paper No. 271*, State University of New York at Buffalo.

Zionts, S. (1977). Integer linear programming with multiple objectives, *Annals of Discrete Mathematics* 1, 551–562.

Zionts, S., and Wallenius, J. (1980). Identifying efficient vectors: some theory and computational results, *Operations Research* 24, 785–793.

Chapter 7
Noninteractive and Interactive Multiobjective Programming Methods

7.1 Introduction

In this chapter, we continue to address multiobjective decision problems in which the alternatives are implicitly given by a set of causally related decision variables. Unlike in Chapter 6, however, we shall go beyond the analyst's role of merely generating noninferior solutions, and discuss methodologies that combine the roles of decision maker and decision analyst so that the latter can assist the former to bring about the "best" alternatives, or what is normally called the best-compromise alternatives. Loosely speaking, the *best-compromise* alternative is the one that satisfies the decision maker most. Assuming no prior preference structure, we can formulate a multiobjective decision problem MDP in general as

$$\mathrm{DR}(f_1(\mathbf{x}),\ldots,f_2(\mathbf{x})) \tag{7.1}$$

$$\text{subject to} \quad \mathbf{x} \in X, \tag{7.2}$$

where

$$X = \{\mathbf{x} \in R^N \,|\, g_i(\mathbf{x}) \leqslant 0,\ i = 1,\ldots,m,\ \mathbf{x} \in S\}, \tag{7.3}$$

S is some subset of R^N, and DR stands for the appropriate decision rules.

A multiobjective decision problem formulated as in (7.1) and (7.2) is read, "Apply the appropriate decision rule(s) and find the best-compromise solution $\mathbf{x}^*$ from the set of alternatives X." As discussed in Chapter 1, it is these underlying decision rules that dictate how best to rank alternatives or to decide which alternative is preferred to another. One decision maker may be a value function or expected utility maximizer. Another may prefer minimization of deviation from goals or ideals, and yet another may prefer to base his judgment on trade-offs. Obviously the type of decision rule used depends as much on the decision maker's preference structure as on the nature of the decision problem itself. It is important to observe that some decision rules lead to a best-compromise solution that is also noninferior, while others may not. Whether we need to ensure noninferiority as a necessary property depends again on the underlying preference structure.

Implicit in the formulation of MDP in (7.1)–(7.3) is the need to bring into the solution process knowledge about the decision maker's preference structure. Information about preference must be elicited (or assumed) and incorporated into search procedures to bring about the best-compromise solutions. Because of the structure of X, methodologies in this chapter will use mathematical programming search procedures. The differences among these methodologies are due to differences in eliciting and using preference. In other words, they differ in the way in which DR in (7.1) is formulated.

Information concerning preference can be elicited from the decision maker either noninteractively or interactively. A *noninteractive technique* requires that preference be elicited only once, either before or after analyzing the system. Mathematical programming methods that incorporate value or utility functions, goal programming, and the surrogate worth trade-off method are examples of noninteractive techniques. On the other hand, an *interactive approach* requires active progressive interaction between the decision maker and the analyst throughout the solution process. An interactive approach is normally characterized by three basic steps:

1. Solve the problem based on some initial set of parameters to obtain a feasible, preferably noninferior, solution.
2. Get the decision maker to react to this solution.
3. Use the decision maker's response to formulate a new set of parameters, forming a new problem to be solved.

Steps (1)–(3) are repeated until the decision maker is satisfied with the current solution or no further action can be taken by the method. Most of the methods to be described in this chapter have these interactive characteristics.

Based on the types of preference information elicited and the ways they are used, we can divide the methodologies in this chapter into three classes: those which use some form of global preference; those which require elicitation of preference through weights, priorities, goals, and ideals; and those that require eliciting preference through trade-offs. These three classes are not meant to be mutually exclusive or complete. We make this classification of methods merely for convenience.

7.2 Methods Based on Global Preference

The methods of this section are based on using value functions, utility functions, or other information about the decision maker's global preference structure to order alternatives completely. This information is either elicited directly or assumed.

7.2.1 Ad Hoc Preference Function Programming Approach

The obvious example of a method based on global preference combines ad hoc direct assessment of value or utility functions described in Section 5.2 with appropriate search procedures. One assesses the value function $v(f_1,\ldots,f_n)$ or the utility function $u(f_1,\ldots,f_n)$ by questioning the decision maker and subsequently translating the decision problem MDP in (7.1)–(7.3) into a surrogate MDP having the mathematical programming form

$$\begin{aligned}&\max \quad v(f_1(\mathbf{x}),\ldots,f_n(\mathbf{x}))\\&\text{subject to} \quad \mathbf{x}\in X\end{aligned} \tag{7.4}$$

in the certainty case or

$$\begin{aligned}&\max \quad E[u(f_1(\mathbf{x}),\ldots,f_n(\mathbf{x}))]\\&\text{subject to} \quad \mathbf{x}\in X\end{aligned} \tag{7.5}$$

in the uncertainty case.

Application of this method requires a decision maker with responsibility for maximizing a value function or expected utility. Otherwise, we must apply a different decision rule DR in the formulation of our multiobjective decision problem (7.1)–(7.3).

After transforming the multiobjective decision problem (7.1)–(7.3) into a surrogate MDP as in either (7.4) or (7.5), the task of finding the best-compromise solution is a matter of merely applying suitable scalar optimization techniques (which are readily available) to find an optimal solution of either (7.4) or (7.5), depending on whether the problem is deterministic or probabilistic. Bell [1977], Keefer and Pollock [1980], Kulikowski [1977], and Keefer [1978a, b] give examples of practical applications of this method.

If the value function or utility function does represent the true preference structure of the decision maker, then the best-compromise solution, according to the value function or expected utility maximizing rule represented by either (7.4) or (7.5), need not be noninferior. This situation arises when $v(\ )$ or $u(\ )$ is not monotonic. For example, when $v(\ )$ is unimodal on the set of alternative X, we may have two feasible alternatives $\mathbf{x}^1$ and $\mathbf{x}^2$ such that $\mathbf{f}(\mathbf{x}^1)\geqslant\mathbf{f}(\mathbf{x}^2)$ and $v(\mathbf{f}(\mathbf{x}^1))>v(\mathbf{f}(\mathbf{x}^2))$. Hence $\mathbf{x}^2$ dominates $\mathbf{x}^1$ (in minimization problems) and yet $\mathbf{x}^1$ is preferred to $\mathbf{x}^2$ since the value function at $\mathbf{x}^1$ is greater than that at $\mathbf{x}^2$. Figure 7.1 illustrates the two-dimensional case.

If the value function is monotonic (increasing or decreasing), however, in the feasible region X, noninferiority can and should be a necessary property of the best-compromise solution. Geoffrion [1967] showed that in the two-objective case under certainty a noninferior solution that maximizes v always exists if we assume that the value function v is monotonic and several other mild assumptions hold. This is true of decision problems with any number of objective functions, as we summarize below.

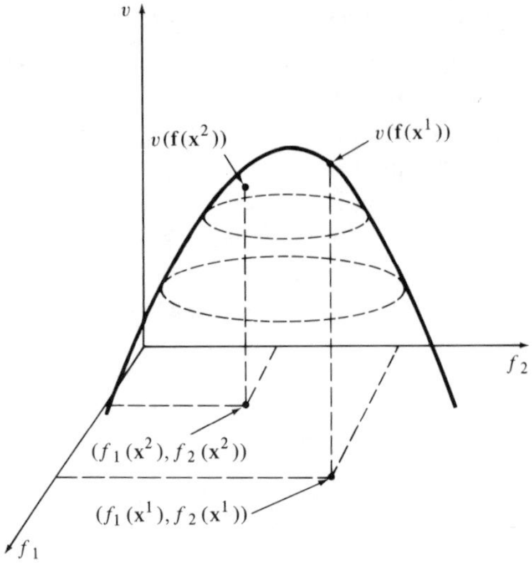

Figure 7.1 Example in which noninferiority may not be necessary.

Let X^* be the set of noninferior solutions of the vector optimization problem VOP:

$$\begin{aligned} &\min \quad (f_1(\mathbf{x}),\ldots,f_n(\mathbf{x})) \\ &\text{subject to} \quad \mathbf{x} \in X \end{aligned} \tag{7.6}$$

and $F=\{\hat{\mathbf{f}} \triangleq \mathbf{f}(\mathbf{x}) | \mathbf{x} \in X\}$. Also let $V(X)$ be the set of optimal solutions of (7.4).

Theorem 7.1 (Geoffrion 1967a). *Assume i) that all f_j and v are continuous functions and X is a compact set and ii) that v is a monotonic decreasing function. Then*

$$V(X) \cap X^* \neq \varnothing. \tag{7.7}$$

This theorem states that in searching for an optimal solution of (7.4), one need only search for the "right" noninferior solution. In special cases this is useful for developing algorithms for solving (7.4) that are not only efficient but also guarantee that the best-compromise solution obtained is noninferior.

7.2.2 Geoffrion's Bicriterion Method

The bicriterion method [Geoffrion 1967a] is applied to problems

1. that are deterministic,
2. that have two objective functions,

3. that have continuous decision variables, and a set of alternatives X of the form (7.3) with $S = \varnothing$,
4. in which each f_j is a continuous convex function, where X is a compact and convex set, and
5. in which v is monotonic and continuous.

According to Theorem 7.1, one need only search among the noninferior solutions of VOP to find the best-compromise solution of MDP. However, according to Theorem 4.5, noninferior solutions for convex problems can always be found by solving the weighting problem $P(\lambda)$, of the form

$$\begin{aligned} &\min \quad \lambda f_1(\mathbf{x}) + (1-\lambda) f_2(\mathbf{x}) \\ &\text{subject to} \quad \mathbf{x} \in X, \end{aligned} \tag{7.8}$$

where $0 \leqslant \lambda \leqslant 1$. Thus, one need merely find the value of λ^* that yields not only a noninferior solution but also an optimal solution of (7.4) when $n = 2$, that is, the best-compromise solution. Geoffrion [1967a] developed the following method to find the desired value of λ:

Theorem 7.2. *For any given λ, let $X^*(\lambda)$ be the set of optimal solutions of $P(\lambda)$ and let*

$$V(\lambda) = \max v(\mathbf{f}(\mathbf{x})), \qquad \mathbf{x} \in X^*(\lambda). \tag{7.9}$$

a. *If λ^* is an optimal solution of*

$$\max_{0 \leqslant \lambda \leqslant 1} V(\lambda), \tag{7.10}$$

then an optimal solution of $P(\lambda^*)$ is an optimal solution of (7.4) *when $n = 2$.*
b. *If $\mathbf{x}(\lambda)$ is a vector-valued function defined on the closed interval $[0,1]$ such that $\mathbf{x}(\lambda)$ is an optimal solution of $P(\lambda)$ and if $\mathbf{x}(\lambda)$ is continuous everywhere except possibly at a finite number of points in $[0,1]$, where $\mathbf{x}(\lambda)$ can have simple discontinuity, then i) for every $\lambda \in [0,1]$ at which $\mathbf{x}(\lambda)$ is continuous*

$$V(\lambda) = v(\mathbf{f}(\mathbf{x}(\lambda))) \tag{7.11}$$

and ii) for every $\hat{\lambda} \in [0,1]$ at which $\mathbf{x}(\ )$ is discontinuous with $\lim_{\lambda \to \hat{\lambda}^-} \mathbf{x}(\lambda) = \mathbf{x}(\hat{\lambda}^-)$ and $\lim_{\lambda \to \hat{\lambda}^+} \mathbf{x}(\lambda) = \mathbf{x}(\hat{\lambda}^+)$, we have

$$V(\hat{\lambda}) = \max_{0 \leqslant \alpha \leqslant 1} \left[v\left(\alpha \mathbf{f}(\mathbf{x}(\hat{\lambda}^-)) + (1-\alpha)\mathbf{f}(\mathbf{x}(\hat{\lambda}^+))\right)\right] \tag{7.12}$$

or equivalently

$$V(\hat{\lambda}) = \max_{0 \leqslant \alpha \leqslant 1} \left[\alpha v\left(\mathbf{f}(\mathbf{x}(\hat{\lambda}^-))\right) + (1-\alpha) v\left(\mathbf{f}(\mathbf{x}(\hat{\lambda}^+))\right)\right]. \tag{7.13}$$

Theorem 7.2 is useful for generating an optimal solution of (7.4) (when $n = 2$) as follows: Part (b) states that if a function $\mathbf{x}(\lambda)$ having the prescribed property can be found by solving $P(\lambda)$, then the function $V(\lambda)$

can also be calculated by means of (7.11)–(7.13). Then, from part (a), λ^*, the "right" value of λ, that yielding the best-compromise solution, can be easily obtained by solving a simple one-dimensional optimization problem (7.10). The main virtue of this approach is that it converts an N-dimensional optimization problem (7.4) into a number of one-dimensional optimization problems (7.8), (7.10), (7.12), and (7.13), which are often easier to solve.

This approach is useful only if $P(\lambda)$ can manageably be solved parametrically to obtain $\mathbf{x}(\lambda)$ and $\mathbf{x}(\lambda)$ is continuous (except possibly at a finite number of points in $[0,1]$). As Geoffrion [1967a] has noted there are three classes of problems for which algorithms exist to solve $P(\lambda)$ parametrically that yield $\mathbf{x}(\lambda)$ continuous (except at a finite number of points):

In *linear problems* f_1, f_2 are linear and X is a convex polyhedron defined by linear constraints. In this case, parametric procedures for two-objective linear problems, or the algorithm described in Section 6.2.3, can be used to solve $P(\lambda)$ and find $\mathbf{x}(\lambda)$ [Gass and Saaty, 1955]. In this type of problem $\mathbf{x}(\lambda)$ is piecewise constant with at most a finite number of discontinuous points on $[0,1]$.

In *partially quadratic problems* f_1 is linear and f_2 is a positive semidefinite quadratic function, and X is a convex polyhedron. In this case Wolfe's parametric algorithm for solving $P(\lambda)$ will yield $\mathbf{x}(\lambda)$ [Wolfe, 1959], which is continuous and piecewise linear on $[0,1)$.

In *strictly convex problems* f_1 and f_2 are locally strictly convex, and X is a convex set satisfying the regularity assumption (see Section 2.3.2). In this case Geoffrion's parametric convex method can be used to solve $P(\lambda)$ [Geoffrion, 1966, 1967b], yielding a continuous function $\mathbf{x}(\lambda)$ on $[0,1]$.

Assuming that $P(\lambda)$ can be solved parametrically for $\mathbf{x}(\lambda)$, a bicriterion algorithm based on Geoffrion's strategy can be sketched as follows:

Step 1: Solve $P(\lambda)$ parametrically and obtain $\mathbf{x}(\lambda)$ and all its points of discontinuity, $0=\lambda_0<\lambda_1<\lambda_2<\cdots<\lambda_p<\lambda_{p+1}=1$, where p is some finite nonnegative integer.

Step 2: For each $0\leqslant i\leqslant p$, use (7.11)–(7.13) to compute $V(\lambda)$ for all $\lambda_i\leqslant\lambda<\lambda_{i+1}$, i.e.,

$$V(\lambda)=\begin{cases} v(\mathbf{f}(\mathbf{x}(\lambda))), & \lambda_i<\lambda<\lambda_{i+1}, \\ \max\limits_{0\leqslant\alpha\leqslant 1}\left[v\left(\alpha\mathbf{f}(\mathbf{x}(\lambda_i^-))+(1-\alpha)\mathbf{f}(\mathbf{x}(\lambda_i^+))\right)\right], & \lambda=\lambda_i, \\ & 1<i\leqslant p. \end{cases} \tag{7.14}$$

Also set $V(0)=v(\mathbf{f}(\mathbf{x}(0)))$ and $V(1)=v(\mathbf{f}(\mathbf{x}(1)))$.

Step 3: Find λ^* by using any appropriate one-dimensional search procedure to solve $\max_{0\leqslant\lambda\leqslant 1}V(\lambda)$.

The above algorithm can be made more efficient if $V(\lambda)$ is unimodal. In that case, the line search in step 3 does not require knowing $V(\lambda)$ completely. We start at any two convenient points[1] $(\lambda^i, \lambda^{i+1})$, and compute and compare $V(\lambda^i)$ and $V(\lambda^{i+1})$. This pairwise comparison tells us in which direction $V(\lambda)$ is increased. In view of the unimodality of $V(\lambda)$, it will also tell us whether the peak of $V(\lambda)$ has been reached or passed. If not, we simply generate another pair of λs, an element of which is a member of the previous pair, and compare the pairs again. We continue until the peak of $V(\lambda)$ is reached or passed and the proper value of λ^* can be determined. To ensure unimodality of $V(\lambda)$, Geoffrion [1967b] also shows that it suffices to assume, in addition to earlier assumptions, that the function v is quasi-concave.[2] Details of this result and appropriate modifications of the above algorithm for linear and partially quadratic problems can be found in Geoffrion [1967b].

Example 1: Consider a two-objective decision problem with $f_1(\mathbf{x})=(x_1-1)^2+x_2^2+(x_3-2)^2$, $f_2(\mathbf{x})=(x_1-2)^2+(x_2-1)^2+x_3^2$, which are to be minimized. The constraint set is given by $X=\{\mathbf{x}\in R^3 \mid g(\mathbf{x})=x_1+x_2+x_3\leqslant 6, x_i\geqslant 0,\ i=1,2,3\}$. Assume also that the value function has also been assessed and is found to be of the additive form $v(f_1,f_2)=-f_1-\sqrt{f_2}$, which is strictly decreasing, but neither concave nor quasi-concave. Consequently the MDP we wish to solve is

$$\max \quad v(f_1,f_2)=-f_1-\sqrt{f_2} \tag{7.15}$$

$$\text{subject to} \qquad g(\mathbf{x})=x_1+x_2+x_3\leqslant 6, \tag{7.16}$$

$$x_1,x_2,x_3\geqslant 0. \tag{7.17}$$

The corresponding parametric problem $P(\lambda)$ is

$$\min \quad \lambda f_1(\mathbf{x})+(1-\lambda)f_2(\mathbf{x}) \tag{7.18}$$

$$\text{subject to} \qquad g(\mathbf{x})=x_1+x_2+x_3\leqslant 6, \tag{7.19}$$

$$x_1,x_2,x_3\geqslant 0. \tag{7.20}$$

We now apply the above algorithm.

STEP 1: For $\lambda\in[0,1]$, as f_1 and f_2 are strictly convex and all other conditions required by Geoffrion's strict convex parametric programming are satisfied, we can apply the algorithm to solve $P(\lambda)$ numerically. For this particular

---

[1]Any two consecutive points of discontinuity $(\lambda_i, \lambda_{i+1})$ in the linear case, or any two consecutive adjacent noninferior points in the partially quadratic case, can be candidates.

[2]A real-valued function $w(y)$ is *quasi-concave* in its domain Y if and only if for any $y_1, y_2\in Y$, $w(\alpha y_1+(1-\alpha)y_2)\geqslant \min[w(y_1), w(y_2)]$.

example we can solve $P(\lambda)$ analytically by applying the Kuhn–Tucker conditions as in the previous chapter, obtaining

$$\mathbf{x}(\lambda)=\mathbf{x}^1+\lambda\mathbf{x}^2, \qquad 0\leqslant\lambda\leqslant 1, \tag{7.21}$$

where

$$\mathbf{x}^1=(2,1,0)^{\mathrm{T}}, \qquad \mathbf{x}^2=(-1,-1,2)^{\mathrm{T}}. \tag{7.22}$$

STEP 2: Since $\mathbf{x}(\lambda)$ is continuous throughout [0, 1], (7.14) yields

$$V(\lambda)=v(\mathbf{f}(\mathbf{x}(\lambda)))=-6(1-\lambda)^2-\sqrt{6}\,\lambda \tag{7.23}$$

for all $\lambda\in[0,1]$.

STEP 3: To find λ^* we solve

$$\max_{0\leqslant\lambda\leqslant 1}\left[-6(1-\lambda)^2-\sqrt{6}\,\lambda\right]. \tag{7.24}$$

Again in practice, any appropriate one-dimensional search algorithm (see, for example, Luenberger [1973, pp. 137–143]) can be applied to solve this type of line search problem, but for illustrative purposes, we solve (7.24) analytically, obtaining

$$\lambda^*=1-\sqrt{6}/12\approx 0.8.$$

Thus, the optimal solution of (7.15)–(7.17), and hence the best-compromise solution of MDP for this problem, is $\mathbf{x}(\lambda^*)=(1.2, 0.2, 1.6)^{\mathrm{T}}$, at which $v(\mathbf{f}(\mathbf{x}(\lambda^*)))=V(\lambda^*)=-0.73$.

Example 2: Consider the two-objective linear decision problem already considered in Example 3 of Chapter 6, where $f_1(\mathbf{x})=-x_1-2x_2$, $f_2(\mathbf{x})=-3x_1-x_2$ are to be minimized and X is given by

$$X=\left\{\mathbf{x}\in R^2 \mid x_1+x_2\leqslant 6,\ 2x_1+x_2\leqslant 9,\ 0\leqslant x_1\leqslant 4,\ 0\leqslant x_2\leqslant 5\right\}.$$

Let the value function be given by $v(f_1,f_2)=-f_1-\sqrt{f_2+17}$. Thus the MDP for this decision problem is

$$\begin{aligned}&\max \quad v(f_1,f_2)=-f_1-\sqrt{f_2+17}\\ &\text{subject to} \quad \mathbf{x}\in X,\end{aligned} \tag{7.25}$$

and the corresponding weighting problem $P(\lambda)$ is

$$\begin{aligned}&\min \quad \lambda f_1+(1-\lambda)f_2\\ &\text{subject to} \quad \mathbf{x}\in X.\end{aligned} \tag{7.26}$$

STEP 1: By either the parametric method of Gass and Saaty [1955], the algorithm described in Section 6.2.3, or the analytical method of Example 3 of Chapter 6, we solve $P(\lambda)$ to find that as λ ranges from 0 to 1 the optimal solution of $P(\lambda)$ traverses lines CB and BA in Figure 6.3 from C to B to A. In fact, if we let $\mathbf{x}^*(\lambda)$ represent the optimal solution of $P(\lambda)$ for any given λ, then from Figure 6.3 we have

$$\mathbf{x}^*(\lambda)=\begin{cases}(4,1)^{\mathrm{T}} & \text{if } 0\leqslant\lambda<\tfrac{1}{4},\\ \alpha(4,1)^{\mathrm{T}}+(1-\alpha)(3,3)^{\mathrm{T}},\quad 0\leqslant\alpha\leqslant 1, & \text{if } \lambda=\tfrac{1}{4},\\ (3,3)^{\mathrm{T}} & \text{if } \tfrac{1}{4}<\lambda<\tfrac{2}{3},\\ \alpha(3,3)^{\mathrm{T}}+(1-\alpha)(1,5)^{\mathrm{T}},\quad 0\leqslant\alpha\leqslant 1, & \text{if } \lambda=\tfrac{2}{3},\\ (1,5)^{\mathrm{T}} & \text{if } \tfrac{2}{3}<\lambda\leqslant 1.\end{cases}$$

Hence we can construct $\mathbf{x}(\lambda)$ as

$$\mathbf{x}(\lambda)=\begin{cases}(4,1)^{\mathrm{T}}, & 0\leqslant\lambda<\tfrac{1}{4},\\ (3,4)^{\mathrm{T}}, & \tfrac{1}{4}\leqslant\lambda<\tfrac{2}{3},\\ (1,5)^{\mathrm{T}}, & \tfrac{2}{3}\leqslant\lambda\leqslant 1,\end{cases}$$

which is piecewise constant with the two points of discontinuity at $\lambda_1=\frac{1}{4}$ and $\lambda_2=\frac{2}{3}$.

STEP 2: $V(\lambda)$ is constructed as follows:

$$V(\lambda)=v(\mathbf{f}(\mathbf{x}(\lambda)))$$

for all $\lambda\neq\lambda_1,\lambda_2$, or

$$V(\lambda)=\begin{cases}4, & 0\leqslant\lambda<\tfrac{1}{4},\\ 9, & \tfrac{1}{4}<\lambda<\tfrac{2}{3},\\ 8, & \tfrac{2}{3}<\lambda\leqslant 1.\end{cases}\tag{7.27}$$

At the points of discontinuity

$$\begin{aligned}V(\tfrac{1}{4})&=\max_{0\leqslant\alpha\leqslant 1}\left[v\left(\alpha\mathbf{f}\left(\mathbf{x}(\tfrac{1}{4}^{-})\right)+(1-\alpha)\mathbf{f}\left(\mathbf{x}(\tfrac{1}{4}^{+})\right)\right)\right]\\ &=\max_{0\leqslant\alpha\leqslant 1}(9-5\alpha)=9;\end{aligned}\tag{7.28}$$

i.e., $\alpha^*=0$. Also

$$\begin{aligned}V(\tfrac{2}{3})&=\max_{0\leqslant\alpha\leqslant 1}\left[v\left(\alpha\mathbf{f}\left(\mathbf{x}(\tfrac{2}{3}^{-})\right)+(1-\alpha)\mathbf{f}\left(\mathbf{x}(\tfrac{2}{3}^{+})\right)\right)\right]\\ &=\max_{0\leqslant\alpha\leqslant 1}\left(11-\sqrt{9-\alpha}\right)=11-\sqrt{8}=8.17.\end{aligned}\tag{7.29}$$

STEP 3: It is clear from (7.27)–(7.29) that λ^*, which maximizes $V(\lambda)$ in $[0,1]$, is any point in the range $\frac{1}{4}\leqslant\lambda<\frac{2}{3}$ and $\mathbf{x}(\lambda^*)=(3,4)^{\mathrm{T}}$ with $V(\lambda^*)=9$.

Because $\mathbf{x}(\lambda)$ is piecewise constant in linear problems, we need not apply a one-dimensional search to find λ^* in step 3. The function $V(\lambda)$ will have only a finite number of values, so simple comparison of these values will suffice to find λ^*.

7.2.3 The Modified PROTRADE Method

Goicoechea et al. [1976, 1979] developed a technique for handling multiobjective programming problems having the following characteristics: i) the objective functions are linear, ii) the coefficients in the objective functions are normally distributed random variables with known means and variances, and iii) the constraint set X is defined as in (7.3), where each $g_i(\mathbf{x})$ is a differentiable convex function, and $S=\varnothing$. This technique uses complete knowledge of the preference structure under uncertainty in the form of the assessed utility function. This technique also uses information concerning trade-offs between the levels of attainment of objectives and the probabilities of attaining those levels, because of which the technique is called the probabilistic trade-off (PROTRADE) method by its developers. This is despite the fact that the method also uses some information about *goals* and *trade-offs*. The trade-offs used here, however, are not trade-offs among objective functions, but rather trade-offs between risk levels and goal attainment levels.

The method, a modified version of that proposed by Goicoechea et al. [1976, 1979], is to use the assessed utility function to determine the best alternative based on Bernoulli's principle (maximizing expected utility). This alternative is then subjected to explicit risk trade-off analysis. A compromise between the goal attainment levels and the probabilities of attaining those levels is brought about by using information obtained from the decision maker regarding the above levels to reduce the constraint set. The steps of this procedure are given more precisely below. Let the objective function f_i, $i=1,\ldots,n$, be defined as

$$f_i(\mathbf{x})=\sum_{j=1}^{N} c_{ij}x_j \tag{7.30a}$$

with

$$c_{ij}\sim N\left(\mu_{ij},\sigma_{ij}^2\right), \tag{7.30b}$$

where μ_{ij} and σ_{ij}^2 are mean and variance of c_{ij}, respectively. Clearly $f_i(\mathbf{x})$ is also a normally distributed random variable with means $\bar{f}_i(\mathbf{x})$ and $\sigma_i^2(\mathbf{x})$, where

$$\bar{f}_i(\mathbf{x})=\sum_{j=1}^{N} \mu_{ij}x_j \tag{7.31a}$$

and

$$\sigma_i^2(\mathbf{x}) = \sum_{j=1}^{N} \sigma_{ij}^2 x_j^2. \tag{7.31b}$$

In view of the above, the procedure can be divided into two phases: The first seeks the best alternative by maximizing the expected utility; the second seeks a compromise solution by explicitly analyzing risk level. In the original method the best alternative in the first phase is produced by solving a weighting problem—apparently, to obtain a solution which is also noninferior. The weight used is apparently not a *global optimal* weight.

The modification presented here makes use of the fact that the assessed utility function already represents complete information about the decision maker's preference structure. It should, thus, provide all information for the first phase and no additional information should be required. The modified PROTRADE method proceeds as follows:

Phase I: Generating the Maximum Expected Utility Alternative

Step 1: Use procedures in Chapter 5 to assess the decision maker's utility function $u(f_1,\ldots,f_n)$.

Step 2: Find $\mathbf{x}^0$ by solving

$$\max_{\mathbf{x}\in X} \quad E\big(u(f_1,\ldots,f_n)\big). \tag{7.32}$$

Then compute $\bar{\mathbf{f}}(\mathbf{x}^0)$.

Phase II: Generating the Best-Compromise Solution Through Explicit Risk Analysis

Step 3: Compute $1-\alpha_i^0$, for each $i=1,\ldots,n$, where

$$P\big(f_i(\mathbf{x}) \leqslant \bar{f}_i(\mathbf{x}^0)\big) = 1-\alpha_i^0. \tag{7.33}$$

Note that $1-\alpha_i^0$ represents the probability that $f_i(\mathbf{x})$ will be less than the best alternative $\bar{f}_i(\mathbf{x}^0)$ obtained from phase I. Thus, α_i^0 can be used as a measure of the actual risk of not being able to attain at most $\bar{f}_i(\mathbf{x}^0)$. Set the iteration number $k=1$ and $X_0 = X$.

Step 4: Ask the decision maker to examine all pairs $(\bar{f}_i(\mathbf{x}^0), 1-\alpha_i^0)$. If the decision maker is satisfied with the levels of $\bar{f}_i(\mathbf{x}^0)$ and with the probability of obtaining $\bar{f}_i$ greater than $\bar{f}_i(\mathbf{x}^0)$, for each $i=1,\ldots,n$, stop. Otherwise, ask the decision maker to select i) the objective function $\bar{f}_{k_1}(\mathbf{x})$, $i \leqslant k_1 \leqslant n$, that is considered most undesirable and ii) the desirable level of $\bar{f}_{k_1}(\mathbf{x})$, $\bar{f}_{k_1}^1$, and the desirable risk level $\alpha_{k_1}^1$ so that

$$P\big(\bar{f}_{k_1}(\mathbf{x}) \leqslant \bar{f}_{k_1}^1\big) \leqslant \alpha_{k_1}^1. \tag{7.34}$$

Equation (7.34) can easily be converted to an ordinary constraint equation:

$$X_k = \{\mathbf{x} | \mathbf{x} \in X \text{ and (7.34) is satisfied}\}.$$

Step 5: Solve

$$\begin{array}{ll} \max & E(u(f_1,\ldots,f_n)) \\ \text{subject to} & \mathbf{x}\in X_{k-1}\cap X_k \end{array} \tag{7.35}$$

to obtain $\mathbf{x}^1$. Also compute $\bar{\mathbf{f}}(\mathbf{x}^1)$ and $1-\alpha_i^1$ for each i that has not been considered previously, so that

$$P(f_i(\mathbf{x})\leqslant \bar{f}_i(\mathbf{x}^1))\leqslant 1-\alpha_i. \tag{7.36}$$

Step 6: Set $k=k+1$. If $k>n$, stop: the last solution from step 5 is the best-compromise solution. Otherwise, go to step 4; the decision maker should only consider $(\bar{f}_i(\mathbf{x}),(1-\alpha_i))$ for each i whose desirable levels of $\bar{f}_i$ and α_i have not previously been considered.

In this algorithm, there is a *double accounting* for risk: when assessing u in the first phase, and when performing explicit risk analysis in the second phase. The utility functions in the first phase take risk into account, but not until the explicit analysis of the second phase can the decision maker assess risk based on the behavior of the system.

7.3 Methods Based on Weights, Priorities, Goals, and Ideals

For certain multiobjective decision problems, particularly in the private sector, weights, priorities, goals, and ideals are used routinely in decision making. The decision maker may feel perfectly comfortable giving his preference in those terms. His concept of best is then defined in terms of how much the actual achievement of each objective deviates from the desired goals or ideals. More precisely, the best-compromise alternative is often defined to have the *minimum combined deviation* from the desired goals or ideals. Using our terminology, the decision rule in (7.1) may read as illustrated in Example 4 of Chapter 1: "Choose an alternative having the minimum combined deviation from the goals $\hat{f}_1,\ldots,\hat{f}_n$, given the weights or priorities of the objective functions."

If the minimum combined deviation is properly defined, this decision rule leads to a well-defined preference structure, characterized by a total preference ordering relation (see Section 3.3) capable of completely ranking the set of alternatives X. Unfortunately, the distance measures that define the minimum combined deviations are not unique. In general, we can use any one of the mathematical weighted norms (weighted l_p norm)

$$d_p(\mathbf{f}(\mathbf{x}),\hat{\mathbf{f}}) \triangleq \left(\sum_{j=1}^{n} w_j|f_j(\mathbf{x})-\hat{f}_j|^p\right)^{1/p}, \tag{7.37}$$

where $1\leqslant p\leqslant\infty$, $\hat{\mathbf{f}}$ is the goal vector, w_j is the weight or priority given to the jth objective, and $d(\ ,\ )$ represents the *distance* between $\mathbf{f}(x)$ and $\hat{\mathbf{f}}$. Using (7.37) as a measure of deviation between $\mathbf{f}(\mathbf{x})$ and $\hat{\mathbf{f}}$ in the decision rule DR specified earlier, our general formulation of the multiobjective decision problem (7.1)–(7.2) becomes a surrogate MDP of the form

$$\min \quad \left\{ d_p(\mathbf{f}(\mathbf{x}),\hat{\mathbf{f}}) \triangleq \left(\sum_{j=1}^{n} w_j |f_j(\mathbf{x}) - \hat{f}_j|^p \right)^{1/p} \right\} \tag{7.38}$$

$$\text{subject to} \quad \mathbf{x} \in X.$$

Conceptually, once $\hat{\mathbf{f}}$ and $\mathbf{w} \triangleq (w_1,\ldots,w_n)$ are given, and (7.38) is formulated for any chosen value of $1 \leq p < \infty$, any proper optimization technique can be applied to the surrogate MDP (7.38) to determine the best-compromise solution of the original MDP. As remarked in Section 4.7, the best-compromise solution obtained this way may not have the noninferiority property. Thus the preference structure underlying goal programming, in most cases, represents a *satisficing* rather than an *optimizing* behavior. As Theorem 4.14 stipulates, only when $\hat{\mathbf{f}} = (f_1^*,\ldots,f_n^*)$ with $f_j^* = \min_{x \in X} f_j(\mathbf{x})$, $1 \leq p < \infty$, and either the solution of (7.38) is unique or $w_j > 0$ for each $j = 1,\ldots,n$ is an optimal solution of the surrogate MDP (7.38) noninferior.

To develop more specific and efficient algorithms, (7.38) can be divided into a number of classes. The following are a few examples that have been treated in the literature:

Case 1. $p = 1$; f_j, $j = 1,\ldots,n$, and g_i, $i = 1,\ldots,m$, are linear and there are no integer variables, i.e., $S = \varnothing$; $\hat{\mathbf{f}}$ is a perceived goal vector given by the decision maker (linear goal programming);

Case 2. similar to case 1 but with integer variables, i.e., $S \subseteq$ set of integers and $S \neq \varnothing$ (integer goal programming);

Case 3. $p = 1$; $f_j, j = 1,\ldots,n$, are nonlinear, X is a convex set, and $S = \varnothing$; $\hat{\mathbf{f}}$ is a perceived goal vector given by the decision maker (nonlinear goal programming);

Case 4. $p = 1$ and $\hat{\mathbf{f}} = \mathbf{f}^*$ (lexicographic programming and HOPE method);

Case 5. $1 \leq p < \infty$ and $\hat{\mathbf{f}} = \mathbf{f}^*$ or a moving target (compromise programming and displaced-ideal method);

Case 6. $p = \infty$, $\hat{\mathbf{f}} = \mathbf{f}^*$, and the weights are computed rather than assessed from information given by the decision maker (STEM method);

Case 7. goals are given as intervals rather than fixed points (SEMOPS and SIGMOPS methods).

7.3.1 Linear Goal Programming

Goal programming was first used for linear problems by Charnes and Cooper [1961]. In fact, as they point out later [Charnes and Cooper, 1975], they developed goal programming in the context of *constrained regression* when they attempted to find a formula for executive compensation in a division of the General Electric Company. There have been numerous subsequent works on goal programming, particularly in the areas of algorithmic development, applications, and extensions (see the survey by Kornbluth [1973], texts on goal programming by Lee [1972] and by Ignizio [1976], and the references therein).

The simplest variation of (7.38) is when i) the absolute value (l_1 norm) is used as the measure of deviation, ii) all objective functions and constraints are linear, and iii) all decision variables are continuous. To be more explicit, let each objective function

$$f_i(\mathbf{x}) = \sum_{j=1}^{N} c_{ij} x_j, \qquad i=1,\ldots,n,$$

each constraint

$$g_i(\mathbf{x}) = \sum_{j=1}^{N} a_{ij} x_j, \qquad i=1,\ldots,m,$$

and the constraint set $X=\{\mathbf{x}\in R^N \mid A\mathbf{x}\leqslant \mathbf{b},\ \mathbf{x}\geqslant \mathbf{0}\}$, where A is the $m\times N$ matrix whose ijth element is a_{ij}, and $\mathbf{b}$ is a constant $m\times 1$ vector.

After substituting $p=1$, the formulation (7.38) becomes

$$\min \quad \sum_{j=1}^{n} w_j |f_j(\mathbf{x}) - \hat{f}_j| \tag{7.39}$$

$$\text{subject to} \qquad A\mathbf{x}\leqslant \mathbf{b}, \quad \mathbf{x}\geqslant \mathbf{0}. \tag{7.40}$$

This formulation is a linear programming problem except for the objective function. It would be quite convenient if such formulation could be converted to an equivalent linear form so that an efficient solution algorithm, such as the simplex method, could then be applied. Fortunately this can be easily accomplished by introducing the variables

$$y_j^+ \triangleq \tfrac{1}{2}\{|f_j(\mathbf{x}) - \hat{f}_j| + [f_j(\mathbf{x}) - \hat{f}_j]\} \tag{7.41}$$

and

$$y_i^- \triangleq \tfrac{1}{2}\{|f_j(\mathbf{x}) - \hat{f}_j| - [f_j(\mathbf{x}) - \hat{f}_j]\} \tag{7.42}$$

for each $j=1,\ldots,n$. We note that

$$y_j^+ + y_j^- = |f_j(\mathbf{x}) - \hat{f}_j|, \tag{7.43}$$

$$y_j^+ - y_j^- = f_j(\mathbf{x}) - \hat{f}_j, \tag{7.44}$$

$$y_j^+ y_j^- = 0, \tag{7.45}$$

and $y_j^+ \geqslant 0$ and $y_j^- \geqslant 0$. Hence (7.39)–(7.40) can be transformed into LGP_1:

$$\min \sum_{j=1}^{n} w_j(y_j^+ + y_j^-) \tag{7.46}$$

$$\text{subject to} \quad f_j(\mathbf{x}) - y_j^+ + y_j^- = \hat{f}_j, \quad j=1,\ldots,n, \tag{7.47a}$$

$$A\mathbf{x} \leqslant \mathbf{b}, \tag{7.47b}$$

$$y_j^+ y_j^- = 0, \quad j=1,\ldots,n, \tag{7.47c}$$

$$\mathbf{x} \geqslant \mathbf{0}, \quad \mathbf{y}^+ \geqslant \mathbf{0}, \quad \mathbf{y}^- \geqslant \mathbf{0}.$$

The linear goal programming formulation LGP_1 in (7.46)–(7.47), although not quite a linear program because of (7.47c), can be handled easily by the simplex method. The nonlinear equality constraint in (7.47c) is dealt with when selecting entering basic variables by ensuring that *y_j^+ and y_j^- cannot become basic variables simultaneously*.

It is instructive to pause to observe the practical significance of y_j^+ and y_j^-. From (7.41) we see that y_j^+ is equal to $f_j(\mathbf{x}) - \hat{f}_j$ if $f_j(\mathbf{x}) \geqslant \hat{f}_j$, and is equal to zero otherwise. We see from (7.42) that y_j^- equals $\hat{f}_j - f_j(\mathbf{x})$ if $\hat{f}_j \geqslant f_j(\mathbf{x})$, and equals zero otherwise. Thus y_j^+ and y_j^- can be interpreted as the *overattainment* and the *underattainment*, respectively, of the jth goal level. Because of this, the variables y_j^+ and y_j^- are often called *deviational variables*. Overattainment and underattainment can clearly not occur simultaneously. That is, if $y_j^+ > 0$, y_j^- must be zero, and vice versa. This fact is reflected by (7.41c) in the LGP_1 formulation. Depending on the decision situation, some decision makers may prefer overattainment whereas others may prefer underattainment. In order to accommodate this preference, weights w_j^+ and w_j^- may be assigned to y_j^+ and y_j^-, respectively. At least one of these weights must be strictly positive and both are nonnegative. If overattainment is considered more desirable than underattainment, then w_j^- / w_j^+ should be large so as to drive the value of y_j^- as small as possible. If on the other hand underattainment is more desirable, then w_j^- / w_j^+ should be between 0 and 1. For example, if each f_j is a *cost-type* objective function (preference decreases as f_j increases) whose goal level is $\hat{f}_j$, overattainment, i.e., $y_j^+ = f_j - \hat{f}_j > 0$, is not desirable. In this case we may set $w_j^+ = 1$ and $w_j^- = 0$ and the LGP_1 formulation in (7.46) and (7.47) becomes LGP_2:

$$\min \sum_{j=1}^{n} w_j y_j^+ \tag{7.48}$$

$$\text{subject to} \quad f_j(\mathbf{x}) - y_j^+ + y_j^- = \hat{f}_j, \quad j=1,\ldots,n, \tag{7.49a}$$

$$A\mathbf{x} \leqslant \mathbf{b}, \tag{7.49b}$$

$$y_j^+ y_j^- = 0, \quad j=1,\ldots,n, \tag{7.49c}$$

$$\mathbf{x} \geqslant \mathbf{0}, \quad \mathbf{y}^+ \geqslant \mathbf{0}, \quad \mathbf{y}^- \geqslant \mathbf{0}.$$

Obviously for benefit-type objective functions, the situation may be reversed. In such a case, we may want to set $w_j^- = 1$ and $w_j^+ = 0$, thereby having $\Sigma_{j=1}^n w_j y_j^-$ replace $\Sigma_{j=1}^n w_j y_j^+$ as the objective function in (7.48). The goal programming formulation as in (7.48)–(7.49) is normally known as the *one-sided* goal programming formulation.

From both a conceptual and an algorithmic standpoint, it is imperative to distinguish between simple weights and the preemptive priorities, although both are used as measures of relative importance among the objective functions. When the relative importance among objectives is measured in an interval scale, the result is usually a set of simple weights w_j with the property $w_j \geqslant 0$ for each $j = 1, \ldots, n$ (often normalized, $\Sigma_{j=1}^n w_j = 1$). When simple weights w_j are used in the LGP formulation (7.46)–(7.47), the objective function becomes an ordinary linear function. Consequently the traditional simplex method can be applied with a slight modification of the entering variable rule to take into account the constraint (7.47c) as described earlier.

On the other hand, measuring the relative importance among objectives in an ordinal scale usually results in a preemptive priority ranking, which divides the objectives $f_1, \ldots, f_n$ into L priority classes, $1 \leqslant L \leqslant n$. Each class is associated with the quantity P_l, $l = 1, \ldots, L$, signifying that the lth class has the lth priority. Preemptive priority ranking is in the same spirit as that used in the lexicographic ordering discussed in Section 5.3. If objective f_j is in the lth priority class, then it has lower priority than those objectives which belong to the first, second, or $(l-1)$th priority class. But at the same time it also has higher priority than those in the $(l+1)$th, $\ldots, L$th priority classes. Although it is not necessary to assign any numerical value to each P_l, it is convenient to think of $P_1, \ldots, P_L$ as a sequence of numbers with the property $P_l \gg P_{l+1}$, for each $l = 1, \ldots, L-1$.

The LGP formulation in (7.46)–(7.47) can thus be modified to a general form LPG, incorporating preemptive priorities and over- and underattainment weights:

$$\min \quad \sum_{l=1}^{L} P_l \left(\sum_{j \in J_l} \left(w_j^+ y_j^+ + w_j^- y_j^- \right) \right) \tag{7.50}$$

$$\text{subject to} \quad f_j(\mathbf{x}) - y_j^+ + y_j^- = \hat{f}_j, \quad j = 1, \ldots, n, \tag{7.51a}$$

$$A\mathbf{x} \leqslant \mathbf{b}, \tag{7.51b}$$

$$y_j^+ y_j^- = 0, \quad j = 1, \ldots, n, \tag{7.51c}$$

$$\mathbf{x} \geqslant \mathbf{0}, \quad \mathbf{y}^+ \geqslant \mathbf{0}, \quad \mathbf{y}^- \geqslant \mathbf{0},$$

where $J_l \neq \varnothing$ is the set of indices of objective functions in the lth priority class. When we have n distinct priority classes (i.e., $L = n$) with f_j belonging to the jth class, then the objective function in (7.50) becomes simply $\Sigma_{j=1}^{n} P_j(w_j^+ y_j^+ + w_j^- y_j^-)$.

Because of the presence of preemptive priorities in (7.50), a strategy for solving LGP_3 in (7.50)–(7.51c) proceeds in much the same way as the lexicographic method described in Section 5.3. That is, we begin by trying to achieve the goals of all objectives in the first priority class. Having done that, we try to satisfy the goals in the second priority class, keeping the goals in the first class satisfied. The process is repeated until either a unique solution is obtained at some stage or all priority classes are considered. In the latter case, if the set of solutions is still not unique, the best-compromise solution can be selected subjectively from the set. This is equivalent to solving at most L linear programming problems sequentially. The simplex method can easily be adapted for this purpose. The only modification to the simplex tableau is to add to the bottom of the tableau $L-1$ additional rows to take into account the $L-1$ additional priority classes. The lth row in the bottom half represents the objective function of the lth subproblem (corresponding to the lth priority class), and its entries are computed in the normal way. We shall describe the modified simplex algorithm for goal programming, first proposed by Lee [1972], in sufficient detail to provide the reader with a working knowledge of the algorithm. Further details, examples, and extensions can be found in the texts of Lee [1972] or Ignizio [1976].

The modified simplex method solves (7.50)–(7.51) as follows:

STEP 1: *Setting up the problem.* Compute the objective function for each lth subproblem corresponding to the lth priority class, $l=1,\ldots,L$, using the formula

$$z_l(\mathbf{x}) = \sum_{j\in J_l} (w_j^+ y_j^+ + w_j^- y_j^-), \qquad l=1,\ldots,L. \tag{7.52}$$

Assume, without loss of generality, that $J_1=\{1\}, J_2=\{2\},\ldots,J_{L-1}=\{L-1\}$, and $J_L=\{L,\ldots,n\}$. Hence

$$z_l(\mathbf{x}) = w_l^+ y_l^+ + w_l^- y_l^-, \qquad l=1,\ldots,L-1$$

and

$$z_L(\mathbf{x}) = w_L^+ y_L^+ + w_L^- y_L^- + w_{L+1}^+ y_{L+1}^+ + w_{L+1}^- y_{L+1}^- + \cdots + w_n^+ y_n^+ + w_n^- y_n^- .$$

The following tableau of Figure 7.2 displays the LGP problem corresponding to the above example.

STEP 2: *Finding the initial basic solution and setting up the initial simplex tableau.* As can be seen from Figure 7.2, if each $\hat{f}_j > 0$, $j=1,\ldots,n$, then $y_1^-,\ldots,y_n^-$ are always eligible to be basic variables. Naturally, if for some $1\leq j\leq n$, $\hat{f}_j<0$, then y_j^+ can be used. The remaining m basic variables can always be found either by inspection or by the usual two-phase procedure in

$$
\begin{array}{llc|ccccccccccccc|c|c}
 & \text{Basic variables} & x_1 & \cdots & x_N & y_1^+ y_1^- & \cdots & y_{L-1}^+ y_{L-1}^- & y_L^+ y_L^- & \cdots & y_n^+ y_n^- & s_1 & \cdots & s_m & \text{Constants} & \\
\hline
 & & c_{11} & \cdots & c_{1N} & (-1)(1) & & & & & & & & & \hat{f}_1 & \\
 & & \vdots & & \vdots & & & \ddots & & & & & & & \vdots & \\
 & \mathbf{x}_B & c_{n1} & \cdots & c_{nN} & & & & & & (-1)(1) & & & & \hat{f}_n & \boldsymbol{\alpha} \\
 & & a_{11} & \cdots & a_{1N} & & & & & & & 1 & & & b_1 & \\
 & & \vdots & & \vdots & & & & & & & & \ddots & & \vdots & \\
 & & a_{m1} & \cdots & a_{mN} & & & & & & & & & 1 & b_m & \\
\hdashline
P_1 & -z_1 & & & & w_1^+ w_1^- & & & & & & & & & -z_1^0 & \\
\vdots & \vdots & & & & & \ddots & & & & & & & & \vdots & \mathbf{z}^0 \\
P_{L-1} & -z_{L-1} & & & & & & w_{L-1}^+ w_{L-1}^- & & & & & & & -z_{L-1}^0 & \\
P_L & -z_L & & & & & & & w_L^+ w_L^- & \cdots & w_n^+ w_n^- & & & & -z_L^0 & \\
\end{array}
$$

Figure 7.2 Tableau displaying initial data for linear goal programming.

linear programming. In Figure 7.2, it is obvious that if all $b_i > 0$, $i = 1,\ldots,m$, the slack variables $s_1,\ldots,s_m$ can always be used as basic variables. Having obtained the initial basic variables $\mathbf{x}_B^0$, the initial simplex tableau can be acquired by performing necessary pivot operations or by using a formula similar to (6.51).

STEP 3: *Solving the lth priority class subproblems.* If we have found a set of solutions that minimize the deviations from the goals in the first to the $(l-1)$th priority class, we now wish to solve the lth priority class subproblem using row P_l as our objective function. A typical tableau to begin this process is

$$
\begin{array}{c}
\text{Basic variables}\\
x_{\bar{1}}\\ \vdots \\ x_{\overline{n+m}} \\ -z_1 \\ \vdots \\ -z_l \\ \vdots \\ -z_L
\end{array}
\quad
\overbrace{\begin{array}{ccc} & & \\ 1 & & \\ & \ddots & \\ & & 1 \\ & & \\ & & \\ & & \\ & & \\ & & \\ & & \end{array}}^{\mathbf{x}_B}
\left|
\overbrace{\begin{array}{ccccc}
\tilde{d}_{1,\overline{n+m+1}} & & \cdots & & \tilde{d}_{1,\overline{N+2n+m}}\\
\vdots & & & & \vdots\\
\tilde{d}_{n+m,\overline{n+m+1}} & & \cdots & & \tilde{d}_{n+m,\overline{N+2n+m}}\\ \hdashline
\tilde{h}_{1,\overline{n+m+1}} & \cdots & \tilde{h}_{1,j} & \cdots & \tilde{h}_{1,\overline{N+2n+m}}\\
\vdots & & \vdots & & \vdots\\
\tilde{h}_{l,\overline{n+m+1}} & \cdots & \tilde{h}_{l,j} & \cdots & \tilde{h}_{l,\overline{N+2n+m}}\\
\vdots & & \vdots & & \vdots\\
\tilde{h}_{L,\overline{n+m+1}} & \cdots & \tilde{h}_{L,j} & \cdots & \tilde{h}_{L,\overline{N+2n+m}}
\end{array}}^{\mathbf{x}_D}
\right|
\quad
\begin{array}{c}
\text{Constants}\\
\tilde{\alpha}_1\\ \vdots \\ \tilde{\alpha}_{n+m} \\ -z_1^0 \\ \vdots \\ -z_l^0 \\ \vdots \\ -z_L^0
\end{array}
$$

The entries in the tableau are computed by normal pivot operations or directly [cf. (6.51)]. This is the initial simplex tableau for solving the lth priority class. The major modifications of the simplex algorithm for solving this problem, apart from the modification of the tableau above, are associated with the rules for selecting the entering and leaving variables.

Rules for Selecting Entering Variables To find the entering variable we look at row P_l of the current nonbasic columns and apply the following rules:

Entering rule a. Find all nonbasic columns j such that $\tilde{h}_{l,j}$ is negative. If there is no such column, solve the $(l+1)$th priority class subproblem since the current subproblem has already been solved. Otherwise, let J_l^- be the index set of those columns, i.e., $J_l^- = \{j \mid j \in \{\overline{n+m+1},\ldots,\overline{N+2n+m}\}, \tilde{h}_{l,j} < 0\}$.

Entering rule b. Find all columns $j \in J_l^-$ such that $\tilde{h}_{p,j} = 0$ for all $p = 1,\ldots,l-1$. If no such column exists, proceed to the next subproblem. Otherwise go to rule c.

Entering rule c. Choose as the entering column a column j from those obtained in rule b which has the most negative value of $\tilde{h}_{l,j}$ (it does not matter if two columns have the same most negative value).

The basic motivation for entering rules a and c is the same as for the ordinary simplex algorithm. The motivation for entering rule b is that in solving the lth priority class, the optimality of all the preceding priority class subproblems must be maintained. Observe that there may be situations where for all columns j such that $\tilde{h}_{l,j}<0$, there is at least one $1 \leqslant p \leqslant l-1$ such that $\tilde{h}_{p,j}>0$. In such a case, rule b dictates the termination of the solution process of the lth subproblem despite the fact that the subproblem has not achieved optimality in the original constraint set. It has, however, achieved optimality in the modified constraint set. This means that at least some of the goals of objectives in the lth priority class cannot be achieved perfectly.

Rule for Selecting the Leaving Variable Once the entering column j has been selected, the leaving variable can be selected using a modification of the simplex algorithm:

Leaving rule a. First we find all rows i, $1 \leqslant i \leqslant n+m$ such that $\tilde{d}_{i,j}>0$. Let I_l^+ denote the index set of these rows, i.e.,

$$I_l^+ = \{i \mid 1 \leqslant i \leqslant n+m,\, d_{i,j}>0\}.$$

Leaving rule b. Choose the basic variable corresponding to the row i that has the lowest value of $\tilde{\alpha}_i / d_{i,j}$ of the rows in I_l^+ and that does not lead to a pair y_j^+, y_j^-, $j=1,\ldots,n$, becoming basic variables together.

Leaving rule c. If no such row exists, we go back to entering rule b and choose the next best entering column and apply all leaving rules again. If leaving rule b fails to produce a leaving variable for all eligible entering columns, the process is terminated and the lth subproblem is taken as the optimum.

The motivation for leaving rule a is the same as the traditional simplex algorithm, while the motivation for leaving rules b and c is to ensure that the constraints (7.47c) in LGP_1 are satisfied.

The steps of a simplex-based algorithm for solving linear goal programming problems of the form (7.50)–(7.51) may now be summarized.

Step 1: Determine the objective functions of the lth priority class subproblem from

$$z_l(\mathbf{x}) = \sum_{j \in J_l} \left(w_j^+ y_j^+ + w_j^- y_j^-\right), \qquad l=1,\ldots,L, \tag{7.53}$$

and collect all data in the tableau form as illustrated in Figure 7.2.

Step 2: Find the initial basic variables $\mathbf{x}_{\mathrm{B}}^0$. Use the variables y_j^- or y_j^+, depending on whether $\hat{f}_j$ is positive or negative, as part of $\mathbf{x}_{\mathrm{B}}^0$. Also use slack variables, if available, to fill the remaining part. Otherwise use the two-phase method. Obtain the corresponding initial tableau and set $l=1$.

Step 3: Solve the lth priority class subproblem. Apply the rules for selecting the entering and leaving variables as described earlier.

Step 4: Stop if either the solution from the lth subproblem is unique or $l=L$. Otherwise set $l=l+1$ and go to step 3.

The following example illustrates the salient features of the algorithm.

Example 3: Consider a three-objective linear problem with

$$f_1(\mathbf{x})=2x_1-x_2,$$
$$f_2(\mathbf{x})=-x_1-2x_2,$$
$$f_3(\mathbf{x})=-3x_1-x_2,$$

and

$$X=\{\mathbf{x}\in R^2|x_1+4x_2\leqslant 16,\ 2x_1+2x_2\leqslant 11,\ 2x_1+x_2\leqslant 10,\ \mathbf{x}\geqslant 0\}.$$

Suppose the decision maker specifies that the first priority goal P_1 is that f_1 not exceed 4, and the second priority goal P_2 is that f_2 and f_3 not exceed -7 and -12, respectively. In addition, the decision maker specifies that he considers f_2 to be four times as important as f_3. We can translate the above priorities and goals as follows:

1. Since we want to minimize overattainment while we are quite willing to accept underattainment, we can set $w_j^-=0$ for all $j=1,2,3$. We can set w_1^+ at any convenient positive value. For simplicity, then, let $w_1^+=1$.
2. Since the goal of f_2 is considered four times as important as that of f_1, we may set $w_2^+=4$, $w_3^+=1$.

Consequently an equivalent goal programming formulation of the above three-objective decision problem can be written

$$\min\quad P_1y_1^+ + P_2(4y_1^+ + y_3^+) \tag{7.54}$$

$$\begin{aligned}
\text{subject to}\quad & f_1: & 2x_1-x_2-y_1^++y_1^- &=4, && (7.55a)\\
& f_2: & -x_1-2x_2-y_2^++y_2^- &=-7, && (7.55b)\\
& f_3: & -3x_1-x_2-y_3^++y_3^- &=-12, && (7.55c)\\
& g_1: & x_1+4x_2+s_1 &=16, && (7.55d)\\
& g_2: & 2x_1+2x_2+s_2 &=11, && (7.55e)\\
& g_3: & 2x_1+x_2+s_3 &=10, && (7.55f)\\
& & y_j^+y_j^-=0,\quad j=1,2,3 & && (7.55g)\\
& & x_1,x_2,y_j^+,y_j^-,s_1,s_2,s_3\geqslant 0. & &&
\end{aligned}$$

We can apply the simplex-based algorithm to solve (7.54)–(7.55).

STEP 1: $z_1(\mathbf{x})$ and $z_2(\mathbf{x})$ were determined as shown in (7.54), and (7.54)–(7.55) can be displayed in tableau form as

Basic variables	x_1	x_2	y_1^+	y_1^-	y_2^+	y_2^-	y_3^+	y_3^-	s_1	s_2	s_3	Constants
	2	−1	−1	1								4
	−1	−2			−1	1						−7
	−3	−1					−1	1				−12
	1	4							1			16
	2	2								1		11
	2	1									1	10
P_1: $-z_1$			1									0
P_2: $-z_2$					4		1					0

STEP 2: Since $\hat{f}_1 > 0$, $\hat{f}_2 < 0$, $\hat{f}_3 < 0$, we clearly select y_1^-, y_2^+, y_3^+ and s_1, s_2, s_3 as the initial basic variables; i.e., $\mathbf{x}_B^0 = (y_1^-, y_2^+, y_3^+, s_1, s_2, s_3)^T$. The initial simplex tableau after necessary pivot operations is

Basic	x_1	x_2 (entering ↓)	y_1^+	y_1^-	y_2^+	y_2^-	y_3^+	y_3^-	s_1	s_2	s_3	Constants
y_1	2	−1	−1	1								4
leaving ← y_2	1	②			1	−1						7
y_3	3	1					1	−1				12
s_1	1	4							1			16
s_2	2	2								1		11
s_3	2	1									1	10
P_1: $-z_1$			1									0
P_2: $-z_2$	−7	−9			4			1				−40

STEP 3: For subproblem P_1, examining the preceding initial tableau reveals that the first priority class subproblem is already optimum at the current basic solution since all reduced cost coefficients in row P_1 are nonnegative. To solve the second priority class subproblem P_2, we observe that the entries in row P_2 at the first and second (nonbasic) columns are negative with the latter column being more negative. Hence we select x_2 as the

entering variable. On examination of the preceding tableau we find y_2^+ should be the leaving variable. Observe that condition (7.55g) is not violated by these choices of leaving and entering variables.

After performing the indicated pivot operation, we obtain the following tableau:

	Basic	x_1	x_2	y_1^+	y_1^-	y_2^+	y_2^-	y_3^+	y_3^-	s_1	s_2	s_3	Constants
						entering ↓							
leaving ←	y_1^-	($\frac{5}{2}$)		-1	1	$\frac{1}{2}$	$-\frac{1}{2}$						$\frac{15}{2}$
	x_2	$\frac{1}{2}$	1			$\frac{1}{2}$	$-\frac{1}{2}$						$\frac{7}{2}$
	y_3^+	$\frac{5}{2}$				$-\frac{1}{2}$	$\frac{1}{2}$	1	-1				$\frac{17}{2}$
	s_1	-1				-2	2			1			2
	s_2	1				-1	1				1		4
	s_3	$\frac{3}{2}$				$-\frac{1}{2}$	$\frac{1}{2}$					1	$\frac{13}{2}$
P_1:	$-z_1$			1									0
P_2:	$-z_2$	$-\frac{5}{2}$				$\frac{9}{2}$	$-\frac{1}{2}$		1				$-\frac{17}{2}$

The second iteration in solving subproblem P_2 leads to the indicated pivot operation, which replaces y_1^- from the basic variable set with x_1. Condition (7.55g) is still satisfied with these choices. Performing the indicated pivoting yields

	Basic	x_1	x_2	y_1^+	y_1^-	y_2^+	y_2^-	y_3^+	y_3^-	s_1	s_2	s_3	Constants
							entering ↓						
	x_1	1		$-\frac{2}{5}$	$\frac{2}{5}$	$\frac{1}{5}$	$-\frac{1}{5}$						3
	x_2		1	$\frac{1}{5}$	$-\frac{1}{5}$	$\frac{2}{5}$	$-\frac{2}{5}$						2
	y_3^+			1	-1	-1	1	1	-1				2
	s_1			$-\frac{2}{5}$	$\frac{2}{5}$	$-\frac{9}{5}$	$\frac{9}{5}$			1			5
leaving ←	s_2			$\frac{2}{5}$	$-\frac{2}{5}$	$-\frac{6}{5}$	($\frac{6}{5}$)				1		1
	s_3			$\frac{3}{5}$	$-\frac{3}{5}$	-2	2					1	2
P_1:	$-z_1$			1									0
P_1:	$-z_2$			-1	1	5	-1	1					-2

Continuing by performing the pivot indicated yields the final tableau:

	Basic	x_1	x_2	y_1^+	y_1^-	y_2^+	y_2^-	y_3^+	y_3^-	s_1	s_2	s_3	Constants
	x_1	1		$-\frac{1}{3}$	$\frac{1}{3}$						$\frac{1}{6}$		$\frac{19}{6}$
	x_2		1	$\frac{1}{3}$	$-\frac{1}{3}$						$\frac{1}{3}$		$\frac{7}{3}$
	y_3^+			$\frac{2}{3}$	$-\frac{2}{3}$			1	-1		$-\frac{5}{6}$		$\frac{7}{6}$
	s_1			-1	1					1	$-\frac{3}{2}$		$\frac{7}{2}$
	y_2^-			$\frac{1}{3}$	$-\frac{1}{3}$	-1	1				$\frac{5}{6}$		$\frac{5}{6}$
	s_3			$-\frac{1}{15}$	$\frac{1}{15}$						$-\frac{5}{3}$	1	$\frac{1}{3}$
P_1:	$-z_1$			1									0
P_2:	$-z_2$			$-\frac{2}{3}$	$\frac{2}{3}$	4			1		$\frac{5}{6}$		$-\frac{7}{6}$

This is clearly the final tableau, even though the entry in column 3 and row P_2 is still negative. To preserve the optimality of subproblem P_1, y_1^+ cannot be made a basic variable, because the entry in the third column of row P_1 is strictly positive. Consequently the current solution, $\mathbf{x}^* = (\frac{19}{6}, \frac{7}{3})$, is the best-compromise solution satisfying the first priority goals, $f_1(\mathbf{x}^*) = 4$. It also satisfies one of the second priority goals, $f_2(\mathbf{x}^*) < -7$. However, as we may observe from the final tableau, $y_3^+ = \frac{7}{6} > 0$, indicating that the other second priority goal is not achieved: $f_3(\mathbf{x}^*)$ overattains the goal by $\frac{7}{6}$.

The goal programming algorithm applied to this example can also be demonstrated graphically, as shown in Figure 7.3. We first draw the original feasible region X in the $x_1 - x_2$ plane.

Solving subproblem P_1 is equivalent to moving the line $f_1(x) = \text{constant}$ with or against its gradient until y_1^+ is minimum. Since $y_1^+ \geqslant 0$, the minimum occurs when the constant is less than or equal to 4, yielding the minimum $y_1^+ = 0$. The shaded region X_1 in Figure 7.3a consists of all feasible points in X that solve subproblem P_1, hence satisfying the first priority goal. Next we need to solve subproblem P_2, in other words, find a point in X_1 that minimizes $4y_2^+ + y_3^+$. We observe from Figure 7.3 that X_2 is the set of feasible points where the first priority goal and the $f_2(\mathbf{x}) \leqslant -7$ goal are both satisfied, while X_3 is the set of feasible points where the $f_3(\mathbf{x}) \leqslant -12$ goal is achieved. Since $X_1 \cap X_3 = \varnothing$, the last goal will never be fully achieved by any solution that attains the first priority goal. By inspection, point A, which lies in X_2 (i.e., $y_1^+ = 0$, $y_2^+ = 0$), is the point in X_2 closest to the line $f_3(\mathbf{x}) = -12$. Thus y_3^-, and hence $4y_2^+ + y_3^+$, are smallest at A, as obtained from the algorithm.

Note that the best-compromise solution A of the above problem lies on the noninferior faces as shown in Figure 7.3a. In general it can be shown for a one-sided goal programming that there always exists a best-compromise

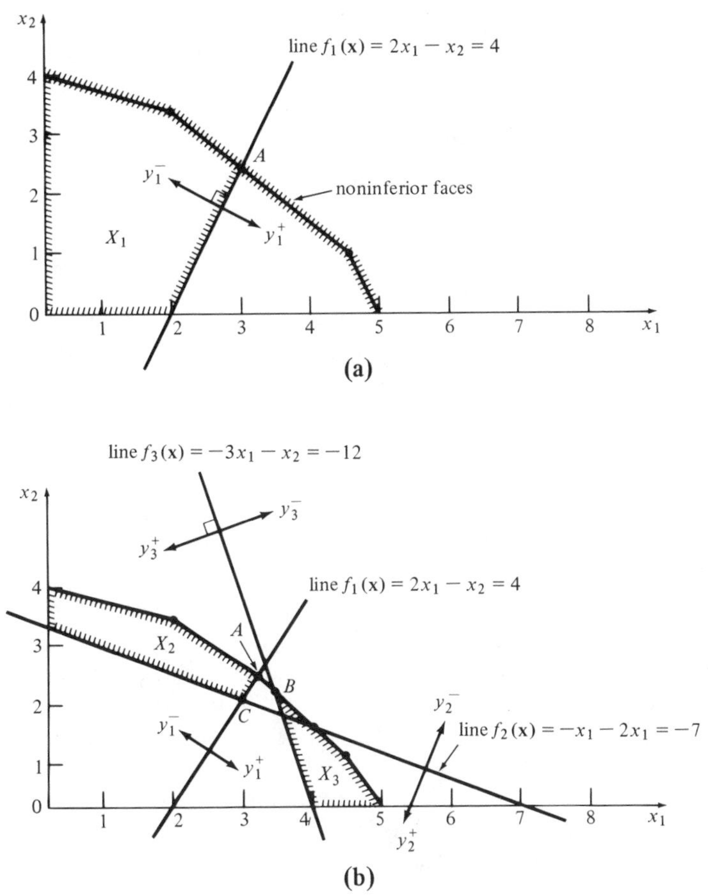

Figure 7.3 Goal programming algorithm.

solution that is also noninferior, but not for a general (two-sided) goal programming. For example, had the second priority goal been changed so that the equivalent P_2 subproblem was to minimize $w_2^+ y_2^+ + w_2^- y_2^- + w_3^+ y_3^+$ for any $w_2^+ > 0$, $w_2^- > w_3^+ > 0$, the best-compromise solution would have been the point C in Figure 7.3b, which is clearly dominated by point A.

A second remark should be familiar to the reader from our discussion of the lexicographic method in Section 5.3. The best-compromise solution based on goal programming is quite sensitive to the priority–goal structure. If, for example, instead of the above structure, the decision maker wants to have $f_3(\mathbf{x})$ not exceeding -12 as the first priority and the other two goals as the second priority, the new best-compromise solution will be point B in

Figure 7.3b. This sensitivity problem is critical since very often the decision maker finds it difficult to give a precise priority–goal structure with a reasonable degree of confidence.

7.3.2 Extensions of Goal Programming

There are two extentions of goal programming that retain the notion of minimizing a function of the deviation variables. The first extension aims to reduce the sensitivity of the solution to the priority–goal structure. This extension provides a mechanism for performing sensitivity analysis on priorities and goal levels in a convenient and systematic way. An interactive approach, now a common strategy in general multiobjective decision making, can be useful for this purpose.

In goal programming, the set of parameters required from the decision maker is the set of priorities, weights, and goal levels necessary to formulate the problem as in (7.50)–(7.51). Lee [1972] proposed an *interactive (linear) goal programming* scheme that fits the above pattern. Given a priority–goal structure, the modified simplex algorithm described in Section 7.3.1 can be used, especially step 1. In order to get the decision maker to react to the currently produced solution in step 2, Lee [1972] suggests the use of goal trade-off information, obtainable from the final simplex tableau, as a means of communicating between the analyst and the decision maker. This goal trade-off reflects the level of sacrificing achieved goals to improve the unachieved goal. For example, in the final tableau of Example 3 we see that the third goal is not achieved while the first and second are. This is evident since $\tilde{h}_{23} = -\frac{2}{3} < 0$. The level by which the third goal is not achieved is read directly from the final tableau as $+\frac{7}{6}$. If we want to force the attainment of the third goal by introducing y_1^+ into the basic variable set, then it is clear that if y_1^+ increases to a positive value, the first goal will not be attained. The goal trade-off between f_1 and f_3 is directly computable from the final tableau as $z_2^0/\tilde{h}_{23} = -\frac{7}{4}$, meaning that if the decision maker wants to achieve the third goal by improving (decreasing) it by $\frac{7}{6}$ units, he has to sacrifice the first goal by letting it be unachieved (increased) by $\frac{7}{4}$ units, a trade-off rate[3] of $h_{23} = -\frac{2}{3}$ units of f_1 per unit of f_3. Based on these and possibly other information (such as probability of goal attainment), it is hoped that the decision maker can restructure his priority–goal structure to yield a new goal programming problem with a better result. Franz and Lee

[3]This conforms to the terminology in Section 7.4.

[1980] computerized this idea together with a scheme to aid in assigning priorities into a preemptive priority-based interactive linear goal programming algorithm and apply it to a hypothetical planning problem.

A different interactive goal programming scheme is proposed by Dyer [1972]. It is primarily designed for one-sided goal programming (linear or nonlinear), with a cardinal weight formulation rather than an ordinal priority-based formulation. The primary objective of the scheme is to provide an effective means of arriving at the optimal set of weights w_j^+ (or w_j^-) through the three-step procedure of interactive techniques discussed in Section 7.1. The dialogue between the decision maker and the analyst in the second step is aimed at eliciting from the decision maker the marginal rate of substitutions (indifference trade-off rates) at the current solution, which will be used as the weights w_j^+ in the next iteration. The mechanism of this interactive scheme is essentially the same as that of Geoffrion, Dyer, and Feinberg in Section 7.4.3.

A different approach to performing the sensitivity analysis on the cardinal weights $w_j^+, w_j^-, j=1,\ldots,n$, in linear goal programming is proposed by Steuer [1979]. It is based on the premise that the deviation variables y_j^+, y_j^-, which are present in the objective function of linear goal programming, as in (7.46)–(7.47), can each be viewed as an objective function to be minimized. Thus the familiar objective function of a linear goal programming problem $\Sigma_{j=1}^n w_j^+ y_j^+ + w_j^- y_j^-$ is merely a weighting representation of second objective functions, where w_j^+, w_j^-, $j=1,\ldots,n$, are the corresponding weights. Without loss of generality it can be assumed that the sum of these weights is equal to unity. If we then allow these weights to vary within their respective ranges between 0 and 1, and study the effects of the solutions obtained, we shall have, in effect, performed the sensitivity analysis of all these weights simultaneously. This is, indeed, the main strength of the method. To carry out this type of sensitivity analysis, it is necessary only to apply Steuer's interval weight technique (Section 6.2.4).

The second extension of goal programming aims to deal with the structure of the problems. Ignizio [1976], Lee and Morris [1977], and Lee [1978] consider the case in which all functions and constraints are linear and some or all of the decision variables are integers. Lee and Morris [1977] then combine the modified simplex method in Section 7.3.1 with the familiar integer programming methods, such as Gomory's cutting plane method, the branch and bound method, and Balas's implicit enumeration method, as means for solving *integer goal programming* problems. They have found Gomery's cutting plane method to be efficient for all-integer goal programming problems. They have also found the adapted branch and bound approach efficient for mixed-integer programming problems and Balas's implicit enumeration method efficient for the 0–1 goal programming problem. Lee [1978] combines the above integer programming approaches with the ideas of interactive goal programming described earlier, to form an interactive goal programming procedure which he applied to assign overlapping shifts for the Nebraska State Patrol.

In *nonlinear* goal programming problems in which all objective functions f_j, $j=1,\ldots,n$, and constraints g_i, $i=1,\ldots,m$, are nonlinear and $S=\varnothing$, the formulation of nonlinear goal programming is the same, namely NGP:

$$\min \quad \sum_{l=1}^{L} P_l\left(\sum_{j\in J_l} \left(w_j^+ y_j^+ + w_j^- y_j^-\right)\right) \tag{7.56}$$

$$\text{subject to} \quad f_j(\mathbf{x}) - y_j^+ + y_j^- = \hat{f}_j, \quad j=1,\ldots,n, \tag{7.57a}$$

$$g_i(\mathbf{x}) \leqslant 0, \quad i=1,\ldots,m, \tag{7.57b}$$

$$\mathbf{y}^+ \geqslant \mathbf{0}, \quad \mathbf{y}^- \geqslant \mathbf{0}.$$

Again J_l is the index set of objectives in the lth priority class. The solution strategy of NGP is clearly the same as that of LGP: A sequence of priority class subproblems is solved successively, starting from the highest priority class.

Starting from $l=1$, we solve the following subproblem:

$$z_l^* = \min \sum_{j\in J_l} (w_j^+ y_j^+ + w_j^- y_j^-) \tag{7.58}$$

$$\text{subject to} \quad \mathbf{x}\in \tilde{X}\cap X_{l-1}, \tag{7.59}$$

where

$$\tilde{X} \triangleq \left\{(\mathbf{x},\mathbf{y}^+,\mathbf{y}^-)\in R^{N+2n} \mid f_j(\mathbf{x}) - y_j^+ + y_j^- = \hat{f}_j,\ j=1,\ldots,n,\ g_i(\mathbf{x})\leqslant 0,\ i=1,\ldots,m\right\},$$

$$X_{l-1} = \left\{(\mathbf{x},\mathbf{y}^+,\mathbf{y}^-)\in R^{N+2n} \,\middle|\, \sum_{j\in J_k} \left(w_j^+, y_j^+ + w_j^- y_j^-\right) \leqslant z_k^* \text{ for all } k=1,\ldots,l-1\right\},$$

$$X_0 = \tilde{X}.$$

The process is terminated whenever X_l, the solution set of the lth priority class subproblem, is a singleton or $l=L$. In the latter case, the best-compromise solution of X_L must be selected subjectively should X_L contain more than one element. Although there is no single concise and efficient tool in nonlinear goal programming that can be used to solve simultaneously the L subproblems of the form (7.58)–(7.59), as there is in the linear case, one need merely apply appropriate optimization algorithms to each of the subproblems in (7.58)–(7.59). Dauer and Krueger [1977], Hwang and Masud [1979], and Ignizio [1976] describe a procedure which employs a modified version of the Hooke and Jeeve method to solve these subproblems, and Ignizio [1976] also describes a procedure which utilizes Griffith–Stewart's linear approximation approach.

Variations of the Goal Programming Approach In the formulation (7.50)–(7.51), if we let $\hat{f}_j = f_j^* \triangleq \min_{\mathbf{x} \in X} f_1(\mathbf{x})$ for all $j = 1, \ldots, n$, then $y_j^+ = 0$, $y_j = f_j(\mathbf{x}) - f_j^*$, and (7.51a) is always satisfied. Consequently, the formulation (7.50)–(7.51) reduces to

$$\min_{\mathbf{x} \in X} \sum_{l=1}^{L} P_l \Big(\sum_{j \in J_l} \big[f_j(\mathbf{x}) - f_j^* \big] \Big)$$

or

$$\min_{\mathbf{x} \in X} \sum_{l=1}^{L} P_l \Big(\sum_{j = J_l} f_j(\mathbf{x}) \Big). \tag{7.60}$$

This is clearly equivalent to the familiar lexicographic method discussed in Chapter 5. Moreover if $L = n$, $J_l = \{l\}$, $l = 1, \ldots, n$, and P_l is a simple cardinal weight w_l, (7.60) becomes

$$\min_{\mathbf{x} \in X} \sum_{j=1}^{n} w_j f_i(\mathbf{x}), \tag{7.61}$$

which is a familiar optimal weight method. If the set of optimal weights is known, a solution of (7.61) represents the best-compromise solution. Eliciting the optimal weight directly is, however, often difficult. Ho [1979] proposed an interactive scheme, the holistic preference estimation (HOPE) method, to systematically determine this set of optimal weights for linear problems. The process requires the decision maker to provide i) a set of ordinal rankings of objectives and ii) the most preferred solution among a subset of noninferior extreme points generated at each iteration. The method successively determines the optimal weights from the smallest up to the largest. The algorithm requires solving a series of linear parametric programming problems. For further details see Ho [1979, 1980].

The *goal attainment method* proposed by Gembicki [1973] and Gembicki and Haimes [1975] is yet another variation of goal programming. In this approach a vector of weights $\mathbf{w}$ relating the relative under- or overattainment of the desired goals must be elicited from the decision maker in addition to the goal vector $\hat{\mathbf{f}}$. To find the best-compromise solution, we solve

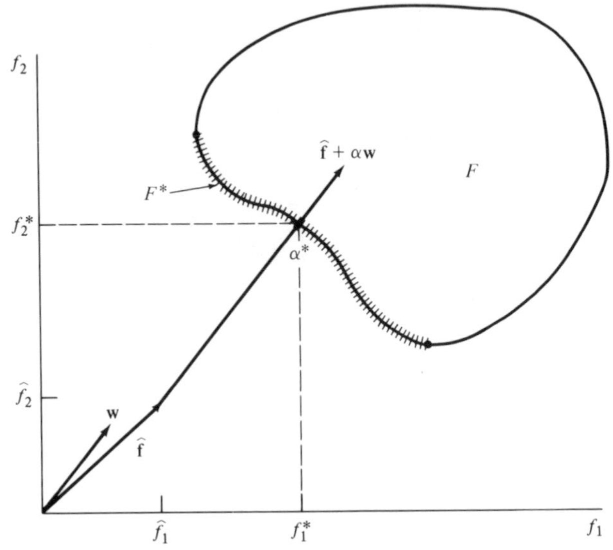

Figure 7.4 The goal attainment method.

the following problem:

$$\min \quad \alpha \tag{7.62}$$

$$\text{subject to} \quad \mathbf{x} \in X, \tag{7.63a}$$

$$\mathbf{f}(\mathbf{x}) - \alpha \mathbf{w} \leqslant \hat{\mathbf{f}}, \quad \mathbf{w} \geqslant \mathbf{0}, \tag{7.63b}$$

where α is a scalar variable unrestricted in sign. This has an advantage over ordinary goal programming in that fewer variables need to be dealt with. It can be easily shown that by setting $\hat{\mathbf{f}} = \mathbf{f}^*$ an optimal solution of (7.62)–(7.63) always exists, given any $\mathbf{w} \geqslant \mathbf{0}$, and that the set of noninferior solutions can be generated by varying $\mathbf{w} \geqslant \mathbf{0}$ even for nonconvex problems. The mechanism by which this method operates is illustrated for the two-objective case in Figure 7.4. Given $\mathbf{w}$ and $\hat{\mathbf{f}}$, the direction of the vector $\hat{\mathbf{f}} + \alpha \mathbf{w}$ can be determined. The problem (7.62)–(7.63) is equivalent to finding a feasible point on this vector in the objective space which is closest to the origin. Clearly this will be the first point at which $\hat{\mathbf{f}} + \alpha \mathbf{w}$ intersects the feasible region F in the objective space. Should this point of intersection exist, it would clearly be a noninferior solution.

Example 4: To illustrate, consider a two-objective nonconvex problem $f_1(\mathbf{x}) = (x_1 - 2)^2 + (x_2 - 1)^2 + 2$, $f_2(\mathbf{x}) = 9x_1 - (x_2 - 1)^2$, and $X = \{\mathbf{x} \in R^2 | \mathbf{x} \geqslant 0\}$. If the decision maker wants to achieve the goals $\hat{\mathbf{f}} = (1, 2)^{\mathrm{T}}$ and considers f_1 to be three times as important as f_2, then $\mathbf{w} = (\frac{3}{4}, \frac{1}{4})^{\mathrm{T}}$. The best-compromise solution, according to the goal attainment method, is given by solving

$$\min \quad \alpha \tag{7.64}$$

$$\text{subject to} \quad (x_1-2)^2 + (x_2-1)^2 + 2 - \tfrac{3}{4}\alpha \leqslant 1, \tag{7.65a}$$

$$x_1 - (x_2-1)^2 - \tfrac{1}{4}\alpha \leqslant 2, \tag{7.65b}$$

$$x_1, x_2 \geqslant 0.$$

Solving (7.64)–(7.65) analytically yields the best-compromise solution $\mathbf{x}^* = (2,1)^{\mathrm{T}}$, with $\alpha^* = \frac{4}{3}$.

7.3.3 Compromise Programming and the Method of the Displaced Ideal

Let us now return to the surrogate formulation of a multiobjective decision problem in (7.38). Here we shall maintain the preference structure which stipulates that the best-compromise solution is one which minimizes the combined deviation $d(\mathbf{f}(\mathbf{x}),\hat{\mathbf{f}})$ from the given levels $\hat{\mathbf{f}}$ as in (7.38).

To use this idea, three elements need to be determined:

i. the goal vector $\hat{\mathbf{f}}$,
ii. the weights of priority structure, and
iii. the choice of p which, in turn, determines the choice of measure of deviation.

We can expect the first two to be meaningfully supplied by the decision maker, although getting them may not be easy. On the other hand, the proper choice of p, and therefore the choice of *deviation* measure, is not at all obvious, due to the abstract nature of $d(\ ,\ )$, which is often difficult to relate to any real construct. In fact, only the absolute value norm (l_1 norm), the Euclidean norm (l_2 norm), and the Tchebycheff norm (l_∞ norm with $p=\infty$) represent geometrical concepts of distance that we may find meaningful. For simplicity, in the goal programming formulations in the preceding sections, only the l_1 norm is used.

Because of the difficulty in choosing p and $d(\ ,\ )$, Yu [1973] and Zeleny [1973] introduced the concepts of compromise solutions and compromise set, which Zeleny [1973, 1974, 1977] later combined with the concept of displaced ideal to form an interactive strategy for reducing a solution set until the best-compromise solution can conveniently be selected.

To employ the compromise solution, it is necessary to set the goal vector $\hat{\mathbf{f}} = \mathbf{f}^* = (f_1^*,\ldots,f_n^*)$, where as usual f_j^* represents the minimum possible value of f_j in the feasible region X (or F in the objective space). If monotonicity of preferences is assumed, i.e., the lower the value of f_j the better, then clearly $\mathbf{f}^*$ should represent an *ideal point* or a *utopia point*. If $\mathbf{f}^*$

is feasible there should be no doubt what the best-compromise solution should be. Such a fortunate case is, however, rare, and we normally have to be content with finding a solution that has the minimum deviation from the ideal $\mathbf{f}^*$.

Given a weight vector $\mathbf{w}$,[4] $\mathbf{x}_w^p$ is a *compromise solution* of an MDP with respect to p if and only if it solves

$$\min_{\mathbf{x}\in X}\left(d_p(\mathbf{f}(\mathbf{x}),\mathbf{f}^*) \triangleq \left\{ \sum_{j=1}^{n} w_j\left[f_j(\mathbf{x}) - f_j^* \right]^p \right\}^{1/p} \right) \tag{7.66}$$

or equivalently, for $1 \leqslant p < \infty$,

$$\min_{\mathbf{x}\in X}\left\{ \tilde{d}_p(\mathbf{f}(\mathbf{x}),\mathbf{f}^*) \triangleq \sum_{j=1}^{n} w_j\left(f_j(\mathbf{x}) - f_j^* \right)^p \right\}. \tag{7.67}$$

We note that (7.66) and (7.67) are equivalent problems for $1 \leqslant p < \infty$ since $d_p(\ ,\ )$ is an increasing function of $\tilde{d}_p(\ ,\ )$. Hence an optimal solution of the former is also optimal solution of the latter and vice versa. The *compromise set* X_w^c, given the weight $\mathbf{w}$, is defined as the set of all compromise solutions $\mathbf{x}_w^p$, $1 \leqslant p \leqslant \infty$. More precisely,

$$X_w^c \triangleq \{\mathbf{x} \in X \,|\, \mathbf{x} \text{ solves (7.66) or (7.67) given } \mathbf{w} \text{ for some } 1 \leqslant p \leqslant \infty\}. \tag{7.68}$$

By Theorem 4.14, if $\mathbf{w} > \mathbf{0}$, $\mathbf{x}_w^p$ is always a noninferior solution for any $1 \leqslant p < \infty$. It can also be shown that at least one $\mathbf{x}_w^\infty$ is noninferior (see Dindelbach and Dürr [1971]). Thus if we include only $\mathbf{x}_w^\infty$, which are noninferior in X_w^c, the compromise set X_w^c is a subset of the set of noninferior solutions X^*.

We can illustrate the compromise set graphically in the two objective linear cases as in Figure 7.5. Note that when equal weights are assigned to all objectives, i.e., $\mathbf{w} = (1/n, \ldots, 1/n)^{\mathrm{T}}$, $\mathbf{x}_w^2$ is the point where the geometrical (Euclidean) distance between $\mathbf{f}(\mathbf{x}_w^2)$ and $\mathbf{f}^*$ is smallest. Observe also that for the linear case, the compromise set X_w^c is completely determined if $\mathbf{x}_w^1$ and $\mathbf{x}_w^\infty$ are known. Indeed, for the two-objective problem with $\mathbf{w} > \mathbf{0}$, X_w^c is a set of points on the noninferior set F^* which lie between $\mathbf{x}_w^1$ and $\mathbf{x}_w^\infty$. For example, if $\mathbf{x}_w^1$ and $\mathbf{x}_w^\infty$ lie on the same noninferior edge, then $X_w^c = \{\mathbf{x} \,|\, \mathbf{x} = \alpha\mathbf{x}_w^1 + (1-\alpha)\mathbf{x}_w^\infty\}$. For problems with three or more objectives, Zeleny

---

[4] For best results it is suggested that the w_j be scaled so that the order of magnitudes of the terms in the summation in (7.66) or (7.67) be the same. For example, if the decision maker gives the weight vectors $\mathbf{w}^0$ with $\Sigma_{j=1}^n w_j^0 = 1$, $w_j \geqslant 0$, then we may, for example, use $w_j = w_j^0 / f_j^*$.

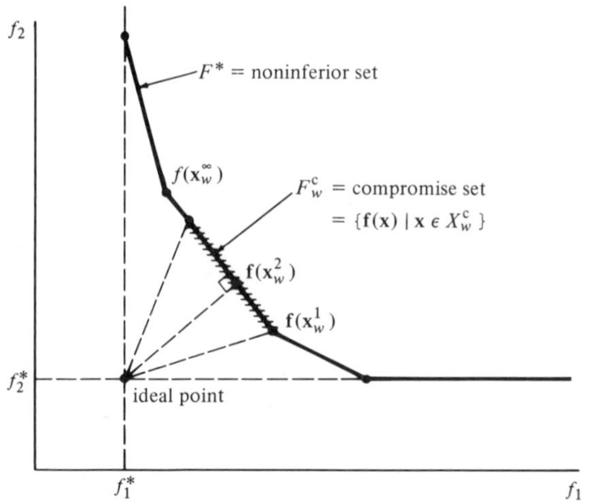

Figure 7.5 The compromise set in the objective space.

[1973] suggests that the compromise set X_w^c be approximated by the noninferior solutions of the following two-objective problem:

$$\min_{\mathbf{x} \in X} \left[\tilde{d}_1(\mathbf{f}(\mathbf{x}), \mathbf{f}^*), d_\infty(\mathbf{f}(\mathbf{x}), \mathbf{f}^*) \right]. \tag{7.69}$$

Note that $d_\infty(\mathbf{f}(\mathbf{x}), \mathbf{f}^*) = \max_{1 \leq j \leq n}\{w_j[f_j(\mathbf{x}) - f_j^*]\}$.

The compromise solution X_w^c is a reduced subset of X^*. Having obtained X_w^c, the assumed preference structure requires that the best-compromise solution be selected from this compromise set. If X_w^c is still too large to select the best-compromise solution from it, it should be reduced further. Zeleny [1973, 1977] suggests a number of complementary ways of reducing the compromise set. The decision maker may be asked to directly eliminate alternatives in X_w^c which appear to him inferior or to estimate a set of intervals $[a_j, b_j]$, $j = 1, \ldots, n$, within which each weight w_j should be. In the latter case, techniques such as Steuer's interval criterion weights method (Chapter 6) can be used to find the reduced set of X^* whose intersection with X_w^c contains the best-compromise solution. If the needed information cannot easily be elicited from the decision maker, the following reduction process, performed mostly by the analyst, is suggested.

First, while the compromise set X_w^c is generated by minimizing the combined distance from the ideal point $\mathbf{f}^*$, a similar compromise set $\overline{X}_w^c$ may also be generated by maximizing the combined distance from the *anti-ideal* or most undesirable point $\mathbf{f}^0$, where $f_j^0 = \max_{\mathbf{x} \in X} f_j(\mathbf{x})$. More precisely,

$$\overline{X}_w^c = \left\{ \mathbf{x} | \mathbf{x} \text{ solves } \max_{\mathbf{x} \in X} \sum_{j=1}^{n} \left(w_j \left[f_j^0 - f_j(\mathbf{x}) \right]^p \right)^{1/p}, \text{ for some } 1 \leq p \leq \infty \right\}. \tag{7.70}$$

The intersection $X_w^c \cap \bar{X}_w^c$ should then furnish a workable reduced compromise set.

The second method, suggested by Zeleny [1976], is based on the so-called displaced ideal. The ideal point $\mathbf{f}^*$ depends as it pragmatically should, among other things, on the set of alternatives X. After the set of alternatives in X to be considered is reduced to the compromise set X_w^c (after having been modified by the above procedures), the ideal point with respect to the new X_w^c should, therefore, displace the previous ideal point. The new ideal point $\tilde{\mathbf{f}}^*$ can be calculated from

$$\tilde{\mathbf{f}}_j^* = \min_{\mathbf{x} \in X_w^c} f_j(\mathbf{x}). \tag{7.71}$$

Using this new ideal point, the new compromise set $\tilde{X}_w^c$ can be constructed similar to the construction of X_w^c.

$$\tilde{X}_w^c \triangleq \left\{ \mathbf{x} | \mathbf{x} \text{ solves either } \min_{\mathbf{x} \in X_w^c} \sum_{j=1}^{n} w_j \left[f_j(\mathbf{x}) - \tilde{f}_j^* \right]^p, \ 1 \leq p < \infty, \right.$$

$$\left. \text{or } \min_{\mathbf{x} \in X_w^c} \max_{1 \leq j \leq n} \left(w_j \left[f_j(\mathbf{x}) - \tilde{f}_j^* \right] \right) \right\}. \tag{7.72}$$

Zeleny [1976] also argues that the relative importance of each objective depends not only on how the decision maker views these objectives in general (as reflected by the given w_js), but also on the context in which these objectives can assume values. This second component of relative importance is thus very much dependent on the set of alternatives we are working with. For possible procedures of modifying $\mathbf{w}$ to be used in (7.72), see Zeleny [1976].

Once a reduced compromise set $\tilde{X}_w^c$ is obtained, a search for the best-compromise solution can proceed again as before. By continuing the reduction of the compromise set using the displaced ideal, the (reduced) compromise set should eventually enclose the new ideal point, thus terminating the process.

To summarize, the method of displaced ideal has the following basic steps:

0. Ask the decision maker to give weights $\mathbf{w}^0$. Set $\tilde{X} = X$.
1. Find the ideal point $\mathbf{f}^*$ by solving $\min_{\mathbf{x} \in \tilde{X}} f_j(\mathbf{x})$ for each $j = 1, \ldots, n$. Then scale the weights $w_j = w_j^0 / f_j^*$.
2. Construct the compromise set X_w^c by finding the set of noninferior solutions of

$$\min_{\mathbf{x} \in \tilde{X}} \ \left(\tilde{d}_1(\mathbf{f}(\mathbf{x}), \mathbf{f}), d_\infty(\mathbf{f}(\mathbf{x}), \mathbf{f}^*) \right).$$

3. If the decision maker is able to select the best-compromise solution from X_w^c, or X_w^c contains $\mathbf{f}^*$, stop; the best-compromise solution is found. Otherwise go to step 4.

4. Reduce X_w^c by various means described earlier including finding the new ideal point by setting $\tilde{X} = X_w^c$, and go to step 1.

Further refinements and details of this method can be found in Zeleny [1976, 1977].

One final remark is noteworthy. Although Zeleny developed this method in the context of linear problems, it seems to be applicable, at least in principle, to general multiobjective decision problems.

7.3.4 The STEP Method

The STEP method (STEM) is perhaps one of the first linear multiobjective techniques to be developed. It was first described as the progressive orientation procedure [Benayoun and Tergny, 1969] and later elaborated by Benayoun et al. [1971].

This technique is based on the premise that the best-compromise solution has the minimum combined deviation from the ideal point $\mathbf{f}^*$, where $f_j^* = \min_{\mathbf{x} \in X} f_j(\mathbf{x})$. However, the method assumes that the decision maker has a pessimistic view or strong dislike of the "worst" component of the objectives. As such, it chooses the worst component of all individual deviations from the ideals of component objectives as the measure of combined deviation from the ideal point $\mathbf{f}^*$. Consequently, for a linear problem with $X = \{\mathbf{x} \in R^N \mid A\mathbf{x} \leqslant \mathbf{b}, \mathbf{x} \geqslant \mathbf{0}\}$ and $f_i(x) = \sum_{j=1}^N c_{ij} x_j$, $i = 1, \dots, n$, the surrogate mathematical programming problem to be solved is

$$\max_{\mathbf{x} \in X} d_\infty(\mathbf{f}(\mathbf{x}), \mathbf{f}^*), \tag{7.73}$$

where $d_\infty(\mathbf{f}(\mathbf{x}), \mathbf{f}^*) \triangleq \max_{1 \leqslant j \leqslant n} \{ w_j [f_j(\mathbf{x}) - f_j^*)] \}$.

Equivalently,

$$\max \quad \alpha \tag{7.74}$$

$$\text{subject to} \quad \mathbf{x} \in X, \tag{7.75a}$$

$$w_j [f_j(\mathbf{x}) - f_j^*] \leqslant \alpha, \qquad j = 1, \dots, n, \tag{7.75b}$$

where the normalized weights are computed from a payoff table (as we shall see shortly).

The STEP method is an interactive scheme that progressively elicits information from the decision maker primarily to modify the constraint set in (7.75a) and to slightly modify the weights w_j. This is done by constructing the so-called payoff table displaying values of objective functions at

$\mathbf{x}^1,\ldots,\mathbf{x}^n$, where $\mathbf{x}^j$ solves $\min_{\mathbf{x}\in X} f_j(\mathbf{x}), j=1,\ldots,n$. A typical payoff table is

	f_1	f_2	$\cdots$	f_j	$\cdots$	f_n
f_1	f_1^*	f_1^2	$\cdots$	f_1^j	$\cdots$	f_1^n
f_2	f_2^1	f_2^*		f_2^j	$\cdots$	f_2^n
$\vdots$	$\vdots$	$\vdots$		$\vdots$		$\vdots$
f_j	f_j^1	f_j^2	$\cdots$	f_j^*	$\cdots$	f_j^n
$\vdots$	$\vdots$	$\vdots$		$\vdots$		$\vdots$
f_n	f_n^1	f_n^2	$\cdots$	f_n^j	$\cdots$	f_n^*

where $f_j^* = f_j(\mathbf{x}^j)$ and $f_j^i = f_j(\mathbf{x}^i)$ for each $j=1,\ldots,n$, $i=1,\ldots,n$, and $i\neq j$. The original set of normalized weights $w_1,\ldots,w_n$ is computed from the payoff matrix by the formula

$$w_i = \mu_i \Big/ \sum_{k=1}^{n} \mu_k, \qquad i=1,\ldots,n, \tag{7.76}$$

where, for each $i=1,\ldots,n$,

$$\mu_i = \left[\left(\hat{f}_i - f_i^*\right)/\bar{f}_i\right]\left(\sum_{j=1}^{N} c_{ij}^2\right)^{-1/2}, \tag{7.77}$$

and where $\hat{f}_i = \max_{1\leqslant j\leqslant n} f_i(\mathbf{x}^j)$ is the maximum entry in row i, and $\bar{f}_i = \hat{f}_i$ if $\hat{f}_i > 0$, otherwise $\bar{f}_i = |f_i^*|$. At the qth iteration, the decision maker is asked to evaluate the solution at the $(q-1)$th iteration, and to compare the values $f_1(\mathbf{x}^{q-1}),\ldots,f_n(\mathbf{x}^{q-1})$ with the ideal $f_1^*,\ldots,f_n^*$. He is asked to indicate which objective can be increased and by how much, so that other objectives can be decreased from the current unsatisfactory levels. Suppose the decision maker chooses to sacrifice the $\hat{j}$ objective $f_{\hat{j}}$ by $\Delta f_{\hat{j}}$. The constraint set for the qth iteration is

$$X^q = X^{q-1}\cap\tilde{X}^q, \tag{7.78}$$

where

$$\tilde{X}^q = \left\{\mathbf{x}\in X \mid f_{\hat{j}}(\mathbf{x}) \leqslant f_{\hat{j}}(\mathbf{x}^{q-1}) + \Delta f_{\hat{j}} \text{ and } f_j(\mathbf{x}) \leqslant f_j(\mathbf{x}^{q-1}) \text{ for each } j\neq\hat{j}\right\}. \tag{7.79}$$

The weights should be modified accordingly by setting

$$w_{\hat{j}} = 0 \qquad \text{and} \qquad w_j = \mu_j \Big/ \sum_{k\neq\hat{j}} \mu_k, \tag{7.80}$$

where μ_k is given in (7.77). Consequently, the linear programming problem to be solved at the qth iteration is

$$\min \quad \alpha \tag{7.81}$$

$$\text{subject to} \quad \mathbf{x} \in X^q, \quad w_j[f_j(\mathbf{x}) - f_j^*] \leqslant \alpha, \qquad j \in J^q, \tag{7.82}$$

where $J^q \triangleq J^0 - \{\hat{j}\}$ and $J^0 \triangleq \{1,2,\ldots,n\}$.

The process is terminated when one of the following occurs: i) the decision maker is satisfied with the current solution, ii) there is no satisfactory objective in the current solution, or iii) when $q = n$. For the last two cases, no best-compromise solution exists. As Cohon and Marks [1975] remark, such an inconclusive result is rather unlikely. The inability of the decision maker to select a final decision does not necessarily mean that there is no best-compromise solution. Perhaps there is a lack of sufficient information available for the decision maker to make the necessary resolution. Even so, the method is simple to understand and to use.

The steps of the STEP method, then, are as follows:

Step 0: Find $f_j^* = \max_{\mathbf{x} \in X} f_j(\mathbf{x})$ for each $j = 1,\ldots,n$. Construct the payoff table and compute the initial set of weights $w_1,\ldots,w_n$. Set $q = 1$, $X^q = X$, and $J^0 = \{1,2,\ldots,n\}$.

Step 1: Formulate (7.81)–(7.82) and solve to obtain $\mathbf{x}_q^*$. Then compute $f_1(\mathbf{x}_q^*),\ldots,f_n(\mathbf{x}_q^*)$.

Step 2: Ask the decision maker to compare $(f_1(\mathbf{x}_q^*),\ldots,f_n(\mathbf{x}_q^*))^{\mathrm{T}}$ with $(f_1^*,\ldots,f_n^*)^{\mathrm{T}}$. a) If the decision maker is satisfied with the current solution, stop—the best-compromise solution has been found. b) If there is no satisfactory objective, stop—no best-compromise solution can be found by this method. c) If there are some satisfactory objectives, ask the decision maker to select one such objective $f_{\hat{j}}$ and the amount $\Delta f_{\hat{j}}$ to be sacrificed (increased) in exchange for an improvement of some unsatisfactory objectives.

Step 3: If $q = n$, stop—no best-compromise solution can be found by this method. Otherwise set $q = q + 1$, compute X^q, and modify the set of weights according to (7.78)–(7.79) and (7.80), respectively. Then go to step 1.

Example 5: Consider again the problem of minimizing

$$f_1(\mathbf{x}) = -x_1 - 2x_2, \qquad f_2(\mathbf{x}) = -3x_1 - x_2,$$

$$X = \left\{\mathbf{x} \in R^2 \,|\, x_1 + x_2 \leqslant 6,\, 2x_1 + x_2 \leqslant 9,\, 0 \leqslant x_1 \leqslant 4,\, 0 \leqslant x_2 \leqslant 5\right\}.$$

We want to solve this problem by the STEP method.

STEP 0: Solving $\min_{\mathbf{x} \in X} f_1(\mathbf{x})$ yields $\mathbf{x}^1 = (1,5)^{\mathrm{T}} \Rightarrow f_1^* = f_1(\mathbf{x}^1) = -11$ and $f_2^1 = f_2(\mathbf{x}^1) = -8$. Solving $\min_{\mathbf{x} \in X} f_2(\mathbf{x})$ yields $\mathbf{x}^2 = (4,1)^{\mathrm{T}} \Rightarrow f_2^* = f_2(\mathbf{x}^2) =$

-13 and $f_1^2 = f_1(\mathbf{x}^2) = -6$. Hence the payoff matrix for this problem is

	f_1	f_2		
f_1	-11	-8	$\rightarrow$	$\bar{f}_1 = \max\{-11, -8\} = -8,$
f_2	-6	-13	$\rightarrow$	$\bar{f}_2 = \max\{-6, -13\} = -6.$

Hence the original set of weights computed from (7.76)–(7.80) is $\mu_1 = 3/11\sqrt{5} \approx 0.122$, $\mu_2 = 7/13\sqrt{10} \approx 0.170$ and $w_1 = \mu_1/(\mu_1 + \mu_2) \approx 0.42$, $w_2 = \mu_2/(\mu_1 + \mu_2) \approx 0.58$.

Iteration 1

STEP 1: The first subproblem to be solved is

$$\min \quad \alpha \tag{7.83}$$

$$\text{subject to} \quad \mathbf{x} \in X^1 = X, \tag{7.84a}$$

$$-0.42x_1 - 0.84x_2 - 4.62 \leqslant \alpha, \tag{7.84b}$$

$$-1.74x_1 - 0.58x_2 - 7.54 \leqslant \alpha. \tag{7.84c}$$

Solving (7.83)–(7.84) using the simplex method yields $\mathbf{x}_1^* = (2.8, 3.2)^T$, $f_1(\mathbf{x}_1^*) = -9.2$, and $f_2(\mathbf{x}_1^*) = -11.6$.

STEP 2: Suppose the decision maker compares $(f_1(\mathbf{x}_1^*), f_2(\mathbf{x}_1^*))$ with the ideals $(-11, -13)$ and is willing to give up (increase) f_2 by one unit from -11.6 to -10.6 to improve f_1.

STEP 3: The new constraint set X^2 becomes

$$X^2 = X^1 \cap X^2 = X \cap X^2,$$

where

$$X^2 = \{\mathbf{x} \in R^2 | (-3x_1 - x_2) \leqslant -10.6, (-x_1, -2x_2) \leqslant -9.2\}.$$

In Figure 7.6 X^2 is shown as the shaded area. We also set the weight $w_2 = 0$; therefore $w_1 = 1$.

Iteration 2

STEP 1: We solve

$$\min \quad \alpha \tag{7.85}$$

$$\text{subject to} \quad \mathbf{x} \in X^2, \quad (-x_1 - 2x_2) - (-11) \leqslant \alpha, \tag{7.86}$$

which yields $\mathbf{x}_2 = (2.3, 3.7)^T$, $f_1(\mathbf{x}^2) = -9.7$, and $f_2(\mathbf{x}^2) = -10.6$.

STEP 2: If the decision maker is satisfied with the current solution, we stop the process, and the best-compromise solution is $\mathbf{x}^2$.

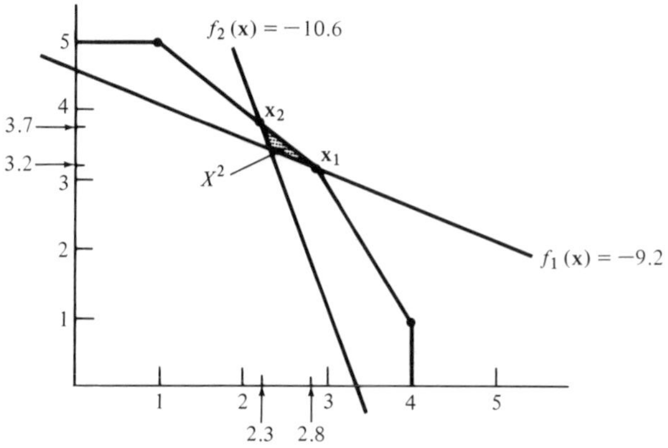

Figure 7.6 Modified constraint set for Example 5.

There have been several variations, extensions, and applications of the STEP method. Fichefet [1976] combined the basic features of goal programming and the STEP method to form the goal programming STEP method. Nijkamp and Spronk [1980] and Spronk and Telgen [1980] developed, respectively, an interactive multiple goal programming and an ellipsoidal interactive multiple goal programming, which exhibit not only the features of goal programming but also some of those of the STEP method. Choo and Atkins [1980] developed a method quite similar to the STEP method for solving multiobjective linear fractional problems. Johnson and Loucks [1980] combined the STEP method with computer display equipment, thereby making the interactive feature of the STEP method not only operational but also convenient. Finally Dinkelbach and Isermann [1980] modified the STEP method and applied it to the planning of an academic department.

7.3.5 The SEMOPS Method

The final method to be discussed in this class is called the *sequential multiobjective problem solving* (SEMOPS) technique, developed by Monarchi et al. [1973]. This is a nonlinear interactive method that relies on the minimization of deviation from the given goal levels. It differs, however, from other methods discussed thus far in that the goal levels elicited from the decision maker may be *intervals* rather than fixed points. Consequently, the measure of deviation from the goals is formulated differently from the *norm* measure used earlier. In fact, the measure is a function of the ratios of the actual levels and of the bounds of those interval goals.

Five types of goal level specifications are permitted and, consequently, five types of measures of deviations are suggested, as summarized in Table

Table 7.1 Suggested Measures of Deviation for Interval Goals

Type of goal specified by DM	Measure of deviation suggested
1. upper bound (at most): $f_j(\mathbf{x}) \leqslant b_j$	$d_j = f_j(\mathbf{x})/b_j$
2. lower bound (at least): $a_j \leqslant f_j(\mathbf{x})$	$d_j = a_j/f_j(\mathbf{x})$
3. equal: $f_j(\mathbf{x}) = A_j$	$d_j = \frac{1}{2}[f_j(\mathbf{x})/A_j + A_j/f_j(\mathbf{x})]$
4. within an interval: $a_j \leqslant f_j(\mathbf{x}) \leqslant b_j$	$d_j = [b_j/(a_j + b_j)](a_j/f_j(\mathbf{x}) + f_j(\mathbf{x})/b_j]$
5. outside an interval: $f_j(\mathbf{x}) \leqslant a_j, f_j(\mathbf{x}) \geqslant b_j,$ $a_j < b_j$	$d_j = [(a_j + b_j)/b_j][a_j/f_j(\mathbf{x}) + f_j(\mathbf{x})/b_j]^{-1}$

7.1. At the qth iteration the decision maker is asked not only to provide the interval goal levels but also to specify which objectives are to be kept strictly within the stated goals. Let $J = \{1,\ldots,n\}$. If the decision maker specifies the index set I^q such that all goals in I^q are to be kept strictly within the specified goals, then the surrogate problem to be solved at the qth iteration is

$$\min \quad \sum_{i \in J^q} d_i^q \tag{7.87}$$

$$\text{subject to} \quad \mathbf{x} \in X^q, \tag{7.88}$$

where $J^q = J - I^q$ and $X^q = \{\mathbf{x} \in X \mid f_j(\mathbf{x})$ are kept strictly within the specified goal levels for each $j \in I^q\}$.

Problem (7.87)–(7.88) is solved for the qth iteration $\mathbf{x}^q$ and $f_1(\mathbf{x}^q),\ldots,f_n(\mathbf{x}^q)$ are calculated. These values of objectives are presented to the decision maker. New goal level specifications and I^{q+1} are then elicited for the next iteration. The process is terminated whenever the decision maker is satisfied with the current solution. As in goal programming, the best-compromise solution obtained by this method is not necessarily noninferior.

Monarchi et al. [1973] also suggested that additional information may also be presented to the decision maker to assist him in finding the new goal levels. This information is obtained by solving as many auxiliary subproblems as the number of members of J^q. Each auxiliary subproblem is formulated as in (7.87)–(7.88), except that a goal on f_j, $j \in J^q$, is now put into the constraint set and the objective function is as in (7.87) minus d_j^q.

Monarchi et al. [1976] also combined the idea of SEMOPS with that of goal programming to develop the sequential information generator for multiple objective problems (SIGMOP), details of which will not be presented here.

7.4 Methods Based on Trade-offs

Like all other methods described in this chapter, the methods in this section require some form of interaction between the decision maker and the analyst, but unlike the others, interactions in this method are based on the concept of trade-off. Because of its importance, we first attempt to put this and some related concepts into perspective.

7.4.1 What Is a Trade-off?[5]

A trade-off, according to Webster's New World Dictionary is "an exchange, especially a giving up of one benefit, advantage, etc. in order to gain another regarded as more desirable." The term has been used freely in various multiobjective decision problems. In Section 4.9, we spoke of total trade-offs, partial trade-offs, and trade-off rates, and we developed expressions for computing these quantities. In Section 5.5, we discussed indifferent trade-offs or marginal rates of substitution. The way these trade-offs differ from one another and the contexts in which they are used are the subject of this section.

Total and Partial Trade-offs When there are more than two objectives (i.e., $n>2$), it is useful to make a distinction between *total* and *partial* trade-offs.

Given two feasible alternatives $\mathbf{x}^0$ and $\mathbf{x}^*$, the corresponding levels of objectives are $f(\mathbf{x}^0)=(f_1(\mathbf{x}^0),\ldots,f_n(\mathbf{x}^0))$ and $f(\mathbf{x}^*)=(f_1(\mathbf{x}^*),\ldots,f_n(\mathbf{x}^*))$, respectively. Denote the ratio of change between f_k and f_j by $T_{kj}(\mathbf{x}^0,\mathbf{x}^*)$, where

$$T_{kj}(\mathbf{x}^0,\mathbf{x}^*)=\left[f_k(\mathbf{x}^0)-f_k(\mathbf{x}^*)\right]/\left[f_j(\mathbf{x}^0)-f_j(\mathbf{x}^*)\right]. \tag{7.89}$$

Definitions. $T_{kj}(\mathbf{x}^0,\mathbf{x}^*)$ is said to be the *partial trade-off* involving f_k and f_j between $\mathbf{x}^0$ and $\mathbf{x}^*$ if $f_l(\mathbf{x}^0)=f_l(\mathbf{x}^*)$ for all $l=1,\ldots,n$, $l\neq k$ or j. On the other hand, if $f_l(\mathbf{x}^0)\neq f_l(\mathbf{x}^*)$ for at least one $l=1,\ldots,n$ and $l\neq k$ or j, then $T_{kj}(\mathbf{x}^0,\mathbf{x}^*)$ is called the *total trade-off* involving f_k and f_j between $\mathbf{x}^0$ and $\mathbf{x}^*$.

[5]This section is adapted from Haimes and Chankong [1979].

The terms "partial" and "total" are used analogously to partial and total derivatives. The partial trade-off can be found, for example, in constructing multiattribute utility functions or in constructing a family of indifference curves. It is also used in the surrogate worth trade-off method [Haimes and Hall, 1974] and in the interactive SWT, which are both discussed in the next chapter. Its principal value is that it enables the decision maker to compare changes in two objectives at a time, thus making it easier to assign preferences. Total trade-off is probably most often used in discrete multiobjective decision problems with a finite number of available alternatives. An interesting example of the total trade-off rate is the *trade-off vector* as described by Isermann [1978] and used in Zionts and Wallenius [1976] in their development of an interactive multiobjective algorithm for solving a linear multiobjective decision problem. Their trade-off vector is a column vector obtained from the reduced costs portion of the optimal multiple objective simplex tableau. Each component of this vector represents the change in each objective level per one unit change in the corresponding nonbasic variables.

For continuous problems, the following concepts are useful.

Definition. $T_{kj}(\mathbf{x}^0,\mathbf{x}^*)$ is said to be a *local total* (*partial*) *trade-off* involving f_k and f_j between $\mathbf{x}^0$ and $\mathbf{x}^*$ if $\mathbf{x}^0 \in X \cap N(\mathbf{x}^*)$ and $T_{kj}(\mathbf{x}^0,\mathbf{x}^*)$ is a total (partial) trade-off involving f_k and f_j between $\mathbf{x}^0$ and $\mathbf{x}^*$.

Definition. Given a feasible alternative $\mathbf{x}^*$ and a feasible direction $\mathbf{d}^*$ emanating from $\mathbf{x}^*$ (i.e., there exists $\alpha_0 > 0$ so that $\mathbf{x}^* + \alpha\mathbf{d}^* \in X$ for $0 \leqslant \alpha \leqslant \alpha_0$), we define the $f_k - f_j$ *total trade-off rate* at $\mathbf{x}^*$ along the direction $\mathbf{d}^*$ as

$$t_{kj}(\mathbf{x}^*,\mathbf{d}^*) = \lim_{\alpha \to 0} T_{kj}(\mathbf{x}^* + \alpha\mathbf{d}^*, \mathbf{x}^*). \tag{7.90}$$

Again a familiar example of this is the trade-off vector used by Isermann [1978] and Zionts and Wallenius [1976]. It represents the total trade-off rate along one of the edges of the feasible region emanating from the extreme point under study.

Assume all $f_j(\mathbf{x}^*)$ are continuously differentiable. It can easily be shown that

$$t_{kj}(\mathbf{x}^*,\mathbf{d}^*) = \left[\nabla f_k(\mathbf{x}^*)\cdot\mathbf{d}^*\right] / \left[\nabla f_j(\mathbf{x}^*)\cdot\mathbf{d}^*\right]. \tag{7.91}$$

If $\mathbf{d}_0^*$ is a feasible direction with the property that there exists $\bar{\alpha} > 0$ such that $f_l(\mathbf{x}^* + \alpha\mathbf{d}_0^*) = f_l(\mathbf{x}^*)$ for all $l \neq k$ or j and for all $0 \leqslant \alpha \leqslant \bar{\alpha}$, then we shall call the corresponding $t_{kj}(\mathbf{x}^*,\mathbf{d}^*)$ the *partial trade-off rate*.

To illustrate these concepts, consider a simplified water resources planning problem conceived by Reid and Vemuri [1971]. A multipurpose dam was to be constructed at a certain site. After preliminary analysis, it was

Table 7.2 Alternatives Appropriate for Final Decision

Alternative	Decision variables		Objective functions		
	x_1	x_2	Cost f_1	Water loss f_2	Storage capacity f_3
A	0.70	22.36	500	250	500
B	116.19	44.72	7,029	1000	3750
C	172.95	44.72	12,500	1000	5000

decided that three main objectives were suitable decision criteria:

to minimize the cost of construction f_1,

to minimize water loss f_2 (volume/year),

to maximize the total storage capacity f_3 of the reservoir.

It was further found that these decision criteria depend mainly on two variables: x_1, the total man-hours devoted to building the dam, and x_2, the mean radius of the lake impounded (in miles). Moreover, relationships between the decision criteria and these decision variables were found to be as follows:

$$f_1(x_1, x_2) = e^{0.01x_1}x_1^{0.02}x_2^2,$$
$$f_2(x_1, x_2) = 0.5x_2^2,$$
$$f_3(x_1, x_2) = e^{0.005x_1}x_1^{0.001}x_2^2.$$

From physical and geological considerations three alternatives, listed in Table 7.2, were considered appropriate candidates for final implementation. The corresponding trade-offs between the pairs of alternatives A/B, A/C, and B/C in Table 7.2 are given in Table 7.3.

To choose among *A*, *B*, and *C*, we compare them pairwise based on subjective value judgments of the trade-offs and the levels of the objective functions. Given an explicit set of alternatives, such as in the above example, trade-offs for each pair of those alternatives can easily be computed. The trade-offs between *A* and *B* and between *A* and *C* are examples of what we defined as total trade-off, since nonzero trade-offs occur for

Table 7.3 Trade-off Values

	f_1/f_2	f_1/f_3
A/B	8.7	2.0
A/C	16.0	2.7
B/C	∞	4.4

both pairs f_1/f_2 and f_1/f_3. Thus both numbers f_1/f_2 and f_1/f_3 must simultaneously play important roles in the subjective value judgment for deciding between A and B and between A and C. On the other hand, the trade-off between B and C is an example of partial trade-off, since $f_1/f_2=\infty$. Consequently, in deciding between B and C, apart from the levels of f_1, f_2, and f_3, only the value of f_1/f_3 is considered.

When alternatives are specified only implicitly, e.g., when there is no information available to limit the set of alternatives to a small finite number as in the above example, it is impractical if not impossible to compute trade-offs between every pair of alternatives. Decision making in this case should be carried out iteratively. Starting from an initial trial point, say $\mathbf{x}^0=(x_1^0, x_2^0)=(0.7, 22.4)$, our objective is to find a new point $\mathbf{x}^1$ that is preferred by the decision maker over $\mathbf{x}^0$. This is equivalent to moving in a certain direction in the x_1-x_2 plane (or decision variable space). Lacking adequate analytical tools, human judgment should be employed in choosing the direction to move, but before judgment can be used, it is necessary to know how the levels of the objective functions f_1, f_2, and f_3 are affected by such moves.

This is where the concept of trade-off rate is useful. The values of trade-off rates depend on the direction in which we move. For example, at $\mathbf{x}^0$, trade-off rates among f_1, f_2, and f_3 in the directions defined by $\mathbf{d}_1=(0.98, 0.19)$, $\mathbf{d}_2=(0.99997, 0.00798)$, and $\mathbf{d}_3=(1,0)$, all emanating from $\mathbf{x}^0$, are given in Table 7.4.

The trade-off rates in directions $\mathbf{d}_1$ and $\mathbf{d}_2$ are examples of total trade-off rates, whereas those in directions $\mathbf{d}_3$ are examples of partial trade-off rates. The trade-off rates in any given trial direction are critically important in presenting alternatives to the decision maker in the interactive phase of the multiobjective decision-making process. The main results of Section 4.9 provide the theoretical basis for computing these trade-off rates.

Intuitively, the term "trade-off" implies in decision making that one factor has to be sacrificed in order to obtain another (hence the negative T_{kj}). This implies the decision-making problem starts with a set of (local or global) noninferior alternatives (i.e., X is the set of local or global noninferior solutions). In comparison, we are generalizing the term to mean the

Table 7.4 Examples of Trade-off Rates

Direction	Trade-off rates f_1/f_2	Trade-off rates f_1/f_3
$\mathbf{d}_1$	5.31	1.46
$\mathbf{d}_2$	81.00	1.96
$\mathbf{d}_3$	∞	2.01

ratio of changes of two objectives; i.e., we allow T_{kj} to be positive for a pair k and j and for a pair $\mathbf{x}^0$ and $\mathbf{x}^*$. From the definitions,

a. $\mathbf{x}^*$ is noninferior in X if and only if for each $\mathbf{x} \in X$, there is at least one pair k and j (both dependent on $\mathbf{x}$) such that $T_{kj}(\mathbf{x}, \mathbf{x}^*)$ is negative; and
b. $\mathbf{x}^*$ is locally noninferior if and only if there exist a $\delta > 0$ such that $\mathbf{x} \in X \cap N(\mathbf{x}^*, \delta)$ and at least one pair k and j such that $T_{kj}(\mathbf{x}, \mathbf{x}^*)$ is negative.

Indifference Trade-off Given two alternatives $\mathbf{x}^0$ and $\mathbf{x}^*$, if $f(\mathbf{x}^0)$ and $f(\mathbf{x}^*)$ lie on the same indifference (isopreference) curve, the corresponding trade-off, whether total or partial, is usually known as the *indifference trade-off* or *marginal rate of substitution*, a term widely used in decision making today (see, for example, Haimes [1977], MacCrimmon and Wehrung [1977], and Section 5.5).

As we noted in Section 5.5, if $v(f_1, \ldots, f_n)$ is the corresponding value function, the family of indifference curves is given by

$$v(f_1, \ldots, f_n) = \text{const.} \tag{7.92}$$

Suppose we want to find the indifference trade-off rate between f_j and f_k at a fixed point $\mathbf{f}^*$ which lies on an indifference curve

$$v(f_1, \ldots, f_n) = v_1. \tag{7.93}$$

We can then reduce one degree of freedom by expressing, say, f_k as an implicit function of the remaining objectives (including f_j):

$$f_k = f_k(f_1, \ldots, f_{k-1}, f_{k+1}, \ldots, f_n). \tag{7.94}$$

Note that the particular functional form of f_k is dependent on the value of v_1. The indifference trade-off rate between f_k and f_j at $\mathbf{f}^*$, m_{kj}, is given by

$$m_{kj} = \left. \frac{\partial f_k(f_1, \ldots, f_{k-1}, f_{k+1}, \ldots, f_n)}{\partial f_j} \right|_{\mathbf{f} = \mathbf{f}^*}. \tag{7.95}$$

Alternatively, after using (7.93) and applying the chain rule, we have

$$m_{kj} \triangleq \frac{\partial v(\mathbf{f}^*)}{\partial f_j} \Big/ \frac{\partial v(\mathbf{f}^*)}{\partial f_k}. \tag{7.96}$$

Note that if m_{kj} is truly to represent a noninferior indifference trade-off rate, it must indeed be negative.

Objective and Subjective Trade-offs The terms "objective" and "subjective" are used to reflect the degree of human involvement in evaluating trade-offs [Ackoff and Sasieni, 1968]. If a trade-off is calculated using solely the internal structure of the system under study and is feasible, it is called an *objective* trade-off (or sometimes marginal rate of transformation). If, on the other hand, the trade-off is determined solely by the decision maker, who at times has to ignore the internal behavior of the system and evaluate trade-offs to satisfy certain preference criteria (e.g., indifference criterion or preferred proportional criterion—see, for example, MacCrimmon and Wehrung [1977]), it is called a *subjective* trade-off. Subjective trade-offs are used most often in decision making based on the concepts of utility function or preference. Geoffrion's interactive procedure [Geoffrion et al., 1972], for example, relies on subjective trade-off analysis; that is, it requires subjective determination of the marginal rate of substitution or indifference trade-off, based on predetermined preference criteria. In contrast, in objective trade-off analysis it is the trade-offs that are chosen in advance, and the preferences are assigned accordingly, generally an easier task. In a large and complex decision-making problem in which the effect of the internal structure on decision making is significant and trade-off values can be obtained in a systematic way, an objective trade-off analysis is naturally preferred. The objectively determined value of a trade-off is more realistic and, most importantly, guaranteed to be feasible, since it is determined from the characteristics of the system itself.

A major obstacle to implementation of objective trade-off analysis arises in problems with a large set of feasible alternatives, e.g., when X is infinite. This is the lack of an easy or systematic way of evaluating the trade-offs required. The theoretical development in Section 4.9, however, allows the systematic determination of objective trade-offs to be not only possible but also convenient for certain types of problems. Zionts and Wallenius [1976] also rely on objective trade-off analysis, as we shall now see.

7.4.2 The Zionts–Wallenius Method

Zionts and Wallenius [1976, 1980] developed an interactive procedure for handling the class of multiobjective decision problems having the following characteristics:

i. the constraint set is defined by linear constraints,
ii. the objective functions are either linear or convex, and
iii. the (implicit) value function is either linearly additive or a concave function of linear objective functions. It is also assumed to be a monotone decreasing function of each objective.

The interactive feature—and hence the best-compromise solution—derives from the use of total trade-offs.

The basic feature of this interactive scheme is best described in terms of linear problems. Let X be a convex polyhedron defined by linear constraints, i.e., $X \triangleq \{\mathbf{x} \in R^N \mid A\mathbf{x} = \mathbf{b},\ \mathbf{x} \geqslant \mathbf{0}\}$, where A is an $m \times N$ matrix of full rank; and let the objective function f_i be linear and defined as $f_i(\mathbf{x}) = \sum_{j=1}^{N} c_{ij} x_j$, $i = 1, \ldots, n$. Also let the (implicit) value function be of a linear additive form:

$$v(f_1,\ldots,f_n) = -\sum_{i=1}^{n} \lambda_i f_i, \tag{7.97}$$

where $\sum_{i=1}^{n}\lambda_i = 1$ and $\lambda_i > 0$, $i=1,\ldots,n$, and are unknown. Note that the negative sign and the positivity of λ_i are necessary to ensure that v is a monotone decreasing function of each f_i. Then the surrogate problem we wish to solve (to find the best-compromise solution) is

$$\max_{\mathbf{x}\in X} v(f_1,\ldots,f_n) = -\sum_{i=1}^{n}\lambda_i f_i(\mathbf{x}) \quad \text{or} \quad \min_{\mathbf{x}\in X} -v(f_1,\ldots,f_n) = \sum_{i=1}^{n}\lambda_i f_i(\mathbf{x}). \tag{7.98}$$

Solving (7.98) is equivalent to finding an optimal weight λ_i^* such that the best-compromise solution is an optimal solution of the familiar weighting problem (7.98) with $\boldsymbol{\lambda}$ being replaced by $\boldsymbol{\lambda}^*$. The basic difference between this and other methods that aim at determining optimal weights (see, for example, the HOPE method of Ho [1979]) is in the type of information exchanged between the decision maker and the analyst, and the way in which it is used to bring about the best-compromise solution.

Even if the exact value of the λ_is is unknown, (7.98) is still nothing more than a linear programming problem with at least one solution lying on one of the extreme points or extreme rays of X. Moreover, since (7.98) is just a weighting problem, its solution must be a noninferior solution of the original multiobjective decision problem (see Theorems 4.5 and 4.6). Consequently, in searching for the best-compromise solution based on (7.98), one need only search the set of all noninferior extreme points or extreme rays of X. The methods of exploring adjacent noninferior extreme points (Section 6.2.3) are quite useful for this purpose.

Now consider a noninferior extreme point $\mathbf{x}^0$ and its corresponding simplex tableau (cf. Section 6.9.3),

$$
\begin{array}{c|cccc|cccc|c}
\text{Basic variables} & & \mathbf{x}_B^0 & & & & \mathbf{x}_D^0 & & & \text{Constants} \\
x_{\bar{1}}^0 & 1 & & & & \bar{a}_{1,\overline{m+1}} & \bar{a}_{1,\overline{m+2}} & \cdots & \bar{a}_{1,\bar{N}} & \bar{b}_1 \\
x_{\bar{2}}^0 & & 1 & & & \bar{a}_{2,\overline{m+1}} & \bar{a}_{2,\overline{m+2}} & \cdots & \bar{a}_{2,\bar{N}} & \bar{b}_2 \\
\vdots & & & \ddots & & \vdots & \vdots & & \vdots & \vdots \\
x_{\bar{m}}^0 & & & & 1 & \bar{a}_{m,\overline{m+1}} & \bar{a}_{m,\overline{m+2}} & \cdots & \bar{a}_{m,\bar{N}} & \bar{b}_m \\
\hline
-f_1 & & & & & \bar{c}_{1,\overline{m+1}} & \bar{c}_{1,\overline{m+2}} & \cdots & \bar{c}_{1,\bar{N}} & -\bar{f}_1 \\
-f_2 & & & & & \bar{c}_{2,\overline{m+1}} & \bar{c}_{2,\overline{m+2}} & & \bar{c}_{2,\bar{N}} & -\bar{f}_2 \\
\vdots & & & & & \vdots & \vdots & & \vdots & \vdots \\
-f_n & & & & & \bar{c}_{n,\overline{m+1}} & \bar{c}_{n,\overline{m+1}} & \cdots & \bar{c}_{n,\bar{N}} & -\bar{f}_n
\end{array}
$$

Let J_D^0 be the set of indices for the nonbasic columns, i.e.,

$$J_D^0=\{\overline{m+1},\overline{m+2},\ldots,\overline{N}\}\subset J\triangleq\{1,2,\ldots,N\}.$$

Then for any nonbasic column $j\in J_D^0$ $\bar{c}_{i,j}$ represents the rate of change of f_i per one unit increase in the nonbasic variable x_j as it enters the basis. Consequently, the column vector $\bar{\mathbf{c}}_j$ represents the total trade-off rate vector along the direction of the extreme edge emanating from $\mathbf{x}^0$ as x_j increases from zero. From (7.91) and (7.97) it is clear that if the decision maker prefers to make this trade (i.e., if he is willing to move from $\mathbf{x}^0$ along the edge resulting from introducing x_j into the basis), then we must have

$$-\sum_{i=1}^{n}\lambda_i\bar{c}_{ij}>0 \tag{7.99}$$

to ensure that v is increasing in that direction. On the other hand, if the decision maker would prefer not to make a trade,

$$\sum_{i=1}^{n}\lambda_i\bar{c}_{ij}<0, \tag{7.100}$$

and if the decision maker is indifferent to the trade,

$$\sum_{i=1}^{n}\lambda_i\bar{c}_{ij}=0. \tag{7.101}$$

With these observations, the basic steps of the method of Zionts and Wallenius should be clear. A summary of the steps follows:

Step 0: Select a convenient value of $\lambda_i>0$ and solve (7.98) to find an initial noninferior extreme point. Set the iteration index $k=0$.

Step 1: Use any method described in Section 6.2.3 or the method Zionts and Wallenius suggest to find all adjacent noninferior extreme points to $\mathbf{x}^k$ that have not been considered before, i.e., find all nonbasic columns which lead to adjacent noninferior extreme points that have not been considered before. Let $J(\mathbf{x}^k)$ be the index set of such nonbasic columns.

Step 2: For each $j\in J(\mathbf{x}^k)$, present the trade-offs given by $\bar{\mathbf{c}}_j^k$ to the decision maker and ask him if he prefers to make the trade. For each yes answer formulate the constraint as in (7.99), for each no answer formulate the constraint as in (7.100), and for each "I don't know," formulate the constraint as in (7.101). If the answer is "no" or "I don't know" for each $j\in J(\mathbf{x}^k)$, stop: The current noninferior extreme point is the best-compromise solution. Otherwise proceed to step 3.

Step 3: Use the simplex method to find a feasible solution of the system of inequalities (7.99)–(7.101) generated during this and all previous iterations and satisfying the conditions

$$\sum_{i=1}^{n} \lambda_i = 1 \qquad \text{and} \qquad \lambda_i > 0, \quad i = 1, \ldots, n. \tag{7.102}$$

Let this feasible solution be $\boldsymbol{\lambda}^{k+1}$. Solve (7.98) when $\boldsymbol{\lambda} = \boldsymbol{\lambda}^{k+1}$ to get $\mathbf{x}^{k+1}$. Set $k = k+1$ and return to step 1.

Example 6: Consider the problem of Example 6 of Chapter 6 where $f_1(\mathbf{x}) = -x_1 - 2x_2$, $f_2(\mathbf{x}) = -x_1 + 2x_3$, and $f_3 = x_1 - x_3$, with $X = \{\mathbf{x} \in R^3 \mid x_1 + x_2 \leqslant 1, x_2 \leqslant 2, -x_1 - x_2 + x_3 = 4, \mathbf{x} \geqslant \mathbf{0}\}$. For illustrative purposes, let us assume that

$$v(f_1, f_2, f_3) = -0.2f_1 - 0.2f_2 - 0.6f_3. \tag{7.103}$$

To apply the algorithm we first select $\boldsymbol{\lambda} = (\frac{1}{3}, \frac{1}{3}, \frac{1}{3})^{\mathrm{T}}$ and solve (7.98) to get the optimal simplex tableau

Basis	x_1	x_2	x_3	x_4	x_5	x_6	Constant
x_1	1		0	1	-1		3
x_2		1	0	0	1		2
x_6			1	1	0	1	1
$-f_1$			0	1	1		7
$-f_2$			2	1	-1		3
$-f_6$			-1	-1	1		-3

The corresponding noninferior extreme point is $\mathbf{x}^0 = (3, 2, 0)^{\mathrm{T}}$. Employing Theorem 6.6 to find the nonbasic columns corresponding to noninferior extreme points leads to the following tableau:

Basis	ε_4	ε_5	ε_6	v_1	v_2	v_3	Constant
ε_3	1			0	-2	1	1
ε_4		1		-1	-1	1	1
ε_5			1	-1	1	-1	1

Each ε_3, ε_4, and ε_5 can be pivoted into the nonbasic set, indicating that each ε_3, ε_4, ε_5 can be made equal to zero. By Theorem 6.6 columns 3–5 in the first tableau lead to adjacent noninferior extreme points. Set $J(\mathbf{x}^0) = \{3, 4, 5\}$. The columns $(0, 2, -1)^{\mathrm{T}}$, $(1, 1, -1)^{\mathrm{T}}$, and $(1, -1, 1)^{\mathrm{T}}$ thus represent the total trade-off rate vectors.

The decision maker is asked if he is willing to make the following trade:

a. Increase f_2 by two units to get a one-unit decrease in f_3, while f_1 remains unchanged. According to (7.103), the decision maker should say yes since $-[0(0.2) + 2(0.2) - 1(0.6)] > 0$, indicating a decrease in value function.

b. Decrease f_3 by one unit for an increase of both f_1 and f_2 by one unit each. Again according to (7.103), the decision maker should say yes since $-[1(0.2)+1(0.2)-1(0.6)]>0$.
c. Decrease f_2 by one unit for an increase of both f_1 and f_3 by one unit each. The decision maker according to (7.103) should answer no since $-[1(0.2)-1(0.2)+1(0.6)]<0$.

We have

$$-\lambda_1-2\lambda_2+\lambda_3>0, \tag{7.104a}$$

$$-\lambda_1-\lambda_2+\lambda_3>0, \tag{7.104b}$$

$$-\lambda_1+\lambda_2-\lambda_3<0, \tag{7.104c}$$

and also

$$\lambda_1+\lambda_2+\lambda_2=1, \qquad \lambda_1,\lambda_2,\lambda_3>0. \tag{7.105}$$

A feasible solution of (7.104)–(7.105) is $\boldsymbol{\lambda}^1=(0.25,0.10,0.65)^T$. We now solve (7.98) using $\boldsymbol{\lambda}=\boldsymbol{\lambda}^1$. The optimal tableau is then

Basis	x_1	x_2	x_3	x_4	x_5	x_6	Constants
x_1	1	1	-1		-1		2
x_2		1	0		1		2
x_4		0	1	1	0	1	1
$-f_1$			-1		1	-1	6
$-f_2$			1		-1	-1	2
$-f_3$			0		1	1	-2

Again using Theorem 6.6, we find that columns 3, 5, and 6 lead to noninferior extreme points but that column 6 leads to the noninferior extreme point already considered, so we consider only columns 3 and 5. Continuing to question the decision maker, we should find that he is unwilling to move along any of the extreme edges offered since

$$-[-1(0.2)+1(0.2)+0(0.6)]=0, \qquad -[1(0.2)-1(0.2)+1(0.6)]<0.$$

Hence the current noninferior extreme point $\mathbf{x}^1=(2,2,0)^T$ can be taken to be the best-compromise solution.

Observe that the convergence property of this method is similar to that of the algorithm for finding noninferior solutions for linear problems described in Chapter 6.

The methods can be extended to convex objective functions or concave value functions of linear objective functions by linear piecewise approximations. The interested reader is referred to Zionts and Wallenius [1976, 1980]. For extensions of the methods to linear problems with discrete variables see Zionts [1975, 1976, 1977a, b] and Villarreal et al. [1980].

7.4.3 Geoffrion's Method and Its Variants

An interactive method first developed by Geoffrion [1970] and further elaborated by Geoffrion et al. [1972] is designed for solving relatively general multiobjective decision problems. Unlike the method discussed in Section 7.4.2, it is predicated on the concept of subjective indifference trade-offs. The existence of a value-function representation of the underlying preference structure is assumed (although its true form is never required), and the surrogate problem to be solved to find the best-compromise solution is

$$\begin{aligned}&\max \quad v(f_1(\mathbf{x}),\ldots,f_n(\mathbf{x}))\\&\text{subject to} \quad \mathbf{x}\in X,\end{aligned} \tag{7.106}$$

where X is the constraint set defined as $X \triangleq \{\mathbf{x}\in R^N \mid g_i(\mathbf{x})\leq 0,\ i=1,\ldots,n\}$. The basic assumptions made for this method are i) all functions are differentiable, ii) X is compact, and iii) v is a concave function on X.

Viewing (7.106) as a nonlinear programming problem, Geoffrion et al. [1972] follow the familiar strategy of nonlinear programming of finding the best direction of search (often the direction of steepest ascent) and the optimal step size in that direction. More specifically, adopting the Frank–Wolfe nonlinear programming algorithm, there are two optimization problems to be solved in the qth iteration, where the current solution is $\mathbf{x}^q$.

1. First we solve the direction-finding subproblem P_1:

$$\begin{aligned}&\max \quad \nabla_x v(f_1(\mathbf{x}^q),\ldots,f_n(\mathbf{x}^q))\cdot\mathbf{y}\\&\text{subject to} \quad \mathbf{y}\in X\end{aligned} \tag{7.107}$$

   to get optimal solution $\mathbf{y}^q$, so that the steepest ascent direction from $\mathbf{x}^q$ can be determined as

$$\mathbf{d}^q=\mathbf{y}^q-\mathbf{x}^q. \tag{7.108}$$

   The compactness of X and the continuity of all functions ensure that P_1 has an optimal solution.

2. Next we solve the step-size subproblem P_2:

$$\max_{1\leq\alpha\leq 1} \quad v(f_1(\mathbf{x}^q+\alpha\mathbf{d}^q),\ldots,f_n(\mathbf{x}^q+\alpha\mathbf{d}^q)) \tag{7.109}$$

   to determine the optimal move along $\mathbf{d}^q$ by obtaining the step size α^q.

The new iteration begins by updating the solution from $\mathbf{x}^q$ to $\mathbf{x}^{q+1}$, where $\mathbf{x}^{q+1}=\mathbf{x}^q+\alpha^q\mathbf{d}^q$. In theory the optimal solution is reached when no improvement in v is achieved in any feasible direction emanating from the current solution. This is equivalent to satisfying the first-order necessary conditions for optimality. Together with the concavity of v this guarantees optimality. In practice, this is whenever the new solution $\mathbf{x}^{q+1}$ does not differ substantially from $\mathbf{x}^q$, i.e., $\|\mathbf{x}^{q+1}-\mathbf{x}^q\|$ is smaller than some specified small positive number. Observe that the best-compromise solution produced by this method is not necessarily noninferior unless v is known to be monotonically decreasing for each f_j, $j=1,\ldots,n$.

The virtue of this approach is that it requires only local knowledge of v, namely, the gradient of v at $\mathbf{x}^q$, or $\nabla_x v(\mathbf{f}(\mathbf{x}^q))$, and the value of v along a certain direction. Getting this local information necessary to solving P_1 and P_2 is where the interactive feature of the method comes into play.

In eliciting necessary information from the decision maker to estimate the gradient $\nabla_x v(\mathbf{f}(\mathbf{x}))$, we observe a close relationship between the gradient and indifference trade-offs defined in (7.96). Clearly the gradient of $v(\mathbf{f}(\mathbf{x}))$ with respect to $\mathbf{x}$ at $\mathbf{x}^q$ is defined as a row vector

$$\nabla_x v(\mathbf{f}(\mathbf{x}^q)) \triangleq \left(\frac{\partial v(\mathbf{f}(\mathbf{x}^q)}{\partial x_1},\ldots,\frac{\partial v(\mathbf{f}(\mathbf{x}^q)}{\partial x_N}\right), \tag{7.110}$$

or, by the chain rule and some simplification,

$$\nabla_x v(\mathbf{f}(\mathbf{x}^q)) = \sum_{i=1}^{n}\frac{\partial v(\mathbf{f}^q)}{\partial f_i}\nabla_x f_i(\mathbf{x}^q). \tag{7.111}$$

Taking f_1 as the reference criterion with $\partial v(\mathbf{f}^q)/\partial f_1 \neq 0$ (the choice of f_1 is arbitrary) and noting (7.96), we can write (7.111)

$$\nabla_x v(\mathbf{f}(\mathbf{x}^q)) = \frac{\partial v(\mathbf{f}^q)}{\partial f_1}\sum_{i=1}^{n} m_{1j}^q \nabla_x f_i(\mathbf{x}^q), \tag{7.112}$$

where m_{1j}^q is the indifference trade-off rate at the qth iteration between f_1 and f_i. The objective function of P_1 is then equivalent to maximizing

$$\sum_{i=1}^{n} m_{1i}^q \nabla_x f_i(\mathbf{x}^q)\cdot\mathbf{y}. \tag{7.113}$$

The only quantities that need to be determined in (7.113) are the indifference trade-offs or marginal rates of substitution m_{1j}^q, $i=2,\ldots,n$. These have to be elicited from the decision maker who, in principle, has to estimate such trade-offs subjectively. In practice, we often find that the decision maker has difficulty accomplishing such a task unaided [Wallenius, 1975]. Realizing this difficulty, Dyer [1972] developed a time-sharing scheme which aims to decrease the difficulty of the problem. Rosinger [1980] suggested a family of alternative procedures for eliciting this type of information.

In solving P_2 the decision maker must also make another value judgment. Geoffrion et al. [1972] suggested that the decision maker be asked to evaluate a two-dimensional diagram—the computed values of $f_j(\mathbf{x}^q+\alpha\mathbf{d}^q)$, $j=1,\ldots,n$, vs α. He is then asked to locate the best α according to his preference. Even with this graphic aid, the decision maker may have difficulty estimating the optimal step size. This coupled with the slow rate of convergence, especially near the optimum (which is a common characteristic of a nonlinear feasible direction algorithm such as in the Frank–Wolfe method), has inspired the development of a few variations of this approach. Two of these, due to Oppenheimer [1978] and Musselman and Talavage [1980], attempt to solve (7.106) relying on subjective indifference trade-offs elicited from the decision maker. They differ, however, in the way in which this information is used to find an improved point for the next iteration.

Instead of solving P_1 and P_2, Oppenheimer [1978] suggested that a proxy function of known form (but with unknown parameter) be used to replace $v(\mathbf{f}(\mathbf{x}))$ locally. This function, denoted $p(\mathbf{f})$, should have the same general characteristics as $v(\mathbf{f}(\mathbf{x}))$ (at least locally at $\mathbf{x}^q$): the function is concave on X, and $\nabla_f p(\mathbf{f})$ is colinear with $\nabla_f v(\mathbf{f}(\mathbf{x}))$ at $\mathbf{x}^q$ and $\mathbf{x}^{q-1}$, implying that

$$m_{1j}^k = \frac{\partial v(\mathbf{f}(\mathbf{x}^k))}{\partial f_j} \Big/ \frac{\partial v(\mathbf{f}(\mathbf{x}^k))}{\partial f_1} = \frac{\partial p(\mathbf{f}(\mathbf{x}^k))}{\partial f_j} \Big/ \frac{\partial p(\mathbf{f}(\mathbf{x}^k))}{\partial f_1} \tag{7.114}$$

for each $j=2,\ldots,n$ and $k=q,\ q-1$. This means that although the form of $p(\mathbf{f})$ may be fixed, its parameters have to be determined at every iteration using knowledge of m_{1j}.

Thus by solving

$$\max_{\mathbf{x}\in X} \quad p(\mathbf{f}(\mathbf{x})) \tag{7.115}$$

to obtain $\mathbf{x}^{q+1}$, it can be shown (see Oppenheimer [1978]) that $v(\mathbf{x}^{q+1}) > v(\mathbf{x}^q)$. Consequently, the method offers an alternative way of generating a sequence of improved solutions which converge to the best-compromise solution. The process is again terminated whenever the new iteration does not produce a solution that is substantially different from the previous one. Convergence of the method to the best-compromise solution has been discussed by Oppenheimer [1978], who suggested using the sum-of-exponents or sum-of-powers for $p(\mathbf{f}(\mathbf{x}))$. For example, we may use a sum-of-exponents function

$$p(\mathbf{f}) = -\sum_{i=1}^{n} \lambda_i e^{+\alpha_i f_i}, \tag{7.116}$$

where λ_1 is set arbitrarily at unity and the remaining $2n-1$ variables are determined from the $2n-2$ equations in (7.114) and an additional equation to be determined from the third point, say $\mathbf{x}^{q-2}$.

A recent variation of the Geoffrion method, which also relies on subjective indifference trade-offs, is due to Musselman and Talavage [1980]. Here the indifference trade-offs obtained from the decision maker are used to define a cutting plane which removes a portion of the feasible region containing points that have lower values of v than at the current point $\mathbf{x}^q$.

Because of the concavity of v,

$$v(\mathbf{f}) \leqslant v(\mathbf{f}^q) + \nabla_{\mathbf{f}} v(\mathbf{f}^q) \cdot (\mathbf{f} - \mathbf{f}^q) \tag{7.117}$$

or

$$\sum_{j=1}^{n} m_{1j}^q (f_j - f_j^q) \geqslant [v(\mathbf{f}) - v(\mathbf{f}^q)] / \alpha^q \tag{7.118}$$

and $\alpha^q = \partial v(\mathbf{f}^q)/\partial f_1$. It is assumed, without loss of generality, that $\alpha^q > 0$.

Since we are interested in finding a better point than the current one, we should henceforth want to move within the region where $v(\mathbf{f}) \geqslant v(\mathbf{f}^q)$. From (7.118), this region is defined by

$$-g_{m+q} \triangleq \sum_{j=1}^{n} m_{1j}^q (f_j - f_j^q) \geqslant 0, \tag{7.119}$$

which defines a cutting plane called the *trade-off cut* by Musselman and Talavage [1980]. Thus, for each iteration, we generate one more constraint of the form (7.119) to reduce the constraint set further. The constraint set to be searched for the $(q+1)$th iteration is then

$$X^q = \{\mathbf{x} \in R^N \mid g_i(\mathbf{x}) \leqslant 0, i = 1, \ldots, m+q\}. \tag{7.120}$$

In finding the next point $\mathbf{x}^{q+1}$ from within X^q the proposed method goes through the two usual steps—finding the direction of search and the step size. The direction of search used here, however, is not the direction of steepest ascent but rather a usable direction of improving v that attempts to move to the center of the region X^q. We wish to make the next trade-off cut as large as possible. The direction is obtained simply by solving a linear programming problem equivalent to the minimax problem:

$$\min \quad \varepsilon \tag{7.121}$$

$$\text{subject to} \quad g_i(\mathbf{x}^q) + \nabla_x g_i(\mathbf{x}^q) \cdot \mathbf{d} \leqslant \varepsilon, \quad i = 1, \ldots, m+q \tag{7.122a}$$

$$-1 \leqslant d_j \leqslant 1, \quad j = 1, \ldots, N. \tag{7.122b}$$

If the optimal $\varepsilon^* \geqslant 0$, then the best-compromise solution is found, since there is no feasible direction in X^q where v can be further improved. If, on the other hand, the optimal $\varepsilon^* < 0$, then the optimal direction $\mathbf{d}^q$ is a feasible movement in X^q; hence, a direction of improving v is ensured by the trade-off cut.

Having found the direction of search $\mathbf{d}^q$, we again have to determine our optimal move along $\mathbf{d}^q$. Methods discussed earlier can be used. Musselman and Talavage [1980] suggest using trial and error. A trial point $\hat{\mathbf{x}} = \mathbf{x}^q + \lambda \mathbf{d}^q$ is selected and the quantity $\beta = \alpha \nabla_x v(\mathbf{f}(\hat{\mathbf{x}})) \cdot \lambda \mathbf{d}^q = \Sigma_{j=1}^n \hat{m}_{1j} \nabla_x f(\hat{\mathbf{x}}) \cdot \alpha(\lambda \mathbf{d}^q)$ is computed by eliciting $\hat{m}_{1j}$ from the decision maker. Then λ is contracted or enlarged by a proper amount, depending on whether $\beta < 0$ or $\beta > 0$, respectively. This is repeated if the peak of v along $\mathbf{d}^q$ is reached or exceeded, that is, if $\beta = 0$ or changes sign, respectively. The corresponding value of λ is noted, and the next point is calculated from $\mathbf{x}^{q+1} = \mathbf{x}^q + \lambda \mathbf{d}^q$. The $(q+1)$th iteration can now begin.

This method, like all of its predecessors, relies heavily on a subjective determination of indifference trade-offs, which has often been questioned from the practical viewpoint. Whether it is a viable method in practice remains to be tested.

7.5 Summary

The multiobjective decision problems treated in this and the previous chapter have two distinguishing characteristics: Two sets of variables—decision variables and decision criteria—are related to one another by a set of means–ends relationships (objective functions), and the set of alternatives is given implicitly in terms of causal relationships and constraints on the decision variables. The techniques presented in this chapter attempt to find the best-compromise solution—that most satisfactory to the decision maker—rather than just noninferior solutions.

We adopted a simple three-way classification based on the type of preference information elicited from the decision maker. In the first group are methods that require complete knowledge of the decision maker's global preference structure, expressed in the form of the value or utility function. An ad hoc integration of multiattribute value or utility functions, appropriate mathematical programming algorithms, and Geoffrion's bicriterion method typify these techniques. The so-called PROTRADE method, developed by Goicoechea et al. [1976, 1977] for problems with normally distributed coefficients in the objective functions, also relies on, among other things, complete knowledge of the multiattribute utility function. Methods in this group are usually noninteractive.

Methods in the second group assume that the decision maker's preference structure is adequately represented by weights, priorities, goals, and ideals and that the best-compromise solution is one that minimizes the combined deviation from goals or ideals. Goal programming and its variations, compromise programming, the method of the displaced ideal, the STEP method, and the SEMOPS method and its variation, are among the most notable examples. Goal programming has both noninteractive and interactive versions, whereas the other methods discussed are interactive.

In the third group, the decision maker's preference is elicited by means of trade-off to arrive ultimately at the best-compromise solution. Different forms of trade-offs—indifference vs feasible trade-offs, total vs partial trade-offs, and objective vs subjective trade-offs—were discussed. The Zionts–Wallenius method, Geoffrion's method, Oppenheimer's proxy method, the Musselman and Talavage trade-off cut method, and the Haimes and Hall surrogate worth trade-off method (to be presented in the next chapter) are representative of this group.

Obviously many other techniques that fall in one of the above three categories have been omitted. Notable among these are techniques due to Savir [1966], Maier–Rothe and Stankard [1970], and Belenson and Kapur [1973], the LINMAP technique [Srinivasan and Shocker, 1973], the boundary point ranking method [Hamming, 1976], the interactive conversion of goals into constraints [Adulphan and DeGuia, 1977], the minimum deviation method [Adulphan and Sukchareonpong, 1978], and the compromise constraint method [Adulphan and Tabuchanon, 1977]. In the next chapter we turn to a further class of methodologies based on the trade-off concept.

References

Ackoff, R. L., and Sasieni, M. W. (1968). *Fundamentals of Operations Research*, Wiley, New York.

Adulphan, P. (1978). Multicriterion optimization models, in *Systems Models for Decision Making* (W. Sharif and P. Adulphan, eds.), Asian Institute of Technology, Bangkok, pp. 385–433.

Adulphan, P., and DeGuia, A. A. (1977). An interactive approach to multicriterion optimization, *Operations Research* 24, suppl. no. 4.

Adulphan, P., and Sukchareonpong, P. (1978). Minimum deviation approach for multiple-objective optimization, presented at the 8th International Conference on IFORS, Toronto, June 19–23.

Adulphan, P., and Tabuchanon, M. T. (1977). Bicriterion linear programming, *International Journal of Computers and Operations Research* 4, 147–153.

Adulphan, P., and Tabuchanon, M. T. (1980). Multicriterion optimization in industrial systems, *Decision Models for Industrial Systems Engineers and Managers* (P. Adulphan and M. T. Tabuchanon, eds.), Asian Institute of Technology, Bangkok, pp. 387–461.

Belenson, S. M., and Kapur, K. C. (1973). An algorithm for solving multicriterion linear programming problems with examples, *Operations Research Quarterly* 24, 65–72.

Bell, D. E. (1977). A decision analysis of objectives for a forest pest problem, in *Conflicting Objectives in Decisions* (D. E. Bell, R. E. Keeney, and H. Raiffa, eds.), Wiley, Chichester, Great Britain, pp. 389–424.

Benayoun, R., Montgolfier, J. de, Tergny, J., and Larichev, O. I. (1971). Linear programming with multiple objective functions: STEP method (STEM), *Mathematical Programming* 1, 366–375.

Benayoun, R., and Tergny, J. (1969). Critères multiples en programmation mathématique: une solution dans le cas lineaire, *RFAIRO* 3, 31–56.

Charnes, A., and Cooper, W. (1961). *Management Models and Industrial Applications of Linear Programming*, Wiley, New York, Vol. 1.

Charnes, A., and Cooper, W. (1975). Goal programming and constrained regression —a comment, *OMEGA* 3, 403–409.

Choo, E. V., and Atkins, D. R. (1980). An interactive algorithm for multicriteria programming, *Computers and Operations Research* 7, 81–88.

Cohon, J., and Marks, D. H. (1975). A review and evaluation of multiobjective programming techniques, *Water Resources Research* 11, 208–220.

Dauer, J. P., and Krueger, R. J. (1977). An iterative approach to goal programming, *Operations Research Quarterly* 28, 671–681.

Dinkelbach, W., and Dürr, W. (1972). Effizienzaussagen bei Ersatzprogrammen zum Vectormaximumproblem, *Operations Research Verfahren* (H. P. Künzi and H. Schubert, eds.), Anton Hain, Meisenheim, Vol. 12, pp. 117–123.

Dinkelbach, W., and Isermann, H. (1980). Resource allocation of an academic department in the presence of multiple criteria—some experience with a modified STEP method, *Computers and Operations Research* 7, 99–106.

Dyer, J. S. (1972). Interactive goal programming, *Management Science* 19, 62–70.

Dyer, J. S. (1973). An empirical investigation of a man–machine interactive approach to the solution of the multiple criteria problem, *Multiple Criteria Decision Making* (J. L. Cochrane and M. Zeleny, eds.), University of South Carolina Press, Columbia, pp. 202–216.

Fichefet, J. (1976). GPSTEM: an interactive multiobjective optimization method, *Progress in Operations Research*, North-Holland, Amsterdam, Vol. 1, pp. 317–332.

Franz, L. S., and Lee, S. M. (1980). An interactive decision support system methodology and applications, paper presented at Multiple Criteria Decision Making Conference at University of Delaware, Newark, August 10–15.

Gass, S., and Saaty, T. (1955). The computational algorithm for the parametric objective function, *Naval Research Logistic Quarterly* 2, 39–45.

Gembicki, F. (1973). Vector optimization for control with performance and parameter sensitivity indices, Ph.D. dissertation, Case Western Reserve.

Gembicki, F., and Haimes, Y. Y. (1975). Approach to performance and multiobjective sensitivity optimization: the goal attainment method, *IEEE Automatic Control* AC-20, No. 6.

Geoffrion, A. M. (1966). Strictly concave parametric programming. Part I—basic theory, *Management Science* 13, 244–253.

Geoffrion, A. M. (1967a). Strictly concave parametric programming. Part II—additional theory and computational experience, *Management Science* 13, pp. 359–370.

Geoffrion, A. M. (1967b). Solving bicriterion mathematical programs, *Operations Research* 15, pp. 39–54.

Geoffrion, A. M. (1970). Vector maximal decomposition programming, Working Paper No. 165, Western Management Science Institute, University of California at Los Angeles.

Geoffrion, A. M., Dyer, J. S., and Feinberg, A. (1972). An interactive approach for multi-criterion optimization with an application to the operation of an academic department, *Management Sciences* 19, 357–368.

Goicoechea, A., Duckstein, L., and Bulfin, R. L. (1976). Multiobjective stochastic programming: the PROTRADE method, paper presented to Operations Society of America, Miami Beach, Nov. 3–5.

Goicoechea, A., Duckstein, L., and Fagel, M. M. (1979). Multiple objectives under uncertainty: an illustrative application of PROTRADE, *Water Resources Research* 15, 203–210.

Haimes, Y. Y. (1977). *Hierarchical Analyses of Water Resources Systems: Modeling and Optimization of Large-Scale Systems*, McGraw-Hill, New York.

Haimes, Y. Y., and Chankong, V. (1979). Kuhn–Tucker multipliers as trade-offs in multiobjective decision-making analysis, *Automatica* 15, 59–72.

Haimes, Y. Y., and Hall, W. A. (1974). Multiobjectives in water resources systems analysis: the surrogate worth trade-off method, *Water Resources Research* 10, 614–624.

Hamming, T. (1976). A new method for interactive multiobjective optimization: a boundary point ranking model, *Multiple Criteria Decision Making*, Jouy-en-Josas, France, 1975 (H. Thiriez and S. Zionts, eds.), Springer, Berlin.

Ho, J. K. (1979). Holistic preference evaluation in multiple criteria optimization, Tech. Rep. No. BNL-25656-AMD-818, Brookhaven National Laboratory, Upton, New York.

Ho, J. K. (1980). An experiment in multiple criteria energy policy analysis, Technical report no. BNL-28154-AMD-858, Brookhaven National Laboratory, Upton, New York, 1980; also presented at Multiple Criteria Decision Making Conference, University of Delaware, Newark.

Hwang, C. L., and Masud, A. S. M. (1979). *Multiple Objective Decision Making—Methods and Applications*, Springer, Berlin.

Ignizio, J. P. (1976). *Goal Programming and Extensions*, Lexington Books, Massachusetts.

Isermann, M. (1978). Duality in multiple objective linear programming, in *Multiple Criteria Problem Solving—Buffalo, New York, 1977* (S. Zionts, ed.), Springer, New York, 1978.

Johnson, L. E., and Loucks, D. P. (1980). Interactive multiobjective planning using computing graphics, *Computers and Operations Research* 7, 89–98.

Keefer, D. L. (1978a). Allocation planning for R&D with uncertainty and multiple competing objectives, *IEEE Transactions on Engineering Management* EM-25, 8–14.

Keefer, D. L. (1978b). Applying multiobjective decision analysis of resource allocation planning problems, in *Multiple Criteria Problem Solving—Buffalo, New York, 1977* (S. Zionts, ed.), Springer, Berlin, pp. 299–300.

Keefer, D. L., and Pollock, S. M. (1980). Approximations and sensitivity in multiobjective resource allocation, *Operations Research* 28, 176–187.

Kornbluth, J. S. M. (1973). A survey of goal programming, *OMEGA* 1, 193–205.

Kulikowski, R. (1977). A dynamic consumption model and optimization of utility functionals, in *Conflicting Objectives in Decisions* (D. E. Bell, R. L. Keeney, and H. Raiffa, eds.), Wiley, Chichester, Great Britain, pp. 223–231.

Lasdon, L., and Waren, A. D. (1978). Generalized reduced gradient software for linearly and nonlinearly constrained problems, in *Design and Implementation of Optimization Software* (H. Greenberg, ed.), Sijthof and Noordhoff, The Netherlands, p. 363.

Lee, S. M. (1972). *Goal Programming for Decision Analysis*, Auerbach, Philadelphia.

Lee, S. M. (1978). Interactive integer goal programming: methods and application, in *Multiple Criteria Problem Solving* (S. Zionts, ed.), Springer, Berlin-Heidelberg, pp. 362–383.

Lee, S. M., and Morris, R. L. (1977). Integer goal programming methods, in *Multiple Criteria Decision Making—TIMS Studies in the Management Sciences* (M. K. Starr and M. Zeleny, eds.), North Holland, Amsterdam, pp. 272–290.

Luenberger, D. G. (1973). *Introduction to Linear and Nonlinear Programming*, Addison-Wesley, Reading, Massachusetts.

MacCrimmon, K. R., and Wehrung, D. A. (1977). Trade-off analysis: the indifference and the preferred proportions approaches, in *Conflicting Objectives in Decisions* (D. E. Bell, R. L. Keeney, and H. Raiffa, eds.), Wiley, Chichester, Great Britain, pp. 123–147.

Maier-Rothe, C., and Stankard, M. F., Jr. (1970). A linear programming approach to choosing between multi-objective alternatives, presented at 7th Mathematical Programming Symposium, the Hague.

Monarchi, D. E., Kisiel, C. C., and Duckstein, L. (1973). Interactive multiobjective programming in water resources: a case study, *Water Resources Research* 9, 837–850.

Monarchi, D. E., Wilser, J. E., and Duckstein, L. (1976). An interactive multiple objective decision making aid using nonlinear goal programming, in *Multiple Criteria Decision Making — Kyoto, 1975* (M. Zeleny, ed.), Springer, Berlin.

Musselman, K., and Talavage, J. (1980). A trade-off cut approach to multiple objective optimization, *Operations Research* 28, no. 6.

Nijkamp, P., and Spronk, J. (1980). Interactive multiple goal programming: an evaluation and some results, in *Multiple Criteria Decision Making: Theory and Applications — Hagen / Königswinter, West Germany, 1979* (G. Fandel and T. Gal, eds.), Springer, Berlin, pp. 278–293.

Oppenheimer, K. R. (1978). A proxy approach to multi-attribute decision making, *Management Science* 24, 675–689.

Reid, R. W., and Vemuri, V. (1971). On the noninferior index approach to large-scale multicriteria systems, *Journal of the Franklin Institute* 291, 241–254.

Rosinger, R. E. (1980). Interactive algorithm for multiobjective optimization, in *Multiple Criteria Decision Making: Theory and Applications — Hagen / Königswinter, West Germany, 1979* (G. Fandel and T. Gal, eds.), Springer, Berlin-Heidelberg, pp. 400–405.

Savir, D. (1966). Multiobjective linear programming, Tech. Rep. No. ORC-66-21, Operations Research Center, College of Engineering, University of California, Berkeley.

Spronk, J., and Telgen, J. (1980). An ellipsoidal interactive multiple goal programming method, presented at Multiple Criteria Decision Making Conference at University of Delaware, Newark, August 10–15.

Srinivasan, V., and Shocker, A. D. (1973). Linear programming for multidimensional analysis of preferences, *Psychometrika* 38, 337–369.

Steuer, R. E. (1979). Goal programming sensitivity analysis using interval penalty weights, *Mathematical Programming* 17, 16–31.

Villarreal, B., Karwan, M. H., and Zionts, S. (1980). An interactive branch and bound procedure for multicriterion integer linear programming, in *Multiple Criteria Decision Making Theory and Applications — Hagen / Königswinter, West Germany, 1979* (G. Fandel and T. Gal, eds.), Springer, Berlin, pp. 448–467.

Wallenius, J. (1975). Comparative evaluation of some interactive approaches to multicriterion optimization, *Management Science* 21, 1387–1396.

Wolfe, P. (1959). The simplex method for quadratic programming, *Econometrica* 27, 382–398.

Yu, P. L. (1973). A class of solutions for group decision problems, *Management Science* 19, 936–946.

Zeleny, M. (1973). Compromise programming, in *Multiple Criteria Decision Making* (J. L. Cochrane and M. Zeleny, eds.), University of South Carolina, Columbia, pp. 373–391.

Zeleny, M. (1974). *Linear Multiple Programming*, Springer, Berlin.

Zeleny, M. (1977). Adaptive displacement of preferences in decision making, in *Multiple Criteria Decision Making—TIMS Studies in Management Science* (M. K. Starr and M. Zeleny, eds.), North-Holland, Amsterdam, pp. 147–158.

Zionts, S. (1976). An interactive method for evaluating discrete alternatives involving multiple criteria, Working Paper No. 271, School of Management, State University of New York at Buffalo.

Zionts, S. (1977a). Multiple criteria decision making for discrete alternatives with ordinal criteria, Working Paper No. 299, School of Management, State University of New York at Buffalo.

Zionts, S. (1977b). Integer linear programming with multiple objectives, *Annals of Discrete Mathematics* 1, 551–562.

Zionts, S., and Wallenius, J. (1976). An interactive programming method for solving the multiple criteria problem, *Management Science* 22, 652–663.

Zionts, S., and Wallenius, J. (1980). An interactive multiple objective linear programming method for a class of underlying nonlinear utility function, Working Paper No. 451, School of Management, State University of New York at Buffalo.

Chapter 8

The Surrogate Worth Trade-off Method and Its Extensions

8.1 Introduction

In this chapter, we present a methodology that combines a number of concepts discussed thus far. First, we have seen that monotonicity of preference is a common property of most multiobjective decision problems, and the method to be presented here requires a best-compromise solution that is also noninferior. Second, the decision maker's task is often made simpler if he is asked to indicate a preference rather than supply estimates of the trade-offs involved, such as the marginal rates of substitution, and this method is based on objective trade-off analysis. Finally, the decision maker is most comfortable, and perhaps consistent, responding to questions that require comparing two objectives at a time, and this method exploits partial trade-offs and partial trade-off rates.

8.2 The SWT Method

We have been describing the *surrogate worth trade-off method* (SWT), originally developed by Haimes and Hall [1974].[1] In its original version, SWT is, in principle, noninteractive and assumes continuous variables and twice differentiable objective functions and constraints. It consists of four steps: 1) generate a representative subset of noninferior solutions, 2) obtain relevant trade-off information for each generated solution, 3) interact with the decision maker to obtain information about preference expressed in terms of *worth*, and 4) retrieve the best-compromise solution from the information obtained.

---

[1]See also Haimes et al. [1975], Hall and Haimes [1976], Haimes [1977], Haimes and Chankong [1979], and Haimes [1980, 1981].

Step 1: Generation of a Representative Subset of Noninferior Solutions While any of the methods discussed in Chapter 6 can be used to generate a representative subset of noninferior solutions, the ε-constraint method is recommended in view of what is required in step 2. We choose a reference objective f_k and formulate the ε-constraint problem $P_k(\boldsymbol{\varepsilon})$:

$$\min \quad f_k(\mathbf{x}) \tag{8.1}$$

$$\text{subject to} \quad \mathbf{x} \in X, \tag{8.2a}$$

$$f_j(\mathbf{x}) \leqslant \varepsilon_j, \quad j=1,\ldots,n, \quad j \neq k. \tag{8.2b}$$

Although there is no rule to specify which objective should be chosen as a reference, a dominant objective, or one in familiar units (such as dollars) and yielding a meaningful trade-off analysis, is recommended.

To generate ad hoc a representative subset of noninferior solutions we simply pick a reasonable number of values for each ε_j and solve $P_k(\boldsymbol{\varepsilon})$ for each combination of these values ($j \neq k$). As a guideline to ensure that $P_k(\boldsymbol{\varepsilon})$ is feasible, each ε_j should be selected in the range $[a_j, b_j]$ where, for each $j=1,\ldots,n, j \neq k$,

$$a_j = \min_{\mathbf{x} \in X} f_j(\mathbf{x}), \qquad b_j = \max_{\mathbf{x} \in X} f_j(\mathbf{x}). \tag{8.3}$$

Step 2: Obtaining Trade-off Information In the process of solving $P_k(\boldsymbol{\varepsilon})$ either analytically or by existing optimization algorithms, the trade-off information can easily be obtained merely by observing the optimal Kuhn–Tucker multipliers corresponding to the ε constraints (8.2b). Let these multipliers be denoted by $\lambda_{kj}(\mathbf{x}^0), j=1,\ldots,n, j \neq k$, where $\mathbf{x}^0$ solves $P_k(\boldsymbol{\varepsilon})$. Assuming all the hypotheses of Theorem 4.30, two cases can occur by virtue of that theorem.

First, if all $\lambda_{kj}(\mathbf{x}^0) > 0$ for *each* $j \neq k$, then the noninferior surface in the objective space around the neighborhood of $\mathbf{f}^0 \triangleq \mathbf{f}(\mathbf{x}^0)$ can be represented by

$$f_k = f_k(f_1,\ldots,f_{k-1}, f_{k+1},\ldots,f_n) \tag{8.4}$$

and

$$\lambda_{kj}(\mathbf{x}^0) = -\left.\frac{\partial f_k}{\partial f_j}\right|_{\mathbf{f}=\mathbf{f}^0} \qquad \text{for each} \quad j \neq k. \tag{8.5}$$

Thus each $\lambda_{kj}(\mathbf{x}^0)$ represents the noninferior partial trade-off rate between f_k and f_j at $\mathbf{f}^0$ when all other objectives are held fixed at their respective values at $\mathbf{x}^0$. The adjective "noninferior" is used to signify that after the trade-off is made the resulting point remains on the noninferior surface.

In case 2, $\lambda_{kj}(\mathbf{x}^0) > 0$ for *some* $j \neq k$, and in addition $\lambda_{kl}(\mathbf{x}^0) = 0$, also for some $l \neq k$. The noninferior surface in the neighborhood of $\mathbf{f}^0$ can then be expressed

$$f_k = \hat{f}_k(\hat{\mathbf{f}}), \tag{8.6}$$

where $\hat{\mathbf{f}}$ is a vector consisting of all f_j with $\lambda_{kj}(\mathbf{x}^0) > 0$. Also, each $\lambda_{kj}(\mathbf{x}^0)$ that is strictly positive can be interpreted as a trade-off rate, as given in Theorem 4.30(c), that exhibits an exchange between f_k and f_j while each objective f_l such that $\lambda_{kl}(\mathbf{x}^0) = 0$ also changes.

We shall put the second case aside until Section 8.7. In other words, of all the noninferior solutions generated in step 1, we shall consider only those whose associated multipliers $\lambda_{kj}(\mathbf{x})$ are all strictly positive. In effect, we have limited ourselves to considering only solutions that are proper and noninferior, as evident from Theorem 4.13(a). In this case, if the primary objective is changed from f_k to f_i, the trade-offs $\lambda_{ij}, j \neq i$, can be determined from the λ_{kj}s by using the formula

$$\lambda_{ij} = \lambda_{ik}\lambda_{kj} \qquad \text{for all} \quad i \neq j \tag{8.7a}$$

and

$$\lambda_{ik} = 1/\lambda_{ki}. \tag{8.7b}$$

Relationships (8.7) follow easily from (8.4), (8.5), and the chain rule.

Step 3: Interacting with the Decision Maker to Elicit Preference The decision maker is supplied with trade-off information from step 2 and the levels of all criteria. He then expresses his ordinal preference on whether or not (and by how much) he would like to make such a trade at that level. The surrogate worth function is then constructed from this information.

Let, for example, $\mathbf{x}^0$ be a noninferior solution generated in step 1 and $\lambda_{kj}(\mathbf{x}^0)$ be a trade-off between f_k and f_j for each $j = 1, \ldots, k-1, k+1, \ldots, n$ (as determined in step 2) when we move from $\mathbf{x}^0$ to some other noninferior solution close to $\mathbf{x}^0$. The decision maker is asked, "How (much) would you like to improve f_k by $\lambda_{kj}(\mathbf{x}^0)$ units per one-unit degradation of f_j while all other objectives remain fixed at $f_l(\mathbf{x}^0)$, $l \neq j, k$? Indicate your preference on a scale of $+10$ to -10, where the values have the following meaning:

$+10$ means you have the greatest desire to improve f_k by $\lambda_{kj}(\mathbf{x}^0)$ units per one-unit degradation of f_j,

0 means you are indifferent about the trade,

-10 means you have the greatest desire to degrade f_k by $\lambda_{kj}(\mathbf{x}^0)$ units per one-unit improvement in f_j.

Values between -10 and 0, and 0 and 10 show proportional desire to make the trade."

The decision maker's response is recorded as $W_{kj}(\mathbf{x}^0)$, called the *surrogate worth* of the trade-off between f_k and f_j at $\mathbf{x}^0$. At a particular noninferior solution, there will be $n-1$ questions to obtain $W_{kj}(\mathbf{x}^0)$ for each $j \neq k$. So that we can measure $W_{kj}(\mathbf{x}^0)$ on a ratio scale, we define the surrogate worth scale for measuring W_{kj}s with the following conventions:

1. Positive numbers will be assigned uniformly to W_{kj} if the decision maker feels a positive preference toward the trade-off between f_k and f_j as posed by the given question.
2. Negative numbers will be assigned uniformly to W_{kj} if the decision maker feels a distinct aversion or a negative preference toward the trade-off between f_k and f_j as posed by the given question.
3. The scale for measuring W_{kj} is bounded from above by $+10$ and from below by -10.
4. A value of $+10$ will be assigned to W_{kj} if the decision maker is completely satisfied with the trade-off between f_k and f_j as posed by the given question.
5. A value of -10 will be assigned to W_{kj} if the decision maker is completely satisfied with the trade-off between f_k and f_j that is the converse of the given question.
6. A value of 0 will be assigned to W_{kj} if the decision maker is genuinely indifferent toward the trade-off between f_k and f_j as posed by the given question.
7. A number between 0 and $+10$ exclusive will be assigned to W_{kj} according to the decision maker's feeling of satisfaction toward the trade-off between f_k and f_j (as posed by the above question). It is assumed he compares this with the remaining trade-offs toward which he would feel genuine indifference or perfect satisfaction.
8. A number between 0 and -10 exclusive will be assigned to W_{kj} according to the decision maker's feeling of satisfaction toward the trade-off between f_k and f_j that is the converse of that posed by the given question. He compares this with the remaining trade-offs toward which he would feel genuine indifference or perfect satisfaction.
9. In two situations with different levels of f_k and two (not necessarily) different trade-offs bëtween f_k and f_j as posed by the given question, the two trade-offs will be assigned an equal value of W_{kj} if and only if the decision maker feels no preference for one situation over the other; and one trade-off will be assigned a higher value of W_{kj} than the other if and only if the decision maker feels a greater level of satisfaction with one than with the other.

These conventions completely define the scale for measuring W_{kj}. If desired, they can be translated into a set of mathematical assumptions that is then amenable to axiomatic treatment. We are, however, only interested in the practical aspects. If all these conventions are successfully implemented by the decision maker, each half of the surrogate worth scale so obtained becomes, in the terminology of the theory of scales in Chapter 2, a ratio scale whose halves are mirror images of each other. Because W_{kj} is measured in such a scale, all arithmetic operations (except multiplying and dividing by each other when they have different signs) can be performed on it without destroying or distorting the relevant information contained therein. A mathematical transformation by a monotone increasing function is also permissible. (See Chapter 2 for a more detailed discussion of scaling theory.)

In practice, however, strict imposition of these conventions may be opposed, particularly by the decision maker, because of the complexity of the assessment process. At the intermediate level, if the continuity of the scale is thought to be too superficial and difficult to obtain, it may be easier to ask the decision maker to grade his preference in discrete categories which can be coded by integers between $+10$ and -10. This can then be taken as an approximation of a ratio scale. Moreover, in this case, a transformation by a monotone function can always be made with complete freedom and without fear of distorting or destroying the information contained in W_{kj}; other arithmetic operations, however must be handled with care. At the very worst, the decision maker may only be willing to assign three values to W_{kj}, showing positive preference for ($W_{kj}>0$), indifference to ($W_{kj}=0$), or aversion to ($W_{kj}<0$) the prescribed trade-off. He may be reluctant to elaborate on the degree of preference or aversion. In this case, the only invariant transformations on W_{kj} are transformations by a monotone increasing function, and only the sign of W_{kj} carries information about the decision maker's preference.

The decision maker's preference embodied in W_{kj} at each generated noninferior solution can be used to determine the best-compromise solution, as described in the next step.

Step 4: Retrieving the Best-Compromise Solution Intuitively, one would expect that a particular noninferior solution $\mathbf{x}^*$ is the best-compromise solution if the decision maker is indifferent to all trade-offs offered from the current point $\mathbf{x}^*$. In other words, $\mathbf{x}^*$ is the best-compromise solution if

$$W_{kj}(\mathbf{x}^*)=0 \qquad \text{for all} \quad j\neq k. \tag{8.8}$$

To justify (8.8) in a more formal manner, assume that the decision maker's preference structure is characterized by a concave value function $v(f_1,\dots,f_n)$. It can be shown that at $\mathbf{x}^*$

$$\lim_{h_j\to 0}\frac{v(f_1^*,\dots,f_k^*-\lambda_{kj}^*h_j,\dots,f_j+h_j,\dots,f_n)-v(f_1,\dots,f_n)}{h_j}$$

$$=\frac{\partial v(f^*)}{\partial f_j}-\frac{\partial v(f^*)}{\partial f_k}\lambda_{kj}^*. \tag{8.9}$$

Clearly the left-hand side of (8.9) reflects, in the limit, the level of desire of the decision maker to improve (or decrease) f_k by $\lambda_{kj}h_j$ units in exchange for a degradation of h_j units of f_j. It is therefore a monotone increasing function of W_{kj}. If $W_{kj}=0$ for all $j \neq k$, it can be shown that $\nabla_f v(\mathbf{f})=\mathbf{0}$. Since v is a concave function, it is clear that $\mathbf{x}^*$ maximizes $v(\mathbf{f}(\mathbf{x}))$. From (8.9), useful relationships among $W_{kj}(\mathbf{x})$, $\lambda_{kj}(\mathbf{x}^0)$, and $m_{kj}(\mathbf{x}^0)$, the indifference trade-off at $\mathbf{x}^0$, can also be developed. These are

$$W_{kj}(\mathbf{x}^0)>0 \quad \Leftrightarrow \quad \alpha^0\left[m_{kj}(\mathbf{x}^0)-\lambda_{kj}(\mathbf{x}^0)\right]>0; \tag{8.10a}$$

$$W_{kj}(\mathbf{x}^0)=0 \quad \Leftrightarrow \quad \alpha^0\left[m_{kj}(\mathbf{x}^0)-\lambda_{kj}(\mathbf{x}^0)\right]=0; \tag{8.10b}$$

$$W_{kj}(\mathbf{x}^0)<0 \quad \Leftrightarrow \quad \alpha^0\left[m_{kj}(\mathbf{x}^0)-\lambda_{kj}(\mathbf{x}^0)\right]<0, \tag{8.10c}$$

where

$$1/\alpha^0=\partial v(f(\mathbf{x}^0))/\partial f_k.$$

Since $\alpha^0 \neq 0$ (barring some peculiar shape of v), (8.10b) and (8.8) imply that $\mathbf{x}^*$ is the best-compromise solution if

$$m_{kj}(\mathbf{x}^0)=\lambda_{kj}(\mathbf{x}^0). \tag{8.11}$$

We can apply condition (8.8) to retrieve the best-compromise solution. If at some generated noninferior solution all the corresponding W_{kj} vanish, that generated point can immediately be chosen as the best-compromise solution. Otherwise we use multiple regression to construct, for each $j \neq k$, the surrogate worth function W_{kj} relating W_{kj} to f_l for all $l \neq k$. Then the system of equations

$$W_{kj}(f_1,\ldots,f_{k-1},f_{k+1},\ldots,f_n)=0, \qquad j \neq k, \tag{8.12}$$

is solved to determine $\boldsymbol{\varepsilon}^*=(f_1^*,\ldots,f_{k-1}^*,f_{k+1}^*,\ldots,f_n^*)^{\mathrm{T}}$. The best-compromise solution $\mathbf{x}^*$ is then found by solving $P_k(\boldsymbol{\varepsilon}^*)$.

The corresponding trade-offs $\boldsymbol{\lambda}^* \triangleq (\lambda_{k1}^*,\ldots,\lambda_{k,k-1}^*,\lambda_{k,k+1}^*,\ldots,\lambda_{kn}^*)$ can also be found. Note that in practice there usually exists an indifference band around a neighborhood of $\boldsymbol{\lambda}^*$ within which the W_{kj}s, $j \neq k$, do not change. The decision maker may be asked additional questions to obtain the indifference band and to improve the accuracy of $\boldsymbol{\lambda}^*$.

Example 1: Consider again Example 8 of Chapter 6, where the objective functions to be minimized are $f_1(\mathbf{x})=(x_1-3)^2+(x_2-2)^2$, $f_2(\mathbf{x})=x_1+x_2$, and $f_3(\mathbf{x})=x_1+2x_2$ and the constraint set is $X=\{\mathbf{x}\in R^2 | x_1, x_2 \geqslant 0\}$.

Let us now apply that SWT method to this problem.

STEP 1: Choosing f_1 as the primary objective, we formulate $P_1(\boldsymbol{\varepsilon})$:

$$\min_{\mathbf{x}\in X} \; f_1(\mathbf{x}) \tag{8.13}$$

$$\text{subject to} \quad f_2(\mathbf{x})=x_1+x_2 \leqslant \varepsilon_2, \tag{8.14a}$$

$$f_3(\mathbf{x})=x_1+2x_2 \leqslant \varepsilon_3. \tag{8.14b}$$

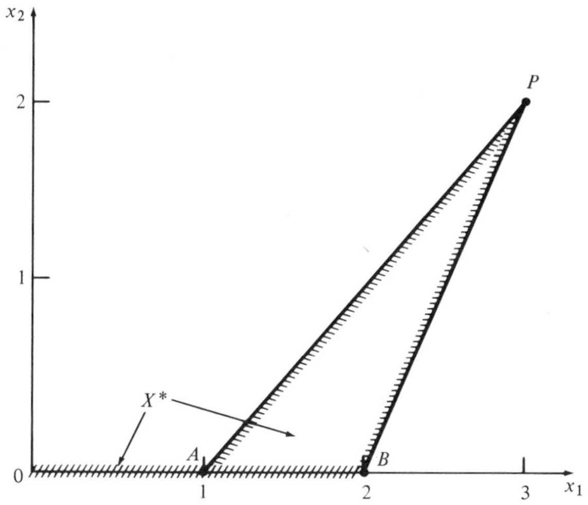

Figure 8.1 Set of noninferior solutions of Example 1.

Because of the simplicity of the problem, we are able to generate the entire set of noninferior solutions, as shown in Figure 8.1 (see for example Figure 4.3).

STEP 2: As noted in Section 4.9.3, only noninferior points in the interior of the triangle PAB are properly noninferior, and corresponding λ_{12} and λ_{13} are both strictly positive in this region. Indeed, it can be easily shown [solving (6.186a) and (6.186b) simultaneously] that

$$\lambda_{12}(x_1, x_2) = 2(x_1 - x_2 - 1), \tag{8.15}$$

$$\lambda_{13}(x_1, x_2) = 2(-2x_1 + x_2 + 4) \tag{8.16}$$

for all $\mathbf{x}$ in the interior of the triangle PAB.

STEP 3: To interact with the decision maker, we prepare Table 8.1, listing a few representative noninferior solutions. We can now go to the decision maker to elicit W_{12} and W_{13} for each noninferior point in Table 8.1. For example, for the first point in the table we ask the decision maker whether he would like to improve f_1 by 0.1 units per one unit degradation of f_2 with f_3 unchanged, given that $f_1 = 0.06$, $f_2 = 4.65$, and $f_3 = 6.45$. The decision maker may have strong adverse feeling about the trade-off. In fact, he really wants to improve f_2 rather than degrade it, so he gives $W_{12} = -10$ at this point.

Table 8.1 Data Generated for Example 1

$\varepsilon_2 = f_2$	$\varepsilon_3 = f_3$	f_1	x_1	x_2	λ_{12}	λ_{13}	w_{12}	w_{13}
4.65	6.45	0.06	2.85	1.8	0.1	0.2	−10	−4
4.30	5.90	0.25	2.70	1.6	0.2	0.4	−9	−4
3.95	5.35	0.56	2.55	1.4	0.3	0.6	−7	−3
3.60	4.80	1.00	2.40	1.2	0.4	0.8	−6	−3
3.25	4.20	1.56	2.25	1.0	0.5	1.0	−4	−2
2.90	3.70	2.25	2.10	0.8	0.6	1.2	−2	−1
2.55	3.15	3.06	1.95	0.6	0.7	1.4	−1	0
2.20	2.60	4.00	1.80	0.4	0.8	1.6	+1	0
1.85	2.05	5.06	1.65	0.2	0.9	1.8	+3	+1

Similar questions are asked to obtain W_{13} at the same point. In this case there are thus two questions to be asked at each point. Suppose we continue this process and get the responses shown in Table 8.1. Next we retrieve the best-compromise solution from this information.

STEP 4: Since there is no point in Table 8.1 where W_{12} and W_{13} equal zero simultaneously, we construct the function $W_{12}(f_2, f_3)$ and $W_{13}(f_2, f_3)$ using the multiple regression method and the data from the table. Carrying out this step, we find that the two functions can be approximated by linear functions of the form

$$W_{12}(f_2, f_3) = 10 - 1.2f_2 - 2.37f_3, \tag{8.17}$$

$$W_{13}(f_2, f_3) = 5 - 1.5f_2 - 0.47f_3. \tag{8.18}$$

Applying condition (8.8), we set $W_{12} = 0$ and $W_{13} = 0$. Solving for f_2, f_3 we find that

$$f_2^* = 2.4 \quad \text{and} \quad f_3^* = 3.0.$$

Setting $\varepsilon_2^* = 2.4$ and $\varepsilon_3^* = 3.0$ in (8.13)–(8.14) and solving for the best-compromise solution yields $\mathbf{x}^* = (1.8, 0.6)^T$.

Example 1 illustrates the salient features of the SWT method. For more examples and applications, see Haimes et al. [1975], Haimes [1977], Haimes and Hall [1977], Sakawa [1978], Cohon [1978], Haimes et al. [1979], Das and Haimes [1980], and Haimes et al. [1980].

In applying the SWT method, two major computational results have become evident: First, the computational effort in generating noninferior solutions is relatively trivial, given access to the generalized reduced gradient algorithm (see Lasdon and Waren [1978]) for solving nonlinear problems and to the simplex routine for solving linear problems. Furthermore, not only is the generation of noninferior solutions simple, but only a representative subset of noninferior solutions is needed in the interaction made with the decision maker.

Second, although the regression analysis is theoretically possible, it is rarely needed in practice. This is primarily because there is a degree of "fuzziness" in the neighborhood of the best-compromise solution, where the decision maker is indifferent. This fact is particularly evident when a wide indifference band exists—a band of preferences where all solutions are equally preferred by the decision maker.

The above conclusions are based on numerous applications of the SWT method, including in the Maumee River basin study, where the overall model has seven objective functions (see, for example, Haimes [1977], Haimes et al. [1979], and Das and Haimes [1980]).

8.3 The SWT Method with Multiple Decision Makers[2]

Many real-world decisions are made not by single individuals but by groups. Whether the group be composed of members of the board of directors of a large corporation, elected representatives in a legislative body, or voters in a political system, the task of dealing with multiple decision makers arises. Multiple decision makers are encountered particularly often in planning problems in the public sector. The analyst must recognize that each decision maker in the group will have his own characteristic interpretation of the significance and relative value of the objectives under consideration. In addition, if a decision maker is a representative of still another group of individuals, he may well be responsive to the views of his constituency.

The analyst's role, then, is to ensure that the decision makers reach the best-compromise solution for the group as a whole. The meaning of "best-compromise" in this sense is not clear, however. One interpretation relies on a notion from welfare economics, that of aggregating the utility functions of individuals into a societal utility function; the preference orderings of individuals could be similarly aggregated. Another interpretation of the problem relies on a notion from game theory concerning the prediction of political outcomes of a bargaining process. In this case the emphasis is placed on determining what alternative will be selected, whereas in the former the emphasis is on what alternative should be selected. Additionally, the criterion for agreement regarding the best-compromise solution is not clear—unanimity, majority voting, and consensus have all been suggested. Although these approaches to the multiple decision maker problem do not exhaust all possibilities, they serve to illustrate the fuzziness of the issue.

Hall and Haimes [1976] address the problem of resolving conflict among decision makers from the point of view of the decision maker's individual

---

[2] This section is adopted from Hall and Haimes [1976], Haimes [1980], Zwick [1981], and Zwick and Haimes [1981].

indifference bands. A decision maker's indifference band is defined to be the subset of the noninferior set in which the improvement of one objective function is equivalent (in the estimation of the decision maker) to the degradation of another. In other words, the indifference band lies within the noninferior set in the vicinity of the best-compromise solution and is composed of solutions of equal worth to the preferred solution. Through interaction with the decision maker, the analyst can use the SWT method to assess an individual decision maker's indifference band as described earlier.

Hall and Haimes [1976] consider three major cases of multiobjective decision problems with multiple decision makers: i) direct group decision making, ii) representative decision making and iii) political decision making. They show how indifference bands can be constructed and how conflicts can be resolved in each of these cases and the role the SWT method plays in these processes. For our discussion it suffices to consider two general cases: the ideal case and the probable case.

In the ideal case the intersection of the decision makers' individual indifference bands is not empty (see Figure 8.2a), reflecting no conflict situation. A noninferior solution agreeable to all can be found within the intersection—this solution can be identified as the best-compromise solution. However, it is more probable that the intersection is indeed empty (see Figure 8.2b), and conflict must thus be resolved through negotiation and compromise if a noninferior solution is to be reached.

Consider the approach of modern welfare economics, that is, the aggregation of individual preferences into a societal preference ordering, also called a social welfare function [Sage, 1977]. In the context of this section the preferences of individual decision makers regarding the location of their indifference bands in the noninferior space would be aggregated into a single location, that of the indifference band for the group, or for society as a whole. However, the work of Arrow [1951, 1963], notably the development of his general possibility theorem, demonstrated that a transitive societal preference ordering is not, in general, possible if that ordering is not imposed. Many authors have sought to relax the transitivity requirement (see Luce and Raiffa [1957] and Kirkwood [1972]). Fleming [1952], Goodman and Markowitz [1952], and Harsanyi [1955] have suggested a group preference structure that is a weighted sum of individual preferences. Sage [1977] has suggested a procedure involving worth assessment and group preference techniques for determining preferences among multiattribute alternatives. Inoue et al. [1981] have introduced a refinement of the weighted preference approach to account for shifting group preferences and variance in their intensity, the extended contributive rule (ECR) method.

Each of these suggested structures suffers from problems arising from the measurement of individual preferences, interpersonal comparison of those preferences, and their aggregation into a social preference structure (see Cohon [1978]). More fundamentally, each of the aggregation methods

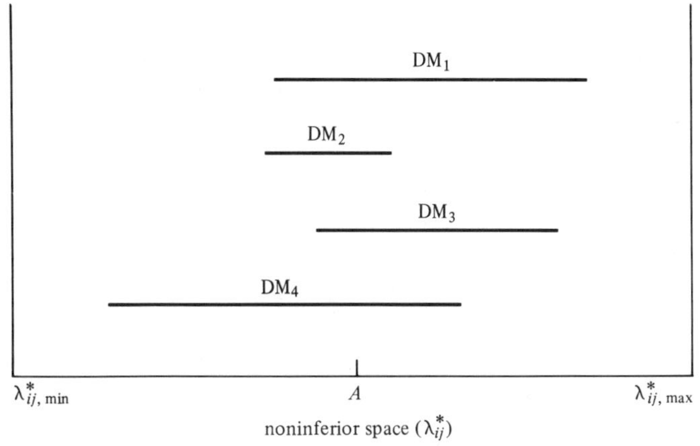

(a)

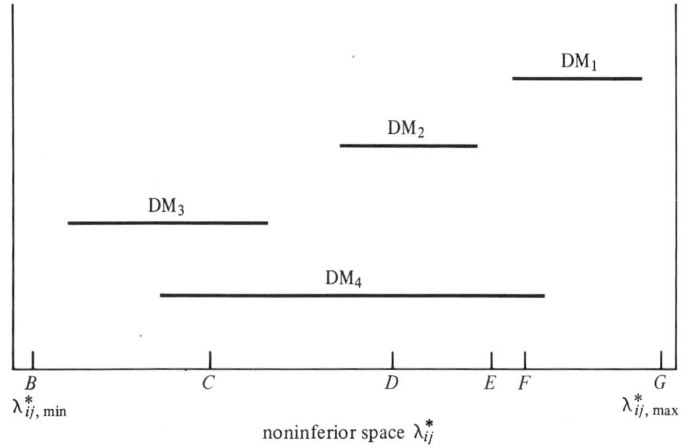

(b)

Figure 8.2 (**a**) Intersecting indifference bands in the ideal case (*after Haimes and Hall* [*1976*]). (**b**) Indifference bands in the probable case.

assumes an a priori justification for directly aggregating individual preferences into a societal preference structure. It is conceivable, however, that what an individual prefers for himself is not indicative of what he prefers for society as a whole. A simple example is the individual who prefers to smoke a certain distinctive brand of cigar but would not prefer all of society to smoke that brand, since it would immediately lose its distinctiveness or become in short supply. However, this shortcoming of the aggregation methods could easily be overcome if the individual were to indicate what he prefers for society rather than for himself.

Consider now an approach to determining an acceptable range (or ranges) of alternatives. For Figure 8.2a the unanimous decision would be to select a range in the vicinity of point *A* which lies within each decision maker's indifference band. In the case depicted in Figure 8.2b, however, the selection is not as obvious. Rietveld [1980] suggested that, faced with the lack of an unanimous agreement on an acceptable range, one should first reject a range of alternatives that is not acceptable to any decision maker. In fact, this decision is a unanimous decision to reject, instead of accept, a range of noninferior alternatives. In Figure 8.2b the ranges outside of points *B* and *G* could be rejected immediately. This leaves us with an acceptable range between points *B* and *G*. If the group wishes to improve its selection further, it must give up the hope of unanimity and resort to voting in order to narrow the range. Although the voting procedure here may also fall victim to the Arrow paradox, the identification of an acceptable range is at least another step in the right direction.

Given the situation in Figure 8.2b, it may yet be possible to reach a unanimous decision. Even should a voting procedure yield votes for ranges in the vicinity of points *C*, *D*, and *F* none of which are preferred by a clear majority of the decision makers, DM_1, DM_2, or both may be persuaded to compromise a small amount in the direction of point *E* such that a majority vote for point *E* is secured. It has been suggested that willingness to expand an indifference band depends on the rate at which each decision maker reaches indifference on the corresponding boundary of his indifference band. This willingness to compromise or cooperate is partly due to the increase in the probability of reaching a decision as one's indifference band expands. When decision makers are reluctant to compromise, Hall and Haimes [1976] have suggested altering the structure of the system's objectives by introducing an additional objective that expresses the probability of reaching a decision in order to precipitate compromise toward a majority decision.

If a majority still cannot be reached, an arbitrative procedure such as the Delphi method [Helmer, 1967] may be employed to arrive at a compromise, although it should be kept in mind that real-world decision makers may be quite reluctant to budge from their original positions owing to political considerations. Indeed, many decison problems of the public sector are subject to an enormous amount of political pressure arising from conflict among special interest groups and politicians (who are often decision makers themselves). Cohon [1978] asserts that if interest groups control public decision making processes, then there is no point in attempting to aggregate the preferences of individuals or in expecting compromise without political bargaining or political interaction among decision makers. Examining predictive decision-making methods that focus on multiple person and cooperative game models ("log rolling" models), Cohon treats decision makers as bargaining with the various interest groups within their constituencies and with other decision makers concerning objectives both relevant and irrelevant to the decision-making system at hand.

The possibility that no solution can be reached must also be recognized. In this case the cause may be the inability of the decision makers to arrive at an agreement either because of a lack of motivation to cooperate or because of a deficiency in the multiple decision-making methodology. Conversely, the information provided by the decision maker to the analyst could be inconsistent, inhibiting convergence to a solution.

Each of the methods discussed in this section tries to effect agreement in the decision makers' indifference bands, which can be generated by the SWT method. Although in practice it may be quite difficult to obtain a solution to this class of problems, the methodology has certain desirable qualities. For example, the indifference band approach may indicate whether any decision can be reached at all, determine in what regions of the noninferior space a possible solution is likely to exist, or provide information useful for a bargaining process.

8.4 The Multiobjective Statistical Method

The *multiobjective statistical method* (MSM) was developed to integrate statistical attributes with multiobjective optimization methodologies, such as the SWT method (see Haimes et al. [1980]).[3] The need for MSM arises with probabilistic multiobjective models.

Let $\mathbf{x}$ denote a vector of decision variables and $\mathbf{f}(\mathbf{y})$ a vector of noncommensurable objective functions with $\mathbf{y}$ the state vector of the system being analyzed. The state vector $\mathbf{y}$ is given by $\mathbf{y}=\mathbf{y}(\mathbf{x};\mathbf{r})$, where $\mathbf{r}$ is a vector of random variables modeling the uncertainties in the system. Let

$$\mathbf{r}=(r_1, r_2,\dots,r_p), \tag{8.19}$$

where each of the r_i, $i=1,2,\dots,p$, are real-valued random variables satisfying

$$\underline{r}_i \leqslant r_i \leqslant \bar{r}_i, \qquad i=1,2,\dots,p. \tag{8.20}$$

Let A_{ij}, $j=1,2,\dots,J_i$, be a collection of subsets of $[\underline{r}_i, \bar{r}_i]$ with probabilities $P(A_{ij})$, $i=1,2,\dots,p$, to be used for a given study. Define the p-fold probabilities

$$p_m=P\left(A_{1j_1}A_{2j_2}\cdots A_{pj_p}\right), \tag{8.21}$$

[3] The outline of MSM presented here is adopted from Haimes et al. [1980] and Haimes [1980].

where $1 \leqslant j_i \leqslant J_i$, $i=1,2,\ldots,p$, and m is an index variable from the set

$$\{1,2,\ldots,M\}, \qquad M=\prod_{i=1}^{p} J_i. \tag{8.22}$$

Here, p_m is the probability that

$$r_i \in A_{1j_1}, \quad r_2 \in A_{2j_2}, \quad \ldots, \quad r_p \in A_{pj_p}.$$

The planning of the system is formulated as the multiobjective optimization problem

$$\min_{\mathbf{x}\in X} \quad \mathbf{f}(\mathbf{y}) \triangleq \begin{bmatrix} f_1(\mathbf{y}) \\ \vdots \\ f_n(\mathbf{y}) \end{bmatrix}. \tag{8.23}$$

For $\hat{\mathbf{x}} \in X$ determine $y_m(\hat{\mathbf{x}}; \mathbf{r}_m)$, where $\mathbf{r}_m$ is the vector of random variables with probability p_m for $m=1,2,\ldots,M$. The most convenient way to define the sets A_{ij} is by dividing the intervals $[\underline{r}_i, \bar{r}_i]$ into J_i discrete subintervals such that

$$\Delta r_i = \frac{\underline{r}_i - \bar{r}_i}{J_i} \quad \text{and} \quad A_{ij} = (\underline{r}_i + (j-1)\Delta r_i, r_i + j\Delta r_i]. \tag{8.24}$$

The components $\underline{r}_m$ are taken to be the midpoints of the appropriate subintervals of $[\underline{r}_i, \bar{r}_i]$ dictated by the index variable m.

To account for the random nature of the state vector $\mathbf{y}$ in the optimization problem, define the quantities $\tilde{f}_l(\mathbf{y}) = E\{f_l(\mathbf{y})\}$, where $l=1,2,\ldots,L$ and $E\{\ \}$ denotes expectation. Then

$$\tilde{f}_l(\hat{\mathbf{y}}) = \tilde{f}_l(\mathbf{y}(\hat{\mathbf{x}})) = \sum_{m=1}^{M} f_l(y(\hat{\mathbf{x}}; r_m))p_m, \tag{8.25}$$

where $\hat{\mathbf{x}} \in X$ represents a fixed set of decisions.

In order to proceed with the optimization problem it is necessary to obtain a functional relationship that maps $\mathbf{x}$ into $\tilde{f}_l(\mathbf{x})$ for each objective function $l=1,2,\ldots,n$. One possible method is to obtain a collection of ordered pairs $\{\hat{\mathbf{x}}, \tilde{f}_l(\hat{\mathbf{x}})\}$ and use a curve-fitting technique to determine the functional relationships $\tilde{f}_l$ for each l.

The problem has now been reduced to

$$\min_{\mathbf{x}\in X} \quad \mathbf{f}(\mathbf{x}), \tag{8.26}$$

which is a deterministic multiobjective optimization problem and can be solved by standard procedures, such as the SWT method, to determine the optimal decision vector $\mathbf{x}^*$.

8.5 Risk and Sensitivity as Multiple Objective Functions

At present, most mathematical models treat important system characteristics such as risk, uncertainty, sensitivity, stability, responsivity, and irreversibility either by means of system constraints or by artificially embedding them in the overall index of performance. The systems analyst (the modeler) assumes the role both of the professional analyst and the decision maker by explicitly or implicitly assigning weights to these and other noncommensurate system characteristics, thus making them commensurate with the performance index (the mathematical model's objective function). Obviously, this process is questionable even where the analyst is the decision maker. When he is not, the result will seldom be the decision maker's optimum.

It is argued elsewhere that these system characteristics can and should be quantified and included in the mathematical models as separate objective functions.[4] These should then be optimized along with the original model's objective function (index of performance) to allow the decison maker(s) to select a preferred policy (solution) from within the Pareto optimal set. Any procedure short of recognizing these characteristics as objective functions in their own right compromises the modeling process.

In previous work a number of questions associated with risk and uncertainty have been tentatively explored to stimulate further analysis and research into the quantifications of these factors for use in multiobjective optimization analysis. A great many problems exist in water resources systems and other civil systems involving resources in which avoidance of risk and uncertainty is often the dominant objective. If suitable quantitative measures of these objectives can be formulated, then SWT or other multiobjective optimization methodologies can determine the optimal, or at least superior, combinations of risk and various forms of return.

This preliminary analysis and discussion indicates that quantitative measures of risk can be defined and used as objectives to be optimized in a multiobjective framework. In some instances uncertainty (unknown probability distribution) can be treated adequately, yet much insight and analysis are required to quantify adequately the major risk factors in such common problems as those involving water resources systems.

The consideration of risk in a multiobjective framework might be used systematically to accomplish several goals. First, it can assist planners, professionals, and decision makers involved in resources planning and management in general, and in water and related land resources management in particular. Second, it can quantify and display the trade-offs involved in reducing risk, sensitivity, irreversibility, and other systems characteristics (viewed as systems objectives) along with reducing cost or

---

[4]See Haimes and Hall [1977], Olenik and Haimes [1979], and Haimes [1980, 1981].

other performance indices, where all these objectives are kept in their noncommensurable units. Third, it can ensure comprehensive consideration of economic issues, social well-being, health hazards, environmental issues, irreversible impacts, and other costs and benefits, regardless of commensurability. Fourth, it can reduce the uncertainty surrounding resources planning and development in general, and water and land resource development and management decisions in particular.

8.5.1 The Uncertainty/Sensitivity Index Method

When potential outcomes cannot be described in objectively known probability distributions, then sensitivity functions can be developed as surrogates for risk functions. This is the idea of the uncertainty/sensitivity index method (USIM).[5]

Let

$f_1(\mathbf{x}, \boldsymbol{\alpha})$ denote the model's single objective function,

$\mathbf{x}$ denote the vector of decision variables,

$\boldsymbol{\alpha}$ denote the vector of exogenous variables,

$y(\mathbf{x}, \boldsymbol{\alpha})$ denote the system model's output, and

$$X = \{\mathbf{x} | \mathbf{x} \in R^N,\, g_i(x, \hat{\boldsymbol{\alpha}}) \leq 0,\, i = 1, 2, \ldots, m\},$$

and let $g_i(\mathbf{x}, \hat{\boldsymbol{\alpha}})$ be the properly defined constraint function. The notation $\hat{\boldsymbol{\alpha}}$ denotes the nominal value of $\boldsymbol{\alpha}$.

Suppose α_1 is a random variable with no known probability distribution function. Then a primitive sensitivity function $f_2(\mathbf{x}, \boldsymbol{\alpha})$, a surrogate for a risk function, can be developed as

$$f_2(\mathbf{x}, \boldsymbol{\alpha}) = \left(\frac{\partial f_1(\mathbf{x}, \boldsymbol{\alpha})}{\partial \alpha_1} \right)^2. \tag{8.27}$$

The overall multiobjective optimization problem in which uncertainty is intrinsically considered in the decision-making process is given by

$$\min_{\mathbf{x} \in X} \begin{pmatrix} f_1(\mathbf{x}, \hat{\boldsymbol{\alpha}}) \\ f_2(\mathbf{x}, \hat{\boldsymbol{\alpha}}) \end{pmatrix}. \tag{8.28}$$

Rarig [1976] and Rarig and Haimes [1982] developed a dispersion index as a measure of uncertainty. Note that the original system model may itself consist of multiple objectives.

---

[5] See Haimes et al. [1975], Haimes and Hall [1977], and Haimes [1981].

8.6. The Hierarchical Multiobjective Approach[6]

Higher-level coordination among the various subsystems in hierarchical structures has commonly been achieved through making commensurable the subsystems' objectives and subsequently applying single-objective optimization techniques. A superior modeling and optimization process involves integrating the hierarchical and multiobjective approaches into a unified framework. This framework combines the strengths of both. The flexibility of hierarchical multiobjective structures makes the modeling process more realistic and understandable to the decision makers—the ultimate users of these models—and the notion of a single "optimal" solution generated in a single-objective model, the cause of skepticism and dismay among executives and decision makers, is replaced with the more realistic concept of Pareto optimality and associated trade-offs.

Integration of the hierarchical and multiobjective approaches may thus result in a hierarchy of noncommensurable objectives at various levels. A large-scale system is likely to be a hierarchical multiobjective structure of four or more levels of objectives and subobjectives (see Figure 8.3).

8.6.1 Problem Formulation

Consider the following multiobjective optimization problem, depicted in Figure 8.4:

$$\min \begin{bmatrix} F_1(\mathbf{f}^1,\ldots,\mathbf{f}^p) \\ \vdots \\ F_n(\mathbf{f}^1,\ldots,\mathbf{f}^p) \end{bmatrix}, \qquad \mathbf{f}^i = \left(f_1^i(\mathbf{x}_i,\mathbf{m}_i,\mathbf{y}_i),\ldots,f_{ni}^i(\mathbf{x}_i,\mathbf{m}_i,\mathbf{y}_i)\right)^{\mathrm{T}} \tag{8.29}$$

$$\text{subject to} \qquad \mathbf{y}_i = \mathbf{H}_i(\mathbf{x}_i,\mathbf{m}_i), \quad i=1,\ldots,p, \tag{8.30}$$

$$\mathbf{x}_i = \sum_{j=1}^{N} C_{ij}\mathbf{y}_j, \quad i=1,\ldots,p \tag{8.31}$$

Here, $\mathbf{y}_i$ is the output vector, $\mathbf{x}_i$ the input vector from other subsystems, and $\mathbf{m}_i$ the decision vector of the subsystem i ($i=1,\ldots,p$). The vector $\mathbf{f}^i$ is the objective vector of subsystem i, n_i being the number of objectives in subsystem i. The overall objectives are functions $F_1,\ldots,F_n$ (not necessarily explicit functions) of the subsystems' objectives, as indicated in (8.29). The subsystems' equations are represented by (8.30), and (8.31) specifies the

[6]This section is adopted from Haimes and Tarvainen [1981], Tarvainen and Haimes [1981, 1982].

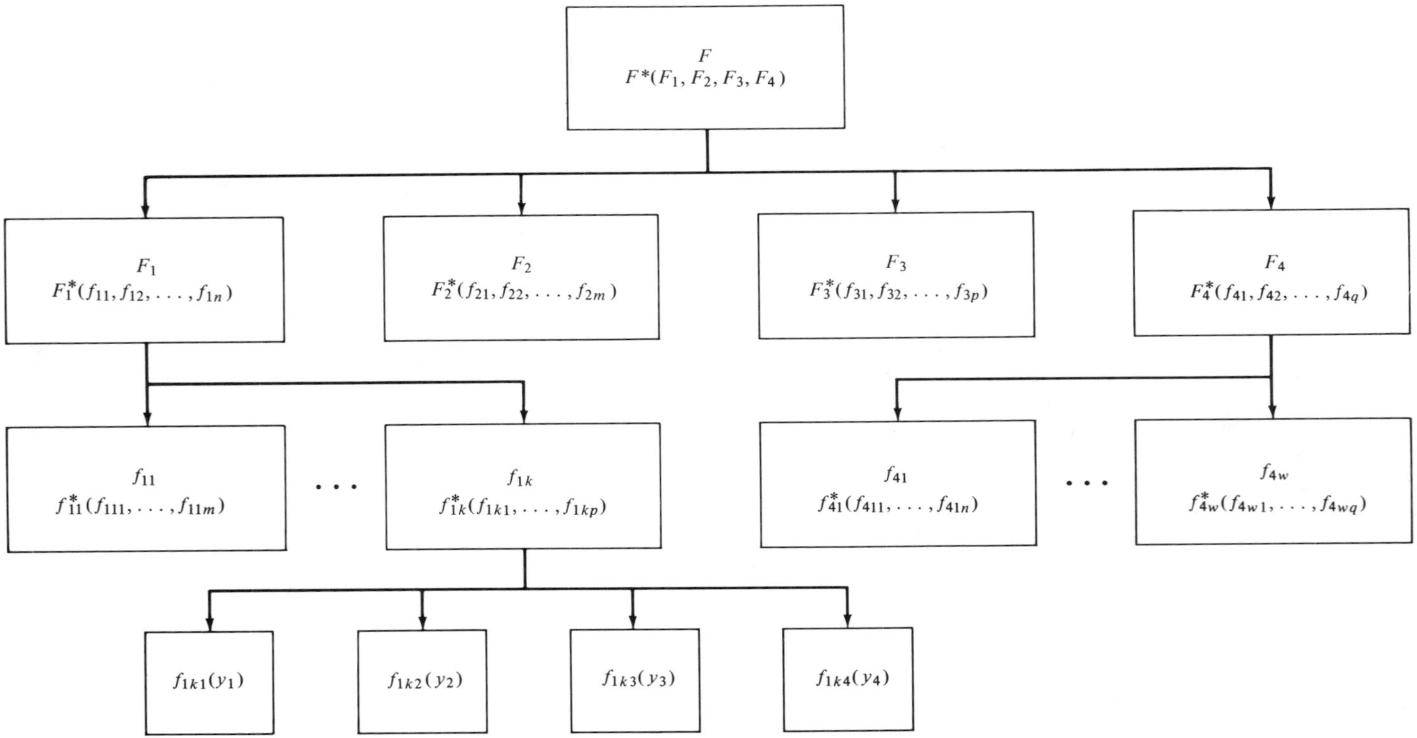

Figure 8.3 Coordination of a hierarchical multiobjective framework.

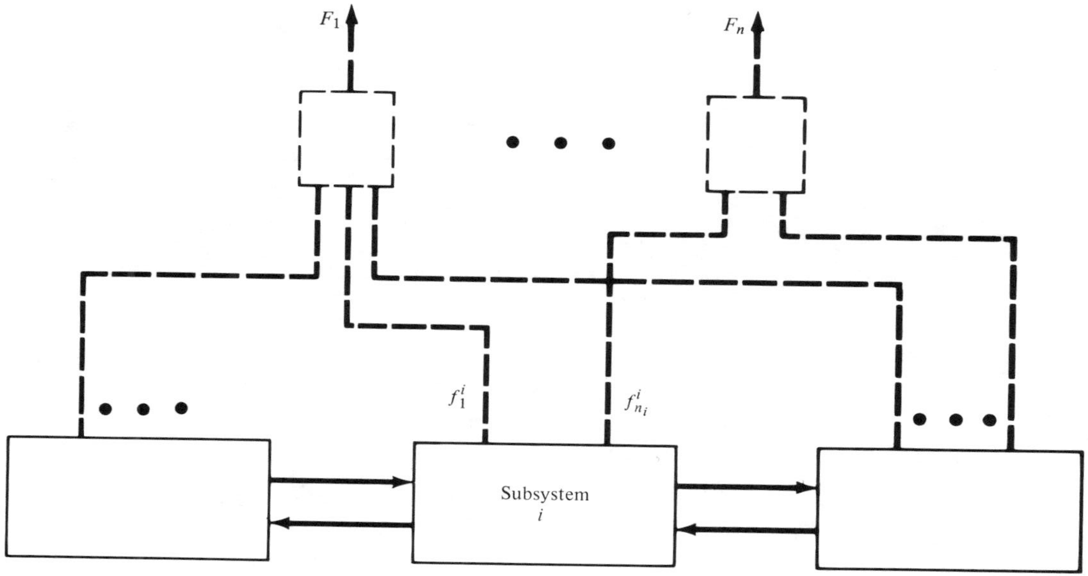

Figure 8.4 Structure of systems and objectives.

interconnections between subsystems, with the C_{ij}s constant matrices. Problem (8.29)–(8.31) is of a rather general form. No principal difficulty is added by including subsystem and overall constraints. A slightly different problem, where the objective structure includes more layers, was studied by Olenik and Haimes [1979]. A case with single objectives in the subsystems is studied in Geoffrion and Hogan [1972].

8.6.2 *The Derivation of Hierarchical Schemes*

As a starting point for developing hierarchical multiobjective schemes, assume that a single decision maker (or a team) obtains the same result when using certain schemes as when solving the problem without decomposition. To establish this equivalence, a characterization of the best-compromise solution is needed. As a means of achieving this characterization, trade-offs are used. In terms of trade-offs, if $\mathbf{z}^0$ is the best-compromise solution of a general multiobjective problem given by

$$\min \quad \{F_1(\mathbf{z}),\ldots,F_n(\mathbf{z})\} \tag{8.32}$$

$$\text{subject to} \quad \mathbf{w}(\mathbf{z}) \leqslant \mathbf{0}, \tag{8.33}$$

then the following set of equations must be satisfied:

$$\boldsymbol{\lambda}^{\mathrm{T}}(\mathbf{F}^0)\frac{\partial \mathbf{F}}{\partial \mathbf{z}}(\mathbf{z}^0)+\boldsymbol{\rho}^{\mathrm{T}}\frac{\partial \mathbf{w}}{\partial \mathbf{z}}(\mathbf{z}^0)=\mathbf{0}, \tag{8.34}$$

$$\boldsymbol{\rho}^{\mathrm{T}}\mathbf{w}(\mathbf{z}^0)=\mathbf{0}, \qquad \boldsymbol{\rho} \geqslant \mathbf{0}, \tag{8.35}$$

$$\mathbf{w}(\mathbf{z}^0) \leqslant \mathbf{0}. \tag{8.36}$$

Here, $\mathbf{F}=(F_1,\ldots,F_n)^{\mathrm{T}}$, $\mathbf{F}^0=\mathbf{F}(\mathbf{z}^0)$, $\boldsymbol{\lambda}(\mathbf{F}^0)=(1,\lambda^*_{12}(\mathbf{F}^0),\ldots,\lambda^*_{1n}(\mathbf{F}^0))^{\mathrm{T}}$ with $\lambda_{ik}(\mathbf{F}^0)$ the indifferent acceptable trade-off between F_1 and F_k $(k=2,\ldots,n)$, $\boldsymbol{\rho}$ is a multiplier vector, and $\partial\mathbf{F}(\ )/\partial\mathbf{z}$ and $\partial\mathbf{w}(\ )/\partial\mathbf{z}$ denote the corresponding Jacobian matrices.

Note that Equations (8.34)–(8.36) are similar to the Kuhn–Tucker conditions for Pareto optimality [Kuhn and Tucker, 1951]. The essential difference is in the use of indifferent trade-offs in (8.34), which makes the above conditions necessary conditions for the best-compromise solution.

A short proof of Equations (8.34)–(8.36) assumes an underlying increasing value function $v(F_1,\ldots,F_n)$, which reaches its maximum at the best-compromise solution. Writing down the single-objective Kuhn–Tucker conditions [Kuhn and Tucker, 1951] for maximizing v subject to Equation (8.33), and taking into account the relations

$$\frac{\partial v}{\partial F_k}\Big/\frac{\partial v}{\partial F_1}=\lambda^*_{1k} \qquad (k=2,\ldots,n)$$

immediately yields conditions (8.34)–(8.36). For a proof without using utility functions, see Tarvainen and Haimes [1982].

With the necessary conditions (8.34)–(8.36), we can proceed as when deriving single-objective hierarchical schemes. That is, we apply the necessary conditions to problem (8.29)–(8.31). Then, some coordination variables are fixed so that the necessary conditions decompose into separate sets of equations, most of which become necessary conditions for respective optimization subproblems. This yields a scheme where an upper level coordinator (or master program) fixes some variables, the subproblems are solved at the lower level, and the rest of the necessary conditions are checked at the upper level; if they are not satisfied, the coordination parameters are modified, and the suboptimizations are repeated until the upper-level conditions are met.

The coordination variables can be chosen in two ways: In the feasible method, they are the physical interaction variables $\mathbf{y}_i$ [when $\mathbf{x}_i$ is determined directly from Equation (8.31)]; in the nonfeasible method they are the ρ multipliers [(8.34)–(8.36)] that relate to Equation (8.31). For a more detailed mathematical explanation of deriving the hierarchical multiobjective schemes, the reader is referred to Tarvainen and Haimes [1982].

Other extensions of the SWT method include the multiobjective optimization of dynamic systems—optimal control problems [Haimes et al., 1975] and the incorporation of the SWT method with a dynamic programming scheme to solve capacity-expansion problems [Chankong et al., 1981]. Nakayama et al. [1980] developed an interactive scheme that is, in principle, similar to an interactive version of the SWT method but invokes (8.10) as the optimality condition. The information obtained from the decision maker at each iteration is $m_{kj}, j \neq k$, rather than W_{kj}. In addition, Seo and Sakawa [1979] proposed a method based on the use of Lagrange multipliers in combination with the component utility function concept. They call it the nested Lagrangian multiplier method.

8.7 The Interactive Surrogate Worth Trade-off Method[7]

8.7.1 Introduction

In this section, we develop an interactive version of the SWT method. As in the development of most of our interactive techniques, the underlying philosophy is to develop a procedure by which the decision maker and the analyst can work in close harmony during the multiobjective decision-making process [MDP]. This procedure allows the complex details of the internal (quantifiable) structure of the multiobjective decision-making problem to be effectively exploited and, at the same time, provides an effective mechanism for treating other important "subjective" elements. The neces-

[7]This section is a condensed version of Chankong and Haimes [1978].

sary theoretical machinery required for developing the ISWT method can be found in Chapter 4. The method is applicable to linear as well as nonlinear multiobjective decision-making problems.

8.7.2 Overview of the ISWT Method

We shall treat multiobjective decision problems of the following form:

Problem 1: Given a multiobjective optimization problem VOP:

$$\min_{\mathbf{x}\in X} \quad \{f_1(\mathbf{x}),\dots,f_n(\mathbf{x})\}, \tag{8.37}$$

$$X=\{\mathbf{x}|\mathbf{x}\in R^N,\, g_i(\mathbf{x})\leqslant 0,\, i=1,\dots,m\}, \tag{8.38}$$

where f_j: $R^N \to R$ for all $j=1,\dots,n$ and g_i: $R^N\to R$ for all $i=1,\dots,m$, find $\mathbf{x}^*\in X^*$, where X^* is the set of noninferior solutions of VOP such that $\mathbf{x}^*$ solves the MDP,

$$\max_{\mathbf{x}\in X^*} \quad v(f_1(\mathbf{x}),\dots,f_n(\mathbf{x})), \tag{8.39}$$

where v, a value function defined on $F=\{f(\mathbf{x})|\mathbf{x}\in X\}$, is assumed to exist and is *known only implicitly to the decision maker* (see the discussion of the value function in Chapter 3).

However, since most scalar optimization techniques can only guarantee local solutions, we shall be content as a solution to Problem 1 with a local noninferior solution of the VOP. We therefore modify Problem 1 to read as follows:

Problem 2: Given a VOP, find $\mathbf{x}^*\in \hat{X}^*$, the set of local noninferior solutions of VOP so that $\mathbf{x}^*$ solves MDP:

$$\max_{\mathbf{x}\in \hat{X}^*} \quad v(f_1(\mathbf{x}),\dots,f_n(\mathbf{x})), \tag{8.40}$$

where $\hat{X}^*$ is the set of local noninferior solutions of VOP. Throughout this section, we make the following assumptions:

Assumption 1. v: $F\to R$ exists and is known only implicitly to the decision maker. Moreover, it is assumed to be continuously differentiable and a monotonic nonincreasing function of f.

Assumption 2. All $f_j, j=1,\dots,n$, and all g_i, $i=1,\dots,m$, are twice continuously differentiable in their respective domains.

Assumption 3. X is compact (so that for every feasible $P_k(\boldsymbol{\varepsilon})$ its solution always exists and is finite).

The ISWT method, like the SWT method, is designed to solve Problem 2. Again, the ε-constraint problem $P_k(\boldsymbol{\varepsilon})$, where $P_k(\boldsymbol{\varepsilon})$ is $\min\{f_k(\mathbf{x})|\, f_j(\mathbf{x})\leqslant \varepsilon_j$

for all $j \neq k$ and $\mathbf{x} \in X\}$, is used as a means of obtaining local noninferior solutions of the VOP.

The proposed method follows the steps of the SWT method up to the point where all the surrogate worth values (W_{kj} for all $j \neq k$) corresponding to a local noninferior solution are obtained from the DM. Careful study reveals that there is close relationship between W_{kj} and the directional derivative of the value function evaluated at the current local noninferior solution and in the direction defined in terms of the associated Kuhn–Tucker multiplier. In light of this relation, a model DM interactive on-line scheme can be constructed in such a way that the values of all W_{kj} are used to determine the direction (in a reduced objective space) in which the value function, although unknown (its true form is never required in the computation), increases most rapidly. In this way we can construct a sequence of locally noninferior points. Each is an improvement (i.e., increases the value function) over the previous one, thereby converging to an unconstrained optimum (i.e., terminates in the indifference band, $W_{kj}=0$ for all $j \neq k$), or a constrained optimum (i.e., the next possible improvement point will be infeasible).

Figure 8.5 depicts in a flow diagram the structure of the ISWT method, which may be outlined as follows:

Step 0: initialization. Select f_k as a primary objective. Guess an initial $\boldsymbol{\varepsilon}^0$.

Step 1: local noninferior solution. With the current $\boldsymbol{\varepsilon}^i$, formulate $P_k(\boldsymbol{\varepsilon}^i)$ and solve for (strict) local solution $\mathbf{x}^i$. Obtain all necessary trade-off information at this point.

Step 2: worth assessments. Exchange information obtained from step 1 with the decision maker and in return obtain the worth values W_{kj}^i for $j \neq k$ from the DM.

Step 3: termination. Check stopping criteria and if not satisfied, proceed.

Step 4: update. Use W_{kj}^i to update $\boldsymbol{\varepsilon}^i \to \boldsymbol{\varepsilon}^{i+1}$ and return to step 1.

The part played by the decision maker (step 2) in dictating the best direction for the search away from the current trial point will be discussed after we describe the method in detail.

8.7.3 Detailed Components of the ISWT Method

The theory required for step 1 of the ISWT method can be found in Chapter 4. We shall describe its use, developing new results as the need arises.

Local Noninferiority For $\mathbf{x}^i$ [which solves $P_k(\boldsymbol{\varepsilon}^i)$] to be a local noninferior solution of a nonlinear MOP, the following conditions should be satisfied: $\mathbf{x}^i$ must be a regular point of the constraints of $P_k(\boldsymbol{\varepsilon}^i)$, second-order sufficiency conditions must be satisfied at $\mathbf{x}^i$, and all binding constraints

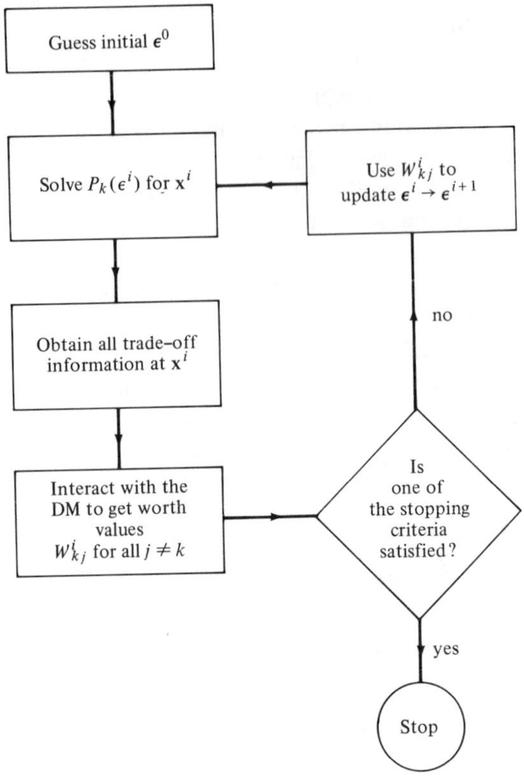

Figure 8.5 The underlying structure of the ISWT method.

must be nondegenerate. Normally we assume that the second-order sufficiency conditions are satisfied (a mild assumption for smooth nonlinear curves). The binding constraints can easily be checked for nondegeneracy. For problems with many more variables than constraints, it is likely that gradients of all constraints at a particular point will be linearly independent, indicating that for such problems the regularity condition is likely to be satisfied at most points. For small problems (i.e., small N), however, the regularity condition should be checked using, for example, the Gaussian elimination process.

For linear problems, only the nondegeneracy condition is required.

Trade-off Information and Assessment of Worth Values Given that $\mathbf{x}^i$ satisfies the conditions in Section 4.9.1, we have established that if λ^i_{kl}, the Kuhn–Tucker multiplier associated with the constraint $f_l(\mathbf{x}) \leqslant \varepsilon^i_l$, is positive for each $l \neq k$, then λ^i_{kl} approximates a local partial trade-off at point $\mathbf{x}^i$. To move from $\mathbf{x}^i$ to some other locally noninferior point in the neighborhood of

$\mathbf{x}^i$, λ^i_{kl} units of f_k will always be given up per one unit gain of f_l (or vice versa), with all other objectives remaining constant at the level of $f_l(\mathbf{x}^i)$, $l \neq k$ and j.

Thus if $\lambda^k_{kl} > 0$ for all $l \neq k$, we ask the decision maker for each $l \neq k$

Question 1. "Given that $f_j = f_j(\mathbf{x}^i)$ for all $j = 1, \ldots, n$, how (much) would you like to decrease f_k by λ^i_{kl} units for each one unit increase in f_l with all other f_j remaining unchanged?"

The decision maker is asked to show his degree of preference in the trade-off by assigning to W^i_{kl} a number between $+10$ and -10. A large positive value of W^i_{kl} indicates a strong preference to make the prescribed exchange and vice versa. If $W^i_{kl} = 0$, the decision maker is indifferent to the prescribed trade. Care should be taken in phrasing the question to the decision maker since an erroneously worded question may affect the sign of W^i_{kl}.

At the end of this questioning period we have a sequence of numbers (integers) representing W^i_{kl} for all $l \neq k$, which will then be used in the *updating* procedure. If some $\lambda^i_{kj} = 0$, according to Theorem 4.30 we would like to have λ^i_{kj} strictly positive for all $j \neq k$ for each generated point $\mathbf{x}^i$ (in order to claim local proper noninferiority for $\mathbf{x}^i$). Unfortunately, such a condition cannot be guaranteed. We can only control the choice of ε. We may therefore have to work with zero-valued Kuhn–Tucker multipliers because of the breakdown of the regularity assumption. (See the example at the end of Chapter 4.)

For convenience, we shall make use of the following notation: $J_k = \{j \mid 1 \leqslant j \leqslant n,\ j \neq k\}$, $J^i_k = \{j \mid j \in J_k,\ \lambda^i_{kj} > 0\}$ and $J_k - J^i_k = \{j \mid j \in J_k,\ \lambda^i_{kj} = 0\}$. When $J_k - J^i_k \neq \varnothing$, if we make a small change of δf_l units in f_l, where $l \in J^i_k$, then f_k changes by $-\lambda^i_{kl}\,\delta f_l$, and each f_j, where $\lambda^i_{kj} = 0$, also changes by $(\nabla f_j(\mathbf{x}^i) \cdot \partial \mathbf{x}(\boldsymbol{\varepsilon}^i)/\partial \varepsilon_l)\,\delta f_l$ units as was shown in Theorem 4.30(c). For this reason, we ask the decision maker (for each $l \in J^i_k$) the following question:

Question 2. "Given that $f_j = f_j(\mathbf{x}^i)$ for all $j = 1, \ldots, n$, how (much) would you like to decrease f_k by λ^i_{kl} units and change f_j by $\nabla f_j(\mathbf{x}^i) \cdot \partial \mathbf{x}(\boldsymbol{\varepsilon}^i)/\partial \varepsilon_l$ units, while increasing f_l by one unit?"

At the end of this questioning period we again have a sequence of numbers representing W^i_{kl} for all $l \in J^i_k$, which will be used in the updating procedure.

Observe that all values required by question 2 are known except $\partial \mathbf{x}(\boldsymbol{\varepsilon}^i)/\partial \varepsilon_l$, $l \in J^i_k$, which may be computed either of two ways:

i. For each $l \in J^i_k$, solve $P_k[\boldsymbol{\varepsilon}^i(l)]$, where $\boldsymbol{\varepsilon}^i(l) = (\varepsilon^i_1, \ldots, \varepsilon^i_{k-1}, \varepsilon^i_{k+1}, \ldots, \varepsilon^i_l + \delta\varepsilon_l, \ldots, \varepsilon^i_n)$ and some small $\delta\varepsilon_l \neq 0$, to get $x[\varepsilon^i(l)]$; then

$$\frac{\partial \mathbf{x}(\boldsymbol{\varepsilon}^i)}{\partial \varepsilon_l} \approx \frac{\mathbf{x}(\boldsymbol{\varepsilon}^i(l)) - \mathbf{x}^i}{\delta \varepsilon_l}. \tag{8.41}$$

ii. Let $\mathbf{H}(\mathbf{x}^i)$ be a vector consisting of all the binding constraints at $\mathbf{x}^i$ arranged such that its last p components are $f_{j_1}(\mathbf{x}^i),\ldots,f_{j_p}(\mathbf{x}^i)$, where $J_k^i=\{j_1,\ldots,j_p\}$. Then for each $1 \leqslant a \leqslant p$, $\partial \mathbf{x}(\varepsilon^i)/\partial \varepsilon_{j_a}$ is given in the ath column of the matrix B, where B is the top right $N \times p$ matrix of the matrix

$$\begin{pmatrix} L(\mathbf{x}^i) & (\nabla h(\mathbf{x}^i))^{\mathrm{T}} \\ \nabla h(\mathbf{x}^i) & 0 \end{pmatrix}^{-1},$$

and $L(\mathbf{x}^i)$ is the Hessian matrix of the Lagrangian of $P_k(\boldsymbol{\varepsilon}^i)$,

$$f_k(\mathbf{x})+\sum_{j\neq k}\lambda_{kj}f_j(\mathbf{x})+\sum_{i=1}^{m}\mu_i g_i(\mathbf{x})$$

[Rarig, 1976]. In any case, estimating $\partial \mathbf{x}(\boldsymbol{\varepsilon}^i)/\partial \varepsilon_l$ is not easy when n and N are large. We should therefore use question 2 as a last resort. A possible alternative to using question 2 is suggested in Chankong [1977].

Updating $\boldsymbol{\varepsilon}^i$ ($\boldsymbol{\varepsilon}^i \to \boldsymbol{\varepsilon}^{i+1}$) After obtaining W_{kj}^i, $j \in J_k^i$, we would like to use them to estimate a new $\boldsymbol{\varepsilon}^{i+1}$ so that $\mathbf{x}^{i+1}$ [which is a solution of $P_k(\boldsymbol{\varepsilon}^{i+1})$] will be an improved point; i.e.,

$$v^i=v\big(f_1(\mathbf{x}^i),\ldots,f_n(\mathbf{x}^i)\big)<v\big(f_1(\mathbf{x}^{i+1}),\ldots,f_n(\mathbf{x}^{i+1})\big)=v^{i+1}.$$

As an illustration of the simplicity of the underlying idea, consider a simple problem with three objective functions $f_1(\mathbf{x})$, $f_2(\mathbf{x})$, and $f_3(\mathbf{x})$. The set of feasible alternatives X is, for simplicity, assumed to be R^2. To generate noninferior solutions, we shall use the constraint problem $P_1(\boldsymbol{\varepsilon})$ defined as

$$\max \quad f_1(\mathbf{x}) \tag{8.42}$$

$$\text{subject of} \quad f_2(\mathbf{x}) \leqslant \varepsilon_2, \tag{8.43a}$$

$$f_3(\mathbf{x}) \leqslant \varepsilon_3, \tag{8.43b}$$

$\mathbf{x} \in X$. For a selected $\boldsymbol{\varepsilon}^0$, let $\mathbf{x}^0$ solve $P_1(\boldsymbol{\varepsilon}^0)$, with $\lambda_{12}^0>0$ and $\lambda_{13}^0>0$ being the corresponding Kuhn–Tucker multipliers of (8.43a) and (8.43b), respectively. Assuming that the regularity and second-order sufficiency conditions are satisfied at $\mathbf{x}^0$, $\mathbf{x}^0$ is then a local noninferior solution. Also $-\lambda_{12}^0$ and $-\lambda_{13}^0$ represent the partial trade-off rates at $\mathbf{x}^0$. This allows us to interact with the decision maker by asking, "Given that $f_i=f_i(\mathbf{x}^0)$, $i=1,2,3$, how (much) would you like to decrease f_1 by λ_{12}^0 units per one unit increase in f_2 while f_3 remains unchanged?"

Suppose the decision maker responds by assigning $W_{12}^0=+8$, indicating that he particularly likes that trade. This means that if we can generate a new point with $f_2=f_2(\mathbf{x}^0)+\delta f_2$ ($\delta f_2>0$), $f_1=f_1(\mathbf{x}^0)+\lambda_{12}^0\,\delta f_2$, and $f_3=f_3(\mathbf{x}^0)$, then this point will be a better point than $\mathbf{x}^0$ according to the decision maker's preference. Intuitively, by the interpretation of λ_{12}^0, one way to obtain an approximation of such a point is to change the right-hand side of (8.43b) from ε_2^0 to $\varepsilon_2^0 + \delta f_2$ (keeping $\varepsilon_3 = \varepsilon_3^0$) and to solve the problem again.

Now the decision maker is asked a similar question that uses λ_{13}^0 and interchanges the roles of f_2 and f_3. Suppose again that the decision maker responds by assigning $W_{13}^0 = -4$ (indicating that he rather prefers although not as enthusiastically as previously) to increase f_1 and decrease f_3 by the approximate ratio of λ_{13}^0 (units f_1/unit f_3) with f_2 unchanged. Thus, if a new point can be found so that at this new point $f_3 = f_3(\mathbf{x}^0) - \delta f_3$ (for some small $\delta f_3 > 0$), $f_1 = f_1(\mathbf{x}^0) + \lambda_{13}\delta f_3$, and $f_2 = f_2(\mathbf{x}^0)$, the decision maker will prefer the new point to $\mathbf{x}^0$. Again a linear approximation of such a point can be obtained by changing the right-hand side of (8.43b) from ε_3^0 to $\varepsilon_3^0 + \delta f_3$ (keeping $\varepsilon_2 = \varepsilon_2^0$) and solving the problem again. Analyzing the decision maker's responses to both questions, one would expect that the solution $\mathbf{x}^1$ of a new problem $P_1(\boldsymbol{\varepsilon}^1)$, where $\varepsilon_2^1 = \varepsilon_2^0 + \delta f_2$ and $\varepsilon_3^1 = \varepsilon_3^0 - \delta f_3$ ($\delta f_2 > 0$ and $\delta f_3 > 0$), would be a better point than $\mathbf{x}^0$ according to the decision maker's preference. This is demonstrated by assuming that the decision maker's structure of preference can be characterized by a monotone nonincreasing value function v.

Under the specified assumptions and if δf_2 and δf_3 are sufficiently small, $\mathbf{x}^1 (\neq \mathbf{x}^0)$ always exists and is unique (hence it is a local noninferior solution). Under the same assumptions, we are able to *independently* control the levels of f_2 and f_3 and still remain on the locally noninferior surface in the neighborhood of $\mathbf{x}^0$ [see Theorem 4.30(a)]. This allows the decision maker to make all necessary assessments and answer the two questions independently.

We have been using the signs of W_{12}^0 and W_{13}^0 as a clue to obtain a new point. The question remains of how much ε_2 and ε_3 should be changed to obtain the best available new point. The clue again lies in the relative values of W_{12}^0 and W_{13}^0 (as well as the scaling factors for f_2 and f_3). In the following development, we shall formalize this idea and extend it to a more general case.

The Relationship Between W_{kj}^i and the Utility Function U We shall assume that the conventions discussed in Section 8.2 can be successfully implemented to obtain values for W_{kj}. Let W_{kj}^i be obtained by means of Question 1. Specifically, the value of W_{kj}^i indicates the degree of decision maker's preference in a ratio scale of -10 to $+10$ for exchanging (decreasing) λ_{kj}^i units of f_k per one-unit increase of f_j, with all other objectives remaining unchanged. On the other hand, we observe that the expression

$$\lim_{h_j \to 0} \frac{v\left(f_1^i, \ldots, f_k^i - \lambda_{kj}^i h_j, \ldots, f_j^i + h_j, \ldots, f_n^i\right) - v\left(f_1^i, \ldots, f_n^i\right)}{h_j} \tag{8.44}$$

also represents the degree of the decision maker's preferences in another ratio scale for the same prescribed trade-off. Correspondingly, given λ^i_{kj} and $f_j^i, j \neq k$, there should be a one-to-one correspondence between W^i_{kj} and the expression (8.44). Moreover as W^i_{kj} vanishes or increases, so does the expression (8.44) and vice versa. Thus, it is reasonable to assume that there exists a monotonically increasing function γ^i_j with $\gamma^i_j(0) = 0$ such that

$$\gamma^i_j\left(W^i_{kj}\right) = \lim_{h_j \to 0} \frac{v\left(f_1^i, \ldots, f_k^i - \lambda^i_{kj} h_j, \ldots, f_j^i + h_j, \ldots, f_n^i\right) - v\left(f_1^i, \ldots, f_n^i\right)}{h_j}. \tag{8.45}$$

For a more formal definition of γ^i_j, see Appendix A.2 of Chankong [1977]. Here we observe that before γ^i_j can be defined the point $(\lambda^i_{kj}, f_1^i, \ldots, f_n^i)$ must be specified. This explains the superscript i in γ^i_j. Likewise the subscript j indicates that γ^i_j is different for each j to be consistent with the right-hand side of (8.45).

By definition the right-hand side of (8.45) is the directional derivative of v in the direction $\mathbf{d}_{kj} \triangleq (0, \ldots, 0, -\lambda^i_{kj}(k\text{th}), 0, \ldots, 0, 1(j\text{th}), 0, \ldots, 0)^{\mathrm{T}}$. With this observation it follows that

$$\begin{aligned}
\lim_{h_j \to 0} & \frac{v\left(f_1^i, \ldots, f_k^i - \lambda^i_{kj} h_j, \ldots, f_j^i + h_j, \ldots, f_n^i\right) - v\left(f_1^i, \ldots, f_n^i\right)}{h_j} \\
& \triangleq \nabla_f v\left(f_1^i, \ldots, f_n^i\right) \cdot \mathbf{d}_{kj} \\
& = \left(\frac{\partial v}{\partial f_j}\right)^i - \left(\frac{\partial v}{\partial f_k}\right)^i \lambda^i_{kj},
\end{aligned}$$

where

$$\left(\frac{\partial v}{\partial f_j}\right)^i \triangleq \frac{\partial}{\partial f_j} v\left(f_1(\mathbf{x}^i), \ldots, f_n(\mathbf{x}^i)\right).$$

Hence

$$\left(\frac{\partial v}{\partial f_j}\right)^i - \left(\frac{\partial v}{\partial f_k}\right)^i \lambda^i_{kj} = \gamma^i_j\left(W^i_{kj}\right). \tag{8.46}$$

For W^i_{kj} obtained by means of question 2, it is reasonable to assume that there exists a monotonically increasing function γ^i_j such that $\gamma^i_j(0) = 0$ and

$$\gamma^i_j\left(W^i_{kj}\right) = \lim_{h_j \to 0} \frac{v\left(f_1^i + b^i_{1j} h_j, \ldots, f_k^i - \lambda^i_{kj} h_j, \ldots, f_n^i + b^i_{nj} h_j\right) - v\left(f_1^i, \ldots, f_n^i\right)}{h_j}, \tag{8.47}$$

where

$$b^i_{lj} = \nabla f_l(\mathbf{x}^i) \cdot \frac{\partial \mathbf{x}(\boldsymbol{\varepsilon}^i)}{\partial \varepsilon_j} \qquad \text{for all} \quad l \neq k, j.$$

(Observe that $b^i_{lj}=0$ for all $l\in J^i_k=\{j|1\leqslant j\leqslant n, \lambda^i_{kj}>0\}$ and $b^i_{jj}=1$.) Since the right-hand side of (8.47) is the directional derivative of v in the direction

$$\mathbf{d}_{kj} \triangleq \left(b^i_{1j},\ldots,b^i_{k-1,j},-\lambda^i_{kj},b^i_{k+1,j},\ldots,b^i_{j-1,j},1,b^i_{j+1,j},\ldots,b^i_{nj}\right)^{\mathrm{T}},$$

and using (8.47), we have

$$\left(\frac{\partial v}{\partial f_l}\right)^i-\left(\frac{\partial v}{\partial f_k}\right)^i\lambda^i_{kl}+\sum_{j\in J_k-J^i_k}\left(\frac{\partial v}{\partial f_j}\right)^i b^i_{jl}=\gamma^i_j\left(W^i_{kj}\right). \tag{8.48}$$

In summary we have established that W^i_{kj} is closely related to a directional derivative of v. When W^i_{kj} is obtained using question 1, (8.46) represents such a relationship. Furthermore, (8.48) represents a similar relation when W^i_{kj} is obtained using question 2. With these relationships we can utilize the information embodied in W^i_{kj} to develop schemes for determining the search direction, step size, and some stopping criteria. For further details, see Chankong [1977].

8.8 Summary

This chapter has presented methods designed for the same class of problems treated in Chapter 7. Like the methods discussed in Section 7.4, the underlying concept for all techniques discussed here is the trade-off. Within this group, the surrogate worth trade-off method forms the nucleus from which other methods are derived. The SWT method, which principally is a deterministic, noninteractive, single-decision-maker technique, has been extended to multiple-decision-maker problems (Section 8.3), stochastic problems (Sections 8.4 and 8.5), hierarchical multiobjective problems (Section 8.6), and interactive features of the method (Section 8.7).

The SWT method and its interactive version can be applied to both linear and nonlinear problems and are based partly on the main results developed in Chapter 4, partly on a relationship between the utility function and the surrogate worth function constructed by interaction with the decision maker. In these methods, the analyst generates noninferior solutions and provides the decision maker with information about local behavior of the model in the form of trade-offs (the values of appropriate Kuhn–Tucker multipliers). The decision maker reacts to such information and provides his preference assessment in the form of surrogate worth. This information is then used to arrive at the best-compromise solution. Other extensions and applications of the SWT method can be found in the literature cited.

References

Arrow, K. J. (1951). *Social Choice and Individual Values*, Wiley, New York.

Arrow, K. J. (1963). *Social Choice and Individual Values*, Yale University Press, New Haven.

Chankong, V. (1977). Multiobjective decision making analysis, Ph.D. thesis, Case Western Reserve University, Cleveland, Ohio.

Chankong, V., and Haimes, Y. Y. (1978). *The Interactive Surrogate Worth Trade-off (ISWT) Method for Multiobjective Decision Making*, Springer, New York.

Chankong, V., Haimes, Y. Y., and Gemperline, D. (1981). Multiobjective dynamic programming for capacity expansion, *IEEE Transactions on Automatic Control* (Bellman's special issue) AC-26, 1195–1207.

Cohon, J. (1978). *Multiobjective Programming and Planning*, Academic, New York.

Cohon, J., and Marks, D. H. (1975). A review and evaluation of multiobjective programming techniques, *Water Resources Research* 11, 208–220.

Das, P., and Haimes, Y. Y. (1980). Multiobjective optimization in water quality and land management, *Water Resources Research* 15(6).

Fleming, M. (1952). A cardinal concept of welfare, *Quarterly Journal of Economics* 66, 336–384.

Geoffrion, A. M., and Hogan, W. W. (1972). Coordination of two-level organizations with multiple objectives, in *Techniques of Optimization* (A. V. Balakrishnan, ed.), Academic, New York, pp. 455–466.

Goodman, I. A., and Markowitz, H. (1952). Social welfare functions based on individual rankings, *American Journal of Sociology* 58, 257–262.

Haimes, Y. Y. (1977). *Hierarchical Analyses of Water Resources Systems: Modeling and Optimization of Large-Scale Systems*, McGraw-Hill, New York.

Haimes, Y. Y. (1980). The surrogate worth trade-off method and its extensions, in *Multiple Criteria Decision Making Theory and Applications — Hagen/Königswinter, West Germany, 1979* (G. Fandel and T. Gal, eds.), Springer, Berlin, pp. 85–108.

Haimes, Y. Y., (1981). Risk benefit analysis in a multiobjective framework, in *Risk/Benefit Analysis in Water Resources Planning and Management* (Y. Y. Haimes, ed.), Plenum, New York, pp. 89–122.

Haimes, Y. Y., and Chankong, V. (1979). Kuhn–Tucker multipliers as trade-offs in multiobjective decision-making analysis, *Automatica* 15, 59–72.

Haimes, Y. Y., and Hall, W. A. (1974). Multiobjectives in water resources systems analysis: the surrogate worth trade-off method, *Water Resources Research* 10, 614–624.

Haimes, Y. Y., and Hall, W. A. (1977). Sensitivity, responsivity, stability, and irreversibility as multiple objectives in civil systems, *Advances in Water Resources* 1, no. 2.

Haimes, Y. Y., Hall, W. A., and Freedman, H. T. (1975). *Multiobjective Optimization in Water Resource Systems: The Surrogate Worth Trade-off Method*, Elsevier, Amsterdam.

Haimes, Y. Y., Das, P., and Sung, K. (1979). Level-B multiobjective planning for water and land, *ASCE Journal of the Water Resources Planning and Management Division* 105, no. WR2.

Haimes, Y. Y., Loparo, K. A., Olenik, S. C., and Nanda, S. K. (1980). Multiobjective statistical method (MSM) for interior drainage systems, *Water Resources Research* 16, 465–475.

Haimes, Y. Y., and Tarvainen, K. (1981). Hierarchical-multiobjective framework for large scale systems, in *Multicriteria Analysis in Practice* (P. Nijkamp and J. Spronk, eds.), Gower, London, pp. 201–232.

Hall, W. A., and Haimes, Y. Y. (1976). The surrogate worth trade-off method with multiple decision-makers, in *Multiple Criteria Decision-Making: Kyoto, 1975* (M. Zeleny, ed.), Springer, New York, pp. 207–233.

Helmer, O., (1967). Analysis of the future: the Delphi method, The RAND Corporation, P-3558.

Harsanyi, J. C. (1955). Cardinal welfare, individualistic ethics, and interpersonal comparison in utility, *Journal of Political Economy* 63, 309–321.

Inoue, K., Tanino, T., Nakayama, H., and Sawaragi, Y. (1981). A trial towards group decision in structuring environmental science, presented at the Fourth Criteria Decision Making Conference, University of Delaware, August 10–15.

Kirkwood, C. W. (1972). Decision analysis incorporating preferences of groups, tech. rep. no. 74, Operations Research Center, Massachusetts Institute of Technology.

Kuhn, H. W., and Tucker, A. W. (1951). Nonlinear programming, *Proceedings of the Second Berkeley Symposium on Mathematics, Statistics, and Probability*, University of California Press, Berkeley, pp. 481–492.

Lasdon, L., and Waren, A. D. (1978). Generalized reduced gradient software for linearly and nonlinearly constrained problems, in *Design and Implementation of Optimization Software* (H. Greenberg, ed.), Sijthof and Noordhoff, The Netherlands, p. 363.

Luce, R. D., and Raiffa, H. (1957). *Games and Decisions: Introduction and Critical Survey*, Wiley, New York.

Nakayama, M., Tanino, T., and Sawaragi, Y. (1980). An interactive optimization method in multicriteria decision making, *IEEE Transactions on Systems, Man, and Cybernetics* SMC-10, 163–169.

Olenik, S. C., and Haimes, Y. Y. (1979). A hierarchical-multiobjective method for water resources planning, *IEEE Transactions on Systems, Man, and Cybernetics* SMC-9, 534–544.

Rarig, H. (1976). Two new measures of performance and parameter sensitivity in multiobjective optimization problems, M.S. thesis, Case Western Reserve University, Cleveland.

Rarig, H., and Haimes, Y. Y. (1982). Risk dispersion index method, *IEEE Transactions on Systems, Man, and Cybernetics* (in press).

Rietveld, P. (1980). *Multiple Objective Decision Methods and Regional Planning*, North Holland, New York.

Sage, A. (1977). *Methodology for Large-Scale Systems*, McGraw-Hill, New York.

Sakawa, M. (1978). Multiobjective optimization by the surrogate worth trade-off method, *IEEE Transactions on Reliability* R-27, 311–313.

Seo, F., and Sakawa, S. M. (1979). A methodology for environmental systems management: dynamic application of the nested Lagrangian multiplier method, *IEEE Transactions on Systems, Man, and Cybernetics* SMC-9, 794–805.

Tarvainen, K., and Haimes, Y. Y. (1981). Hierarchical-multiobjective framework for energy storage systems, in *Organizations: Multiple Agents with Multiple Criteria* (J. Morse, ed.), Springer, Berlin, pp. 424–446.

Tarvainen, K., and Haimes, Y. Y. (1982). Coordination of hierarchical-multiobjective systems: theory and methodology, *IEEE Transactions on Systems, Man, and Cybernetics* (in press).

Zwick, P. D. (1981). Coordination in a hierarchical multiobjective framework: application to energy storage systems, Master's thesis, Department of Systems Engineering, Case Western Reserve University, Cleveland.

Zwick, P., and Haimes, Y. Y. (1981). Computational aspects of hierarchical multiobjective coordination, Technical memo no. LSSPA-81-2, Center for Large Scale Systems and Policy Analysis, Case Western Reserve University, Cleveland.

Chapter 9
Comparative Evaluation and Comments

9.1 Introduction

We have, with few exceptions, avoided until now evaluating the methods discussed. In this chapter, we aim to compare the merits of the methods. To do so, we must evaluate from two points of view: the decision maker's and the analyst's.

The decision maker's participation and cooperation in the solution process is essential. Moreover, the decision maker's trust in the reliability of the method and the outcome and his willingness to act on it are imperative if the method is to have any worth. The analyst must make the necessary preparations, formulations, and analysis in conformity with the requirements of the particular methodology. It follows that a complete evaluation considers both subjective and objective merits. The former is concerned with how a particular method is perceived and received by the users, particularly the decision makers. The latter, on the other hand, is related to such objective criteria as the type and amount of input required, the type and quality of output produced, as well as those criteria which reflect the logical structure and internal consistency of a particular method itself.

9.2 Evaluation by Classification Scheme: An *ex ante* Evaluation

When various multiobjective decision making methods are classified according to a particular scheme, certain of their characteristics are highlighted. These characteristics often reflect the situations in which a particular method is applicable, the way in which it should be used, and the type and quality of product one can expect.

Examples of the many classification schemes which have been proposed[1] are presented here:

1. Classification schemes based on the manner in which the decision maker participates in the solution process include, for example, the noninteractive–interactive and a priori–"progressive"–a posteriori articulation of preferences (see Cohon and Marks [1975] and Hwang and Masad [1979]).
2. Classification schemes based on the types of preference information given to or elicited from the decision maker include, for example, global preference function, priorities, goals and ideals, and trade-offs and preferences (see Ho [1979] and also Chapter 7).
3. Discipline-oriented classification schemes include, for example, group methods such as mathematical economics, psychometric analysis, mathematical optimization, cost-effectiveness and cost-benefit analysis, and decision analysis (suggested by Bell et al. [1977]).
4. Classification schemes may be based on the number of decision makers (e.g., Cohon [1978] and Rietveld [1980]).
5. Classification schemes may be based on decision situations according to the types of variables, the states of nature, and the description of the set of alternatives [Zionts, 1980].
6. Classification schemes may be based on the type of input, instruments or throughput, and output [Despontin and Spronk, 1979; Rietveld, 1980].

In accordance with Chapter 1, we have throughout Part II followed a classification strategy based on the following two groups of criteria:

A. *Decision Situation or Problem Structure.* This includes the
   - A1. type of decision variables and attributes (discrete or continuous),
   - A2. level of measurement of the above variables (nominal, ordinal, interval, or ratio scales),
   - A3. state of nature (deterministic or probabilistic),
   - A4. description of the set of alternatives (explicit or implicit; if explicit and finite, is it large or small?), and
   - A5. type of causal and means–ends relationships (linear, convex, or nonlinear).

B. *Decision Rule or Preference Modeling.* This signifies the type of preference information required. It includes three main classes:
   - B1. global preference functions;
   - B2. priorities, weights, goals, and ideals; and
   - B3. trade-offs and preferences.

---

[1] See, for example, MacCrimmon [1973], Cohon and Mark [1975], Bell, Keeney, and Raiffa [1955], Starr and Zeleny [1977], Cohon [1978], Hwang and Masud [1979], Despontin and Spronk [1979], Ho [1979], Zionts [1980], and Rietveld [1980].

In addition, we can subclassify methods in each of the above classes using the following additional groups of criteria.

C. *Input Required by the Method.* This can be further categorized as
   C1. data requirement (types, amount, and accuracy),
   C2. the manner and extent of the decision maker participation, and
   C3. the number of decision makers.
D. *Output or Product of the Method.* This includes the following options:
   D1. the best-compromise solution that is also noninferior,
   D2. the best-compromise solution that may not be noninferior, and
   D3. a list of ranked alternatives.

In view of these classification criteria, which can also serve as evaluation criteria, we now give a capsule *ex ante* evaluation of various methods discussed in this book. Some of the statements contained herein are based on our own value judgments, experience, and knowledge of the methods.

9.2.1 Criterion A: Problem Structure or Decision Situation

Subcriterion A1: Type of Decision Variables and Attributes (Discrete or Continuous) The multiattribute value and utility function, the lexicographic, and the ELECTRE methods can be used for either discrete or continuous problems, whereas the construction procedures for the indifference curve method are mainly for continuous variables. Generating techniques and other mathematical programming techniques are generally designed for continuous problems. Any of these methods can also be applied to discrete problems if i) there exist appropriate solution techniques for solving associated scalar optimization problems and ii) the method does not depend on concepts related to derivatives such as the trade-off rate.

Subcriterion A2: Level of Measurement of the Variables (Nominal, Ordinal, Interval, or Ratio Scales) The lexicographic and ELECTRE methods can handle problems with variables measured in ordinal scales. All other methods discussed in the text require variables to be measured in at least interval scales. In theory, however, one can also find an ordinal value function to rank order alternatives in multiobjective decision problems with variables being measured in ordinal scales. However, the construction of such functions for a particular problem is often not practical, with the possible exception of single-objective decision problems having a small number of alternatives.

Subcriterion A3: State of Nature (Deterministic or Probabilistic) The multiattribute utility function approach and the PROTRADE approach were developed exclusively for decision problems under uncertainty. The remaining techniques were designed primarily for deterministic problems. Yet risk elements can clearly be explicitly incorporated as an additional objective function (see Chapter 8). Maximization of expected value can also be incorporated as an objective function in those techniques that can handle nonlinear objectives and constraints, such as the lexicographic, nonlinear goal programming, Geoffrion et al., and Haimes–Hall SWT methods. For an example of this extension in the case of the SWT method, see Chapter 8.

Subcriterion A4: Description of the Set of Alternatives (Explicit or Implicit; if Explicit and Finite, Is It Large or Small?) All assessment techniques discussed in Chapter 5 are for decision problems whose set of alternatives is given explicitly, whereas the generating and mathematical programming techniques discussed in Chapters 6–8 are for problems with an implicitly defined set of alternatives. The ELECTRE method in particular is suitable for problems in which the set of alternatives is finite and not too large.

Subcriterion A5: Type of Causal and Means – Ends Relationships (Linear, Convex, or Nonlinear) Simplex-based generating techniques, Steuer's method (the interval weight method), the NISE generating method, linear goal programming and most of its extensions and variants, the STEP method, and the method of Zionts and Wallenius are all designed exclusively for linear multiobjective decision problems. The remaining techniques, such as the SWT method, are applicable to both linear and nonlinear problems.

9.2.2 *Criterion B: Decision Rule or Preference Model*

Which type of decision rule or preference model is to be used by a certain method should be clear from the text. For example, the multiattribute value or utility function method, the indifference curve method, and the PROTRADE method require complete knowledge of the global preference structure in the form of value functions, utility functions, or indifference curves. In the lexicographic method, preference is modeled partly by priority structure and partly by value or utility function for each individual attribute. For the ELECTRE method, the modeling of preference is in terms of the so-called outranking relation, which is not necessarily transitive or complete. A partial decision rule inherent in all generating techniques is that the best-compromise solution should be noninferior. Goal programming and all its extension and variants, compromise programming and the method of the displaced ideal, the STEP method and its variants, and the SEMOPS and SIGMOP methods are examples of methodologies that model preference by means of weights, priorities, goals, and ideals. The modeling of preference through trade-offs and direct preference is exemplified in the Zionts–Wallenius method, Geoffrion's method, Oppenheimer's proxy method, the Musselman–Talavage trade-off cut method, and the Haimes–Hall surrogate worth trade-off method and its extensions.

9.2.3 Criterion C: Input

Subcriterion C1: Data Requirement (Types, Amount, and Accuracy) In general all assessment methods discussed in Chapter 5 require moderate data. This, however, assumes that all preliminary analyses have been carried out. In particular, such analyses should ensure that whenever the value of any particular attribute corresponding to a certain alternative and a state of nature is required, such information is readily available.

For the generating and mathematical programming techniques discussed in Chapters 6–8, where the set of alternatives is given in terms of causal relationships, an extensive amount of data is usually required in large scale problems to formulate and calibrate the causal relationships.

Subcriterion C2: The Manner and Extent of the Decision Maker's Participation The assessment methodologies discussed in Chapter 5 (except the ELECTRE method), like traditional goal programming and the original surrogate worth trade-off method, typify noninteractive methods. Of those just mentioned, the SWT method involves a posteriori articulation of preference while the rest are based on a priori articulation of preference. All other methods discussed are interactive, which means progressive articulation of preference is required. Interactive schemes usually require less effort by the decision maker, for they are designed to move from one potential candidate for best-compromise solution to another in some efficient and systematic way. Most of these schemes also have been claimed to provide a good learning process for the decision maker as well as the analyst.

Methods based on a priori articulation of preference have often been criticized as being too rigid in the sense that changes, particularly in connection with the decision maker's preference, are not easily accounted for. Because a priori articulation of preference is normally carried out with a minimum of information about the system, such "changes" in preference judgment should be expected as the decision maker learns about the system's behavior. For related comments on this issue, see Starr and Zeleny [1977].

Subcriterion C3: The Number of Decision Makers. Most methods discussed in this book are designed primarily for decision problems with a single decision maker. Some however, are quite amenable to problems with multiple decision makers. For example, individual value functions can be combined to form a group value function if certain conditions concerning interpersonal comparison are satisfied (see, for example Kirkwood [1972]).

As another example, the surrogate worth trade-off method is easily adapted to multiple decision makers (see Hall and Haimes [1976], Haimes [1977], and Chapter 8).

9.2.4 Criterion D: Output

With the possible exception of the ELECTRE method, the indifference curve method, the generating techniques, compromise programming, and the method of the displaced ideal, all methods discussed aim at producing the best-compromise solution. Of these, the SWT method and its extensions are the most effective at emphasizing and guaranteeing that the best-compromise solution obtained is noninferior.

Among the exceptions, generating techniques produce a set or approximate set of unranked noninferior solutions. Compromise programming and the method of the displaced ideal, used together, not only can produce the best-compromise solution that is noninferior, they also yield a series of reduced sets of noninferior solutions called compromise sets. The compromise solutions within each compromise set are, however, unranked. The ELECTRE and indifference curve methods yield a list of indifference classes based on the outranking relation and the weak preference ordering relation, respectively (see Section 3.3 for the definitions).

9.3 Some *ex post* Evaluations

As Rietveld [1980] observed, *ex ante* evaluations give only a tentative or partial picture of how these methods may perform in practice. To provide a complete picture, *ex post* evaluations need to be carried out.

An *ex post* evaluation may be based on such subjective criteria as

- how the method is received by the users, particularly the decision makers;
- the ability of the method to produce final products that truly reflect the decision maker's preference;
- the ability of the method to assist the decision maker to learn more about the system's behavior and about the consequences of possible alternative actions;
- the formal knowledge and experience required on the part of the analyst;
- the formal knowledge and experience required from the decision maker(s); and
- the ease of use.

Some objective criteria, such as the computational efforts and time and financial resources required, are also relevant. Other evaluation criteria can be found in Fandel and Wilhelm [1976] and Voogd [1976].

The best way of carrying out such an evaluation is in a properly designed comparative evaluation study in a practiced situation using real decision makers. Unfortunately, studies of this type are still fragmentary. Some preliminary results can be found in Cohon and Marks [1975], Wallenius [1975], Wallenius and Zionts [1976], Tell [1976], Karwan and Wallace [1980], Schomaker [1980a–c], Rietveld [1980], and Khairullah and Zionts [1980]. Unless major efforts are devoted to this type of evaluation, the direction of further developments in the field of multiobjective decision making will be dictated primarily by the individual interests of researchers.

References

Bell, D. E., Keeney, R. E., and Raiffa, H. (1977). Introduction and overview, in *Conflicting Objectives in Decisions*, Wiley, Chichester, pp. 1–16.

Cohon, J. L. (1978). *Multiobjective Programming and Planning*, Academic, New York.

Cohon, J. L., and Marks, D. H. (1975). A review and evaluation of multiobjective programming techniques, *Water Resources Research* 11, pp. 208–220.

Despontin, M., and Spronk, J. (1979). Comparison and evaluation of multiple criteria decision models: first results of an international investigation, *Report 4923/A*, Center for Research in Business Economics, Department of Business Finance and Portfolio Investment, Erasmus University, Rotterdam.

Fandel, G., and Wilhelm, J. (1976). Rational solution principles and information requirements as elements of a theory of multiple criteria decision making, in *Multiple Criteria Decision Making—Jouy-en-Josas, France, 1975* (H. Thiriez and S. Zionts, eds.), Springer, Berlin, pp. 215–231.

Haimes, Y. Y. (1977). *Hierarchical Analyses of Water Resources Systems*, McGraw–Hill, New York.

Hall, W. A., and Haimes, Y. Y. (1976). The surrogate worth trade-off method with multiple decision makers, in *Multiple Criteria Decision Making: Kyoto 1975* (M. Zeleny, ed.), Springer, Berlin, pp. 207–233.

Hwang, C. L., and Masud, A. S. M. (1979). *Multiobjective Decision Making: Methods and Applications*, Springer, Berlin.

Ho, J. K. (1979). Multiple criteria optimization: a unified framework, presented at the Conference on Human Aided Optimization, August 6–8, 1980, the Wharton School, Philadelphia; also Rep. No. ADM820–BNL26594, Applied Mathematics Department, Brookhaven National Laboratory, Upton, New York.

Karwan, K. R., and Wallace, W. A. (1980). An evaluation of conjoint analysis as an alternative to goal programming, in *Multiple Criteria Decision Making: Theory and Applications—Hagen/Königswinter, West Germany*, 1979 (G. Fandel and T. Gal, eds.), Springer, Berlin, pp. 135–149.

Khairullah, Z. Y., and Zionts, S. (1980). An experiment with some approaches for solving problems with multiple criteria, in *Multiple Criteria Decision Making: Theory and Applications—Hagen/Königswinter, West Germany, 1979* (G. Fandel and T. Gal, eds.), Springer, Berlin, pp. 150–159.

Kirkwood, C. W. (1972). Decision analysis incorporating preferences of groups, Tech. Rep. No. 74, Operations Research Center, Massachusetts Institute of Technology.

MacCrimmon, K. R. (1973). An overview of multiple objective decision making, in *Multiple Criteria Decision Making* (J. Cochrane and M. Zeleny, eds.), University of South Carolina Press, Columbia, pp. 18–44.

Rietveld, P. (1980). *Multiple Objective Decision Methods and Regional Planning*, North Holland, Amsterdam.

Schomaker, P. J. M. (1980a). An experimental comparison of various approaches to determining weights in additive utility models, Center for Decision Research, Graduate School of Business, University of Chicago.

Schomaker, P. J. M. (1980b). On the determinacy of von Neumann–Morgenstern utility functions, *Proceedings of the American Institute for Decision Sciences*, Las Vegas.

Schomaker, P. J. M. (1980c). Philosophical and behavioral issues in multiattribute utility analysis, Center for Decision Research, Graduate School of Business, University of Chicago.

Starr, M. K., and Zeleny, M. (eds.) (1977). *Multiple Criteria Decision Making — TIMS Studies in the Management Sciences*, North Holland, Amsterdam.

Tell, B. (1976). A comparative study of four multiple criteria methods, *Multiple Criteria Decision Making — Jouy-en-Josas, France 1975* (H. Thiriez and S. Zionts, eds.), Springer, Berlin, pp. 183–198.

Voogd, J. M. (1976). Methoden en Technieken betreffende Evaluatie, Planologisch Studiecentrum, TNO, Delft.

Wallenius, J. (1975). Comparative evaluation of some interactive approaches of multicriterion optimization, *Management Science* 21, 1387–1396.

Wallenius, J., and Zionts, S. (1976). Some tests of an interactive programming method for multicriterion optimization and an attempt at implementation, in *Multiple Criteria Decision Making — Jouy-en-Josas, France, 1975* (M. Thiriez and S. Zionts, eds.), Springer, Berlin, p. 319.

Zionts, S. (1980). Methods for solving management problems involving multiple objectives, in *Multiple Criteria Decision Making: Theory and Application — Hagen / Königswinter, West Germany, 1979* (G. Fandel and T. Gal, eds.), Springer, Berlin, pp. 540 – 558.

Appendix

Trade-off Interpretation in the Minimax Multiobjective Problem

Since the minimax and maximin functions are very common in modeling systems with multiple objectives, we shall place our discussion in a generic setting. Consider a multiobjective problem whose objectives (all to be minimized) are $f_1(\mathbf{x}),\ldots,f_n(\mathbf{x})$, where

$$f_n(x) = \max_{1 \leq l \leq p} f_{nl}(x),$$

where f_j, $j=1,\ldots,n-1$, and f_{nl}, $l=1,\ldots,p$, are continuously differentiable real-valued functions defined on some subset of R^N. Even with these differentiability assumptions it is not certain that $f_n(x)$ will always be differentiable at all points where it is defined. In fact, the following results, which we shall prove in this appendix, give some of the necessary and sufficient conditions for f_n to be differentiable at a given point.

Lemma 1. *Define F: $X \rightarrow R$ as $F(\mathbf{x}) = \max_{j \in J} f_j(\mathbf{x})$, where each f_j is a continuously differentiable real-valued function defined on a subset X of R^N and $J = \{j \mid 1 \leq j \leq p\}$. Also define for each $\mathbf{x}^0 \in X$ $J^0 = \{j \mid j \in J, F(\mathbf{x}^0) = f_j(\mathbf{x}^0)\}$. Then*

a. *the directional derivative of $F(\mathbf{x})$ at $\mathbf{x}^0$ exists in all directions in X; more precisely, for any feasible direction* $\mathbf{d}$

$$\lim_{\alpha \rightarrow 0^+} \frac{F(\mathbf{x}^0 + \alpha\mathbf{d}) - F(\mathbf{x}^0)}{\alpha} = \max_{j \in J^0} \left(\nabla f_j(\mathbf{x}^0) \cdot \mathbf{d}\right);$$

b. *F is differentiable at $\mathbf{x}^0$ if J^0 is a singleton; and*

c. *F is not differentiable at $\mathbf{x}^0$ if J^0 is not a singleton and for some $1 \leq i \leq N$, $\partial f_j(\mathbf{x}^0)/\partial x_i$ are not equal for all $j \in J^0$.*

For general problems, it is very possible that condition c will apply. Despite the apparent difficulty that $f_n(\mathbf{x})$ may not be differentiable at some points, the ISWT (or SWT) method can still be used to solve the problem without undue effort.

The first phase (i.e., generating noninferior solutions) remains unchanged; i.e., we solve the ε-constraint problem $P_1(\boldsymbol{\varepsilon})$:

$$\begin{aligned} &\min \quad f_1(\mathbf{x}) \\ &\text{subject to} \qquad f_j(\mathbf{x}) \leq \varepsilon_j, \quad j=2,\ldots,n-1, \\ &\qquad\qquad\qquad f_n(\mathbf{x}) \leq \varepsilon_n, \end{aligned}$$

$\mathbf{x} \in X$, which is equivalent to solving $\hat{P}_1(\boldsymbol{\varepsilon})$:

$$\begin{aligned} &\min \quad f_1(\mathbf{x}) \\ &\text{subject to} \qquad f_j(\mathbf{x}) \leq \varepsilon_j, \quad j=2,\ldots,n-1, \\ &\qquad\qquad\qquad f_{nl}(\mathbf{x}) \leq \varepsilon_n, \quad l=1,\ldots,P, \end{aligned}$$

$\mathbf{x} \in X$. The functions in $\hat{P}_1(\boldsymbol{\varepsilon})$ are all continuously differentiable and thus can be easily solved numerically.

In the second phase we need noninferior trade-off information between f_1 and f_n in order to interact with the DM. The following result (whose proof is to be presented subsequently) will show how such information can be obtained from the solution of $\hat{P}_1(\boldsymbol{\varepsilon})$.

Lemma 2. *For some given* $\boldsymbol{\varepsilon}^0 = (\varepsilon_2^0, \ldots, \varepsilon_n^0)$, *let* $\mathbf{x}^0$ *solve* $\hat{P}_1(\boldsymbol{\varepsilon}^0)$ *with the following properties*:

i. $\mathbf{x}^0$ *is a regular point of the constraints of* $\hat{P}_1(\boldsymbol{\varepsilon})$,
ii. *the second-order sufficiency condition is satisfied at* $\mathbf{x}^0$, *and*
iii. *there is no degenerate constraint at* $\mathbf{x}^0$.

Define $J = \{j | 2 \leq j \leq n-1\}$, $J^0 = \{j | 2 \leq j \leq n-1, \lambda_{1j}^0 > 0\}$, *and* $L_n^0 = \{l | 1 \leq l \leq p, \lambda_{1nl}^0 > 0\}$.

a. *If* $L_n^0 \neq \varnothing$ *then, on the locally noninferior surface,* f_1 *is a function of* f_i, $j \in J^0$, *and* f_n, *where*

$$\left.\frac{\partial f_1}{\partial f_n}\right|_{\mathbf{f}=\mathbf{f}^0} = -\sum_{l \in L_n^0} \lambda_{1nl}^0,$$

and $(\partial f_1/\partial f_n)|_{\mathbf{f}=\mathbf{f}^0}$ *is the partial derivative of* f_1 *with respect to* f_n, *holding all* f_j, $j \in J^0$, *constant at* $f_j(\mathbf{x}^0)$ *and all* ε_j, $j \in J - J^0$, *constant at* ε_j^0.

REMARK: $(\partial f_1/\partial f_n)|_{\mathbf{f}=\mathbf{f}^0}$ always exists under the above hypotheses despite the fact that f_n itself may or may not be differentiable (at $\mathbf{x}^0$) with respect to $\mathbf{x}$.

b. *If $L_n^0=\varnothing$, then if f_j, $j\in J^0$, changes by some small amount $\delta\varepsilon_j$ from its present value, then to stay in the locally noninferior surface f_n will also change by $\delta\varepsilon_n$ from $f_n(\mathbf{x}^0)\neq\varepsilon_n^0$, where*

$$\delta\varepsilon_n=\sum_{j\in J^0}\max_{l\in J_n'}\left(\nabla f_l(\mathbf{x}^0)\cdot\frac{\partial\mathbf{x}(\boldsymbol{\varepsilon}^0)}{\partial\varepsilon_j}\right)\partial\varepsilon_j+O_j\left(|\delta\varepsilon_j|^2\right),$$

$$\lim_{\delta\varepsilon_j\to 0}O_j\left(|\delta\varepsilon_j|^2\right)=0,$$

$$J_n'=\left\{l\,|\,1\leq l\leq p,\, f_n(\mathbf{x}^0)=f_{nl}(\mathbf{x}^0)\right\},$$

and $\mathbf{x}(\boldsymbol{\varepsilon})$ is the solution of $\hat{P}_1(\boldsymbol{\varepsilon})$ for any given $\boldsymbol{\varepsilon}$ in some neighborhood $N(\boldsymbol{\varepsilon}^0)$ of $\boldsymbol{\varepsilon}^0$.

REMARK: The result in Lemma 2(a) says that, after solving $\hat{P}_1(\boldsymbol{\varepsilon}^0)$ [with conditions (i)–(iii) being satisfied], if one of the constraints $f_{nl}(\mathbf{x})\leq\varepsilon_n^0$ is binding (for at least one $1\leq l\leq p$), then so is the constraint $f_n(\mathbf{x})\leq\varepsilon_n^0$ in $P_1(\boldsymbol{\varepsilon}^0)$ at the current solution point. It further implies that the *noninferior local trade-off rate* between f_1 and f_n is the negative sum of all the positive optimal Lagrange multipliers corresponding to the constraints $f_{nl}(\mathbf{x})\leq\varepsilon_n^0$ in $\hat{P}_1(\boldsymbol{\varepsilon}^0)$.

On the other hand, Lemma 2(b) says that if none of the constraints $f_{nl}(\mathbf{x}^0)\leq\varepsilon_n^0$ in $\hat{P}(\boldsymbol{\varepsilon}^0)$ are binding at the solution point, neither is the constraint $f_n(\mathbf{x})\leq\varepsilon_n$ in $P_1(\boldsymbol{\varepsilon})$. Hence at the current solution point f_n cannot be changed independently; in other words, such an independent change may lead to an inferior solution. Changes in f_n should be made as they depend on changes in other constraint objectives f_j (which appear in the constraints $f_j(x)\leq\varepsilon_j$, $j=2,\dots,n-1$) that are binding at that point.

PROOF OF LEMMA 1:

(a) Note that J^0 must contain at least one element. We want to construct a neighborhood of $\mathbf{x}^0$ such that for all $\mathbf{x}\in N(\mathbf{x}^0)\cap\mathbf{X}$, $F(\mathbf{x})=f_j(\mathbf{x})$ for some $j\in J^0$. When $J=J^0$, any neighborhood of $\mathbf{x}^0$ can be used. When $J\neq J^0$, let

$$\eta=F(\mathbf{x}^0)-\max_{j\in J-J^0}f_j(\mathbf{x}^0)>0.$$

Using continuity of all f_j, we have the following: for each $j\in J$, there exists $\varepsilon_j>0$ such that $|f_j(\mathbf{x}^0)-f_j(\mathbf{x})|<\eta/2$ for all $\mathbf{x}\in X$ such that $\|x-x_0\|<\varepsilon_j$. Thus if we take $\delta=\min_{j\in J}\varepsilon_j$, then $N(x^0)=\{\mathbf{x}|\|\mathbf{x}-\mathbf{x}_0\|<\delta\}$ is the required neighborhood, since for each $\mathbf{x}\in N(x^0)\cap X$ and for any $l\in J-J^0$ and $j\in J^0$, we have

$$\begin{aligned}f_l(\mathbf{x})&<f_l(\mathbf{x}^0)+\tfrac{1}{2}\eta\leq f_l(\mathbf{x}^0)+\tfrac{1}{2}\left[F(\mathbf{x}^0)-f_l(\mathbf{x}^0)\right]\\&=F(\mathbf{x}^0)-\tfrac{1}{2}\left[F(\mathbf{x}^0)-f_l(\mathbf{x}^0)\right]\leq f_j(\mathbf{x}^0)-\tfrac{1}{2}\eta<f_j(\mathbf{x}).\end{aligned}$$

Thus for all $\mathbf{x}\in N(\mathbf{x}^0)\cap X$, $F(\mathbf{x})=\max_{j\in J^0}f_j(\mathbf{x})$.

Consider a point $\mathbf{x} \in N(\mathbf{x}^0) \cap X$ and write $\mathbf{x} = \mathbf{x}^0 + \alpha \mathbf{d}_x$, where $0 < \alpha < \varepsilon$ and $\mathbf{d}_x$ is a unit vector in R^N. Using the mean value theorem we can write,

$$F(\mathbf{x}) = \max_{j \in J^0} f_j(\mathbf{x}) = \max_{j \in J^0} \left\{ f_j(\mathbf{x}^0) + \alpha \nabla f_j\left(\mathbf{x}^0 + \hat{\alpha} d_x\right) \cdot \mathbf{d}_x \right\} \qquad (0 \leqslant \hat{\alpha} \leqslant \alpha)$$

$$= F(\mathbf{x}^0) + \alpha \max_{j \in J^0} s_j(\alpha, \mathbf{d}_x), \tag{A.1}$$

where $s_j(\alpha, \mathbf{d}_x) = \nabla f_j(\mathbf{x}^0 + \hat{\alpha}\mathbf{d}_x) \cdot \mathbf{d}_x$. Owing to the continuity of $\nabla f_j(\mathbf{x})$ at $\mathbf{x}^0$ (for all $j \in J$), $s_j(\alpha, \mathbf{d}_x)$ is also a continuous function of α for each fixed $\mathbf{d}_x$. Consequently, $\lim_{\alpha \to 0} s_j(\alpha, \mathbf{d}_x) = \nabla f_j(\mathbf{x}^0) \cdot \mathbf{d}_x$. Moreover there must exist a small number α^0, $0 < \alpha^0 \leqslant \varepsilon$, and at least one $j \in J^0$, say j_1, such that for all $0 \leqslant \theta \leqslant \alpha^0$

$$\max_{j \in J^0} s_j(\theta, \mathbf{d}_x) = s_{j_1}(\theta, \mathbf{d}_x).$$

Hence for all $0 \leqslant \theta \leqslant \alpha^0$

$$\lim_{\theta \to 0^+} \frac{F\left(\mathbf{x}^0 + \theta \mathbf{d}_x\right) - F(\mathbf{x}^0)}{\theta} = \lim_{\theta \to 0^+} \max_{j \in J^0} s_j(\theta, \mathbf{d}_x) = \lim_{\theta \to 0^+} s_{j_1}(\theta, \mathbf{d}_x)$$

$$= \nabla f_{j_1}(\mathbf{x}^0) \cdot \mathbf{d}_x = \max_{j \in J^0} \left(\nabla f_j(\mathbf{x}^0) \cdot \mathbf{d}_x \right). \tag{A.2}$$

Hence the directional derivative of $F(\mathbf{x})$ at $\mathbf{x}^0$ in any feasible direction $\mathbf{d}$ exists and is equal to

$$\max_{j \in J^0} \nabla f_j(\mathbf{x}^0) \cdot \mathbf{d}.$$

(b) If J^0 is a singleton, i.e., the element of J^0 is j_1 (say), then from (A.1) $F(\mathbf{x}) = f_{j_1}(\mathbf{x})$ for all $\mathbf{x} \in N(\mathbf{x}^0) \cap X$ and must therefore be differentiable at $\mathbf{x}^0$ since f_{j_1} is.

(c) Let J^0 contain more than one element and let $\partial f_j(\mathbf{x}^0)/\partial x_{i_1}$ be unequal for all $j \in J^0 (1 \leqslant i_1 \leqslant N)$. To show the nondifferentiability of $F(\mathbf{x})$ at $\mathbf{x}^0$, we need merely show that $\partial F(\mathbf{x}^0)/\partial x_{i_1}$ does not exist. To show this, we apply (A.2) to the direction $\mathbf{e}_{i_1} = (0, \ldots, 0, 1, 0, \ldots, 0)$ and to $-\mathbf{e}_{i_1}$, yielding

$$\lim_{\theta \to 0^+} \frac{F\left(\mathbf{x}^0 + \theta \mathbf{e}_{i_1}\right) - F(\mathbf{x}^0)}{\theta} = \max_{j \in J^0} \nabla f_j(\mathbf{x}^0) \cdot \mathbf{e}_{i_1} = \max_{j \in J^0} \frac{\partial f_j(\mathbf{x}^0)}{\partial x_{i_1}},$$

$$\lim_{\theta \to 0^-} \frac{F\left(\mathbf{x}^0 - \theta \mathbf{e}_{i_1}\right) - F(\mathbf{x}^0)}{\theta} = \max_{j \in J^0} - \nabla f_j(\mathbf{x}^0) \cdot \mathbf{e}_{i_1} = - \min_{j \in J^0} \frac{\partial f_j(\mathbf{x}^0)}{\partial x_{i_1}}.$$

However,

$$\lim_{\theta\to 0^-}\frac{F(\mathbf{x}^0+\theta\mathbf{e}_{i_1})-F(\mathbf{x}^0)}{\theta}=\lim_{\theta\to 0^+}\frac{F(\mathbf{x}^0-\theta\mathbf{e}_{i_1})-F(\mathbf{x}^0)}{-\theta}=\min_{j\in J^0}\frac{\partial f_j(\mathbf{x}^0)}{\partial x_{i_1}}$$

$$\neq\max_{j\in J^0}\frac{\partial f_j(\mathbf{x}^0)}{\partial x_{i_1}}=\lim_{\theta\to 0^+}\frac{F(\mathbf{x}^0+\mathbf{e}_{i_1})-F(\mathbf{x}^0)}{\theta}.$$

Hence $\partial F(\mathbf{x}^0)/\partial x_{i_1}$ does not exist at $\mathbf{x}^0$. ■

PROOF OF LEMMA 2:

(a) Using the result in Theorem 4.4(a) and the given hypotheses of this lemma, we can conclude that there exists a neighborhood $N(\boldsymbol{\varepsilon}^*)$ of $\boldsymbol{\varepsilon}^0$ such that the local noninferior solution surface of $\hat{P}_1(\boldsymbol{\varepsilon})$ around $\mathbf{x}^0$ can be parametrically described by

$$\mathbf{x}=\mathbf{x}(\varepsilon_2,\ldots,\varepsilon_n), \tag{A.3a}$$

$$f_1(\mathbf{x})=\hat{f}_1(\varepsilon_1,\ldots,\varepsilon_n), \tag{A.3b}$$

$$f_j(\mathbf{x})=\varepsilon_j,\qquad j\in J^0, \tag{A.3c}$$

$$f_{nl}(\mathbf{x})=\varepsilon_n,\qquad l\in L_n^0, \tag{A.3d}$$

for some $\boldsymbol{\varepsilon}\in N(\boldsymbol{\varepsilon}^0)$ with $\mathbf{x}^0=\mathbf{x}(\boldsymbol{\varepsilon}^0)$ and $f_1^0=\hat{f}_1(\boldsymbol{\varepsilon}^0)$.

Equivalently, the local noninferior surface around $\mathbf{x}^0$ as generated by $P_1(\boldsymbol{\varepsilon})$ can be parametrically described by

$$f_1(\mathbf{x})=\hat{f}_1(\varepsilon_2,\ldots,\varepsilon_n), \tag{A.4a}$$

$$f_j(\mathbf{x})=\varepsilon_j,\qquad j\in J^0, \tag{A.4b}$$

$$f_n(\mathbf{x})=\varepsilon_n, \tag{A.4c}$$

for some $\boldsymbol{\varepsilon}\in N(\boldsymbol{\varepsilon}^0)$ with $f_1^0=\hat{f}_1^0(\boldsymbol{\varepsilon}^0)$, $f_j^0=\varepsilon_j^0$, and $f_n^0=\varepsilon_n^0$.

Hence,

$$\left.\frac{\partial f_1}{\partial f_n}\right|_{x=x^0}=\left.\frac{\partial f_1}{\partial \varepsilon_n}\right|_{\varepsilon=\varepsilon^0}=\lim_{\delta\varepsilon_n\to 0}\frac{\hat{f}_1(\varepsilon_2^0,\ldots,\varepsilon_{n-1}^0,\varepsilon_n^0+\delta\varepsilon_n)-\hat{f}_1(\varepsilon_2^0,\ldots,\varepsilon_n^0)}{\delta\varepsilon_n}. \tag{A.5}$$

Now observe that $\hat{P}_1(\boldsymbol{\varepsilon})$ is a special case of the following problem:

$$\begin{aligned}&\min\quad f_1(\mathbf{x})\\&\text{subject to}\quad f_j(\mathbf{x})\leqslant\varepsilon_j,\quad j=2,\ldots,n-1,\\&\qquad\qquad\quad f_{nl}(\mathbf{x})\leqslant\varepsilon_{nl},\quad l=1,\ldots,p,\end{aligned}$$

$\mathbf{x}\in X$. Again the local noninferior solution surface of $\overline{P}_1(\boldsymbol{\varepsilon})$ is parametrically described by the parameters $\bar{\boldsymbol{\varepsilon}}=(\varepsilon_2,\ldots,\varepsilon_{n-1},\varepsilon_{n1},\ldots,\varepsilon_{np})$ in a neighborhood

$N(\bar{\varepsilon}^0) = N(\varepsilon_2^0, \ldots, \varepsilon_{n-1}^0, \varepsilon_n^0, \ldots, \varepsilon_n^0)$ of $\bar{\varepsilon}^0$ as

$$\mathbf{x} = \bar{\mathbf{x}}(\varepsilon_2, \ldots, \varepsilon_{n-1}, \varepsilon_{n1}, \ldots, \varepsilon_{np}),$$
$$f_1(\mathbf{x}) = \bar{f}_1(\varepsilon_2, \ldots, \varepsilon_{n-1}, \varepsilon_{n1}, \ldots, \varepsilon_{np}),$$
$$f_j(\mathbf{x}) = \varepsilon_j, \qquad j \in J^0,$$
$$f_{nl}(\mathbf{x}) = \varepsilon_{nl}, \qquad l \in L_n^0.$$

From Luenberger's sensitivity theorem, $\partial \bar{f}_1(\mathbf{x}^0)/\partial \varepsilon_{nl} = -\lambda_{\ln l}^0$ for all $l \in L_n^0$. Consider a subset A of $N(\bar{\varepsilon}^0)$, where

$$\mathbf{A} = \left\{ \bar{\varepsilon} = (\varepsilon_2, \ldots, \varepsilon_{n-1}, \varepsilon_{n1}, \ldots, \varepsilon_{np}) | \bar{\varepsilon} \in N(\bar{\varepsilon}^0) \text{ and } \varepsilon_{n1} = \varepsilon_{n2} = \cdots = \varepsilon_{np} \right\}.$$

Clearly there is a one-to-one correspondence between each member of $N(\boldsymbol{\varepsilon}^0)$ (modified if necessary) and each member of A; i.e., for each $\boldsymbol{\varepsilon} \in N(\boldsymbol{\varepsilon}^0)$, there exists $\bar{\varepsilon} \in A$ (and vice versa) such that $\hat{f}_1(\boldsymbol{\varepsilon}) = \bar{f}_1(\bar{\varepsilon})$, and obviously $\hat{f}_1(\boldsymbol{\varepsilon}^0) = \bar{f}_1(\bar{\varepsilon}^0)$.

Hence for all $|\delta\varepsilon_n| < \bar{\delta\varepsilon}_n$, where $\bar{\delta\varepsilon}_n$ is some small positive number,

$$\begin{aligned}
&\hat{f}_1(\varepsilon_2^0, \ldots, \varepsilon_{n-1}^0, \varepsilon_n^0 + \delta\varepsilon_n) - \hat{f}_1(\varepsilon_2^0, \ldots, \varepsilon_{n-1}^0, \varepsilon_n^0) \\
&= \bar{f}(\varepsilon_2^0, \ldots, \varepsilon_{n-1}^0, \varepsilon_{nl}^0 + \delta\varepsilon_n, \ldots, \varepsilon_{np}^0 + \delta\varepsilon_n) - \bar{f}(\varepsilon_2^0, \ldots, \varepsilon_{n-1}^0, \varepsilon_{n1}^0, \ldots, \varepsilon_{np}^0) \\
&= \sum_{l=1}^{p} \left(\frac{\partial \bar{f}(x^0)}{\partial \varepsilon_{nl}} \delta\varepsilon_n \right) + O(|\delta\varepsilon_n|^2) \\
&= -\left(\sum_{l \in L_n^0} \lambda_{nl}^0 \right) \delta\varepsilon_n + O(|\delta\varepsilon_n|^2).
\end{aligned}$$

Therefore,

$$\begin{aligned}
\left. \frac{\partial f_1}{\partial f_n} \right|_{x = x^0} &= \lim_{\delta\varepsilon_n \to 0} \frac{\hat{f}_1(\varepsilon_2^0, \ldots, \varepsilon_{n-1}^0, \varepsilon_n^0 + \delta\varepsilon_n) - \hat{f}_1(\varepsilon_2^0, \ldots, \varepsilon_{n-1}^0, \varepsilon_n^0)}{\delta\varepsilon_n} \\
&= -\sum_{l \in L_n^0} \lambda_{nl}^0
\end{aligned}$$

as required.

(b) This result is analogous to Theorem 4.30, and the proof is similar. The only significant departure is that we need to replace the term

$$\nabla f_j(\mathbf{x}^0) \cdot \frac{\partial \mathbf{x}(\boldsymbol{\varepsilon}^0)}{\partial \varepsilon_l},$$

which is the directional derivative of f_j in the direction $\partial \mathbf{x}(\boldsymbol{\varepsilon}^0)/\partial \varepsilon_l$, by the term

$$\max_{l \in J_n^1} \left(\nabla f_l(\mathbf{x}^0) \cdot \frac{\partial \mathbf{x}(\boldsymbol{\varepsilon}^0)}{\partial \varepsilon_j} \right),$$

which is, by Lemma 1(a), the directional derivative of $f_n(\mathbf{x})$ in the direction $\partial \mathbf{x}(\boldsymbol{\varepsilon}^0)/\partial \varepsilon_j$. ■

Author Index

Subject Index

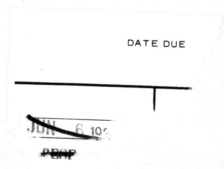